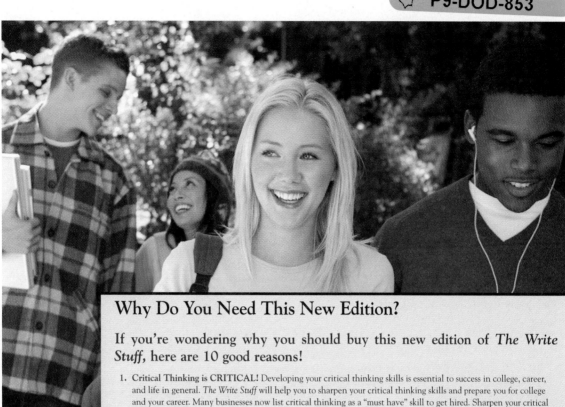

Why Do You Need This New Edition?

If you're wondering why you should buy this new edition of *The Write Stuff*, here are 10 good reasons!

1. **Critical Thinking is CRITICAL!** Developing your critical thinking skills is essential to success in college, career, and life in general. *The Write Stuff* will help you to sharpen your critical thinking skills and prepare you for college and your career. Many businesses now list critical thinking as a "must have" skill to get hired. Sharpen your critical thinking skills now!

2. **Spotlight on Critical Thinking!** A new feature called *Spotlight on Critical Thinking* enables you to develop the basic skills you'll need for successful college writing, reading, and thinking—skills you will continue to use after college, in your career, and beyond.

3. **Critical Thinking Toolbox and Visuals:** *The Write Stuff* introduces a Critical Thinking Toolbox and uses visuals throughout that adhere to the skills and concepts presented in that particular feature. Thus, it makes *The Write Stuff* and the critical thinking concepts presented in it easy to utilize and implement throughout the semester!

4. **A Valuable Resource:** *The Write Stuff* is a resource you can refer to again and again throughout your college career! Keep this book at arm's length even after you pass the course!

5. **Transferability:** *The Write Stuff* teaches you to think critically/analytically, enabling you to transfer those vital skills to all your future college courses.

6. **Move Forward:** *The Write Stuff* fosters discovery and experimentation rather than plain instruction and abstract discussions.

7. **Student Success and Self Discovery:** Student Success Tips will help you to uncover and develop your own personal reading and writing processes.

8. **Vocabulary Development:** Checking Vocabulary exercises after reading selections will help you to expand your vocabulary and be your own thesaurus!

9. **New Readings!** 35% of the readings in *The Write Stuff* are new, including **Texting: Blessing or Curse?** *Matthew Zellmer;* **Business School Makes PowerPoint a Prerequisite,** *Justin Pope;* **Making the Pitch in Print: Advertising,** *Courtland L. Bovée, John V. Thill, George P. Dovel, and Marian Burk Wood;* **Fairy Tales and Modern Stories,** *Bruno Bettelheim; and* **Can You Be Educated from a Distance?** *James Barszcz.*

10. **Chapter Objectives & MyWritingLab:** Each chapter in *The Write Stuff* now opens with a list of chapter objectives and ties them into the most powerful online writing tool on the planet with Pearson's **MyWritingLab** (www.mywritinglab.com). Now you can truly grasp chapter content and test your understanding of that content with MyWritingLab in a more meaningful way!

PEARSON

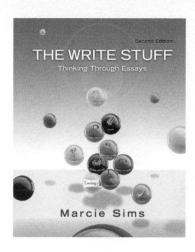

How important is critical thinking to the writing course?

- *Critical thinking is the foundation for everything in the writing course.*
- *Critical thinking should be applied to every writing and reading assignment.*
- *Critical thinking would be even more important in the course if it were easy to implement.*

The Write Stuff: Thinking Through Essays focuses on teaching students the critical thinking skills they need to interpret and analyze information and express their ideas clearly and logically in writing. Critical thinking provides the theme that integrates the instruction throughout the text.

Critical thinking is the foundation for everything in the writing course.

"The focus on critical thinking and its inextricable connection to good college writing is a necessary emphasis and one which many texts do not include"

—**Gina Masucci-MacKenzie,** *Community College of Philadelphia*

▪ **Part I: Critical Thinking.** The two critical thinking chapters of Part I lay the foundation of *The Write Stuff.* Chapter 1 (Critical Thinking in Reading and Writing) defines critical thinking and explains the meaning and function of specific critical thinking terms and tools used throughout the book. Subsequently, Chapter 2 (Critical Thinking and Reading Techniques) equips developing writers with the critical thinking skills they need to interpret and analyze information so they can understand information presented to them.

▪ **Chapter Openers/Thinking Critically questions.** Each chapter opens with an image accompanied by questions and/or prompts to get students thinking critically. This gives students a way to think about the chapter material before they use it and helps engage them with the chapter.

THE WRITE STUFF
Thinking Through Essays

Second Edition

Marcie Sims

Critical thinking should be applied to every writing assignment.

"Too often, students learn about critical thinking without the practice of relevancy and application. The Write Stuff bridges the gap between merely giving a vocabulary list of critical thinking terms and illustrating their importance in the writing process"

— **Peter Francev,** *Mt. San Antonio College*

- **Critical Thinking Checklists.** Featured in the writing chapters, these checklists reinforce the critical thinking–writing connection and ensure that students are thinking critically about all the elements of their essays.

- **Applying Critical Thinking boxes.** These boxes either briefly define the critical thinking tools relevant to specific sections of the chapter (and explain how students can apply them) or demonstrate practical applications of the tools. In the writing chapters, students are taught to think critically about writing structures and how to express ideas clearly. In the grammar chapters, students are prompted to think critically about key sentence elements.

- **Step-by-step writing instruction in the modes.** The writing chapters each contain sections ("Before Writing . . ."; "Writing . . ."; "Structuring . . . ") that isolate the phases of the process, getting students to think critically about the importance of this phase, and how to put the phases together in the culminating writing activities.

- **Spotlight on Critical Thinking features.** The "Spotlight on Critical Thinking" feature in each of the modes chapters (7 – 16) is a stand-alone box element that discusses how critical thinking skills may be applied in the kinds of courses and professions (healthcare, culinary) that are particularly relevant to that mode. The feature will focus on how students can apply particular critical thinking techniques from chapter 2 into those courses/professions. Each spotlight provides specific examples of how to apply specific critical thinking skills.

SPOTLIGHT ON CRITICAL THINKING

Narration is a skill you will need to use both in college and in your career.

Writing narratives: You will have to write narratives with detailed descriptions of events from time to time. For example, in college writing classes, students are often asked to write a narrative essay about a significant day in their lives. In your career, you might have to write a narrative report about a series of events for a coworker or supervisor. For example, in a career in the culinary arts, you may have to write a narrative about how you made that perfect flan.

Use your **analysis** skills to check the **purpose** and **conclusions** in your narrative writing for college classes and later in your writing for your career. Develop your **purpose, ideas,** and **support** based on the critical thinking tips in Chapter 1.

Reading narratives: Use the Six Steps to Active Reading and the T-KED method for annotating as you read (both explained in Chapter 2) in your courses and in your career. For example, if you are reading a narrative case study in a psychology class, you will have to read carefully and annotate as you read in order to analyze the nuances of the case. On the job, if you were reading a proposal from a potential client, then you would need to read actively and annotate with questions and feedback as you read (see Chapter 2 for help).

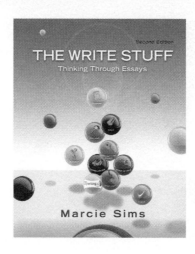

Second Edition

THE WRITE STUFF
Thinking Through Essays

Marcie Sims

Critical thinking would be even more important if I could easily integrate it into my course.

"I never knew how to use critical thinking skills. This text spells it out perfectly so that even a person who has been out of school for YEARS can understand and grasp the concepts."

—**Patricia Cunningham,** *Student*

Visual cues throughout the text. Critical thinking terms may be unfamiliar to many students and seem abstract and hard to grasp. In order to make the connection between these terms and their application to writing essays that clearly articulate and support ideas and arguments, the author has assembled a "Critical Thinking Toolbox" in which each of the critical thinking terms is linked to a specific tool icon. This provides students with visual cues that identify critical thinking tools they can use whenever they embark on a writing assignment.

Critical Thinking and your course. The 41-page Instructor's Guide located in the Instructor's Resource Manual (isbn # 0205029558) includes help on integrating critical thinking into your classroom through small group work, in-class activities, peer review, portfolios, student seminars, projects, games, and more.

The Write Stuff: Thinking Through Essays Reviewers

The author and Pearson-Prentice Hall would like to thank the following instructors who have helped craft *The Write Stuff: Thinking Through Essays*. The reviewers below often reviewed multiple stages of the manuscript, helping the author refine and improve upon instructional content for the second edition. We are most grateful for their comments.

Joseph Antinarella
Tidewater Community College

Linda Barnes
Vance-Granville Community College

Michael Bodek
Bergen Community College

Sharon Bone
Ivy Tech Community College

Barbara Brown
Olive Harvey College

J. Kevin Bruce
Southern State Community College

Kristin Brunnemer
Pierce College

Jessica Carroll
Miami Dade College

Janet Cutshall
Sussex Community College

Neomi Daniels
West Hills Community College

Patrick Ellingham
Broward Community College

Janice Filer
Shelton State Community College

Karen Fleming
Sinclair Community College

Gina Masucci-MacKenzie
Community College of Philadelphia

Jeffrey Simon
University of Maryland

Wendy-Jean Frandsen
Vance-Granville Community College

Shonette Grant
Northern Virginia Community College

Aileen Gum
City College

Ann Habmlin
Amarillo College

Carrie Harrison
Pittsburgh Technical Institute

Elaine Herrick
Temple College

Sue Hightower
Tallahassee Community College

Carlotta Hill
Oklahoma City Community College

Tina Hultgren
Kishwaukee College

Lennie Irvin
San Antonio College

Billy Jones
Miami Dade College

Mandy Kallus
Kingwood College

Kelli Keener
Dalton State College

Tina Bodenheimer
Southwest Tennessee Community College

Emily Lesman
Illinois Valley Community College

Dimitri Keriotis
Modesto Junior College

Gina Ladinsky
Santa Monica College

Anastasia Lankford
Eastfield College

Audry Lynch
Mission College

Elizabeth Marsh
Bergen Community College

Paula McGrew
West Virginia Wesleyan College

Patrick McMahon
Tallahassee Community College

Mary Mears
Macon College

Nancy Meyer
DeVry University-Colombus

Carissa Morris
Georgia Perimeter College

Debbie Naquin
Northern Virginia Community College

Luis Nazario
Pueblo Community College

David Nelson
Glendale Community College

Peter Francev
Mt. San Antonio College

Kirsten Higgins
Green River Community College

Mary Nielsen
Dalton State College

Elaine Pierce Chakonas
Northeastern Illinois University

Anne Marie Prendergast
Bergen Community College

Jonas Prida
Harford Community College

Dunia Ritchey
Virginia College Online

Christine Ross
Northeast Iowa Community College

Harvery Rubinstein
Hudson County Community College

Jennifer Sorenson
Western Wyoming Community College

Chrishawn Speller
Seminole Community College

Sharon Taylor
Western Wyoming Community College

Sharisse Turner
Tallahassee Community College

Maria Villar Smith
Miami Dade College

Hank Galmish
Green River Community College

Susan Gronert
Daytona State College

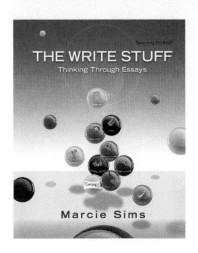

Praise for
The Write Stuff: Thinking Through Essays

Throughout the entire four-year writing and development process, reviewers liked what they saw. Below is just a sample of what was said.

"[Chapter 1] draws a clear bridge between critical thinking skills and the modern day benefits of such a skill."
—Maria Villar-Smith, *Miami Dade College*

"I like the looks of this book in that it is clear and explains how to critically think. . . . I like the 'steps' that are clearly explained and that ask for students to respond."
—Gina Ladinsky, *Santa Monica College*

"I liked the approach, especially the emphasis on critical thinking. With today's under-prepared student, this is increasingly important."
—David Nelson, *Glendale Community College*

"TWS is better than our current text, which is intentionally bland. The readings are solid, the discussion of the writing process is useful, and the focus on critical inquiry is obvious. . .the discussion of in-class exams alone makes it better than most texts out there."
—Jonas Prida, *Harford Community College*

"Students, especially developing writers, lack critical thinking skills. They absolutely need work in this area. A grammatically correct paper that lacks logic is worthless for all involved."
—Anne Pendergast, *Bergen Community College*

THE WRITE STUFF
Second Edition
Thinking Through Essays

Marcie Sims

How would you define the skill of critical thinking in your course?

In the summer of 2008, Pearson-Prentice Hall surveyed instructors about the importance of critical thinking. In addition to saying it is very important that a writing text provide a framework for critical thinking, instructors offered definitions for us to consider.

> *"Critical thinking is integral to (students') ability to analyze readings, to their ability to write thoughtful essays, and to investigate their own strengths. Thus, I would define it as students' ability to be conscious thinkers as they read, write, and plan."*
>
> —**Chae Sweet,** *Hudson County Community College*

> *"... I find that today's students tend to want to read their instructor's mind and give her the answer they think she is looking for rather than seriously approaching the topic as a way to provide their perspective, which should bring something new to the discussion."*
>
> —**Sheila Antley Counts,** *Spartanburg Community College*

> *"I want the students to be able to understand complex arguments, to take into account the counter arguments, to identify lapses in logic, to identify bias, and to apply these skills to their own writing of arguments."*
>
> —**Monica Bosson,** *City College of San Francisco*

> *"The continued emphasis on critical thinking serves to remind students that the concept isn't something to be learned and then discarded at the end of the course."*
>
> —**Mary Nielsen,** *Dalton State College*

> *"I like the author's pedagogical approach to teaching writing, and specifically the emphasis on critical thinking. Critical thinking should be the cornerstone of a liberal arts education."*
>
> —**Jeffrey Simon,** *University of Maryland*

Second Edition

THE WRITE STUFF
Thinking Through Essays

Marcie Sims
Green River Community College

Prentice Hall

Boston   Columbus   Indianapolis   New York   San Francisco   Upper Saddle River
Amsterdam   Cape Town   Dubai   London   Madrid   Milan   Munich   Paris   Montreal   Toronto
Delhi   Mexico City   Sao Paulo   Sydney   Hong Kong   Seoul   Singapore   Taipei   Tokyo

Senior Acquisitions Editor: Matthew Wright
Development Editor: Paul Sarkis
Senior Marketing Manager: Thomas DeMarco
Senior Supplements Editor: Donna Campion
Senior Media Producer: Stefanie Liebman
Editorial Assistant: Samantha Neary
**Project Coordination, Text Design, and Electronic
  Page Makeup:** Laserwords Maine

Art Director, Cover: Anne Nieglos
Cover Designer: Ilze Lemesis
Cover Illustration: Slamer/Shutterstock
Photo Researcher: Jodie Hein
Senior Manufacturing Buyer: Mary Ann Gloriande
Printer and Binder: Quad Graphics-Taunton
Cover Printer: Lehigh-Phoenix Color Corporation

For permission to use copyrighted material, grateful acknowledgment is made to the copyright holders on page 703, which is hereby made part of this copyright page.

1 2 3 4 5 6 7 8 9 10—QGT—13 12 11 10

Student Edition

ISBN-13: 978-0-205-02952-5
ISBN-10: 0-205-02952-3

Annotated Instructor's Edition

ISBN-13: 978-0-205-02954-9
ISBN-10: 0-205-02954-X

Prentice Hall
is an imprint of

www.pearsonhighered.com

Brief Contents

Contents

PART II — WRITING EXPOSITORY PARAGRAPHS AND ESSAYS   39

3 Writing Expository Paragraphs   39

4 Essays: Building Blocks   57

PART III WRITING AND CRITICAL THINKING IN THE MODES   123

To the Instructor

The Write Stuff: Thinking Through Essays, Second Edition, is an all-in-one writing text designed for upper developmental and beginning-level composition courses. *The Write Stuff* provides all the information students need to build their analytical reading and writing skills, as well as the information and practice they need for doing so using correct grammar and an appropriate style. Most be-

ginning composition texts do not provide the basic instruction and exercises needed while at the same time developing more difficult-to-grasp analytical skills: interpretation and analysis. This text not only provides students with the basic tools for writing well organized and developed essays that are grammatically and mechanically correct, but it also focuses on teaching students the critical thinking skills they need to interpret and analyze information and express their ideas clearly and logically in writing. Critical thinking provides the

theme that integrates the instruction throughout the text.

Students in developmental and entry-level composition courses need detailed instruction on how to write paragraphs and essays; how to spot and correct their spelling, usage, and sentence-level errors; and how to include quotes correctly from other writers. They also need instruction on how to interpret what they read, how to go deeper into the topics they've chosen to write about, how to choose the best approach for communicating their ideas to their target audience, and how to pull all of these aspects together into a meaningful purpose for writing. *The Write Stuff* encourages students to engage in an active critical thinking process during all stages of reading and writing and helps them to move beyond defending the obvious in their understanding of others' ideas as well as their own.

The tone and level of *The Write Stuff* speaks to students who are on the cusp of college-level reading and writing. The user-friendly tips and exercises help students develop the tools they need to succeed in reading and writing, and the critical thinking focus throughout the book helps them move past rote learning and summary into true interpretation and analysis of what they are reading or what they are writing about.

CRITICAL THINKING IN *THE WRITE STUFF*

Critical thinking, the unifying theme of *The Write Stuff*, is defined in Chapter 1, which also includes clear explanations of the meaning and function of specific critical thinking terms and tools that are used in almost every chapter of the book. These terms include *purpose, ideas, support, assumptions and biases, conclusions, point of view,* and *analysis.*

Critical thinking terms may be unfamiliar to many students and seem abstract and hard to grasp. In order to make explicit the connection between these terms and their application to writing essays that clearly articulate and support ideas and arguments, the concept of a critical thinking toolbox is used. Each of the terms listed above is linked to a specific tool icon. The idea is to provide students with visual cues that identify critical

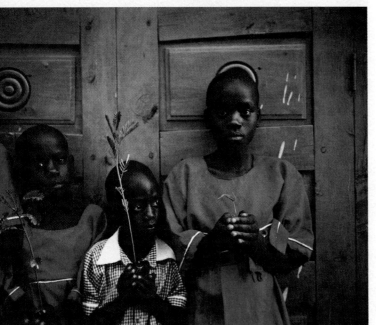

thinking tools they can use whenever they embark on a writing or reading assignment. For example, blueprints are used to represent purpose, and beams to represent the main ideas expressed in topic sentences to support a thesis. Nails are used to represent the support (examples, details, facts) a writer uses to underpin ideas, while a magnifying glass represents the importance of looking closely at and analyzing the elements of an argument, an essay, or even an individual sentence.

These icons are used consistently throughout the text to make explicit to students the connection between the critical thinking tools they have learned about in Chapter 1 and their application to real-world writing. The icons work not only on a visual identification level, alerting students that a specific tool is being used, but on a subliminal level, so that students begin automatically to connect the icons with important critical thinking concepts. As they progress through the text, students will become increasingly familiar with these critical thinking concepts and tools and develop confidence in using them in their writing assignments.

CONTENT

The Write Stuff focuses on upper developmental writing, reading, and analysis skills, and it works well for both developmental and entry-level composition classes. It includes the following features:

- **Critical thinking skills defined and applied** with critical thinking pointers, prompts, and exercises throughout the text
- **Critical reading and analysis techniques** for reading college-level assignments, including visual aids
- **Applying Critical Thinking boxes** that either briefly define the critical thinking tools relevant to specific sections of these chapter and explain in concrete terms how students can apply them, or demonstrate practical applications of these tools
- **Spotlight on Critical Thinking features** that provide real-world examples of how students can apply these skills in college, their career, and beyond
- **Critical thinking icons** that keep terminology and tools discussed in Chapter 1 fresh in students' minds, integrating them into the ongoing instruction, and showing them to have practical use in all aspects of essay writing
- Clearly defined and attainable chapter learning objectives that tie into MyWritingLab (www.mywritinglab.com).
- A review of the basics for writing paragraphs
- Thorough coverage of the basics for writing essays
- Separate chapters on each of the modes, including argument
- Professional reading selections, with writing prompts, for analysis
- Annotated student essays that provide achievable models for student writers
- Two chapters that cover how to find, evaluate, summarize, analyze, and cite sources, and how to use MLA documentation style
- A section on sentence construction and common sentence construction errors with ample practice exercises
- A handbook that provides information and helpful tips on correct use of grammar, spelling, vocabulary, and style, plus plentiful sentence and paragraph length exercises
- A chapter on analyzing visuals
- A chapter on writing about stories

ORGANIZATION

Part I introduces students to the concept of critical thinking, defines important terms, and outlines critical thinking skills and how they apply to reading and writing.

In Part II, students are given a review of how to write expository paragraphs and essays. They learn about paragraph and essay structure, and how to generate ideas, clarify their purpose for writing, assess their audience, and customize their approach to a topic. They are introduced to the essay writing process, shown how to organize and provide details and support for their essay's purpose, and learn about the importance of order, unity, and coherence.

In Part III, students learn about various modes, or essay types, including narration, description, process, classification, definition, example/illustration, cause and effect, comparison and contrast, and argument and persuasion, as well as how to combine them. Each chapter contains critical thinking pointers, specific instruction on how to write in a particular mode, an annotated student essay that provides a realistic and level-appropriate model, an annotated professional sample of the mode with exercises, and tips for possible mode combinations depending on essay purpose and assignment. The section ends with a chapter that provides tips on writing timed essays and essay exams.

In Part IV of *The Write Stuff,* students learn how to write from sources including readings, articles, literature, and visuals, as well as how to summarize, paraphrase, and analyze other writers' work. They learn how to find sources to support their own ideas (research), how to evaluate these sources, and how to cite them correctly in their own writing (MLA citation format).

In Part V, students learn how to write about visual forms of communication, including paintings, photos, and sculpture, as well as film, TV, and advertisements. Moreover, they get a selection of readings for analysis with comprehension and critical thinking questions and writing prompts. The essay modes chapters provide annotated sample student essays as well as professional reading selections for students to practice their critical reading skills. All of the reading selections have exercises and writing prompts that emphasize critical thinking and encourage deeper understanding and analysis by students.

Part VI provides a review of sentence parts and common sentence construction errors and contains tips and exercises for avoiding sentence fragments, run-ons, and comma splices.

Part VII, a grammar handbook, covers the following topics and provides a wealth of sentence- and paragraph-level exercises for each:

- Punctuation
- Common shift and construction errors (with tips for spotting and fixing them)
- Spelling and mechanics
- Tone, style, diction, and usage
- ESL tips
- Tips for building vocabulary and using context clues to figure out unfamiliar words

Hopefully, you and your students will find that this text provides *the right stuff* to help them develop critical thinking abilities and learn how to apply them in every aspect of writing and reading.

ACKNOWLEDGMENTS

I am grateful to all of my students, colleagues, friends, and family who have supported me in the process of writing *The Write Stuff: Thinking Through Essays.*

First, I would like to thank my editors, Matthew Wright, Paul Sarkis, and Gillian Cook, for their support, vision, and encouragement throughout the development of this text. Kudos to Bruce Hobart and all the staff at Laserwords for their careful attention to and formatting of *The Write Stuff.*

Thanks also to Tom DeMarco for all his support and vision, and to all the editorial assistants, design staff, marketing support, and representatives at Pearson.

I am also grateful to all my colleagues who helped review chapters or preliminary editions and those who adopted *The Write Stuff.* Thanks also to my colleagues at Green River Community College for their support and encouragement as I wrote this text.

Another thanks to the artists and photographers who let me feature their beautiful visuals in this text: I am especially indebted to Tom Shugrue, Wayne Buck, Annie Musselman, Trudy Lary, Steve Corvelo, Cindy Small, Patrick Navin, Paul Metivier, Hank Galmish, Douglas L. Cole, and the other artists featured in the book.

Furthermore, I am extremely grateful to my students, past and present, who have inspired me in the classroom and who inspired me to begin writing textbooks in the first place. Thank you also to those students who have given me permission to use their work and to those who provided their feedback on this text and its exercises. *The Write Stuff* would not be if not for you.

Finally, I want to thank my family for their patience and support as I worked on this text. Special thanks to my sons, Marcus and Thomas. Thanks also to my mother, Delores Sims, and to my brothers and sister and their families: Nick, Charlie, Dolly, Diana, Jerith, Mathew, Krysta, and Ashley Sims. Thanks also to Douglas T. Cole; Sharon Thornton and Fumitaka Matsuoka; Doug and Nancy Cole; Halvor and Ilona Cole; Traci Cole and David and Rachel Haygood; Katharine deBaun; Sandy Johanson; Jaeney Hoene; Tom Clarke; Jennifer Whetham; Hank Galmish; Julie Moore; Brad Johnson; Jim Wood; Neal Vasishth; Richard, Cara, and Josh Berman; Jeb, Darci, Levi, and Jaspar Wyman; Tom and Hannah Shugrue; and all of my extended family across the country.

ABOUT THE AUTHOR

Marcie Sims has been teaching pre-college and college-level composition for 20 years. She is the author of *The Write Stuff: Thinking Through Essays* and *The Write Stuff: Thinking Through Paragraphs* (Pearson). She is a tenured faculty member at Green River Community College in Auburn, Washington. She lives in Seattle, Washington, with her two sons Marcus and Thomas.

Picture by Jennifer Whetham

SUPPLEMENTS AND ADDITIONAL RESOURCES

Pearson Resources for Instructors and Students

Book-Specific Ancillary Material

Annotated Instructor's Edition for The Write Stuff: Thinking Through Essays, 2/e
ISBN 020502954X
The *AIE* offers in-text answers to all exercises and includes valuable information on using MyWritingLab (www.mywritinglab.com) in and out of the classroom! It is a valuable resource for experienced and first-time instructors alike.

Instructor's Resource Manual for The Write Stuff: Thinking Through Essays, 2/e
ISBN 0205029558
The IRM offers a 41-page guide on strategies for integrating critical thinking into the classroom, sample syllabi, and a detailed essay on meeting the needs of nonnative speakers of English. It also contains chapter summaries, additional quizzes, and PowerPoint slides for every major topic. This valuable resource is exceptionally useful for adjuncts who might need additional support and advice in setting up their courses.

Additional Resources

Pearson is pleased to offer a variety of support materials to help make teaching writing easier for teachers and to help students excel in their coursework. Many of our student supplements are available free or at a greatly reduced price when packaged with *The Write Stuff: Thinking Through Essays*. Visit www.pearsonhighereducation.com, contact your local Pearson sales representative, or review a detailed listing of the full supplements package in the *Instructor's Resource Manual* for more information.

MEDIA RESOURCES mywritinglab

MyWritingLab: Where better practice makes better writers!
www.mywritinglab.com
MyWritingLab, a complete online learning program, provides better practice exercises to developing writers.
What makes the practice in MyWritingLab better?

- **Diagnostic Testing**
- **Progressive Learning**
- **Online Gradebook**
- **eTextbook**

Preface to the Student

USE THIS TEXT AS A RESOURCE

The Write Stuff is a tool, so remember to use it in a way that best serves your purpose. You don't need to read the chapters in sequence. Read them in the order assigned by your instructor, but don't forget to use the index to look up what you need help with in your own writing and to answer questions that arise as you study. Throughout the book, notes in the margin will direct you to where you can find related information or expanded explanations for specific topics.

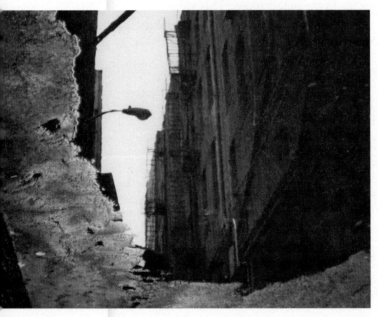

The Write Stuff weaves critical thinking practice throughout the sections. You will learn about the basic components of critical thinking in Chapter 1. In Chapter 2, you'll learn how to apply critical thinking skills to reading. Then, in the chapters on writing essays, the chapters related to reading and analysis skills, and in the reading selections themselves, you will find critical thinking questions and writing prompts to hone your analysis skills as you read. There are critical thinking tips and icons in every chapter to motivate and guide you in your critical thinking. You'll also find spotlight icons that provide real-world examples of how you can apply critical thinking skills in your courses and your career.

The critical writing and reading skills you learn here will help you do better in courses you will take throughout your college career (not just in English or writing classes).

ORGANIZATION

The Write Stuff is designed to provide the basic skills you'll need for success-ful college writing, reading, and critical thinking—skills you will continue to use after college, in your career, and beyond. Throughout the text, you will find helpful Applying Critical Thinking boxes, Spotlight on Critical Thinking boxes, and visual icons to help you apply critical thinking skills in your reading and writing.

Part I of *The Write Stuff* provides an overview of critical thinking skills, including a definition of critical thinking and of the specific tools and terms you can use to apply critical thinking analysis to your own writing and the writing of others. It also provides step-by-step instruction in how to engage your critical thinking skills and read analytically.

Part II of the text provides a review of writing paragraphs, a general in-troduction to the writing process, and step-by-step guidance through the process of writing expository essays.

Part III introduces different modes or types of essays and discusses how to choose which mode to use, when to use one mode over another, and when to use a combination of two or more modes. It provides the tools you need to write a clear argument and to read and evaluate the arguments of others.

In Part IV, you will learn how to paraphrase and summarize what you read as well as additional techniques for writing about what you read. You will find out how to evaluate and use outside sources in your writing and be introduced to the MLA (Modern Language Association) format for documenting sources correctly and avoiding plagiarism. Part V of this text includes a chapter that describes techniques and critical analysis skills for writing about visuals, and provides a selection of professional and student sample readings for analysis, critical thinking, and writing tasks. Part VI focuses on sentence construction and common sentence er-rors, and Part VII features a grammar, mechanics, and style handbook with user-friendly explanations of the most common grammar and usage, tone, and style errors with exercises for practice. This part of the text also has a chapter on how to build your vocabulary and how to figure out words you don't know from their context in a reading. This last part of the text provides tips for typing and word processing. This all-in-one textbook provides what you'll need to succeed in your college writing and reading tasks.

STUDENT SUCCESS TIPS

In order to do well in any course, not just an introduction to writing course, it helps to know some basic tips for succeeding as a college student.

Before Your Course(s) Begins

1. **When registering for courses, first check with an advisor and/or research your campus's college catalog (usually available online).** You want to make sure the courses you are registering for are the correct ones for your intended degree or certificate, and to make sure you have satisfied all prerequisites for the course.

2. **Locate your classroom(s) before the first day of class so you won't get lost and be late on your first day of classes.** First impressions are important, and it is a stressful experience to be late to class.

3. **Get to your campus bookstore and purchase all of your course textbook(s) at least a week before classes begin.** If you order your books online or from another source, then be sure to check with your instructor(s) first to get the exact book information you need, including the edition number, and allow time for delivery.

4. **After you have purchased your textbooks, review them before classes begin** to familiarize yourself with the material you will be learning and to get a sense of the purpose and direction of your courses.

5. **Research on-campus tutoring facilities.** Visit your campus writing center or tutoring locations to see what is available to you once your classes begin. Visit your campus library to get a sense of the tools and resources available to you. Research any other on-campus resources that may help you with particular needs: the financial aid department, the career center, student programs, the women's center, the advising and counseling center, the disabled students resource center, and so on. Depending on your circumstances, you could be eligible for additional support, which often is free.

The First Week of Class

1. **Review the course syllabus** (the handout that is an overview of the course, usually distributed on the first or second day of class) carefully for each class you take. Be sure you understand all of the learning objectives and requirements for the course as well as the grading policies. The course syllabus is like an agreement—a contract—between you

and the instructor. If you stay in the course, you are agreeing to the terms of this contract.

2. **Make a connection with at least one other student from class.** Exchange phone numbers and email addresses (if you choose to). Later, if you miss a class, you can get information and notes from your contact, and vice versa.

3. **Create a calendar of due dates for papers, projects, and exams.** Post the calendar in your room or place it in the front of your notebook so you are aware of these dates and won't procrastinate. You should arrange your work and outside schedules carefully, especially on the days that come before a major test or due date for an essay assignment.

Throughout the Class

1. **Find a "study buddy" or, even better, form a study group with three or more classmates.** Be careful, though, not to share homework or writing assignments. Do your own work. Study groups are for studying together for tests or special projects. When it comes to individual homework or essay assignments, they must be done on your own. You can, however, peer critique each other's work afterwards or go to the on-campus tutoring or writing center for help in reviewing your drafts. Studies have shown that when students form connections with other students on campus, it increases their chances of being successful, and they are more likely to stay and complete their degree.

2. **Complete your work on time and submit it in a professional format.** You're in college now, so be sure that the quality of your work reflects that. You are responsible for knowing due dates and assignment requirements and accomplishing them on time.

3. **Keep copies of all the work you submit.** It is your responsibility to be able to reproduce any lost or misplaced work. Also, keep all graded work turned back to you until you have received your final grade. Even the most organized instructors can make a mistake in their grading records and miss recording, or record incorrectly, a score for an assignment or essay.

4. **Take notes in class.** Many students don't take notes during class, yet this is an integral part of student success and leads to increased comprehension and retention of material.

5. **If you need to communicate with your instructor, make an appointment.** Do not assume that an instructor is "on call" at all times, either in person,

by phone, or via email. Instructors usually teach around 70–150 students per quarter or semester, so be respectful of their time and request an appointment if an issue or question arises that can't be answered by another classmate. Do not approach your teachers to ask for something at the beginning of class, or worse, to say "Did I miss anything?" if you missed the previous class. Of course you missed something! Get the information from a classmate first; if you need a handout from an instructor, approach him or her after class to get that handout, or see the instructor during scheduled office hours to get missed handouts.

6. **Take care of yourself.** College is stressful, so be sure to eat well, exercise, and remember to get enough sleep. Even the most conscientious students can't succeed if they become ill and can't make it to class or do their work.

7. **Keep a positive attitude and keep your goals in mind.** Remember why you are in college in the first place. These college years are ones that you will most likely look back upon fondly later, so keep your goals in mind and be proud of your accomplishments. Keeping a sense of humor helps too. Remember, you learn from mistakes, so do what you can to remedy them, and, most important, learn the lessons that they give you and grow as a result. After all, some of the best learning in college doesn't come out of lectures or assignments. It comes out of life experiences and working with others.

1 Critical Thinking in Reading and Writing

LEARNING OBJECTIVES

In this chapter, you will learn to

LO 1 Define and understand critical thinking.

LO 2 Distinguish the tools for critical thinking.

LO 3 Understand critical thinking terms.

LO 4 Practice and apply critical thinking skills.

THINKING CRITICALLY

Look at the picture above. Then answer the questions that follow.

1. On first glance, what do you think this image is? What do you see?

_____

_____

2. Now take a closer look, paying attention to each detail of the photograph. Look at the outside of the picture. Look at the details. Look at the *point of view* it is taken from. Do you know what it is yet? The title of the photograph is "Puddle Reflection." Now do you know what it is? This is a picture of a puddle on the ground with the reflection of a building and the sky. How long did it take you to figure out (if

Continued ▶

at all)? Was your first *assumption* about the picture correct? Did your *conclusion* hold up when you carefully examined the evidence?

_____

_____

The italicized terms above are critical thinking terms: Look for detailed explanations of them in this chapter.

LO 1 CRITICAL THINKING

Critical thinking is a term you will hear quite a bit in college because it refers to the kind of thinking you'll be asked to do in your courses and later in your career. You'll be happy to know that you are already a critical thinker! You engage your critical thinking skills every day. Whenever you make a decision, solve a problem, or prioritize tasks, you are using critical thinking. For instance, when you choose your classes each term, you have to think carefully about your schedule: What classes are open this term? Which classes count toward your degree or certificate goals? How many classes can you take in one term and still be successful? Which classes are most important for you to take first? Engaging in the process of making these decisions, weighing the choices, and prioritizing all involve critical thinking. Even on a day-to-day basis, you engage your critical thinking skills. When you shop for groceries, when you decide which bills you should pay first on a limited budget, when you work out problems and arguments between you and your friends or you and your coworkers, you are being a critical thinker.

This chapter will define critical thinking in the context of using critical thinking skills to perform college tasks. It will provide you with tools and tips designed to help you read and write analytically (to read looking for answers to questions and to draw some conclusions about your topic) and to evaluate your own reading and writing processes. The skills involved in thinking critically are essential to effective reading and writing. Good thinking and good writing go hand in hand.

Critical thinking in society and education is not a new concept. The process of evaluating one's own thinking process has been around since human history began. Critical thinking was an essential part of ancient cultures, including the Egyptian (3150 BC), Sumerian (2900 BC), and Babylonian (2300 BC) cultures and later was an integral skill and focus for the ancient Greek philosophers. Socrates (469–399 BC) is known for teaching his students how to analyze their critical thinking processes. In fact, the word *critical* comes from the Greek word *kritikos*, meaning "to question" or "to analyze."

Various experts define critical thinking differently, but critical thinking is always a process that involves actively thinking through and evaluating all the steps in your own thinking process or the thinking process of others. Many teachers and experts emphasize the importance of critical thinking in college courses. Richard Paul is one of today's most well known scholars of critical thinking skills. According to Paul, critical thinking involves a "mode of thinking—about any subject, content, or problem—in which the thinker improves the quality of his or her thinking by skillfully taking charge" of each step in the process of thinking and the conclusions reached as a result of that thinking (Foundation for Critical Thinking, www.criticalthinking.org).

The bottom line is that you must be aware of your own thoughts and how they affect your conclusions. There are different skills and tools you can use to improve your thinking process as you read and write. You can use these critical thinking skills to understand and evaluate the writings of others and to discover the strengths and weaknesses in their reasoning or arguments. As you learn these skills, your own thinking and writing skills will improve. Develop the habit of a step-by-step process of thinking about each part of an argument or idea. Critical thinking skills are essential for clear, fair-minded, analytical writing as well as for good analytical reading. Once you get hooked on the power that comes from using your critical thinking skills, you may not be able to stop—you will find yourself using them everywhere: while reading the newspaper, listening to the radio, reading a novel, or even watching a movie.

Think of each step in the critical thinking process as a domino in a long line of dominoes set up to fall in a certain pattern and to end in a specific place. Knock over one domino, and it will knock over the next. But if one domino is out of place, it will keep all the others that follow it from falling correctly. In the same way, one error in your reasoning can throw off your whole chain of thinking and interrupt the flow and logic of your ideas. So line up each step in your critical thinking process carefully: Weigh each piece of evidence you provide, think about your reasons and conclusions, and make sure no point you make is out of line. Otherwise, your chain of thought and evidence will be thrown off, and your end result will be derailed. You want your dominoes to fall into place perfectly, one idea sparking the next: a perfect process.

LO 2 CRITICAL THINKING TOOLS

The following critical thinking tools—terms and elements of argument—are used throughout this textbook to help you evaluate your thinking, reading, and writing processes; to explore your ideas, arguments, and conclusions; and to analyze the arguments and writing decisions of other writers. The icons (pictures) that accompany these key critical thinking tools will alert you to when they are being used in the text and remind you when to use them yourself as you read selections and practice your writing skills.

CRITICAL THINKING TOOLBOX

Icons	Critical Thinking Terms	Definitions	Writing Terms
PURPOSE (Blueprints/plans)	Purpose	What you want to say about your topic: the point(s) you are making. The purpose is the plan or blueprint for what you want to say in your essay.	Thesis statement
IDEAS (Support/beams)	Ideas	The foundation for your argument: Ideas develop your purpose. They form the structure of your overall sentences (beams), develop your thesis (plans), and hold up your conclusion.	Topic sentences
SUPPORT (Nails)	Support	Examples, details, and evidence illustrate the ideas you use to support your purpose. They provide support (nails) for the ideas (beams) that support your purpose.	Major and minor details
ASSUMPTIONS BIASES (Tape measure)	Assumptions and Biases	Assumptions (information you take for granted) and biases (personal beliefs you have about particular topics) can be a helpful tool or they can throw a wrench into your thinking if they are not valid. Always evaluate them when making an argument.	
CONCLUSIONS (Finished house)	Conclusions	The results of your argument or purpose. The result of carefully building your argument (using plans, beams, and nails) is a well-thought-out conclusion (house).	Conclusion
POINT OF VIEW (Camera)	Point of View	How you see the subject you are discussing.	
ANALYSIS (Magnifying glass)	Analysis	Breaking down an idea and working out the meaning of the individual parts and how they relate to the whole: You look at the overall meaning and the connections between the parts.	

These critical thinking terms are essential to the critical thinking process, but they are also the tools of argument. In some ways, *most college writing contains some level of argument:* You always have a purpose to put forth to your readers.

Now read the following more detailed explanations of each of these terms, and consider the questions related to them that you should ask yourself as you read and write in order to think more critically and analyze more thoroughly.

1. **Purpose.** When you write, your purpose—the point(s) you want to make—should be clear and consistent from the beginning to the end of your essay or paragraph. Everything you include should develop that purpose. This is the argument you put forth to your readers.

    When you read, ask yourself:

    ■ What is the author's purpose for writing?

    ■ What argument(s) is the author putting forth?

    ■ What *direct or implied questions* is he or she addressing?

    When you write, ask yourself:

    ■ What is my purpose in this writing assignment?

    ■ What is my argument for this topic?

    ■ What conclusion(s) have I reached related to it?

    ■ How will I argue this conclusion or these conclusions?

2. **Ideas and Information.** You develop your purpose using your own ideas, personal knowledge, and information. Your ideas and background information are specific branches of the tree that forms your purpose—they expand upon it. Later, you develop these individual ideas, or branches, using examples, ideas, details, and commentary.

    When you read, ask yourself:

    ■ What ideas does the author include to support his or her purpose?

    ■ What background information does he or she provide?

When you write, ask yourself:

- What ideas do I want to include to support my purpose?
- What background or personal information can I use to develop the purpose?

SUPPORT

3. **Support.** You need to provide information to support your purpose, ideas, and conclusions on a subject. You can draw on your personal experiences or those of others, use facts and statistics you have researched if your instructor allows research for the particular assignment you are working on, provide examples and specific details, or supply information provided by your instructor to support your reasoning. Always evaluate the information provided by other writers. Include commentary about the examples and details you provide.

When you read, ask yourself:

- What evidence or examples is the author using to support his or her reasoning?
- Are the examples and support believable and clearly explained?
- Do they adequately support the author's purpose?

When you write, ask yourself:

- What evidence or examples can I provide to back my ideas?
- Are they believable and clearly explained?
- Do they support my purpose?

ASSUMPTIONS
BIASES

4. **Assumptions and Biases.** Be sure that the assumptions you or another author make about a topic or idea are not flawed or based on misinformation. Check for any errors in ideas resulting from an unfounded bias in your thinking process or that of an author. Any mistakes in the concepts or ideas that your reasoning is based on can cause problems in your argument. So, although assumptions and biases are helpful tools, they can throw a *wrench* in your thinking if they are unfounded.

When you read, ask yourself:

- Is there an error in the idea the author is explaining?
- Does the author include assumptions or biases that are flawed or unfair?

When you write, ask yourself:

- Is there an error in the idea I'm explaining?
- Are the assumptions I made or the biases I brought into thinking about my topic based on false information?

5. **Conclusions, Implications, and Consequences.** A conclusion is the final point in your argument, the place you reach after discussing the ideas that support your purpose, your argument. Consequences *are the results* of a point you have argued. Implications are more subtle: They are the possible results of an argument that you have inferred (or an author has implied). Be sure to look at all the possible consequences of your argument. For instance, if you argue that the music program should be canceled at your school and the money should be used to add more parking spaces at your campus, be sure to address all the implications and consequences of canceling the music program. You need to be aware that you are implying that having more parking spaces is more important to your school than having a music program. The consequences could be a loss in the artistic identity of your school, fewer students who wanted to focus on music would apply to your college, and so on.

When you read, ask yourself:

- What are the implications of the author's ideas in this reading?
- Are the consequences of his or her arguments acceptable?

When you write, ask yourself:

- What are the implications of my ideas in this paper?
- Are the consequences of my ideas acceptable and clearly thought out?

Back to the domino idea again: Think of the concluding argument in your writing not as the last domino falling over in the chain but as one near the end. The consequences of your argument are the last few dominoes that follow that one. They might not be directly stated in your paper: You'll have to imagine those last dominoes falling and what they mean. For instance, will the canceling of the music program lead to a decrease in enrollment and hurt the overall budget at the school and the quality of the education provided?

6. **Point of View.** Your point of view is your perspective on a topic. Be sure to check the assumptions your point of view is based upon and whether your point of view is unreasonably biased.

When you read, ask yourself:
- What point of view does the author have on his or her topic?
- Did he or she consider other points of view that might be relevant?
- Is the point of view one-sided or biased?

When you write, ask yourself:
- What is my point of view on the topic?
- Have I considered other points of view that might be relevant?
- Is my point of view too biased for my intended audience?

7. **Analysis.** Analysis involves breaking down an idea and working out the meaning of the individual parts and how they relate to the whole. It is an in-depth look at every detail of an idea or argument, like using a magnifying glass to examine something up close and carefully.

When you read, ask yourself:
- What is the author saying?
- Does the author develop his or her ideas well using specific ideas, support, and analysis?

When you write, ask yourself:
- What am I saying, and how can I explain it?
- Do I develop all the ideas well using specific ideas, support, and analysis?

Using the critical thinking tools for reading and writing will help you focus on the basic parts of your written arguments. With practice, these skills will become an automatic and natural part of your reading and writing processes.

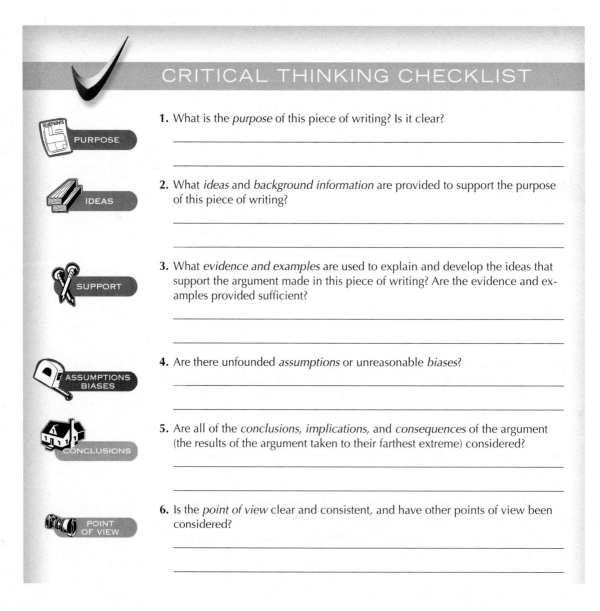 LO 3 CRITICAL THINKING CHECKLIST

The critical thinking skills defined in this chapter can help you get into the habit of analyzing and evaluating the ideas and techniques you and other writers use to present arguments. Throughout this book, you will see critical thinking questions based on the concepts covered here. Be sure to use the general Critical Thinking Checklist below to evaluate your critical thinking process or the process of another writer.

CRITICAL THINKING CHECKLIST

PURPOSE

1. What is the *purpose* of this piece of writing? Is it clear?

_____

_____

IDEAS

2. What *ideas* and *background information* are provided to support the purpose of this piece of writing?

_____

_____

SUPPORT

3. What *evidence and examples* are used to explain and develop the ideas that support the argument made in this piece of writing? Are the evidence and examples provided sufficient?

_____

_____

ASSUMPTIONS BIASES

4. Are there unfounded *assumptions* or unreasonable *biases*?

_____

_____

CONCLUSIONS

5. Are all of the *conclusions, implications,* and *consequences* of the argument (the results of the argument taken to their farthest extreme) considered?

_____

_____

POINT OF VIEW

6. Is the *point of view* clear and consistent, and have other points of view been considered?

_____

_____

ANALYSIS

7. Using these critical thinking tools, *analyze* the overall structure of this essay and the strength of the author's argument, ideas, and support. Was the author successful in accomplishing the purpose? Why, or why not?

_____

_____

(LO 4) CRITICAL THINKING IN ACTION

In order for these tools to become second nature, you need to practice using them in your own writing and when you read others' work. Practice these skills on the following reading.

ACTIVITY 1-1   Using the Critical Thinking Checklist

Directions, Part 1:   *Review the critical thinking terms, and read the article "Texting: Blessing or Curse?" Then, answer the seven questions in the Critical Thinking Checklist after the article.*

READING

Texting: Blessing or Curse?

Matthew Zellmer
Journal-Sentinel Online, March 10, 2009

Sports fans do it from their seats. Millions do it to help choose the next "American Idol." President Barack Obama even used it to give supporters the scoop on his choice for a running mate. Indeed, text messaging is everywhere, and it's here to stay. It's equal parts communication tool and cultural phenomenon. Depending on whom you ask, texting might be the greatest innovation since the Internet. But its ubiquitousness is hardly met with universal love.

The criticisms are many. Among them: Texting is expensive, it distracts us from daily work, it feeds our destructive need for instant gratification, it encourages short attention spans and, lastly, it's making us dumb.

Full disclosure: Since I have a disability that limits motor functioning, I find texting tedious and use it only in crowded, noisy environments when absolutely necessary. But I typically have dismissed most of the above objections as overblown, given all the worse bad habits one can name. But the recent arrest of a 14-year-old Wauwatosa East High School student made me reconsider.

According to a Journal Sentinel report, the student disobeyed a teacher's order to stop texting and denied she had a phone, forcing the school's resource officer to search the room. A police officer discovered the phone in the student's pants while the student laughed. School officials suspended the student for a week, and she was cited twice for trespassing on school grounds.

School officials were quick to say the arrest was for the girl's behavior toward the teacher and police officer, not the act of texting. However, while classroom disruption takes many forms, texting was the means in this case. As someone too old to have texted in high school, I sought counsel from some teacher friends. I already knew that cell phones aren't allowed in classrooms, so I wondered how often students smuggle them in.

Predictably, my friends told me phones frequently are confiscated. One said his school district requires parents to pick up their child's phone in person after it has been taken away and that a second violation results in the school keeping the phone for the remainder of the academic year. Unfortunately, the prevalence of texting may pose an even more substantive problem for educators: an erosion of students' writing skills.

The consensus among the teachers I spoke with was that the texting culture of abbreviation and brevity makes for poorer quality work and worsens grades, especially in the first weeks of school before correct grammar and proper mechanics can be instilled. These problems usually are overcome easily but not without "whining and disregard for directions," according to one. Allegedly "complete" assignments are sometimes three sentences. One suggestion has been to require writing in all subjects, including math.

This seems like a worthy idea, as kids must be taught the importance of writing skills in the professional world. Parents and educators are uniquely qualified to do so by any reasonable method necessary. Except, of course, text messaging.

Part 2:   *What effect did knowing that you would have to answer critical thinking questions afterwards have on the way you read the article?*

_____

_____

_____

_____

_____

_____

_____

_____

_____

_____

_____

_____

_____

_____

_____

_____

_____

CRITICAL THINKING CHECKLIST

PURPOSE

1. What is the *purpose* of this piece of writing? Is it clear?

_____

_____

IDEAS

2. What *ideas* and *background information* are provided to support the purpose of this piece of writing?

_____

_____

SUPPORT

3. What *evidence* and *examples* are used to explain and develop the ideas that support the argument made in the piece of writing? Are the evidence and examples provided sufficient?

_____

_____

ASSUMPTIONS
BIASES

4. Are there unfounded *assumptions* or unreasonable *biases*?

_____

_____

Continued ▶

5. Are all of the *conclusions, implications,* and *consequences* of the arguments (the results taken to their farthest extreme) considered?

_____

_____

6. Is the *point of view* clear and consistent, and have other points of view been considered?

_____

_____

7. Using these critical thinking tools, *analyze* the overall structure of this essay and the strength of the author's arguments, ideas, and support. Was he or she successful in accomplishing the purpose? Why, or why not?

_____

_____

ACTIVITY 1-2   Checking Your Critical Thinking Skills

Directions, Part 1:   *Read the article below, and draw icons from the Critical Thinking Toolbox in the left or right margin next to the places where the writer uses those tools. Don't worry about your drawing skills.*   Answers will vary.

READING

Business School Makes PowerPoint a Prerequisite

Justin Pope
Seattle Times Online, July 31, 2007

Chicago business-school administrator Rose Martinelli says PowerPoint presentations permit potential students to demonstrate creativity that might not come through in traditional applications. At business meetings the world over, PowerPoint-style presentations are often met with yawns and glazed eyes.

But at one of the world's top business schools, such slide shows are now an entrance requirement. In a first, the University of Chicago will begin requiring prospective students to submit four pages of PowerPoint-like slides with their applications this fall.

The new requirement is partly an acknowledgment that Microsoft's PowerPoint, along with similar but lesser-known programs, has become a ubiquitous tool in the business world. But Chicago says so-called "slideware," if used correctly, also can let students show off a creative side that might not reveal itself in test scores, recommendations and even essays.

By adding PowerPoint to its application, Chicago thinks it might attract more students who have the kind of cleverness that can really pay off in business, and fewer of the technocrat types who sometimes give the program a bad name. "We wanted to have a free-form space for students to be able to say what they think is important, not always having the school run that dialogue," said Rose Martinelli, associate dean for student recruitment and admissions.

Online applications are already the norm, and it's not uncommon for colleges to let students submit extra materials such as artwork. Undergraduate and graduate applications also are beginning to ask for more creative and open-ended essays. Partly that's to better identify the students with a creative spark. Partly it's to fend off the boredom of reading thousands of grinding, repetitive responses to "Why is University X right for you?" But asking for four electronic slides appears to be a new idea.

Chicago's new requirement may provoke groans from some quarters. It could be called corporate America's final surrender to a technology that, in the name of promoting the flow of information, often gums it up by encouraging bureaucratic jargon and making colorful but useless graphics just a little too easy to produce.

Nonetheless, PowerPoint has become the lingua franca of business meetings worldwide. Its 500 million copies are used (or misused) in 30 million presentations per day, Microsoft has estimated.

Technology isn't a hurdle for most University of Chicago applicants, but "other schools might have to think about that," said Nicole Chestang, chief client officer for the Graduate Management Admission Council, a worldwide group of management programs that oversees the GMAT entrance exam.

It's also business schools that traditionally have the most boring essays, focusing on workplace accomplishments rather than passions or unusual talents, which are increasingly interested in creativity. Michael Avidan, a second-year Chicago MBA student, predicts some applicants will be turned off by the requirement but says it's an opportunity for clever students whose test scores and other application materials might not stand out to shine.

Part 2: *Write a few sentences about what effect looking for these specific critical thinking tools had on the way you read and understood this article.*

Answers will vary.

_____

_____

_____

_____

Part 3: *On a separate sheet of paper, answer the seven Critical Thinking Checklist questions for this article.*   *Answers will vary.*

Glossary of Critical Thinking Terms

Here is a glossary of critical thinking terms to help you in your reading and writing. Some of these terms have already been covered in the chapter, and some of them are new but will also help you in using your critical thinking skills.

ANALYSIS Analysis involves breaking down an idea and working out the meaning of the individual parts and how they relate to the whole. For example, if you were asked to analyze a paragraph or a poem, you would go through each line or sentence and figure out what each individual part is saying; then you'd look at the overall meaning and the connections between the parts.

Cross Reference
See Chapter 15 for information on writing argument essays.

ARGUMENT In most college writing, you are making some type of argument(s) and presenting a conclusion about a topic using reason and evidence to convince your readers of your point. Arguments in writing can be casual and entertaining (such as arguing for the best place in town to go on a first date), or they can be more formal and structured (such as arguing for the need for a new science building on your campus).

ASSUMPTION An assumption is a belief or claim that you take for granted or that society, a particular people, or an author you are reading takes for granted without providing or asking for evidence or proof to support the idea. Almost everything you believe and do is based on assumptions; for instance, you assume the sun will rise each morning and set each evening. Some, however, are more individual assumptions that you take for granted but that not everyone would agree with. It is important to learn to separate the assumptions that have a basis in fact from ones that don't. When reading other people's writing, look carefully for the assumptions, the ideas they take for granted, and consider whether these are undeniable truths.

BIAS Bias is a particular viewpoint that you or an author has about an idea or a topic. All ideas or opinions reflect a bias. Sometimes you (or an author) are conscious of the biases in your ideas, and sometimes you are not. Having biases is not necessarily a bad thing (it is inevitable), but when one's biases are founded on misinformation or unrealistic assumptions, they can get in the way of good critical thinking.

CONCLUSION A conclusion is the end result of an argument. It is the main point you make in your paper and should be the logical result of the reasons you provide to support your argument. When you read an author's argument, you are looking for his or her conclusion about the chosen topic and how well it has been developed using reasons, examples, and details as support.

EVALUATION Evaluation is looking at the strength of your reasoning, support, and conclusions (or those of another writer) and how well those ideas are developed and explained. Evaluate the arguments you put forth and how well you supported them with examples, reasons, and details. Also, consider the counterarguments—what people who argue for a different stand might say against your conclusion on the issue—and evaluate how well those arguments are constructed.

IMPLY/IMPLICATION *To imply* means "to hint that something is so, to say it indirectly." For instance, if your aunt visits you and says, "My, aren't you looking *filled out* these days!" she may be implying, or hinting, that you need to go on a diet.

INFERENCE Inference involves tapping into your ability to read between the lines and figure out, or infer, what someone means based on clues in what they say or write. For instance, in the example above, your aunt has *implied* that you are getting fat, and you, in receiving those clues from her language, have *inferred* her meaning.

INTERPRETATION Interpretation involves decoding an idea so you understand its meaning. When you interpret an author's idea, you decode it using your own words. You need to interpret and understand an author's ideas before you can analyze their meanings and evaluate them.

OPINION Your opinion is what you (or another writer) believe about an idea, question, or topic. Opinion involves thinking about an idea or question and coming to your own conclusions about it. An opinion is based on weighing information and deciding where you stand on a question.

POINT OF VIEW Point of view in critical thinking refers to the perspective you are coming from in your reasoning and writing (or the perspective of the author you are reading). Be aware of your own point of view and the biases, assumptions, and opinions that make up that point of view, and be prepared to think of potential points of view that differ from yours (or from the views of the author you are reading).

PURPOSE The term *purpose* refers to the reason you are writing a piece in the first place. What have you (or the author you are reading) set out to explain or prove to your readers? Sometimes the purpose of your writing is directly stated, as in a thesis statement, and sometimes it is implied by the arguments and reasons you provide throughout your writing.

SYNTHESIS Synthesis involves pulling together your ideas, and sometimes the ideas of others, in order to make or support an argument. Often, in writing, synthesis involves pulling together ideas from different authors that connect on a particular subject or argument to give a bigger picture.

ACTIVITY 1-3   Critical Thinking Review and Practice

Directions: *Answer the following questions.*

1. Reread the definition for critical thinking on page 2. Then write a definition of critical thinking using your own words.   *Answers will vary.*

    _____

    _____

    _____

    _____

2. List three assumptions you had about college before you began. Then write a line or two about whether each assumption ended up being valid (true) or invalid (not true or unfounded).   *Answers will vary.*

    Assumption 1: _____

    _____

    _____

    True or unfounded: _____

    Assumption 2: _____

    _____

    _____

    True or unfounded: _____

Assumption 3: _____

_____

_____

True or unfounded: _____

3. List two benefits you predict you will gain from learning and applying
    the critical thinking tools and terms explained in this chapter.
    Answers will vary.

    1. _____

    _____

    _____

    2. _____

    _____

    _____

ACTIVITY 1-4   Critical Thinking Terms and Tools

Directions: *Answer the following true/false, multiple choice, and matching questions to test your understanding of the terms and concepts discussed in this chapter.*

1. T/F ___F___ Critical thinking is a new concept from the last 10 years
   or so.

2. T/F ___T___ We engage critical thinking skills in college and also in
   our day-to-day decisions in life.

3. T/F ___F___ It is always a bad idea to have a *bias* in your ideas or
   views of a subject.

4. T/F ___T___ An assumption that you have as the foundation of your
   thinking can be an accurate assumption or a false
   assumption.

5. T/F ___T___ *Inference* means the ability to read between the lines and
   figure out what an author means using clues in the text.

6. T/F ___F___ *Synthesis* means adding supporting examples.

7. ___c___ Which of the following critical thinking terms **best**
   matches the term *thesis statement*?

   a. bias

   b. support

   c. purpose

   d. point of view

Matching Terms to Definitions: *Draw the tool icon (for example, hammer, nails, and so on) for each term on the line provided next to it. Then, match each term to its definition.*

_a_   **8.** Analysis   _____   a. Looking at the individual parts closely to assess the whole purpose or argument

_d_   **9.** Bias   _____   b. The end result of an argument

_h_   **10.** Support   _____   c. A belief or claim one takes for granted without providing or asking for evidence or proof to support the idea

_f_   **11.** Ideas   _____   d. The perspective you (or the author) are coming from in your reasoning and writing

_b_   **12.** Conclusion   _____   e. A particular viewpoint that you (or an author) have about an idea or a topic

_g_   **13.** Purpose   _____   f. Personal knowledge and information (specific branches of the tree that form your purpose)

_e_   **14.** Point of view   _____   g. The reason you are writing a piece in the first place; what you (or the author you are reading) set out to explain or prove to the readers

_c_   **15.** Assumption   _____   h. Personal experiences or those of others, facts and statistics you have researched, examples and specific details to develop your purpose

IN SUMMARY

Be sure to refer to the critical thinking terms and tools provided in this chapter, whenever necessary, as you work through different sections of this text. You will see these tools and terms used in different places throughout the book (watch for the icons), and you will need to use some or all of them in the writing assignments, reading selection activities, and grammar exercises. Also, critical thinking skills are essential to developing good *arguments* in paragraphs and essays. Finally, you'll need to engage critical thinking skills to evaluate the writing of others: classmates, professional authors you read for class, and any sources you consult. As with any new language, the language of critical thinking gets easier with familiarity and practice. Training yourself to use critical thinking skills is challenging, but using these skills will significantly improve your reading and writing abilities, and it may become a treasured, lifelong habit.

To check your progress in meeting this chapter's objectives, log in to www.mywritinglab.com, go to the **Study Plan** tab, click on **Critical Thinking** and choose **Critical Thinking: Responding to Text and Visuals** from the list of subtopics. Read and view the resources in the **Review Materials** section, and then complete the **Recall, Apply,** and **Write** sets in the **Activities** section.

2 Critical Thinking and Reading Techniques

THINKING CRITICALLY

Good reading skills and good critical thinking skills go hand-in-hand. Have you ever read an article or a chapter of a book, or part of an article or chapter, and then not remembered or absorbed anything that you read? Before you read this chapter, what do you think you can do to increase your retention of information as you read? List some ideas in the lines below.

_____

_____

_____

LO 1 CRITICAL THINKING AND THE READING PROCESS

The critical thinking tools discussed in Chapter 1 can help you go beyond basic comprehension of what you read. If you get into the habit of asking critical thinking questions as you read a selection, you will be able to understand it better and reach deeper analytical conclusions. Not only will you be able to assess the arguments an author is making in a story or essay, you will also be able to recognize the writing techniques used and the ideas on which the author is building arguments and conclusions. You can also check to see if the author makes any errors in the introduction or conclusion to the piece.

LO 2 ACTIVE READING

To become a better reader, you must engage in active versus passive reading. Developing active reading habits helps you read critically and engage in thoughtful analysis as you read. The difference between *passive* and *active* reading is like the difference between *hearing* and *listening*. You can hear what someone says without listening to the words, and you can read words passively without actively engaging in understanding what they mean. Good listening takes concentration, and so does active reading. Active reading involves communication between you and the text: It's a dialogue, not a monologue.

Once you develop a system for reading actively that works for you, use it regularly. Many of the assigned readings you'll have in college require you to think critically and analyze the ideas and arguments, the techniques, and the reasoning of the author. Try out the following active reading systems to see which one works best for you, or combine and customize these techniques into a system of your own. As with developing any new habit, it takes a commitment up front, but the time you spend pays off in a more thorough understanding of what you read and an increased ability to remember what you have learned.

LO 3 SIX STEPS TO ACTIVE READING

Use the following six steps to turn your reading process into an active engagement between you and the text instead of a passive process that leaves you bored or keeps you from understanding and remembering what you read. First, buy a notebook to keep as your Reader's Log. For each textbook chapter, article, or essay you read, follow the six steps below, and record them in your Reader's Log. Start each entry in your log with the date, title of the

APPLYING CRITICAL THINKING

PURPOSE   IDEAS   SUPPORT   ASSUMPTIONS BIASES   CONCLUSIONS   POINT OF VIEW   ANALYSIS

Here are some questions you can ask as you read in order to think critically about what an author is saying.

1. What is the author's **purpose** or **goal** in this reading selection? What does he or she set out to explain, argue, or prove?

2. What are the **implied** or **stated** questions being addressed in this reading selection?

3. What **ideas** and **support** (evidence, data, experience, or facts) does the author use to develop a purpose or goal for the reading? Is the support adequate? Convincing?

4. Does the author present alternative **points of view** when needed?

5. What **assumptions** does the author make in this reading selection? (Assumptions are ideas or reasons the author takes for granted and upon which he or she bases judgments or develops his or her reasoning.) Are the assumptions valid?

6. What are the **implications** or **consequences** of the author's reasoning and/or ideas and arguments (direct or implied) in this selection? What **conclusions** does the author reach?

chapter or article, and the page numbers of the reading. The entries in the sample student log that follow are based on the reading "A Whole Lot of Cheatin' Going On," by Mark Clayton on page 426.

Reading Log

Date: 10-8-10

Reading: "A Whole Lot of Cheatin' Going On" by Mark Clayton, pp. 426–430.

Step One: Preview the Reading

Previewing what's coming in a chapter or article helps increase your retention as you read—it's like glancing at a whole picture before you study its individual parts.

Preview the entire chapter or article before you begin reading it, and be sure to do the following:

1. Read the chapter or article title and any subtitles.
2. Read the introduction (or at least the first paragraph of the chapter or article if there is no formal introduction).
3. Read the first sentence of each paragraph. In textbooks, this is often the topic sentence and will tell you the main point of the paragraph.
4. Look for text that is in boldface or italic font, underlined, or presented in a bulleted or numbered format. Key words that are defined in the text are often in boldface, and authors use italics or underlining to emphasize important information.
5. Look at any photographs, graphs, charts, diagrams, or other visual aids, as these are included to provide additional information that supports and illustrates the text.
6. Read the summary at the end of the chapter or article (if there is no summary, then read the last paragraph).

Step Two: Think About What You Already Know About the Topic

After you have previewed the reading, *ask yourself what you already know about the topic.* Chances are you have heard or read some things about it before reading the piece. What can you tap into in your memory or knowledge that will help you better understand this new reading? If you don't know anything about the specific topic, what do you know about related topics, subtopics, or ideas within the article? For instance, if the article is about how to fly fish successfully, but you've never fly fished, have you fished with a rod at all? Have you seen someone fish with a rod on TV? What do you know about fishing in general? Even a little bit of background helps you feel more comfortable and retain new information better, so take a moment to scan your knowledge about the topic itself or background information related to the topic.

Reading Log

Date: 10-8-10

Reading: "A Whole Lot of Cheatin' Going On" by Mark Clayton, pp. 426–430.

Prior knowledge/background: I know that cheating is a problem that has gotten worse in both high schools and colleges and that many schools are trying to crack down on cheaters. I also know that the Internet makes it easier to cheat and even has lots of sites devoted to getting papers written by other people (to copy).

Step Three: Create Questions to Begin Your Dialogue with the Text

Creating questions keeps you active and engaged in your reading as you look for answers. Turn the title and subheadings into questions before you read, and then look for answers to them as you read the whole selection. This active process will help you build a more detailed picture of the reading. Write the questions that you create from the title and subtitles in your Reading Log and leave space beneath your questions to fill in your answers after you read (Step Four).

Then, create a few more questions of your own that come to mind based on your preview of the chapter or article (e.g., What is osmosis? Why do volcanoes erupt? How does the American jury system work?) and write them in your log.

Reading Log

Date: 10-8-10

Reading: "A Whole Lot of Cheatin' Going On" by Mark Clayton, pp. 426–430.

Prior knowledge/background: I know that cheating is a problem that has gotten worse in both high schools and colleges and that many schools are trying to crack down on cheaters. I also know that the Internet makes it easier to cheat and even has lots of sites devoted to getting papers written by other people.

Questions made from title and subtitles:
1. Why is a "whole lot of cheatin' going on"?
2. How are "colleges watching more closely"?
3. How is technology contributing to both the problem and the solution?
4. What does the "expectation of honesty" mean?

Step Four: Read in Blocks

Either read from one subtitle to the next, or if there are no subtitles, read one or two paragraphs at a time, and then, after each section, complete Step Five.

> ▶ **NOTE**   Reading in blocks instead of straight through a chapter without stopping keeps you focused and careful. It helps prevent the "I just read the whole chapter or article, and I have no idea what I read" syndrome.

Step Five: Write in Your Reader's Log

Write the following in your Reader's Log for each of the blocks of text you read:

1. **A two to three sentence summary of the main ideas from each section** or one or two paragraph block(s) as you finish it.
2. **The answers to the questions from Step Three** as you discover them—or amend your questions if you find your questions were off track.
3. **Any vocabulary words** from each block that you don't know. If you can't figure out their meanings by the end of the block, then look them up after finishing the block (not understanding a key word or term can sabotage your understanding of that section).

Once you are sure you have understood the section you have read, place a check mark at the end of it, and move on to the next one.

Reading Log

Summary of Section 2: This section explains the kinds of technology students are using to cheat, such as sites like cheater.com where they can download essays. Also, it talks about how librarians are using technology to spot the downloaded essays by collecting examples and using a database that stores these lifted essays.

How are "colleges watching more closely"?

They are using technology and special programs to spot plagiarized work.

How is technology contributing to both the problem and the solution?

Students are using the Internet to cheat, and librarians are keeping track of the sites available and using software that detects stolen work.

Vocabulary: There were no words in this section that I didn't know.

Step Six: Review and Answer

When you've finished reading the article or essay and writing your summary statements, answers, and new vocabulary for each block of the chapter or article, go back and read (review) them all.

Next, in your Reader's Log, review all the questions and your answers from Step Three without looking at the chapter or article or your notes from Step Five. If you can't remember the answers easily without looking, or if you are unsure of your answers, then review your Step Five notes and, if necessary, the relevant sections of the reading selection.

▶ **FINAL NOTE**   If you follow all these steps, you will have engaged in an active reading process. Also, you will have notes for review to use later for class discussions, tests, or writing assignments. At first, the Six Steps for Active Reading will take longer than passively reading straight through a chapter or article. However, with practice, you will be able to go through these steps quickly, sometimes doing Steps One, Two, and Six completely in your head as you get into the habit of reading as a dialogue. Finally, this process can actually *save you time* by preventing you from having to reread whole chapters or articles because you didn't understand or retain information.

Example of the Six Steps in Action

Read through the excerpt below from an article in the *Christian Science Monitor* about the icecaps melting and global warming, and see how the Six Steps process works for one student.

Reading Log

Step One: I have previewed the entire article and read the title, introduction, first sentence of each paragraph, and the last paragraph.

Step Two: I already know that the nations of the world are competing for the limited supply of oil in the world and that there are restrictions on where nations can drill. I also know that global warming has contributed to the melting of the icecaps and a changing environment in the Arctic.

READING

As Icecaps Melt, Russia Races for Arctic's Resources

Fred Weir
The Christian Science Monitor, July 31, 2007

MOSCOW—As global warming makes exploration of the Arctic sea floor possible for the first time, Russia has launched a massive expedition to help secure the region's vast resources.

In the next few days, two manned minisubs will be sent through a hole blasted in the polar ice to scour the ocean floor nearly three miles below. They will gather rock samples and plant a titanium capsule containing the Russian flag to symbolize Moscow's claim over 460,000 square miles of hitherto international territory—an area bigger than France and Germany combined in a region estimated to contain a quarter of the world's undis-
✓ covered oil and gas reserves.

The issue of who owns the North Pole, now administered by the International Seabed Authority, has long been regarded as academic since the entire region is locked in year-round impenetrable ice. But probably not for much longer.

The area of the Arctic Ocean covered by ice has been shrinking since the early 20th century and the change has accelerated in the past decade, according to the U.S. National Oceanic and Atmospheric Administration. Some scientists blame the shrinkage on the effects of human-driven cli-
✓ mate change.

As the Arctic's ice recedes, its waters are becoming more navigable—and its riches more accessible to a resource-hungry world. "The No. 1 reason for the urgency about this is global warming, which makes it likely that a very large part of the Arctic will become open to economic exploitation in coming decades," says Alexei Maleshenko, an expert with the Carnegie Center in Moscow. "The race for the North Pole is becoming
✓ very exciting."

Step Three, Question 1:
Why are the icecaps melting, and why and how is Russia racing for the Arctic's resources? What resources? Racing against whom?

Step Three, Question 2:
Is Russia the first and only country starting this process?

Step Three, Question 3:
How will the countries decide who owns the North Pole?

Step Three, Question 4:
Why is it shrinking, and how will that change things?

Step Three, Question 5:
Will all this oil be collectable, and who will get it?

The U.S. Geological Survey estimates that 25 percent of the world's undiscovered oil and gas reserves lie beneath the Arctic Ocean. Experts at the Russian Institute of Oceanology calculate that the saddle-shaped territory that Russia is planning to claim may contain up to 10 billion tons of petroleum, plus other mineral resources and vast, untapped fishing stocks.

The 1982 Law of the Sea Convention establishes a 12-mile offshore territorial limit for each country, plus a 200-mile "economic zone" in which it has exclusive rights. But the law leaves open the possibility that the economic zone can be extended if it can be proved that the seafloor is actually an extension of a country's geological territory. In 2001, Russia submitted documents to the United Nations claiming that the Lomonosov Ridge, which underlies the Arctic Ocean, is an extension of the Siberian continental shelf and should therefore be treated as Russian territory. The case was rejected.   ✓

Step Three, Question 6:
Is it attached to Russia?

Step Four: I went through
the article and read in
blocks (see check marks)

Reading Log

Step Five, Summary: This section of the article is about the Arctic icecap beginning to melt, which will make it easier for humans to explore and have access to its resources. Russia is exploring the area now in an attempt to get the oil. There are questions about whether or not Russia or anyone else can claim the area exclusively.

Answers, Question 1: Global warming is melting the icecaps in the Arctic, and Russia is racing against other nations to get the oil that is under the ice there. **Question 2:** So far, Russia is the first country to explore getting the oil from there. **Question 3:** There is not yet a process for deciding who owns the North Pole, but now that it is reachable, there may be a battle coming. **Question 4:** Human-driven climate change has made the icecaps melt, and the melting will start a battle over who owns the North Pole and its resources. **Question 5:** It looks like it will be collectable, billions of gallons. It is not clear yet who owns it. **Question 6:** So far, the United Nations has rejected Russia's claim.

Vocabulary words: titanium, impenetrable, accelerated.

Step Six: My answers to the questions were accurate, so I will review them. Vocabulary words mean (1) titanium: a type of metal, (2) impenetrable: impossible to get through, (3) accelerated: sped up.

ACTIVITY 2-1   Six Steps Practice

Directions, Part 1:   *Apply the Six Steps method to the next section of the ice-caps article. Write your questions in the margin of the reading; place check marks after each section after you have read and understood it; and write the answers to your questions, your summary, and any unfamiliar vocabulary words in your Reader's Log or on a separate sheet of paper.*

READING

As Icecaps Melt, Russia Races for Arctic's Resources (*continued*)

But a group of Russian scientists returned from a six-week Arctic mission in June insisting that they had uncovered solid evidence to support the Russian claim. That paved the way for the current expedition, which includes the giant nuclear-powered icebreaker Rossiya, the huge research ship Akademik Fyodorov, two Mir deep-sea submersibles—previously used to explore the wreck of the Titanic—and about 130 scientists.

The subs were tested Sunday, near Franz-Joseph Land in the frozen Barents Sea, and found to be working well. "It was the first-ever dive of manned vehicles under the Arctic ice," Anatoly Sagelevich, one of the pilots, told the official ITAR-Tass agency. "We now know that we can perform this task."

The upcoming dive beneath the North Pole will be far more difficult, and involve collecting evidence the about age, sediment thickness, and types of rock, as well as other data—all of which will be presented to the United Nations Commission on the Limits of the Continental Shelf (a body of scientists chosen by parties to the Law of the Sea Convention) to support Russia's claim to the territory.

The longer-term goal, Sagelevich says, is to get used to permanently working in that environment. . . . Nations that border the Arctic are concerned about security as well as energy. The U.S. Navy and Coast Guard co-sponsored a symposium in Washington this month titled "The Impact of an Ice-Diminishing Arctic on Naval and Maritime Operations." . . .

Some experts fear the potential for conflict over Arctic territory and resources, and the Russian media highlighted reports of a "U.S. spy plane" that allegedly shadowed the North Pole expedition this week. But others say existing international law is adequate to enable boundaries of influence to be negotiated between the key players as global warming unlocks the north's treasures.

"I don't see why this issue should worsen relations between Russia and other countries," says Pavel Zolotaryov, deputy director of the official Institute of USA-Canada Studies in Moscow. "We can solve our differences on the basis of information. And after this expedition, Russia will be able to say that we've been there and conducted the research" to bolster Russia's claims in the region.

Part 2:   *Write a few sentences describing the effect using the Six Steps for reading actively had on the way you read the section and on your understanding of it.*
Answers will vary.

_____

_____

_____

_____

ACTIVITY 2-2 More Six Steps Practice

Directions: *Pick an article or essay from the reading section of this textbook, from outside of class, or from a chapter in a textbook from one of your other classes, and apply the Six Steps method. Explain below what effect this process had on the way you read the chapter, article, or essay, and your understanding of its content.* *Answers will vary.*

_____

_____

_____

_____

LO 4 THE T-KED METHOD FOR MARKING TEXTBOOKS AND ARTICLES

To be a good reader, you also need to know how to annotate (mark, highlight, and make notes) throughout your assigned reading. The T-KED method is a system designed to help you mark your text as you read. It gives you codes you can use, in addition to highlighting and using regular symbols (see examples on p. 36). It works best for nonfiction articles, textbook chapters, or essays. The process involves marking the **thesis** (**T**) or main point of the article or essay; the **key ideas** (**K**) in each body paragraph; the **examples** (**E**) that provide major support for those key ideas; and the minor **details** (**D**) that support those examples. By marking these elements as you read, you will increase your comprehension and your ability to distinguish main ideas and arguments from major and minor supporting examples and details.

T = Thesis

The **thesis** is the main idea, argument, or point of an article or essay. It is the purpose statement of a piece. A thesis can be one sentence, or it can be a few sentences, depending on the length and complexity of the piece. Usually, the thesis is located in the first or second paragraph of an article or essay, but sometimes it is stated at the end.

On rare occasions, the thesis is never stated and is only implied by a series of arguments and examples. In an implied thesis, the author doesn't directly state the final conclusion or argument he or she is making in a sentence in the introduction, though it sometimes is stated fairly clearly in the conclusion. Instead, the author will provide many ideas, examples, and details about a subject that will lead you to a conclusion about the topic. The author provides hints through the kind of examples and information given about the subject and leads you through the article or essay in a way that makes you come to the desired conclusion on your own. If you find that the thesis is implied instead of directly stated in an article you read, write a sentence of your own that explains what the main idea or argument of the reading is *after* you have read all the information and examples (as clues).

Try this: After reading the first two paragraphs of an article or essay, **circle** the one to three sentences that you think state the main argument. **Mark a T** in the left margin next to the sentences you have circled as the thesis statement.

> ▶ **NOTE**   As you read through the article or essay, you may find you were wrong about the thesis statement and will have to mark the correct one. Or if it turns out the thesis was implied, you might have to write it in yourself.

K = Key Idea

For each paragraph of the article or essay, **underline** the one to two sentence key idea for that paragraph. **Mark a K** in the left margin next to each underlined key idea. The **key idea** is the *topic sentence* for the paragraph.

Try this: As you read the article, underline the key idea (topic sentence) in each paragraph.

▶ **TIP**   Read the entire paragraph before you underline the key idea. Often the key idea or topic sentence for a paragraph is the first or second sentence of the paragraph, but sometimes it's in the middle or even at the end of the paragraph.

E = Examples

In each paragraph, **put an E** over each sentence or part of a sentence that provides a **major supporting detail** or **major example to support** the key idea or topic sentence of that paragraph.

D = Details

In each paragraph, **put a D** over any **minor detail that supports** a major detail or example used to support the paragraph's key idea or topic sentence.

T (again!)

Doublecheck your T (thesis) to make sure it still works as the main idea of the article or essay. If not, circle the real thesis, or write in the implied thesis of the article.

▶ **TIP**   What was the essay or article trying to explain or show through implied ideas or prove though evidence? The answer to that question is the thesis.

LO 5   ANNOTATE AS YOU READ

Whether or not you choose to use one of the specific active reading systems discussed earlier when you read, you need to get in the habit of using high-lighting or underlining, codes, and other annotating methods.

Highlighting and underlining are ways to separate the main ideas from the rest of the sentences in a reading. Use highlighting or underlining on the thesis, topic sentences, and major ideas for each section. You can also use a highlighter to mark words you don't know and then fill in their definitions in the margins.

Be sure to use the margins to write notes to yourself throughout the reading. You can use the margin spaces for the following purposes:

1. To write what you already know about the subject or any insights that you have as you read

2. To number subpoints or examples given in support of the main idea of a paragraph or of the reading as a whole

3. To write in definitions of unfamiliar vocabulary words you've marked

4. To write in questions you have as you read

5. To make comments about illustrations

6. To make comments when you notice an author's biases or assumptions

7. To add codes (see some suggestions below)

8. To note any other reminders to yourself that will help your understanding when you review later

Codes You Can Use

You can customize your own list of symbols and codes to use to annotate text as you read. Here are a few common symbols or codes you can use:

?	Use a question mark whenever you don't understand a term or a concept in a particular section. It will remind you later to doublecheck that part to increase your understanding.
□	Draw boxes around key words—you can write the definitions for those in the margins.
O	Or draw circles around key terms, and add the definitions in the margins.
1, 2	Use numbers to indicate listed points that are not already numbered, or use numbers to mark the numbers of examples given for each main idea.
☆, *, ☺	Use symbols such as stars, asterisks, or smiley faces to indicate important points or sections you particularly enjoyed.

Example of Using T-KED, Highlighting, and Codes as You Read

Note the codes, highlighting, and T-KED notations in tan and blue in the following excerpt from Mark Clayton's "A Whole Lot of Cheatin' Going On" (p. 426) with the thesis, a key idea, an example, and a detail noted.

> Sitting in the glow of his computer screen at 2 a.m. on Oct. 26, 1998, John Smolik, a University of Texas freshman, fires off an e-mail message to an online debate over academic cheating on the Austin campus.
>
> Many of the 100-plus student messages argue that cheaters only hurt themselves. Not so, says Mr. Smolik's missive, labeled "reality check!" ☺ "Cheating is an answer," he writes. "It might not be a good answer, but nonetheless it is an answer."
>
> Actually, Smolik "disagrees with cheating" and was simply playing devil's advocate, he said in a recent interview. But he allows that his provocative message put forward a widely shared view. And researchers agree.
>
> *T*   Across America, college students and college-bound high-schoolers appear to be cheating like there's no tomorrow, student surveys show. **
>
> *K*   Whether copying another student's homework, cheating on a test, or plagiarizing an essay, cheating is limited only by imagination—and
>
> *E*   technology. Some program their calculators with formulas, but rig them to show an empty memory if an instructor checks.
>
> Mr. Krouse taps adult behavior as a factor. "Because adults and role models in society do it, some students may have used those examples to rationalize cheating," he says.
>
> *D*   In a survey conducted in 1997–98, he also found that 66 percent of the parents of these top students said cheating was "not a big deal."

ACTIVITY 2-3   T-KED Practice

Directions: *Pick a chapter from this text, an article from outside of class, or a chapter from a textbook from one of your other classes, and read and apply the T-KED method to it. Then explain what effect this process had on the way you read the chapter or article and your understanding of the chapter or article.*

Answers will vary.

_____

_____

_____

_____

USE THE CRITICAL THINKING CHECKLIST

Remember to apply the questions from the Critical Thinking Checklist in Chapter 1 to all the articles you read for a class. You can weave these questions into your active reading process by asking and answering them when you have completed the Six Steps for Active Reading or the T-KED Method to make sure you are reading with a critical mind.

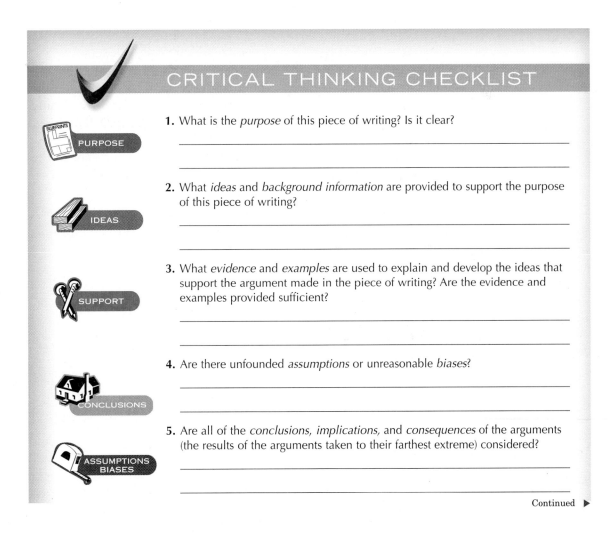

CRITICAL THINKING CHECKLIST

PURPOSE

1. What is the *purpose* of this piece of writing? Is it clear?

IDEAS

2. What *ideas* and *background information* are provided to support the purpose of this piece of writing?

SUPPORT

3. What *evidence* and *examples* are used to explain and develop the ideas that support the argument made in the piece of writing? Are the evidence and examples provided sufficient?

CONCLUSIONS

4. Are there unfounded *assumptions* or unreasonable *biases*?

ASSUMPTIONS BIASES

5. Are all of the *conclusions, implications,* and *consequences* of the arguments (the results of the arguments taken to their farthest extreme) considered?

Continued ▶

6. Is the *point of view* clear and consistent, and have other points of view been considered?

_____

_____

7. Using these critical thinking tools, *analyze* the overall structure of this essay and the strength of the author's arguments, ideas, and support. Was he or she successful in accomplishing the purpose? Why, or why not?

_____

_____

PEARSON
mywritinglab To check your progress in meeting this chapter's objectives, log in to **www .mywritinglab.com**, go to the **Study Plan** tab, click on **Critical Thinking** and choose **Critical Thinking: Responding to Text and Visuals** from the list of subtopics. Read and view the resources in the **Review Materials** section, and then complete the **Recall, Apply,** and **Write** sets in the **Activities** section.

3 Writing Expository Paragraphs

LEARNING OBJECTIVES

In this chapter, you will learn to

LO 1 Write expository paragraphs.

LO 2 Apply tips for a good topic sentence.

LO 3 Add support: examples, details, and analysis.

LO 4 Use various paragraph structures.

LO 5 Use self- and peer assessment techniques.

THINKING CRITICALLY

Look at the picture above. Then answer the questions that follow.

1. When you first looked at the picture, were you immediately aware of what it was a picture of?

_____

_____

Writing a paragraph involves putting the parts in order so that you can effectively communicate your point to your intended audience. Just like the parts of a picture, the parts of a paragraph should not be arranged in a random order, or your readers will be disoriented and have difficulty understanding your point.

APPLYING CRITICAL THINKING

PURPOSE   IDEAS   SUPPORT   ASSUMPTIONS / BIASES   CONCLUSIONS   POINT OF VIEW   ANALYSIS

In this chapter, you will use critical thinking to determine your **purpose** for writing a paragraph, the **argument** you want to make, the **support** you will provide, and the **conclusion** you will reach. To write an effective paragraph, you will need to consider the following:

- What is your **point of view**? What do you think or believe about the topic?
- What are your **assumptions** or **biases**? What do you take for granted about the topic? Is your point of view based on correct information?
- What is your **analysis** of the topic? Have you broken the topic down so that you understand it? Have you examined your argument to make sure it is clear and based on solid evidence?

PARAGRAPH TO ESSAY

It is essential to understand the structure of a paragraph in order to understand how to write essays. The major components of a paragraph are also present in an essay. Both feature a statement of purpose. Both include examples, details, and analysis to support and develop the purpose statement, and both include a conclusion that reiterates the purpose and wraps up the topic.

> ### The Paragraph Format
>
> **Topic sentence (topic + purpose)**
> **Support (examples and details)**
> **Analysis and interpretation**
> **Concluding sentence**

Paragraph to Essay: Pattern Similarities

As you can see in the following chart, both the paragraph and the essay begin with an introduction that sets up the topic and purpose. They both include supportive examples, details, and analysis and interpretation of those examples and details. Both use transitions between major points to maintain flow and coherence, and, finally, both have a conclusion that reiterates the statement of purpose and provides a closing remark or idea for further thought.

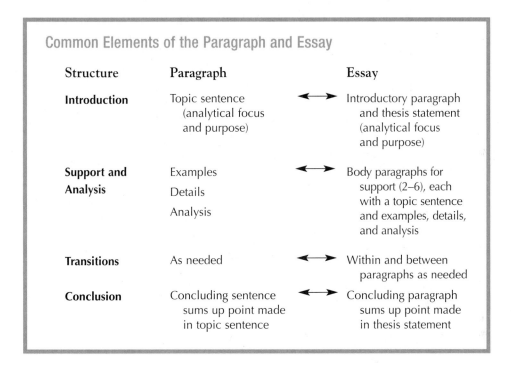

Common Elements of the Paragraph and Essay

Structure	Paragraph	Essay
Introduction	Topic sentence (analytical focus and purpose)	← → Introductory paragraph and thesis statement (analytical focus and purpose)
Support and Analysis	Examples Details Analysis	← → Body paragraphs for support (2–6), each with a topic sentence and examples, details, and analysis
Transitions	As needed	← → Within and between paragraphs as needed
Conclusion	Concluding sentence sums up point made in topic sentence	← → Concluding paragraph sums up point made in thesis statement

LO 1 WRITING EXPOSITORY PARAGRAPHS

The word *expository* is derived from a Latin term meaning "to explain." So, an **expository paragraph** always has a purpose or message that it tries to explain. Therefore, you need to engage your critical thinking skills and use the critical thinking tools described in Chapter 1 to make sure that your writing has something meaningful to explain. Even if you are writing an essay in which you describe something that you witnessed, you usually have a critical point you want to make about that experience, something you want to convey to your readers. Many expository paragraphs contain an

argument, a point the writer is putting forth to readers, that needs evidence and support to back it up.

Since in your expository paragraphs you are attempting to persuade readers to see the conclusions you've come to on your topic or to buy into your opinion, you need to provide evidence and support for your arguments in order to develop your paragraphs. The **evidence** you use can come in the form of personal experience, the experience of others, research, facts, statistics, or quotes from assigned readings. You also need to engage your critical thinking skills to evaluate the strength of your arguments and ideas and the way you've organized your ideas and support for your purpose.

Paragraphs can be stand-alone units of writing, or they can be building blocks in an essay. For shorter writing assignments about specific topics, a paragraph is a helpful writing tool for organizing and developing your ideas about a topic. Paragraphs can be customized, depending on the purpose of your assignment, your topic, and your audience, the same way essays can.

However, all paragraph types share the same basic elements:

- A topic sentence
- Support statements, examples, and details
- Opinion and analysis
- A concluding sentence
- Transitions to maintain the flow from sentence to sentence

LO2 THE TOPIC SENTENCE

Before you begin your paragraph, you need to narrow down your topic so it has a specific focus, and you need to be clear about the point you want to make about the topic. Then, you can create a good topic sentence to set up your paragraph.

Topic   →   Topic Sentence

The **topic sentence** is the *controlling idea* of a paragraph: It establishes the paragraph's topic and purpose. Ask yourself, "What point do I want to make about this topic? What opinion do I want to put forth about this topic?" Your topic sentence should be more than just a fact or detail: It should be a conclusion you've reached related to the topic. Your topic sentence should state your opinion about your topic, and the goal of your paragraph should be to convince your readers of the truth or validity of your opinion by supporting it with examples and details that prove your point.

A topic sentence is *too broad* if it is too generalized or too large in scope to develop and support in one paragraph. A topic sentence is *too narrow* if it is just a fact or detail and not an opinion that can be supported and developed. For instance, if your topic is tennis, you need to think of something you want to say about the sport. If you begin with a topic sentence that is too broad, like "Tennis is a popular sport," it will be hard to make a specific point in the space of a paragraph. What aspect of tennis are you going to address? How popular is it as a spectator sport? How many people like to play tennis as a leisure activity? How many young people take it up in school and college? Make sure your topic sentence isn't too narrow or limited either. You don't want just to state a fact or detail, like "One common stroke in tennis is the forehand," because then there is nothing else for you to discuss in the paragraph. Try to come up with a focus and an opinion that needs to be developed through examples and details. For instance, *Tennis is a sport that requires both physical and mental training.*

Topic Sentence Revision:

Too Broad: Tennis is a popular sport.

Too Narrow: One common stroke in tennis is the forehand.

Just Right: Tennis is a sport that requires both physical and mental training.

Too Broad: Weather is important.

Too Narrow: Storms usually bring rain.

Just Right: Assessing weather conditions is an important factor in driving safely.

Too Broad: There are lots of choices of what to drink in the morning.

Too Narrow: Coffee is a breakfast beverage.

Just Right: People have different favorites for the right morning drink, including coffee, tea, and juice.

ACTIVITY 3-1   Creating a Good Topic Sentence

Directions: *Mark the following topic sentences as TB (too broad), TN (too narrow) or TS (good topic sentence). If a topic sentence is too broad or too narrow, rewrite it on the line provided so that it makes a specific point you can support in the space of a paragraph. Revised sentences will vary.*

Example: TV is entertaining.

TB: Cartoon Network is a network dedicated to entertaining children

and adults alike by providing 24-hour-a-day cartoons.

_TB_   **1.** Sports are part of our culture.

_____

_____

_TN_   **2.** One piece of equipment needed for soccer is shin guards.

_____

_____

_TS_   **3.** Skiing is an expensive hobby.

_____

_____

_TB_   **4.** Snowboarding is a popular sport.

_____

_____

_TS_   **5.** Snowboarding and skiing have strong similarities.

_____

_____

_TN_   **6.** A warm hat and gloves are helpful when skiing.

_____

_____

_TN_   **7.** Soccer is usually called "football" in Europe.

_____

_____

_TS_   **8.** Soccer requires speed and agility.

_____

_____

_TS_   **9.** Baseball represents American values.

_____

_____

_TN_   **10.** A baseball game usually has nine innings.

_____

_____

(LO 3) SUPPORT AND ANALYSIS

You need to provide support and analysis to develop your paragraph's purpose and topic sentence. You can use your own knowledge about and personal experience with your subject to provide support, and you can use examples from other people or writers (major supporting details). Examples are most convincing when you include specific minor details about them that further demonstrate your point. If you use quotes or facts from a source, be sure to acknowledge that source (see Chapter 19). After you provide examples and details, explain what purpose they serve. _Analyze_ their significance in proving the point you set out to make in your topic sentence.

Support → Examples → Details → Comments/Analysis

For instance, if you state that tennis strokes are some of the most important elements of the game, you want to give some examples of the different types of strokes and some details that explain what they are and how they work. In the following excerpt from a paragraph on tennis, the writer provides examples of the kinds of strokes a player needs to learn (serve, volley, backhand, and lobs), details about the serve, and then analysis of what the player must do to gain these skills. Finally, you need to use transitional words or phrases between one example and the next to keep your paragraph flowing smoothly from sentence to sentence, example to example.

Cross Reference
See pp. 114–116 for examples of transitions you can use.

> The most important physical skills tennis players must learn are the serve, the volley, forehand and backhand strokes, and the lob. The serve, for example, has several components such as the toss, form, speed, and technique. Therefore, tennis players must work on their technical skills in order to improve their game. Moreover, besides the physical demands of tennis, players must work on their mental game to become great at the sport. So much of tennis is psychological.

Note how the sentences in the excerpt build on each other to provide support (examples and details) and analysis, and see how transition words such as _also_, _for example_, and _moreover_ help move the reader from one point to the next smoothly.

ACTIVITY 3-2   Providing Support: Examples, Details, and Comments/Analysis

Directions: *Provide a* specific example *to illustrate each of the topic sentences below. Then, provide at least* one detail *about the example and* one comment *analyzing the significance of the example and detail.*   *Answers will vary.*

Example:

Topic Sentence: Severe weather can cause many problems with traffic.

Specific example/s: *For instance, extremely cold temperatures after a lot of rain can cause particularly dangerous road conditions.*

Concrete detail/s: *One of the most dangerous effects of cold after rain is black ice on the roads.*

Comment analyzing the significance of the example and detail provided to support the topic sentence:

Ice on roads, particularly hard-to-see black ice, causes some of the worst conditions for drivers and leads to many car accidents due to loss of control.

1. Most holidays feature some sort of special food that is served in celebration.

   Specific example: _____

   _____

   Concrete detail/s: _____

   _____

   Comment analyzing the significance of the example and detail provided to support the topic sentence:

   _____

   _____

2. Fruit is nutritious, but it is also a great choice because of its variety of textures and flavors that appeal to the senses.

   Specific example: _____

   _____

   Concrete detail/s: _____

   _____

Comment analyzing the significance of the example and detail provided to support the topic sentence:

_____

_____

3. Cats make great house pets for several reasons.

   Specific example/s: _____

   _____

   Concrete detail/s: _____

   _____

   Comment analyzing the significance of the example and detail provided to support the topic sentence:

   _____

   _____

4. Music is often closely tied to special memories.

   Specific example/s: _____

   _____

   Concrete detail/s: _____

   _____

   Comment analyzing the significance of the example and detail provided to support the topic sentence:

   _____

   _____

5. College helps provide career opportunities for students who graduate.

   Specific example/s: _____

   _____

   Concrete detail/s: _____

   _____

   Comment analyzing the significance of the example and detail provided to support the topic sentence:

   _____

   _____

The Concluding Sentence

A paragraph ends with a **concluding sentence** that re-emphasizes the topic sentence's focus and *purpose*. Be careful not to just restate your topic sentence. Instead, end with a closing thought related to your topic sentence but with an idea for further thought on the topic. Be careful not to introduce a completely new argument or purpose in your concluding sentence that changes the focus of your original topic sentence. Sometimes, the concluding sentence in a paragraph can serve as a transition to the next paragraph if you are writing several paragraphs or an entire essay. In the case of the tennis paragraph, a good concluding sentence might be, "Indeed, tennis is a sport that requires players to have both physical and mental discipline in order to be at the top of their game."

ACTIVITY 3-3   Creating a Good Concluding Sentence

Directions: *For each of the five topic sentences in Activity 3-2, create a concluding sentence that connects to the topic sentence; highlights the examples, details, and comments you added; and leaves the reader with an ending thought.*   Answers will vary.

Example:

Topic sentence: Severe weather can cause many problems with traffic.

Concluding sentence: *As you can see, bad weather has disastrous effects on the roads and consequently also on the drivers who face dangerous conditions and slower traffic.*

1. _____

   _____

2. _____

   _____

3. _____

   _____

4. _____

   _____

5. _____

   _____

Model Paragraph

Here is the full paragraph on playing tennis. It has been annotated to show all the elements of an effective paragraph: topic sentence, support (examples, details, and analysis), and concluding sentence. Transitions are highlighted in blue.

Tennis is a sport that requires dedication. To begin with, tennis requires a player to be in good shape. Tennis demands speed and agility. For instance, a player must be able to run from the baseline to the net very quickly. He or she must also learn the most important physical skills such as the serve, the volley, forehand and backhand strokes, and the lob. The serve, for example, has several components such as the toss, form, speed, and technique. Therefore, tennis players must work on technical skills to improve their games. Moreover, besides the physical demands of tennis, players must work on their mental game to become great at the sport. So much of tennis is psychological. If a player loses mental focus during a match, his or her strokes and techniques begin to fall apart. For example, if a player loses mental focus while serving, the first skill to go is the toss. Then it's easy for the player to begin double faulting. A double fault is when the server misses both serves and loses that point. *Indeed, tennis is a sport that requires the players to have discipline and dedication in order to be at the top of their game.*	Topic sentence Supporting example Specific detail Supporting example Specific detail Supporting example Supporting example Supporting example Supporting example Specific detail Concluding sentence

PARAGRAPH STRUCTURE

The classic paragraph form is often shown as an inverted triangle: The topic sentence comes first; the middle provides examples, details, and analysis; and the end features the concluding sentence. In most cases, this pattern will be your best bet when writing an individual paragraph or a couple of paragraphs. It is also the most common pattern for body paragraphs within essays.

Sample Paragraph

Reality TV is really more about escaping reality than capturing it. The whole point of reality TV is supposed to be capturing real life on screen. However, most people watch reality TV to escape from the reality and	Topic sentence

Supporting example   predictability of their own lives. My friends tell me they watch reality TV to "chill," to get away from the day-to-day activities of their normal lives. The "real" people in reality TV shows are put into artificial situations and are supposed to act normally. But who could act normally in such ex-

Supporting example   treme conditions? One reality show, for instance, focuses on people surviving for a month on a remote island, living off their wits and the land.

Specific detail   Some of the contestants resort to eating bugs, strange plants, and anything that will help them get the nutrition they need. But with camera crews filming every move, how could the people on the show ever be real or natural? Maybe they could ask the camera crew for a sandwich! Other reality

Supporting example   shows feature artificial living situations where extremely diverse personalities are forced to live together. For instance, a show might feature a German sports star forced to live with a rapper from New York City. Again, with the cameras rolling, no one is acting as he or she would in normal life. So why do people watch these unrealistic reality shows? *They watch them because they provide a brief escape from their very real lives and so they*

Concluding sentence   *can indulge in a false reality.*

However, there are a couple of variations in the placement of the topic sentence that are available as alternatives to the classic pattern.

Variation One

Instead of the topic sentence being at the beginning of the paragraph, it comes at the end. The paragraph starts out with general information or a personal story to set up the purpose; then it builds to the controlling idea (topic sentence). The topic sentence, then, serves double duty as the concluding sentence as well. This variation on the typical pattern is best represented by the triangle below.

Sample Paragraph: Variation One

There are many different types of toys on the market today. There are

Supporting example   still many action figures that let children use their imagination to role play.
Supporting example   For instance, superhero figures still spark the imagination. Spiderman is an
Specific detail   example of an action figure that many children like to use to "save the
Supporting example   day." Also, many puzzle games and strategy board games are still popular and help children build their math and logic skills. For example, the clas-
Specific detail   sic game Battleship is available in peg form and electronic form: Both

forms build prediction and math skills. Another popular type of toy is one that lets children construct shapes and objects. For instance, Legos are more popular than ever. They even have Star Wars–based Legos that allow children to play out Star Wars stories. Legos also help children build their analysis and hand–eye coordination skills. *Overall, there are many toys on today's market that help build children's imagination and physical and intellectual skills.*

Specific detail

Topic sentence

Variation Two

In this pattern, the topic sentence comes in the middle of the paragraph. The paragraph begins with a more generalized and elaborate setup for the main purpose. Then, in the middle, the topic sentence states the paragraph's controlling idea or purpose. Finally, the paragraph moves into broader examples and analysis again. There may or may not be a specific concluding sentence in this pattern. This variation is best represented by a diamond shape.

Sample Paragraph: Variation Two

There are many different types of toys on the market today. There are still many action figures that let children use their imagination to play roles. For instance, superhero figures still spark the imagination. Spiderman is an example of an action figure that many children like to use to "save the day." Also, many puzzle games and strategy board games are still popular and help children build their math and logic skills. For example, the classic game Battleship is available in peg form and electronic form: Both forms build prediction and math skills. *In fact, there are many toys on today's market that help build children's imagination and physical and intellectual skills.* Another popular type of toy is one that lets children construct shapes and objects. For instance, Legos are more popular than ever. They even have Star Wars–based Legos that allow children to make stories from the Star Wars stories and also help them to build their analytical and hand–eye coordination skills.

Supporting example
Supporting example
Specific detail
Supporting example

Topic sentence

Supporting example
Specific detail

APPLYING CRITICAL THINKING

You need to engage your critical thinking skills to check the parts of your paragraph to ensure you have developed your **purpose** and provided enough **ideas**, **support**, and **analysis**. Here are some tips you can use to write effective paragraphs.

Tip One: Avoid awkward announcements. Don't announce what you are going to write about: Just say it.

> **Announcement:** In this paragraph I will show that shopping can be an addiction.
> **Revised:** Shopping can be an addiction.

Tip Two: Delete *It seems, I think,* or *I feel* statements in paragraphs. They weaken your voice and argument.

> *I think* **statement:** I think credit card companies should be monitored more closely.
> **Revised:** Credit card companies should be monitored more closely.

Tip Three: Avoid the common pitfalls of introducing new ideas or contradicting yourself in the conclusion: the "shoot yourself in the foot" effect.

> **"Shot in the foot" conclusion:** Another addiction that's worse though is food addiction.
> **Revised conclusion sentence:** Shopping can, in fact, be a serious addiction with negative consequences.

Tip Four: Choose the appropriate paragraph length based on your topic and purpose. The number of sentences in a body paragraph varies, depending on the topic sentence and its scope. The length of a paragraph is also affected by how many support examples and details are needed to develop the purpose. On average, most body paragraphs range from 4 to 15 sentences. Decide carefully how much support and how many examples your purpose and topic will need.

Tip Five: Be sure to check that you have provided enough support, using examples and details, and that you have framed your examples with analysis and interpretation when needed.

Tip Six: Make sure you provide transitions to keep your sentences flowing smoothly from one to the next.

LO 5 SELF- AND PEER ASSESSMENT

Self-assessment and peer assessment of drafts empower you to evaluate the effectiveness of your writing and to go through it, step by step, and look at the separate elements that contribute to the success of your paragraph. Think of these elements *before* you begin an actual draft, and use the following self-assessment checklist to make sure you have addressed them well. Then you can have your peers (classmates, friends, or even tutors) use the peer-assessment checklist to critique your paragraph. Check to make sure critical thinking tools were used in your writing and were used to assess the writing of others, too.

PARAGRAPH CHECKLIST

Self-Assessment Version

| BLUEPRINTS PURPOSE | IDEAS | SUPPORT | ASSUMPTIONS BIASES | CONCLUSIONS | POINT OF VIEW | ANALYSIS |

_____ Do you have a topic sentence (**idea**) for your paragraph that develops your **purpose** and includes an opinion and not just a fact or detail?

_____ Did you make sure that your topic sentence is not too narrow or too broad to accomplish your goal in a paragraph?

_____ Do you provide adequate **support** for your topic sentence (examples, details, and analysis)? Review the critical thinking skills in Chapter 1 for deeper **analysis**.

_____ Do you have a **concluding** sentence for your paragraph that supports your topic sentence and pulls together the examples and details for that paragraph? Did you avoid bringing in a new idea?

_____ Do you include transitions between sentences when necessary (either at the end of one or the beginning of the next) to help lead the reader smoothly from one support idea to the next?

_____ Did you proofread, edit, and revise your paragraph for organization, style, unity, sentence variety, grammar, and spelling?

Other problems or needs you noticed that need attention in the next draft:

_____

_____

_____

_____

PARAGRAPH CHECKLIST

Peer-Assessment Version

| PURPOSE | IDEAS | SUPPORT | ASSUMPTIONS BIASES | CONCLUSIONS | POINT OF VIEW | ANALYSIS |

_____ Does the writer have a topic sentence (**idea**) for the paragraph that develops the **purpose** and includes an opinion and not just a fact or detail?

_____ Is the topic sentence too narrow or too broad to accomplish the goal of the paragraph?

_____ Did the author provide adequate **support** for the topic sentence (examples, details, and analysis)? Review the critical thinking skills in Chapter 1 for deeper **analysis** suggestions.

_____ Does the **concluding** sentence support the topic sentence and pull together the examples and details for that paragraph? Did the author avoid bringing in a new idea?

_____ Did the author include transitions between sentences when necessary (either at the end of one or the beginning of the next) to help lead the reader smoothly from one support idea to the next?

_____ List suggestions for improvement in organization, style, unity, sentence variety, grammar, and spelling.

Other comments for the author:

_____

_____

_____

_____

ACTIVITY 3-4   Paragraph Practice

Directions: *Choose one of the following topics and narrow it down to a focused topic you can write a paragraph about. Then, using the steps outlined below, create a paragraph, one element at a time. Answers will vary.*

Topics

- Grocery shopping
- Downloading music from the Internet
- Marriage
- Funerals
- Holiday rituals

Step One: Choose one of the topics above, and write a list of three to five possible focus topics on the subject.

Topic: _____

Focused topics: _____

_____

Step Two: Create a **topic sentence** that is neither too broad nor too narrow and includes an opinion about the topic.

_____

_____

Step Three: Provide a **supporting example and a detail** to illustrate that example.

Supporting example (one or two sentences):

_____

_____

Detail to illustrate and develop the example (one or two sentences):

_____

_____

Step Four: Provide a **second supporting example and detail**. Be sure to include a **transitional word or phrase** to move smoothly from the first example to this one.

Transitional word or phrase and supporting example (one or two sentences): _____

_____

Detail to illustrate and develop the example (one or two sentences): _____

_____

Step Five: Provide a **concluding sentence** that pulls your ideas together and/or leaves the reader with further thought on the topic. Remember to avoid bringing in a completely new opinion or idea.

_____

_____

Step Six: Review and revise what you have written. Read the entire paragraph and see if you need to fix the language or add transitions between the parts to make sure your writing flows smoothly from one point to the next. You should now have a solid draft of a complete paragraph.

ACTIVITY 3-5   More Paragraph Practice

Directions: *Choose one of the topics below to write a paragraph about. Be sure to include the essential elements of a paragraph, and choose the best paragraph structure (see pages 49–52) for your narrowed topic. Be sure to have a clear topic sentence, specific examples and details to illustrate your points, transitions when needed, and a concluding sentence.* *Answers will vary.*

Topics

- Equipment needed for camping
- Taking care of a family pet
- Learning to ride a bicycle
- Preparing for a job interview
- The funniest show on TV

Paragraph: _____

_____

_____

_____

_____

_____

_____

To check your progress in meeting this chapter's objectives, log in to www.mywritinglab.com, go to the **Study Plan** tab, click on **Writing Expository Paragraphs and Essays** and choose **Recognizing the Essay, The Topic Sentence** and **Developing and Organizing a Paragraph** from the list of subtopics. Read and view the resources in the **Review Materials** section, and then complete the **Recall**, **Apply**, and **Write** sets in the **Activities** section.

Silhouette   Wayne Buck

LEARNING OBJECTIVES

In this chapter, you will learn to

 LO 1 Write expository essays.

LO 2 Write introductory, body, and concluding paragraphs.

LO 3 Use the building blocks of an essay.

 LO 4 Write thesis statements with purpose.

THINKING CRITICALLY

Look at the picture. Then answer the questions that follow.

When you first looked at this photo, what did you notice? What caught your eye? How does the background affect the figure in shadow? How does the title help you understand the picture's subject and purpose?

_____

_____

Continued ▶

57

Writing an essay involves having a clear purpose; providing support in the form of examples, details, and comments; and arranging the essay parts in an effective order so that you can clearly communicate your point to your intended audience. Just like the photo above, you want the overall shape and structure of your essay to be clear. The parts of an essay should not be arranged in a random order, or your readers will have difficulty understanding your point.

(LO 1) EXPOSITORY ESSAYS

An **expository essay** has a specific format that allows you to focus on your topic and the point you want to make about it. Like a paragraph, it has a clear statement of purpose (thesis statement); is developed using examples, details, and analysis; has a strong conclusion; uses an organized pattern to convey information; and includes clear transitions to maintain the flow of ideas from sentence to sentence and paragraph to paragraph.

First, you need to know the audience for your essay, and you need to know your subject; then you need to narrow that subject to a manageable topic. The **subject** is the general topic you are writing about, which you need to focus into a manageable topic for the length of your essay. The **purpose** is what you want to explain or prove related to that topic, so your thesis is a statement of purpose of your overall goal. Your **audience** is the intended reader(s) of your essay—who you are addressing—so you'll need to customize both your tone (casual, informal, or more formal and academic) and the amount and types of information you include, depending on the intended audience.

An expository essay includes an **introductory paragraph** (or paragraphs, depending on the length and style of the essay); **body paragraphs**, which develop the thesis statement (purpose); and a **concluding paragraph**, which restates the purpose and adds closing remarks.

The number of paragraphs in an essay varies, depending on the scope of your topic and the goal(s) of your thesis statement. Most essays have at least four paragraphs and can have as many as needed to achieve the established goals of the topic and purpose. Let your topic, goals, and the guidelines of your instructor's assignment set the length and number of paragraphs you will need. Do not rely on a formula with a set number of paragraphs that might limit your ideas and the goals for your essay.

Writing any type of essay involves using a general format and organizational pattern, and all essays benefit from the writer engaging in some form of writing process to achieve the best results. The process for writing

Cross Reference
See Chapter 5 for information on generating ideas, assessing audience, and narrowing topic.

an essay is covered in Chapter 5. Many assignments will require you to blend the skills of two or more essay modes (particular types of essays with a specific expository purpose or approach). For instance, you might combine three modes: argument with comparison/contrast and narration in an argument/persuasion essay on which car to buy as a college student. Rarely does an essay feature one mode only, though there are exceptions (such as a process essay for a biology lab class that provides a report on the steps in an experiment and its results). Most essays use a combination of modes, often with one dominant, for example, argument or description. Specific modes and their elements are covered in detail in Chapters 7–15.

Use the following essay format as a guideline:

THE ESSAY FORMAT

INTRODUCTORY PARAGRAPH

Opening Line/Attention Grabber: Designed to draw in your readers

General Background for the Topic: The setup

Thesis Statement (or Statement of Purpose): Your **thesis statement** states the purpose of your essay. It outlines what you plan to explain to your readers about your subject; it's the conclusion you've reached about the topic.

Ask yourself these questions to get to a strong thesis statement:

- **What** am I writing about?
- **How** will I demonstrate my purpose? What is my plan of development?
- **So What?** What is the main conclusion I've reached on my topic? What do I want my readers to know?

BODY PARAGRAPHS

Topic Sentence: Main idea for the paragraph and develops the thesis

Support: Backs up your topic sentence idea with a statement of support, fact, or opinion (1–3 support statements per body paragraph)

- **Examples:** One or two examples to illustrate each idea
- **Details:** One or more details to illustrate and explain each example
- **Analysis/Commentary:** Analysis and commentary on the importance of the supporting examples and details and how they illustrate the topic sentence

- ■ **Concluding Sentence:** Sums up the main idea from the topic sentence, and/or provides ideas for further thought, or serves as transition to next paragraph

Include these elements in each body paragraph in your essay. You should use transitions at the end of one body paragraph or at the beginning of the next to make your essay flow smoothly.

CONCLUDING PARAGRAPH

Re-emphasizes your essay's thesis without re-stating it: Reminds your reader of your thesis and sums up your main points

- ■ Sums up your analytical conclusions
- ■ Ends with closing ideas for further thought
- ▶ **NOTE**   Do not introduce any contradictory ideas in the concluding paragraph (ideas that go against your previous opinions or purpose)

A well written essay has **coherence:** It flows smoothly from one point to the next and from one paragraph to the next. To achieve good coherence in your essay, make sure that your ideas are developed in a logical order, that you provide support and examples in the best order possible, and that you use transitional words or phrases that move your readers smoothly from one idea or paragraph to the next. **Transitions** are discussed in depth on page 66.

LO 3 THE BUILDING BLOCKS OF AN EXPOSITORY ESSAY

Following is a detailed description of the basic building blocks of an essay: the title, the introduction and thesis, the body paragraphs, and the conclusion. The sample topic is parking problems on campus.

ESSAY TITLE

The title for your essay is the key to introducing your topic and drawing in your reader. Try titles that are clear, yet interesting. You can start with a working title before you begin writing your essay, or you may not come up with a title until you have finished your first draft. Either way, the title is an important part of drawing in your reader when your essay is finished.

Example: Pesky Parking Problems at Our Campus

Title Format

Your title should be centered with no extra spaces (stay in double-space format throughout your essay). Do not use a larger font than the one for the body of your paper. Do not use bolding, underlining, or quotation marks (unless you have a quotation within your title). If you have a title with a subtitle, use a colon between the two parts.

Cross Reference
See Chapter 19 for more on typing format.

> **Example:** Too Many Students, Not Enough Spaces: The Parking Problem at Our Campus

ACTIVITY 4-1 Creating Catchy Titles

Directions: *For each of the following statements of purpose for an essay, come up with a working title that would help draw the interest of your audience.*
Answers will vary.

1. College students easily fall prey to fad diets.

   Working title: _____

2. Traveling to another country is a great way to learn about one's own culture.

   Working title: _____

3. Standardized testing in elementary school causes several problems.

   Working title: _____

INTRODUCTORY PARAGRAPH(S)

The purpose of your introduction is to draw in your reader, establish your topic, and explain the purpose you want to develop—the argument or "take" on the subject you want to communicate. Your introduction establishes the style and tone of your essay and the kind of language and "voice" you will use. To create a successful introduction, include the following elements:

Opening Line(s)/Attention Grabber

The first sentence or two of your essay should intrigue your readers, draw them in, and introduce the subject of your paper. Here are some techniques for accomplishing this goal:

1. **Begin with a rhetorical question:**

   > **Example:** "When was the last time you spent over 20 minutes trying to find on-campus parking?"

▶ **NOTE**   Usually, it is best to avoid second person ("you") point of view in an essay, but opening an essay with a rhetorical question is a widely accepted exception.

2. **Begin with a declaration:**

   Example: "Campus parking has gotten out of hand."

3. **Begin with a definition, a statistic, or a quotation**: Define a key term, present a powerful statistic related to your topic, or use an intriguing quotation to hook your readers.

   Example: "There is one parking spot for every ten students at our campus."

   ▶ **NOTE**   If you use a definition, statistic, or quotation from a source, you must cite it (see Chapter 19 for help).

4. **Begin with a poignant detail or example:**

   Example: "Most students at our campus wait at least 20 minutes for a parking space if they arrive between the hours of 9:00 AM and noon."

   ▶ **NOTE**   If it is a detail you learned through research, you'll have to cite your source.

5. **Begin with a creative scenario or anecdote:**

   Example: "Imagine your first day at a new college. You pull into the main parking lot 15 minutes before your first class is scheduled to begin. However, as soon as you enter, you see at least 20 cars circling the very full lot."

Again, remember to be cautious with using the second-person point of view—"you"—in your essay.

▶ **NOTE**   Avoid using a generalized dramatic statement for your opening line. For instance, "All people feel the need to drive their own cars." You may be wrong, and this statement is too broad. Also, avoid formulaic introductory sentences such as "In today's society" or "Throughout history . . ." or "According to the dictionary. . . ."

General Background on the Topic

Provide some general information about your topic. Begin narrowing down to your focused thesis statement. Sometimes you need to provide background information about the problem or subject for your audience and give a brief history of the issue to give context for the point you want to make. For instance, if you were writing about the parking problem at your campus for an audience from your campus only, you may need just a little background, more of a reminder really, of the parking problem itself. However, if your audience is the general public, with many readers who don't attend your campus, you'd have to give specific details and background history on the growth and severity of the parking issue at your campus.

LO 4 Thesis Statement

A good thesis statement establishes the narrowed scope of your topic, provides at least one controlling idea or analytical purpose it will develop, and gives a basic "map" to let your readers know how you will structure and develop your ideas.

You want to write a thesis statement that explains exactly the purpose for your essay. A thesis statement has a message to convey: It is making a claim. A thesis always involves your opinion, not just facts or details. Your thesis statement is the conclusion you've come to about your topic; therefore, it is what you most want to convey to your readers. *It is what you want them to understand about your topic.*

APPLYING CRITICAL THINKING

Engaging your critical thinking skills will help you develop a **purpose** or **blueprint** for constructing your essay. Your purpose should be clear and consistent from the beginning to the end of your essay. Everything you include should develop that purpose. Knowing what you want to say will help you write a clear, precise thesis statement. Ask yourself these questions to determine your purpose for writing:

1. What is my **point of view**? What do I think or believe about this topic? What do I want to explain or prove to my reader?

2. What **assumptions** or **biases** do I have about the topic? What ideas do I take for granted? Is my point of view based on correct information?

3. Have I **analyzed** the topic so that I understand it?

4. Do I have a clear **point** or **argument** to make about the topic?

Most thesis statements for essays that range from one to four pages in length will be one sentence. Generally a good thesis statement will address the following questions:

1. *What* is the purpose of my essay?
2. *How* will I develop it?
3. *So what* do I want to explain or prove to my readers through this essay?

Asking and answering these questions forces you to create a specific and well developed thesis statement that addresses *what* the purpose of your essay is, *how* the essay will be developed (plan of development or essay map), and *so what*—the main point you want to prove. Here is a thesis statement that includes the answers to the *what*, *how*, and *so what* questions:

> **Example:** [*What?*] "Our campus has a serious parking problem [*How?*] since we have far more students than spots, [*So what?*] so our campus needs to build a second parking lot."

Remember, though, that your thesis statement should not be a question or a series of questions; it should be your *answers* to the questions you want to address on the topic. Also, avoid awkward announcements such as "In this essay, I will attempt to show you that parking is a serious problem at our campus." Instead, jump right to your point: "Parking is a serious problem at our campus." In fact, throughout your essay, delete all statements that begin with *I believe, I feel, I think,* or *I will explain* and weak statements such as "It seems that . . . ," etc. You can use "I" in expository essays, but use it only when you are giving a personal example for support. For instance, "I once drove around the parking lot for over 30 minutes."

Also, your thesis needs to be narrow enough to be developed thoroughly in the essay, but it cannot be too broad to be covered in sufficient detail.

ACTIVITY 4-2 Thesis Practice

Directions: *Create a thesis statement that is neither too broad nor too narrow and that provides an opinion and purpose to pull together the three supporting points listed for each of the following thesis statements.* Answers will vary. Sample answers are provided.

Example:

Thesis: <u>Small-breed dogs share many characteristics with their larger-</u>
<u>breed counterparts.</u>

a. Chihuahuas may be tiny, but they tend to form packs like bigger dogs.

b. Miniature greyhounds are fast, like their larger-version breed.

c. Toy poodles, like the standard poodle, are dogs with strict rules for breeding.

1. **Thesis:** *Different cultures showcase particular spices.*

   a. Mexican food features lots of cumin and fresh cilantro.

   b. Italian dishes often include fresh oregano and basil.

   c. Indian cuisine is rich with coriander, hot chilies, and star anise.

2. **Thesis:** *Sports are great for one's health.*

   a. Tennis provides an excellent source of cardiovascular activity.

   b. Playing basketball gets the heart pumping and the blood flowing.

   c. Skiing burns calories and provides a great workout.

3. **Thesis:** *Anime is now an important part of American culture.*

   a. Japanese anime is a specialized cartoon style that was first popular in Japan.

   b. Now, Americans have become huge anime fans, both watching and creating their own versions.

   c. Anime often features both male and female protagonists who strive to become better individuals.

BODY PARAGRAPHS

The function of body paragraphs is to develop the purpose and arguments set up in your introduction and thesis statement. Each body paragraph has a subtopic or idea derived from the thesis that it develops and supports with examples, details, and analysis. The purpose of the body of your paper is to provide the evidence to back up the arguments in your thesis. The number of sentences in a body paragraph varies, depending on the topic sentence and its scope; on average, most body paragraphs range from 4 to 15 sentences in length. The number of body paragraphs in an essay varies based on the topic, your purpose, your plan for development or essay map, and the

IDEAS

SUPPORT

ANALYSIS

tasks and page requirements of your writing assignment. Be sure that your body paragraphs provide the following:

Cross Reference

See Chapter 6 for more about unity, development, coherence, and transitions.

- **Development:** Elaboration on your purpose, ideas, and analysis
- **Support:** Ample examples and evidence for and analysis of your ideas
- **Unity:** Each sentence helping to support the topic sentence
- **Coherence:** The sentences and ideas flowing smoothly from one to the next with a logical order and appropriate transitions between sentences, if needed, and between body paragraphs

Transitions are words, phrases, or sometimes even complete sentences that help move the reader smoothly from one point to the next. They point the reader in the direction you want to take them. Transitions are necessary both *within* paragraphs and *between* them. When a transitional word, phrase, or sentence is used to connect one paragraph to the next, the transition can come at the end of the previous paragraph or at the beginning of the next, whichever works best for your purpose and organization.

ACTIVITY 4-3   Improving Coherence

Directions: *Read the following list of sentences about starting an on-campus club. Next, arrange the list of sentences into the most logical order, and then create a paragraph with those sentences using transitional words and phrases when needed to help the flow.* Paragraphs will vary, but the order should be logical, usually by time order: The most likely order is 3, 5, 8, 2, 4, 1, 7, 6.

1. Create officer positions with clear job descriptions.
2. Find a faculty advisor.
3. Find out if other students are interested in starting up the club with you.
4. Write a mission statement and/or definition of vision for your club.
5. Create and post fliers to recruit more members.
6. Plan activities for the year.
7. Have an election to choose officers for your club after you have created the descriptions of duties.
8. Find a meeting time that works for all members, and set a regular time.

_____

_____

_____

_____

_____

_____

Topic Sentence

The topic sentence is the **main idea** for each body paragraph. It is like a mini-thesis for that paragraph. Like a thesis statement, a topic sentence should involve an *analytical point* that you want to make, not just a fact or detail. It is the blueprint for that paragraph's purpose. Therefore, the topic sentence provides not only your topic for that paragraph but the opinion, argument, or analytical point you plan to make about that topic.

> **Example:** "To begin with, due to a growth in student enrollment, we have more students than we have parking spaces, and this imbalance has caused many problems."

The part about more students than spots would be just a detail or fact, but as soon as your opinion about this imbalance and its effects are added, you have set up an idea that you will demonstrate throughout the paragraph with support and analysis. Use your critical thinking analysis skills to assess your topic sentence. Is it an idea or opinion and not just a fact or detail?

ACTIVITY 4-4 Topic Sentence Practice

Directions: *Create three topic sentences for each of the thesis statements provided below.* Answers will vary.

Example:

Thesis: Traveling to foreign countries calls for an open mind and sense of adventure.

Topic sentence 1: *To begin with, you may have to learn the basics of another language and be willing to sound silly trying it out.*

Topic sentence 2: *Also, you may be exposed to new and unusual foods as you travel.*

Topic sentence 3: *You may experience differences in customs and behaviors that require an open mind and a good sense of humor.*

1. **Thesis:** Getting along well with one's neighbors requires a conscious effort.

    Topic sentence 1: _____

    _____

    Topic sentence 2: _____

    _____

    Topic sentence 3: _____

    _____

2. **Thesis:** There are several ways one can work on remembering important events.

    Topic sentence 1: _____

    _____

    Topic sentence 2: _____

    _____

    Topic sentence 3: _____

    _____

3. **Thesis:** Limiting the amount of television children watch provides several benefits.

    Topic sentence 1: _____

    _____

    Topic sentence 2: _____

    _____

    Topic sentence 3: _____

    _____

Support for Your Topic Sentence

After you have set up your paragraph's purpose with a topic sentence, you will need to support your topic sentence idea. Engage your critical thinking skills to choose the best supporting ideas and examples for your purpose. You can support your topic idea with the following:

1. **Examples:** Give two to four specific examples to support your topic sentence.

> **Example:** Over the past 40 years, since the existing parking structures were first built, our campus enrollment has nearly doubled.

2. **Details:** Give a concrete detail or two to support each of your examples.

> **Example:** According to our campus's *New Student Handbook*, we have over 10,000 students; however, we have only 5,000 parking spaces.

3. **Analysis:** After you have given examples and details to support your topic sentence, be sure to *interpret the significance* of your examples and details with an analytical statement. Don't assume that the facts will speak for themselves: Most readers need and want commentary from you that explains the significance of the details and examples you've provided and their relevance to your argument.

> **Example:** When we look at the numbers, we can see that the growth of our campus has created the current parking crisis: We simply have not kept up with the pace of population growth.

Concluding Sentence

The concluding sentence sums up the purpose and main idea of a body paragraph. It pulls all your ideas and purpose together in a finished product. It may also include a transition to your next body paragraph, although usually the transition appears at the beginning of the next paragraph.

> **Example:** As you can see, the current parking situation has gotten out of hand at our campus.

Sometimes the concluding sentence in a body paragraph is a way to move to the next idea you want to develop: a sentence doing double duty as a close for one paragraph and idea and an introduction to the next example, idea, or concept you want to discuss.

Providing Support in the Best Way

Be sure to engage your critical thinking analysis skills as you provide meaningful support for your ideas.

Cross Reference
See Chapter 20 for more
on the ice cream sandwich.

Creating an Analytical Ice Cream Sandwich

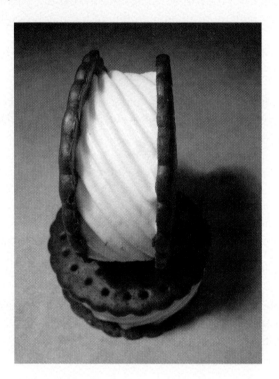

An ice cream sandwich has two chocolate cookies that surround an ice cream filling. Think of the facts, examples, or details you include in your paragraphs as the ice cream filling. You need to surround that filling with two cookies to hold it together. The top cookie is your topic sentence, which sets up the point you want to make in the paragraph, and the bottom cookie is your concluding sentence, which frames your examples with interpretation and analysis.

The Analytical Ice Cream Sandwich

Top cookie: Topic sentence (controlling idea of paragraph)

Ice cream filling: Facts, examples, or details (support to develop the topic sentence)

Bottom cookie: Concluding sentence (interpretation and analysis of the examples and details and how they support the topic sentence)

Ice Cream Sandwich Example:

Top cookie: The parking problem has gotten worse due to the growth of student population.

Ice cream filling: Over the last five years, the student population has grown by over 3,000 students.

Bottom cookie: This large increase has put an unmanageable burden on existing parking lots and parking staff.

ACTIVITY 4-5 Ice Cream Sandwich Practice

Directions: *Choose one of the topic sentences you created in Activity 4-4 and create a full ice cream sandwich to support that topic sentence.* *Answers will vary.*

Top cookie: _____

_____

Ice cream filling (example/detail): _____

_____

Bottom cookie (concluding sentence—interpretation and analysis): _____

_____

_____

Concluding Paragraph

The concluding paragraph sums up the main purpose of your essay, re-emphasizing your thesis (without repeating it word for word) and providing an overall sense of conclusion. Most successful concluding paragraphs are at least three sentences long, but they can be several sentences longer than that, depending on the scope of the thesis and assignment. Regardless, they should be succinct and end with a "Ta Da!"—an overall sense of wrapping up with a bang and reiterating your essay's purpose.

▶ **NOTE** Be sure to avoid the common pitfall of introducing a new idea or contradicting yourself in the conclusion: the "shoot yourself in the foot" effect.

Example: As you can see, the parking problem at our campus is bad, but the lack of class offerings at night is an even worse problem.

Ouch! You just shot yourself in the foot and belittled the importance of the topic you chose and developed throughout your essay by introducing a whole new topic out of the blue.

PUTTING IT ALL TOGETHER

Once you are familiar with all the building blocks of an essay, you can put them together in the best possible way to develop your purpose and engage your audience. After you have written a complete draft of an essay, use the following checklist to make sure you have included all the necessary building blocks:

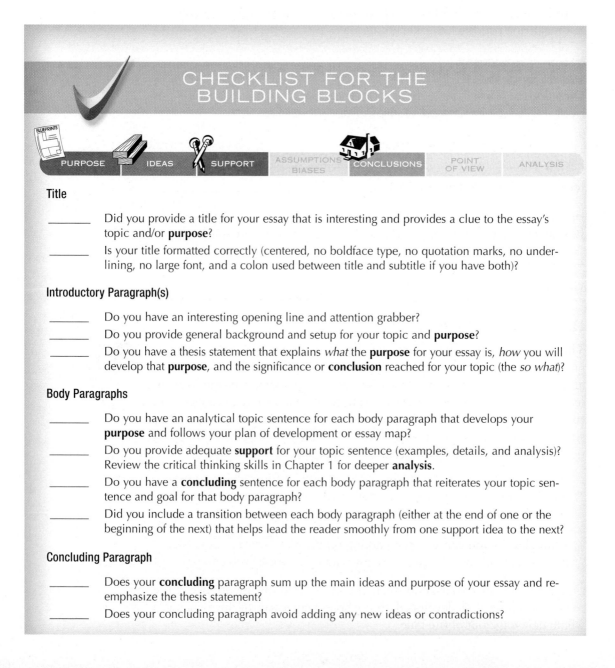

CHECKLIST FOR THE BUILDING BLOCKS

PURPOSE   IDEAS   SUPPORT   ASSUMPTIONS BIASES   CONCLUSIONS   POINT OF VIEW   ANALYSIS

Title

_____   Did you provide a title for your essay that is interesting and provides a clue to the essay's topic and/or **purpose**?

_____   Is your title formatted correctly (centered, no boldface type, no quotation marks, no underlining, no large font, and a colon used between title and subtitle if you have both)?

Introductory Paragraph(s)

_____   Do you have an interesting opening line and attention grabber?

_____   Do you provide general background and setup for your topic and **purpose**?

_____   Do you have a thesis statement that explains *what* the **purpose** for your essay is, *how* you will develop that **purpose**, and the significance or **conclusion** reached for your topic (the *so what*)?

Body Paragraphs

_____   Do you have an analytical topic sentence for each body paragraph that develops your **purpose** and follows your plan of development or essay map?

_____   Do you provide adequate **support** for your topic sentence (examples, details, and analysis)? Review the critical thinking skills in Chapter 1 for deeper **analysis**.

_____   Do you have a **concluding** sentence for each body paragraph that reiterates your topic sentence and goal for that body paragraph?

_____   Did you include a transition between each body paragraph (either at the end of one or the beginning of the next) that helps lead the reader smoothly from one support idea to the next?

Concluding Paragraph

_____   Does your **concluding** paragraph sum up the main ideas and purpose of your essay and re-emphasize the thesis statement?

_____   Does your concluding paragraph avoid adding any new ideas or contradictions?

Now that you know the basic parts, or building blocks, for an expository essay, Chapter 5 will guide you through the process for generating a polished essay, from ideas to final product. For specific types of essays or approaches, see Chapters 7–15.

To check your progress in meeting this chapter's objectives, log in to www .mywritinglab.com, go to the **Study Plan** tab, click on **Writing Expository Paragraphs and Essays** and choose **Recognizing the Essay, Essay Introductions, Conclusions, and Titles** and **Thesis Statement** from the list of subtopics. Read and view the resources in the **Review Materials** section, and then complete the **Recall**, **Apply**, and **Write** sets in the **Activities** section.

5 Essays: Process

Atlantic City, NJ, Boardwalk

LEARNING OBJECTIVES

In this chapter, you will learn to

LO 1 Plan and write essays.

LO 2 Narrow a subject, find your purpose, and determine your audience.

LO 3 Use the 10-step guide for writing essays.

LO 4 Practice writing essays through a model.

LO 5 Use self- and peer assessment for essays.

THINKING CRITICALLY

Look at the picture. Then answer the questions that follow.

1. What habits do you already have when you sit down to do any kind of writing?

_____

_____

2. Of those habits, which are most effective for you and why and which are not and why?

_____

_____

Writing a focused essay involves a journey from planning to final revision and polishing.

LO 1 PLANNING AND WRITING EXPOSITORY ESSAYS

Writing an expository essay involves a process in which you engage your critical thinking skills and develop your ideas in stages. Basically, the writing process includes five major stages:

1. **Prewriting:**   Generate ideas and your paper's purpose.

2. **Organizing:**   Develop a plan for presenting your purpose and ideas.

3. **Drafting:**   Create a first draft of your essay based on your plan and the pattern(s) of organization you have chosen; develop support for your essay's purpose.

4. **Revising:**   Reassess the draft for content, development, organization, and support (examples and details).

5. **Editing:**   Check for sentence-level effectiveness, style, diction, grammar, and spelling errors.

This process will be broken down in detail later in this chapter. To begin, though, you must figure out your assignment and decide on your subject, purpose, and audience. From these three elements, you will develop a more specific topic, thesis, plan for development, and appropriate tone and style for your essay. Remember that you can change the order of these steps—this process is a tool—and decide what works best for you in each writing task.

Most writers figure out what writing process works best for them and which steps of the writing process they can switch, modify, or even skip completely. You may modify the process differently from assignment to assignment; however, until you have developed a writing process that works for you and produces fully developed, well-organized, well-written essays, try this traditional approach to the stages of the writing process. The key is to analyze what works and be actively involved in the process of thinking critically about your ideas and how best to develop them in your essay.

LO 2 SUBJECT, PURPOSE, AND AUDIENCE

Once you have determined the *subject* you will write about (based on an assignment or your own subject choice), you must narrow your subject to a manageable topic, come up with a *purpose* for writing about it, and adjust your approach and overall tone to suit your intended *audience*.

Use the flow chart on page 76 to help you move from *subject*, *purpose*, and *audience* to *topic*, *thesis*, and *tone* and *approach*.

Subject, Purpose, and Audience

Subject

A broad subject that you chose or is assigned to you.

For example: "Music"

Purpose

What do you want to *explain* or *prove* about your topic?

What point do you want to make? What is your opinion on the topic? What will you argue?

Audience

Who is your target audience? Instructor? Classmates? Other?

Modify your approach (tone, style, ideas, and support) so it is appropriate to the target audience.

▼   ▼   ▼

Topic

A narrowed aspect of your subject, e.g., "Lipsyncing at Concerts"

Thesis

What is your point?

How will you develop it?

So what? What is the significance of your conclusion or argument?

Tone/approach

Modify your tone and your approach based on your audience.

Narrowing Subject to a Topic

Use your critical thinking tools to figure out a good topic that is narrow enough for the scope of your essay's purpose. Before you can write well on a subject, you need to narrow your topic to a sufficiently specific focus that you can develop well in a short essay. For instance, if you begin with a broad subject such as "parks in our city," then you need to figure out what aspects of parks (size, location, amenities) or what kind of parks (theme parks, recreational parks, green zones) you want to focus on before you come up with exactly what you want to say (purpose).

If you have a subject assigned to you, or if you come up with a subject out of an interest of your own, you need to narrow the focus of your essay's scope and purpose before you begin writing. If your subject is too broad (the scope is too big), you won't be able to cover the nuances of the topic in depth, and your essay will stay too general and gloss the surface instead of delving deeper into the topic. For instance, the topic "baseball" is too broad: Can you imagine trying to cover everything about this game in one essay? You could narrow this broad topic down to the idea of free agents in baseball. If your topic is *too narrow*, it will not be a big enough issue or question to address in your essay, so make sure your proposed topic is not a detail or fact that doesn't need development. For instance, if your topic was "the baseball is a specific kind of ball used in the game," it would be very hard to come up with enough description and information for a full essay.

APPLYING CRITICAL THINKING

| PURPOSE | IDEAS | SUPPORT | ASSUMPTIONS BIASES | CONCLUSIONS | POINT OF VIEW | ANALYSIS |

Ways to Narrow a Broad Subject to a Manageable Topic

Here are a few techniques that can help you move from a broad subject to a narrowed topic. They include brainstorming, which is a way to get your ideas flowing, and asking questions that help you **analyze** the subject—break it down into its different parts. The more you think about a broad subject and analyze what it is about, the better able you will be to narrow it down to a workable topic.

The subject of *volunteering* is used here to demonstrate how you can narrow a subject to a topic that would work well for a focused expository essay.

Broad Subject: Volunteering

1. Brainstorm a list of issues related to, ideas about, or types of volunteering.

   Volunteering: community service, Girl Scouts, tutoring, cleanup in neighborhood, school aide, hospitals, nursing homes, types of volunteering, benefits of volunteering

2. Ask yourself why you thought of this topic in the first place—why is it interesting or important to you?

   School aides: I am sad and surprised that local schoolteachers are not getting the support they need to help our children learn.

3. Generate a question or several questions related to the topic you chose.

   How can I get teachers at my son's school the help they need to provide successful classroom experiences? How can I get more people in our community to volunteer their time for our schools?

4. Start with a problem related to the topic.

   My son's third-grade class has not been able to go on field trips or have arts and crafts time because there is only one teacher and 30 students.

Continued ▶

5. Start with a point or purpose in mind.

I want to convince the other parents from my PTA that we need parents to get involved in the classrooms and take a more active role in helping our teachers.

ACTIVITY 5-1   Narrowing Your Topic

Directions: *The following subjects are too broad to develop into successful thesis statements. Use one or more of the techniques given to create two more focused subtopics for each broad topic listed.*   Answers will vary.

Example:

Topic: Television

Subtopic 1:   *The unrealistic side of reality TV*

Subtopic 2:   *Television as an addiction*

1. **Topic:** Sports

    Subtopic 1: _____

    Subtopic 2: _____

2. **Topic:** Movies

    Subtopic 1: _____

    Subtopic 2: _____

3. **Topic:** Transportation

    Subtopic 1: _____

    Subtopic 2: _____

4. **Topic:** Music

    Subtopic 1: _____

    Subtopic 2: _____

5. **Topic:** Pets

    Subtopic 1: _____

    Subtopic 2: _____

6. **Topic:** Education

   Subtopic 1: _____

   Subtopic 2: _____

7. **Topic:** Travel

   Subtopic 1: _____

   Subtopic 2: _____

8. **Topic:** Nutrition

   Subtopic 1: _____

   Subtopic 2: _____

9. **Topic:** Politics

   Subtopic 1: _____

   Subtopic 2: _____

10. **Topic:** Cities

    Subtopic 1: _____

    Subtopic 2: _____

Purpose and Approach

Sometimes, just narrowing your topic using one of the techniques listed in the Critical Thinking box will lead you to your essay's purpose, and you'll be able to create a thesis statement effortlessly. Otherwise, once you have narrowed your subject to a manageable topic, the next step is to come up with your essay's purpose (what you want to explain to your readers about your topic) and how you will approach it. In order to do this, ask yourself the following questions:

Cross Reference
Review pp. 63–64 of Chapter 4 on creating a good thesis statement.

1. What is my *purpose* or *goal* for writing an essay on this topic?
2. What *questions* do I want to address in the essay?
3. Is there a *problem* (or problems) I want to solve in the essay? If so, what is it?
4. What *evidence* (support) can I use to back up my ideas and purpose (e.g., personal experience, facts, outside evidence or research)?
5. What point of view (perspective) do I have about the topic, and what assumptions or biases do I have about it?

ACTIVITY 5-2   Identifying Your Purpose and Approach to a Topic

Directions: *Choose one of the narrowed topics you came up with in Activity 5-1. Answer the following questions to go deeper and develop a sense of what your purpose would be for writing about the topic and how you would approach it. (Refer to Chapter 1, if necessary, for a review of the critical thinking process.)*
Answers will vary.

1. Based on the narrowed idea you chose from Activity 5-1, what would be your purpose or goal if you wrote an essay on this topic?

    _____

    _____

    _____

2. What *questions* would you attempt to address in the essay?

    _____

    _____

    _____

3. Is there a *problem* (or problems) you'd attempt to solve or address in the essay? If so, what are they?

    _____

    _____

    _____

4. What *evidence* (support) could you use to back your ideas and purpose (e.g., personal experience, facts, outside evidence, or research)?

    _____

    _____

    _____

5. What point of view (perspective) would you be coming from in the essay, and what assumptions or biases do you already have related to the subject?

    _____

    _____

    _____

Once you have thought about your purpose and approach for an essay on your chosen topic, come up with support that will illustrate and explain your purpose. Can you provide any personal examples that would help illustrate your ideas? Are there examples from your community or your knowledge of culture that would support your ideas? Should you provide some data and facts to support your ideas? (Be sure to check with your instructor before conducting and using research.)

Review your answer to question 4 above, then complete the next activity.

Cross Reference
Review Chapter 4 for more information about including support in your essay.

ACTIVITY 5-3 Developing Support for Your Topic

Directions: *Using the same narrowed topic you chose for Activity 5-2, provide some examples you could use for support.* *Answers will vary.*

1. Example 1: _____

_____

2. Example 2: _____

_____

3. Example 3: _____

_____

Assessing Your Audience

Another aspect you should consider before writing your first draft is the audience for your essay:

Who are you writing it for?

What do you want them to understand?

Once you have identified your audience, you can make choices about the best approach to take and how much background information or explanation to include about your topic. For instance, if you are writing about ceramics for a general audience, you would have to add more definitions and in-depth explanations. If your audience is academic, your tone and vocabulary should be more formal. An academic audience would also expect supporting evidence, definitions, and examples to back your arguments. If your audience is specialized—for example, if you were writing an essay about ceramics for other artists who work in the field—your tone would be semi-formal and your vocabulary could get specialized. If you are writing an essay for another group of students on a whimsical or humorous topic, then your tone and vocabulary can be more informal.

Cross Reference
See Chapter 30 for help in choosing the right tone and style to match your audience.

Types of Audience

General—all types of people

Academic—college students and faculty

Specialized—specific to a certain field or background, such as nursing
students or the instructor for a content class you are taking

Ask yourself what the target audience for your essay is. Then use the
answer to assess how much background information on the topic you will
have to provide, what level of vocabulary you will use (and how much you'll
need to define specialized terms), what approach and tone (more serious/
formal, casual/playful, or somewhere in between) would work best, and how
much evidence you'll need to provide to persuade your readers.

ACTIVITY 5-4   Adjusting Your Approach
for an Intended Audience

Topic: *Increasing violence on college campuses*
  Audience 1: Other college students
  Audience 2: Parents of college students
  Audience 3: State legislators

Directions: *How would you need to adjust your tone, approach, inclusion of
background information, and even purpose for these three different audiences? Be
sure to look at Chapter 30 for more detailed information about style and tone if
you need help with this exercise.* Answers will vary.

_____

_____

_____

_____

_____

After you have determined the target audience for your essay, choose an
appropriate tone, and choose sentence structures and vocabulary that match it.

ACTIVITY 5-5   Finding the Right Tone

Directions: *For each of the topics given, determine a suitable audience. Then
explain the type of tone you would use (formal or informal), and briefly explain
why.* Answers will vary.

Example:

Topic: Lack of hospitals in our state

Potential target audience: _The state legislature (senators)_____

Best tone choice: _Formal, because I would be making a formal proposal_

_to lawmakers and need to be taken seriously_____

1. **Topic:** The need for a new stop sign in our neighborhood

   Potential target audience: _____

   Best tone choice and reason: _____

   _____

2. **Topic:** How to treat an infection

   Potential target audience: _____

   Best tone choice and reason: _____

   _____

3. **Topic:** Tips for downloading songs onto an iPod

   Potential target audience: _____

   Best tone choice and reason: _____

   _____

4. **Topic:** The need to expand the campus bookstore's hours of operation

   Potential target audience: _____

   Best tone choice and reason: _____

   _____

5. **Topic:** The best dog-friendly parks in our city

   Potential target audience: _____

   Best tone choice and reason: _____

   _____

Once you have a topic, know your purpose, have identified your audience, and know what you want to say about your topic, you are ready to craft your statement of purpose—your **thesis**. A thesis statement should be a

Cross Reference
See Chapter 4,
pp. 63–64, for how to
write a strong thesis.

complete sentence that narrows the topic and provides your opinion about that topic. It is what you want to explain or prove about your topic: the argument you put forth. Make sure your thesis statement is broad enough that it can be developed but not so broad that it can't be developed well in a short essay.

ACTIVITY 5-6   Writing Your Thesis Statement

Directions: *Choose two of the topics from Activity 5-5 for which you assessed an audience, and write a one-sentence thesis statement in a tone that is appropriate for that audience.* *Answers will vary.*

1.   Thesis: _____

_____

_____

2.   Thesis: _____

_____

_____

You are now ready to start the process of writing an essay, going from prewriting to a final, polished paper. Here is a 10-step guide to the writing process. Some writers use every step, some use some of the steps, and some change the order of the steps. Try out the process, and figure out what works best for you. Be sure to use your critical thinking skills throughout the process to make the best choices about your subject, your purpose for writing about it, and the audience you want to reach.

LO 3   A 10-STEP GUIDE FOR WRITING AN EXPOSITORY ESSAY

These steps are designed to break the writing process down into manageable stages. Feel free to change the order and continually test what works best for you and your individual learning style. Sometimes your needs change depending on an individual assignment. Remember, all formulas and step-by-step processes are tools designed to help you achieve the standards required for expository essays. Don't let the tools control you: Use them, customize them, or abandon them if you need to for your own needs and purpose.

APPLYING CRITICAL THINKING

| PURPOSE | IDEAS | SUPPORT | ASSUMPTIONS BIASES | CONCLUSIONS | POINT OF VIEW | ANALYSIS |

Your critical thinking skills should be engaged in all stages of the writing process. As you go through these 10 steps, be sure to keep in mind your **purpose**, the information (**ideas**, **support**) you will need to develop that purpose, the implications of your ideas and arguments, the **assumptions** you make, the **point of view** you are expressing, and the audience you are writing for.

Let's say you choose to write an essay on the topic of adopting versus buying a pet: You could use the following steps to develop your ideas, outline an organizational plan, identify your audience, and clarify your purpose for writing the essay.

GENERATE IDEAS AND PREWRITE

Step One: Generate Ideas

You can use several techniques to generate ideas, narrow your topic, determine your purpose, and organize your ideas. The techniques include thinking about your topic, freewriting, mapping, brainstorming, clustering, and journaling. Everyone's writing process develops individually; try these techniques, and figure out which ones work best for you. Some people prefer to do their prewriting on paper using a pen or pencil, and some prefer to use their computer to type brainstorm lists or rough outlines. Others like to use the columns function in their word processing program to create categories and brainstorm directly below the separate categories. Discover what works for you. You may want to change the order or skip some steps, which is fine: These are tools, and you are the essay's carpenter.

Thinking and Talking

As soon as you get your assignment or choose your topic, begin thinking about it. Some prewriting happens in your head before you even put pen to paper. Talk it out with a classmate or friend if you can. Ask yourself, "What do I want to accomplish in this paper?" "What do I have to say about this subject?" "What aspect of this subject am I most interested in, and how do I want to narrow it down to a manageable topic?" "What are some questions or issues I can address related to this subject?"

Freewriting

Freewriting is a popular technique for generating ideas and narrowing your topic. When you **freewrite,** you just put pen to paper and let the ideas flow out of you without worrying about spelling, grammar, or "dumb" ideas. When you freewrite, turn off your inner editor, and just let the ideas flow out of you. Later you can sort out the good and the bad stuff.

> **Example:** I know I want to write about adopting an unwanted pet instead of buying one at the pet store . . . let me see . . . I have lots of reasons why I feel this way . . . hmmm some of them include all the unwanted animals that get put down or go without companionship, oh yeah, also, the money for adopting pets goes into spaying and neutering cats and dogs so there are not even more unwanted pets created

Mapping

Mapping is a way to literally map out your essay plan and how you will structure your essay. You can map using boxes and arrows, a flow chart, or whatever works best for your style.

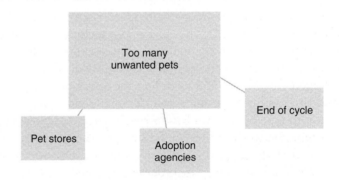

▶ **TIP** Computer software designed for generating ideas and mapping is available on most college campuses.

Brainstorming

Brainstorming is a free-flowing, free-association list of words or ideas that you crank out on paper to get the ideas flowing. As in freewriting, you need to turn off your inner editor and just storm your brain for as many ideas and details or even associations as you can related to your subject or assigned writing prompt.

Example: Unwanted pets, pets for profits, unspayed or neutered pets, animals put to sleep, dogs, cats, rabbits, hamsters, rats, mice, ferrets, adoption agencies, pet stores, choosing to get pets from rescue centers over pet stores, ending the cycle

Clustering

Clustering is another way to represent your ideas visually. You can circle your main subject and then draw lines and add further clusters or circles around connected ideas or subtopics that you generate.

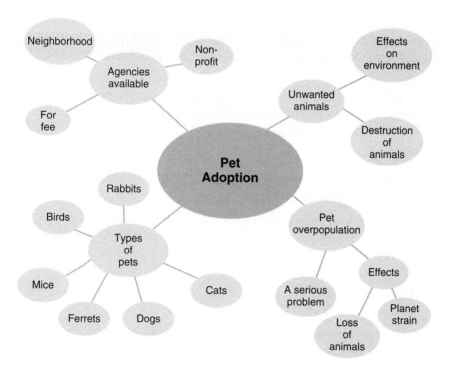

Journaling

Journaling involves writing your thoughts down in a journal. Some instructors will require you to keep a writer's journal for jotting down ideas and recording the steps in your writing process. Or you can start a journal on your own to write ideas as they come to you—that way, your thoughts can be collected in one place as they come to you in bits and pieces over the course of a few days.

ACTIVITY 5-7   Generating Ideas

Directions: *On a separate sheet of paper, practice using the prewriting tech-niques described to generate some ideas and subtopics for the topics provided.*
Answers will vary.

1. Tips for new college students
2. Finding information for your courses (research)
3. Shopping for food
4. Clothes and personalities
5. Modes of transportation

Step Two: Organize Your Ideas

Now take the ideas you've generated in the prewriting stage and come up with a way to organize and develop them. You need to create a basic plan for your essay, and generate examples and details to support your topic. Here is what to do to create that plan:

1. **Think about your purpose.** Ask yourself, "What do I want to explain or prove with this essay about my topic?"
2. **Create questions about the topic.** After you have generated more ideas by prewriting on your subject, use them to come up with some questions that you could address or answer in your essay related to the topic.
3. **Delete ideas.** Delete any ideas or subtopics you generated that don't fit your topic or seem off base or tangential.
4. **Add ideas.** As you review your prewriting, add new ideas or subtopics that didn't occur to you before.
5. **Re-brainstorm.** Brainstorm more ideas, now that your focus is more manageable.
6. **Re-freewrite.** Freewrite again now that your ideas are more focused.

Now you are ready to create a rough outline of your ideas and subtopics to see how they could be put together in a first draft. Here is an example of a rough outline that is based on the previous prewriting about the advantages and disadvantages of getting a pet from a pet store or a shelter:

Example Rough Outline

Topic: Adopting pets versus buying in a pet store

I. Disadvantages of pet stores
   A. For profit—therefore do not always have the best interests of pets in mind
   B. Encourage the creation of more pets for profit
   C. Favor pedigreed breeds over mixed-breed pets
II. Advantages of adoption
   A. Spaying and neutering are guaranteed
   B. Saves the lives of unwanted animals
   C. Discourages creating pets for profit
   D. Helps stop the cycle of unwanted pets

▶ **NOTE**   Your campus may have software available for help in creating outlines.

Cross Reference
See Chapter 6 for detailed explanation of outline format.

ACTIVITY 5-8   Creating a Rough Outline

Directions: *Choose one of the topics you did prewriting for in the earlier activities, and generate a working thesis. Then on a separate sheet of paper, write a rough outline for an essay based on your thesis using the numbered list above.*
Answers will vary.

_____

_____

Step Three: Establish Your Topic, Purpose, and Audience

Now you need to determine the purpose for your topic, the audience you are writing for, and how you want to approach it. (Refer to pp. 79 and 81, if necessary, where these concepts are explored more fully.) Remember these elements:

1. **Narrow your topic:** Use the strategies on pages 76–78 to narrow your subject into a focused, manageable topic.

2. **Purpose:** Be clear about what you want to explain, show, or prove in your essay.

3. **Audience:** Think about your target audience. What approach and tone should you use to best address it?

ACTIVITY 5-9   Topic, Purpose, and Audience

Directions: *Using the rough outline you created in Activity 5-8, answer the following questions.* Answers will vary.

1. What is your *narrowed topic*—the specific question or idea you will be addressing?

   _____

   _____

2. What is your *purpose* for writing this essay? What do you intend to explain or prove to your audience?

   _____

   _____

3. Who is your intended *audience?*

   _____

   _____

WRITE A FIRST DRAFT

Step Four: Start Your First Draft

Just dive in. Although this step is often the one where many students begin in their writing process, you shouldn't write an actual draft until you have accomplished the three steps above. Otherwise, you run the danger of wasting a lot of time and effort figuring out your purpose or rambling through the first page (or even longer) of your essay. Also, while writing your first full draft, don't worry about spelling and grammar: You will only lose your train of thought and become derailed from the points you are making. Instead, check grammar and spelling later in the editing stage.

ACTIVITY 5-10 Write a First Draft

Directions: *Use the ideas you generated from prewriting, your rough outline, and your answers to Activity 5-9 to write a rough draft of your essay (1½ to 2 pages), and give it a working title.*

REVISE

Step Five: Reorganize for Order, Unity, Coherence, and Sentence Variety

Revision is the most crucial stage of the writing process, yet the one that students try to skip more than any other. Few writers are such naturals that they crank out perfect essays and sentences in a first draft. Most writers need several drafts to accomplish a well-designed, well-written, and well-supported essay. Many students mistakenly confuse the term "revision" with "edit" or "proofread." Revision focuses on organization, style, and content, while proofreading and editing, which will be explained in the next stage, focus on fixing grammar and spelling errors.

Engage your critical thinking tools as you revise: Essay writing is recursive (a process of going back and reworking what you have written): Revision is the key to excellence in content and delivery. During revision, check the order of your paragraphs and the details within them; move things that need to be moved, and delete things that don't belong. Make sure your paragraphs have enough support from examples and details to develop their topic sentences. Check that each paragraph develops the thesis of your paper and each sentence in each paragraph develops the topic sentence. If it doesn't, get it out of there. Ensure your essay flows smoothly by adding appropriate transitional words or phrases where needed, and check to make sure that you have varied your sentence lengths and sentence types.

Cross Reference
See Chapter 6 for more information on order, coherence, unity, and sentence variety.

Use the following checklist to make sure you revise all the elements of your essay:

Revision Checklist

1. Restructure paragraph order, if needed.
2. Delete unnecessary words, sentences, ideas, or details.
3. Add more support (examples and details) to fully develop your topic sentences.

4. Add transitions between paragraphs and between sentences where needed (see Transitions and Coherence, Chapter 6).

5. Check for sentence variety (see Chapter 24).

ACTIVITY 5-11   Revision

Directions: *On a separate sheet of paper, revise your essay draft using the Revision Checklist in Step Five.*

Step Six: Fine-Tune Thesis and Topic Sentences

Make sure that your thesis statement is analytical, with a clear opinion or argument that you want to explain or prove. Check to make sure that your topic sentences are also ideas and not just facts or details, and make sure that they support and develop your thesis statement.

Step Seven: Provide Support—Add More Examples, Details, and Analysis

Be sure that each body paragraph has at least two statements of support for the idea set out in the topic sentence. Include examples to illustrate your point, as well as corresponding details and analysis of the examples and details in relation to your essay's purpose.

ACTIVITY 5-12   Providing Supporting Examples

Directions: *Come up with at least one new example to provide support for each of the topic sentences in your essay draft. Answers will vary.*

Supporting example for topic sentence 1: _____

_____

Supporting example for topic sentence 2: _____

_____

Supporting example for topic sentence 3: _____

_____

Supporting example for topic sentence 4: _____

_____

ACTIVITY 5-13   Supporting Details

Directions: *Come up with two supporting details or facts to further define, illustrate, or explain the examples you created in Activity 5-12.* *Answers will vary.*

1. Detail 1: _____

    Detail 2: _____

2. Detail 1: _____

    Detail 2: _____

3. Detail 1: _____

    Detail 2: _____

4. Detail 1: _____

    Detail 2: _____

ACTIVITY 5-14   Creating Ice Cream Sandwiches for Your Examples

Cross Reference
See Chapter 4, pp. 70–71, for more about ice cream sandwiches.

Directions: *Choose a topic sentence from your essay draft, and use it to create a full ice cream sandwich.* *Answers will vary.*

Top cookie: Your original topic sentence. _____

_____

Ice cream filling: Provide at least one supporting example and one detail to illustrate that detail.

Example(s): _____

_____

Supporting detail(s): _____

_____

Bottom cookie: Provide a sentence that interprets the importance of the examples and details and what they illustrate.

_____

_____

PROOFREAD AND EDIT

After you have revised for style and content, you need to proofread your essay for grammar and spelling errors. Turn on your inner editor at this stage of the writing process. Many students fall into the procrastination trap and run out of time to proofread and edit their drafts. It is important to turn in professional quality work; don't let minor errors and typos sabotage the thought behind your ideas, arguments, and support. It helps if you can put your final essay draft aside for a day before you complete this stage; that way you can spot those simple errors and typos that are invisible to your brain in the first few hours after you finish your paper (because you just wrote the sentences and know what they are *supposed* to say). Also, be sure to have your textbook and a dictionary handy as you go through your essay. Remember this rule of thumb as you proofread: When in doubt, look it up.

Step Eight: Check Spelling

Cross Reference
See Chapter 29 for commonly confused words.

Use a dictionary or spell-check to check the spelling of any words you are unsure about, and also check for words that you might have used incorrectly.

ACTIVITY 5-15   Check Spelling

Directions: *Check the Commonly Confused Words list on pages 620–634 to see if you have committed any of these common mistakes in word choice. Then, use a dictionary or spell-check to doublecheck your spelling—when in doubt, look it up.*

Step Nine: Check Word Usage, Word Choices, Tone, and Style

Cross Reference
See Chapter 30 for help in all of these categories.

Use a thesaurus to find synonyms (words that mean the same thing) to avoid overusing particular words. Check for slang, biased language, clichés, and inappropriate tone or changes in tone.

ACTIVITY 5-16 Check Usage and Tone

Directions: *Go through your essay draft, and make sure you have used a consistent and appropriate tone throughout. Also, check word choices, and revise any inappropriate dialect, slang, or clichés.*

Step Ten: Check for Sentence-Level Errors

1. Check especially for fragments, run-ons, and comma splices (see Chapter 25).
2. Check for incorrect comma use, point of view shifts, pronoun agreement, subject–verb agreement, pronoun reference fault errors, semicolon and colon use, apostrophe use, faulty parallelism, dangling or misplaced modifiers, and unnecessary passive voice constructions (these common errors are covered in the handbook section of this text).

ACTIVITY 5-17 Grammar Review and Final Revision

Directions: *Go through your essay, and check for the common sentence-level grammar errors summarized in Step Ten. Correct any errors you find. Then use the following Revision Checklist to evaluate the basic elements of your essay:*

REVISION CHECKLIST

_____ Check for a clear and interesting title in correct format.
_____ Check for an interesting introductory paragraph that sets up your purpose and leads into your thesis.
_____ Check for purpose and a clear thesis statement.
_____ Check that you have used appropriate vocabulary, tone, and approach for your target audience.
_____ Check to make sure that you have organized your paper logically, with clear topic sentences in the body paragraphs and transitions.
_____ Check to make sure you have maintained unity—all sentences and paragraphs help develop your purpose and thesis.
_____ Check to make sure you have included enough support in your essay to develop your purpose. Do you need more examples and details?
_____ Check to make sure that your sentence structure and your vocabulary choices are varied and interesting.

Continued ▶

_____ Check for a strong concluding paragraph that sums up the analytical conclusion (purpose) established in your thesis.

_____ Check for complete sentences (eliminate fragments, run-ons, or comma splices).

_____ Check for correct punctuation throughout the paper (commas, semicolons, colons, other punctuation marks).

_____ Check for mechanics (spelling, capitalization, underlining, italics, abbreviations, numbering) using the grammar section of this text and a dictionary.

LO 4 A SAMPLE ESSAY: MODELING THE PROCESS

It helps sometimes to see another student go through a draft and revise an essay in stages. As the student goes through various drafts of her paper on the following pages, look at the annotated changes in the drafts.

Step One: Prewriting

Student: I've been assigned to write something about the city I live in. Hmmm. I live in Seattle; there's so much to say about it. Maybe I'll begin with a brainstorm list to narrow my topic. I'll remember to let everything just flow here and list everything that comes to mind without any judgment or editing at this point.

Let's see . . .

Topic: Seattle

I'll just brainstorm a list of what comes to mind on this topic:

Rain, trees, Space Needle, Mt. Rainier, ferries, coffee, music, grunge, restaurants, people, diversity, fish, the aquarium, the Waterfront, downtown, Woodland Park Zoo, University of Washington, community colleges, rhododendrons, parks, beaches, Alki, Golden Gardens, flannel, tourists . . .

OK, OK, I'll stop here. I already have plenty of topic ideas.

I'll pick Seattle's downtown Waterfront as my narrowed topic, and next, I'll do a cluster to generate ideas for an essay on this topic:

Narrowed Topic: Seattle's downtown Waterfront

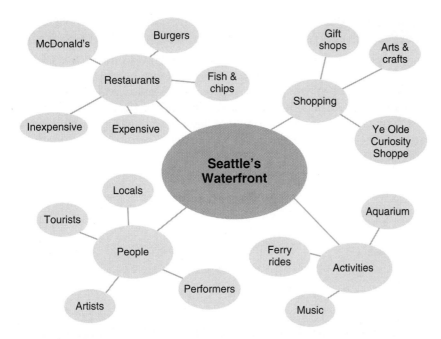

Step Two: Organizing

OK, next, I'll develop the categories/subtopics I've developed in the cluster above.

First, I'll create a rough outline for my paper based on my cluster.

Seattle's Waterfront

   I. Restaurants
      A. Casual/affordable
      B. Fancy/pricey

   II. Shopping
      A. Cheap or tourist-based
      B. Expensive/exclusive/specialized

   III. Activities
      A. Entertainment
      B. Activities/attractions

   IV. People
      A. Tourists
      B. Locals
      C. Street performers

▶ **NOTE** Here the student could go back and brainstorm again for each subcategory to develop additional examples and ideas. Check your campus for helpful software available for creating outlines in correct formats.

Cross Reference

See Chapter 6 for outline format and outline critique form.

Step Three: Drafting

OK, let me see, my *audience* is my classmates and my instructor. My *subject* is narrowed to the *topic* of Seattle's downtown Waterfront. What is my *purpose*? What do I want to explain, show, or prove about Seattle's Waterfront?

Looking at my categories and my rough outline, I can see that I will be focusing on what to do and see on the Waterfront. So maybe my working thesis or statement of purpose will be something like: *There are many things to do on Seattle's Waterfront.*

OK, here goes my first draft . . .

Seattle's Waterfront

There are so many things to do in the Seattle area. One of my favorite places to go in Seattle is its downtown Waterfront. I always take visiting relatives there too. I like the variety of choices I have when I go there. Seattle's Waterfront offers many things to see and do.

First, there are lots of good restaurants on Seattle's Waterfront. If you don't have a lot of money and want a casual experience, try good old McDonald's. Also, there is a hotdog stand that is open all year. There are lots of places that sell fish and chips to go for not very much money. If you want to go fancier, then there's a great range, there's a Red Robin with a medium priced menu that offers anything from hamburgers to salads. If you want to go even fancier, try one of the many nice Seafood restaurants along the piers. For instance, Elliott Bay Fishhouse or Ivar's.

There is great shopping at the Waterfront. If you want a great spot for souveneers or little trinkets, go to Ye Olde Curiousity Shoppe. It's also a very entertaining place and kind of a tourist attraction all on its own. You can buy anything from candy, shells and "Seattle" pens and cups to strange stuff that will amaze your friends—even gag gifts. If you want a nicer gift, there are many clothes and gift shops that offer nicer gifts, there are also art galleries that sell to the public.

There is also the aquarium, with all kinds of fish and sea animals. There is the Cinemax/Omni theater that shows movies. There is also an arcade with all kinds of games and prizes, and even a carousel. There are lots of street performers too, musicians, comedians, jugglers, etc. You can take a ferry ride or a boat cruise from the pier.

There are lots of people at Seattle's Waterfront. There are tourists from all over the United States and even all over the world. But not only the tourists come to the Waterfront, locals like it too. You can see whole families out for some fun on the pier or in the arcade. You can see couples strolling along the walkway after a romantic dinner for two. You can also see local musicians and street vendors trying to make some money.

So, next time you go to downtown Seattle, be sure to visit it's waterfront. There is so much to do including great restaurants, shopping, activities and people to see.

Step Four: Revision

1. Reorganize for unity, coherence, and sentence variety.

I need to check whether every sentence or example in my body paragraphs belongs there—are they in the right spots? Does anything need to be deleted? Do I need transitions? Do I have sentence variety? I'll work on making these changes in the next draft.

2. Fine-tune thesis and topic sentences.

Ok, I can see that both my thesis and my topic sentences could be improved. Let me go back to the Building Blocks advice from Chapter 4 on thesis statements and topic sentences.

Thesis—Let me use the *what, how,* and *so what* questions.

What is the purpose of my essay: Seattle's Waterfront offers many things to see and do (my existing thesis works perfectly as a "what").

How will I develop it: The waterfront has a great variety of restaurants, shopping, activities, and types of people. (I used my categories to create a plan of development, a map for how I will develop my thesis.)

So what is the main point I want to prove: Therefore, the waterfront is an ideal place to spend a full day in Seattle, as it provides anything you could want in a perfect Seattle experience.

Topic Sentences: OK, when I look at my topic sentences, I see that they are a bit broad and don't offer any real point or main idea. They should be more of an opinion than just a fact or detail. Let me try to rewrite each of them with more of an analytical message and a bit more focus.

Topic Sentence 1: First, there are lots of good restaurants on Seattle's Waterfront.
Revision: To begin with, Seattle's Waterfront offers a variety of restaurants to suit any palate and any budget.

Topic Sentence 2: There is great shopping at the Waterfront.
Revision: Also, there are several great shopping opportunities on the Waterfront, from kitsch to classy.

Topic Sentence 3: There is also the aquarium, with all kinds of fish and sea animals. (This is not really a topic sentence, since it is not the main idea for my paragraph; it's an example with details to support an idea for things to do. I'll change it.)
Revision: The Waterfront is a great place to go for activities and entertainment.

Topic Sentence 4: Finally, there are lots of people at Seattle's Waterfront.
Revision: Finally, Seattle's Waterfront provides the best people watching in the city.

3. Add more support, examples, and details.

In this draft, I'm going to add my new thesis statement and topic sentences and see where I can provide more supporting examples and details.

▶ **NOTE**   Changes made by the student in the second draft, including reorganization for unity, coherence, and sentence variety, a new thesis and topic sentences, have been underlined and annotated. Transitions are highlighted in blue.

Seattle's Waterfront

There are so many things to do in the Seattle area. For instance, one of my favorite places to go in Seattle is its downtown Waterfront. I always take visiting relatives there too since I like the variety of choices I have when I go there. No matter what you want, Seattle's Waterfront offers many things to see and do. The waterfront has a great variety of restaurants, shopping, activities, and types of people. *Therefore, the waterfront is an ideal place to spend a full day in Seattle as it provides anything you could want in a perfect Seattle experience.*

Thesis statement

TS   *To begin with, Seattle's Waterfront offers a variety of restaurants to suit any palate and any budget.* If you don't have a lot of money and want a casual experience, try good old McDonald's. McDonald's offers many full-meal options for under five dollars. For instance, you can get a Big Mac, fries, and a Coke for less than five dollars. Also, there is a hotdog stand that is open all year and has great dogs and Polish sausages for under three dollars, and there are lots of places that sell fish and chips to go for not very much money. Ivar's is the most famous place to get fish and chips to go. You can get a full order of fish and chips for six dollars or less. If you want to go fancier, then there's a great range, there's a Red Robin with a medium priced menu that offers anything from hamburgers to salads. Most burgers there, along with unlimited French fries, cost less than eight dollars. They also have a full range of desserts and the best two-dollar shake in town. If you want to go even fancier, try one of the many nice seafood restaurants along the piers. For instance, Elliott Bay Fishhouse, which has fresh salmon and other grilled fish entrées, ranging from thirteen to twenty dollars and has a fancier atmosphere with candles and white tablecloths or Ivar's, the indoor restaurant which serves the full entrée and salad plates for about the same

Supporting example
Supporting detail
Supporting example

Supporting example
Supporting detail

Supporting example
Supporting detail

Supporting example

Supporting detail

Supporting example

Concluding sentence

range. Both of these restaurants are a more romantic atmosphere with higher-priced and more elaborate menus. <u>The Waterfront has any type of dining experience you could want.</u>

TS

<u>Also, there are several great shopping opportunities on the Waterfront, from kitsch to classy.</u> If you want a great spot for souvenirs or little trinkets, go to Ye Olde Curiosity Shoppe. It's also a very enter-taining place and kind of a tourist attraction all on its own. In this

Supporting example

shop, you can buy anything from candy, shells and "Seattle" pens and cups to strange stuff that will amaze your friends—even gag gifts. For

Supporting detail

instance, you can get soap that turns your friends' hands black when they use it and disappearing ink. If you want a nicer gift, there are many clothes and gift shops that offer nicer gifts, for instance, there are

Supporting example

art shops with beautiful Native American carvings and paintings there are also art galleries that sell to the public, most of these feature local

Concluding sentence

artists and include paintings, carvings, and glassworks. <u>It's a place where you can find anything.</u>

TS

<u>Moreover, the Waterfront is a great place to go for activities and entertainment.</u> There is the aquarium, with all kinds of fish and sea

Supporting example

animals. You can see seals and otters, and you can touch live sea urchins in a touching tank. There is also the Cinemax/Omni theater

Supporting example

that shows movies, an arcade with all kinds of games and prizes, and

Supporting detail

even a carousel. The carousel is a refurbished, old-fashioned carousel with elaborately painted and decorated horses. There are lots of street performers too, musicians, comedians, jugglers, etc. Furthermore, you can take a ferry ride or a boat cruise from the pier. Some of these

Supporting example

cruises include dinner and dancing as you cruise the Puget Sound. There are even formal Summer Concerts at the Pier concerts that

Supporting detail

Concluding sentence

feature famous R&B and rock artists such as BB King and the Indigo Girls. <u>As you can see, there are lots of entertaining attractions on the waterfront.</u>

TS   Finally, Seattle's Waterfront provides the best people watching
in the city. There are tourists from all over the United States and
even all over the world. On any given day in the summer, you can see   Supporting example
tourists from the Midwest, from Japan, China, Africa, India, and
many other countries from around the world. But not only the
tourists come to the Waterfront, locals like it too. You can see whole
families out for some fun on the pier or in the arcade; also, you can
see couples strolling along the walkway after a romantic dinner for
two. You can also see local musicians and street vendors trying to
make some money. Some musicians play solo, usually with a guitar or   Supporting example
a drum, and some musicians include complete bands, with a singer
and sometimes even a whole sound system. All types of people like   Concluding sentence
the waterfront.

So, next time you go to downtown Seattle, be sure to visit it's   Concluding paragraph
waterfront. There is so much to do including eating at great restau-
rants, shopping, doing activities and watching people.

Step 5: Editing

1. Check spelling.

I'm a pretty good speller. But I've been burned by spell-check before. I'll just
doublecheck the words I'm not one hundred percent sure of with a dictionary. Also, I'm going to glance through the Commonly Confused Words section of my text (Chapter 29) to see if I have misused any of those.

2. Check word usage, word choices, tone, and style.

I see that I have repeated some words a lot and that some of the words are
slang terms. The tone is also too informal. I'll check a thesaurus for synonyms I can use. I used the second person ("you") too much in my essay,
so I'll change the point of view to third person. I have quite a few "There are"
or "There is" statements or "is" and "has" verbs, so I'll try and make them
into more active verb constructions. Also, I think now that the title is too
broad, so I'll add a subtitle.

3. Check for sentence-level errors.

Now I'll go through the whole paper checking for each of the common errors listed in Step Ten of "A 10-Step Process for Writing an Essay." (See p. 84.)

The Final Version

▶ **NOTE**   All of the changes in this final version have been underlined and annotated.

Allegria 1

Debra Allegria

Professor Edelstein

English 095

23 May 2010

Seattle's Waterfront: Fun and Adventure for All

The Seattle area is full of great things to do. For instance, one of my favorite places to go in Seattle is its downtown waterfront. I always take visiting relatives there, too, since I like the variety of choices I have when I go there. In fact, Seattle's waterfront in particular offers many things to see and to do. The waterfront offers a great variety of restaurants, shopping, activities, and types of people. *Therefore,* the

Thesis statement · *waterfront is an ideal place to spend a full day in Seattle as it provides anything one could want in a perfect Seattle experience.*

To begin with, Seattle's waterfront offers a variety of restaurants to

Topic sentence · *suit any palate and any budget.* If a person does not have a great deal of money to spend and wants a casual experience, he or she can go to reliable McDonald's on the waterfront. McDonald's offers many full-meal options for under five dollars. For instance, a shopper can get a Big Mac, fries, and a Coke for less than five dollars. Also, the waterfront boasts a famous hotdog stand that is open all year and has great dogs

Allegria 2

and Polish sausages for under three dollars. Moreover, several places along the waterfront sell fish and chips to go for not very much money. Ivar's is the most famous place to get fish and chips to go. A hungry visitor can get a full order of fish and chips for six dollars or less.

If a person wants to go to a fancy restaurant on the waterfront, *then there's a great range.* Red Robin features a medium-priced range menu that offers anything from hamburgers to salads. Most burgers there, along with unlimited French fries, cost less than eight dollars. Red Robin also offers a full range of desserts and the best two-dollar shake in town. If one wants to go even fancier, he or she can try one of the many nice seafood restaurants along the pier. For instance, Elliott Bay Fishhouse has fresh salmon and other grilled fish entrées, ranging from thirteen to twenty dollars, and has a nicer atmosphere with candles and white tablecloths. Also, Ivar's provides an indoor restaurant that serves full entrée and salad plates for about the same range. Both of these restaurants boast a more romantic atmosphere and feature higher-priced and more elaborate menu options. Indeed, Seattle's waterfront has any type of dining experience one could want.

Also, Seattle's waterfront offers *great shopping opportunities with* *all kinds of merchandise, from kitsch to classy.* If a visitor wants a great spot for souvenirs or little trinkets, he or she can go to Ye Olde Curiosity Shoppe, a very entertaining place and kind of a tourist attraction all on its own. In this shop, one can buy anything from candy, shells, and "Seattle" pens and cups to strange stuff that will amaze one's friends—even gag gifts. For instance, one can get soap that turns friends' hands black when they use it and infamous disappearing ink. If a shopper desires a nicer gift, many clothes and gift shops offer nicer gifts; for instance, the waterfront sports art shops with beautiful Native American carvings and paintings and art galleries that sell to

[New paragraph started]

Topic sentence

Concluding sentence

Topic sentence

Allegria 3

Concluding sentence

the public; most of these feature local artists and include paintings, carvings, and glassworks. Truly, the waterfront is a place where experienced shoppers can find anything.

Topic sentence

Moreover, the waterfront is a great place to go for activities and entertainment. In the Seattle Aquarium, with all kinds of fish and sea animals, guests can see seals and otters and can touch live sea urchins in an open tank. Also, the Cinemax/Omni Theater shows movies and features an arcade with all kinds of games and prizes, and even a carousel. The carousel is a refurbished, old-fashioned merry-go-round with elaborately painted and decorated horses. Street performers frequent the waterfront too: musicians, comedians, jugglers, etc. Furthermore, one can take a ferry ride or a boat cruise from the pier. Some of these cruises include dinner and dancing as they cruise the Puget Sound. Finally, the summer weather brings Summer Concerts at the Pier, which feature famous R&B and rock artists such as BB King and the Indigo Girls. As you can see, several entertaining attractions

Concluding sentence

exist on the waterfront.

Topic sentence

Finally, Seattle's waterfront provides the best people watching in the city. Tourists from all over the United States and even all over the world visit the waterfront. On any given day in the summer, one can see tourists from the Midwest and from Japan, China, Africa, India, and many other countries from around the world. However, not only the tourists come to the waterfront; locals like it, too. Whole families come out for some fun on the pier or in the arcade; also, couples regularly stroll along the walkway after a romantic dinner for two. Moreover, local musicians and street vendors are prominent on the waterfront. Some musicians play solo, usually a guitar or a drum, and some musicians have complete bands, including a singer and sometimes even a whole

Allegria 4

sound system. All types of people like the waterfront, <u>making it the best</u>   Concluding sentence
<u>spot to be seen and do some people watching.</u>

  <u>As you can see, Seattle's waterfront offers the best of all possible</u>   Restatement of thesis
<u>spots to squeeze in a full day of activities. No other spot can offer so</u>
<u>much in one place, including a wealth of great restaurants, shopping,</u>
<u>activities, and people to see.</u>

Each person will have a different experience using the 10-step process, which can also differ from assignment to assignment, but following it will help you write an effective essay and ensure that it contains all the elements of a good essay.

ACTIVITY 5-18   **More Practice Writing an Essay**

Directions: *Choose from the following broad topics, or choose one of your own, to practice using the Building Blocks (Chapter 4) and 10 steps to writing an essay.*

Topic choices:

1. Music in advertising
2. Uses for the Internet
3. Traveling to a foreign country
4. Finding a good apartment
5. Riding the subway versus riding the bus

 Topic of your own: _____

LO 5 SELF- AND PEER ASSESSMENT OF WRITING

Self- and peer assessment of essay drafts lets you evaluate the effectiveness of your writing and go through, step by step, and look at the separate elements that contribute to the success of your essay and achieving your purpose. If you know the criteria used by instructors for grading essays *before* you begin an actual draft, you'll be sure to focus on those elements as you write it; then you can self-assess to see if you addressed those elements well. Finally, you can have your peers (classmates, friends, or tutors) critique your essay using the checklist in this chapter on p. 95.

To check your progress in meeting this chapter's objectives, log in to www .mywritinglab.com, go to the **Study Plan** tab, click on **Writing Expository Paragraphs and Essays** and choose **Prewriting, The Writing Process, Revising the Essay,** and **Editing the Essay** from the list of subtopics. Read and view the resources in the **Review Materials** section, and then complete the **Recall, Apply,** and **Write** sets in the **Activities** section.

6 Essays: Order, Unity, and Coherence

Flamingos   Wayne Buck

THINKING CRITICALLY

Look at the picture. Then answer the questions that follow.

When you first looked at this photo, what did you notice? Could you tell what the objects in the picture were at first glance? Did the individual flamingos stand out, or did they blend into one larger image?

_____

_____

Just like the photo above, you want the overall shape and structure of your essay to have unity, coherence, and a smooth order that come together to make a great overall whole.

⬤ TYPES OF ORDER

Think about the best order pattern for your purpose. There are several ways to organize an essay. It's important to choose an order of development that best suits your purpose. The order pattern you choose to organize your essay helps your readers follow your ideas and your support for those ideas.

Here are a few of the most effective essay order patterns and some suggestions for when to use them:

Time Order

Cross Reference

See Chapters 7 and 9 on how to write narration and process essays.

Time order, also called *chronological order,* is most often used in narration and process essays. This order pattern is used to tell what happened in the order it happened (narrative) and to explain how to do a step-by-step process (process).

> **Narration time order example:** Yesterday, I went to the store. Then, after the store, I had to stop and get gas for my car. Next, I stopped at the post office to pick up my mail . . .
>
> **Process time order example:** To make chocolate chip cookies, first, you will need to gather all the necessary ingredients. After you have assembled the required ingredients, measure the butter and sugar in a large glass bowl. Next, cream together the sugar and butter to make a smooth paste . . .

Order of Importance

Cross Reference

See Chapters 7, 13, 14, and 15 for descriptions of each of these essay types.

Order of importance is most often used in description, narration, cause and effect, comparison/contrast, or argument essays when the writer wants to emphasize *the most to least important ideas* or *the least to most important ideas.*

> **Most to least important order example:** When we get to Disneyland, there are several rides we just have to ride. We should start with the best so we have enough time to ride our favorites. First, we have to ride the Pirates of the Caribbean. After all, it is the best ride in the park. Next, we should go straight to The Haunted Mansion. Following that, we should go to Space Mountain . . .

Least to most important order example: There are several important things to keep in mind when buying a house. First, find a real estate agent you like. Also, set up tours of the houses you like the look of from the real estate website. It's very important to set up an inspection of the house you are interested in to make sure it is safe and in the condition the seller says it is. Finally, and most important, check that the houses are in your price range by figuring out your finances and loan possibilities before you start looking seriously for a new home.

▶ **NOTE**   Refer to the transitions section later in this chapter (p. 114) for more information on how to make your order flow more smoothly.

Spatial Order

Spatial order is used when you are describing a place, such as a town, city, or room in your house. Using spatial order helps you describe what something looks like: a messy room, a float in a parade, a neighbor's garden. Spatial order helps create a mental picture for your reader of the space you are describing. For instance, if you were describing your room, you could start from front to back, top to bottom, or side to side. One part at a time, describe the space to give the whole picture.

Spatial order example: Gill's garden was beautiful. Front and center was a pool with a fountain in the shape of a little boy in the middle surrounded by water lilies. Immediately behind the pool was a dark green hedge with a wooden bench in front of it. Rising behind the hedge was a line of graceful willow trees whose long drooping branches brushed the top of the bench.

Cross Reference
See Chapters 7–15 for customized forms of order and patterns of development designed for particular essay types and purposes.

ACTIVITY 6-1   Patterns of Order

Directions: *Which order pattern would you choose for each of the following essay topics? Some topics may work with more than one order pattern; if so, pick the best one for this topic.   Answers may vary.*

1. Finding your way around campus _____*spatial order*_____
2. Steps for making a peanut-butter-and-jelly sandwich ____*time order*____

3. How to get the most out of college _____ *order of importance* _____

4. A typical morning for a college student _____ *time order* _____

5. The many skills of a great teacher _____ *order of importance* _____

6. How to train a new pet _____ *order of importance* _____

7. The health risks of smoking _____ *order of importance* _____

8. Steps for changing your car's oil _____ *time order* _____

9. Reasons we need a stop sign on our street _____ *order of importance* _____

10. A description of our house _____ *spatial order* _____

LO 2 UNITY AND THE ART OF ACHIEVING COHERENCE WITH TRANSITIONS

Good writing flows smoothly from one point to the next with nothing out of place. When writing an essay, it is important to maintain both **unity** (every detail belongs) and **coherence** (smooth flow from one point to the next). Transitional words, phrases, or sentences provide the bridges needed to keep the flow smooth from sentence to sentence or paragraph to paragraph.

Unity

Unity means that each sentence you've included in your essay helps develop the point you have set out to make. In order to achieve unity, each paragraph must support and develop your essay's thesis statement. Also, within the paragraphs, each sentence must develop or support the topic sentence or controlling idea of that paragraph. For example, which sentence in this paragraph does not belong?

> (1) Italian food is comfort food. (2) To begin with, most Italian food is loaded with carbohydrates, which are fundamental for that feeling of comfort from food. (3) Pasta, a main staple in Italian food, is full of carbohydrates and is satisfying and delicious. (4) Spaghetti, for instance, is one of the most famous Italian pasta dishes. (5) Moreover, lasagna is a delicious pasta dish, and it satisfies the cheese lover, too. (6) Enchiladas, though a Mexican dish, are a great comfort dish, too. (7) Also, ravioli, one of my favorite Italian specialties, is an excellent comfort food choice. Indeed, most pasta dishes confirm the belief that Italian food equals comfort food.

Did you spot the sentence that didn't belong in this paragraph? The sentence that does not support the topic sentence (and interferes with the unity of this paragraph) is sentence number 6. Enchiladas are a Mexican dish, and, therefore, this sentence does not support the idea of Italian food as comfort food. Not all unity errors will be this easy to spot. Sometimes, you will find you have changed direction or switched focus in a very subtle way during the process of writing your first draft.

ACTIVITY 6-2   Test for Unity

Directions: *Read the following paragraph and underline the two sentences that do not belong (do not directly support and develop the topic sentence). Then explain briefly, on the lines provided, why they don't belong in this paragraph.*

(1) Taking classes online provides the opportunity for students who work full time or are stay-at-home parents to complete their educational goals. (2) Before distance learning and online class offerings, students had no choice but to physically attend college classes or try to find limited choices for old-fashioned correspondence courses. (3) With the arrival of the Internet age, students with limited schedules or children at home have more opportunities to attend college. (4) For instance, students who work full time can sign up for an online class and "attend" the course on their own schedule. (5) Employers will be happy, too, with more flexible scheduling hours. (6) Moreover, online classes give parents at home more chances to take college courses without worrying about expensive daycare costs. (7) Stay-at-home moms and dads can take the college courses they need while still being home with their children. (8) Some fathers even choose to be the main at-home parent. (9) The Internet and distance-learning opportunities have made scheduling classes for students who work or who are parents much easier.

Sentences that don't belong: _5 & 8_____

Explain why: _Answers will vary._____

_____

_____

To check your own writing for unity, go through your entire first draft to make sure that each sentence belongs in each particular paragraph and in the essay as a whole. To help you accomplish this task, ask yourself the following questions:

1. Does every sentence in each paragraph specifically support or develop the topic sentence?

2. Does each paragraph in my essay support my thesis?

3. Are there any sentences in this draft that don't develop my thesis statement?

If you answer no to any of these questions, go back to your essay and revise or delete the sentences and/or paragraphs that don't directly support your thesis or topic sentences.

Coherence and Transitions

Coherence means that every sentence in each paragraph and each paragraph in an essay flow smoothly from one point to the next. Coherence relates to the order of development you choose for your paragraph or essay and involves the use of transitions between key sentences and between paragraphs in an essay. **Transitions** are words, phrases, or sometimes even complete sentences that help move the reader smoothly from one point to the next. They point the reader in the direction you want to take them. Transitions are necessary both *within* paragraphs and *between* them. When a transitional word, phrase, or sentence is used to connect one paragraph to the next, the transition can come at the end of the previous paragraph or at the beginning of the next, whichever works best for your purpose and organization.

Here is a list of transitional words or phrases categorized by type for easy use in paragraphs and essays:

TRANSITIONS TO . . .

Show Addition of Another Point

again	but also	in addition	nor
also	equally important	last	plus the fact
and	finally	lastly	secondly
and then	first	likewise	then too
another	further	moreover	thirdly
besides	furthermore	next	too

Show Contrast or a Change in Idea

although	even though	instead	on the other side
anyhow	for all that	nevertheless	otherwise
at the same time	however	notwithstanding	regardless
but	in any event	on the contrary	still
despite this	in contrast	on the other hand	yet

TRANSITIONS TO . . .

Show a Comparison

in like manner	in the same way	likewise	similarly

Show Summary or Repetition

as has been noted	in closing	in other words	on the whole
as I have said	in conclusion	in short	to conclude
in brief	in essence	in summary	to sum up

Illustrate or Give Examples/Specifics

a few include	essentially	in particular	the following
an example	for example	let us consider	specifically
especially	for instance	the case of	you can see this in

Strengthen a Point

basically	indeed	truly	without a doubt
essentially	irrefutably	undeniably	without question

Result and/or Cause/Effect Relationships

accordingly	consequently	since	therefore
as a result	for this reason	so	thereupon
because	hence	then	thus

Purpose

all things considered	for this reason	to accomplish	with this in mind
for this purpose	in order to	to this end	with this objective

Place (Usually Prepositions)

above	beside	inside	outside
across	between	nearer	over
adjacent to	beyond	nearly	there
below	farther	next to	through
beneath	here	opposite	under

Continued ▶

TRANSITIONS TO . . .

Show Time

after	before	in the meantime	not long after
afterwards	between	later	soon
at last	first	meanwhile	then
at length	immediately	next	while

Show Amount

a great deal	less than	most	smaller
few	many	over	some
greater	more than	several	under

ACTIVITY 6-3   Provide Transitions

Directions: *Choose transitions from the tables above, or use a transition of your own, to fill in the blanks below and help this paragraph flow more smoothly.*
Answers will vary. Possible answers provided.

Advertisements often convey messages that negatively affect women's self-esteem. _____For instance_____, advertisements in magazines often depict women as extremely thin. _____Therefore_____, the message is women must be thin to be beautiful. _____Moreover_____, television commercials often depict women in the home using some form of cleaning product. _____For example_____, one commercial has a woman dancing romantically with her mop in a perfectly clean kitchen.

_____Thus_____, the message to men and women is that women should do the cleaning. _____Also_____, they should enjoy the cleaning.

_____Furthermore_____, many magazine and television ads push cosmetics and hair products and feature glamorous, heavily made-up women.

_____As a result_____, women feel pressured to buy these products to match the images of the women in these ads. These forms of advertising, _____consequently_____, convey messages to women that can hurt their self-worth and perception of themselves.

LO3 OUTLINES: PERFECTING YOUR ESSAY'S ORDER OF DEVELOPMENT

One of the best ways to ensure a well-organized essay and an order of development that best illustrates your essay's purpose is to write an outline of your essay. Some writers begin with a rough outline of their papers before they've written a draft. However, even if you didn't *start* with an outline, it is a powerful tool to use *after you have written your first draft* to check and revise the organization and structure of ideas.

Outline Format

An outline helps you to order your thoughts: It creates a plan for your essay's development. It's like a table of contents for each component of your essay. Outlines allow you to order your main ideas and supporting examples and details in the most logical way and, therefore, most effectively develop your essay's purpose.

An outline has a consistent format, with the main ideas placed closest to the far left margin. Then the subpoints, examples, and details used to develop those main ideas are indented; the farther right your ideas are placed, the more specific or detailed is the support they provide. If you have four main sections to develop in your essay, you'll have four main ideas. Then you can add as many subpoints, examples, and details as needed for each section to fully develop those ideas. Here are some guidelines for writing an outline.

Guidelines for Writing an Outline

1. Thesis Statement: Write your thesis statement at the top of the outline, but do not include the general introduction that will come before your thesis statement.

2. Main Ideas: List the main ideas (concepts for each **topic sentence**) that will be developed in the body paragraphs of your essay using Roman numerals to label them (I, II, III, and so on). Use a phrase of just a few words, not a complete sentence, to explain each main idea. Think of these, instead, as titles for each paragraph of your paper. The main ideas are formatted in the left margin.

3. Subpoints:

List the **subpoints** you will use to support the main idea/topic sentence of each paragraph using capital letters (A, B, C, and so on). Use short phrases to represent each subpoint. These subpoints are formatted one tab right from the left margin.

▶ **NOTE**   You must have at least two subpoints: If you have an "A" then you must have at least a "B." If you have only one subpoint, then combine it with the main idea phrase, or develop a second subpoint.

4. Support:

List supporting examples and details below each subpoint. The next level of detail is labeled with numbers (1, 2, 3, and so on). If you have details to illustrate these examples, they are labeled with lowercase letters (a, b, c, and so on). If you have even another level of details to develop those, label them with numbers followed by a single parenthesis [1), 2), 3), and so on]. Each level of detail will also progressively tab right.

▶ **NOTE**   You must have at least two of each supporting levels of information, so if you have a "1" you need at least a "2"; if you have an "a" detail under "1" then you also need a "b." If you do not have a second detail at the same level, create one, or wrap the single detail into the previous example.

5. Conclusion:

Provide a brief statement of conclusion at the end of your outline.

▶ **NOTE**   Check your campus for helpful software that is available for creating outlines in the correct format automatically. These tools and programs make your job easier and ensure that your format is correct.

Sample Outline

Debra Allegria

Professor Edelstein

English 095

20 May 2010

Thesis: Seattle's waterfront is an ideal place to spend a full day in the city, since it provides everything one could want to do for a perfect Seattle experience.

   I. Seattle's Waterfront: Restaurants

      A. Affordable restaurants

         1. McDonald's

            a. extra value meals

            b. several meals under $5

         2. fish and chips shop

            a. full meal under $5

            b. outdoor seats/no tipping

      B. Fancy/higher budget restaurants

         1. Red Robin

            a. medium to higher price items

            b. good comfort food

         2. Elliot Bay Fishhouse

            a. higher priced seafood entrees

            b. full view

         3. Ivar's Restaurant

            a. higher-priced seafood items

            b. full view

  II. Waterfront shopping

      A. Ye Olde Curiosity Shoppe

Continued ▶

        1. gags

          a. magic tricks

          b. gag/joke gifts

        2. artwork

          a. carvings

          b. Native American paintings

    B. Street vendors

        1. T-shirts

        2. Seattle mementos

III. Activities and Entertainment

    A. Seattle Aquarium

        1. sea animals

        2. gift shop

    B. Street performers

        1. musicians

        2. comedians

        3. jugglers

    C. Summer concerts

IV. People watching

    A. Tourists

        1. U.S. tourists

        2. International tourists

    B. Local artists and musicians

Conclusion: The waterfront offers the best of all possible spots to squeeze in a full day of activities.

Here are some questions you can ask as you develop your outline to ensure you have thought critically about what you want to say and how you want to say it.

CRITICAL THINKING QUESTIONS TO ASK AS YOU DESIGN YOUR OUTLINE

PURPOSE

IDEAS

SUPPORT

ANALYSIS

1. What is the main point or conclusion I've made about my topic? What **purpose** do I want to convey to my readers? (In the above outline, it would be where to go to experience the full Seattle experience.)

2. What are the main **ideas** and **support** I will use in my paper, and in what order do I want to present them? Which evidence and examples are main examples and which are supporting details?

3. Do I have any claims that may need more support to convince my readers of my point?

4. How will I order my reasons for support and main body paragraphs? What is the best order of development to successfully argue my conclusions and present my evidence?

5. **Analyze** to see if there are there any parts that need to be deleted, expanded upon, or rearranged.

Finally, use the Outline Critique Form below to self-review or peer-review your outline.

OUTLINE CRITIQUE FORM

1. Does the outline start with a thesis statement? _____

2. Is the thesis statement an idea or opinion that can be developed through examples and details? Is there a clear message or point being made? _____

3. Did the author use correct outline format (see the format above for outline rules)? _____

4. Are the subtopics/sections/categories clear and explained with a short phrase? _____

5. Are the categories and subpoints detailed enough to be clear but not overly detailed? _____

6. If there is a "1" or an "A" in a category or subpoint, is it followed by at least one more point ("2" or "B," and so on)? _____

7. If secondary sources are included in the outline, can you tell how they will be used as support? _____

Continued ▶

Comments and suggestions for revision:

_____

_____

_____

_____

_____

To check your progress in meeting this chapter's objectives, log in to **www .mywritinglab.com**, go to the **Study Plan** tab, click on **Writing Expository Paragraphs and Essays** and choose **Essay Organization** from the list of subtopics. Read and view the resources in the **Review Materials** section, and then complete the **Recall, Apply,** and **Write** sets in the **Activities** section.

Día de Los Muertos

THINKING CRITICALLY

Look at the picture above. Then answer the questions that follow.

1. *Describe* this photograph in your own words using as many specific, descriptive words as possible.

   _____

   _____

2. *Narrate* a short, one-paragraph story about this image; use your imagination.

   _____

   _____

ESSAY MODES

Essay **modes** are types of essays designed to address specific purposes. You can use different modes, or specific patterns of writing, to write about the same topic: It all depends on your purpose and your intended audience. Some essays will benefit from the use of a specific mode or pattern, while others will benefit from a combination of several different modes, and some will do better with no formal structure at all. The dominant mode you choose, the choice to combine modes, or the decision to reject using a specific mode depends on the purpose of your writing. Engage your critical thinking skills and carefully assess your topic, purpose, and audience to make the best choice.

Whether you choose to use a single mode, combine modes, or not to use mode structures at all will be based on several key factors:

1. Your instructor's assignment or specific request for a mode essay
2. The purpose of your essay and decisions you make for how to structure it in the most efficient way
3. Your intended audience and the best combination of modes to illustrate and develop your intended purpose

CHOOSING THE RIGHT APPROACH

All essays should have an **expository purpose,** a point they wish to explain. You have a choice in how you structure your essay, and there are specialized modes you can use or combine to do this. Review the critical thinking tools in Chapter 1 to figure out your essay's purpose and to choose the best way to organize and develop that purpose. Although each mode explained in the following chapters has a specialized purpose and format, they can all be used to make an *argument* or *analytical point.* Many professional essays feature a dominant mode approach but also tap into one to three other modes to develop their purpose. There are nine commonly used essay modes:

Narration:	Telling a story using narrative details and description (see Chapter 7).
Description:	The art of using vivid details to paint a picture with words (see Chapter 8).
Process:	Describing a step-by-step process or a series of steps one must take to accomplish a task (see Chapter 9).
Classification:	Sometimes also called "classification and division." Categorizing people, things, or concepts into particular groups in order to draw conclusions about them (see Chapter 10).

Definition: Defining an item or a concept (see Chapter 11).

Example and illustration: Providing examples in order to illustrate an idea or set of ideas (see Chapter 12).

Cause and effect: The relationship between causes (reasons) and effects (results) (see Chapter 13).

Comparison and contrast: Similarities and differences between two subjects or among several subjects (see Chapter 14).

Argument or persuasion: Persuading an audience to agree with a particular viewpoint or arguing for a change in the status quo (see Chapter 15).

Some essay assignments will call for one of the above modes, and some will require you to use a combination of modes to complete your purpose. Many times your essay will have a dominant mode, a particular approach such as argument, but will still tap into several other modes for support such as narration, examples, comparison and contrast, and so on. All the essay modes follow a simple template for developing a purpose:

Cross Reference
Review Chapters 4–6 for a detailed review of basic essay structure.

1. They begin with an introductory paragraph that introduces the topic and presents the purpose of the essay in an analytical thesis statement.

2. They develop the thesis statement with body paragraphs using clear topic sentences and supporting examples and details.

3. They end with a concluding paragraph that restates or sums up the main purpose and sometimes comments on it.

Choosing Dresses for the Dance   Ashley Sims

LEARNING OBJECTIVES

In this chapter, you will learn to

 Write narrative essays.

LO 2 Structure a narrative essay.

LO 3 Use dialogue in narrative essays.

LO 4 Use complementary modes for narrative essays.

THINKING CRITICALLY

Look at the photograph above. Then on a separate piece of paper, write a brief story explaining what is going on in the picture. Use your imagination, and include as many specific details about the situation and the subjects as you can. Answer the questions that follow.

1. What did you focus on when you wrote the story?

   _____

   _____

2. What effect did looking at a concrete (actual) image have on the way you wrote your story and the details you included?

   _____

   _____

LO 1 NARRATIVE ESSAYS

In a **narrative essay,** you recount an event, story, or series of events in order to explain some insight or truth gained from an experience. Although some narrative essays are less formal and involve a straightforward telling of a story or event, most narrative essay assignments include a more analytical purpose: They have a point, a plot, a lesson, or a message to impart to the reader through telling a story or recounting an event and framing it with analysis.

Critical Thinking and Narration

It is the *inclusion of a lesson* that distinguishes the expository narrative essay from a merely narrative description of events. Expository narrative essays feature a lesson or clear message, implied or directly stated, that is conveyed to the reader through the recounting of events. This analytical purpose is stated in the first paragraph of the essay in the *thesis* (or *purpose statement*). This lesson or message is then restated in the conclusion as well.

Because analytical, or expository, narrative essays have a more intentional purpose, they require more thought than an essay that merely recounts an event. You must engage your critical thinking skills and figure out what you

APPLYING CRITICAL THINKING

PURPOSE   IDEAS   SUPPORT   ASSUMPTIONS BIASES   CONCLUSIONS   POINT OF VIEW   ANALYSIS

In order to determine your **purpose** for writing—the message you want to convey in your narrative essay—use the following questions to help you clarify what you learned from the experience you are writing about and what point you want to convey based on what you learned:

1. What is my **analysis** of the story? What have I learned or what do I want my readers to learn from the story I am telling?

2. What is my plan for my narrative? What point do I want to make through telling this story? How will I convey that message in my essay?

3. What **ideas** will I include? What **support** (facts, examples, evidence) can I include to illustrate and explain the point of my narrative?

want to say about the event, how you want to say it, how you'll organize your ideas, and how you'll weave in analysis and commentary about the actual event.

BEFORE WRITING A NARRATIVE ESSAY

Before you begin to write a narrative essay on an assigned topic, or one you have chosen, start by asking yourself these questions:

1. What did I learn from the experience?
2. What do I want my readers to learn or understand after reading about the event I experienced or witnessed?
3. How can I re-create the event vividly in my readers' heads? What examples and details should I use to re-create the story?
4. How should I organize my paragraphs after my introduction and thesis, and how can I move smoothly from one event or detail to the next?
5. What's the best way to conclude my essay?

Answering these questions will lead you to an expository thesis statement, help you decide which examples and details to include for support, and give you a general idea of how you want to organize and conclude your essay.

ACTIVITY 7-1   Outlining a Specific Event

Directions: *Think of an event you witnessed or a specific happy or sad event in your own life. Then answer the following questions about that event:*

1.   What happened? (Describe briefly in one paragraph.)

   _____

   _____

   _____

   _____

   _____

2.   What did you learn about yourself and/or others that day, and why?

   _____

   _____

   _____

3. What would you want your readers to understand after reading about the event? _____

_____

_____

4. What specific details and examples could you use to re-create the event and vividly tell the story? _____

_____

_____

5. What critical thinking tools could you use to plan, support, organize, and develop the purpose of the narration? _____

_____

_____

WRITING A NARRATIVE ESSAY

The structure of a narrative essay is usually less formal than for other types of essays. Often the essay tells a story about an event, or series of events, in chronological order, the order in which they occurred.

The *point of view* in narrative essays is usually *first person*. Therefore, it is perfectly appropriate to use the word "I" throughout a narrative essay. For example:

Cross Reference
See Chapter 28 for more about point of view.

> "When I was 12 years old, I learned a valuable lesson about the dangers of playing with fire. It all started when my brother and I found a lighter in our backyard."

You should develop your narrative essay using *descriptive details*. Include specific details about the setting and detailed descriptions of the people and their actions. Choose words that conjure up vivid images, not vague descriptors such as "beautiful."

> **Vague descriptors:** The cake was *beautiful* and looked *delicious*.
>
> **Revised:** The wedding cake was three layers high and snowy white, covered with fluffy whipped cream and delicate pastel pink roses made of butter cream frosting.

Use real dialogue, as far as you can remember it from the event, to make the scene(s) come alive on paper. When you use *dialogue* in a narration essay, it serves as a great way to provide supporting details in the body paragraphs to help develop the message or overall *expository purpose* of your essay. For information on how to use dialogue correctly, see pages 136–137 later in this chapter.

The chart below provides a brief overview of the structure of a narrative essay.

BASIC STRUCTURE FOR A NARRATIVE ESSAY

INTRODUCTORY PARAGRAPH

Sets up background for the event or story.

Thesis statement: A statement that describes what you are trying to explain, show, prove, or argue in your narrative essay; what you learned from the experience.

BODY PARAGRAPHS (Two to five, depending on assignment and purpose)

Develop the narrative of the event using time order.

Use transitions within and between paragraphs to emphasize time changes and/or significant turns in the narrative.

Provide concrete details and description.

Use as many senses as possible in your description (sight, sound, smell, touch, and taste).

Add dialogue when appropriate.

Add commentary and analysis about the details and descriptions to help develop the expository purpose/thesis statement.

Explain what you were thinking and feeling as the events took place.

CONCLUDING PARAGRAPH

Sum up and re-emphasize the thesis: the **lesson learned** and message of the story you've told in your narrative essay.

 LO 2 STRUCTURING A NARRATIVE ESSAY

Topic

If you have been assigned a narrative topic by your instructor, be sure to read the assignment carefully to determine the requirements of the assignment and how to best create your thesis and analytical purpose. If you are choosing your own topic, prewrite about possible events using a technique, or techniques, that work for you in order to generate a topic and details to include in your essay. Focus on what happened and what you learned from it. Many events stand out in people's memories as pivotal points in their lives.

A Few Topic Possibilities

Here is a list of some topics you could write a narrative essay about: the birth of a child; the happiest day of your life; an accident; a tragedy; an embarrassing event; your first day on a job; the death of a loved one; the saddest day of your life; a surprise; a celebration; a proud moment; your first day at college.

Thesis Statements

The thesis statement in a narrative essay contains the lesson learned from the event. Engage your critical thinking skills to figure out why the event or story you've chosen to write about stood out to you. What can readers learn from your experience? If you have been assigned a specific narrative essay task, be sure to include key words from the assignment to fulfill the assignment's purpose. If you are generating your own topic and purpose, be sure to use the prewriting techniques from Chapter 5 to come up with ideas, details, and a purpose for telling a story about this event. For instance, if you decided to write about the death of someone you loved, you'd need to explain how you felt and what you learned about yourself, about the nature of life, and so on. Use your critical thinking and analysis skills to explain the significance of the event. Also, be sure to look back at the information on thesis statements in Chapters 4 and 5.

The easiest way to generate a meaningful thesis statement for your narrative essay is to begin with the event that is your topic, come up with a point you want to convey to your readers about the event, and then create a thesis statement that directly states the conclusion you've come to about what you learned that day. Here are some examples of that process:

Topic = My vacation to Italy

A point I want to convey = How I learned to be flexible and open minded

> **Thesis:** Last year, during my vacation in Italy, I learned to not expect everything to be the same as it is in my country and that I need to be open-minded, flexible, and respectful when I travel to other countries.

Topic = Trying out for the football team

A point I want to convey = How it felt when I didn't get picked and dealing with that

> **Thesis:** When I tried out for the football team this fall and didn't get picked, I learned a lesson about humility and carrying on.

Topic = The birth of my child

A point I want to convey = Changing priorities

> **Thesis:** The day my daughter was born, my priorities changed completely.

ACTIVITY 7-2   Creating Thesis Statements

Directions: *For each of the following narrative topics, create a one-sentence thesis statement. Make sure the thesis statement has a clear message or lesson to convey about what you learned from the experience.* Answers will vary.

1. **Topic:** My earliest memory

    Thesis statement: _____

    _____

2. **Topic:** My first experience with death or illness

    Thesis statement: _____

    _____

3. **Topic:** The happiest day of my life

    Thesis statement: _____

    _____

4. **Topic:** The first time I [choose an event such as "drove a car"]

    Thesis statement: _____

    _____

5. **Topic:** The most embarrassing thing that ever happened to me

    Thesis statement: _____

    _____

Introductory Paragraph

Begin your narrative essay with a general introduction to draw the reader in and set up the event you will be recounting. You may need to provide some background information to contextualize the event and its importance. End the introductory paragraph with your thesis statement.

Body Paragraphs

Body paragraphs in a narrative essay develop details and description to recount an event vividly and support the purpose for telling the story in the first place. Often, the topic sentences in narrative essays are less formal or analytical than in other types of essays. Topic sentences in narrative essays often set up the next stage in a sequence of events using a clear time order and transitions. Sometimes, though, a topic sentence in a narrative essay can be a more traditional analytical statement that you develop with examples and details. For instance, for the thesis related to traveling to Italy, you could have topic sentences that are analytical setups for each point, or you could use time and event topic sentences that set up the next stage of what happened in the event you are writing about. For example:

> **Thesis:** Last year, during my vacation in Italy, I learned to not expect everything to be the same as it is in my country and that I need to be open-minded, flexible, and respectful when I travel to other countries.
>
> **Analytical statement topic sentence for this thesis:** First, I learned that day that I need to be open-minded when traveling outside my own country.
>
> **Time and event topic sentence for the same thesis:** In the morning, I encountered a situation that made me rethink my previous beliefs.

ACTIVITY 7-3   Creating Topic Sentences

Directions: *Choose one of the thesis statements you developed in Activity 7-2 and write two possible topic sentences that could set up two body paragraphs in support of that thesis.* Answers will vary.

Thesis statement: _____

Topic sentence 1:

_____

_____

Topic sentence 2:

_____

_____

ACTIVITY 7-4   Providing Examples and Details

Directions: *Now, using the two topic sentences you created in Activity 7-3, provide a specific example and a supporting detail for each.* *Answers will vary.*

Topic sentence 1:

_____

_____

Supporting detail to demonstrate/develop the example:

_____

_____

Topic sentence 2:

_____

_____

Supporting detail to demonstrate/develop the example:

_____

_____

ACTIVITY 7-5   Abstract to Specific

Directions: *Translate the following abstract descriptive words bolded in each sentence into concrete, specific descriptions of the thing or person in the sentence.* *Answers will vary.*

> **Example:** It was a **big** house.
> The house was <u>three stories high</u> and had a <u>three-car garage</u>, a <u>wraparound porch</u>, and a <u>one-acre lawn</u>.

1. She is a **beautiful** woman.

_____

_____

2. It was an **awesome** action scene in the movie.

   _____

   _____

3. Her dress was **indescribable**.

   _____

   _____

4. The crowd was **unbelievable**.

   _____

   _____

5. The party was **fantastic**.

   _____

   _____

When you recount an event in time order, be sure to include transitional words and phrases to move from one point in time to another. Here are some common transitions used to convey time order:

TRANSITIONS TO . . .

Show Time

after	before	in the meantime	not long after
afterwards	between	later	soon
at last	first	meanwhile	then
at length	immediately	next	while

"*After* we returned from the hospital, I went straight to bed."

"*Next*, my husband went to pick up the kids."

"*Later*, we showed them their new baby brother."

See Chapter 6 (pages 114–116) for other transitions commonly used with narration, including those that show addition of a point, summary, examples, purpose, or place.

Concluding Paragraph

The concluding paragraph for a narrative essay is basic: Restate the thesis statement, focusing on the purpose for recounting the event. Be sure not to use the same sentence you used in your introductory paragraph, though.

CONCLUSIONS

Explain what you learned from the experience, and reiterate the purpose required by the specific assignment (if there is one).

ACTIVITY 7-6   Writing a Conclusion

Directions: *Using the thesis, topic sentences, and examples you chose for the last three activities, write a three- to five-sentence conclusion for the topic as if you had written the entire essay.*

_____

_____

_____

_____

LO 3 DIALOGUE

As discussed earlier in this chapter, dialogue can play an important part in a narrative essay. Here are some tips to keep in mind when you include dialogue in a narrative essay.

Tips for Correct Use of Dialogue in Narrative Essays

1. **Use tags and quotation marks.** When you use dialogue, you need a tag to indicate who is speaking and quotation marks around the words they are saying.

> **Tag:** Bob said,
> **Quotation Marks:** "I have to leave this party early."
> **Used Together:** Bob said, "I have to leave this party early."

Cross Reference
See Chaper 27 for more about quotation marks.

Tag placement can also come in the middle or at the end of the dialogue:

> "Today," **Bob said,** "is the first day of the rest of my life."
> "Today is the first day of the rest of my life," **Bob said.**

2. **Use correct punctuation.** Start sentences of dialogue within quotation marks with a capital letter.

> Andrea sighed, "Yes, I know it's time to leave."

Punctuation goes inside the quotation marks (except when using in-text citation in documented papers).

> "The key point," Dominic said, "is to listen first."

3. Tab (indent five spaces) every time you switch speakers in dialogue.

> Mary asked Bob, "Will you change jobs, too?"
> "Yes," Bob responded, "I will."
> "And how will you afford the rent until you get settled?" Mary asked sharply, unable to mask her concern.
> "I'll just figure it out as I go along," Bob responded, shaking his head and smiling at Mary's worried frown.

4. Weave descriptions of the characters and their actions into blocks of dialogue. When you have blocks of dialogue in your essay, weave in descriptions of the characters and their movements or actions as they speak. Create a "movie" of the scene by including details of what they are saying and what they are doing as they say it. Again, the key to good narrative writing is concrete description. Look again at the dialogue exchange between Mary and Bob above in tip 3 for an example of weaving description into dialogue.

5. Don't let the dialogue take over. Use dialogue as a supporting detail in your essay, not as the main vehicle for imparting your story and your story's message. Be sure to *frame your dialogue with analysis*, the realizations you came to and what you were feeling and thinking as the words were said during the incident—always re-emphasize your *analytical purpose*.

> She screamed, "No, I refuse to leave. I can't. I won't!"
>
> Until that moment, I hadn't realized how hard it was for her to leave the house in which she had spent her entire life.

ACTIVITY 7-7   Writing Dialogue

Directions:

1. On a separate sheet of paper, write a short dialogue, including at least two turns speaking for each person. You can use an actual dialogue that occurred between you and someone else (as clearly as you can remember it), or you can make up a dialogue between two fictional characters.

2. *Be sure to include tags, start a new paragraph whenever you switch speakers, and include some physical motion or description of the characters as they speak. Review the tips on using dialogue for help.*

Use the critique form below to check for the basics in your narration essay draft.

NARRATIVE ESSAY CRITIQUE FORM

PURPOSE   IDEAS   SUPPORT   ASSUMPTIONS BIASES   CONCLUSIONS   POINT OF VIEW   ANALYSIS

Use the following critique form to check for the basics in a narrative essay draft.

Overall

	Done well	Needs work

1. Does the essay tell a story using description that has a clear **purpose** (lesson(s) learned from the experience)?

2. Does the essay use time order in the body paragraphs?

3. Are the paragraphs broken up well, and are they about the right length?

Introduction

4. Is the title interesting and in the correct format?

5. Is there a general introduction that gives the background for the story (the events that led up to the event/day described)?

6. Is there a clear thesis statement that explains the message of the story being told—the lesson learned or expository purpose?

Body

7. Do the **ideas** in the body paragraphs develop the story logically and flow smoothly?

8. Are transitions used between and, when needed, within the paragraphs?

9. Do the body paragraphs include **support** and descriptive details that enhance the story?

10. Does the writer use as many sensory details as possible in the description of what happened and how it made the writer feel?

11. Does the body of the paper include some dialogue to bring the action to life?

12. Is **analysis** woven throughout the body to emphasize the significance of the story and develop the thesis of the lesson(s) learned from the event? Are critical thinking tools engaged?

Conclusion   Done well   Needs work

13. Does the **concluding** paragraph sum up the story with an analytical
frame that re-emphasizes the introductory paragraph and thesis, without
adding new ideas?   _____   _____

Editing

14. Circle the following errors you think you see in this draft: spelling errors, fragments, run-ons/comma
splices, errors in comma and semicolon/colon use, pronoun disagreement, reference fault errors,
and errors in parallelism, apostrophe use, verb use/tense, and passive voice construction. (See the
handbook section of the text for help in identifying and correcting these errors.)

15. Other types of grammar or sentence-level errors:

_____

Comments:

_____

_____

LO 4 COMPLEMENTARY MODES FOR NARRATIVE ESSAYS

When writing a narrative essay, you can tap into several other modes described
in the following chapters that combine well to create a powerful narration.

- **Description:** Description is essential in narration for adding concrete
  details and vivid description.
- **Illustration and example:** Most good narrative essays include specific
  illustration and examples to develop the purpose of the writing.
- **Process:** Process focuses on narrating a series of steps to accomplish
  something and can be used to narrate a particular ritual or process.
- **Cause and effect:** You can describe an event in detail and employ
  cause-and-effect analysis to look at the consequences of the actions that
  take place.
- **Comparison/contrast:** A great way to narrate something is to compare
  or contrast it with another event.
- **Argument:** Sometimes your reason for narrating an event in detail is to
  persuade your readers to learn a particular lesson or feel a particular way:
  You are combining argument techniques within your narration.

Sample Student Essay

The dominant mode used in this student's paper is narration. Look for other modes used in this essay, such as description, illustration and example, and cause-and-effect analysis (marked in the essay).

Jamie Grant

Professor Nolan

English 100

20 April 2010

Learning Through Loss

A few years ago, my beloved grandmother, Belle, died after a sudden and severe illness. At first I was devastated by the loss.

Thesis statement

However, after a while, I found that I could honor her life by living my life based on her example of keeping our family connected and being generous, and by appreciating my life and my family while I can because life is short and therefore precious.

Topic sentence

My grandmother was beautiful to me both inside and out. She was a tiny woman who was somewhat hunched over, her back round from osteoporosis. Her face was lined, and the backs of her hands were spotted and shiny, the skin fragile and paper-like. Her hair was a stunning silver and soft and wispy. She was also the best and

Concluding sentence

wisest person I've ever known. Through her life and my times with her, she taught me the importance of family and the importance of giving to others.

Topic sentence

Our family has always been close, and my grandmother was the matriarch who kept our family connected and whose life was a model for all of us. She actively invited all of her grandchildren, including me and my brother, to visit regularly. My brother and I would spend long summers at my grandmother's lake property. She

Grant 2

made sure that my parents sent us to visit, and she invited our cousins who we rarely saw over for visits while we were there; she believed that connecting with family is a vital and active process. She told us regularly that nothing is more important than family.

Concluding sentence

Topic sentence

Furthermore, my grandmother gave to her community. She volunteered for the local Red Cross, and she helped with the local food bank every week. Once, when I was eight years old and visiting her, I went with her to help give out food to the needy. I asked her, "Why do you do this every week, Grandma, even when you are tired?"

"It's important to give back to your community, to do something selfless for the good of others without expecting something in return," she said. She then winked at me as she passed her rough fingers through her silver hair.

"Oh," I said, knitting my brow in concentration. Even though I was young, I remember thinking about how wise and generous she was. Now that I'm older and she is gone, I appreciate her true wisdom and admirable character even more.

Concluding sentence

A week prior to her death, my brother and I visited her at the lake property and had a special time as usual. I didn't know it then, but that would be the last time I saw her. She became severely ill a few days later and was taken to the hospital. On September 21, 2005, at five a.m., we got a call from her doctor who told us she had passed away. We were all shocked and heartbroken. Though she was ill, we never thought she would pass away that soon. I had never experienced death before, and I didn't really know what to do. I was sad and grieving at first, but I began to understand that my grandmother had had a full life, and that she could live on in our thoughts and in our actions. I could become the kind of charitable

Continued ▶

Grant 3

Topic sentence

person she was. I could help keep our family close in her absence. In addition, I began to understand that life is short and that I need to cherish my family and my life now, like my grandmother did.

Restatement of thesis

The death of my grandmother taught me to appreciate my life and my loved ones and to live a life that gives to others. Though she is gone and I'm sad for the loss of her physical presence, I keep her in my heart and thoughts, and I use her model of love of family and giving to others to be a better person in my life.

This student's draft has a good basic narrative structure and organization and a strong message or lesson learned. This draft also includes some dialogue. The next draft would need more descriptive details and concrete images of the grandmother and the setting. Also, the essay would be stronger with more examples, sentence variety, and changes in style and vocabulary.

ACTIVITY 7-8   Thinking Critically About the Student Essay

Directions: *Analyze the essay to identify the features and details characteristic of the narrative mode. Mark them on the essay. Then, reread the essay, and make a list of specific revisions you would make to correct any problems with content, organization, transitions, and style.*

PROFESSIONAL NARRATIVE ESSAY

Only Daughter

Sandra Cisneros

Sandra Cisneros, born in Chicago in 1954, was the only daughter raised in a Mexican-American family with six brothers. She has a B.A. in English from Loyola University and an M.F.A. in Creative Writing from the University of Iowa. Her first book, *The House on Mango Street* (1984), features short vignettes related to Latina women in America. Later publications include *My Wicked, Wicked Ways* (1987), *Woman Hollering Creek* (1991), and *The Future is Mestizo: Life Where Cultures Meet* (2000). "Only Daughter" is an essay first published in *Glamour*.

1   Once, several years ago, when I was just starting out my writing career, I was asked to write my own contributor's note for an anthology. I wrote: "I am the only daughter in a family of six sons. *That* explains everything."

2   Well, I've thought that ever since, and yes, it explains a lot to me, but for the reader's sake I should have written: "I am the only daughter in a *Mexican* family of six sons." Or even: "I am the only daughter of a Mexican father and a Mexican-American mother." Or: "I am the only daughter of a working-class family of nine." All of these had everything to do with who I am today.

3   I was/am the only daughter and *only* a daughter. Being an only daughter in a family of six sons forced me by circumstance to spend a lot of time by myself because my brothers felt it beneath them to play with a *girl* in public. But that aloneness, that loneliness, was good for a would-be writer—it allowed me time to think and think, to imagine, to read and prepare myself.

4   Being only a daughter for my father meant my destiny would lead me to become someone's wife. That's what he believed. But when I was in the fifth grade and shared my plans for college with him, I was sure he understood. I remember my father saying, *"Que bueno, mi'ja,* that's good." That meant a lot to me, especially since my brothers thought the idea hilarious. What I didn't realize was that my father thought college was good for girls—good for finding a husband. After four years in college and two more in graduate school, and still no husband, my father shakes his head even now and says I wasted all that education.

5   In retrospect, I'm lucky my father believed daughters were meant for husbands. It meant it didn't matter if I majored in something silly like English. Alter all, I'd find a nice professional eventually, right? This allowed me the liberty to putter about embroidering my little poems and stories without my father interrupting with so much as a "What's that you're writing?"

6   But the truth is, I wanted him to interrupt. I wanted my father to understand what it was I was scribbling, to introduce me as "My only daughter, the writer." Not as "This is my only daughter. She teaches." *Es maestra—teacher.* Not even *profesora.*

7   In a sense, everything I have ever written has been for him, to win his approval even though I know my father can't read English words, even though my father's only reading includes the brown-ink *Esto* sports

magazines from Mexico City and the bloody *¡Alarma!* magazines that feature yet another sighting of *La Virgen de Gaudalupe* on a tortilla or a wife's revenge on her philandering husband by bashing his skull in with a *molcajete* (a kitchen mortar made of volcanic rock). Or the *fotonovelas,* the little picture paperbacks with tragedy and trauma erupting from the characters' mouths in bubbles.

8   A father represents, then, the public majority. A public who's disinterested in reading, and yet one whom I am writing about and for, and privately trying to woo.

9   When we were growing up in Chicago, we moved a lot because of my father. He suffered bouts of nostalgia. Then we'd have to let go of our flat, store the furniture with my mother's relatives, load the station wagon with baggage and bologna sandwiches and head south. To Mexico City.

10   We came back, of course. To yet another Chicago flat, another Chicago neighborhood, another Catholic school. Each time, my father would seek out the parish priest in order to get a tuition break, and complain or boast: "I have seven sons."

11   He meant *siete hijos,* seven children, but he translated it "sons." "I have seven sons." To anyone who would listen. The Sears Roebuck employee who sold us the washing machine. The short-order cook where my father ate his ham-and-eggs breakfasts. "I have seven sons." As if he deserved a medal from the state.

12   My papa. He didn't mean anything by the mistranslation, I'm sure. But somehow I could feel myself being erased. I'd tug my father's sleeve and whisper: "Not seven sons. Six! and one *daughter.*"

13   When my oldest brother graduated from medical school, he fulfilled my father's dream that we study hard and use this—our heads—instead of this—our hands. Even now my father's hands are thick and yellow, stubbed by a history of hammer and nails and twine and coils and springs. "Use this," my father said, tapping his head, "and not this," showing us those hands. He always looked tired when he said it.

14   Wasn't college an investment? And hadn't I spent all those years in college? And if I didn't marry, what was it all for? Why would anyone go to college and then choose to be poor? Especially someone who has always been poor.

15   Last year, after ten years of writing professionally, the financial rewards started to trickle in. My second National Endowment for the Arts Fellowship. A guest professorship at the University of California, Berkeley. My book, which sold to a major New York publishing house.

16   At Christmas, I flew home to Chicago. The house was throbbing, same as always; hot *tamales* and sweet *tamales* hissing in my mother's pressure cooker, and everybody—my mother, six brothers, wives, babies, aunts,

cousins—talking too loud and at the same time, like in a Fellini film, because that's just how we are.

17   I went upstairs to my father's room. One of my stories had just been translated into Spanish and published in an anthology of Chicano writing, and I wanted to show it to him. Ever since he recovered from a stroke two years ago, my father likes to spend his leisure hours horizontally. And that's how I found him, watching a Pedro Infante movie on Galavision and eating rice pudding.

18   There was a glass filled with milk on the bedside table. There were several vials of pills and balled Kleenex. And on the floor, one black sock and a plastic urinal that I didn't want to look at but looked at anyway. Pedro Infante was about to burst into song, and my father was laughing.

19   I'm not sure if it was because my story was translated into Spanish, or because it was published in Mexico, or perhaps because the story dealt with Tepeyac, the *colonia* my father was raised in and the house he grew up in, but at any rate, my father punched the mute button on his remote control and read my story.

20   I sat on the bed next to my father and waited. He read it very slowly. As if he were reading each line over and over. He laughed at all the right places and read lines he liked out loud. He pointed and asked questions: "Is this So—and—so?" "Yes," I said. He kept reading.

21   When he was finally finished, after what seemed like hours, my father looked up and asked: "Where can we get more copies of this for the relatives?"

Reading Reflection Questions *Answers will vary. Sample answers provided.*

1. What are the direct or indirect (implied) messages in this story?

   In general, the message is that even though her father thought she was

   less capable in some ways because she was a daughter and not a son,

   she found a way through her writing to impress him.

2. What does Sandra Cisneros mean by her statement, "I was/am the only daughter and *only* a daughter" (paragraph 3)?

   The second "only" relates to the idea of a daughter being less capable

   than a son.

3. In paragraph 2, Cisneros adds details to her self-description of being one daughter among six sons. Name one of the details. What effect does her including these details have on you as a reader? *Answers will vary.*

   _____

   _____

   _____

Objective Questions

4. T/F ____F____ Cisneros doesn't feel there are any advantages to being a daughter.

5. T/F ____F____ Her father didn't want her to go to college.

6. T/F ____T____ Her father often announces that he has seven sons (not specifying that one of his children is a female).

7. List two examples of details Cisneros includes in this essay that illustrate how she felt treated differently by her father because she is a daughter. *Answers will vary.*

_____

_____

Checking Vocabulary

Define the following in your own words, or provide a dictionary definition if you don't know the word.

8. retrospect: *looking back* _____

9. philandering: *cheating/having affairs* _____

10. vials: *bottles* _____

CRITICAL THINKING CHECKLIST

PURPOSE

1. What is the **purpose** of this piece of writing? Is it clear?
   Answers will vary.

_____

_____

IDEAS

2. What **ideas** and **background information** are provided to support the purpose of this piece of writing?

_____

_____

SUPPORT

3. What **evidence** and **examples** are used to explain and develop the ideas that support the argument made in the piece of writing? Are the evidence and examples provided sufficient for **support**?

_____

_____

4. Are there unfounded **assumptions** or unreasonable **biases**?

_____

_____

5. Are all of the **conclusions**, **implications**, and **consequences** (the results of the arguments taken to their farthest extreme) of the arguments considered?

_____

_____

6. Is the **point of view** clear and consistent, and have other points of view been considered?

_____

_____

7. Using these critical thinking tools, **analyze** the overall structure of this essay and the strength of the author's arguments, ideas, and support. Was he or she successful in accomplishing the purpose? Why, or why not?

_____

_____

Essay Assignments

1. Write an essay using the thesis statement, topic sentences, supporting examples, and concluding paragraph you wrote about in the activities in this chapter.

2. Write an analytical essay about an incident that happened to you (or that you witnessed) that had a significant impact on you. Describe what happened using specific details, and explain the impact. What lesson did you learn that day (about yourself, others, your culture, other)?

   a. The organization for this essay involves a general introduction that explains the incident briefly and includes a thesis statement, which tells exactly what lesson(s) you learned from the experience.

   b. The body paragraphs should use time order to tell what happened. Be sure to include some dialogue to make the event come alive for your readers; follow the tips for using dialogue correctly earlier in this chapter.

   c. When describing the incident, include specific details and descriptions, using as many senses as possible (sight, sound, touch, smell, taste). Review Chapters 4, 5, and 6 for essay writing basics and the writing process.

  d. In the conclusion, sum up the lesson(s) you learned and how you feel now about the incident.

  After you finish your first draft of this essay, use the narrative essay critique form to check for the basics. You can also have a classmate or friend check your draft using the checklist. Then review your essay.

3. Write a narrative essay about your first day of college.

4. Write a narrative essay about your first day on a job.

5. Write a narrative essay about an event that taught you something about yourself that you hadn't realized before.

6. Write a narrative essay about an occurrence related to your losing trust in someone.

7. Write a narrative essay about a complex or difficult situation and how you got through it.

SPOTLIGHT ON CRITICAL THINKING

Narration is a skill you will need to use both in college and in your career.

Writing narratives: You will have to write narratives with detailed descriptions of events from time to time. For example, in college writing classes, students are often asked to write a narrative essay about a significant day in their lives. In your career, you might have to write a narrative report about a series of events for a coworker or supervisor. For example, in a career in the culinary arts, you may have to write a narrative about how you made that perfect flan.

Use your **analysis** skills to check the **purpose** and **conclusions** in your narrative writing for college classes and later in your writing for your career. Develop your **purpose, ideas,** and **support** based on the critical thinking tips in Chapter 1.

Reading narratives: Use the Six Steps to Active Reading and the T-KED method for annotating as you read (both explained in Chapter 2) in your courses and in your career. For example, if you are reading a narrative case study in a psychology class, you will have to read carefully and annotate as you read in order to analyze the nuances of the case. On the job, if you were reading a proposal from a potential client, then you would need to read actively and annotate with questions and feedback as you read (see Chapter 2 for help).

To check your progress in meeting this chapter's objectives, log in to www .mywritinglab.com, go to the **Study Plan** tab, click on **Writing and Critical Thinking in the Modes** and choose **Essay Development—Narrating** from the list of subtopics. Read and view the resources in the **Review Materials** section, and then complete the **Recall, Apply,** and **Write** sets in the **Activities** section.

8 Description

Garden Pan   Hank Galmish

THINKING CRITICALLY

Look at the picture above. Then perform the following task.

Describe this photograph in your own words, using specific details that include colors, shapes, contrasts, and content.

_____

_____

_____

_____

_____

_____

_____

_____

150

LO 1 DESCRIPTIVE ESSAYS

Descriptive essays describe people, places and settings, things, or whole narrative scenes using as many of the senses as possible—*sight, sound, touch, smell, and taste*—and as many concrete, descriptive words as possible.

Critical Thinking and Description

Like all essays, descriptive essays should have a clear purpose: to inform, to narrate, to convince your readers to do something or believe something, and so on. For instance, you could describe a particular computer system in order to convince your readers that it is the best buy when shopping for a new computer.

BEFORE WRITING A DESCRIPTIVE ESSAY

Before you begin to write a descriptive essay on an assigned topic, or one you have chosen, start by asking yourself these questions:

1. What exactly am I describing?
2. What kind of language and details should I include to best describe the object, place, or person I am describing?
3. How should I organize my paragraphs after my introduction and thesis, and how can I move smoothly from one descriptive detail to the next?
4. Why am I writing this description? What is my purpose for describing this person, place, or thing? What do I want my readers to learn or understand from reading this description?
5. How should I conclude this essay?

Answering these questions will lead you to an expository thesis statement, help you determine which language and details will provide vivid description and images for support, and give you a general idea of how you want to organize your essay.

APPLYING CRITICAL THINKING

| PURPOSE | IDEAS | SUPPORT | ASSUMPTIONS BIASES | CONCLUSIONS | POINT OF VIEW | ANALYSIS |

Specific, or concrete, details and images provide important **support** in a descriptive essay. Use the following tips to write clear, vivid descriptions:

1. Choose words that conjure vivid images, not vague descriptors such as "pretty" or "nice."

    Vague descriptors: She had a pretty face and nice hair.

    Revised: Her face was oval and pleasantly rosy, and her hair was sleek and golden.

2. Use words related to the senses (sight, hearing, touch, taste, and smell) when you describe a person, place, or thing to create a picture in your reader's mind. For instance, in describing a room, include visual details (light streaming through the window), sounds (wind in the trees outside), taste (if possible—e.g., a taste in the air), smells (of clean laundry), touch (the texture of a blanket), and the overall atmospheric feel.

3. Use similes (comparisons of one thing to another that begin with the words "like" or "as") or metaphors (comparisons in which one thing is described as being another thing). For instance, you can use a simile to help someone get a better image of your grandmother's hands by writing,

    My grandmother's hands were *as rough as a lizard's shedding skin.*

    Or you can use a metaphor to describe your grandmother's hands:

    Her hands were *gentle spiders* playing with the edge of the quilt.

    Be careful, though, not to resort to common clichés in your description such as "He looked like a Greek god." Such phrases do not create vivid images because they are overused.

Cross Reference
See Chapter 30 for more about clichés.

ACTIVITY 8-1   Practicing Description

Directions: *Briefly describe the following topics using* concrete *language (precise and vivid words) and specific details. Then provide a purpose for describing the object, place, or person:* Answers will vary.

   1. Briefly describe your grandmother (or a grandmother-like person).

_____

_____

_____

_____

_____

Purpose: _____

_____

_____

_____

2. Briefly describe your bedroom.

_____

_____

_____

_____

Purpose: _____

_____

_____

_____

3. Briefly describe your car (or the car owned by someone you know).

_____

_____

_____

_____

Purpose: _____

_____

_____

_____

WRITING A DESCRIPTIVE ESSAY

The structure of a descriptive essay is usually based on the object, place, or person you are describing. In a descriptive essay, you will often use spatial order to focus on one aspect at a time. Another common pattern is order of importance, in which you list characteristics of the person, place, or thing in the order of most to least important or vice versa (for instance, starting

Cross Reference

See Chapter 6 for more about spatial order and order of importance.

with a description of your mother's face and eyes before moving on to her body type, voice, and other characteristics).

Be sure to include transitional words and phrases as you move from one characteristic to another. For instance, "In one corner of my room, there is a big, overstuffed chair upholstered with material with small blue flowers. <u>In the opposite</u> corner stands the bureau my mother used when she was a child."

Organize your descriptive essay based on the best choice for the object, place, or person you are describing (arrange spatially or by order of importance) and based on your description's purpose, the message of the essay. Engage your critical thinking skills to make a choice for the best order and plan.

The chart below provides a brief overview of the structure of a descriptive essay.

BASIC STRUCTURE FOR A DESCRIPTIVE ESSAY

INTRODUCTORY PARAGRAPH

Sets up background for describing the person, place, or thing that leads into the thesis; statement of purpose.

Thesis statement: Presents what you are trying to explain, show, prove, or argue through the description of this subject; what you want your readers to understand about it.

BODY PARAGRAPHS
(Two to five, depending on assignment and purpose)

Develop the description in spatial order or order of importance. Descriptive essays often have simple topic sentences that introduce the next aspect being described.

Use transitions within and between paragraphs to emphasize the transition from one detail or part to the next.

Provide concrete details and description.

Use as many senses as possible in your description (sight, sound, smell, touch, and taste).

Use comparisons and similes to describe the subject.

Add commentary about the details and descriptions to develop the expository purpose/thesis statement.

Create a concrete visual image that allows the readers to form a visual in their minds.

CONCLUDING PARAGRAPH

Sum up **and** re-emphasize the thesis, the purpose for your description in the first place.

LO 2 STRUCTURING A DESCRIPTIVE ESSAY

Topic

If you do not have a topic assigned by your instructor for your descriptive essay, then brainstorm ideas for things, places, or people you might want to describe. Then come up with some ideas for a purpose for describing the topic you have chosen. What do you want your readers to understand through your description?

A Few Topic Possibilities

Here is a list of some topics you could use for a descriptive essay: your car, your family, your campus, your pet, your workplace, your favorite restaurant, your street, your room, a particular friend, your classroom, your computer, your favorite meal, your local movie theater, and so on.

Thesis Statements

In a descriptive essay, you can reach some kind of judgment based on your detailed description, argue for a particular preference, critique an object or person, or just describe something in order to inform your readers about it. You state the purpose in your thesis statement. In order to come up with a good thesis statement for your descriptive essay, you'll need to do some form of prewriting on your subject. Try brainstorming a list of details and ideas about your topic, or cluster to generate details and ideas in order to determine the purpose for your description. Here are some examples:

Cross Reference
See Chapter 5 for a review of prewriting techniques.

Topic:	Wooden kayaks
Purpose:	My goal is to describe a wooden kayak in detail in order to prove that a kayak is as much a work of art as it is a boat for actual use.
Thesis:	A wooden kayak is a detailed and elaborate boat that is as much a work of art as it is a utilitarian object.
Topic:	My science professor
Purpose:	To describe my unusual science teacher and to show my readers how her strange outfits and eccentric personality are all part of her teaching approach.
Thesis:	My science teacher is an eccentric instructor who wears elaborate and bizarre outfits every day with her lab coat and acts a bit crazy, all for the sake of improving her students' learning.

ACTIVITY 8-2   Creating Thesis Statements

Directions: *Using the topics listed below, cluster on a separate sheet of paper to generate ideas, and then create a one-sentence thesis statement for each general topic. Make sure the thesis has a clear message or purpose to convey about the subject you are describing.* Answers will vary.

1. Topic: Your school

Thesis: _____

_____

2. Topic: Your street/neighborhood

Thesis: _____

_____

3. Topic: A favorite item of clothing

Thesis: _____

_____

4. Topic: Your best friend

Thesis: _____

_____

5. Topic: A flower garden

Thesis: _____

_____

Introductory Paragraph

Begin your descriptive essay with a general introduction that sets up the topic of your description and intrigues your readers. End the introductory paragraph with your thesis statement.

Body Paragraphs

The body paragraphs in a descriptive essay focus on developing specific details and concrete examples to describe your topic. They also comment on the description and your emotional or intellectual response to the subject you are describing. *Topic sentences* in a descriptive essay focus on describing a particular quality or area of the subject you are describing.

Topic Sentence Example: (based on the kayak sample thesis):
The most important element that makes a wooden kayak a work of art
is the fact that it is hand crafted from beautiful, carefully prepared wood.

ACTIVITY 8-3 Creating Topic Sentences

Directions: *Now create a topic sentence you could use to develop a body paragraph
for each of the thesis statements you created in Activity 8-2.* *Answers will vary.*

1. Your school: _____

   _____

   _____

2. Your street/neighborhood: _____

   _____

   _____

3. A favorite item of clothing: _____

   _____

   _____

4. Your best friend: _____

   _____

   _____

5. A flower garden: _____

   _____

   _____

   Details are particularly important in a descriptive essay. Details can be
objective (factual descriptions without feelings, judgments, or biases), or
they can be **subjective** (details that relate to your own biases, judgments, or
emotions).

Sample objective detail for the kayak topic: Any wood used to create
a wooden boat must be specifically treated to ensure that it is water safe
and will not warp.

Sample subjective detail for the kayak topic: Though many hardwoods
work well for building a kayak, the most beautiful wood to use is maple.

ACTIVITY 8-4   Providing Details

Directions: *Now provide at least three vivid, descriptive details you would use for the topic sentences you created in Activity 8-3. Then decide if your descriptions are objective, subjective, or both.* Answers will vary.

1. Your school: _____

   _____

   _____

   Objective, subjective, or both: _____

2. Your street/neighborhood: _____

   _____

   _____

   Objective, subjective, or both: _____

3. A favorite item of clothing: _____

   _____

   _____

   Objective, subjective, or both: _____

4. Your best friend: _____

   _____

   _____

   Objective, subjective, or both: _____

5. A flower garden: _____

   _____

   _____

   Objective, subjective, or both: _____

ACTIVITY 8-5   Abstract to Vivid Language

Directions: *Translate the abstract descriptive words that are bolded in each sentence into vivid, specific descriptions of the thing or person in the sentence. Try to include sensory description when possible (sight, touch, smell, sound, taste).* Answers will vary.

Example: The food was **bland**.

The food tasted like cardboard mixed with mashed potatoes without salt.

_____

1. It is a **typical** house on a typical street.

_____

_____

2. My friend is **odd looking**.

_____

_____

3. It was the **ugliest** cat I had ever seen.

_____

_____

4. The room was **huge**.

_____

_____

5. The car was **old**.

_____

_____

One way to add more specific description is to use comparisons such as similes and metaphors.

ACTIVITY 8-6   Creating Comparisons (Similes and Metaphors)

Directions: *Come up with a simile or metaphor for each of the objects below to help your readers get a good visual or sensory image of it. Try not to use a clichéd, commonly used simile or metaphor.* Answers will vary.

Example:

Blue eyes

Simile: *eyes as blue as a spring sky*

Metaphor: *faded denim eyes*

1. A nice face

   Simile: _____

   Metaphor: _____

2. Green

   Simile: _____

   Metaphor: _____

3. Happy

   Simile: _____

   Metaphor: _____

4. Hairy

   Simile: _____

   Metaphor: _____

5. Crazy

   Simile: _____

   Metaphor: _____

Transitions that are useful in writing descriptive essays include those showing comparison, examples, place, or amount (see Chapter 6, pages 114–116).

Concluding Paragraph

The concluding paragraph for a descriptive essay should remind your readers what the purpose of your description was—why you described this person, place, or object in the first place.

ACTIVITY 8-7 Writing a Conclusion

Directions: *Choose one of the topics you have been developing in the previous activities, and write a three- to five-sentence concluding paragraph for it.* Answers will vary.

_____

_____

_____

_____

_____

Remember, it's important to avoid using abstract descriptors in your essay. Instead, use vivid, specific descriptions, language, and examples.

ACTIVITY 8-8   Describe a Monster

Directions: *This activity requires two people, so work with a partner. It is a classic description exercise that is a fun way to practice using specific and concrete description, and it is a great way to increase your awareness of your reader's need to visualize what you are describing.*

Step One: On a sheet of paper, draw a monster. Be creative, and enjoy yourself. Don't let anyone see your monster drawing; turn it over on your desk.

Step Two: Now, on a separate sheet of paper, write a one-paragraph description of your monster using specific, concrete descriptive words.

Step Three: Exchange your written description only with your partner. Keep your monster drawing upside down so that your partner doesn't see it.

Step Four: Read your partner's written description of his or her monster. Then, on a separate sheet of paper, draw the monster based on the description given.

Step Five: Compare the original drawing to the one created based on the written description.

Step Six: Answer the following questions. *Answers will vary.*

1. Did the drawings look close to the original? (Ignore drawing talent differences; focus on basic structures such as number of eyes, legs, overall shape, and so on.)

_____

_____

2. What problems arose from details missing in the description?

_____

_____

3. What would you do differently now if you were asked to rewrite your description of your monster?

_____

_____

_____

Use the critique form on page 162 to check for the basics in your descriptive essay draft.

DESCRIPTIVE ESSAY CRITIQUE FORM

PURPOSE IDEAS SUPPORT ASSUMPTIONS BIASES CONCLUSIONS POINT OF VIEW ANALYSIS

Use the following critique form to check for the basics in your descriptive essay draft.

Overall   Done well Needs work

1. Does the essay describe a person, place, or thing with an analytical **purpose** (e.g., to help clarify, narrate, inform, convince)? _____ _____

2. Does the essay use a logical order in the body paragraphs (with an analytical setup and concluding paragraph)? _____ _____

3. Are the paragraphs broken up well and about the right length? _____ _____

Introduction

4. Is the title interesting and in the correct format? _____ _____

5. Is there a general introduction that sets up the thesis? _____ _____

6. Is there a clear thesis statement that explains the significance of the person, place, or thing being described? _____ _____

Body

7. Do the **ideas** in the body paragraphs develop logically and flow smoothly? _____ _____

8. Are transitions used between and, when needed, within the paragraphs? _____ _____

9. Do the body paragraphs include **support** and descriptive details and concrete images? _____ _____

10. Does the writer use as many senses as possible in the description? _____ _____

11. If similes or metaphors are used, are they fresh and effective? _____ _____

Conclusion

12. Does the **concluding** paragraph sum up the **purpose** and **analysis** of the description? _____ _____

Editing

13. Circle the following errors you think you see in this draft: spelling errors, fragments, run-ons/comma splices, errors in comma and semicolon/colon use, pronoun disagreement, reference fault errors, and errors in parallelism, apostrophe use, verb use/tense, and passive voice construction. (See the handbook section for help in identifying and correcting these errors.)

14. Other types of grammar or sentence-level errors:

_____

Comments:

_____

_____

(LO 3) COMPLEMENTARY MODES FOR DESCRIPTIVE ESSAYS

When writing a descriptive essay, you can tap into several other modes described in other chapters that combine well to create a powerful description.

- **Narration:** Narration is essential in description for adding concrete details and vivid word pictures.
- **Illustration and example:** Most good descriptive essays include specific illustrations and examples to develop the purpose of the writing.
- **Process:** Process focuses on describing a series of steps to accomplish something and can be used to describe a particular ritual or process.
- **Cause and effect:** You can describe an event in detail and employ cause-and-effect analysis to look at the consequences of the actions that take place.
- **Comparison/contrast:** A great way to describe something or someone is to compare (or contrast) them to something or someone else.
- **Argument:** Sometimes, your reason for describing something or someone in detail is to persuade your readers to learn a particular lesson or feel a particular way: You are combining argument techniques with your description. For instance, you could describe a particular object, such as a car or computer, in order to convince your readers to purchase one.

Sample Student Essay

Hill 1

Lynne Hill

Professor Lib

English 090

3 February 2008

My Husband's Guitar

My husband plays guitar everyday. I have gotten used to hearing its music move through our house, especially in the early morning and late evening. My husband's guitar is a beautiful and important part of

Continued ▶

Hill 2

Thesis statement

our lives together. His guitar is a beautiful object in and of itself; however, it is more than a thing: it is also an extension of my husband himself, and the music it makes reflects his moods and serves as a tribute to our lives together.

Topic sentence

Descriptive details

Concluding sentence

My husband's guitar is a classically styled acoustic guitar. It is made of wood and has six metal strings. The front of the guitar is a lovely honey-amber color, with fine-lined grain and a high-polish shine. The surface feels smooth, slick, and cool to the touch. There is a black plastic, kidney-shaped back plate where he strums the strings. The sides, back, and neck of the guitar are a darker colored wood, the color of strong coffee. Also, the long neck has six metal strings, four of them copper colored and two of them the color of steel. Besides the strings, the neck has 20 fret lines and six mother-of-pearl inset dots. Both of these features help him play correct chords and guide his fingers to the right places on the strings when he plays. Finally, six knobs that look a little like keys or small handles sit at the top of the neck that the strings are wrapped around. When he turns these knobs, the stings are adjusted, and he can get his guitar in perfect tune. As you can imagine, the guitar is a beautiful object, and even if I never heard my husband play, I would still find it admirable.

Topic sentence

Concluding sentence

However, it is when my husband plays that the life and beauty of his guitar really shine. His music is rich and comforting. The sound is like a comforting humming. His songs and chords reflect the moods and best moments of his personality and of our marriage. He plays happy songs with faster, more upbeat chords, and he plays slower songs with more somber chords for the sadder or more serious times of our lives. In fact, I can usually guess my husband's mood by the type of song or the chords he is playing on his guitar.

Hill 3

My husband's guitar is like an extension of himself and our relationship. It is a beautiful object with a lovely message to convey to anyone who takes the time to listen. I cherish its presence in our home and
the music my husband makes with it.

Restatement of thesis

ACTIVITY 8-9 Thinking Critically About the Student Essay

Directions: **Analyze** *the essay to identify the features and details characteristic
of the descriptive mode. Mark them on the essay. Then, reread the essay, and
make a list of specific revisions you would make to correct any problems with content, organization, transitions, and style.*

PROFESSIONAL DESCRIPTIVE ESSAY

More Room

Judith Ortiz Cofer

Judith Ortiz Cofer was born in Hormigueros, Puerto Rico, in 1952 and
emigrated with her family to the United States in 1954. She is the
author of *The Line of the Sun*; *The Latin Deli: Prose and Poetry*; *Silent
Dancing: A Partial Remembrance of a Puerto Rican Childhood*; and two
books of poetry: *Reaching for the Mainland* and *Terms of Survival*. Her
work has appeared in *Glamour*, *The Georgia Review*, *Kenyon Review*, and
other journals. Currently, she is a professor of English and Creative
Writing at the University of Georgia. Her most recent book is *An
Island Like You: Stories of the Barrio*.

1   My grandmother's house is like a chambered nautilus; it has many
rooms, yet it is not a mansion. Its proportions are small and its design simple. It is a house that has grown organically, according to the needs of its
inhabitants. To all of us in the family it is known as *la casa de Mama*. It is
the place of our origin; the stage for our memories and dreams of Island life.

2   I remember how in my childhood it sat on stilts; this was before it had a downstairs. It rested on its perch like a great blue bird, not a flying sort of bird, more like a nesting hen, but with spread wings. Grandfather had built it soon after their marriage. He was a painter and house builder by trade, a poet and meditative man by nature. As each of their eight children were born, new rooms were added. After a few years, the paint did not exactly match, nor the materials, so that there was a chronology to it, like the rings of a tree, and Mama could tell you the history of each room in her *casa,* and thus the genealogy of the family along with it.

3   Her room is the heart of the house. Though I have seen it recently, and both woman and room have diminished in size, changed by the new perspective of my eyes, now capable of looking over countertops and tall beds, it is not this picture I carry in my memory of Mama's *casa.* Instead, I see her room as a queen's chamber where a small woman loomed large, a throne-room with a massive four-poster bed in its center which stood taller than a child's head. It was on this bed where her own children had been born that the smallest grandchildren were allowed to take naps in the afternoons; here too was where Mama secluded herself to dispense private advice to her daughters, sitting on the edge of the bed, looking down at whoever sat on the rocker where generations of babies had been sung to sleep. To me she looked like a wise empress right out of the fairy tales I was addicted to reading.

4   Though the room was dominated by the mahogany four-poster, it also contained all of Mama's symbols of power. On her dresser instead of cosmetics there were jars filled with herbs: *yerba buena, yerba mala,* the making of purgatives and teas to which we were all subjected during childhood crises. She had a steaming cup for anyone who could not, or would not, get up to face life on any given day.

5   If the acrid aftertaste of her cures for malingering did not get you out of bed, then it was time to call *el doctor.*

6   And there was the monstrous chifforobe she kept locked with a little golden key she did not hide. This was a test of her dominion over us; though my cousins and I wanted a look inside that massive wardrobe more than anything, we never reached for that little key lying on top of her Bible on the dresser. This was also where she placed her earrings and rosary at night. God's word was her security system. This chifforobe was the place where I imagined she kept jewels, satin slippers, and elegant sequined, silk gowns of heartbreaking fineness. I lusted after those imaginary costumes. I had heard that Mama had been a great beauty in her youth, and the belle of many balls. My cousins had other ideas as to what she kept in that wooden vault: its secret could be money (Mama did not hand cash to strangers, banks were out of the question, so there were

stories that her mattress was stuffed with dollar bills, and that she buried coins in jars in her garden under rosebushes, or kept them in her inviolate chifforobe); there might be that legendary gun salvaged from the Spanish-American conflict over the Island. We went wild over suspected treasures that we made up simply because children have to fill locked trunks with something wonderful.

7   On the wall above the bed hung a heavy silver crucifix. Christ's agonized head hung directly over Mama's pillow. I avoided looking at this weapon suspended over where her head would lay; and on the rare occasions when I was allowed to sleep on that bed, I scooted down to the safe middle of the mattress, where her body's impression took me in like a mother's lap. Having taken care of the obligatory religious decoration with a crucifix, Mama covered the other walls with objects sent to her over the years by her children in the States. *Los Nueva Yores* were represented by, among other things, a postcard of Niagara Falls from her son Hernán, postmarked, Buffalo, N.Y. In a conspicuous gold frame hung a large color photograph of her daughter Nena, her husband and their five children at the entrance to Disneyland in California. From us she had gotten a black lace fan. Father had brought it to her from a tour of duty with the Navy in Europe (on Sundays she would remove it from its hook on the wall to fan herself at mass). Each year more items were added as the family grew and dispersed, and every object in the room had a story attached to it, a *cuento* which Mama would bestow on anyone who received the privilege of a day alone with her. It was almost worth pretending to be sick, though the bitter herb purgatives of the body were a big price to pay for the spirit revivals of her story-telling.

8   Mama slept alone on her large bed, except for the times when a sick grandchild warranted the privilege, or when a heartbroken daughter came home in need of more than herbal teas. In the family there is a story about how this came to be.

9   When one of the daughters, my mother or one of her sisters, tells the *cuento* of how Mama came to own her nights, it is usually preceded by the qualifications that Papa's exile from his wife's room was not a result of animosity between the couple, but that the act had been Mama's famous bloodless coup for her personal freedom. Papa was the benevolent dictator of her body and her life who had had to be banished from her bed so that Mama could better serve her family. Before the telling, we had to agree that the old man was not to blame. We all recognized that in the family Papa was as an *alma de Dios,* a saintly, soft-spoken presence whose main pleasures in life, such as writing poetry and reading the Spanish large-type editions of *Reader's Digest,* always took place outside the vortex of Mama's crowded realm. It was not his fault, after all, that every year or so he planted

a baby-seed in Mama's fertile body, keeping her from leading the active life she needed and desired. He loved her and the babies. Papa composed odes and lyrics to celebrate births and anniversaries and hired musicians to accompany him singing them to his family and friends at extravagant pig-roasts he threw yearly. Mama and the oldest girls worked for days preparing the food. Papa sat for hours in his painter's shed, also his study and library, composing the songs. At these celebrations he was also known to give long speeches in praise of God, his fecund wife, and his beloved island. As a middle child, my mother remembers these occasions as a time when the women sat in the kitchen and lamented their burdens, while the men feasted out in the patio, their rum-thickened voices rising in song and praise for each other, *compañeros* all.

10   It was after the birth of her eighth child, after she had lost three at birth or in infancy, that Mama made her decision. They say that Mama had had a special way of letting her husband know that they were expecting, one that had begun when, at the beginning of their marriage, he had built her a house too confining for her taste. So, when she discovered her first pregnancy, she supposedly drew plans for another room, which he dutifully executed. Every time a child was due, she would demand *more space, more space*. Papa acceded to her wishes, child after child, since he had learned early that Mama's renowned temper was a thing that grew like a monster along with a new belly. In this way Mama got the house that she wanted, but with each child she lost in heart and energy. She had knowledge of her body and perceived that if she had any more children, her dreams and her plans would have to be permanently forgotten, because she would be a chronically ill woman, like Flora with her twelve children: asthma, no teeth, in bed more than on her feet.

11   And so, after my youngest uncle was born, she asked Papa to build a large room at the back of the house. He did so in joyful anticipation. Mama had asked him special things this time: shelves on the walls, a private entrance. He thought that she meant this room to be a nursery where several children could sleep. He thought it was a wonderful idea. He painted it his favorite color, sky blue, and made large windows looking out over a green hill and the church spires beyond. But nothing happened. Mama's belly did not grow, yet she seemed in a frenzy of activity over the house. Finally, an anxious Papa approached his wife to tell her that the new room was finished and ready to be occupied. And Mama, they say, replied: "Good, it's for *you*."

12   And so it was that Mama discovered the only means of birth control available to a Catholic woman of her time: sacrifice. She gave up the comfort of Papa's sexual love for something she deemed greater: the right to own and control her body, so that she might live to meet her

grandchildren—me among them—so that she could give more of herself to the ones already there, so that she could be more than a channel for other lives, so that even now that time has robbed her of the elasticity of her body and of her amazing reservoir of energy she still emanates the kind of joy that can only be achieved by living according to the dictates of one's own heart.

Reading Reflection Questions   *Answers will vary. Sample answers provided.*

1. What are the direct or indirect (implied) messages in this story?

   That this girl respected her grandmother for all she did and how she

   took back her freedom and control of her body to focus on her family

2. Why do you think the grandmother keeps demanding more room?

   To match the number of children and to give her more space of her own

   _____

3. What does the extra space represent for her?

   Freedom and autonomy

   _____

Objective Questions

Answer the following true/false questions by writing T for true or F for false.

4. T/F ___F___ The husband, Cofer's grandfather, doesn't want to grant the request for more room.

5. T/F ___F___ The grandmother didn't really have a hot temper when she was pregnant.

6. T/F ___T___ The author understands her grandmother's needs and reasons for more room.

7. List two specific examples of descriptive details used in this story that gave readers a vivid image. *Answers may vary.*

   _____

   _____

Checking Vocabulary

Define the following in your own words or provide a dictionary definition if you do not know the word.

8. malingering: *feigning illness*

9. fertile: *easily impregnated*

10. elasticity: *flexibility—ability to stretch*

CRITICAL THINKING CHECKLIST

Answers will vary.

1. What is the **purpose** of this piece of writing? Is it clear?

_____

_____

2. What **ideas** and **background information** are provided to support the purpose of this piece of writing?

_____

_____

3. What **evidence** and **examples** are used to explain and develop the ideas that support the argument made in the piece of writing? Are the evidence and examples provided sufficient for **support**?

_____

_____

4. Are there unfounded **assumptions** or unreasonable **biases**?

_____

_____

5. Are all of the **conclusions**, **implications**, and **consequences** of the arguments (the results of the arguments taken to their farthest extreme) considered?

_____

_____

6. Is the **point of view** clear and consistent, and have other points of view been considered?

_____

_____

7. Using these critical thinking tools, **analyze** the overall structure of this essay and the strength of the author's arguments, ideas, and support. Was he or she successful in accomplishing her purpose? Why, or why not?

_____

_____

Essay Assignments

1. Using one of the topics you developed in this chapter, write a complete descriptive essay on that topic. Use the critique form to check your draft.

2. Describe a room in your house or apartment using as many senses as possible. Use specific, concrete details as opposed to abstract descriptions such as "large" or "beautiful." Create a picture of the room in your readers' minds by painting a picture with details and sensory descriptions. Finally, come up with an expository purpose: a conclusion you've reached upon examining this room.

3. Describe a particular spot on your college campus. Pick a space no larger than 25′ × 25′ so you can include concrete, specific descriptive details. Be sure to incorporate as many senses as possible in your description. Then create a thesis statement that has the purpose of establishing what kind of atmosphere this place has and what mood it evokes.

4. Describe one of the following people, using concrete, specific nouns and adjectives and including as many of the senses as possible. Avoid vague, abstract descriptions such as "beautiful," "handsome," and so on. Create a vivid picture of this person by developing a portrait with a description in words. Be sure to include a thesis statement that puts forth a purpose to develop: what you want to show a reader or a conclusion you have reached about this person.

your mother	your father	your best friend
your grandmother	your grandfather	a sibling

SPOTLIGHT ON CRITICAL THINKING

Description is a skill you will need to use both in college and in your career.

Writing descriptive pieces: You may have to write detailed descriptions of lab results in a science class. Similarly, in careers in the sciences, you might have to describe a product to clients in exact detail. Use your **analysis** skills to check the **purpose** and **conclusions** in your descriptive writing for college classes and later in your writing for your career. For instance, if you are in the field of nursing, you may have to describe in detail the condition of a patient. Develop your **purpose, ideas,** and **support** based on the critical thinking tips in Chapter 1.

Reading descriptive pieces: Use the Six Steps to Active Reading and the T-KED method for annotating as you read (both explained in Chapter 2) in your courses and in your career. For example, if you are reading a description of a crime scene in a criminal justice course, you would need to pay special attention to all the details and clues and annotate as you read. On the job, if you were reading descriptions of various computer software for your company, then you would need to read actively and annotate with questions and feedback as you read (see Chapter 2 for help).

To check your progress in meeting this chapter's objectives, log in to www .mywritinglab.com, go to the **Study Plan** tab, click on **Writing and Critical Thinking in the Modes** and choose **Essay Development—Describing** from the list of subtopics. Read and view the resources in the **Review Materials** section, and then complete the **Recall, Apply,** and **Write** sets in the **Activities** section.

9 Process

Korean Fishing Boat

Tom Shugrue

THINKING CRITICALLY

Look at the pictures above. Then answer the questions that follow.

1. In your own words, describe the process that is demonstrated in these two images.

_____

_____

2. If you had to write a short essay describing a process that you perform routinely at home or work, how would you organize the essay?

_____

_____

3. What are some reasons for writing a description of a specific process? Provide an example.

_____

_____

(LO 1) PROCESS ESSAYS

Process essays tell people how things work (e.g. a combustion engine or the digestive system), how to do something (bake a cake, get legislation through Congress, find a job), or how to analyze a process to see how efficient it is or to explain a better alternative (for example, how a traditional combustion engine works, how this contributes to pollution, and how a hybrid engine works and decreases pollution). Process writing is very common in business, in science and math classes, and in careers that involve many process-related tasks.

Critical Thinking and Process

Be sure to make the purpose of your process essay clear: to inform, to critique, and to propose an alternative process after describing the status quo (the way things are now). Think carefully about the best way to describe the process and demonstrate the purpose for your essay: What do you want your readers to learn about this process besides how to do it? How can you best structure the essay to achieve your goal, and what details will you include?

BEFORE WRITING A PROCESS ESSAY

Before you begin to write a process essay on an assigned topic, or one you have chosen, start by asking yourself these questions:

1. What process am I describing?
2. What specific steps, examples, and details should I use to describe the process?
3. How should I organize my paragraphs after my introduction and thesis statement, and how can I move smoothly from one step or detail to the next?
4. What is my purpose for writing this process description (to describe how something works, to tell someone how to accomplish a task, to critique a process and provide a better alternative, other)?
5. What do I want my readers to learn and understand after reading about this process? Who is my intended audience, and how much will they already know about my topic?

Answering these questions will lead you to an expository thesis statement, help you determine what examples to use, and give you a general idea of how you want to organize your essay.

ACTIVITY 9-1   Steps in a Process

Directions: *Briefly describe the major steps in each of the following common processes. Then come up with a purpose for writing about such a process (what you would want your readers to understand or learn through your description of the process).* Answers will vary.

1. Brushing teeth properly: _____

   _____

   _____

   Purpose: _____

   _____

2. Making a sandwich: _____

   _____

   _____

   Purpose: _____

   _____

3. Registering for classes: _____

   _____

   _____

   Purpose: _____

   _____

4. Grocery shopping: _____

   _____

   _____

   Purpose: _____

   _____

5. Reading a textbook chapter: _____

   _____

   _____

   Purpose: _____

   _____

WRITING A PROCESS ESSAY

The structure of a process essay is usually based on chronological order, describing one step at a time, in the order it happens. For example, if you were telling your readers how to properly make a bed, you might describe it like this:

> To make your bed in the best possible way, start by taking your fitted sheet and putting one corner tightly over the top left corner of your bed. Next, put the other top corner of the fitted sheet on the top right corner of your bed. Carefully pull the bottom two corners of the sheet to the bottom of your bed, and do the same process with the two bottom corners of your mattress. Next, get your flat sheet ready . . .

A process essay can also be organized by order of importance of the individual steps if the process doesn't require a particular sequence of steps. For example, if you were describing the process of applying for a new job, you might choose order of importance to list the steps involved and include paragraphs on how to list qualifications, how to update a resumé, how to write an application letter, and how to present oneself in an interview.

Decide what your *expository purpose* or message is for writing a process description (to evaluate a process, to teach or instruct, to propose an alternative process, other). Be sure to describe the steps in chronological order or order of importance and to include *descriptive details* that explain and illustrate each one. Then make sure that your essay's conclusion reiterates the purpose of your process description or analysis. The following chart provides a brief overview of the structure of a process essay.

BASIC STRUCTURE FOR A PROCESS ESSAY

INTRODUCTORY PARAGRAPH

Sets up background for the process and why you are describing it.

Thesis statement: A statement that describes what you are trying to explain, show, prove, or argue through describing a process. Do you want to instruct someone in how to perform a specific task? Do you want to explain how a process works? Or do you want to critique a process and propose an alternative?

BODY PARAGRAPHS (two to five, depending on assignment and purpose)

Develop the process of the event using time order or order of importance. Topic sentences should clarify the type of order and the categories or major stages of the process.

Use transitions within and between paragraphs to emphasize switching to the next step.

Provide concrete details and description.

Define terms when necessary, especially if your process involves parts or tools.

Add commentary and analysis about the steps, details, and descriptions to help develop the expository purpose/thesis statement.

CONCLUDING PARAGRAPH

Sum up and re-emphasize the thesis: the **purpose** for describing this process in the first place.

STRUCTURING A PROCESS ESSAY

Topic

If you do not have a topic assigned by your instructor for your process essay, then brainstorm ideas for a process you might want to describe. Then come up with some ideas for a purpose for describing the topic. What do you want your readers to understand through your description of the process?

A Few Topic Possibilities

You could write about the following: a scientific or natural process you have learned about through other courses; a daily ritual such as getting ready for school, making your lunch, or studying for a test in order to show what you think is the best approach to accomplishing it; or the best way to accomplish a specific goal such as saving money for college.

Thesis Statements

The thesis statement in a process essay establishes what process you are describing or analyzing and for what purpose. For instance, if you were writing a basic essay in order to explain how to do a task step by step, then the thesis statement would establish that very simply.

> **Example:** In order to make a perfect homemade cake, complete each of the following steps in order, and you will succeed.

If you were critiquing an existing process and proposing an alternative, you would set out both of these goals in your thesis statement.

> **Example:** The combustion engine has been in use for over a century, but it is inefficient and bad for the environment; therefore, the hybrid engine's process of using gas to start and electricity for driving makes it better for the environment and an overall better choice for a new car.

The thesis statement, then, in a process essay describes the process and your purpose for writing about it: what you want your readers to understand about the targeted process after reading your essay.

ACTIVITY 9-2   Creating Thesis Statements

Directions: *Create a one-sentence thesis statement for each general topic. Make sure the thesis has a clear message or lesson to convey about why you would describe each process.* Answers will vary.

1. **Topic:** Choosing a new wardrobe for school or work

   Thesis sentence: _____

   _____

2. **Topic:** Writing an essay

   Thesis sentence: _____

   _____

3. **Topic:** Choosing a movie to see

   Thesis sentence: _____

   _____

4. **Topic:** Finding an apartment to rent

   Thesis sentence: _____

   _____

5. **Topic:** Finding a part-time job

   Thesis sentence: _____

   _____

Introductory Paragraph

Begin your process essay with a general introduction that sets up the process you'll be describing. End the introductory paragraph with your thesis statement.

Body Paragraphs

The body paragraphs in a process essay can be arranged in time order or order of importance, depending on the decision you have made about the most efficient way for you to explain the purpose of your thesis statement. Topic sentences should clarify the type of order and the categories or major stages of the process. You can describe one step in each paragraph, or you can arrange the body paragraphs so you describe the process, critique it, and then propose an alternative. When you use any of these organizational patterns, you need to include specific examples and definitions as needed. Particularly useful transitions for process essays are those relating to the addition of another point (see below). Other transitions you will find useful include those used to strengthen a point and to show a summary, examples, purpose, place, and time (see Chapter 6, pages 114–116).

TRANSITIONS TO . . .

Show Addition of Another Point

again	but also	in addition	nor
also	equally important	last	plus the fact
and	finally	lastly	secondly
and then	first	likewise	then too
another	further	moreover	thirdly
besides	furthermore	next	too

ACTIVITY 9-3   Creating Topic Sentences

Directions: *Create one possible topic sentence for each of the thesis statements you created in Activity 9-2.* Answers will vary.

1. **Topic:** Choosing a new wardrobe for school or work

   Topic sentence: _____

   _____

2. **Topic:** Writing an essay

   Topic sentence: _____

   _____

3. Topic: Choosing a movie to see

Topic sentence: _____

_____

4. Topic: Finding an apartment to rent

Topic sentence: _____

_____

5. Topic: Finding a part-time job

Topic sentence: _____

_____

Support for your topic sentences should include examples, specific details that explain the process and all of its steps, and definitions of terms when needed.

APPLYING CRITICAL THINKING

| PURPOSE | IDEAS | SUPPORT | ASSUMPTIONS BIASES | CONCLUSIONS | POINT OF VIEW | ANALYSIS |

When you write a process essay, do not assume your reader will know what you mean. **Analyze** the steps involved carefully. Make sure you include them all, and describe exactly how they are performed. For instance, if you are describing making a peanut butter sandwich and say, "Spread the peanut butter on the bread," you may want to add "using a knife," or the reader could use a bare hand. Obviously, most people will know you assume they will use a knife in a common process such as making a sandwich, but in more complex processes, such as the way a nuclear power plant works, you will need to be specific and define any technical terms you use in order for a general audience to understand you.

ACTIVITY 9-4   Using Examples, Definitions, and Other Details

Directions: *Now provide at least three possible examples or details you would include for each of the topic sentences you created in Activity 9-3.* Answers will vary.

1. Topic: Choosing a new wardrobe for school or work

Examples: _____

_____

2. Topic: Writing an essay

   Examples: _____

   _____

3. Topic: Choosing a movie to see

   Examples: _____

   _____

4. Topic: Finding an apartment to rent

   Examples: _____

   _____

5. Topic: Finding a part-time job

   Examples: _____

   _____

Concluding Paragraph

The concluding paragraph in a process essay should restate both the process being described and the purpose for describing it: to instruct the reader on how to do something; to describe how a machine, experiment, or system works; to critique the way something works and propose an alternative; and so on.

CONCLUSIONS

ACTIVITY 9-5   **Writing a Concluding Paragraph**

Directions: *Choose one of the topics from the previous activities, and write a three- to five-sentence concluding paragraph for the topic. Be sure to reiterate what you set up in the thesis.* Answers may vary.

_____

_____

_____

_____

_____

_____

Use the critique form on the following page to check for the basics in your process essay draft.

PROCESS ESSAY CRITIQUE FORM

PURPOSE   IDEAS   SUPPORT   ASSUMPTIONS BIASES   CONCLUSIONS   POINT OF VIEW   ANALYSIS

Overall

	Done well	Needs work

1. Does the essay clearly describe a process with an **analytical** purpose (e.g., to inform, critique, etc.)?   _____ _____

2. Does the essay use time order or order of importance in the body paragraphs?   _____ _____

3. Are the paragraphs broken up well and about the right length?   _____ _____

Introduction

4. Is the title interesting and in the correct format?   _____ _____

5. Is there a general introduction that sets up the thesis?   _____ _____

6. Is there a clear thesis statement that explains the purpose of the process being described?   _____ _____

Body

7. Do the body paragraphs develop the process logically and flow smoothly?   _____ _____

8. Are transitions used between and, when needed, within the paragraphs?   _____ _____

9. Do the **ideas** in the body paragraphs include **support**—descriptive details to show the process?   _____ _____

Conclusion

10. Does the **concluding** paragraph sum up the process and re-emphasize the **purpose** set up in the introductory paragraph and thesis, without adding new ideas?   _____ _____

Editing

11. Circle the following errors you think you see in this draft: spelling errors, fragments, run-ons/comma splices, errors in comma and semicolon/colon use, pronoun disagreement, reference fault errors, and errors in parallelism, apostrophe use, verb use/tense, and passive voice construction. (See the handbook section for help in identifying and correcting these errors.)

12. Other types of grammar or sentence-level errors:

_____

Comments:

_____

_____

(LO 3) COMPLEMENTARY MODES FOR PROCESS ESSAYS

When writing a process essay, you can tap into several other modes described in other chapters that combine well to create an effective process essay.

- **Narration and description:** These modes are often combined with process due to the need for specific description and details and sometimes retelling of stories.
- **Examples and illustration:** Most good process essays focus on providing specific examples and illustration to develop their purpose.
- **Cause and effect:** Cause-and-effect analysis can be used to look at the reasons for and results of each step in a process.
- **Comparison/contrast:** This mode can be used to compare or contrast the individual stages or tasks in a process.
- **Argument:** Sometimes your reason for describing a process is to persuade your readers to learn a particular process or to critique an existing process and convince your readers to use it or avoid it.

Sample Student Essay

Rooney 1

Michelle Rooney

Professor Hernandez

English 100

28 February 2010

How to Pick the Right Courses

Being a college student poses many difficult challenges. One of the toughest parts of being in school is knowing which classes to take and knowing how to go about registering for the right courses once you have determined them. It is essential to plan ahead and research options, know your goals, and register on time if you want to succeed in picking the right courses for your degree in a timely manner.

Thesis statement

Continued ▶

Rooney 2

Topic sentence   To begin with, many students make the mistake of waiting to the last minute to think about their courses for the next semester or quarter. However, it is essential to plan ahead. Choosing the right courses for your goals and your target degree is not a matter that should be taken lightly or put off to the last minute. Begin thinking about the next quarter or semester's course offerings and what you might want to take at least two weeks before your scheduled registration date. You have to find out what the registration date is, or if it is open registration, when that begins. Then, you need to mark your calendar and begin the next steps of getting ready to register.

Topic sentence   The next major component to picking your classes is to research your options carefully. Get a copy of the course schedule as soon as it becomes available. Then, research which courses you still need to take to achieve your education or degree goals. Also, research if any of the courses you are interested in need a prerequisite course first. You may have to take a required course before you can take the course you have in mind. Also, you will need to check the available times for the courses you need and make sure they do not conflict with each other or with your work schedule if you work.

Topic sentence   Finally, the last step involved in getting the courses you need is to register on time and not procrastinate. For some students, this step will first require having enough money to afford tuition, but other students who have their financial needs met still make the mistake of putting off registering and therefore risk not getting the classes they want and need. Remember, classes get full, and the longer you wait, the more you increase your chances of not getting your first choices for classes. Be sure to have some back-up courses in mind. For instance, if you plan to take a biology lab course, be prepared to take a geology lab course if biology is full.

Rooney 3

If you follow these steps and avoid procrastination, you should   Restatement of thesis

be successful in your quest for the right classes. College is stressful

enough, so why make the process for registering for classes another

source of tension? Prepare, be ready, and register on time.

ACTIVITY 9-6   Thinking Critically About the Student Essay

Directions: *Analyze the essay to identify the features and details characteristic of the process mode. Mark them on the essay. Then, reread the essay, and make a list of specific revisions you would make to correct any problems with content, organization, transitions, and style.*

MAKING THE PITCH IN PRINT

Advertising

Courtland L. Bovée, John V. Thill, George P. Dovel, and Marian Burk Wood

COPYWRITERS AND COPYWRITING

1   Given the importance of copy, it comes as no surprise that copywriters are key players in the advertising process. In fact, many of the most notable leaders and voices in the industry began their careers as copywriters, including Jane Maas, David Ogilvy, Rosser Reeves, Leo Burnett, and William Bernbach. As a profession, copywriting is somewhat unusual because so many of its top practitioners have been in their jobs for years, even decades (rather than moving up the management ranks as is usual in many professions). Copywriters can either work for agencies or set themselves up as freelancers, selling their services to agencies and advertisers. Because it presents endless opportunities to be creative, copywriting is one of those rare jobs that can be fresh and challenging year after year.

2   Although successful copywriters share a love of language with novelists, poets, and other writers, copywriting is first and foremost a business function, not an artistic endeavor. The challenge isn't to create works of literary merit, but to meet advertising objectives. This doesn't mean that copywriting isn't an

art, however; it's simply art in pursuit of a business goal. Nor is it easy. Such noted literary writers as Stephen Vincent Benét, George Bernard Shaw, and Ernest Hemingway tried to write ad copy and found themselves unable to do it effectively. It's the combined requirements of language skills, business acumen, and an ability to create under the pressure of tight deadlines and format restrictions (such as the limited number of words you have to work with) that make copywriting so challenging—and so endlessly rewarding.

3   Copywriters have many styles and approaches to writing, but most agree on one thing: copywriting is hard work. It can involve a great deal of planning and coordinating with clients, legal staffers, account executives, researchers, and art directors. In addition, it usually entails hammering away at your copy until it's as good as it can be. David Ogilvy talked about doing 19 drafts of a single piece of copy and writing 37 headlines for a Sears ad in order to get 3 possibilities to show to the client. Actually, the chance to write and rewrite that many times is a luxury that most copywriters don't have; they often must produce copy on tight schedules with unforgiving deadlines (such as magazine publication deadlines).

4   The task of copywriting is most often associated with the headlines and copy you see in an ad, but copywriters actually develop a wide variety of other materials, from posters to catalogs to press releases, as well as the words you hear in radio and television commercials.

PRINT COPY

5   Copywriters are responsible for every word you see in print ads, whether the words are in a catchy headline or in the fine print at the bottom of the page. The three major categories of copy are headlines, body copy, and slogans.

HEADLINES

6   The *headline,* also called a *heading* or a *head,* constitutes the dominant line or lines of copy in an ad. Headlines are typically set in larger type and appear at the top of the ad, although there are no hard-and-fast rules on headline layout. *Subheads* are secondary headlines, often written to move the reader from the main headline to the body copy.

7   Even if there is a pageful of body copy and only a few words in the headline, the headline is the most important piece of copy for two reasons: First, it serves as the "come-on" to get people to stop turning the page and check out your ad. Second, as much as 80 percent of your audience may not bother to read the body copy, so whatever message these nonreaders carry away from the ad will have to come from the headline.

8   Copywriters can choose from a variety of headline types, each of which performs a particular function.

- **News headlines.** News headlines present information that's new to the audience, such as announcing a new store location, a new product, or lower prices. This approach is common because potential customers are often looking for new solutions, lower prices, and other relevant changes in the marketplace. For example, a newspaper ad from the Silo home electronics chain announced a recent sale using a news headline: "Everything on Sale! 4 Days Only! 5–20% Off Everything!" Headlines like this are typical in local newspaper advertising.
- **Emotional headlines.** The emotional appeal described earlier in the chapter is represented by emotional headlines. The quotation headline "I'm sick of her ruining our lives" was used in an ad for the American Mental Health Fund to echo the frustration some parents feel when they can't understand their teenagers' behavior. Combined with a photo of a sad and withdrawn teenage girl, the headline grabs any parent who has felt such frustration, and the body copy goes on to explain that families shouldn't get mad at people with mental illnesses but should help them get treatment for their conditions.
- **Benefit headlines.** The benefit headline is a statement of the key customer benefit. An ad for Quicken personal finance software used the question-form headline: "How do you know exactly where your money goes and how much you have?" followed by "It's this simple" above a photograph of the product package. The customer benefit is keeping better track of your money, and Quicken is the solution offered.
- **Directive headlines.** Headlines that direct the reader to do something, or at least suggest the reader do something, can motivate consumer action. Such headlines can be a hard sell, such as "Come in now and save," or they can be something more subtle, such as "Just feel the color in these black and whites," the headline in an ad for Ensoniq keyboards.
- **Offbeat and curiosity headlines.** Humor, wordplay, and mystery can be effective ways to draw readers into an ad. An ad promoting vacation travel to Spain used the headline "Si in the dark," with a photo of a lively nighttime scene. The word *Si* is catchy because it first looks like an error, until the reader reads the body copy to learn that the ad is talking about Spain (*si* is Spanish for "yes").
- **Hornblowing headlines.** The hornblowing headline, called "Brag and Boast" heads by the Gallup & Robinson research organization, should be used with care. Customers have seen it all and heard it all, and "We're the greatest" headlines tend to sound arrogant and self-centered. This isn't to say that you can't stress superiority; you just need to do it in a way that takes the customer's needs into account, and the headline must be honest. The headline "Neuberger & Berman Guardian Fund" followed by the subhead "#1 Performing Growth and Income Fund"

blows the company's own horn but also conveys an important product benefit. Since investors look for top-performing mutual funds, the information about being number one is relevant.

- **Slogan, label, or logo headlines.** Some headlines show a company's slogan, a product label, or the organization's logo. Powerful slogans like Hallmark's "When you care enough to send the very best" can make great headlines because they click with the reader's emotions. Label and logo headlines can build product and company awareness, but they must be used with care. If the label or logo doesn't make some emotional or logical connection with the reader, the ad probably won't succeed.

8   Headlines often have maximum impact when coupled with a well-chosen graphic element, rather than trying to carry the message with words alone. In fact, the careful combination of the two can increase the audience's involvement with the ad, especially if one of the two says something ironic or unexpected that has to be resolved by considering the other element. A magazine ad for Easter Seals had the headline "After all we did for Pete, he walked out on us." At first, you think the birth-defects organization is complaining. Then you see a photo of Pete with new artificial legs, walking away from a medical facility. It's a powerful combination that makes the reader feel good about the things Easter Seals can do for people.

Checklist for Producing Excellent Copy

- ❏ **A.** Avoid clichés.
    - Create fresh, original phrases that vividly convey your message.
    - Remember that clever wordplay based on clichés can be quite effective.
- ❏ **B.** Watch out for borrowed interest.
    - Make sure you don't use inappropriate copy or graphics since they can steal the show from your basic sales message.
    - Be sure nothing draws attention from the message.
- ❏ **C.** Don't boast.
    - Be sure the ad's purpose isn't merely to pat the advertiser on the back.
    - Tout success when you must convince nonbuyers that lots of people just like them have purchased your product; this isn't the same as shouting "We're the best!"
- ❏ **D.** Make it personal, informal, and relevant.
    - Connect with the audience in a way that is personal and comfortable. Pompous, stiff, and overly "businesslike" tends to turn people away.
    - Avoid copy that sounds like it belongs in an ad, with too many overblown adjectives and unsupported claims of superiority.
- ❏ **E.** Keep it simple, specific, and concise.

- Make your case quickly and stick to the point. This will help you get past all the barriers and filters that people put up to help them select which things they'll pay attention to and which they'll ignore.
- Avoid copy that's confusing, meandering, too long, or too detailed.
❑ **F.** Give the audience a reason to read, listen, or watch.
- Offer a solution to your audience's problems.
- Entertain your audience.
- Consider any means possible to get your audience to pay attention long enough to get your sales message across.

BODY COPY

9   The second major category of copy is the *body copy,* which constitutes the words in the main body of the ad, apart from headlines, photo captions, and other blocks of text. The importance of body copy varies from ad to ad, and some ads have little or no body copy. Ads for easy-to-understand products, for instance, often rely on the headline and a visual such as a photograph to get their point across. In contrast, when the selling message needs a lot of supporting detail to be convincing, an ad can be packed full of body copy. Some advertisers have the impression that long body copy should be avoided, but that isn't always the case. The rule to apply here is to use the "right" number of words. You might not need many words in a perfume ad, but you might need a page or two to cover a complex industrial product.

10   As with headlines, body copy can be built around several different formats. *Straight-line copy* is copy that takes off from the headline and develops the selling points for the product. *Narrative copy,* in contrast, tells a story as it persuades; the same selling points may be covered, but in a different context. *Dialog/monolog copy* lets one or two characters in the ad do the selling through what they are saying. *Picture-and-caption copy* relies on photographs or illustrations to tell the story, with support from their accompanying captions.

SLOGANS

11   The third major category of copy includes *slogans,* or *tag lines,* memorable sayings that convey a selling message. Over the years, Coca-Cola has used such slogans as "Coke is it," "It's the real thing," and "Always Coca-Cola." Slogans are sometimes used as headlines, but not always. Their importance lies in the fact they often become the most memorable result of an advertising campaign. You've probably got a few slogans stuck in your head. Ever heard of "Quality is job number 1," "Don't leave home without it," or "Melts in your mouth, not in your hand"?

12   The Korean automaker Hyundai recently switched back to the slogan "Cars that make sense," which is a great way of expressing its desired

positioning as a lower cost but still reliable alternative to Japanese and U.S. cars. For several years, the company had used "Hyundai. Yes, Hyundai," but "Cars that make sense" has proved to be a much more effective way to define the value it offers consumers.

Reading Reflection Questions *Answers will vary. Sample answers are provided.*

1. What is the main purpose in this article? Explain in your own words.

   to explain the process and tips for writing print advertising

   _____

2. Explain how this article is an example of a process essay. What are some characteristics that distinguish it as describing a process?

   the article gives step-by-step explanation of the process of copywriting

   including the how to's

3. ___*T*___ T/F According to the article, copywriters write all the words you see in print ads.

4. According to the article, the three major categories of copy editing include the following: *[answer: c]*

   a. Titles, information, and small print

   b. Slogans, titles, and print

   c. Headlines, body copy, and slogans

   d. Details, captions, and images

5. ___*F*___ T/F According to the article, most readers read all the body copy or words of an ad.

6. List two examples from the article of famous slogans for brands.

   e.g., Coke is it, melts in your mouth not in your hand, cars that make sense

7. ___*F*___ T/F According to the article, using clichés is a good practice for producing good copy writing.

Checking Vocabulary

Define each of the following words by figuring out their meaning using context clues in the reading selection. If you cannot work out the meaning of a word, use a dictionary.

8. practitioners (paragraph 1): *people who perform a particular task*

9. headline (paragraph 6): *a dominant line in copy ads—like a title line*

10. slogans (paragraph 11): *tag lines or memorable sayings that convey a*

    selling message

CRITICAL THINKING CHECKLIST

Answers will vary.

PURPOSE

1. What is the **purpose** of this piece of writing? Is it clear?

_____

_____

IDEAS

2. What **ideas** and **background information** are provided to support the purpose of this piece of writing?

_____

_____

SUPPORT

3. What **evidence**, **support**, and **examples** are used to explain and develop the ideas that support the argument made in the piece of writing? Are the evidence and examples provided sufficient?

_____

_____

ASSUMPTIONS BIASES

4. Are there unfounded **assumptions** or unreasonable **biases**?

_____

_____

CONCLUSIONS

5. Are all of the **conclusions**, **implications**, and **consequences** (the results of the arguments taken to their farthest extreme) of the arguments considered?

_____

_____

POINT OF VIEW

6. Is the **point of view** clear and consistent, and have other points of view been considered?

_____

_____

ANALYSIS

7. Using these critical thinking tools, **analyze** the overall structure of this essay and the strength of the author's arguments, ideas, and support. Was he or she successful in accomplishing the purpose? Why, or why not?

_____

_____

Essay Assignments

1. Use one of the topics you developed in this chapter, and write a complete process essay on that topic. Use the critique form to check your draft.

2. Write a process description for making your favorite dish or sandwich. Include all the details you can, be very specific, and use the exact order for re-creating the process you go through when making this item.

3. Pick a routine you know well from everyday experience, and write a process essay that would show someone else who has never done this activity step by step how to accomplish it (for example, how to make the bed, how to change oil in the car, how to clean the bathroom, how to do a task you complete routinely for your job, and so on).

4. Write a process description of how to apply and interview for a job.

SPOTLIGHT ON CRITICAL THINKING

Writing about **processes** is something you will do often in college, your career, and everyday life.

Writing processes: For example, in culinary arts, you need to learn how to write a clear and precise process to create a good recipe. In everyday life or your career, you might need to teach someone how to do a specific task, and you'll need to write clear, step-by-step directions. When training coworkers, you'll often have to transfer a process you know well into step-by-step written directions for a new coworker. Use your **analysis** skills to check the **purpose** and **conclusions** in your process writing for college classes and later in your writing for your career. Develop your **purpose, ideas,** and **support** based on the critical thinking tips in Chapter 1.

Reading processes: In biology and chemistry lab courses, you'll need to read step-by-step process directions and follow them well. On the job, you'll have many occasions when you need to read directions for a process and follow them closely. For example, if you are learning how to run a printing press, you'll have an elaborate process in writing to learn. Use the Six Steps for Active Reading in Chapter 2 to be a more careful and interactive reader.

To check your progress in meeting this chapter's objectives, log in to **www.mywritinglab.com**, go to the **Study Plan** tab, click on **Writing and Critical Thinking in the Modes** and choose **Essay Development—Process** from the list of subtopics. Read and view the resources in the **Review Materials** section, and then complete the **Recall, Apply,** and **Write** sets in the **Activities** section.

10 Classification

Gorilla   Wayne Buck

THINKING CRITICALLY

Look at the picture above. Then answer the question that follows.

Classification is a great way to sort out the different categories within a group. Gorillas are mammals, like humans. Looking at the picture above, what similarities do you see between humans and gorillas that demonstrate their same categorization?

_____

_____

_____

_____

LO 1 CLASSIFICATION ESSAYS

Classification (sometimes also called "division") involves grouping, or dividing items into categories. It involves using common characteristics to define categories within groups. You use classification skills all the time in your daily life. When you write a grocery list, you separate items into categories such as dairy, fruits and vegetables, frozen foods, and so on. In the academic world, classification comes in handy for subdividing larger groups in order to analyze them or some aspect of them. Classification mode is often used in argument essays and story analysis essays (categorizing an author's techniques or characters). Classification writing is also common in the workplace: Many tasks involve sorting items or people into particular groups or classifications for marketing or analysis purposes.

Critical Thinking and Classification

Be sure you know your purpose in choosing to classify information. Decide on the criteria you are going to use, and then sort, or *classify*, items accordingly. *Division* involves specifically dividing items into distinct groupings. When dividing and classifying, look at specific qualities of the people or items being classified. Then use those qualities as a basis for making your classification decisions. For instance, if you were classifying movies, you could sort them by genre: horror, action, adventure, romantic comedy, and so on.

Then you could subdivide each category, for instance:

Analysis involves breaking down an idea and working out the meaning of the individual parts and how they relate to the whole. When you are classifying people or items, you want to look at the whole group and think carefully about what broad categories you could use to organize them accurately and then how you could break those categories down into more specific subgroups you can write about.

BEFORE WRITING A CLASSIFICATION ESSAY

Before you begin to write a classification essay on an assigned topic, or one you have chosen, start by asking yourself these questions:

1. What basis or principles will I use to classify the topic?

2. How can I subdivide my categories or classifications?

3. What do I want to explain or prove as a result of this classification and division?

4. Have I unfairly or inaccurately classified my subjects or oversimplified complex divisions?

5. What do I want my readers to learn or understand after reading this essay?

Answering these questions will lead you to a thesis statement, help you determine what examples and details to include for support, and give you a general idea of how you want to organize your essay.

ACTIVITY 10-1   Practicing Classification

Directions: *For each topic, list two or three ways you could subdivide or classify it into categories.*   Answers will vary.

Example:

Topic: Carbohydrates

Categories: *Pasta, bread, crackers* _____

1. **Topic:** American cars

    Categories: _____

2. **Topic:** Dog breeds

    Categories: _____

3. **Topic:** TV shows

    Categories: _____

4. **Topic:** Sports

    Categories: _____

5. **Topic:** Types of dwellings/places to live

    Categories: _____

WRITING A CLASSIFICATION ESSAY

The paragraph structure of a classification essay is based on sorting a group into its particular parts in order to understand the whole better. For instance, you could choose to classify and divide college students on the basis of their age, gender, race, economic backgrounds, and academic backgrounds. After classifying and studying the various parts of the college student body, you could reach a better understanding of the whole group. The purpose of a classification essay may also be to *critique* the categories set by someone else and argue against the constructions and decisions made in the process of categorizing those items or people. Often, classification essays involve a great deal of comparison and contrast, description, and narration, and they serve the purpose of making an argument to persuade a reader to agree with the writer's point.

When you classify, think about what point you want to make about the group you've chosen for your topic and the best way to subdivide that group into categories. For instance, if you want to write about online classes, you might want to first subdivide online classes into specific types: online composition classes, online history classes, and online math classes, for instance. Be careful to avoid biased classifications that do not fairly represent the members of each subgroup or misrepresent the items, thoughts, or people within those groups. For instance, you wouldn't want to claim that online students have particular habits or faults that on-campus students don't, if you didn't have legitimate support for such a claim. Also, don't oversimplify your subdivisions into groups that don't fully represent the complexities of the subjects.

APPLYING CRITICAL THINKING

| PURPOSE | IDEAS | SUPPORT | ASSUMPTIONS BIASES | CONCLUSIONS | POINT OF VIEW | ANALYSIS |

Classification is something you do to make sense out of groups of things and people around you. When you classify, be extra careful not to overgeneralize, and be aware of your **biases** and **assumptions**.

1. A **bias** is a particular viewpoint that you have about an idea or a topic. Sometimes you are conscious of the biases in your ideas, and sometimes you are not. Having biases is not necessarily a bad thing, but when they are founded on misinformation they can get in the way of good critical thinking. When you classify people or things, think carefully about what ideas you already have about the group(s) you are discussing and whether they are based on fact.

   Example of unfounded bias: Girls are not as good at solving math problems as are boys.

2. An **assumption** is a belief or claim that you take for granted. Almost everything you believe and do is based on assumptions. Some assumptions, however, are ones that you take for granted but not everyone would agree with. It is important to learn to separate the assumptions that have a solid basis in fact from the ones that don't when you are making decisions about classifying information.

   Example of unfounded assumption: Computer Science majors are nerds.

In your introductory paragraph, identify your topic, and explain how you will divide and classify it. For instance, you could introduce the category of online classes and then divide and classify subsets of those. Also, clearly establish your purpose for classifying this group. What conclusion did you reach through the process of subdividing the group? Then, in the body paragraphs, focus on one subgroup at a time. Be sure to use transitions that show comparisons and contrasts. You may even subdivide the subcategories using separate paragraphs. Finally, in the concluding paragraph, re-emphasize the method of classification you used, state the conclusions you reached by subdividing the group, and emphasize the point you want to express to your readers. The chart below provides a brief overview of the structure of a classification essay.

BASIC STRUCTURE FOR A CLASSIFICATION ESSAY

INTRODUCTORY PARAGRAPH

Sets up the categories/subdivisions of the larger topic you will discuss in your thesis.

Thesis statement: A statement that describes what you are trying to explain, show, prove, or argue by using classification—and what conclusions you reached by subdividing your topic.

BODY PARAGRAPHS (Two to five, depending on assignment and purpose)

Develop the separate subcategories, maybe even subdividing and classifying them—indicate with your **topic sentences.**

Use transitions within and between paragraphs to make the paragraphs flow smoothly.

Provide concrete examples/details and description about the categories.

Analyze the examples.

CONCLUDING PARAGRAPH

Sum up and re-emphasize the thesis: the conclusions reached by classifying your topic.

LO 2 STRUCTURING A CLASSIFICATION ESSAY

Topic

To generate your topic and purpose for your classification essay, use the guidelines specified by your instructor's assignment. If you do not have a specific classification assignment, come up with a topic idea through brainstorming and decide how you could classify it into groups.

A Few Topic Possibilities

You can write a classification essay that groups together types of people, types of classes, cars, exercise, music, films, and so on. Many groups call for classification and division in order to understand the nuances and complexities within them. Be sure to have a purpose in mind for categorizing: a conclusion related to the classifications you made that you want to explain to your readers.

ACTIVITY 10-2   Breaking a Topic into Categories

Directions: *For each of the topics below, use one of the ways of classifying it that you chose in Activity 10-1 and come up with a list of subcategories.* Answers will vary.

Example:

Topic: Carbohydrates

Category: Pasta

Subcategories: *spaghetti, lasagna, macaroni* _____

1. **Topic:** American cars

   Category: _____

   Subcategories: _____

2. **Topic:** Dog breeds

   Category: _____

   Subcategories: _____

3. **Topic:** TV shows

   Category: _____

   Subcategories: _____

4. **Topic:** Sports

   Category: _____

   Subcategories: _____

5. **Topic:** Types of dwellings/places to live

   Category: _____

   Subcategories: _____

Thesis Statements

If you have a specific classification assignment that dictates what you will be trying to explain or prove through your essay, then customize your thesis using key words from the assignment itself. For instance, if you were asked to classify colleges and universities in order to explore which options were best for you, your thesis would specify which categories you have chosen to use and what conclusion you've reached as a result of this classification.

> College students fall into certain groups when it comes to their living options—those who live in on-campus dorms, those who share an apartment or house with other students, or those who stay with their parents while in college to save money—and each category has its own advantages and disadvantages.

ACTIVITY 10-3   Creating Thesis Statements

Directions: *Using the categories and subcategories you generated in Activities 10-1 and 10-2, create a one-sentence thesis statement for three of the general topics. Make sure the thesis statement has a clear message or lesson to convey about what conclusion you reached using classification.* Answers will vary.

1. Topic: _____

    _____

    _____

    _____

2. Topic: _____

    _____

    _____

    _____

3. Topic: _____

    _____

    _____

    _____

Introductory Paragraph

In the introductory paragraph of your classification essay, provide general information about the topic, the larger group that will be classified. Then present the subcategories you will use to create your classification. Finally, in the thesis statement, explain the purpose for your classification essay: what point you want your readers to see as a result of your classification process.

Body Paragraphs

In your body paragraphs, individually develop each subcategory you created through your classification of your general topic into groups. Provide clear topic sentences that present each subcategory. Then, add specific examples and details to explain and develop the subcategories. You may need to add subcategories for your subcategories, too. Use transitions when needed both within and between your paragraphs. Contrast and comparison transitions are particularly useful in classification essays; you can also use transitions that show addition of points and purpose (see Chapter 6, pages 114–116).

TRANSITIONS TO . . .

Show Contrast or a Change in Idea

although	even though	instead	on the other side
anyhow	for all that	nevertheless	otherwise
at the same time	however	notwithstanding	regardless
but	in any event	on the contrary	still
despite this	in contrast	on the other hand	yet

Show a Comparison

in like manner	in the same way	likewise	similarly

ACTIVITY 10-4 Creating Topic Sentences

Directions: *Now create two topic sentences for each of the thesis statements you created in Activity 10-3, addressing the different categories you would discuss in each paragraph.* Answers will vary.

1. Topic: _____

   _____

   _____

2. **Topic:** _____

_____

_____

3. **Topic:** _____

_____

_____

Definitions and Examples

Because in classification essays you are explaining and discussing a category in each paragraph, you need to provide clear definitions and examples to illustrate the differences and similarities between the categories. For instance, if you were taking a biology class, you might be asked to classify trees into groups. You might use *evergreen* and *deciduous* as two of your sub-categories, and then you would need to define both these terms and provide examples of the types of trees they refer to:

TREES	
Deciduous	**Evergreen**
(Leaves fall off in winter)	(Leaves/needles stay on year round)
Maple	Cedar
Oak	Fir
Elm	Pine

ACTIVITY 10-5   Providing Examples

Directions: *Now provide at least three possible examples or details you would include for three of the topic sentences you created in Activity 10-4. Answers will vary.*

1. **Topic:** _____

_____

_____

2. **Topic:** _____

_____

_____

3. Topic: _____

_____

_____

Concluding Paragraph

In your concluding paragraph, restate your thesis statement emphasizing what conclusions you reached by classifying your topic. Touch on the categories you used to classify your topic and the main point you want your readers to realize after they read your essay.

ACTIVITY 10-6   **Writing a Conclusion**

Directions: *Choose one of the topics you've been developing in the preceding activities, and write a three- to five-sentence concluding paragraph that re-emphasizes the classification categories and the purpose you want to get across by using the classification process you have chosen.* Answers will vary.

_____

_____

_____

_____

_____

Use the following critique form to check for the basics in your classification essay draft.

CLASSIFICATION ESSAY CRITIQUE FORM

PURPOSE   IDEAS   SUPPORT   ASSUMPTIONS BIASES   CONCLUSIONS   POINT OF VIEW   ANALYSIS

Overall   Done well   Needs work

1. Does the essay categorize two or more subjects with specific characteristics?   _____   _____

2. Does the essay use specific categories consistently and clearly?   _____   _____

3. Are the paragraphs broken up well and about the right length?   _____   _____

Continued ▶

Introduction

4. Is the title interesting and in correct format?   _____ _____
5. Is there a general introduction that sets up the thesis and categories?   _____ _____
6. Is there a clear thesis statement that explains the **purpose** of the classifications being made?   _____ _____

Body

7. Do the **ideas** in the body paragraphs develop the categories and flow smoothly?   _____ _____
8. Are transitions used between and, when needed, within the paragraphs?   _____ _____
9. Do the body paragraphs include **support** (descriptive details and examples)?   _____ _____

Conclusion

10. Does the **concluding** paragraph sum up the categories with **analysis** and re-emphasize the purpose developed in the introductory paragraph and thesis, without adding new ideas?   _____ _____

Editing

11. Circle the following errors you think you see in this draft: spelling errors, fragments, run-ons/comma splices, errors in comma and semicolon/colon use, pronoun disagreement, reference fault errors, and errors in parallelism, apostrophe use, verb use/tense, and passive voice construction. (See the handbook section for help in identifying and correcting these errors.)
12. Other types of grammar or sentence-level errors:

_____

Comments:

_____

_____

LO 3 COMPLEMENTARY MODES FOR CLASSIFICATION ESSAYS

Classification mode combines well with several other modes.

- **Narration** and **description** can be used to develop the categories.
- **Illustration and examples** will further elaborate on the classifications.
- You can look at the **causes and effects** of classifications and divisions.
- You can **compare and contrast** among the categories.
- You can use classification to prove an **argument** or **persuade** your readers to agree with a particular point of view.

Sample Student Essay

Hill 1

Lynne Hill

Professor Martinez

English 100

23 November 2010

TV People, Movie People, and Book People

Do you know people who love to watch TV, who go to the movies as much as possible, or who read books voraciously? Several of my friends fall into one of these categories, and some of them are so deeply devoted to their need for TV, movies, or books that that connection has become part of who they are. These people, let us call them the "TV people," "movie people," and "book people," have particular characteristics and particular personalities.

The TV people like to stay home on most nights, arranging their schedules as they consult the TV Guide. They hate the sound of silence if they are home. They are drawn as if by a magnet to the lure of the box in the corner, calling them like a siren: "Come turn me on . . . you can watch just for a little while . . . Oprah misses you. . . . " The devoted TV people will forgo housecleaning, homework, and any type of creative project to ensure they do not miss a chance for some good passive TV watching. The TV people have a master plan for avoiding engaging with their lives: They can let the shows do the thinking, and the living, for them.

The movie people are one step above the TV people when it comes to social engagement. At least they will step out of their homes in the evenings from time to time . . . to see a movie. Some movie people have even studied cinematography and consider their fascination with movies a sign of their expertise;

Thesis statement

Topic sentence

Topic sentence

Continued ▶

Hill 2

some will even actively critique the films—true artists in their medium. There are subcategories of movie people: the loner movie people, the social movie people, and the snobby movie people versus the non-discriminating movie people. The loner movie people prefer to watch movies by themselves. They are easily irritated by friends who make comments during the show, and they are distracted by the sounds of people eating popcorn or snacks. The social movie people choose not to go to movies alone: they passively watch with someone or several people. Then, they like to engage in dialogue about the movies afterwards. The snobby movie people will see only the highly critically acclaimed, "artsy" movies, while the non-discriminating movie people will see anything—and love it! It's pricier to be a movie person than a TV person. Movies and the nearly mandatory accompanying snacks from the snack bar can set a person back $20 at a time.

Topic sentence

Finally, the book people are often the most creative, intelligent, and self-sufficient category; however, that does not guarantee that they win in the social graces department. The book people are creative: they create movies in their own heads from the books they read, casting their own actors and blocking their own scenes. They are actively engaged in the stories they read, not just passive viewers. Also, book people are smart and can be great conversationalists, if you can tear them away from whatever current book they are engaged in. In fact, book people can be downright anti-social on vacations, sneaking off to a beach or back room alone to delve back into whatever juicy book they are reading.

Restatement of thesis

It's predictable that there are all levels of TV people, movie people, and book people out there. Certainly, each of these types has their own distinguishing characteristics. Which category do you fit in most closely?

ACTIVITY 10-7   Thinking Critically About the Student Essay

Directions: *Analyze the essay to identify the features and details characteristic of the classification mode. Mark them on the essay. Then, reread the essay, and make a list of specific revisions you would make to correct any problems with content, organization, transitions, and style.*

Race in America

George Henderson

George Henderson is Dean of the College of Liberal Arts at the University of Oklahoma, where he is also a professor of Human Relations, Education, and Sociology. Henderson has served as a race relations consultant to many national and international organizations. He is author of *Our Souls to Keep: Black/White Relations in America* (1999) and coeditor with Grace Xuequin Ma of *Rethinking Ethnicity and Health Care: A Sociocultural Perspective* (1999). This essay appeared in a special issue on race in America in the spring 2000 issue of *National Forum.*

Note: Some of the vocabulary in this essay is very high-level, so make sure to use context clues and to consult a dictionary when you need to.

1   Because of intermarriage, most Americans have multiple ethnic and racial identities. Some persons of mixed lineage prefer to assume culturally nondescript identities. For example, they have become "white people," "black people," "Indians," "Latinos," "Asians," or just plain "Americans" in order to somehow deflect from themselves any connection with their ancestors. The task of tracing their families has become too taxing or too insignificant. Even so, the effects of ethnicity and race are pervasive: disparate patterns of community relationships and economic opportunities haunt us. At some time in their history, all ethnic groups in the United States have been the underclass. Also, at different times, all ethnic groups have been both the oppressed and the oppressors.

2   Ethnicity is the most distinguishing characteristic of Americans, where we are sorted primarily on the basis of our cultural identities or nationalities. An ethnic group is a culturally distinct population whose members share a collective identity and a common heritage. Historically, the overwhelming majority of ethnic groups emerged in the United States as a result of one of several responses to the following processes: (1) migration, (2) consolidation of group forces in the face of an impending threat from an aggressor, (3) annexation or changes in political boundary lines, or

(4) schisms within a church. Hence, "ethnic minority" presupposes people different from the mainstream or dominant cultured persons.

3   But it is the erroneous belief that people who come to America can be placed in categories based on their unique gene pools that has resulted in the most blatant instances of discrimination. Races, however defined, do not correspond to genetic reality because inbreeding world populations share a common gene pool. A much more practical dictum, and one that has often been ignored throughout American history, is that all people belong to the same species. Unfortunately, too few individuals believe that the only race of any significance is the human race.

A BRIEF HISTORY

4   At the time of the American Revolution, the American population was largely composed of English Protestants who had absorbed a substantial number of German and Scotch-Irish settlers and a smaller number of French, Dutch, Swedes, Poles, Swiss, Irish, and other immigrants. The colonies had a modest number of Catholics, and a smaller number of Jews. Excluding Quakers and Swedes, the colonists treated Native Americans with contempt and hostility, and engaged in wars against them that bordered on genocide. They drove natives from the coastal plains in order to make way for a massive white movement to the West. Although Africans, most of whom were slaves, comprised one-fifth of the American population during the Revolution, they, similar to Indians, were not perceived by most white colonists as being worthy of assimilation.

5   The white peoples of the new nation had long since crossed Caucasian lines to create a conglomerate but culturally homogeneous society. People of different ethnic groups—English, Irish, German, Huguenot, Dutch, Swedish—mingled and intermarried. English settlers and peoples from western and northern Europe had begun a process of ethnic assimilation that caused some writers to incorrectly describe the nation as melted into one ethnic group: American. In reality, non-Caucasian Americans were not included in the Eurocentric cultural pot.

6   During the 150 years immediately following the Revolution, large numbers of immigrants came to the United States from eastern European countries. They were the so-called "new immigrants." During the latter part of that period, slaves were emancipated, numerous Indian tribes were conquered and forced to relocate to reservations, portions of Mexico's land were taken, and Asians began emigrating to the United States. The English language and English-oriented cultural patterns grew even more dominant. Despite a proliferation of cultural diversity within the growing ethnic enclaves, Anglo-conformity ideology spawned racist

notions about Nordic and Aryan racial superiority. This ideology gave rise to nativist political agendas and exclusionist immigration policies favoring western and northern European immigrants.

7   Non-English-speaking western Europeans and northern Europeans were also discriminated against. The slowness of some of those immigrants, particularly Germans, to learn English, their tendency to live in enclaves, and their establishment of ethnic-language newspapers were friction points. Such ethnic-oriented lifestyles prompted many Americanized people to chide: "If they don't like it here, they can go back to where they came from." But that solution was too simplistic. Immigrants from all countries and cultures, even those who were deemed socially and religiously undesirable, were needed to help build a nation—to work the farms, dig the ore, build railroads and canals, settle the prairies, and otherwise provide human resources.

8   Beginning in the 1890s, immigrants from eastern and southern Europe were numerically dominant. That set the stage for racist statements about inferior, darker people threatening the purity of blond, blue-eyed Nordics or Aryans through miscegenation. Intermixture was perceived as a deadly plague. Although the immigrants from eastern and southern Europe were not suitable marriage partners, their critics stated, they could be properly assimilated and amalgamated. This kind of ethnocentrism prevented large numbers of other immigrants and indigenous peoples of color from becoming fully functioning citizens. And the legacy for the children of people denied equal opportunities was second-class citizenship. We can easily document the negative effects of second-class citizenship: abhorrent inequalities, unwarranted exclusions, and atmospheres of rejection.

9   Immigrants who lived in remote, isolated areas were able to maintain some semblance of being ethnic nations within America. But the growth of cities brought about the decline of farming populations and ethnic colonies. A short time was required for the white immigrants who settled in cities to discard their native languages and cultures. But it is erroneous to think of any ethnic group as melting away without leaving a trace of its cultural heritage. All ethnic groups have infused portions of their cultures into the tapestry of American history.

10   Early twentieth-century eastern European immigrants were a very disparate mixture of peoples. They came from nations that were trying to become states—Poland, Czechoslovakia, Lithuania, and Yugoslavia; from states trying to become nations—Italy, Turkey, and Greece; and from areas outside the Western concept of either state or nation. All of them included people such as Jews who did not easily fit into any of those categories. Through social and educational movements, laws, and superordinate goals such as winning wars and establishing economic world superiority,

eastern Europeans and other white ethnic groups were able to enter mainstream America.

11   The cultures and colors of Third World ethnic groups were in stark contrast to European immigrants. Those differences became obstacles to assimilation and, more importantly, to people of color achieving equal opportunities. Nonwhite groups in the United States occupied specific low-status niches in the workplace, which in turn resulted in similarities among their members in such things as occupations, standard of living, level of education, place of residence, access to political power, and quality of health care. Likenesses within those groups facilitated the formation of stereotypes and prejudices that inhibited the full citizenship of nonwhite minorities.

12   Immigrants who held highly esteemed occupations—lawyers, artists, engineers, scientists, and physicians—became Americanized much faster than those who held less esteemed positions—unskilled laborers, farm workers, coal miners, and stock clerks. But even in those instances there were pro-European biases and stereotypes. For example, French chefs, Italian opera singers, Polish teachers, German conductors, and Russian scientists were more highly recruited than Africans, Hispanics, and Asians who had the same skills. Racial and quasi-racial groups—including American Indians, Mexican Americans, Asian Americans, African Americans, and Puerto Ricans—were not nearly so readily absorbed as various Caucasian ethnic groups. And that is generally the situation today. Despite numerous and impressive gains during the past century, a disproportionate number of peoples of color are still treated like pariahs.

WHAT DOES THE FUTURE HOLD?

13   If U.S. Census Bureau population projections are correct, our nation is undergoing mind-boggling demographic changes: Hispanics will triple in numbers, from 31.4 million in 1999 to 98.2 million in 2050; blacks will increase 70 percent, from 34.9 million to 59.2 million; Asians and Pacific Islanders will triple, from 10.9 million to 37.6 million; Native Americans and Alaska Natives will increase from approximately 2.2 million to 2.6 million. During the same period, the non-Hispanic white population will increase from 196.1 million to 213 million. Also, the foreign-born population, most of them coming from Asia and Latin America, will increase from 26 million to 53.8 million. The non-Hispanic white population will decrease from 72 percent of the total population in 1999 to 52 percent in 2050, and the nation's workforce will be composed of over 50 percent racial and ethnic minorities and immigrants. Who then will be the pariahs?

14   Without equal opportunities, the melting pot will continue to be an unreachable mirage, a dream of equality deferred, for too many people of color. This does not in any way detract from the significance of the

things minorities have achieved. Ethnic-group histories and lists of cultural contributions support the contention that each group is an integral part of a whole nation. Although all American ethnic minority groups have experienced continuous socioeconomic gains, the so-called "playing field" that includes white participants is not yet level. Simply stated, the rising tide of economic prosperity has not yet lifted the masses of people of color. Whatever our life circumstances, the citizens of the United States are bound together not as separate ethnic groups but as members of different ethnic groups united in spirit and behavior and locked into a common destiny.

15 There is little doubt that our nation is at a crossroads in its race relations. Where we go from here is up to all of us. We can try segregation again, continuance of the status quo, silence in the face of prejudice and discriminatory practices, or activism. The choice is ours.

16 Segregation of ethnic minorities is not a redeeming choice for the United States. It did not work during earlier times, and it will not work now. There have never been separate but equal majority-group and minority-group communities in the United States. And the pretense of such a condition would once again be a particularly pernicious injustice to all citizens. Racial segregation diminishes both the perpetrators and their victims. Preserving the status quo in education, employment, health care, and housing, which so often is little more than codified racial discrimination, is not justice for minorities either.

17 Inaction by people who witness oppressive acts is equally unacceptable. Even though they may be shocked and frustrated by the problems, standing in wide-eyed horror is not an adequate posture to assume. While they may be legally absolved of any wrongdoing, these silent people must come to terms with what others believe to be their moral culpability. Of course, silence may be prudent. Usually, there is a high price to be paid by those who would challenge racism in community institutions. Friends, jobs, promotions, and prestige may be lost. Furthermore, few victories come easily, and most of the victors are unsung heroes.

18 Individuals who choose to challenge purveyors of bigotry and unequal opportunities must also take care that in their actions to redress racial injustices, they do not emulate the oppressors whom they deplore. That might makes right, that blood washes out injustices—these too are false strategies for achieving justice. "It does not matter much to a slave what the color of his master is," a wise black janitor once said. We, the descendants of migrants, immigrants, and slaves, can build a better nation—a place where all people have safe housing, get a top-quality education, do meaningful work for adequate wages, are treated fairly in criminal-justice systems, have their medical needs met, and in the end die a timely death unhurried by bigots. This is the kind of history that should be made.

Reading Reflection Questions *Answers will vary. Sample answers are provided.*

1. What are the direct or indirect (implied) messages in this essay?

   To explore the history of race, classification of different racial groups, and

   discrimination in America; to comment on the current and future problems

   related to race; and to encourage a positive change in attitudes and

   approaches to race

2. What techniques, organization patterns, and details distinguish this as a *classification* essay? *The clear categorizations of subgroups and races*

3. In your own words, what is Henderson's view of people who identify themselves by race? *That they should see themselves first and foremost*

   as part of the human race

Objective Questions

4. T/F __F__ As early white settlers in America, the Quakers treated Native Americans badly.

5. T/F __F__ The author believes that segregation by race can be beneficial to society.

6. T/F __T__ Nonwhite immigrants with higher-prestige jobs such as doctors or lawyers became Americanized faster.

7. Provide two examples of injustices that have happened in American society as a result of racial differences as mentioned by Henderson.

   Colonists treating Native Americans badly, African Americans being kept

   as slaves

Checking Vocabulary

Define the following in your own words, or provide a dictionary definition if you don't know the word.

8. ethnicity: *racial/cultural background*

9. migration: *moving from one country to another*

10. ethnocentrism: *belief that one's own ethnic group is better than other*

    ethnic groups

CRITICAL THINKING CHECKLIST

PURPOSE

Answers will vary.

1. What is the **purpose** of this piece of writing? Is it clear?

_____

_____

IDEAS

2. What **ideas** and **background information** are provided to support the purpose of this piece of writing?

_____

_____

SUPPORT

3. What **evidence** and **examples** are used to explain and develop the ideas that support the argument made in the piece of writing? Are the evidence and examples provided sufficient?

_____

_____

ASSUMPTIONS BIASES

4. Are there unfounded **assumptions** or unreasonable **biases**?

_____

_____

CONCLUSIONS

5. Are all of the **conclusions**, **implications**, and **consequences** of the arguments (the results of the arguments taken to their farthest extreme) considered?

_____

_____

POINT OF VIEW

6. Is the **point of view** clear and consistent, and have other points of view been considered?

_____

_____

ANALYSIS

7. Using these critical thinking tools, **analyze** the overall structure of this essay and the strength of the author's arguments, ideas, and support. Was he or she successful in accomplishing the purpose? Why, or why not?

_____

_____

Essay Assignments

1. Write a classification essay using any of the topics you developed in the activities in this chapter.

2. Classify college students into at least four categories (think of stereotyping them into particular *types* of students). Then come up with an analytical conclusion based on the categories or stereotypes.

3. Pick one of the following types of establishments, and then categorize the types within those establishments. Use specific examples and details. Then come to an analytical conclusion related to these categories.

   a. Fast food restaurants

   b. Coffee shops

   c. Department stores

4. Categorize your coworkers as to skill levels and efficiency. Then come to an analytical conclusion as a result of your categories and criteria.

5. Categorize teachers at your college into types. Then come to an analytical conclusion related to teachers and the categories they fall into.

6. Categorize American cars versus imported cars. Then come to an analytical conclusion related to the details and categories you come up with.

SPOTLIGHT ON CRITICAL THINKING

We **classify** people, things, and ideas everyday both in college and in careers.

   Writing classifications: For example, in science classes, you will write essays or reports that classify plants and organisms into particular categories and classes. On the job, you may have to write summaries that classify clients and coworkers into specialized groups based on common characteristics that they share. Use your **analysis** skills to check the **purpose** and **conclusions** in your classification writing for college classes and later in your writing for your career. Develop your **purpose, ideas,** and **support** based on the critical thinking tips in Chapter 1.

   Reading classifications: In sociology and anthropology classes, people will be classified by groups in articles and studies that you read. Use your critical thinking skills from Chapter 1 and your Active Reading Skills from Chapter 2 to question and critique as you read. On the job, you'll have many occasions to read classifications of products or clients. If you were selling someone a new copy machine, for instance, you'd need to first classify the types of products you have to sell them and read all about their functions beforehand. Use the Six Steps for Active Reading in Chapter 2 to be a more careful and interactive reader.

To check your progress in meeting this chapter's objectives, log in to www .mywritinglab.com, go to the **Study Plan** tab, click on **Writing and Critical Thinking in the Modes** and choose **Essay Development—Division/Classification** from the list of subtopics. Read and view the resources in the **Review Materials** section, and then complete the **Recall, Apply,** and **Write** sets in the **Activities** section.

11 Definition

Patrick Navin

THINKING CRITICALLY

Look at the picture above. Then do the tasks that follow.

1. Define the object above. Use specific descriptive words, as if your audience has no idea what this thing is and cannot see it for themselves.

   _____

   _____

   _____

Continued ▶

2. Now briefly define the symbolic significance of this object. Explain any associations and connections to its cultural identity.

_____

_____

_____

DEFINITION ESSAYS

Definition essays explain, define, and clarify items, terms, and concepts. They are used to tell the reader what something is or what something means. Though you may need to use some description in a definition essay, make sure that when you are defining an object or concept you don't merely describe the subject: _Defining_ must explain what it _is_ and what it _means_, not just what it looks like.

Critical Thinking and Definition

The purpose for a definition essay can range from providing a straightforward definition of a term or concept in order to increase your reader's understanding of it to a definition that includes the symbolic meaning or cultural

APPLYING CRITICAL THINKING

| PURPOSE | IDEAS | SUPPORT | ASSUMPTIONS BIASES | CONCLUSIONS | POINT OF VIEW | ANALYSIS |

You define words and concepts to make it easier to communicate with others. Some definitions are straightforward and rely on facts and dictionaries, while some require more **analysis** and explanation on your part—and maybe even some creative thought and comparisons. To write an effective definition essay, you will need to consider the following questions:

1. What is my **purpose** and plan for this definition essay? What point do I want to make? How will I convey that message?

2. What **ideas** should I include to make my definition clear to my reader? What **support** (descriptive details, terms, examples, creative comparisons) will help me develop my definition and its purpose?

and historic relevance of an item or idea. For instance, you might define a "tamale" as a type of food composed of corn *masa* (ground corn flour) and fillings, such as meats, vegetables, or fruit, that is popular in countries such as Mexico and El Salvador. Then you could move on to define what this particular food represents in terms of the history, culture, or traditions of these countries. Definition essays are commonly used in reports to classmates and coworkers or to define specific terms or processes in a particular field or for a particular audience.

An **extended definition** consists of one or more paragraphs that explain a complex term. In an extended definition, you might use synonyms (words that have the same or similar meanings), give examples, discuss the term's origins, provide comparisons, explain what the word is not, or create an anecdote to show the word in action. You can consult a dictionary, but do not use a dictionary quotation as the main part of your definition. You may, however, integrate information you learn from the dictionary into your extended definition (check with your instructor). Extended definitions can employ other methods of development—narration, description, process analysis, illustration, classification, comparison and contrast, and cause and effect. Often, they also define by negation, by explaining what the term *does not mean*. Extended definitions can be purely personal, or they can be largely objective. A personal definition explains how a writer is using the term and allows the reader to see a word in a different light.

BEFORE WRITING A DEFINITION ESSAY

Before you begin to write a definition essay on an assigned topic, or one you have chosen, start by asking yourself these questions:

1. What is the object or concept I want to define?
2. What general category does my subject fall into?
3. What distinguishing characteristics does it have?
4. Can I compare it with something similar to define it?
5. Can I explain it by saying what it is not?
6. Why am I defining this subject, and what purpose can it serve?
7. What do I want my readers to learn or understand after reading this essay?

Answering these questions will lead you to an expository thesis statement, help you determine examples and details to include for support, and give you a general idea of how you want to organize your essay.

APPLYING CRITICAL THINKING

PURPOSE   IDEAS   SUPPORT   ASSUMPTIONS BIASES   CONCLUSIONS   POINT OF VIEW   ANALYSIS

To define your subject, you can draw on your own personal knowledge of the subject. If you are defining an object, you can have it in front of you to help create your definition. Be careful, though, not to slip into merely describing the object. Define what it is, its purpose, how it is used or what it is used for, or what relationship it has to society and human use. Use your well founded **assumptions** and **biases** to help you. Ask your instructor if you are allowed to look up definitions for an object or concept you are assigned to define. If you are allowed to include researched definitions from dictionaries, encyclopedias, or the Internet, then make sure to give credit to any outside sources you use.

ACTIVITY 11-1 Practicing Definition

Directions: *Prewrite on the following topics for a definition essay by brain-storming or clustering. Use a separate sheet of paper.* Answers will vary.

1. Family
2. Tradition
3. Global warming
4. Discrimination
5. Globalization
6. Favoritism
7. Home
8. Logo of your choice
9. Meditation
10. Ceremony

WRITING A DEFINITION ESSAY

In your introductory paragraph, identify the topic you will be defining. Then, on the basis of your prewriting, explain in your thesis statement how you will define the subject and what your purpose is for defining it.

In the body of your essay, you can define the item, term, or concept you have chosen by first discussing how your subject fits into a general category. Then you can write about its distinguishing features in order to define it more specifically. For instance, if you had to define a mango, you might first put it into the general category of an exotic or tropical fruit. Then you would get specific about the mango's distinguishing qualities: its taste, color, shape, size, texture, and so on.

In order to define your subject more precisely, you can also compare it with similar things. For instance, you could compare a hammer with a mallet, as they are similar kinds of tools, but emphasize how they differ. Or you could compare something unfamiliar (the item you are defining) with something familiar to your audience. For example, you could explain that bouillabaisse is like a beef stew but made from several types of fish and shellfish. You can also define a term by saying what it is not. For instance, you could define the term "obesity" by saying what it is not: It is not being just a couple of pounds overweight.

You might also want to talk about subcategories within the term you are defining. If you were defining the term *schizophrenia* for a psychology course, you might want to talk about different types of schizophrenia such as disorganized, paranoid, and catatonic. Conclude your definition essay by summing up what you have defined and your purpose for defining it. Here is a sample definition paragraph that provides a simple, clear definition of the term "flag." The topic sentence is in italics.

> *A flag is an object that is made of fabric and includes colors and possibly shapes, letters, or figures to represent a group, team, or even a country.* For example, many sports teams have flags dedicated to them that feature the team name and a picture of the team mascot. The Chicago Bulls, for instance, have a team flag that is red and black and has a picture of a bull's head along with the team name. Flags can also represent a country; for instance, the flag of the United States is red, white, and blue, with bold red and white stripes and a square shape in the corner that is dark blue with 50 white stars representing the 50 states.

If you wanted to add the dimension of cultural or symbolic significance to your paragraph, then you might make the topic sentence more analytical and add some examples of what the flag represents and what kind of symbolic weight it carries. For instance:

> *The American flag is more than just a cloth representation of the United States: It is also a symbol of our country's values, history, and identity.* The 50 stars that represent each state also represent America as a country made up of unique states that form a union. This unity is especially important symbolically, given the history of this country and the American Civil War that nearly tore the northern and southern states apart.

The chart below provides a brief overview of the structure of a definition essay.

BASIC STRUCTURE FOR A DEFINITION ESSAY

INTRODUCTORY PARAGRAPH

Sets up background for your definition.

Thesis statement: States how you will define your chosen topic and your purpose for defining it.

PURPOSE

BODY PARAGRAPHS (Two to five, depending on assignment and purpose)

Develop your definition through identifying the group the item or concept belongs to and discussing its distinguishing characteristics.

Topic sentences will set up the structure of your definition in each paragraph.

Provide concrete examples to illustrate and define your topic. Provide definitions of any unfamiliar terms you use in your explanation of your topic. **Analyze** the examples.

Use transitions within and between paragraphs to make the paragraphs flow smoothly.

IDEAS

SUPPORT

ANALYSIS

CONCLUDING PARAGRAPH

Sums up and re-emphasizes the thesis statement: the **conclusions reached** through your definition.

CONCLUSIONS

STRUCTURING A DEFINITION ESSAY

Topic

If you do not have a topic assigned by your instructor for your definition essay, then brainstorm ideas for things, places, or people you might want to define. Then come up with some ideas for a purpose for defining the topic. What do you want your readers to understand through your definition?

A Few Topic Possibilities

You can define a complex term or process you learned about in another class. You can define a term, position, or item from your job. Basically, anything you would need to define to your audience in order to make a point would constitute the need for an in-depth definition.

Thesis Statements

The thesis statement for a definition essay states what item, concept, or term you are going to define and establishes your purpose for writing about it. Your purpose may be simply to define an object or concept for an audience unfamiliar with your subject.

> A mitral valve prolapse is a specific type of heart murmur that exhibits several distinct characteristics.

Often, though, a definition essay's purpose is to define something in order to reach a more complex conclusion related to the subject. For instance, in the tamale example earlier in this chapter, the writer could first define what a *tamale* is and then use tamales as a cultural symbol of the tastes and traditions of the countries that prize them.

> The tamale is an important part of Mexican holiday traditions: It is more than a favorite food, since it is part of a cultural tradition.

In your introductory paragraph, set up the overall topic you will be defining. Then on the basis of your prewriting, establish how you will define the subject and what the purpose is for defining it so as to come up with the right thesis statement for your topic and purpose.

ACTIVITY 11-2   Creating Thesis Statements

Directions: *Choose three of the topics from Activity 11-1 that you brainstormed about and two topics of your own choice (such as terms from other classes you've had), and create a one-sentence thesis statement for each. Make sure each thesis statement identifies the item, concept, or term being defined and your purpose for defining it.* Answers will vary.

1. Item, concept, or term: _____

    Thesis statement: _____

    _____

2. Item, concept, or term: _____

    Thesis statement: _____

    _____

3. Item, concept, or term: _____

Thesis statement: _____

_____

4. Item, concept, or term: _____

Thesis statement: _____

_____

5. Item, concept, or term: _____

Thesis statement: _____

_____

Introductory Paragraph

Begin your definition essay with a general introduction to the subject or term you are defining. End with a thesis statement that sets up the purpose for your definition essay.

Body Paragraphs

After creating a strong thesis statement for a definition essay, you need to organize your body paragraphs in the best way to develop your definition. For instance, using the tamale example from earlier in the chapter, you could use the body paragraphs and topic sentences to further define the tamale and then develop the tamale's significance symbolically, giving specific details and explaining the traditions and cultural history that relate to the tamale in separate paragraphs. Comparison, contrast, and example transitions are particularly useful in definition essays; you could also use transitions to show contrast and purpose (see Chapter 6, pp. 114–116).

TRANSITIONS TO . . .			
Show Contrast or a Change in Idea			
although	even though	instead	on the other side
anyhow	for all that	nevertheless	otherwise
at the same time	however	notwithstanding	regardless
but	in any event	on the contrary	still
despite this	in contrast	on the other hand	yet

TRANSITIONS TO . . .

Show a Comparison

| in like manner | in the same way | likewise | similarly |

Illustrate or Give Examples/Specifics

a few include	essentially	in particular	the following
an example	for example	let us consider	specifically
especially	for instance	the case of	you can see this in

ACTIVITY 11-3   Creating Topic Sentences

Directions: *Choose three of the thesis statements you created in Activity 11-2, and write two topic sentences for each that could be used to develop two of the body paragraphs for that thesis statement in an essay.* *Answers will vary.*

1. Thesis statement: _____

    _____

    Topic sentence 1: _____

    _____

    Topic sentence 2: _____

    _____

2. Thesis statement: _____

    _____

    Topic sentence 1: _____

    _____

    Topic sentence 2: _____

    _____

3. Thesis statement: _____

    _____

    Topic sentence 1: _____

    _____

    Topic sentence 2: _____

    _____

Next, develop your body paragraphs by providing concrete details and examples.

ACTIVITY 11-4 **Supporting Details**

Directions: *Now, provide at least three possible examples or details you would include for three of the topic sentences you created in Activity 11-3.* Answers will vary.

1. Topic sentence: _____

   _____

   Example/detail 1: _____

   _____

   Example/detail 2: _____

   _____

   Example/detail 3: _____

   _____

2. Topic sentence: _____

   _____

   Example/detail 1: _____

   _____

   Example/detail 2: _____

   _____

   Example/detail 3: _____

   _____

3. Topic sentence: _____

   _____

   Example/detail 1: _____

   _____

   Example/detail 2: _____

   _____

   Example/detail 3: _____

   _____

Concluding Paragraph

The concluding paragraph in a definition essay should redefine the object or concept briefly and sum up your purpose for defining it to your reader.

ACTIVITY 11-5   Concluding Paragraphs

Directions: *Choose one of the topics you've been developing in the preceding activities, and write a three- to five-sentence concluding paragraph that re-emphasizes the definition and your purpose for defining it.*   Answers will vary.

_____

_____

_____

_____

_____

Use the critique form below to check for the basics in your definition essay draft.

DEFINITION ESSAY CRITIQUE FORM

| PURPOSE | IDEAS | SUPPORT | ASSUMPTIONS BIASES | CONCLUSIONS | POINT OF VIEW | ANALYSIS |

Overall   Done well   Needs work

1. Does the essay clearly define the subject?   _____   _____
2. Does the essay use specific details and **ideas** consistently and clearly?   _____   _____
3. Are the paragraphs broken up well and about the right length?   _____   _____

Introduction

4. Is the title interesting and in correct format?   _____   _____
5. Is there a general introduction that gives background for the subject and the **purpose** for the definition?   _____   _____
6. Is there a clear thesis statement that explains the **purpose** of the definition?   _____   _____

Body

7. Do the body paragraphs develop the definition and flow smoothly? _____ _____
8. Are transitions used between and, when needed, within the paragraphs? _____ _____
9. Do the body paragraphs include **support** (descriptive details
and examples)? _____ _____

Conclusion

10. Does the **concluding** paragraph sum up the definition with **analysis** and
re-emphasize the **purpose** developed in the introductory paragraph and
thesis, without adding new ideas? _____ _____

Editing

11. Circle the following errors you think you see in this draft: spelling errors,
fragments, run-ons/comma splices, errors in comma and semicolon/colon
use, pronoun disagreement, reference fault errors, and errors in parallelism,
apostrophe use, verb use/tense, and passive voice construction.
(See the handbook section for help in identifying and
correcting these errors.)
12. Other types of grammar or sentence-level errors:

_____

Comments:

_____

_____

LO 3 COMPLEMENTARY MODES FOR DEFINITION ESSAYS

When definition mode is used in an essay, it is often combined with several
other modes.

- **Narration** and **description** can be used to develop a definition.
- **Illustration and examples** can be further used to elaborate on the defin-
ition of a subject.
- **Classification** is usually part of the definition process itself: You have to
classify items into broader groups to define them specifically.
- You can **compare and contrast** items as you define your subject.
- You can use the definition to prove an **argument** or **persuade** your
readers to a particular point of view.

Sample Student Essay

Figueroa 1

Rosie Figueroa

Professor Rosen

English 100

15 March 2010

The Importance of a Quinceañera

Thesis statement

Many cultures have traditional rituals to represent a coming of age. In America, girls often celebrate their sixteenth birthday with a "Sweet 16" party. In Jewish culture, boys and girls celebrate their thirteenth birthday with a Bah or Bat Mitzvah. In my culture, which is Mexican-American, when girls turn fifteen they have an elaborate party called a quinceañera. This party and the rituals involved are a very important part of my culture and an important part of becoming a young woman.

Topic sentence

A quinceañera is a specialized birthday celebration. The word "quinceañera" comes from the Spanish word "quince" which means "fifteen"; therefore, it is literally a celebration of a girl's fifteenth birthday. In some ways, it is more like a wedding than a normal birthday party. For example, in a quinceañera, the girl wears a beautiful white dress and usually a tiara. Also, like in a wedding, she chooses friends (up to 14 of them to make a total of 15) to be part of her quinceañera. If her court is made up of girls, these girls wear special matching dresses, much like bridesmaids, and are part of the formal ceremony acknowledging her coming of age before the reception to celebrate her coming out as a young woman to society. Sometimes, the formal ceremony is held in a church with a priest who gives a blessing, and sometimes it is held at a home or community hall. Always, family and friends are there to celebrate this special birthday.

Concluding sentence

Figueroa 2

The last part of the quinceañera celebrates the importance of the
girl's family and friends in her transition from childhood to adulthood
and involves sharing good food, music, and dancing. Usually, close
family members and godparents contribute money toward the
celebration. Much planning goes into arranging the religious blessing
part of the ceremony as well as the reception afterwards that provides
food and entertainment for all the guests. Moreover, special invitations
are sent out in advance, and these parties can be huge with hundreds
of guests. That's why there are websites dedicated to buying supplies
for a quinceañera celebration. Quinceañeras feature a banquet, often
with rice, beans, carne asada, tamales, and enchiladas. Also, a mariachi
band usually plays traditional Mexican dance music, and everyone,
young and old, dances to celebrate the girl's coming out into society as
a young adult. It's a great chance to connect with family and friends
and to celebrate Mexican traditions, food, music, and overall culture.

The quinceañera is more than just a birthday party: it is an
important part of my Mexican cultural identity. Young girls look
forward to this special day, and family and friends see it as a way to
celebrate both the girl's birthday and their pride in their culture's
traditions and heritage. It celebrates the girl's transition into adulthood
with the best combination of food, music, dancing, and family.

Topic sentence

Concluding sentence

Restatement of thesis

ACTIVITY 11-6   **Thinking Critically About the Student Essay**

*Directions: Analyze the essay to identify the features and details characteristic
of the classification mode. Mark them on the essay. Then, reread the essay, and
make a list of specific revisions you would make to correct any problems with content, organization, transitions, and style.*

PROFESSIONAL DEFINITION ESSAY

Discrimination Is a Virtue

Robert Keith Miller

Robert Keith Miller is the author of several books, including many books on the craft of writing and handbooks for grammar and usage. He is also the author of a book called *Mark Twain*, about Twain's work and his life. Miller is an active scholar in the field of college writing.

1   When I was a child, my grandmother used to tell me a story about a king who had three daughters and decided to test their love. He asked each of them "How much do you love me?" The first replied that she loved him as much as all the diamonds and pearls in the world. The second said that she loved him more than life itself. The third replied "I love you as fresh meat loves salt."

2   This answer enraged the king; he was convinced that his youngest daughter was making fun of him. So he banished her from his realm and left all of his property to her elder sisters.

3   As the story unfolded it became clear, even to a 6-year-old, that the king had made a terrible mistake. The two older girls were hypocrites, and as soon as they had profited from their father's generosity, they began to treat him very badly. A wiser man would have realized that the youngest daughter was the truest. Without attempting to flatter, she had said, in effect, "We go together naturally; we are a perfect team."

4   Years later, when I came to read Shakespeare, I realized that my grandmother's story was loosely based upon the story of King Lear, who put his daughters to a similar test and did not know how to judge the results. Attempting to save the king from the consequences of his foolishness, a loyal friend pleads, "Come sir, arise, away! I'll teach you differences." Unfortunately, the lesson comes too late. Because Lear could not tell the difference between true love and false, he loses his kingdom and eventually his life.

5   We have a word in English which means "the ability to tell differences." That word is *discrimination*. But within the last twenty years, this word has been so frequently misused that an entire generation has grown up believing that "discrimination" means "racism." People are always proclaiming that "discrimination" is something that should be done away with. Should that ever happen, it would prove to be our undoing.

6   Discrimination means discernment; it means the ability to perceive the truth, to use good judgment and to profit accordingly. The *Oxford English Dictionary* traces this understanding of the word back to 1648 and demonstrates that, for the next 300 years, "discrimination" was a virtue, not a vice. Thus, when a character in a nineteenth-century novel makes a happy marriage, Dickens has another character remark, "It does credit to your discrimination that you should have found such a very excellent young woman."

7   Of course, "the ability to tell differences" assumes that differences exist, and this is unsettling for a culture obsessed with the notion of equality. The contemporary belief that discrimination is a vice stems from the compound "discriminate against." What we need to remember, however, is that some things deserve to be judged harshly: we should not leave our kingdoms to the selfish and the wicked.

8   Discrimination is wrong only when someone or something is discriminated against because of prejudice. But to use the word in this sense, as so many people do, is to destroy its true meaning. If you discriminate against something because of general preconceptions rather than particular insights, then you are not discriminating—bias has clouded the clarity of vision which discrimination demands.

9   One of the great ironies of American life is that we manage to discriminate in the practical decisions of daily life, but usually fail to discriminate when we make public policies. Most people are very discriminating when it comes to buying a car, for example, because they realize that cars have differences. Similarly, an increasing number of people have learned to discriminate in what they eat. Some foods are better than others—and indiscriminate eating can undermine one's health. Yet in public affairs, good judgment is depressingly rare. In many areas which involve the common good, we see a failure to tell differences.

10   Consider, for example, some of the thinking behind modern education. On the one hand, there is a refreshing realization that there are differences among children, and some children—be they gifted or handicapped—require special education. On the other hand, we are politically unable to accept the consequences of this perception. The trend in recent years has been to group together students of radically different ability. We call this process "mainstreaming," and it strikes me as a characteristically American response to the discovery of differences: we try to pretend that differences do not matter.

11   Similarly, we try to pretend that there is little difference between the sane and the insane. A fashionable line of argument has it that "everybody is a little mad" and that few mental patients deserve long-term hospitalization. As a consequence of such reasoning, thousands of seriously ill men and

women have been evicted from their hospital beds and returned to what is euphemistically called "the community"—which often means being left to sleep on city streets, where confused and helpless people now live out of paper bags as the direct result of our refusal to discriminate.

12   Or to choose a final example from a different area: how many recent elections reflect thoughtful consideration of the genuine differences among candidates? Benumbed by television commercials that market aspiring officeholders as if they were a new brand of toothpaste or hair spray, too many Americans vote with only a fuzzy understanding of the issues in question. Like Lear, we seem too eager to leave the responsibility of government to others and too ready to trust those who tell us whatever we want to hear.

13   So as we look around us, we should recognize that "discrimination" is a virtue which we desperately need. We must try to avoid making unfair and arbitrary distinctions, but we must not go to the other extreme and pretend that there are no distinctions to be made. The ability to make intelligent judgments is essential both for the success of one's personal life and for the functioning of society as a whole. Let us be open-minded by all means, but not so open-minded that our brains fall out.

Reading Reflection Questions *Answers will vary. Sample answers are provided.*

1. What are the direct or indirect (implied) messages in this essay?

That the word "discrimination" has been reduced to just one specific

meaning; it has lost its other, original meanings "choosing well" or "being

discriminating"

2. Why do you think the author began this article with the story he did (King Lear)?

To give an example of a person who did not use discrimination in his

judgment.

3. How is discrimination related to prejudice according to the author?

It is one negative example of discrimination—if your view is tainted by

prejudice, then you discriminate in a negative way.

Objective Questions

4. T/F ___T___ Discrimination means "the ability to tell differences."

5. T/F ___F___ Discrimination also means "racism," according to the author.

6. T/F ____*T*____ The author believes that the real purpose of discrimination—discernment—is an important and valuable skill.

7. Provide two examples the author uses to support his purpose.

   Discriminating choices for education, choosing good candidates in

   elections

Checking Vocabulary

Define the following in your own words, or provide a dictionary definition if you don't know the word.

8. discernment: *careful distinction/judgment*

9. obsessed: *overly focused on something*

10. prejudice: *unfair bias against another*

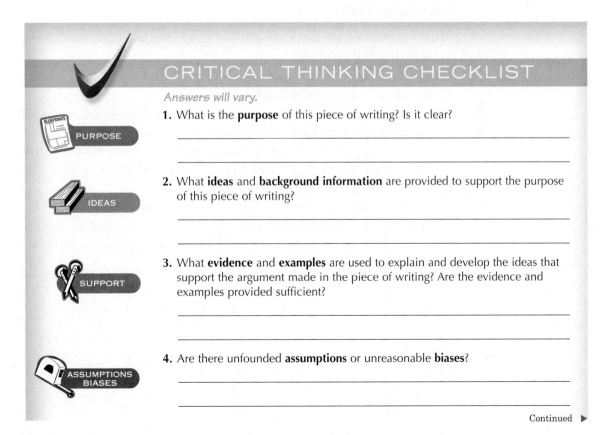

CRITICAL THINKING CHECKLIST

Answers will vary.

PURPOSE

1. What is the **purpose** of this piece of writing? Is it clear?

   _____

   _____

IDEAS

2. What **ideas** and **background information** are provided to support the purpose of this piece of writing?

   _____

   _____

SUPPORT

3. What **evidence** and **examples** are used to explain and develop the ideas that support the argument made in the piece of writing? Are the evidence and examples provided sufficient?

   _____

   _____

ASSUMPTIONS BIASES

4. Are there unfounded **assumptions** or unreasonable **biases**?

   _____

   _____

Continued ▶

5. Are all of the **conclusions**, **implications**, and **consequences** of the arguments (the results of the arguments taken to their farthest extreme) considered?

_____

_____

6. Is the **point of view** clear and consistent, and have other points of view been considered?

_____

_____

7. Using these critical thinking tools, **analyze** the overall structure of this essay and the strength of the author's arguments, ideas, and support. Was he or she successful in accomplishing the purpose? Why, or why not?

_____

_____

Essay Assignments

1. Write a definition essay using any of the topics you developed in the activities in this chapter.

2. Define a concept from one of your other classes (for instance, a term from economics, history, or biology).

3. Combine definition with one other mode from these chapters on modes and write an essay related to some aspect of your college campus. Narrow your topic down to some aspect of your campus that needs definition first: the interlibrary loan option, the Career Center, the Writing Center, the Financial Aid Office, and so on.

4. Provide your own extended definition of the "ideal family."

5. Define the word "patriotism" using a dictionary definition of the word as well as the connotations it carries and your own personal associations with and opinions of the word.

SPOTLIGHT ON CRITICAL THINKING

Definitions help people understand your ideas and the ideas and objects around them.

Writing definitions: In college, you will be asked to define terms and to explain them in a way that your audience will understand. For example, in a criminal justice program, you may have to write a report or summary that defines terms used in the field for a more general audience. On the job, you may be asked by coworkers and clients to write a guideline that defines terms from your industry and to share your expertise in a clear and digestible way. For instance, if you are a nurse, you may train others to fulfill the necessary recordkeeping requirements for patient information. Use your **analysis** skills to check the **purpose** and **conclusions** in writing definitions for college classes and later in your writing for your career. Develop your **purpose, ideas,** and **support** based on the critical thinking tips in Chapter 1.

Reading definitions: In medical terminology courses, you will have to memorize long lists of terms and definitions. Use your critical thinking skills from Chapter 1 and your Active Reading Skills from Chapter 2 to learn the terms and know the differences. On the job, you'll have many occasions to read definitions of terms or concepts. If you were a legal assistant or a lawyer, you would have to read and define legal terms regularly. You would also need to tap into the critical reading skills you mastered in Chapter 2 to get the most out of what you read. Use the Six Steps for Active Reading to be a more careful and interactive reader.

To check your progress in meeting this chapter's objectives, log in to www .mywritinglab.com, go to the **Study Plan** tab, click on **Writing and Critical Thinking in the Modes** and choose **Essay Development—Definition** from the list of subtopics. Read and view the resources in the **Review Materials** section, and then complete the **Recall, Apply,** and **Write** sets in the **Activities** section.

12

Example and Illustration

Windsurfer   Mark Johnson

LEARNING OBJECTIVES

In this chapter, you will learn to

LO 1 Write example essays.

LO 2 Structure example essays.

LO 3 Use complementary modes for example and illustration essays.

THINKING CRITICALLY

Look at the picture above. Then answer the questions that follow.

1. What is this picture an example of?

_____

2. How could this picture be used to illustrate the thrills of windsurfing?

_____

_____

(LO 1) EXAMPLE ESSAYS

Example/illustration essays use examples to clarify, explain, and support the purpose of the essay. Examples include facts, expert testimony, and personal experience. They can be used in combination to support a thesis; or a single, extended example can be used to develop a point.

Critical Thinking and Example

Before you begin generating examples, you need to assess your audience and determine the message you want to get across to them.

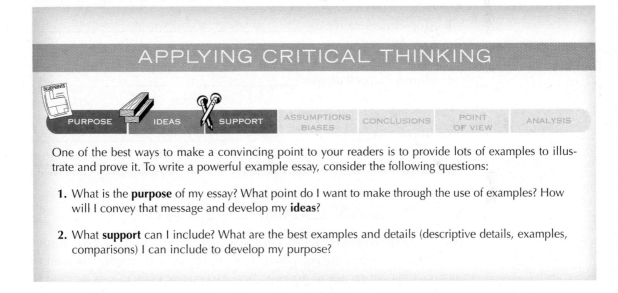

APPLYING CRITICAL THINKING

PURPOSE   IDEAS   SUPPORT   ASSUMPTIONS BIASES   CONCLUSIONS   POINT OF VIEW   ANALYSIS

One of the best ways to make a convincing point to your readers is to provide lots of examples to illustrate and prove it. To write a powerful example essay, consider the following questions:

1. What is the **purpose** of my essay? What point do I want to make through the use of examples? How will I convey that message and develop my **ideas**?

2. What **support** can I include? What are the best examples and details (descriptive details, examples, comparisons) I can include to develop my purpose?

BEFORE WRITING AN EXAMPLE ESSAY

Before you begin to write an example essay on an assigned topic, or one you have chosen, start by asking yourself these questions:

1. What point am I trying to make?
2. Which examples can I include to illustrate my purpose clearly?
3. What facts, testimony, and experiences can I tap into to develop my purpose in this essay?

4. What details should I provide to further illustrate my examples?

5. How should I organize this essay, and how should I conclude it?

ACTIVITY 12-1   Choosing Examples

Directions: *For each of the following topics, list three examples you could use to develop it.* *Answers will vary.*

1. **Topic:** Diet fads _____

   _____

2. **Topic:** Flowers _____

   _____

3. **Topic:** A great meal _____

   _____

4. **Topic:** Natural disasters _____

   _____

5. **Topic:** Peer pressure _____

   _____

WRITING AN EXAMPLE ESSAY

It's important to understand that all essays depend on examples and illustrations to develop and support their thesis statements. Examples are used to support topic sentences in an essay, and extended examples can be used to develop the thesis statement of an essay.

Providing concrete examples to your readers is one of the best ways to convince them about the point you want to make. In your introductory paragraph, set up the overall purpose of your essay, and in your thesis statement, explain, what you will be illustrating through examples, your analytical purpose. Organize your paper in a way that highlights your examples in the most powerful way to get your purpose across. For instance, you might choose to provide your examples for support in a most to least important order (or vice versa), or chronological order.

In the body paragraphs, develop several simple examples or one or more extended examples to develop your thesis. For instance, if you were explaining how a typical wedding from your culture usually works, you could use several different weddings you've attended as examples, or you could choose to use your own wedding—or the wedding of someone close to you—as an extended example of a typical wedding from your culture. Your examples should be vivid and interesting but not unfamiliar to your readers. Most important, the examples must clearly demonstrate the point(s) your thesis sets out to make. Be sure to incorporate as many details and concrete images as possible into your examples. Use transitions between examples within your body paragraphs and between paragraphs for separate examples. Include key words and transitional phrases such as "for example," "to illustrate," and "for instance" to set up the examples you provide to make your points. Finally, in the concluding paragraph, re-emphasize the purpose you want to express to your readers though the examples.

The chart below provides a brief overview of the structure of an example/illustration essay.

BASIC STRUCTURE FOR AN EXAMPLE/ILLUSTRATION ESSAY

INTRODUCTORY PARAGRAPH

Sets up your subject and your purpose.

Thesis statement: A statement that defines your purpose and what example(s) you'll be using to illustrate it.

BODY PARAGRAPHS (Two to five, depending on assignment and purpose)

Topic sentences set up the organization and focus of your examples or extended example.

Develop the examples, illustrations, and details. **Analyze** their significance.

Use transitions within and between paragraphs to make the paragraphs flow smoothly.

CONCLUDING PARAGRAPH

Sums up and re-emphasizes the thesis.

STRUCTURING AN EXAMPLE ESSAY

Topic

If you do not have a topic assigned by your instructor for your illustration/example essay, then brainstorm ideas for things, places, or events you might want to describe. Come up with some ideas for a purpose for describing the topic. What do you want your readers to understand through your use of example?

A Few Topic Possibilities

Many topics work well for writing an example essay. You could write about the kinds of cars you can buy in America, the variety of food and interesting cuisines in this country, the types of clothing that are popular this decade, and so on.

Thesis Statements

A thesis statement for an example or illustration essay clarifies your purpose for including specific examples or illustrations. It states what you want your readers to understand after reading your examples, the message you want to impart.

> Sports fans go to many extremes to show support for their favorite teams.
>
> Technology has made being a college student easier in the last decade.

ACTIVITY 12-2   Creating Thesis Statements

Directions: *Create a thesis statement for each of the topics listed. Make sure that the thesis is something that will need to be demonstrated through examples.* Answers will vary.

1. **Topic:** Prejudice

   Thesis sentence: _____

   _____

2. **Topic:** Interesting hobbies

   Thesis sentence: _____

   _____

3. **Topic:** Food rituals

   Thesis sentence: _____

   _____

4. **Topic:** Natural disasters

   Thesis sentence: _____

   _____

5. **Topic:** Video games

   Thesis sentence: _____

   _____

Introductory Paragraph

Begin your example/illustration essay with a general introduction to the topic for which you are providing examples to illustrate your conclusion. End with the thesis statement to set up the purpose of your example essay.

Body Paragraphs

The body paragraphs in an example/illustration essay provide specific details and examples organized to illustrate your purpose. For instance, in an essay about appropriate birthday parties for people of different ages, you could organize the examples chronologically and create topic sentences for each age-specific type of party. Or you might choose to organize your body paragraphs on the basis of the relevance of each example: least to most important, or vice versa. Your topic sentences should set up each specific example and its relevance to your thesis statement's purpose.

Body paragraphs can be divided into separate examples or can be parts of an extended example. For instance, the following brief outline focuses on birthday parties for three different age groups, and each topic sentence would need at least two examples and your **analysis** to illustrate it.

Thesis: Birthday parties should be age appropriate.

Topic sentence 1: Birthday parties for elementary school-aged children should have interactive games that are supervised by adults.

Topic sentence 2: For middle school-aged children, birthday parties should skip organized games and focus on the kids just hanging out together, gifts, and food.

Topic sentence 3: For high school kids, birthday parties are usually held at a place outside the home, a get-together at a restaurant, for instance, and with a smaller group of close friends.

ACTIVITY 12-3   Creating Topic Sentences

Directions: *For three of the thesis statements you created in Activity 12-2, create topic sentences that could be used to support them.*   *Answers will vary.*

1. **Topic:** _____

    Thesis statement: _____

    Topic sentence: _____

    _____

2. **Topic:** _____

    Thesis statement: _____

    Topic sentence: _____

    _____

3. **Topic:** _____

    Thesis statement: _____

    Topic sentence: _____

    _____

ACTIVITY 12-4   Providing Examples

Directions: *Based on your answers in Activity 12-3, provide three examples that would provide support for each topic sentence.*   *Answers will vary.*

1. **Topic:** _____

    Topic sentence: _____

    Examples: _____

    _____

2. **Topic:** _____

    Topic sentence: _____

    Examples: _____

    _____

3. **Topic:** _____

   Topic sentence: _____

   Examples: _____

   _____

Although example transitions are especially useful in example/illustration essays, other helpful transitions include those that strengthen points and show addition of points or purpose (see Chapter 6, pages 114–116).

TRANSITIONS TO . . .

Illustrate or Give Examples/Specifics

a few include	essentially	in particular	the following
an example	for example	let us consider	specifically
especially	for instance	the case of	you can see this in

Concluding Paragraph

The concluding paragraph for your example essay should recap your purpose and intended message for the examples and illustrations you provided in the essay.

ACTIVITY 12-5   Writing a Conclusion

Directions: *Based on your answers to Activities 12-2, 12-3, and 12-4, write a three- to five-sentence concluding paragraph that would work for one of the topics you worked on.* Answers will vary.

_____

_____

_____

_____

_____

Use the critique form on page 244 to check for the basics in your example essay draft.

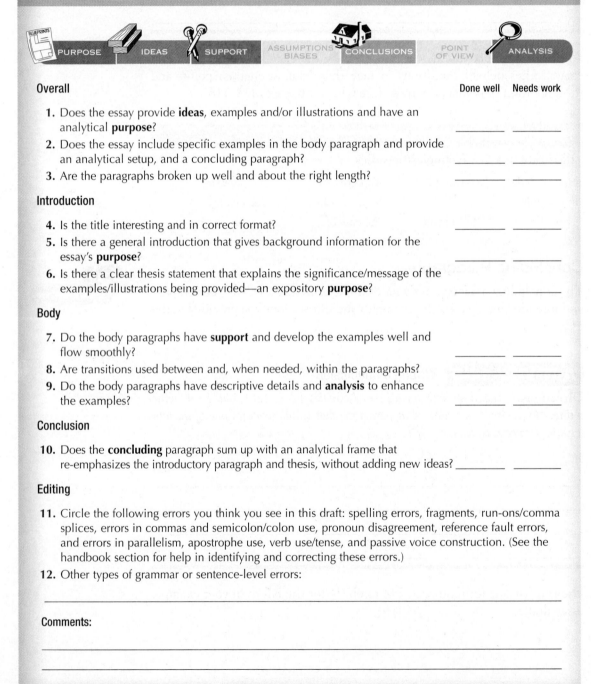

EXAMPLE ESSAY CRITIQUE FORM

PURPOSE | IDEAS | SUPPORT | ASSUMPTIONS BIASES | CONCLUSIONS | POINT OF VIEW | ANALYSIS

Overall

	Done well	Needs work

1. Does the essay provide **ideas**, examples and/or illustrations and have an analytical **purpose**?

2. Does the essay include specific examples in the body paragraph and provide an analytical setup, and a concluding paragraph?

3. Are the paragraphs broken up well and about the right length?

Introduction

4. Is the title interesting and in correct format?

5. Is there a general introduction that gives background information for the essay's **purpose**?

6. Is there a clear thesis statement that explains the significance/message of the examples/illustrations being provided—an expository **purpose**?

Body

7. Do the body paragraphs have **support** and develop the examples well and flow smoothly?

8. Are transitions used between and, when needed, within the paragraphs?

9. Do the body paragraphs have descriptive details and **analysis** to enhance the examples?

Conclusion

10. Does the **concluding** paragraph sum up with an analytical frame that re-emphasizes the introductory paragraph and thesis, without adding new ideas?

Editing

11. Circle the following errors you think you see in this draft: spelling errors, fragments, run-ons/comma splices, errors in commas and semicolon/colon use, pronoun disagreement, reference fault errors, and errors in parallelism, apostrophe use, verb use/tense, and passive voice construction. (See the handbook section for help in identifying and correcting these errors.)

12. Other types of grammar or sentence-level errors:

_____

Comments:

_____

_____

(LO 3) COMPLEMENTARY MODES FOR EXAMPLE ESSAYS

Example mode is often combined with several other modes.

- **Narration** and **description** can be used to develop the analysis of the examples.
- **Definition** mode can be used to help explain objects or concepts used in the examples provided.
- **Cause-and-effect analysis** will further elaborate on the examples.
- You can **compare and contrast** examples as you analyze your subject.
- You can use **argument** to persuade your readers to agree with the point of view you are using examples to support.

Sample Student Essay

Tobias 1

Brian Tobias

Professor Jacobson

English 100

26 September 2010

Seattle's Grunge Bands

Seattle has always been recognized for having great musicians, but in the late '80s and the early '90s, Seattle became the forefront for a new style of rock called grunge. Grunge combined elements of heavy metal, punk, and pop. The music featured screaming guitars, dissonant sounds, and wailing vocals, and it helped bring alternative rock into the mainstream. Pearl Jam, Soundgarden, and Nirvana are some of the best known grunge bands, opening the path to similar bands in the 1990s and making a name for Seattle in music history.

Pearl Jam consisted of Eddie Vedder (lead vocals and guitar), Stone Gossard (rhythm guitar), Jeff Ament (bass guitar), Mike

Thesis statement

Topic Sentence

Continued ▶

Tobias 2

McCready (lead guitar), and Dave Krusen (drummer), later replaced by Dave Abbruzzese. *Ten,* their first album, contained songs about loneliness, murder, suicide, and depression. The sound was a combination of classic rock, howling guitars, and Eddie Vedder's distinctive vocals. Pearl Jam released four other albums throughout the '90s: *Vs., Vitalogy, No Code,* and *Yield.* Pearl Jam outsold Nirvana, making them the top selling grunge band. Although they were criticized for cashing in on the popularity of alternative rock, they did not play by the rules, refusing to make music videos and boycotting Ticketmaster.

Concluding sentence

Topic sentence

    Another great band formed in Seattle was Soundgarden. In 1984, Kim Thayil (lead guitar), Hiro Yamamoto (bass), Scott Sundquist (drummer), replaced in 1986 by Matt Cameron, and Chris Cornell (lead singer, drummer) formed Soundgarden. Their music was a mix of punk, heavy metal, powerful guitar riffs, clear melodies, and the extraordinary and haunting vocals of Cornell. Since 1984, the band has recorded seven albums including *Screaming Life, FOPP, Ultramega OK, Louder than Love, Badmotorfinger, Superunknown,* and *Down on the Upside.* On April 9, 1997, Soundgarden broke up due to fighting among band members. Still, they will always remain an example of one of Seattle's finest grunge bands, with a sound all their own.

Concluding sentence

Topic sentence

    Finally, Nirvana is one of the best known names in the grunge world. Nirvana consisted of Kurt Cobain (singer/guitarist), Chris Novolesic (bass), and Aaron Burkhart (drummer). Burkhart was replaced by Chad Channing in 1986, who was himself replaced by Dave Grohl in 1990. Their music was a powerful combination of hard rock, high-energy pop, strong melodies, screaming guitars, and Cobain's powerful and varied vocals. The band produced several albums between 1989 and 1996 including *Bleach, Silver Dive, Nevermind, Incesticide, In*

Tobias 3

Utero, and *From the Muddy Banks of the Wishkah. Nevermind* was their breakthrough album. By Christmas of 1991, 400,000 copies of the CD were being sold each week, and it became number one on the Billboard charts in January 1992. Nirvana's performances here and abroad were sold out. Then, on April 8, 1994, Kurt Cobain was found dead in his home with a self-inflicted gunshot wound. The band members disbanded in 1996. However, Nirvana will always remain the ultimate Northwest grunge band example.

  In conclusion, Pearl Jam, Soundgarden, and Nirvana were instrumental in starting the grunge era. Each one of the bands had its own style, which laid the foundation for the bands that followed them. They put Seattle on the musical map

Concluding sentence

Restatement of thesis

ACTIVITY 12-6   **Thinking Critically About the Student Essay**

Directions: *Analyze the essay to identify the features and details characteristic of the example/illustration mode. Mark them on the essay. Then, reread the essay, and make a list of specific revisions you would make to correct any problems with content, organization, transitions, and style.*

PROFESSIONAL EXAMPLE ESSAY

Fairy Tales and Modern Stories

Bruno Bettelheim

1 The shortcomings of the realistic stories with which many parents have replaced fairy tales is suggested by a comparison of two such stories—"The Little Engine That Could" and "The Swiss Family Robinson"—with the fairy tale of "Rapunzel." "The Little Engine That Could" encourages the child to believe that if he tries hard and does not give up, he will finally succeed. A

young adult has recalled how much impressed she was at the age of seven when her mother read her this story. She became convinced that one's attitude indeed affects one's achievements—that if she would now approach a task with the conviction that she could conquer it, she would succeed.

2   A few days later, this child encountered in first grade a challenging situation: she was trying to make a house out of paper, gluing various sheets together. But her house continually collapsed. Frustrated, she began to seriously doubt whether her idea of building such a paper house could be realized. But then the story of "The Little Engine That Could" came to her mind; twenty years later, she recalled how at that moment she began to sing to herself the magic formula "I think I can, I think I can, I think I can . . ." So she continued to work on her paper house, and it continued to collapse. The project ended in complete defeat, with this little girl convinced that she had failed where anybody else could have succeeded, as the Little Engine had. Since "The Little Engine That Could" was a story set in the present, using such common props as engines that pulled trains, this girl had tried to apply its lesson directly in her daily life, without any fantasy elaboration, and had experienced a defeat that still rankled twenty years later.

3   Very different was the impact of "The Swiss Family Robinson" on another little girl. The story tells how a shipwrecked family manages to live an adventurous, idyllic, constructive, and pleasurable life—a life very different from this child's own existence. Her father had to be away from home a great deal, and her mother was mentally ill and spent protracted periods in institutions. So the girl was shuttled from her home to that of an aunt, then to that of a grandmother, and back home again, as the need arose. During these years, the girl read over and over again the story of this happy family who lived on a desert island, where no member could be away from the rest of the family.

4   Many years later, she recalled what a warm, cozy feeling she had when, propped up by a few large pillows, she forgot all about her present predicament as she read this story. As soon as she had finished it, she started to read it over again. The happy hours she spent with the Family Robinson in that fantasy land permitted her not to be defeated by the difficulties that reality presented to her. She was able to counteract the impact of harsh reality by imaginary gratifications. But since the story was not a fairy tale, it merely gave her a temporary escape from her problems; it did not hold out any promise to her that her life would take a turn for the better.

5   Consider the effect that "Rapunzel" had on a third girl. This girl's mother had died in a car accident. The girl's father, deeply upset by what had happened to his wife (he had been driving the car), withdrew entirely into himself and handed the care of his daughter over to a nursemaid, who was little interested in the girl and gave her complete freedom to do as she

liked. When the girl was seven, her father remarried, and, as she recalled it, it was around that time that "Rapunzel" became so important to her. Her stepmother was clearly the witch of the story, and she was the girl locked away in the tower. The girl recalled that she felt akin to Rapunzel because the witch had "forcibly" taken possession of her, as her step-mother had forcibly worked her way into the girl's life. The girl felt impris-oned in her new home, in contrast to her life of freedom with the nursemaid. She felt as victimized as Rapunzel, who, in her tower, had so little control over her life. Rapunzel's long hair was the key to the story. The girl wanted her hair to grow long, but her stepmother cut it short; long hair in itself became the symbol of freedom and happiness to her. The story convinced her that a prince (her father) would come someday and rescue her, and this conviction sustained her. If life became too difficult, all she needed was to imagine herself as Rapunzel, her hair grown long, and the prince loving and rescuing her.

6   "Rapunzel" suggests why fairy tales can offer more to the child than even such a very nice children's story as "The Swiss Family Robinson." In "The Swiss Family Robinson," there is no witch against whom the child can discharge her anger in fantasy and on whom she can blame the father's lack of interest. "The Swiss Family Robinson" offers escape fantasies, and it did help the girl who read it over and over to forget temporarily how diffi-cult life was for her. But it offered no specific hope for the future.

7   "Rapunzel," on the other hand, offered the girl a chance to see the witch of the story as so evil that by comparison even the "witch" stepmother at home was not really so bad. "Rapunzel" also promised the girl that her res-cue would be effected by her own body, when her hair grew long. Most important of all, it promised that the "prince" was only temporarily blinded—that he would regain his sight and rescue his princess. This fantasy continued to sustain the girl, though to a less intense degree, until she fell in love and married, and then she no longer needed it. We can understand why at first glance the stepmother, if she had known the meaning of "Rapunzel" to her stepdaughter, would have felt that fairy tales are bad for children. What she would not have known was that unless the stepdaughter had been able to find that fantasy satisfaction through "Rapunzel," she would have tried to break up her father's marriage and that without the hope for the future which the story gave her she might have gone badly astray in life.

8   It seems quite understandable that when children are asked to name their favorite fairy tales, hardly any modern tales are among their choices. Many of the new tales have sad endings, which fail to provide the escape and conso-lation that the fearsome events in the fairy tale require if the child is to be strengthened for meeting the vagaries of his life. Without such encouraging conclusions, the child, after listening to the story, feels that there is indeed no

hope for extricating himself from his despairs. In the traditional fairy tale, the hero is rewarded and the evil person meets his well-deserved fate, thus satisfying the child's deep need for justice to prevail. How else can a child hope that justice will be done to him, who so often feels unfairly treated? And how else can he convince himself that he must act correctly, when he is so sorely tempted to give in to the asocial proddings of his desires?

Reading Reflection Questions   *Sample answers are provided.*

1. What is the main purpose in this article? Explain in your own words.

   To explain that fairy tales can be more comforting than other modern

   "sensible" stories

2. Explain how this article is an example of a illustration essay. What are some characteristics that distinguish it as illustrating examples of some argument or purpose?

   The article gives three specific examples of fairy tales or modern stories

   and their effects on the children who read them

3. In addition to providing examples of fairy tales and modern stories, what is Bettleheim's main argument or conclusion about the two types of stories?

   That fairy tales provide more hope and comfort than other modern

   "sensible" stories

4. ___F___ T/F According to the essay, "The Swiss Family Robinson" is an example of a helpful fairy tale.

5. ___T___ T/F According to the essay, the fairy tale about Rapunzel helped one girl cope with the harsh realities of her family life.

6. In your own words, explain why the author favors fairy tales for providing hope for children.

   E.g., the fairy tales have happy and just endings that provide hope and a

   sense of justice and allow a true coping mechanism for their challenges

7. ___T___ T/ F According to the essay, in fairy tales, the hero is usually rewarded, and the evil person meets his or her well-deserved fate.

Checking Vocabulary

Define each of the following words by figuring out their meanings, using context clues in the reading selection. If you cannot work out the meaning of a word, use a dictionary.

8. rankled (paragraph 1): *continued irritation or resentment*

9. idyllic (paragraph 2): *charmingly simple or rustic*

10. consolation (paragraph 5): *providing comfort or solace*

CRITICAL THINKING CHECKLIST

Answers will vary.

1. What is the **purpose** of this piece of writing? Is it clear?

_____

_____

2. What **ideas** and **background information** are provided to support the purpose of this piece of writing?

_____

_____

3. What **evidence** and **examples** are used to explain and develop the ideas that support the argument made in the piece of writing? Are the evidence and examples provided sufficient?

_____

_____

4. Are there unfounded **assumptions** or unreasonable **biases**?

_____

_____

5. Are all of the **conclusions**, **implications**, and **consequences** of the arguments (the results taken to their farthest extreme) considered?

_____

_____

6. Is the **point of view** clear and consistent, and have other points of view been considered?

_____

_____

7. Using these critical thinking tools, **analyze** the overall structure of this essay and the strength of the author's arguments, ideas, and support. Was he or she successful in accomplishing the purpose? Why, or why not?

_____

_____

Essay Assignments

1. Choose one of the topics you developed in the activities in this chapter, and write a full example/illustration essay on that topic.

2. Write an essay about some type of music genre (e.g., jazz, hip-hop, rap, classical, rock, country), and provide several examples to illustrate your point about the genre. Be sure to come up with an analytical thesis you want to explain or prove in this essay.

3. Write an essay about fast-food restaurants. Include an analytical purpose, and provide specific examples to illustrate your point.

4. Write an essay about a particular sport, and include specific examples to illustrate the analytical purpose you set up in your introduction.

SPOTLIGHT ON CRITICAL THINKING

The most common way we can support our ideas and conclusions—whether it is in college, our careers, or just everyday interactions with others—is to provide examples.

Writing illustration essays: If you write an essay in a class, you'll need to provide examples to support your thesis. For example, in a history class, you'll need to provide examples and details to illustrate any conclusion you make regarding a particular event in history. On the job, you might have to provide written examples regarding how your products are used or to explain tasks you have completed. Use your **analysis** skills to check the **purpose** and **conclusions** in your writing for college classes and later in your writing for your career. Develop your **purpose, ideas,** and **support** based on the critical thinking tips in Chapter 1.

Reading illustrative writing: When you read college textbooks, you are reading an author's use of examples to develop their ideas. If a journalism class asks you to read a local newspaper for examples of public interest stories, use your critical thinking skills from Chapter 1 and your Active Reading Skills from Chapter 2 to be a more careful reader. On the job, you'll have many occasions when you need to read examples or illustrations. If you work in the medical field, you'll need to read carefully about case studies, which are examples of sets of symptoms that patients may exhibit in order to help your determination of their medical issues. You'll need to tap into your critical reading skills from Chapter 2 to get the most out of what you read. Use the Six Steps for Active Reading to be a more careful and interactive reader.

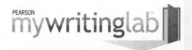

To check your progress in meeting this chapter's objectives, log in to www .mywritinglab.com, go to the **Study Plan** tab, click on **Writing and Critical Thinking in the Modes** and choose **Essay Development—Illustrating** from the list of subtopics. Read and view the resources in the **Review Materials** section, and then complete the **Recall, Apply,** and **Write** sets in the **Activities** section.

13

Cause and Effect

Orangutan Rescue

Annie Musselman

LEARNING OBJECTIVES

In this chapter, you will learn to

 Write cause-and-effect essays.

 Structure cause-and-effect essays.

 Use complementary modes for cause-and-effect essays.

THINKING CRITICALLY

Look at the picture above. Then answer the questions that follow.

1. What **causes** do you think have contributed to these baby orangutans needing help?

_____

_____

2. What **effects** do you think civilization has on forests and on the wild creatures in them?

_____

_____

LO 1 CAUSE-AND-EFFECT ESSAYS

A **cause-and-effect essay** analyzes causes (what led to certain results or *why* something happens) and their effects (the consequences or the *results* of an action or event). Cause-and-effect analysis comes in handy in many aspects of academic and workplace writing to determine what led to a particular event and the consequences of that event.

Cause-and-effect essays examine causes that lead to specific results. They may discuss a single cause and a single effect, a series of effects resulting from a single cause, or a series of causes that led to a particular effect. For instance, a new hair style could be the single cause that leads to a compliment (single effect) from a coworker, or overeating (single cause) could lead to several negative effects such as self-esteem issues, diabetes, back pain, and heart problems. Rainfall and dropping temperatures are two causes that lead to icy roads (single effect), and so on.

> ▶ **LANGUAGE TIP**   Use the word *effect* (a **noun**) when you are writing about results: She could immediately see the *effect* of her actions. Use the word *affect* (a **verb**) when you are writing about the action of the cause: The weather *affected* our travel plans. Though "effect" is sometimes used as a transitive verb, too, that use is not as common, such as "The citizens *effected* a new law." In most cases, "affect" is used as a verb and "effect" is used as a noun: "When you *affect* a situation, you have an *effect* on it."

Critical Thinking and Cause and Effect

Cause-and-effect analysis is useful for helping your readers understand complicated events. The careful examination of the befores and afters of a specific event, for instance, can help readers understand why it happened and how it could be avoided or maybe repeated in the future. The analysis can also help convince your readers of an argument you want to get across, for instance, that they should stop smoking because of the health consequences or help stop the building of a new parking garage that will negatively affect local wetlands.

APPLYING CRITICAL THINKING

| PURPOSE | IDEAS | SUPPORT | ASSUMPTIONS BIASES | CONCLUSIONS | POINT OF VIEW | ANALYSIS |

You see the causes and effects of actions and events around you all the time. You forget to put money in the parking meter (cause) and you get a ticket (effect). When analyzing a cause-and-effect pattern, you need to break down the parts of the cause(s) and the effect(s) of your topic. For example, maybe you forgot to put money in the meter because you saw someone fall while in a crosswalk and ran to help. Perhaps the ticket was waived because you took in the newspaper clipping applauding your rescue of the elderly woman who was almost run over by a truck. To write an effective cause-and-effect essay, you need to **analyze** all the *befores* and *afters* of an event.

BEFORE WRITING A CAUSE-AND-EFFECT ESSAY

Before you begin to write a cause-and-effect essay on an assigned topic, or one you have chosen, start by asking yourself these questions:

1. What process or event is the subject of my cause-and-effect analysis?
2. What are the benefits of doing a cause-and-effect analysis of my chosen topic?
3. Why did this process or event happen—what was the original cause(s)?
4. What is the result(s) (effect/s) of this process or event?
5. What do I want my readers to learn from reading about the cause(s) and/or effect(s) of this event or process?
6. How will I conclude this essay?

Answering these questions will lead you to an expository thesis statement, help you determine the causes and effects you want to focus on, the examples and details to include for support, and a general idea of how to organize your essay.

ACTIVITY 13-1 Prewriting

Directions: *Prewrite on the following broad subjects to come up with some ideas of causes and effects that could be analyzed in relation to each.* Answers will vary.

Example:

Topic: Discrimination
Self-esteem issues, unfair work practices, learned behavior, ignorance, school problems, therapy, cycle of discrimination, institutionalized discrimination, education.

1. **Topic:** Obesity _____

   _____

   _____

2. **Topic:** Eating disorders _____

   _____

   _____

3. **Topic:** Bankruptcy _____

   _____

   _____

4. **Topic:** A promotion _____

   _____

   _____

5. **Topic:** Being fired from a job _____

   _____

   _____

ACTIVITY 13-2   Cause and Effect

Directions: *For each of the topics below, create a flowchart that provides at least one* before *and after* **cause** *and* **effect** *for the subject in the middle.* *Answers will vary.*

Example:

exercise	←	better sleep	→	_better health_
1. _____	←	exhaustion	→	_____
2. _____	←	prejudice	→	_____

3. _____ ← skin damage → _____

4. _____ ← good grades → _____

5. _____ ← tooth decay → _____

6. _____ ← riots → _____

7. _____ ← caffeine addiction → _____

8. _____ ← paying bills → _____

9. _____ ← laughing → _____

10. _____ ← tears → _____

WRITING A CAUSE-AND-EFFECT ESSAY

The point of analyzing causes and effects is to look at the reasons why things happen and/or the results of them happening in order to understand them better and possibly to take action. When analyzing related events, you first need to make sure there is a causal relationship. Did one idea or event lead to another? What was the cause, and what was the effect? After you determine there is a cause-and-effect relationship in your topic, then you need to determine what you want to explain to your readers about it. Do you want to explain the causes and effects in order to inform your readers of a process or to critique the effects or the causes? For example, if you were writing about health and exercise, you could explain the effects of exercise on one's health in order to convince your readers to engage in more exercising. Or you could focus on the negative effects of too little exercise to accomplish the same goal.

Be sure to organize your essay in the best way to build the analytical conclusion you establish in your thesis statement and introduction. When looking at the effects of one particular event or incident, it may help to think of the domino effect (see page 3): The dominos are lined up; then one is knocked over, and they fall one by one leading to an overall change in the structure. The initial push of the first domino is the initial cause, and the dominos that fall one by one are the effects. It is a chain reaction: cause–effect–cause–effect.

Depending on the assignment, you may analyze one cause and several effects, one effect and several causes, or several causes and several effects.

In each of the patterns diagrammed, your body paragraphs would focus on the individual causes and/or effects you have established in your introduction. Use transitional words and phrases between the causes and/or effects you are providing as examples.

The chart below provides a brief overview of the structure of a cause and effect essay.

BASIC STRUCTURE FOR A CAUSE-AND-EFFECT ESSAY

INTRODUCTORY PARAGRAPH

Sets up background for your cause/effect analysis.

Thesis statement: Establishes the causes and effects you will explain and your purpose for analyzing them.

BODY PARAGRAPHS (Two to five, depending on assignment and purpose)

Topic sentences set up the cause-and-effect subcategories.

Develop your analysis of the causal relationship by providing specific examples of the cause(s) and effect(s) and critiquing their importance.

Provide concrete examples and details.

Use transitions within and between paragraphs to make the paragraphs flow smoothly.

CONCLUDING PARAGRAPH

Sums up and re-emphasizes the thesis statement: the conclusions reached through your cause-and-effect analysis.

STRUCTURING A CAUSE-AND-EFFECT ESSAY

Topic

If you do not have a topic assigned by your instructor for your cause-and-effect essay, then brainstorm ideas for events or processes you might want to describe. Then come up with some ideas for a purpose for describing the topic. What do you want your readers to understand through your cause-and-effect essay?

A Few Topic Possibilities

You can write an essay looking at the causes of pollution, a medical condition, depression, or any other cause that leads to a particular result. Or you can look at the effects of an event or condition such as a hurricane or other natural disaster, a medical condition, eating habits, or any action or event that leads to a particular result. The key is to look at what caused something to occur, what happened after something occurred, or both.

Thesis Statements

The thesis statement in a cause-and-effect essay establishes whether you are focusing on just the causes of something, just the effects of something, or both. It also establishes the purpose for the cause-and-effect analysis: what you want your readers to understand. For example, if you were writing about diet and exercise, your thesis might establish both a causal relationship and an argument:

> Watching your diet and increasing your weekly exercise will create significant positive results within weeks of changing your habits.

ACTIVITY 13-3 Creating Thesis Statements

Directions: *Come up with a possible thesis statement for each of the topics you brainstormed in Activity 13-1. Be sure the thesis focuses on the causes, effects, or both related to the topic and has a purpose to convey.* Answers will vary.

1. **Topic:** Obesity

    Thesis statement: _____

    _____

2. **Topic:** Eating disorders

    Thesis statement: _____

    _____

3. **Topic:** Bankruptcy

    Thesis statement: _____

    _____

4. **Topic:** A promotion _____

    Thesis statement: _____

    _____

5. **Topic:** Being fired

    Thesis statement: _____

    _____

Introductory Paragraph

Begin your cause-and-effect essay with a general introduction to the topic, and end your introductory paragraph with a thesis statement that sets up the purpose for your essay.

Body Paragraphs

The body paragraphs and topic sentences set up the order and the examples you will develop for your cause-and-effect analysis. You could arrange the causes and/or effects in separate paragraphs from least to most important (or vice versa) or arrange them in the order in which they take place (chronologically). For instance, if you were writing about Hurricane Katrina, you could look at the effects chronologically (by which place was hit first, second, and so on) or by order of importance (such as "New Orleans is the city that suffered the most loss," and so on). Use transitional words and phrases to lead your readers from one cause or effect to the next. As well as the cause-and-effect transitions shown here, those showing examples and purpose are also useful (see Chapter 6, pages 114–116).

TRANSITIONS TO . . .

Show Result and/or Cause-and-Effect Relationships

accordingly	consequently	since	therefore
as a result	for this reason	so	thereupon
because	hence	then	thus

Be sure to use plenty of specific examples and details to illustrate the particular causes (high winds and torrential rainfall) or effects (such as the breaking of the levees in New Orleans, the loss of property, and so on) in your body paragraphs. Your topic sentences will indicate which causes or effects you will be explaining in each paragraph.

In New Orleans, many lifetime residents lost their homes in the floods.

ACTIVITY 13-4   Creating Topic Sentences

Directions: *Create a possible topic sentence for each of the thesis statements you generated in Activity 13-3. You will need to decide if you will focus on causes, effects, or both if you were writing this essay.*   Answers will vary.

1. **Topic:** Obesity

    Topic sentence: _____

    _____

2. **Topic:** Eating disorders

   Topic sentence: _____

   _____

3. **Topic:** Bankruptcy

   Topic sentence: _____

   _____

4. **Topic:** A promotion

   Topic sentence: _____

   _____

5. **Topic:** Being fired

   Topic sentence: _____

   _____

After you have come up with your topic sentences, you need to support them with examples and details to illustrate your points.

ACTIVITY 13-5 Providing Examples

Directions: *For three of the topic sentences you generated above, provide at least two examples that would help demonstrate your cause and/or effect analysis.* Answers will vary.

1. **Topic:** _____

   Examples: _____

   _____

2. **Topic:** _____

   Examples: _____

   _____

3. **Topic:** _____

   Examples: _____

   _____

Concluding Paragraph

Your essay will need a concluding paragraph that briefly recaps the cause-and-effect analysis and the purpose for studying the causal relationship. Re-emphasize what you want your readers to realize about the cause-and-effect connections after they've read your essay.

ACTIVITY 13-6   Concluding Paragraphs

Directions: *Create a three- to six-sentence concluding paragraph for any one of the topics from the previous activities.* Answers will vary.

Topic chosen: _____

Concluding paragraph: _____

_____

_____

_____

Use the following critique form to check for the basics in your cause-and-effect essay draft.

CAUSE-AND-EFFECT ESSAY CRITIQUE FORM

| BLUEPRINTS PURPOSE | IDEAS | SUPPORT | ASSUMPTIONS BIASES | CONCLUSIONS | POINT OF VIEW | ANALYSIS |

Overall   Done well   Needs work

1. Does the essay clearly develop cause-and-effect **analysis** with a clear **purpose**?   _____   _____
2. Does the essay use a clear order in the body paragraphs?   _____   _____
3. Are the paragraphs broken up well and about the right length?   _____   _____

Introduction

4. Is the title interesting and in correct format?   _____   _____
5. Is there a general introduction that gives the **purpose** for the cause-and-effect **analysis**? Is the process clear?   _____   _____
6. Is there a clear thesis statement that explains the results of the cause(s) and effect(s) and the overall **purpose**?   _____   _____

Body

7. Do the body paragraphs develop the **ideas** and **analysis** well and flow smoothly?   _____   _____
8. Are transitions used between and, when needed, within the paragraphs?   _____   _____

9. Do the body paragraphs include **support** and descriptive details
for development?   _____ _____

10. Does the essay demonstrate the relationship of the cause(s)
and the effect(s) and the importance of their interrelatedness?   _____ _____

Conclusion

11. Does the **concluding** paragraph sum up the essay with an analytical
frame that re-emphasizes the introductory paragraph and thesis, without
adding new ideas?   _____ _____

Editing

12. Circle the following errors you think you see in this draft: spelling errors, fragments, run-ons/comma
splices, errors in comma and semicolon/colon use, pronoun disagreement, reference fault errors,
and errors in parallelism, apostrophe use, verb use/tense, and passive voice construction.
(See the handbook section for help in identifying and correcting these errors)

13. Other types of grammar or sentence-level errors:

_____

Comments:

_____

_____

LO3 COMPLEMENTARY MODES FOR CAUSE-AND-EFFECT ESSAYS

Cause-and-effect mode is often combined with several other modes.

- **Narration** and **description** can be used to develop the analysis.
- **Definition** mode can be used to help explain objects or concepts used
  in the cause-and-effect analysis.
- **Illustration and examples** can further elaborate on the cause-and-effect
  analysis of the subject.
- **Classification** is usually part of the causal process itself: You have to
  classify items into broader groups to analyze them specifically.
- You can **compare and contrast** items or the causes or effects themselves
  as you analyze your subject.
- You can use **argument** to persuade your readers to accept a particular
  point of view related to the cause-and-effect analysis.

Sample Student Essay

Michelle Kunitz

Professor Archer

English 100

3 November 2010

The Dangers of Too Much TV

Television is a great invention, and it is a great element of most homes, as long as it is watched in moderation. Unfortunately, these days, too many children are watching too much TV every day. Studies show that students watch an average of two to four hours of TV a day. **Thesis statement** There are several negative effects of watching too much TV.

Topic sentence The first negative effect for children who watch too much TV is lack of exercise due to sitting passively in front of the tube all day. Unfortunately, many children do not spend as much time outside playing with their friends as they did in the past. With the constant availability of kid's programming, such as cartoons played 24 hours a day, more children choose to stay on the couch watching shows than **Concluding sentence** going outside and playing with their friends. It used to be that cartoons were only available at certain times, so the fact that they are on 24/7 may have added to the increase in TV watching.

Topic sentence A direct result of increased TV watching has been the increase in childhood obesity in America. Many children are more inactive due to increased TV watching, and, in addition, they tend to snack more when **Concluding sentence** indoors watching TV all day. Both of these reasons lead to increased weight in a child.

Topic sentence Another negative effect of too much TV is a decrease in reading and imaginative play by children. When children spend hours watching TV, then they spend a lot less time reading or engaging in imaginative

Kunitz 2

play. For instance, many children these days rarely play board games or work on puzzles. These interactive types of play are much more intellectually stimulating than passive TV viewing.

Overall, the increase in TV viewing by children over the last couple of decades has led to negative consequences for many of them. Their health and intelligence are put in jeopardy when they watch too much TV. Hopefully, parents will take these negative effects seriously and take action to decrease the amount of time their kids spend in front of the tube and strongly encourage them to participate in physical activities, imaginative play, and reading.

ACTIVITY 13-7   Thinking Critically About the Student Essay

Directions: *Analyze the essay to identify the features and details characteristic of the cause-and-effect mode. Mark them on the essay. Then, reread the essay, and make a list of specific revisions you would make to correct any problems with content, organization, transitions, and style.*

PROFESSIONAL CAUSE-AND-EFFECT ESSAY

The Columbine Syndrome: Boys and the Fear of Violence

William S. Pollack

William S. Pollack is Assistant Clinical Professor in the Department of Psychiatry at Harvard Medical School and a clinical psychologist. He is the author of *Real Boys: Rescuing Our Sons from the Myths of Masculinity* (1999), *Real Boys' Voices* (2000), and *Real Boys Workbook* (2001). Pollack serves as an advisor to the President's

National Campaign against Youth Violence. This essay appeared in the fall 2000 issue of the *National Forum.*

> "I don't want to be that type of kid who comes to school and just takes out a gun and starts shooting."—*Bobby, age 12, from a city in the West*

> "The other day I walked into school and a girl was carrying balloons and one of them popped. Everyone in the whole school got really terrified."—*Errol, age 17, from a suburb in the West*

> "I think there are people at my school who have the potential for doing something similar."—*Jules, age 17, from a suburb in the South*

> "People were coming up to me and begging me not to kill them. I felt like telling them: 'Cut it out; I'm not going to do anything.'"—*Cody, age 14, from a suburb in New England*

> "You can't say 'them' or 'you.' You have to say 'us.'"—*Jimmy, age 16, from a small town in the West*

1   Probably no risk other than violence has made America more afraid of boys and made boys more afraid of being male and living in this country. Though it has been understood for decades that the perpetrators of most violent crimes in our nation are male, the recent spate of school shootings, culminating in the heinous massacre of teachers and students recently carried out in suburban Littleton, Colorado, has made the public even more frightened and confused about the threat of extreme violence and its connection, in particular, with boys. Boys of adolescent age, boys just like the ones who have contributed to my research, are the ones pulling the triggers and injuring, sometimes killing, their peers and school teachers. What many people do not realize—and what the media isn't following as well as they might—is that most of the victims of teenage violence, indeed the vast majority, are also boys.

CONSEQUENCES OF THE COLUMBINE SYNDROME

2   In my travels across our country, listening to boys and doing research for my latest book, *Real Boys' Voices* (Random House, 2000), I have come to see that the effect of these terrible crimes has been immense. It has led to the "Columbine Syndrome": Across our nation students, parents, and teachers are absolutely terrified—sometimes to an extreme degree—about which boys amongst them are violent, who the next perpetrators might be, and who their victims will become. Paranoia is rampant. School children and the adults around them are constantly canvassing the student body and worrying, often inappropriately, that particular students may be murderous.

Grady, age seventeen, from a school in the South says, "When a kid's wearing a trenchcoat and he's going for something in his jacket, you learn from watching the news that more than likely he might have a gun."

3   The consequence is that boys themselves are becoming increasingly afraid. They are frightened not only of being victimized by the rage and violence of other boys, but also of being accused, or falsely accused, of having the disposition it takes to snap into hyper-violent action and embark on a murderous rampage. Boys fear that despite their true nature, they will automatically, because they are boys, be seen as somehow toxic, dangerous, and culpable. As one young preadolescent boy said, "I think women like small kids. Girls like newborn babies. They don't like big people. We bigger guys scare everybody, and then we get blamed even when we've done nothing wrong."

4   Boys are also afraid of the violence they may feel inside themselves and of whether it is safe to talk with us about it. As they internalize this fear of being misunderstood—and of being charged with having a violent temperament they genuinely do not have—boys themselves are beginning to worry if maybe, just maybe, the demon is within, if lurking underneath their conscious understanding of themselves are uncontrollable urges to do depraved, violent acts. The Columbine Syndrome means that America's boys today are as confused about violence as they are afraid of it. They fear each other and they fear their own selves.

THE "BOY CODE"

5   While the statistics indicate that teenage boys not only commit a considerable percentage of the nation's violent juvenile crimes but also become the frequent victims of those crimes, in reality there seems to be no inherent biological factor that makes boys more violent than their female counterparts. Violence committed by and acted out upon boys seems to stem, more often than not, from what we teach (or do not teach) boys about the behavior we expect from them. It comes from society's set of rules about masculinity, the Boy Code that says, "To be a man, you must show your strength and your power. You must show that you can hold your own if challenged by another male. You can show your rage, but you must not show any other emotions. You must protect your honor and fight off shame at all costs."

6   Think of it yourself. A boy gets slightly angry as a way to express his pain, and there will be mixed emotions. Some of us may show some fear, but if the anger is in control, we are unlikely to respond in a drastic manner. So long as it is "within bounds," society tends to approve of, if not encourage, aggression by and among boys. Violence in boys is widely

(although, as I have said, incorrectly) seen as inevitable, if not biologically pre-ordained. As long as nobody is seriously hurt, no lethal weapons are employed, and especially within the framework of sports and games—football, soccer, boxing, wrestling—aggression and violence are widely accepted and even encouraged in boys. Boys are constantly trying to prove their masculinity through aggression, and society is complicit; winning a game, or even a fight, helps many boys gain society's respect.

7   The corollary to this message, simply enough, is that soft, gentle, non-violent boys are "feminine" and therefore losers. While we often pay lip service to helping boys "put feelings into words" and even create multi-million dollar educational programs to address this, if you're "a big guy" and start to express your vulnerable emotions too openly, people crawl back in fear. Or imagine the boy who misses a goal and bursts into tears on the soccer field. He is not considered masculine. Peers call him a "girl," "sissy" or "fag." Parents cringe. It is precisely in this environment that even the most hearty boy soon learns to avoid showing his pain in public. He may want to cry, he may wish he could speak of his fear, sadness, or shame; but he holds it back. He resists. Instead, the boy displays anger, aggression, and violence.

8   Perhaps it should not shock us, then, when we hear from the boys who say that while they overwhelmingly condemn extreme violence, and to a large extent do not engage in it, they can understand, empathize with the boys who hit, hurt, and even kill. They tell us about what the teasing and razzing "can do to your head," how alone and isolated some boys can become, and how rage is indeed often the only sanctioned emotion that does not bring further ridicule to them. We are all afraid of boys and violence, but boys, it turns out, are the most in fear. Gun detectors, violence screening tools or "profiles," armed guards, and "zero tolerance" only goad our sons into the very aggression we, and they, are afraid of; by expecting boys to be angry, rambunctious, and dangerous, we push boys to fulfill these prophecies. This is the essence, I believe, of the Columbine Syndrome. By living in fear and expecting danger, that is exactly what we produce.

9   To compound the risk to all of us, society is now giving boys another complex and confusing message, what I call the "No Black Shirts" response. Because the Columbine killers were outcast boys, spiteful nonconforming boys who wore dark clothing and were estranged from their peers, society has now rushed to the conclusion that adolescent boys who seem "different," especially ones who seem quiet, distant, and in pain, are the likely perpetrators of the next ghastly Columbine-like crime. Sadly, what the huge majority of outcast boys needs most—in fact what many so-called "popular" boys, boys on the "inside" often desperately need as well—is not to have their pain suppressed and disregarded, but rather to have it listened to and understood.

CURBING THE SYNDROME

10   Boys in pain require immediate intervention. As soon as we detect that a boy is experiencing emotional distress, we need to stop what we are doing, turn towards him, and hear him out. Whether he is wearing a black hood or Brooks Brothers sweater, whether he is well-liked or an outcast, he needs us to come toward him, embrace and affirm him, and assuage his hurt feelings before they push him to the edge. Boys are simply not inherently violent or dangerous, and the emotional distress that they may feel, in the first instance, does not make them any more so. But if we continue to give boys the message that expressing their distress is forbidden, that we will ignore their vulnerable feelings when we see them, and that we actually expect them to act out angrily and violently, we should not be surprised that the world becomes, for all of us, a mighty frightful place.

11   As the voices I heard (sampled in brief above) and published in detail in *Real Boys' Voices* exemplify, only a tiny percentage of boys are capable of egregious acts of violence. In truth, as aggressive as they can perhaps be pushed to become, most boys are quite anxious about and revolted by the prevalence of violence in society. They feel powerless to do anything about it, though, because they simply feel too much shame, too concerned about how other people will respond to their confessions of fear.

12   The solution, I believe, is for society to commit to a whole new way of seeing boys and violence. First, as a society we need to decide, unequivocally, that as much as we will not exalt boys who fight, we also will not punish or ostracize those who show their vulnerability. By defending and actually providing positive reinforcement to boys who openly exhibit their moments of fear, longing, anxiety, and despair, by telling these boys and men that they are fully "masculine" no matter what emotions they share with us, we can help them avoid the repression and resistance that may make them bottle up their emotions and then spill them out in irrational acts. Second, because society may not change overnight, we need to be on the lookout for the signs of sadness and depression that in boys and men so often seem harder to see, or more difficult to believe and accept. In my book, I outlined these many signs. If we are attentive to them, and if we help boys overcome the pain and disaffection that gives rise to them, much of the aggression and violence we now see will evaporate, or be directed towards safe, appropriate channels.

13   Finally, we must simply decide, as a society, that most boys, as angry or aggressive as they may become, are highly unlikely to become dangerous in any way. The. boys' voices quoted at the beginning of this piece are overwhelming proof that most of our sons have a non-violent nature and that, in reality, their greater struggle is with sadness and the fear of violence

rather than with violence itself. Together we must create prophecies that their gentle nature will triumph over old pressures to act tough and lash out. Perhaps if we hear boys' fears about violence in a new light, read their stories with a new empathy, we may be able to reach across the boundaries of fear and create a new dialogue of peace. For boys and for the rest of us, the only cure for the Columbine Syndrome, in the end, is to develop safe spaces that are friendly to boys and thereby create genuine security. The time is now!

Reading Reflection Questions *Answers will vary. Sample answers are provided.*

1. What are the direct or indirect (implied) messages in this story? *that even though boys are the ones who commit the majority of violent crimes, they are also victims to this perception and are hurt by society's code of being tough and the perception of them as dangerous*

2. In your own words, define what the author means by the "Columbine Syndrome." *a syndrome where we fear boys if they look to us like they could be a threat*

Objective Questions

3. T/F ___*T*___ Most of the perpetrators and victims of teenage violence are boys.

4. T/F ___*T*___ Many boys are afraid of their own potential for violence.

5. T/F ___*F*___ Many boys are afraid they will be feared just for being boys.

6. Explain what the author means by the "Boy Code." *that boys must always be tough*

7. What solution does this author propose to this problem? *immediate interaction, encouraging boys to express their feelings, affirming them and comforting them*

Checking Vocabulary

Define the following in your own words, or provide a dictionary definition if you don't know the word.

8. heinous: *very wicked or wrong*

9. perpetrators: *those who commit harmful or illegal acts*

10. corollary: *an idea that directly relates to another*

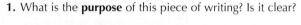

CRITICAL THINKING CHECKLIST

Answers will vary.

PURPOSE

1. What is the **purpose** of this piece of writing? Is it clear?

_____

_____

IDEAS

2. What **ideas** and **background information** are provided to support the purpose of this piece of writing?

_____

_____

SUPPORT

3. What **evidence** and **examples** are used to explain and develop the ideas that support the argument made in the piece of writing? Are the evidence and examples provided sufficient?

_____

_____

ASSUMPTIONS
BIASES

4. Are there unfounded **assumptions** or unreasonable **biases**?

_____

_____

CONCLUSIONS

5. Are all of the **conclusions**, **implications**, and **consequences** of the arguments (the results of the arguments taken to their farthest extreme) considered?

_____

_____

POINT
OF VIEW

6. Is the **point of view** clear and consistent, and have other points of view been considered?

_____

_____

ANALYSIS

7. Using these critical thinking tools, **analyze** the overall structure of this essay and the strength of the author's arguments, ideas, and support. Was he or she successful in accomplishing the purpose? Why, or why not?

_____

_____

Essay Assignments

1. Write an essay that illustrates the negative effects of stress on a college student.

2. Write an essay that focuses on the causes of stress for college students.

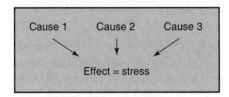

3. Write an essay that explores a chain reaction, or domino effect, where there is a sequence of one cause leading to an effect that starts a second cause that leads to a second effect, and so on.

4. Write a cause-and-effect essay on any of the subjects you worked on in the activities in this chapter.

SPOTLIGHT ON CRITICAL THINKING

We are asked all the time to evaluate the reasons and results of actions or words.

Writing cause-and-effect essays: Cause-and-effect analysis is a common approach in science and social science classes. In sociology, you may be asked to write about the causes and effects of gender stereotyping. On the job, you may have to evaluate the causes and effects of an increase or a decrease in the price of your company's stock. Use your **analysis** skills to check the **purpose** and **conclusions** in your writing for college classes and later in your writing for your career. Develop your **purpose, ideas,** and **support** based on the critical thinking tips in Chapter 1.

Reading cause-and-effect analyses: In many classes, you'll be asked to analyze the causes and effects of an event you read about. For example, in environmental science, you may be asked to evaluate the effects of pollution by reading about several local pollution-causing events that have affected the community. As a biologist or environmental scientist, you may have to test water quality and read reports that analyze of the causes and effects of the changes you document. Use the Six Steps for Active Reading to be a more careful and interactive reader.

To check your progress in meeting this chapter's objectives, log in to www.mywritinglab .com, go to the **Study Plan** tab, click on **Writing and Critical Thinking in the Modes** and choose **Essay Development—Cause and Effect** from the list of subtopics. Read and view the resources in the **Review Materials** section, and then complete the **Recall**, **Apply**, and **Write** sets in the **Activities** section.

14 Comparison and Contrast

Jumping Rocks

Steve Corvelo

LEARNING OBJECTIVES

In this chapter, you will learn to

LO 1 Write comparison and contrast essays.

LO 2 Structure a comparison and contrast essay.

LO 3 Use complementary modes for comparison and contrast essays.

THINKING CRITICALLY

Look carefully at the two photos of children at play above. List some of the similarities and differences between the two pictures.

Similarities: _____

_____

Differences: _____

_____

LO 1 COMPARISON AND CONTRAST ESSAYS

Comparison essays look at the *similarities* between two subjects, and **contrast essays** look at the *differences* between two subjects. A comparison *and* contrast essay looks at both the similarities and differences between two subjects.

Critical Thinking and Comparison and Contrast

There will be many instances in college and in the work world where you will need to use your comparison and contrast analysis skills. You may need to compare and contrast two politicians running for office, two periods of history, two literary characters, two theories, two formal speeches, two potential job opportunities, or two houses or apartments for rent—the possibilities are endless.

BEFORE WRITING A COMPARISON/ CONTRAST ESSAY

Before you begin to write a comparison/contrast essay on an assigned topic, or one you have chosen, start by asking yourself these questions:

1. What two objects, people, or concepts am I going to compare and/or contrast?
2. Are they in the same general category?
3. Am I going to focus on similarities, differences, or both? Are the two subjects mostly alike, mostly different, or some of each?
4. How will I set up my comparisons/contrasts, and how will I structure my paragraphs?
5. What examples and details should I include for support?
6. What do I want my readers to learn or understand after reading this comparison and/or contrast essay?
7. How will I conclude my essay?

Answering these questions will lead you to an expository thesis statement, help you determine what you will be comparing and/or contrasting, help you develop examples and details to include for support, and give you a general idea of how you want to organize your essay.

APPLYING CRITICAL THINKING

PURPOSE   IDEAS   SUPPORT   ASSUMPTIONS BIASES   CONCLUSIONS   POINT OF VIEW   ANALYSIS

We use comparisons and contrasts to make sense of the world and put things into perspective. Comparing is a way to find the familiar through looking at the similarities between things, and contrasting helps us to see the differences between things in order to better understand them. To write an effective comparison/contrast essay, you need to use your **analytical** skills to identify how things are similar and different, determine your **purpose** for writing about those similarities and differences, and decide which **ideas**, **support**, and details will best illustrate and explain the point you want to make.

For example, if you were comparing two grocery stores, what similarities would you point out? What differences? What possible **conclusions** could you reach? Will your comparison lead to a recommendation?

ACTIVITY 14-1   Generating Topics for a Comparison/Contrast Essay

Directions: *Generate three possible topics for a comparison/contrast essay: List the two items, concepts, people, and so on. Then explain whether you would focus on similarities, differences, or both.*   *Answers will vary.*

1. Two subjects: _____

    Similarities, differences, or both: _____

    _____

2. Two subjects: _____

    Similarities, differences, or both: _____

    _____

3. Two subjects: _____

    Similarities, differences, or both: _____

    _____

WRITING A COMPARISON/CONTRAST ESSAY

First, make sure that the two subjects you compare and/or contrast are in the same general group or category. The old cliché "It's like comparing apples and oranges" doesn't really fit, since you could compare an apple with an orange: They are both in the "fruit" category, and they have both similarities and differences. However, you probably wouldn't want to write a compare/contrast essay about an orange and your best friend, unless your best friend is particularly orange and round: After that, there probably wouldn't be enough categories in common to make for an interesting or developed analytical comparison.

Once you have chosen your subjects, you need to decide whether you are focusing on similarities, differences, or both and determine the purpose of your essay. Then you have to choose an organizational plan for your comparison/contrast essay. There are two ways to organize comparison/contrast essays. You can choose a subject-by-subject approach, or you can choose a point-by-point approach.

Subject-by-Subject Organization Pattern

In a **subject-by-subject** organization pattern, you first present all aspects of one subject; then you transition and present all aspects of the second subject. For example:

Subject A = compact cars   Subject B = SUVs

> **Point 1** = Size/comfort
> **Point 2** = Gas mileage/cost
> **Point 3** = Image/personality

An outline of a paper on compact cars versus SUVs, using this pattern, would look like this:

General introductory comments

Thesis: Compact cars and SUVs offer very different options for a consumer when it comes to size and comfort, gas mileage and cost, and the type of image or personality the cars project.

Subject A: Compact Cars
> **Point 1:** Compact cars' size and comfort
> **Point 2:** Compact cars' gas mileage and cost
> **Point 3:** Compact cars' image and personality

Subject B: SUVs

    Point 1: SUVs' size and comfort

    Point 2: SUVs' gas mileage and cost

    Point 3: SUVs' image and personality

Conclusion: Re-emphasize thesis. Provide closing comments.

Point-by-Point Organization Pattern

In a **point-by-point** organization pattern, you discuss both subjects at the same time, categorized point by point. For example:

	Subject A: Compact cars	**Subject B: SUVs**
Point 1	Size/comfort	Size/comfort
Point 2	Gas mileage/cost	Gas mileage/cost
Point 3	Image/personality	Image/personality

An outline of a paper on compact cars versus SUVs, using this pattern, would look like this:

General introductory comments

Thesis: Compact cars and SUVs offer very different options for a consumer when it comes to size and comfort, gas mileage and cost, and the type of image or personality the cars project.

Point 1: Size and comfort for subjects A and B (compact cars and SUVs)

Point 2: Gas mileage and cost for subjects A and B (compact cars and SUVs)

Point 3: Image and personality for subjects A and B (compact cars and SUVs)

Conclusion: Re-emphasize thesis. Provide closing comments.

▶ **NOTE**   These patterns do not necessarily indicate the number of paragraphs you would use in an essay. It might take more than one paragraph to develop each point.

Pick the organizational pattern that works best for your subject and purpose. Also, be sure that you give a balanced comparison, and provide an equal number of details to support both subjects. Create topic sentences that will highlight the categories for comparison or contrast and the points you want to make. Provide plenty of examples and details to illustrate these points in the body paragraphs. Use transitions between paragraphs or examples when needed to help the flow of your essay.

Finally, be sure that you reach an analytical conclusion through your comparison/contrast and that your thesis and your concluding paragraph sum up that analytical conclusion.

The chart below provides a brief overview of the structure of a comparison and contrast essay.

BASIC STRUCTURE FOR A COMPARISON/CONTRAST ESSAY

INTRODUCTORY PARAGRAPH

Sets up your subject and your purpose.

Thesis statement: A statement that defines your purpose and what example(s) you'll be using to illustrate it.

BODY PARAGRAPHS (Two to five, depending on assignment and purpose)

Choose subject-by-subject or point-by-point organization pattern.

Create **topic sentences** to support your thesis.

Develop the comparisons and contrasts through illustrations, details, and **analysis**.

Provide examples and concrete details to illustrate vividly the examples.

Use transitions within and between paragraphs to make the paragraphs flow smoothly.

CONCLUDING PARAGRAPH

Sums up and re-emphasizes the thesis.

LO 2   STRUCTURING A COMPARISON/ CONTRAST ESSAY

Topic

If you do not have a topic assigned by your instructor for your comparison/contrast essay, then brainstorm ideas for things, places, people, or ideas you might want to compare and contrast. Then come up with some ideas for a purpose for comparing/contrasting your subjects. What do you want your readers to understand through your comparison/contrast?

A Few Topic Possibilities

Any two subjects that you want to look at side by side to emphasize similarities or differences or both make for a good topic for this type of essay. You could compare and contrast two historical figures, two political figures, two people you know, two restaurants, two musicians, two paintings, two photographs, two cities, and so on. Just make sure they have enough in common in the first place to make for good explorations.

Thesis Statements

After you have done some prewriting and determined your subjects and whether you will focus on similarities, differences, or both, come up with the purpose for your comparison/contrast essay and write your thesis statement. What conclusion did you reach by comparing and contrasting these subjects? What do you want your readers to understand after reading this essay?

> The Xbox game system is very different from the Wii game system as far as style and technology are concerned.
>
> Home cooking and going out to restaurants to eat result in diverse dining experiences.

ACTIVITY 14-2   Creating Thesis Statements

Directions: *For each of the topics you generated in Activity 14-1, create a thesis statement. Answers will vary.*

1. **Topic:** _____

   Thesis statement: _____

   _____

2. **Topic:** _____

   Thesis statement: _____

   _____

3. **Topic:** _____

   Thesis statement: _____

   _____

Introductory Paragraph

Begin your comparison/contrast essay with a general introduction of the two subjects you are comparing/contrasting in order to demonstrate your analytical conclusion. End with the thesis statement to set up the purpose for your comparison/contrast essay.

Body Paragraphs

The body paragraphs in a comparison/contrast essay are structured either by focusing on one subject at a time or on one category or point for both of the subjects one paragraph at a time. Be sure you have a clear topic sentence that spells out the subject(s) and category you are exploring for each paragraph and the point you want to make. Then, use specific evidence and examples to illustrate the comparisons or contrasts. Analyze the examples. Use comparison and contrast transitions to show your readers when you are comparing and contrasting items. (Other helpful transitions that show summary, example, and purpose are listed on pages 114–116.) Then frame your examples with a concluding sentence that ties in to your topic sentence.

TRANSITIONS TO . . .

Show Contrast or a Change in Idea

although	even though	instead	on the other side
anyhow	for all that	nevertheless	otherwise
at the same time	however	notwithstanding	regardless
but	in any event	on the contrary	still
despite this	in contrast	on the other hand	yet

Show a Comparison

in like manner	in the same way	likewise	similarly

ACTIVITY 14-3   Creating Topic Sentences

Directions: *Create one topic sentence for each of the thesis statements you generated in Activity 14-2. Answers will vary.*

1. **Topic:** _____

   Topic sentence: _____

   _____

2. **Topic:** _____

Topic sentence: _____

_____

3. **Topic:** _____

Topic sentence: _____

_____

After you have created your topic sentences, develop the ideas using examples and details for support.

ACTIVITY 14-4   Providing Details

Directions: *Now, come up with at least two examples or details you could include in a body paragraph developing each of the topic sentences you came up with in Activity 14-3.* Answers will vary.

1. **Topic:** _____

Examples: _____

_____

_____

2. **Topic:** _____

Examples: _____

_____

_____

3. **Topic:** _____

Examples: _____

_____

_____

Concluding Paragraph

The concluding paragraph for a comparison/contrast essay should remind your readers what the purpose of your comparison/contrast was—why you compared and/or contrasted the subjects you chose.

ACTIVITY 14-5   Writing a Conclusion

Directions: *Now choose one of the topics you've been developing in the previous activities, and write a three- to six-sentence concluding paragraph that could finish that essay.* Answers will vary.

_____

_____

_____

_____

Use the critique form below to check for the basics in your comparison and contrast essay draft.

COMPARISON/CONTRAST ESSAY CRITIQUE FORM

PURPOSE   IDEAS   SUPPORT   ASSUMPTIONS BIASES   CONCLUSIONS   POINT OF VIEW   ANALYSIS

Overall   Done well   Needs work

1. Does the essay clearly develop comparison and/or contrast **analysis** with a clear **purpose**/analytical conclusion?   _____   _____

2. Does the essay use a clear order (subject by subject or point by point or an effective combination of the two) in the body paragraphs with an analytical conclusion drawn from the comparison or contrast?   _____   _____

3. Are the paragraphs broken up well and about the right length?   _____   _____

Introduction

4. Is the title interesting and in correct format?   _____   _____

5. Is there a general introduction that gives the purpose for the comparison and contrast analysis? Is the process and organization clear?   _____   _____

6. Is there a clear thesis statement that explains the purpose of the comparisons and/or contrasts and the overall purpose?   _____   _____

Body

7. Do the body paragraphs develop the **ideas** and **analysis** well and flow smoothly?   _____   _____

8. Are transitions used between and, when needed, within the paragraphs?   _____   _____

Continued ▶

Done well   Needs work

9. Do the body paragraphs include **support** and descriptive details for development?   _____ _____

10. Does the writer demonstrate the significance of the similarities and differences (both or just one of the two)?   _____ _____

Conclusion

11. Does the **concluding** paragraph sum up the essay with an analytical frame that re-emphasizes the introductory paragraph and thesis, without adding new ideas?

Editing

12. Circle the following errors you think you see in this draft: spelling errors, fragments, run-ons/comma splices, errors in comma and semicolon/colon use, pronoun disagreement, reference fault errors, and errors in parallelism, apostrophe use, verb use/tense, and passive voice construction. (See the handbook section for help in identifying and correcting these errors.)

13. Other types of grammar or sentence-level errors:

_____

Comments:

_____

_____

LO 3 COMPLEMENTARY MODES FOR COMPARISON/CONTRAST ESSAYS

Compare/contrast mode is often combined with several other modes.

- **Narration** and **description** can be used to develop the analysis.
- **Definition** mode can be used to help explain objects or concepts used in the examples provided.
- **Examples** help illustrate the comparisons.
- **Cause-and-effect analysis** will further elaborate on the examples.
- **Classification** is usually part of the comparison itself: You have to classify items into broader groups to analyze them specifically.
- You can engage **argument** mode to persuade your readers to agree with particular point of view related to the comparison and contrast analysis.

Sample Student Essay

White 1

Todd White

Professor James

English 100

23 May 2010

Softball and Baseball: Serious Differences

Softball and baseball are both popular sports in America. At first glance, they seem very similar. However, there are some major differences between the two sports, not just in how they are played, but also in how much respect and attention sports fans give them.

Both sports use similar equipment, but there are differences in their design. Softball equipment is very basic. The ball is the size of a grapefruit and somewhat soft. The bats and gloves are a little larger than those used in baseball. Baseball is also played with a ball, a bat, and gloves. However, there are some differences in the equipment. To begin with, the baseball itself is smaller and harder than a softball. The baseball is the size of a small orange and it is much harder than a softball. The gloves are similar to softball gloves, but a bit smaller and the bats are a bit narrower than the ones used for softball.

In both softball and baseball, players hit the ball and run from base to base, and the goal of the game is to get as many players as possible into home base to score runs and therefore points. A major difference between these two sports is how the pitcher pitches the ball. In softball, the pitcher pitches underhand. There is slow-pitch softball and fast-pitch softball. Though both pitches are done underhand, the slow-pitch has a much higher arch. Moreover, in softball, there are not different types

Thesis statement

Topic sentence

Topic sentence

Continued ▶

White 2

of pitches: The throw is consistently the same. In baseball, the pitcher throws overhand, and it is always fast-pitch. Also, in baseball, there are many types of pitches, for instance, a curve ball, a slider, and so on. Much of baseball depends on the speed and unpredictability of the pitch.

Concluding sentence

Finally, the most interesting difference between softball and baseball is the amount of recognition, popularity, and respect the two sports receive. Though both are enjoyed and played at most high schools and colleges, baseball is far more popular and is funded and attended at much higher levels. Also, there are more major and minor leagues for baseball, but there are no major leagues for softball. Most importantly, baseball is often called "America's pastime" and is considered a major component of our American heritage. The same prestige is not attributed to softball.

Topic sentence

Concluding sentence

Restatement of thesis

Obviously, there are major differences between softball and baseball, even though these two sports seem so close on the surface. Most likely, softball will never reach the level of esteem that baseball has earned as a beloved part of our American culture. It just doesn't have the history. However, both of these sports are played everyday on fields and in parks around the country.

ACTIVITY 14-6   Thinking Critically About the Student Essay

Directions: *Analyze the essay to identify the features and details characteristic of the comparison and contrast mode. Mark them on the essay. Then, reread the essay, and make a list of specific revisions you would make to correct any problems with content, organization, transitions, and style.*

PROFESSIONAL COMPARE AND CONTRAST ESSAY

American Space, Chinese Place

Yi-Fu Tuan

Yi-Fu Tuan was born in 1930 in Tientsin, China. He received his Ph.D. in 1957 from the University of California, Berkeley, in Geography. He is a retired professor emeritus of the University of Wisconsin, Madison. One of his most important publications is the book *Place, Art and Self.* In his book *Space and Place: The Perspective of Experience*, Tuan explores human movement from place to place and the need for a place to also have a sense of space.

1   Americans have a sense of space, not of place. Go to an American home in exurbia, and almost the first thing you do is drift toward the picture window. How curious that the first compliment you pay your host inside his house is to say how lovely it is outside his house! He is pleased that you should admire his vistas. The distant horizon is not merely a line separating earth from sky, it is a symbol of the future. The American is not rooted in his place, however lovely: his eyes are drawn by the expanding space to a point on the horizon, which is his future. By contrast, consider the traditional Chinese home. Blank walls enclose it.

2   Step behind the spirit wall and you are in a courtyard with perhaps a miniature garden around the corner. Once inside the private compound you are wrapped in an ambiance of calm beauty, an ordered world of buildings, pavement, rock, and decorative vegetation. But you have no distant view: nowhere does space open out before you. Raw nature in such a home is experienced only as weather, and the only open space is the sky above. The Chinese is rooted in his place. When he has to leave, it is not for the promised land on the terrestrial horizon, but for another world altogether along the vertical, religious axis of his imagination.

3   The Chinese tie to place is deeply felt. Wanderlust is an alien sentiment. The Taoist classic *Tao Te Ching* captures the ideal of rootedness in place with these words: "Though there may be another country in the neighborhood so close that they are within sight of each other and the crowing of cocks and barking of dogs in one place can be heard in the other, yet there is no traffic between them; and throughout their lives the two peoples have nothing to do with each other." In theory if not in practice, farmers have ranked high in Chinese society. The reason is not only

that they are engaged in the "root" industry of producing food but that, unlike pecuniary merchants, they are tied to the land and do not abandon their country when it is in danger.

4   Nostalgia is a recurrent theme in Chinese poetry. An American reader of translated Chinese poems will be taken aback—even put off—by the frequency as well as the sentimentality of the lament for home. To understand the strength of this sentiment, we need to know that the Chinese desire for stability and rootedness in place is prompted by the constant threat of war, exile, and the natural disasters of flood and drought. Forcible removal makes the Chinese keenly aware of their loss. By contrast, Americans move, for the most part, voluntarily. Their nostalgia for home town is really longing for childhood to which they cannot return: in the meantime the future beckons and the future is "out there," in open space. When we criticize American rootlessness we tend to forget that it is a result of ideals we admire, namely, social mobility and optimism about the future. When we admire Chinese rootedness, we forget that the word "place" means both location in space and position in society: to be tied to place is also to be bound to one's station in life, with little hope of betterment. Space symbolizes hope; place, achievement and stability.

Reading Reflection Questions   *Answers will vary. Sample answers are provided.*

1. What are the direct or indirect (implied) messages in this story?

   Americans have a sense of space, whereas Chinese are tied to a particular

   place—it is a cultural difference.

2. List two characteristics of this article that distinguish it as a contrast article.

   It looks at similarities and differences between Chinese and American

   views of place/space; it presents a purpose and goal for a comparison

   and contrast between them

3. Who do you think the main intended audience is for this article, Americans or Chinese? Why? *Americans: It is written in English in America; it*

   provides more cultural background and explanations of Chinese customs

4. Provide one reason suggested in the article for the different perspectives of the Chinese and Americans toward their homes. *The Chinese are deeply*

   rooted in place and do not usually move voluntarily. Americans decide to

   move and see opportunities in space.

Objective Questions

5. T/F ____T____ The author suggests that Americans love open spaces.

6. T/F ____F____ The author suggests that Americans are more rooted to their homes than are the Chinese.

7. T/F ____T____ The author suggests that the American desire for home is really longing for a return to childhood.

Checking Vocabulary

Define the following in your own words, or provide a dictionary definition if you don't know the word.

8. ambiance: *atmosphere/mood*

9. wanderlust: *the desire to travel*

10. pecuniary: *involving money*

CRITICAL THINKING CHECKLIST

Answers will vary.

PURPOSE

1. What is the **purpose** of this piece of writing? Is it clear?

_____

_____

IDEAS

2. What **ideas** and **background information** are provided to support the purpose of this piece of writing?

_____

_____

SUPPORT

3. What **evidence** and **examples** are used to explain and develop the ideas that support the argument made in the piece of writing? Are the evidence and examples provided sufficient?

_____

_____

ASSUMPTIONS
BIASES

4. Are there unfounded **assumptions** or unreasonable **biases**?

_____

_____

Continued ▶

5. Are all of the **conclusions**, **implications**, and **consequences** of the arguments (the results of the arguments taken to their farthest extreme) considered?

_____

_____

6. Is the **point of view** clear and consistent, and have other points of view been considered?

_____

_____

7. Using these critical thinking tools, **analyze** the overall structure of this essay and the strength of the author's arguments, ideas, and support. Was he or she successful in accomplishing the purpose? Why, or why not?

_____

_____

Essay Assignments

1. Write a comparison/contrast essay on two teachers you've had. Determine at least three points you want to use for your comparison/contrast. Pick either subject-by-subject or point-by-point organization to construct your essay.

2. Compare and contrast two musicians (or musical groups). Determine at least three points you want to use for your comparison/contrast. Pick either subject-by-subject or point-by-point organization to construct your essay.

3. Compare and contrast two restaurants in your neighborhood. Determine at least three points you want to use for your comparison/contrast. Pick either subject-by-subject or point-by-point organization to construct your essay.

4. Choose any of the subjects you worked on in the activities from this chapter, and write a complete comparison/contrast essay on that topic.

SPOTLIGHT ON CRITICAL THINKING

Comparing and contrasting ideas, objects, and people are natural and effective ways to draw conclusions.
   Writing comparisons/contrasts: In history classes, you often must write essays that compare and contrast events, cultures, or countries. In your career, you may be asked to compare and contrast two products, coworkers, or even our own company with a competitor. Use your **analysis** skills to check the **purpose** and **conclusions** in your writing for college classes and later in your writing for your career. Develop your **purpose**, **ideas**, and **support** based on the critical thinking tips in Chapter 1.
   Reading comparison/contrasts: In political science classes, you will often read accounts of world leaders that compare and contrast their leadership skills or their policies. If you hire and evaluate employees as part of your career, you will read reports that compare and contrast employees' work performances. Use the Six Steps for Active Reading from Chapter 2 to be a more careful and interactive reader.

To check your progress in meeting this chapter's objectives, log in to www .mywritinglab.com, go to the **Study Plan** tab, click on **Writing and Critical Thinking in the Modes** and choose **Essay Development—Comparing and Contrasting** from the list of subtopics. Read and view the resources in the **Review Materials** section, and then complete the **Recall, Apply,** and **Write** sets in the **Activities** section.

15 Argument and Persuasion

LEARNING OBJECTIVES

In this chapter, you will learn to

LO 1 Write argument and persuasion essays.

LO 2 Recognize errors in logic when constructing arguments.

LO 3 Structure argument and persuasion essays.

LO 4 Use complementary modes for argument and persuasion essays.

THINKING CRITICALLY

Look at the advertisment above. Then complete the task that follows.

Most advertisements have arguments embedded within them: The most common argument, of course, is "buy me!" Often other arguments are hinted at, too, for example, if you buy a certain car, you'll seem more good looking. Or, as in this Tommy Hilfiger ad, that if you wear their clothes, you will be part of a large, happy, ethnically diverse family of interesting people.

Choose a magazine, television, or billboard advertisement you've seen recently. Briefly describe the advertisement and what it is trying to persuade you to buy. Then list any secondary arguments the ad is suggesting.

ARGUMENT AND PERSUASION ESSAYS

Argumentative and persuasive writing is one of the most common types of writing you will be asked to do in college. You will be asked to write argumentative and persuasive pieces in the workplace, too. Even a memo to your boss asking for a raise is a type of argument essay. Becoming skilled in clear, logical reasoning and arguments will help you see through the faulty arguments and logic in books, newspaper articles, political speeches, and other kinds of persuasive writing you encounter in the everyday world.

Critical Thinking and Argument

Argument essays involve stating a claim, supporting the claim with valid and fair-minded reasoning, providing examples and evidence to support your argument, and providing an even-handed presentation of counterarguments to your proposed solution.

Providing **counterarguments** (what others would say in response to your arguments) or alternative solutions to a problem shows that you are being fair-minded and not presenting an issue in a biased way. Evidence and support can include facts, statistics, detailed examples, firsthand accounts and/or interviews, and observations. Counterarguments require careful critical thinking. You have to anticipate what others would say against your argument.

APPLYING CRITICAL THINKING

PURPOSE   IDEAS   SUPPORT   ASSUMPTIONS BIASES   CONCLUSIONS   POINT OF VIEW   ANALYSIS

To write an effective argument essay, you will need to consider the following questions:

1. What is my **purpose** for writing this essay? What **ideas** and point or points do I want to make to my audience?

2. What **biases** and **assumptions** do I have? What are they based on? Are they logical? What biases or assumptions might my audience have that I will need to address as I make my arguments?

Continued ▶

3. What is my **point of view** on the subject? Is it based on credible information? How will I best present it?

4. Have I thoroughly **analyzed** my argument? How will I break it down into its basic parts, and how will I present them?

5. What **support** do I need to include? What details (descriptive details, facts, evidence, examples) can I include to develop my argument(s)?

BEFORE WRITING AN ARGUMENT ESSAY

Before you begin to write an argument essay on an assigned topic, or one you have chosen, start by asking yourself these questions:

1. What is my stand on this issue?
2. Is there a plan of action I can propose to solve a problem?
3. Who would disagree with my stand or solution, and why? (What are the counterarguments?)
4. What examples and evidence can I provide to support my arguments and claims?
5. How will I organize my arguments and evidence?
6. How will I conclude my essay?

Answering these questions will lead you to an expository thesis statement, help you determine which language and details will provide vivid description and images for support, and give you a general idea of how you want to organize your essay.

ACTIVITY 15-1   Brainstorming for Potential Arguments

Directions: *Brainstorm a list of problems that exist in your neighborhood or in the country as a whole that need action to resolve them. Answers will vary.*

> **Example:** Need more bus routes in my town, need more stoplights in my district, neighbors need to curb their dogs, welfare reform in America.

_____

_____

_____

_____

_____

WRITING AN ARGUMENT ESSAY

Some students hear the term "argument paper" and assume that they will have to use anger and harsh tones to get their message across. However, in good argument and persuasive writing, you should use logic and fair-minded appeals to your audience in order to sway them to your point of view on a subject. The purpose of an argument/persuasion essay is to develop an *argument* or *claim* about a topic and support it with logical and valid reasons in order to persuade your readers to agree with your position.

Often, instructors will ask you to take a stand on a particular issue and then argue for the stand you take. You will need to provide reasons to support your position on the subject. You will also need to address possible counterarguments both to your overall stand and to the individual reasons or support statements and examples in your paper.

In some argument/persuasion essays, you will be arguing for a proposed *solution* to a perceived *problem*. This type of argument paper goes beyond just explaining your stand on an issue and your reasons for that stand; it also adds the element of proposing an action—arguing for a change to address a perceived problem. Often the thesis statement for an argumentative paper will include the words "should," "needs to," "ought to," or "must" as part of the proposed change.

When writing an argument paper, you must know your audience and customize your approach based on your target audience. For instance, if you were writing a position paper on the issue of gun control, your approach would need to be modified depending on your audience. How you would present your views to a parent-teacher association would be very different from how you would present them to the National Rifle Association.

Also, in all argument/persuasion essays, your tone should be respectful and fair-minded. Of course, you will have a bias: That is the nature of an argument paper. Your stand on the issue must be clear from beginning to end, but do not make the mistake of oversimplifying the counterarguments or underestimating your readers' positions or knowledge on the issue. You may even point out the costs of your solution and the merits of others' arguments against it in order to convince your readers that your position is still the better solution.

LO 2 ERRORS IN LOGIC WHEN CONSTRUCTING ARGUMENTS

Be careful: Argument essays are the easiest essays in which to fall prey to logical fallacies (common errors in logic that weaken your reasoning—list and definitions follow) and the use of emotion over reason. The tone and fair-minded logic of your essay's arguments are essential to persuading your readers of your point and maintaining your credibility. Of course, you are arguing on the basis of your own opinion, but your reasoning should be detailed, logical, and free from fallacies. You need to assess your intended audience carefully in order to choose the most effective tone, approach, and evidence to provide in support of your claims and arguments. Moreover, you need to make sure you haven't oversimplified the subject, your arguments, or your opposition's arguments. You also need to engage your critical thinking skills to evaluate the assumptions and biases built into your arguments and to make sure you haven't committed any logical fallacies in your arguments or in your counterarguments.

Logical Fallacies

Here are some of the most common **logical fallacies**, or errors in reasoning, that students commit in argument essays (they are also common in speeches and debates). Check to make sure you haven't damaged your credibility by including any of these fallacies in your paper.

Ad hominem fallacy: "Ad hominem" is a Latin phrase that means "to the man" and involves *attacking a specific person or group of people* attached to an issue or point of view that opposes one's own position instead of arguing against their claims, reasoning, or evidence.

> **Example:** Those tree-hugging hippies should stop interfering with progress.

Post hoc fallacy: "Post hoc" is a Latin phrase that means "after this." This fallacy involves thinking that because one event happened first, it must be the cause of the event that followed it. It is an unsupported claim that something is the result of something else. One should not make a cause-and-effect analysis without providing evidence to support the connection between two events.

> **Example:** I decided to wear my striped shirt the day I aced my chemistry exam, so if I wear it again today, I should do great in my English test.

Hasty generalization fallacy: In this fallacy, the writer jumps to a conclusion without providing the evidence and reasoning that led to that conclusion.

> **Example:** I'm certain the students' lack of motivation is related to changes in modern music.

Begging the question fallacy: This fallacy involves stating and repeating claims but never giving support or evidence to develop them.

> **Example:** Good parenting would have prevented all of these social problems. All of our society's major problems are a direct result of bad parenting.

Equivocation: "Equivocation" means "using vague words or phrases that mislead the reader." A writer may also use *euphemisms* (words or phrases used to soften the effect of a more direct word) to avoid addressing the severity of an issue or to soften harsher truths. For instance, the words "passed away" or "moved on" are euphemisms for "dead," and "victims of friendly fire" is a euphemism for soldiers killed by their own side.

> **Example:** There were several *casualties* as a result of *friendly* fire.

Red Herring fallacy: This fallacy occurs when a writer uses details, examples, or other language that distract the reader from the real argument.

> **Example:** I hear that many soldiers suffer from depression after returning home from Iraq. Has anyone looked into why these soldiers signed up for the military in the first place?

False dilemma fallacy: This fallacy is also known as the either/or fallacy. The writer presents only two sides to a complex issue that may have many sides. "You're either with us or against us" is a classic false dilemma: One may actually be somewhere in the middle.

> **Example:** If you don't support our request for more library funding, then you are anti–student success.

APPLYING CRITICAL THINKING

Besides being aware of the type of errors in logic you can make while writing a persuasion or argument essay, there are some other basic tips you should you keep in mind as you begin your essay writing process.

Ten Argument Basics

1. Clearly define your argument and **purpose**.

2. Be aware of your audience, and adjust your style and tone appropriately; use tactful and fair language.

3. Provide evidence, **ideas**, examples, **support**, and **conclusions** for your claims and arguments.

4. Check for logical fallacies and oversimplifications in your reasoning.

5. Acknowledge and **analyze** differing **points of view** and present counterarguments.

6. Point out common ground, and, when appropriate, point out the merits of another view, or make a concession to a well-put counterargument.

7. Refute (address and disagree with) counterarguments and claims from the opposing view—again using fair and respectful language.

8. Use the Critical Thinking Checklist from Chapter 1 to check for your own **assumptions**, **biases**, and inferences, and for the consequences of your argument, and overall point of view.

9. Use the critique form later in this chapter to check the structure and components of your essay.

10. Revise and proofread your argument essay carefully.

LO3 STRUCTURING AN ARGUMENT ESSAY

Your argument essay will begin with a call to action or some other type of attention grabber to interest your readers in your subject and your argument. Then you will need to narrow down to your actual argument. Your thesis statement should explain exactly what you are arguing for and why. If your argument involves proposing a change in how things are, remember using the words "should" or "must" or the phrase "needs to" helps your reader know that you are arguing for a change.

> **Example:** My neighborhood needs to petition for speed bumps, and the city should respond to our neighborhood's request.

In your body paragraphs, you'll provide reasons, evidence, and examples to support your proposed argument. The topic sentences will set up those reasons and your examples for support. Also, in these paragraphs, be sure to present the major counterarguments to your point of view, what others might say against your plans or reasoning. Be fair-minded and thorough to maintain integrity and your readers' respect. Address those counterarguments, and explain why you don't agree with them.

Finally, the concluding paragraph will come back and recap the argument you want to convince your readers about. The chart below provides a brief overview of the structure of an argument essay.

BASIC STRUCTURE FOR AN ARGUMENT ESSAY

INTRODUCTORY PARAGRAPH

Sets up and background for the problem or need.

Thesis statement: Presents what you are arguing for: what you want to persuade your readers about

BODY PARAGRAPHS (Two to five, depending on assignment and purpose)

Create topic sentences to develop your thesis.

Develop your arguments with reasoning and evidence.

Use transitions within and between paragraphs to emphasize the transition from one argument or part to the next.

Provide examples and concrete details for support.

Present counterarguments to be fair minded.

Add analysis and commentary about the example used to help develop the arguments/thesis statement.

CONCLUDING PARAGRAPH

Sums up and re-emphasizes the thesis: your arguments and reasons.

STRUCTURING YOUR ARGUMENT ESSAY

Topic

The only real rule for topics for argumentative essays is that you must be trying to persuade your readers about something. You also may be arguing for a change in the status quo, so don't argue for something that already exists (though you could argue that an existing policy or situation is not effective).

A Few Topic Possibilities

▶ NOTE   Be sure to narrow these broad subjects down to manageable topics.

AIDS*	genetic engineering	multiculturalism
animal testing	globalization	issues
assisted suicide	global warming	NAFTA**
beauty contests	homelessness	nuclear energy/
cars/auto culture	hunger	nuclear weapons
censorship	infant mortality	obesity
chemical fertilizers	inflation	ozone layer
child custody/laws	industrial waste	police searches
city sprawl	illegal drugs/laws	pesticide use
city housing	littering/fines	racism
clearcutting	loss of farmland	rainforests
eating disorders	malnutrition	sexism in laws
gender issues	migration	war

*acquired immune deficiency syndrome
**North American Free Trade Agreement

ACTIVITY 15-2   Narrowing Argument Topics

Directions: *Choose three of the broad subjects listed on page 300, and do a cluster, or brainstorm on a separate sheet of paper to narrow them down into more manageable topics. Then, choose a broad topic of your own, and narrow it down in the same way.* Answers will vary.

Subject 1: _____

Possible narrowed topics: _____

_____

_____

Subject 2: _____

Possible narrowed topics: _____

_____

_____

Subject 3: _____

Possible narrowed topics: _____

_____

_____

Subject 4, your choice: _____

Possible narrowed topics: _____

_____

_____

Introductory Paragraph

You will need an introduction of one or two paragraphs. The introduction should start with an attention grabber that introduces your topic. It can be a rhetorical question (a question you ask your readers to set up the topic) or a powerful statement. Next, you need to give a two- or three-sentence general explanation of your argument and any background information the readers would need in order to understand it. Here are some examples of attention grabbers:

Attention Grabber

1. **Rhetorical question:** "Have you ever experienced the frustration of driving around looking for a parking spot?"

2. **A powerful piece of information or fact:** "On an average, a quarter's worth of books will cost a student $100–$200."

3. **An anecdote or story:** "When I started college, I only had $100 set aside for buying my books . . . "

4. **A call to action:** "It's time that students took an active part in dealing with bookstore prices."

5. **A background/explanation of the problem:** "For over twenty years, our campus bookstore has charged too high a profit percentage on our textbooks."

Thesis Statements

Write one to three sentences that contextualize the problem and give the basic facts. Your thesis will be a plan for solving the problem (the proposed change or plan for solution you are arguing for). Try using "should," "must," or "needs to" in your plan of action to indicate the argument.

My employer should contribute half of the cost of my family's health care.

My local grocery store needs to offer a greater selection of organic produce.

ACTIVITY 15-3   Creating Thesis Statements

Directions: *Create a thesis statement for each of the topics you narrowed down in Activity 15-2. Answers will vary.*

1. Subject 1: Thesis statement: _____

   _____

2. Subject 2: Thesis statement: _____

   _____

3. Subject 3: Thesis statement: _____

   _____

4. Subject 4: Thesis statement: _____

   _____

Body Paragraphs

The first body paragraph should explain in more detail the problem you
see and what you are arguing for. Give specific examples and details to
illustrate the problem. The following body paragraphs should explain how
your plan for a solution will solve the problem or at least be the first step
toward changing the problem. Predict, evaluate, and address what people
might say *against* your plan (the counterargument[s]). Many counterarguments have to do with who will *pay* for the changes if the solution involves
spending money. So be sure to address *who* would pay and *how* the money
would be raised. If the counterarguments are about something other than
money such as a moral concern or a political difference, make sure that
you present the counterargument(s) fairly and thoroughly. If you discount
the real counterarguments, your paper loses credibility. Transitions showing purpose and those strengthening a point are useful in argument essays.
Other helpful transitions include those that show summary or example
(see Chapter 6, pages 114–116).

TRANSITIONS TO . . .			
Show Addition of Another Point			
again	but also	in addition	nor
also	equally important	last	plus the fact
and	finally	lastly	secondly
and then	first	likewise	then too
another	further	moreover	thirdly
besides	furthermore	next	too
Show Purpose			
all things considered	for this reason	to accomplish	with this in mind
for this purpose	in order to	to this end	with this objective

ACTIVITY 15-4   Creating Topic Sentences

Directions: *Create a possible topic sentence you could use to develop a body paragraph that would provide reasons and support for each of the thesis statements you created in Activity 15-3.* Answers will vary.

1. Subject 1: Topic sentence: _____

    _____

2. Subject 2: Topic sentence: _____

    _____

3. Subject 3: Topic sentence: _____

    _____

4. Subject 4: Topic sentence: _____

    _____

ACTIVITY 15-5   Providing Support

Directions: *Provide one specific reason that provides support for each of the topic sentences you created in Activity 15-4.* Answers will vary.

1. Subject 1: Reason to support topic sentence: _____

    _____

2. Subject 2: Reason to support topic sentence: _____

    _____

3. Subject 3: Reason to support topic sentence: _____

    _____

4. Subject 4: Reason to support topic sentence: _____

    _____

Concluding Paragraph

The conclusion should sum up the problem and re-explain your plan for solving the problem and how effective it will be. Be sure not to introduce any new ideas, arguments, or evidence in the conclusion.

ACTIVITY 15-6   Writing a Conclusion

Directions: *Now choose one of the topics you've been developing in these activities, and write a three- to six-sentence concluding paragraph for that topic/argument.* Answers will vary.

_____

_____

_____

_____

_____

Use the following critique form to check for the basics in your argument essay draft.

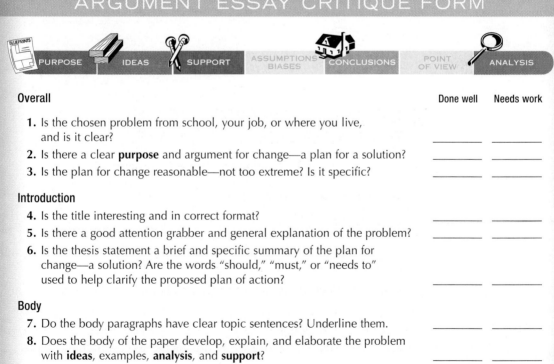

ARGUMENT ESSAY CRITIQUE FORM

PURPOSE   IDEAS   SUPPORT   ASSUMPTIONS BIASES   CONCLUSIONS   POINT OF VIEW   ANALYSIS

	Done well	Needs work
Overall		
1. Is the chosen problem from school, your job, or where you live, and is it clear?	_____	_____
2. Is there a clear **purpose** and argument for change—a plan for a solution?	_____	_____
3. Is the plan for change reasonable—not too extreme? Is it specific?	_____	_____
Introduction		
4. Is the title interesting and in correct format?	_____	_____
5. Is there a good attention grabber and general explanation of the problem?	_____	_____
6. Is the thesis statement a brief and specific summary of the plan for change—a solution? Are the words "should," "must," or "needs to" used to help clarify the proposed plan of action?	_____	_____
Body		
7. Do the body paragraphs have clear topic sentences? Underline them.	_____	_____
8. Does the body of the paper develop, explain, and elaborate the problem with **ideas**, examples, **analysis**, and **support**?	_____	_____

Continued ▶

9. Does the body explain in detail exactly how the plan for change
will resolve the problem and make a positive change?   _____ _____

10. Does the solution include all details for *who, how,* and *why* the solution
will work (including where the money will come from, if necessary)? _____ _____

11. Does each body paragraph have a good concluding sentence?   _____ _____

12. Are transitions used well both within and between paragraphs?   _____ _____

Conclusion

13. Does the **concluding** paragraph sum up well without adding new ideas?   _____ _____

Editing

14. Circle the following errors you think you see in this draft: spelling errors, fragments,
run-ons/comma splices, errors in comma and semicolon/colon use, pronoun disagreement,
reference fault errors, and errors in parallelism, apostrophe use, verb use/tense, and passive
voice construction. (See the handbook sections for help in identifying and correcting
these errors.)

15. Other types of grammar or sentence-level errors:

_____

Comments:

_____

_____

LO 4 COMPLEMENTARY MODES FOR ARGUMENT ESSAYS

Argument mode is often combined with several other modes.

- **Narration** and **description** can be used to develop the argument(s).
- **Definition** mode can be used to explain objects or concepts used in the examples provided.
- **Examples and illustrations** are essential to providing good reasoning and support for your argument.
- **Cause-and-effect analysis** will further elaborate on the arguments and reasons.
- **Description** helps explain the problem(s) and potential solutions.
- You can **compare and contrast** your arguments and counterarguments.

Sample Student Essay

Julie Beeds

Professor Furness

English 101

25 January 2010

Danger Around Every Corner

Have you ever heard the screech of car tires in front of your house, the kind that makes your heart instantly skip a beat or two? We send our children out to play in our front yards. We tell them not to talk to strangers and to watch for cars. I used to think that in most neighborhoods, drivers watch for children, and they drive slower down residential streets just in case a child runs out between two parked cars. However, in my neighborhood, the number of speeding cars is staggering. My neighborhood, specifically my street, has many families with children. However, even though children are on the sidewalks at all times of the day, cars race down our street in excess of 30 mph. It is time to take action and get our neighborhood to petition for speed bumps or a round-about in order to slow cars down and increase our children's safety. Our neighborhood needs to take action to protect the safety of our families: We need to petition for speed bumps or a round-about, and our city needs to listen to and then respond to our concerns and make the required changes.

Thesis statement

The risk of a child on my street being hurt by a car on any given day, at any given time, day or night, is high: I hear cars speeding down my street at all hours. In reaction, some of my neighbors have walked door-to-door asking people to slow down

Topic sentence

Continued ▶

Beeds 2

as they drive on our street. The response seemed good at first; however, the speeding started again soon afterward. I can thankfully say that no child has been hurt yet, but there have been too many narrow escapes.

Concluding sentence

Topic sentence

Even my own family has had a close call. Early this year when we had snow, my daughter and I were sledding down a hill half a block from our home. We had a terrific time playing in the snow until, as we were walking back to our house, a car slid around the corner almost hitting us as we were crossing the street. Even though we are very aware of the dangers on our street, the car came so fast that we had to jump out of its path. The most troubling part was that not only did we come close to getting hurt, the driver never looked back to see if we were okay.

Concluding sentence

Topic sentence

These scary near-misses happen frequently on our block. On one sunny day this summer, my daughter and her friend were rollerblading on the sidewalk across from my house. My daughter's friend hit a rock, tripped, and fell partially into the street. At the same time, a car came down the street, swerved to miss a dog and nearly hit her. The girl's experience of nearly being hit by the car was far more traumatic than the fall she had experienced. Sadly, the driver did not look back or stop to see if there were any injuries. I asked myself, "Do people just not care anymore?"

Topic sentence

However, several people in my neighborhood do care and are ready to take action. Some neighbors have attempted to solve the issue in less than desirable ways. Two doors down from me, my neighbor rolled a tire out into the street when a repeat offender sped down our street at what had to be 40 mph. The tire hit the car on the driver's door and the scene got ugly. A fist fight broke out on

Beeds 3

the sidewalk. When the fight ended, each man went to his corner, and, needless to say, those neighbors to this day do not speak to each other. Even though I do not agree with the tactics my neighbor used, that driver does not speed down the street anymore. However, Concluding sentence we do not want to be vigilantes: we just want our children safe.

Topic sentence Instead of resorting to violent or ugly acts, we have other means of dealing with this issue. My neighbors and I have been working on getting signatures for a petition to put in speed bumps and/or a round-about on our street. The irony of getting signatures is that some of the people that are signing the petition are some of the people that are speeding down the streets in the first place. From what I have researched and been told, getting the signatures will be the easiest part. Having the petition approved and asking the city to allocate money for this project will be the difficult part, Concluding sentence but all of the residents are committed to this project succeeding.

Topic sentence In order to get the Department of Transportation to pay for a speed bump or round-about, a survey of the street or streets in question must occur. The Department of Transportation will evaluate the areas in three categories. The categories are number of accidents, volume of traffic, and average speed of the drivers. The Department of Transportation's evaluation will directly influence how much money they will allocate to the project. If the Department of Transportation allocates half, one quarter, or no Counter-argument money, the neighborhood will have to pay the costs to complete the project, which will be $8,000 to $14,000 depending on which speed control device the Department of Transportation advises. Many would argue that that is a lot of money, but the value of our children's lives far outweighs this cost. Also, with a neighborhood

Continued ▶

Beeds 4

Concluding sentence

fundraiser, the price per person could be quite small. At this stage, our neighborhood must wait its turn for the construction of the speed bumps or round-about.

Restatement of thesis

To summarize, our goal is to keep our children safe. Our neighborhoods and our homes should be where we can feel safe, and our children need to be able to walk, run, and play outside their homes in a safe environment. Installing speed bumps and/or a round-about is an inexpensive deterrent for speeders especially when one weighs it against the possible loss of a child's life. Our lives are not that busy, nor is what we have to do that important or urgent. Do you remember the old commercial "Speed Kills"? We must take action in our neighborhood before we get to that point.

ACTIVITY 15-7   Thinking Critically About the Student Essay

Directions: *Analyze the essay to identify the features and details characteristic of the argument/persuasion mode. Mark them on the essay. Then, reread the essay, and make a list of specific revisions you would make to correct any problems with content, organization, transitions, and style.*

PROFESSIONAL SAMPLE ARGUMENT ESSAY

Can You Be Educated from a Distance?

James Barszcz

1   By almost any measure, there is a boom in Internet-based instruction. In just a few years, thirty-four percent of American colleges and universities have begun offering some form of what's called "distance learning" (DL),

and among the larger schools, it's closer to ninety percent. If you doubt the popularity of the trend, you probably haven't heard of the University of Phoenix. It grants degrees entirely on the basis of online instruction. It en-rolls 90,000 students, a statistic used to support its claim to be the largest private university in the country.

2   While the kinds of instruction offered in these programs will differ, DL usually signifies a course in which the instructors post syllabi, reading as-signments, and schedules on websites, and students send in their written assignments by e-mail. Other forms of communication often come into play, such as threaded messaging, which allows for posting questions and comments that are publicly viewable, as a bulletin board would, as well as chat rooms for real-time interchanges. Generally speaking, face-to-face communication with an instructor is minimized or eliminated altogether.

3   The attraction for students might at first seem obvious. Primarily, there's the convenience promised by courses on the Net: you can do the work, as they say, in your pajamas. But figures indicate that the reduced effort results in a reduced commitment to the course. While the attrition rate for all freshmen at American universities is around twenty percent, the rate for online students is thirty-five percent. Students themselves seem to under-stand the weaknesses inherent in the setup. In a survey conducted for eCornell, the DL division of Cornell University, less than a third of the respondents expected the quality of the online course to be as good as the classroom course.

4   Clearly, from the schools' perspective, there's a lot of money to be saved. Although some of the more ambitious programs require new invest-ments in servers and networks to support collaborative software, most DL courses can run on existing or minimally upgraded systems. The more stu-dents who enroll in a course but don't come to campus, the more the school saves on keeping the lights on in the classrooms, paying custodi-ans, and maintaining parking lots. And, while there's evidence that instruc-tors must work harder to run a DL course for a variety of reasons, they won't be paid any more, and might well be paid less.

5   But as a rule, those who champion distance learning don't base their arguments on convenience or cost savings. More often, they claim DL sig-nals an advance in the effectiveness of education. Consider the vigorous case made by Fairleigh Dickinson University (FDU), in Madison, New Jer-sey, where students—regardless of their expectations or desires—are now required to take one DL course per year. By setting this requirement, FDU claims that it recognizes the Internet as "a premier learning tool" of the current technological age. Skill in using online resources "prepares our students, more than others, for life-long learning—for their jobs, their careers, and their personal growth."

6   Moreover, Internet-based courses will connect FDU students to a "global virtual faculty," a group of "world-class scholars, experts, artists, politicians, and business leaders around the world."

7   Sounds pretty good. But do the claims make much sense? First, it should be noted that students today and in the future might well use the Internet with at least as much facility as the faculty. It's not at all clear that they need to be taught such skills. More to the point, how much time and effort do you suppose "world-class scholars" (much less politicians and business leaders) will expend for the benefit of students they never meet or even see? Probably a lot less than they're devoting to the books, journal articles, and position papers that are already available to anyone with access to a library.

8   Another justification comes from those who see distance learning as the next step in society's progress toward meritocracy. A recent article in *Forbes* magazine cites Professor Roger Schank of Northwestern University, who predicts that soon "students will be able to shop around, taking a course from any institution that offers a good one . . . . Quality education will be available to all. Students will learn what they want to learn rather than what some faculty committee decided was the best practical compromise." In sum, says Professor Schank, who is also chairman of a distance-learning enterprise called CognitiveArts, "Education will be measured by what you know rather than by whose name appears on your diploma."

9   Statements like these assume education consists in acquiring information ("what you know"). Accept that and it's hard to disagree with the conclusions. After all, what does it matter how, or through what medium, you get the information? But few truly educated people hold such a mechanistic view. Indeed, traditionally, education was aimed at cultivating intellectual and moral values, and the "information" you picked up was decidedly secondary. It was commonplace for those giving commencement speeches to note that, based on etymology, education is a drawing out, not a putting in. That is, a true education *educes,* or draws out, from within a person qualities of intellect and character that would otherwise have remained hidden or dormant.

10   Exactly how this kind of educing happens is hard to pin down. Only in part does it come from watching professors in the classroom present material and respond to student questions, the elements of education that can be translated to the Net with reasonable fidelity. Other educational experiences include things like watching how professors joke with each other (or not!) in the hallways, seeing what kinds of pictures are framed in a professor's office, or going out for coffee after class with people in your dorm. Such experiences, and countless others, are sometimes labeled (and

dismissed) as "social life on campus." But they also contribute invaluably to education. Through them, you learn a style, in the noblest sense of that term, a way of regarding the information you acquire and the society you find yourself in. This is what the philosopher Alfred North Whitehead meant when he called style the ultimate acquisition of a cultivated mind. And it's the mysterious ways of cultivating that style that the poet Robert Frost had in mind when he said that all that a college education requires is that you "hang around until you catch on."

11   Hang around campus, that is, not lurk on the Net.

Reading Reflection Questions *Sample answers are provided.*

Answers will vary.

1. What is the main purpose in this article? Explain in your own words.

   To argue that distance learning is inferior to taking classes on campus

2. ___*T*___ T/ F According to the essay, the drop out (attrition) rate for distance learning (online) students is higher than traditional students.

3. What counterarguments does Barszcz provide to his arguments against distance learning (what his opponents might say in defense of distance learning)?

   Cost effectiveness, more effective education, Internet as a premier

   learning tool, and skill in the technological age

4. Give an example of one of the author's refutations to one of the counter-arguments (he addresses counterarguments with refutations).

   E.g., students are familiar with the Internet already, and usually

   their skills are higher than those of their teachers, no real time with

   instructors, and the value of being there, and social skills, attrition

   rates, etc.

5. ___*F*___ T/ F The author agrees that good education is mostly about "what you know" or acquiring facts and information.

6. ___*T*___ T/ F The author thinks that education expands beyond learning information and that even an instructor's office and hallway behavior can be educational.

7. In your own words, what does the author mean, in the last paragraph of the article, when he talks of the importance of learning a "style" in college?

   That students learn how to be a better person in the world through the

   experience of college, that they "catch on"

Checking Vocabulary

Define each of the following words by figuring out their meaning using context clues in the reading selection. If you cannot work out the meaning of a word, use a dictionary.

8. distance learning (paragraph 1): _courses taken entirely online_

9. minimized (paragraph 2): _to reduce to the smallest amount or degree_

10. attrition (paragraph 3): _a reduction in numbers (dropouts)_

CRITICAL THINKING CHECKLIST

Answers will vary.

1. What is the **purpose** of this piece of writing? Is it clear?

_____

_____

2. What **ideas** and **background information** are provided to support the purpose of this piece of writing?

_____

_____

3. What **evidence** and **examples** are used to explain and develop the ideas that support the argument made in the piece of writing? Are the evidence and examples provided sufficient?

_____

_____

4. Are there unfounded **assumptions** or unreasonable **biases**?

_____

_____

5. Are all of the **conclusions**, **implications**, and **consequences** of the arguments (the results of the arguments taken to their farthest extreme) considered?

_____

_____

6. Is the **point of view** clear and consistent, and have other points of view been considered?

_____

_____

ANALYSIS

7. Using these critical thinking tools, **analyze** the overall structure of this essay and the strength of the author's arguments, ideas, and support. Was he or she successful in accomplishing the purpose? Why, or why not?

_____

_____

Essay Assignments

1. Choose one of the subjects listed on page 300 for an argument essay, and narrow that subject to a manageable topic. Then, take a stand on that issue (for or against or proposing a change). Be sure to include the opposition's view and counterarguments, and address them thoroughly. Don't do any secondary research unless you are instructed to do so by your instructor. If you do include secondary research, be sure to use the research techniques and MLA documentation sections (see Chapters 18 and 19) to find and cite your sources correctly.

2. Choose a problem from the following list to create your argument (plan for change or solution):

  a. A problem you see at your school (such as parking, bookstore prices, cafeteria prices and offerings, class scheduling)

  b. A problem where you work (such as parking, scheduling of shifts, problems with coworkers, pay)

  c. A problem from your neighborhood that you'd like to see fixed (such as a needed stop sign/stoplight, parking problems, a needed park)

  After you have chosen a problem related to one of these three choices, you'll need to come up with a plan for a solution. This plan will become your thesis: It is what you'll be arguing for. Remember, using the words "should" or "must" or the phrase "needs to" helps your reader know that you are arguing for a change and helps make sure that you have developed a specific plan of action.

  After you finish your draft of this essay, use the critique form for self- and peer reviews of your essay draft.

3. Choose a topic from one of the activities you worked on in this chapter, and write an argument essay on it.

4. Other possible subjects to narrow down and write an argument essay about:

drunk driving laws	prescription drug costs
sex offender laws	medication/medical costs
smoking laws	steroid use
gas prices	traffic problems
tuition costs	mandatory foreign language classes
immigration laws	obesity in children
overfishing	overpopulation

SPOTLIGHT ON CRITICAL THINKING

As soon as we learn a language, we start learning how to use argument and persuasion to influence others.

Writing argument papers: In many college classes across disciplines, you will be asked to write persuasion essays, arguing a particular position on an issue. For example, in an ethics course, you may be asked to write a position paper arguing for or against the death penalty. On the job, you often must write persuasive advertisements for your products to convince your customers to buy your product. Use your **analysis** skills to check the **purpose** and **conclusions** in your writing for college classes and later in your writing for your career. Develop your **purpose**, **ideas**, and **support** based on the critical thinking tips in Chapter 1.

Reading argument papers: Use your critical reading skills from Chapter 2 to carefully evaluate the arguments and the reasoning of others. You will find that many advertisements that you encounter contain embedded logical fallacies. Also, if you work in the insurance industry, you will have to evaluate written claims that argue for compensation.

To check your progress in meeting this chapter's objectives, log in to www.mywritinglab.com, go to the **Study Plan** tab, click on **Writing and Critical Thinking in the Modes** and choose **Essay Development—Argument** from the list of subtopics. Read and view the resources in the **Review Materials** section, and then complete the **Recall, Apply,** and **Write** sets in the **Activities** section.

THINKING CRITICALLY

Look at the photo above. Then answer the following questions related to taking essay exams and writing under pressure.

1. What effect does writing with a specific time limit have on your ability to perform well?

_____

_____

2. How can you condense the writing process to make the most of your limited writing time?

_____

_____

Continued ▶

3. What can you do to generate ideas quickly and get a focus?

_____

_____

4. How much time out of an hour of writing would you allow for generating ideas and planning?

_____

_____

_____

_____

5. How much time would you dedicate out of that hour to proofread and revise your draft?

_____

_____

LO 1 STRATEGIES FOR TAKING ESSAY EXAMS OR TIMED ESSAYS

Essay exams and timed in-class essays have the same basic rules as take-home essays. The added pressure, of course, is the time restriction and the nervousness factor. Timed essays or in-class essay exams provide great practice for writing under pressure in the real world and your future career. Often, prospective employers will ask you to write something for them during the interview process, and in many jobs, you'll need to be able to crank out a memo or other important forms of writing on the spot.

Like all essays, a timed essay or a focused essay exam with a prescribed instructor prompt will ask you to narrow your focus and state a purpose. You need to stay focused and organized and provide adequate support and examples to illustrate your points. The basic structure is the same, too: a focused introduction that states the purpose for your essay, body paragraphs that develop your thesis and focus on particular aspects of your topic, and a conclusion that wraps up your points in a concise way without introducing any new ideas.

LO 2 Critical Thinking and Timed Essays

You'll do much better in a timed in-class essay if you engage your critical thinking skills from the moment you get your writing prompt. First, you need to interpret and analyze what the writing prompt is asking you to write about. You need to assess the clues buried in the writing assignment or prompt itself: Check for specific directions as well as key words. Then, you need to come up with a thesis statement (a purpose to explain in your timed essay) and a plan for writing your essay. It helps to brainstorm first and jot down a brief outline. Finally, you need to leave some time to critically assess what you've written and make needed revisions before submitting your essay.

LO 3 Before the Essay Exam or Timed Essay

One of the best ways to improve your skills in writing timed essays or taking essay exams is to reduce the panic factor. For many students, the idea of a timed essay causes the same kind of test anxiety that a complicated multiple choice test conjures. In order to alleviate that panic, you need to do some of the same things you do to perform well on a regular exam.

Study and Prepare in Advance

First, be sure that you are well prepared by reading any required materials before the day of the test. If the timed essay is an analysis of assigned readings, you'll have to study them and prepare notes as you would for any exam. If the essay prompt is one that requires no prereading assignments, then prepare by reviewing your writing textbook for the basics of essay writing.

Also, be sure to get a good night's sleep the night before an essay exam or timed in-class essay. If you are exhausted, it is harder to concentrate and think clearly, and your essay will suffer. Finally, be on time to class on the day; arrive early if possible, since anxiety increases if you are running late or get behind. Sometimes instructors provide verbal directions right at the beginning of class; if you are late, you could miss crucial directions or tips.

What You Will Need to Bring to Class

1. **Pens/pencils**, unless you will be writing directly on a computer. It is still a good idea to have a pen or pencil for brainstorming or in case of printer/computer problems. Most instructors prefer black or blue ink. Avoid unusual colors such as purple or green.
2. **Paper or a composition folder**, unless paper is provided by the instructor or you will be typing in a computer lab or classroom.
3. **A dictionary**, if it is allowed by the instructor; check beforehand.

4. **A memory stick or disk**, if you will be writing on a computer in class—always save a copy of your work, and save regularly as you type your essay, every 10 minutes or so.

5. **A watch**, if there is no clock in your classroom, so you can monitor your time as you write.

LO 4 During the Essay Exam or Timed Essay

If you are particularly nervous before the exam, try some relaxation techniques such as deep breathing before you go into the classroom. Use positive thinking to tell yourself you are ready. After all, you've studied, right?

The same basic writing process you learned in Chapter 5 applies to in-class essays or essay exams, too. The five basic steps of the writing process still apply in an essay exam:

1. **Prewriting:** Generates ideas and your paper's purpose

2. **Organizing:** Develops a plan for presenting your purpose and ideas

3. **Drafting:** Creates a first draft of your essay based on your plan and the pattern(s) of organization you have chosen; develops support for your essay's purpose

4. **Revising:** Re-assesses the draft for content, development, organization, and support (examples and details)

5. **Editing:** Checks for sentence-level effectiveness, style, diction, grammar, and spelling errors

Remember to quickly assess your subject, purpose, and audience from the writing prompt. The **subject** of your essay is the topic you are writing about, which you need to focus into a manageable **topic** for the length of your essay. The **purpose** is what you want to explain or prove related to that topic, so your **thesis** is a statement of your overall goal. Your **audience** is the intended reader(s) for your essay—who you are addressing, so you'll need to customize both your tone (such as casual/informal or more formal/academic) and the amount and types of information you include, depending on the intended audience.

LO 5 Common Terms Used in Writing Prompts

As you review your writing prompt or question, check for indicator words that are clues for specific tasks your instructor wants you to accomplish in the essay. Here are some of the common terms used in writing prompts that are clues that you are being asked to provide specific information.

Analyze: Interpret the significance of something; divide the topic into individual components and analyze its parts; look at cause-and-effect relationships; look for purpose, messages, or meanings.

Argue: Take a stand on an issue, and develop your argument with reasoning and support.

Compare/contrast: Explore similarities and/or differences among two or more subjects.

Defend: Provide evidence to support a stand or conclusion.

Define: Provide a definition (or set of definitions).

Discuss: Talk about (write!) the subject—be sure to focus on a particular purpose and not just randomly brainstorm on the topic.

Enumerate: Number off specific points, ways of doing something, steps in a process.

Examine: Analyze and explore an issue thoroughly.

Identify: Specifically list or identify what is required.

Illustrate: Show with examples, support, and analysis.

Interpret: Translate and analyze the significance of the material.

List/include: Provide a list of examples, support, and/or reasons.

Provide/support: Provide examples and details for support and explanation.

Summarize: Summarize the main ideas in your own words.

Trace: In chronological order, detail events or situations related to the subject.

APPLYING CRITICAL THINKING

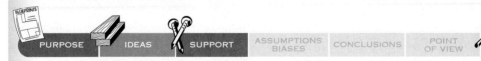

PURPOSE   IDEAS   SUPPORT   ASSUMPTIONS BIASES   CONCLUSIONS   POINT OF VIEW   ANALYSIS

The best way to make the most of your limited time in an exam situation is to do the following:

1. **Make sure that you understand the prompt, or question**, that has been given to you for your writing task. Read it carefully (see the list of terms that follow for clues to what you are being asked to do in the prompt). It helps to revise the given *question* into a thesis statement *answer* before you prewrite.

Continued ▶

2. **Allow at least five minutes for brainstorming** after you get your topic or prompt. Brainstorm on paper with a pen or pencil or on the computer, depending on your preference or the instructor's directions. If you prefer, you can freewrite instead. Develop **support**, **purpose**, and **analysis** in your essay.

3. **Come up with a brief plan for organization**: Try a rough outline to organize your ideas.

4. **Focus more on ideas and details**, and try not to obsess about spelling and style (although do use complete sentences and paragraph structure).

5. **Allow at least five minutes for a quick review/flash revision** of glaring problems after you write your essay. Be sure to check for spelling (this is the time to use the dictionary you brought) or grammar mistakes, and check your tone and diction choices.

Use the revision checklist below as a guideline for what you should look for as you do a quick revision.

REVISION CHECKLIST

_____   Check that you have addressed the prompt and accomplished the tasks set out in the directions and in the clue words.

_____   Check for an interesting introductory paragraph that sets up your purpose and leads into your thesis.

_____   Check for purpose and a clear thesis statement.

_____   Check that you have used appropriate vocabulary, tone, and approach for your target audience.

_____   Check to make sure that you have organized your paper logically with clear topic sentences in the body paragraphs and transitions.

_____   Check to make sure you have maintained unity—all sentences and paragraphs help develop your purpose and thesis.

_____   Check to make sure you have included enough support in your essay to develop your purpose. Do you need more examples and details?

_____   Check to make sure that your sentence structure and your vocabulary choices are varied and interesting.

_____   Check for a strong concluding paragraph that sums up your analytical conclusion (purpose) established in your thesis.

_____   Check for complete sentences (eliminate fragments, run-ons, or comma splices).

_____   Check for correct punctuation throughout the paper (commas, semicolons, colons, other punctuation marks).

_____   Check for conventional rules of mechanics (spelling, capitalization, underlining, italics, abbreviations, numbering) using the grammar section of this text and a dictionary.

ACTIVITY 16-1   Identifying Word Clues in Prompts

Directions: *In each of the following sample essay prompts, identify what the italicized words are asking the writer to do in his/her essay.* Answers will vary.

1. Write a two- to three-page essay that *defines* civic duty and *examines* why people tend to uphold it.

     _____

     _____

2. *Identify* a recurring problem in your neighborhood, and then *illustrate* why it is a problem.

     _____

     _____

3. *Trace* the events that led to the creation of the North Atlantic Treaty Organization (NATO).

     _____

     _____

4. *Examine* the following poem, and *interpret* the meaning and messages within it.

     _____

     _____

5. *Summarize* a current debate or controversy in the news, and then *argue* your stand on the controversy.

     _____

     _____

LO 6 PRACTICE WITH TIMED IN-CLASS ESSAYS AND ESSAY EXAMS

ACTIVITY 16-2   Timed Essay Practice I

Directions: *Give yourself one hour to write this essay from start to finish.*

Prompt Questions: *Write about a time when someone treated you unfairly. Explain what happened. How did it make you feel, and why? Examine your memories of the experience. Interpret this event's significance in your life and to your* *identity. Provide specific examples. What did you learn from this experience? (What you learned will become the thesis statement of your essay.)*

Complete the following:

1. *Brainstorm, prewrite, and outline for five minutes to find a thesis and generate ideas.*
2. *Begin with an introductory paragraph to set up your thesis, and then provide a thesis statement that addresses the topic questions above.*
3. *Set up the rest of your paragraphs to develop your points, and describe what happened. Use narration and description to develop your thesis idea.*
4. *Write a concluding paragraph that sums up your experience.*
5. *Do a quick review for needed organization and details; check quickly for spelling and grammar errors.*

ACTIVITY 16-3   Timed Essay Exam Practice II

Directions: *Write for one hour on the following prompt: Do you think that cigarette smoking should be illegal? Why, or why not? Be sure to argue reasons for your position, define and analyze the counterarguments or positions, and provide support and examples for the reasons for your position on the issue.*

ACTIVITY 16-4   Self-Assessment Essay

Directions: *Write a short one or two page self-assessment essay. In the essay, address the following questions.*

1. *Assess your improvement over the span of this writing course in planning, drafting, and revising essays. How exactly has your essay writing improved? Be specific. Some of the categories to consider include organization, details and examples, development, flow/coherence/transitions, introductory paragraphs and thesis statements, concluding paragraphs, and, finally, grammar and editing (spelling, fragments, run-ons, comma splices, commas, semicolon/colon use, pronoun agreement, reference fault errors, parallelism, apostrophe use, verb use/tense, passive voice construction, and others).*
2. *In your opinion, what are your strengths as a writer? What do you do well in essay writing?*
3. *In your opinion, what are your weaknesses in writing essays? What do you need to continue to work on in the future?*
4. *Anything else you've noticed?*

SPOTLIGHT ON CRITICAL THINKING

Unfortunately, you will often have a limited time to organize your ideas and support into a concise essay, both in college and on the job.

Writing timed essays: Many classes assign in-class written essay tests across disciplines to assess students' understanding of a unit in a course. Many history classes, for instance, will assign short answer or essay tests at the end of a unit. Also, some jobs now ask potential employees to write a short essay during their interview process because these employers value strong written skills. Use your **analysis** skills to check the **purpose** and **conclusions** in your writing for college classes and later in your writing for your career. Develop your **purpose**, **ideas**, and **support** based on the critical thinking tips in Chapter 1.

17 Paraphrase, Summary, and Analysis

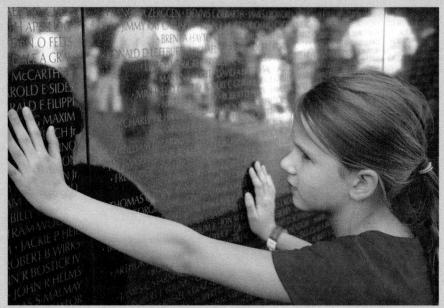

Vietnam War Memorial

LEARNING OBJECTIVES

In this chapter, you will learn to

LO 1 Use six steps to paraphrase material.

LO 2 Use eight steps to summarize material.

LO 3 Combine summary and analysis.

LO 4 Apply the Ice Cream Sandwich technique to frame facts and sources.

THINKING CRITICALLY

Look at the picture above. Then complete the task that follows.

In your own words, summarize what is happening in this picture. Describe the scene and the main action.

_____

_____

_____

You just wrote a summary of one picture's story. Both paraphrase and summary are tools for concisely conveying the main points made by an author. When writing about someone else's writing, you can bring in direct quotes, you can summarize the main ideas of the piece, or you

Continued ▶

can paraphrase a specific part (a couple of sentences). Most likely, you will use some combination of all three techniques.

Engage your critical thinking skills when writing about sources to make the best choices about when and how to combine summary, paraphrase, and direct quotations.

PARAPHRASE

A **paraphrase** involves using one's own words to *rephrase* a sentence or two of an original piece of writing. A paraphrase should be about the same length and contain about the same amount of detail as the original sentence(s) you are paraphrasing. Paraphrasing is like doing a phrase-by-phrase translation of an author's words into your own words. Make sure that you change both the word choice and the sentence structure of a paraphrase so you are not plagiarizing, and give the original author credit.

The purpose of a paraphrase is to provide a *detailed description or translation in your own words* of the original written material, and it should be very short. If you paraphrase more than a few sentences, you are running dangerously close to plagiarizing the author's writing. Summarize the main ideas in a general way instead and only paraphrase (rephrase) the sentences that need to be given in detail—again using only your own words, not the original author's. It is essential to be objective in your paraphrasing of an author's ideas. Do not add your bias, opinion, or personal reaction to the material. *A paraphrase is much more detailed than a summary* because you are literally rephrasing a sentence or two with the same level of detail, and it may end up being the same length or longer than the original piece of writing. Here are the six steps for writing a complete and accurate paraphrase.

Six Steps for Paraphrasing Material

Step One: Read the sentences you want to paraphrase carefully before writing anything (if it is a section from a longer piece, be sure to read the whole piece before paraphrasing the passage to be sure you understand the excerpt). Use the T-KED reading system or one of the Six Steps to Active Reading from Chapter 2 to gain a thorough understanding of the work. It is essential to understand an author's main and supporting points in a work before you can paraphrase them.

Step Two: In your first sentence, provide the author's full name and the name of the work you are paraphrasing from. If it is an excerpt, provide the entire title of the story, essay, or article in quotation marks; if it is from a book or play, underline or use italics for the title, depending on your instructor's preference.

Step Three: Then paraphrase the sentence(s). You may combine two or more sentences into one concise, paraphrased sentence of your own.

Step Four: Write the paraphrase *using your own words*, not the words of the author (no direct quotations in a paraphrase). Also, be sure to use your own sentence structures and style—not too close to the original.

▶ **TIP**   In order to avoid writing the paraphrase in the same words or same style as the original author, try not looking at the original and writing a sentence or two paraphrasing the sentences you have just read. Look at the text again and be sure you included all of the author's main ideas and details. It also helps to verbally explain the author's ideas and support to a friend first, using your own words, before you write a paraphrase.

Step Five: Stay objective. Do not offer your opinion in the paraphrase. Add no interpretation. Do not agree or disagree: Just paraphrase objectively. Read over your paraphrase to check for accuracy. Did you present the author's main ideas and details without adding your own bias or opinion?

Cross Reference

See Chapter 18 for more on avoiding plagiarism and Chapter 19 for correct MLA citation format.

Step Six: Include a page citation and/or publication information when needed. Even paraphrased references to a text in an essay you are writing need citations; otherwise you are guilty of plagiarism (not giving credit to the original author).

Sample Paraphrase

Paragraph excerpt from "Supersize Me" by Greg Critser, in Chapter 22.

Original Paragraph

Many franchisees wanted to take the concept even further, offering large-size versions of other menu items. At this sudden burst of entrepreneurism, however, McDonald's mid-level managers hesitated. Many of them viewed large-sizing as a form of "discounting," with all the negative connotations such a word evoked. In a business where "wholesome" and "dependable" were the primary PR watchwords, large-sizing could become a major image problem. Who knew what the franchisees, with their primal desires and shortcutting ways, would do next? No, large-sizing was something to be controlled tightly from Chicago, if it were to be considered at all.

Paraphrase of the First Two Sentences

In Greg Critser's article, "Supersize Me," he points out that many of the McDonald's franchisees decided to try offering other supersized items after the success of supersized fries. However, managers at the McDonald's headquarters began to worry about what the individual franchise owners were planning (Critser 1).

Use this checklist to ensure that you have accurately paraphrased the original sentence(s).

CHECKLIST FOR A GOOD PARAPHRASE

1. Check to make sure that you paraphrased the ideas in the original sentence(s) in the same order they were presented.

2. Check to make sure the paraphrase includes all of the main ideas and main examples for support from the original sentence(s).

3. Check to make sure that the paraphrase is in your own words and that there are no significant phrases that were in the original sentence(s) (no direct quotes, not even partial quotes).

4. Check to make sure that the paraphrase is accurate in its restatement of the original material and that you have not added any reaction to or opinion about the material (the restatement is objective).

5. Make sure you have included the author's name and the title of the original piece at the beginning of your paraphrase and included a citation of the source at the end.

ACTIVITY 17-1 Paraphrasing

Directions: *Pick a reading from another text or from Chapter 22 (or your instructor might assign a passage), and write a paraphrase of one to three sentences from that reading on a separate sheet of paper, following the Six Steps for Paraphrasing Material above.*

▶ **NOTE**   *You may want to use the T-KED reading system or Six Steps for Active Reading for a thorough understanding of the passage; you must completely comprehend a reading before you can accurately paraphrase it.*

Then, explain below what effect writing your paraphrase had on your overall understanding of the ideas contained in the reading.   Answers will vary.

_____

_____

_____

_____

SUMMARY

A **summary** is an objective, condensed description of an original work (an article, text chapter, story, etc.). Summarizing involves using your own words to describe the main ideas of a piece of writing. It is usually a much shorter (about one quarter or less of the original's length as a rule of thumb) presentation of the concepts of the original piece. A summary should not include direct quotations. The purpose of a summary is to provide a brief description of a longer work, and it should include the author's *main ideas* and the most prominent support for those ideas. It is essential to be objective in your summary of the author's ideas. Add no bias, opinion, or personal reaction to the material.

Here are eight steps for writing a complete and effective summary. *Be sure to read all eight steps before you begin, since some of these steps overlap.*

Eight Steps for Writing a Summary

Step One: Read the entire work (article, essay, short story, novel) at least twice before you write your summary. Be sure to use the T-KED reading system or the Six Steps to Active Reading from Chapter 2 in order to gain a thorough understanding of the work. It is essential first to understand an author's main points and supporting points in a work before you can summarize them.

Step Two: Be brief; a summary is a condensed form of the work's main ideas. Usually a summary uses about one paragraph for each two or three pages of original text. A rule of thumb is that a summary should be about one-quarter the length of the original work.

Step Three: Write the summary in your own words, not the words of the author. Do not use direct quotations in a summary. Be sure to give page citations and/or publishing information after summarized text if your summary is part of a longer paper.

Cross Reference
See Chapter 19 for how to cite sources.

▶ **TIP**   To avoid writing a summary using the same words or style as the original author, reread one section of the work at a time (a couple of paragraphs to a page or so), and then, while not looking at the original work, write a few lines of summary for the section you read. Then, look at the text again, and ensure your summary includes all of the author's main ideas from that section. It also helps to verbally explain the author's ideas and support to a friend first, using your own words, before you write a paraphrase.

Step Four: Stay objective. Do not offer your opinion. Add no interpretation. Do not agree or disagree with the author: Just summarize objectively. Read over your summary to check for accuracy. Did you represent the author's main ideas without adding your own bias or opinion?

Step Five: In your first sentence, provide the author's full name and the name of the work you are summarizing. The titles of stories, essays, articles, and poems should be presented in quotation marks, and books or play titles should be italicized or underlined. Also, provide a general statement about the topic of the selection.

Step Six: State the author's main idea—the author's overall thesis— using your own words. You can identify the thesis by answering the question, What is the main message of this work?

▶ **NOTE**   This step can be combined with Step Five above. However, your summary of the author's thesis should be in the first or second sentence of your summary.

Step Seven: Summaries longer than 200 words should be divided into two or more paragraphs. Use a natural break or change of main idea focus to decide on where paragraph breaks should occur; add a transitional word, phrase, or sentence if you break your summary into two or more paragraphs.

Step Eight: Evaluate, revise, and edit the summary. Go back and reread the work while doublechecking your summary for accuracy. Check to make sure you covered all the main ideas or arguments and all the main subtopics, and that you haven't included any minor supporting details that are not needed. Check to make sure you consistently used your own words and that you did not offer any judgment or opinion in the summary. Finally, check for grammar errors, spelling errors, and overall sentence variety as well as needed transitions so your summary has a nice flow and doesn't sound choppy.

▶ **TIP**   Try putting your summary away for a day or two. Then come back to it, and *read it aloud*. Listen to make sure that it flows smoothly and captures the author's main ideas in a clear and accurate way.

▶ **NOTE**   Some instructors will ask for a summary assignment that *begins* with pure summary and then adds the element of critical analysis *after* summarizing the assigned reading. Most assignments that require analyzing an assigned reading usually require some amount of summary and then critical analysis. See the section Combining Summary and Analysis on p. 334 for further information.

Here is a sample summary of Greg Critser's article "Supersize Me" from Chapter 22. Read the selection carefully before reading this summary. Then note how the summary keeps the same order of ideas as the article, provides the major ideas and the examples used for support of those ideas, remains objective in its presentation of the ideas, and uses transitions to flow smoothly from one idea to the next.

Sample Summary

Greg Critser's article "Supersize Me" defines and gives the history of the supersize craze and how it began as a way for fast-food executives to increase their profits and has now spread into other aspects of American society. Critser describes how David Wallerstein, a McDonald's executive, came to the realization that people want to know they are getting more for their money and would be willing to pay more for supersized meal deals. After surveying customer behavior in a Chicago-area McDonalds's, Wallerstein presented his findings to Ray Kroc, McDonald's founder. Wallerstein's findings were that consumers were eating the entire bag of French fries and then they would look like they wanted more. Wallerstein realized that people did not want to appear gluttonous but would be happy to pay a little more and get bigger portions, so he increased the size of portions and raised the cost slightly so customers would see this move as a bargain.

Finally, Kroc agreed to serve supersized portions, and, after only months, sales were up, which meant profits were up. Then, Max Cooper, another McDonald's executive, built on Wallerstein's idea by packaging a burger, fries, and drink at a cost less than if all three were bought separately: what is called the value meal now. His original thoughts were to cut costs or prices, but, in the end, packaging a meal to make consumers think they were getting a deal is what turned a profit.

Next, the supersize meal concept spread to other fast-food chains. However, these supersized meals have had an effect on American's eating habits. Recent studies have looked at our culture and eating habits including appetite, meal size, and caloric intake. The studies are finding that appetites increased when larger portions were introduced. Finally, according to Critser, the supersize obsession has spread to other aspects of American society: The craze of buying large has spread to homes, clothes, and vehicles. Consumers now go by the adage that bigger is better.

Use this checklist to ensure that you have accurately summarized an article, essay, or textbook chapter.

CHECKLIST FOR A GOOD SUMMARY

Check to make sure that:

1. You summarized the ideas in the original work in the same order they were presented.

2. The summary includes all of the main ideas and examples for support from the passage.

3. The summary is in your own words and there are no significant phrases that were in the original passage (no direct quotes, even partial quotes).

4. The summary is accurate in its condensing of the original material's ideas and you have not added any reaction to or opinion of the material (the summary is objective).

5. You have included the author's name and the name of the original piece and included a citation at the end of your summary of the article if it is part of a paper you are writing and not a stand-alone summary.

ACTIVITY 17-2   Summarizing

Directions: *Pick a reading from another text or from Chapter 22 (or your instructor might assign a reading for you to summarize), and, on a separate sheet of paper, summarize it, following the Eight Steps for Writing a Summary.*

▶ **NOTE**   *You may want to use the T-KED reading system as you read or the Six Steps for Active Reading from Chapter 2 for a thorough understanding of the material: You must completely comprehend a reading before you can accurately summarize it. Then, in the lines provided, explain what effect following this process of summarizing had on your overall understanding of the original work.*   Answers will vary.

_____

_____

_____

_____

LO 3   COMBINING SUMMARY AND ANALYSIS

Cross Reference
Review Chapter 1 for more explanation of the terms *analysis* and *interpretation*.

After you have mastered summarizing an original work using your own words, you are ready to analyze the meaning and significance of the piece. A **summary** explains *what* the author is saying; an **analysis** explains *what he or she means*.

APPLYING CRITICAL THINKING

| PURPOSE | IDEAS | SUPPORT | ASSUMPTIONS BIASES | CONCLUSIONS | POINT OF VIEW | ANALYSIS |

Summary versus Analysis: Know Your Purpose

Summary and ***analysis*** are two very different skills. In a *summary*, you restate in a condensed form what an author says in an article, essay, or other piece of writing using your own words without adding interpretation, commentary, or opinions on the material. *Analysis* involves using your critical thinking skills to *interpret* the important ideas in a piece of writing and to critique the techniques an author uses to present them. Some assignments only require you to summarize assigned material, while others do not require any summary and focus only on analysis and interpretation of the message in an assigned reading. Some assignments, however, require a synthesis of both skills.

To analyze a work well, you need to include some summary of the original ideas and arguments in an unbiased (fair) way. Then you add your own opinion and engage your analytical skills to interpret the direct and implied messages and to critique the author's techniques and style choices. You learned how to write an unbiased summary of an article, textbook chapter, or story earlier in this chapter using the Eight Steps for Writing a Summary (p. 330). Here are two additional steps that you would use after completing the first eight, in order to add analysis to your summary.

Steps 9 and 10 for Writing Critical Analysis

Step Nine: Interpret the language and techniques used by the author to make his or her point. Use specific examples from the text to illustrate your interpretation or to demonstrate the writing or style choices the author has made and what effect those have on the reader and on delivering the message(s) in the writing. See The Ice Cream Sandwich: Framing Facts and Sources on p. 336 for information on how to integrate paraphrases, summaries, or quotations into your analysis.

Step Ten: Analyze the author's purpose in the piece. What are his or her main messages? What are the direct messages or points made, and what indirect messages are implied? What are his or her biases?

Here is a paragraph that uses Steps 9 and 10 to add critical analysis to the end of the summary of Critser's article on page 328.

Sample Critical Analysis

Critser's argument that changing the portion size of McDonald's items has led to an increase in people's appetite is a frightening concept. He argues that as the portions increase, so do appetites (Critser 2). The more that people are offered, the hungrier they seem to be. It is a never-ending cycle. Now the supersize portions are bigger than ever, with more calories per value meal than in any time in McDonald's history. I agree that with this increase in portion size comes an increase in appetite, but more than that, there's an increase in acceptance of overeating in America. Critser's article "Supersize Me" captures a serious problem in the American fast-food industry that needs to be addressed.

ACTIVITY 17-3   Summary and Analysis

Directions: *Choose one of the readings from Chapter 22 and write a two-paragraph critique of it that includes both a summary of the main ideas and specific analysis and critical responses to the ideas in the reading (The Eight Steps plus Steps Nine and Ten—summary plus critical analysis). After you've finished, describe below what effect the process of summarizing and analyzing this reading had on your overall comprehension of the author's ideas.* Answers will vary.

_____

_____

_____

_____

_____

ACTIVITY 17-4   Adding Analysis

Directions: *Review the summary you wrote for Activity 17-2, and add Steps Nine and Ten to make it a summary with critical analysis. After you finish, describe below how your thinking process was different from what it was when you were writing pure summary. How did you have to think differently in order to add analysis?* Answers will vary.

_____

_____

_____

_____

LO 4   THE ICE CREAM SANDWICH: FRAMING FACTS AND SOURCES

The ice cream sandwich system that was briefly described in Chapter 4 is a great technique to help you create analytical frames for your text references. The ice cream sandwich concept is the building block for good analytical writing. Whenever you are given an assignment that involves text analysis, use this ice cream sandwich idea to ensure that each time you bring in a text reference (a paraphrase, summary, or a direct quote), you frame it with your own analytical interpretation of what is being said by the author and your analysis of the significance and the implied or directly stated message(s) of

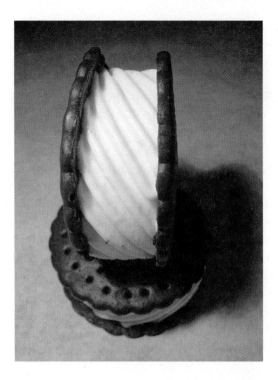

the author. You should also critique the author's technique (style, writing, tone, and language) and choices for how his or her point(s) were developed or crafted.

The Ice Cream Sandwich at a Glance

Top Cookie: A sentence or two to introduce the point you want to make or critique

Ice Cream Filling: The text reference that supports your point. Be sure to put summaries and paraphrases into a sentence of your own:

- Summary
- Paraphrase → plus page number (in parentheses)
- Direct quote

Bottom Cookie: Interpretation and analysis

- Interpretation (what is being said—define key terms when necessary)
- Analysis (what the messages are and a critique of the author's ideas, writing style, or techniques)

Top Cookie (introduction): Start with a sentence or two that introduces the point you want to make using the author for support, or a point you want to critique using an example from the author.

> **Example:** Kim Smith feels that the influence of pop culture over young minds is unavoidable, and she doesn't hold much hope of teens breaking away from this influence.

Ice Cream Filling (paraphrase, summary, or quotation): After introducing the concept you will be discussing, bring in a specific idea or example from the author in the form of a paraphrase, summary, or direct quote from the reading. A paraphrased line or passage or a summarized idea or section from the reading can be integrated into your own sentence, but you need to put in a page number citation after the part of your paragraph that was paraphrased or summarized. If you use a direct quotation from the reading, it can't float in the paper by itself: Attach it to what you are saying. There are three ways to weave a **quote** into your own sentence correctly:

1. **Use a tag line.**

   > **Example:** Kim Smith claims, "The infiltration of pop culture is inevitable" (22).

2. **Weave the quotation into a sentence of your own:**

   > **Example:** We find that the "infiltration of pop culture" (Smith 22) is destined to happen.

3. **Set up the quote with an analytical sentence of your own,** and then use a colon before you provide the quote to illustrate your point:

   > **Example:** The process is inevitable in American pop culture: "Teens will always be influenced by the media machine" (Smith 23).

Then be sure to add a *citation* in the assigned documentation format.

▶ **NOTE**   The punctuation goes outside the parentheses.

Bottom Cookie (analysis): Analytically interpret what the paraphrased, summarized, or quoted passage from the author is saying, making sure to break down each part of a complex quote and defining terms when needed. Then, give an *analytical response* to the idea the

Cross Reference
See Chapter 19 for a detailed explanation of the MLA documentation format.

quote is making: Agree with, disagree with, elaborate on, or critique the ideas or the logic of the arguments.

> **Example:**
>
> **Analytical interpretation:** Smith is saying that it is natural and predictable that the ideas of popular culture will seep into the tastes and values of teenagers.
>
> **Analytical response:** However, she doesn't say whether or not it is a positive phenomenon or if there is a way to fight the effects of this infiltration.

ACTIVITY 17-5   Analytical Ice Cream Sandwich Exercise

Directions: *Pick a one- to two-sentence direct quotation from one of the readings included in this text and write a full analytical Ice Cream Sandwich for that quote.* Answers will vary.

Top Cookie:

_____

_____

Ice Cream Filling (the quote itself):

_____

_____

Add the page number citation: (_____).

Bottom Cookie:

Analytical interpretation: _____

_____

Analytical reaction and/or critique: _____

_____

ACTIVITY 17-6   Creating Ice Cream Sandwiches in Essays

Directions: *Choose a reading from Chapter 22 or another article that you have found or that your instructor has assigned, and write a short essay that includes a summary of the reading and a critical analysis. Make sure that the thesis defines the main message/purpose of the reading, and make sure to include at least one "ice cream sandwich" in each body paragraph.*

To check your progress in meeting this chapter's objectives, log in to www .mywritinglab.com, go to the **Study Plan** tab, click on **Using Sources with Integrity** and choose **Summary Writing** from the list of subtopics. Read and view the resources in the **Review Materials** section, and then complete the **Recall**, **Apply**, and **Write** sets in the **Activities** section.

Finding, Evaluating, and Using Sources

THINKING CRITICALLY

Look at the picture above. Then answer the questions that follow.

1. How do you think using sources can help your essays?

_____

_____

2. What cautions do you think you need to exercise when using sources?

_____

_____

LO 1 CRITICAL THINKING AND THE RESEARCH PROCESS

Often, writing for college, your workplace, or even for the general public involves conducting research and adding sources to a paper to support your thesis. Depending on your purpose and target audience, you will adjust your research process and writing style. Most documented papers include both primary and secondary sources.

Primary sources are original or first-hand materials. They include speeches, first-hand accounts of events, stories, essays, poems, novels, autobiographies, journals, blogs, and e-mails. If you conduct interviews, studies, or surveys, these also count as primary sources, as do poetry, fiction, or artwork you create yourself. **Secondary sources** consist of information written about primary sources. They include summaries, bibliographies, encyclopedia entries, news articles about events, commentaries such as reviews or critiques, and any other material studied and/or interpreted by others.

Using primary sources is essential in your research process, as they provide direct information on your topic. Using secondary sources is also important. However, this means using information from other writers, so be especially aware of their biases, and use your critical thinking skills to evaluate the credibility of their interpretations and evaluations (see Finding, Evaluating, and Integrating Sources later in this chapter).

LO 2 Documented Papers and Research Papers

A **documented paper** requires you to use secondary sources to support and document your essay's arguments and conclusions. You use sources to strengthen and support your own ideas. You first write your own arguments and ideas and then you research ideas and support to illustrate them.

> **Documented paper:** Write your own arguments/conclusion →
> research for support → integrate sources

A **research paper's** purpose, in contrast, is to summarize and present secondary sources in order to draw conclusions from them or to inform your readers about a specific subject. A research paper's main purpose is to provide answers to a research question (or set of questions) designed by you or assigned by your instructor. For instance, you might begin with the question, "What is acid rain, and why do we need to know about it?"

Research paper: Question(s) → research information/answers → conclusion(s)/findings

The nature of your assignment and the goals of your essay dictate the role of secondary research in your paper. Is your purpose to argue your own viewpoint and conclusions and bring in experts to back up your arguments? Or are you using secondary research to inform your audience and present facts and information? Or are you doing both? Even when your paper is research based, you need to draw conclusions based on the research you gathered. You can begin with an argument and then research for support, or you can begin with a question, research answers, and present your conclusions.

BEFORE STARTING RESEARCH

When you begin the process of writing a documented or research paper, spend some time thinking about what you want to accomplish and the assumptions and biases you already have on the subject. Ask yourself the following questions before you begin your research:

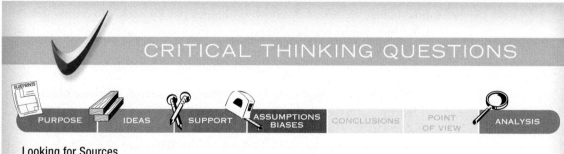

CRITICAL THINKING QUESTIONS

BLUEPRINTS   PURPOSE   IDEAS   SUPPORT   ASSUMPTIONS BIASES   CONCLUSIONS   POINT OF VIEW   ANALYSIS

Looking for Sources

1. What do I want to explain, show, or prove related to my topic? What are my goals? What is my **purpose**?
2. What information, **ideas**, and **support** do I need to develop my argument?
3. What concepts will I need to define in this paper?
4. How shall I assess the **assumptions and biases** of the sources I use?
5. Where should I look for the kinds of information I need, and how will I know if those sources are reliable? How do I **analyze** them?

LO3 FINDING, EVALUATING, AND INTEGRATING SOURCES

When you conduct research, you first need to decide how and where to find the sources you need. Then, you need to evaluate whether those sources, and the information they provide, are reliable and credible. Finally, you need to integrate the sources into your paper and document them correctly.

Finding Sources

These days, students are fortunate to have easy access, at home or on campus, to an amazing source of information: the Internet. However, don't forget that some of the old-fashioned techniques for finding sources still have merit. Your campus or local library, databases, and personal interviews are all excellent resources, too.

Libraries

Due to the seductive powers of the Internet and the ease of online research, many students have forgotten the value of a good library. Books and reference texts (such as specialized dictionaries and encyclopedias) as well as periodicals, magazines, and newspapers are a treasure that you'll find in any library. But libraries also hold valuable collections of DVD, CD-ROM, print, and database resources. Moreover, libraries pay for access to online databases that you might not be able to access from your home computer or would be charged for doing so.

Libraries offer two major options that can make your research easier:

1. **Web sites designed to help you efficiently search all their holdings (print, CD-ROM, database, online subscriptions, and so on).** Often, you can access your college library's Web site from home, using your student ID and password. College library Web sites also include helpful links to other online resources that you might not have found on your own. Both college and local library Web sites have search engines designed to help you customize a search through their holdings (and even the holdings of other local libraries in your area) for the topic you are writing about. Another common feature on a library Web site is an Ask a Librarian link that will allow you to post questions to the librarian on duty, who will get back to you with help.

2. **Helpful staff and trained research librarians who are expert at customized searches and can help you find what you are looking for in a fraction of the time it would take you on your own.** It's not cheating to get help from your librarians: That's what they're there for. Most of

the time they are eager, like library detectives, to help you dig for the perfect sources for your topic. They can even help you narrow and fine-tune the scope of your topic and the purpose for your research. It helps to have completed your brainstorming and have a preliminary outline of ideas for your paper before you visit your local or college librarian. You can also check to see if your college or local libraries have online access to librarians so that you can e-mail questions from home.

Databases

Databases are collections of information. They can be available on CD-ROMs and stored in libraries, or they can be online databases, accessible through your library's subscription service. Go to your local and college libraries to check which databases they subscribe to (or check online on their Web sites). The value of databases is that they are field or subject specialized and have search functions that allow for quick and easy access to reliable, credible sources for your paper. For instance, Infotrac is a database that provides articles on academic subjects either by a subject search or by an author search. All college libraries feature paid subscription services such as Infotrac, ProQuest, EbscoHost, and CQ Researcher. These resources are the first place you should check, since they are already filtered and established credible sources (unlike what you will have to sort through on the Internet). Ask a librarian at your school which services your library subscribes to.

Interviews with Experts

You can conduct interviews in person, by telephone, or via e-mail with experts on the subject you are writing about. Be sure to check with your instructor first to see if interviews from experts are allowed as a source in your paper. Be sure that the person interviewed is a credible expert in the field or subject. Evaluate your interviewee by asking if that person has the right credentials for the subject you are writing about: What degree does he or she hold? What has he or she published in relation to the subject? Is he or she a known authority on the subject?

The Internet and Search Engines

The Internet puts a wealth of information at your fingertips and is accessible from the comfort of your own home, your campus, or your local coffee shop. The World Wide Web has changed the way we conduct research and has opened up possibilities we never dreamed of. The easiest way to navigate the Web and find sources related to your subject is to use a search engine.

A **search engine** allows you to use key words to search a database or the Web for information on specific topics. Some of the more prominent search engines include the following:

Google (www.google.com)

Google Scholar (www.scholar.google.com)

Yahoo (www.yahoo.com)

AltaVista (www.altavista.com)

Ask.com (www.ask.com)

Bing (www.bing.com)

MSN (www.msn.com)

Dictionary.com (www.dictionary.com)

You can do either a basic search using a key word or phrase, or you can do an **advanced search** that allows you to customize your search and target more specific articles for your paper. All of the sites listed, as well as more specialized discipline-specific databases, provide information on how to search most effectively. For example, to the right of the search box on the Google homepage, there is a link called Advanced Search that takes you to a page where you can focus your search efforts and also learn tips for using the search engine to your advantage. If you get more than 500 "hits" (articles or entries related to the key word or phrase you entered) when you do a basic search on your topic, do an advanced search to narrow the scope of the search to articles that more specifically address your topic.

APPLYING CRITICAL THINKING

| PURPOSE | IDEAS | SUPPORT | ASSUMPTIONS BIASES | CONCLUSIONS | POINT OF VIEW | ANALYSIS |

Use your critical thinking and **analysis** skills when you search on the Internet. The use of the Internet for research has led to some of the most serious errors and academic offenses in student papers. The two most prominent problems that arise from students using the Internet to conduct research are the following:

1. **The use of sources that are not legitimate or credible**.

2. **An increase in plagiarism** (using someone else's ideas or words without giving that person credit), both "accidental" and intentional.

The Internet is a gold mine of legitimate, up-to-date, and easily accessible sources for your paper. However, there are many Web sites, articles, studies, and other sources of information available on the Internet that are not legitimate or are even false. You must be on guard particularly when evaluating a source or study online (see the questions on the next page for evaluating your sources). Throughout the country, instances of plagiarism have increased, in large part due to the ease of having information available at the click of a mouse (see How to Avoid Plagiarism on p. 356).

Cross Reference
See Mark Clayton's "A Whole Lot of Cheatin' Going On" in Chapter 22 for a discussion of plagiarism in colleges nationally.

Sample Hit Page from a Google Search for "Search Engines"

Sign in

Google

Web   Images   Video^New!   News   Maps   **more »**

| search engines | Search |

Advanced Search
Preferences

Web   Results **1 - 10** of about **294,000,000** for search engines. (**0.10** seconds)

Sponsored Link

All Major Search Engines
www.registereverywhere.com   Get more traffic and higher ranking in **search engines**. No monthly fees!

Search Engine Watch: Tips About Internet **Search Engines** & Search ...

Search Engine Watch is the authoritative guide to searching at Internet **search engines** and **search engine** registration and ranking issues.
searchenginewatch.com/ - 56k - Sep 8, 2006 - Cached - Similar pages

Search Engines

Offers free tips, site analysis, optimization, submission and maintenance services. Chicago, Illinois.
www.**searchengines**.com/ - 12k - Cached - Similar pages

Dogpile Web **Search** Home Page

Dogpile.com makes searching the Web easy, because it has all the best **search engines** piled into one. So you get better results from more of the web.
www.dogpile.com/ - 23k - Sep 8, 2006 - Cached - Similar pages

Wikipedia: **Search Engine**

Article in the online collaborative encyclopedia, describing the history and mechanisms of Web **search engines**.
en.wikipedia.org/wiki/**Search**_engine - 54k - Cached - Similar pages

MetaCrawler Web **Search** Home Page

MetaCrawler **Search**. **Search** the **Search Engines**. Including Google, Yahoo!, MSN **Search** and Ask. ...
www.metacrawler.com/ - 24k - Sep 8, 2006 - Cached - Similar pages

Google

Enables users to **search** the Web, Usenet, and images. Features include PageRank, caching and translation of results, and an option to find similar pages.
www.google.com/ - 5k - Sep 8, 2006 - Cached - Similar pages

GO.com - Official Home Page

Discover how GO.com can launch your online experience with **Search**, fun stuff to do, and the latest Sports, News, Entertainment, and Movies from the top ...
www.go.com/?page=Home.html - 58k - Cached - Similar pages

AltaVista

AltaVista provides the most comprehensive **search** experience on the Web! ... **SEARCH**:

Worldwide or Select a country RESULTS IN: All languages ...
www.altavista.com/ - 10k - Cached - Similar pages

Homepage HotBot Web **Search**

Offers a **search** powered by a choice of Google or AskJeeves. There are options to block offensive language, customize **search** results, and skins.
www.hotbot.com/ - 6k - Cached - Similar pages

Search Engines

Features of best **search engines** in table format. ... **Search engines** have become a little bit standardized, allowing us to use some of the same **search** ...
www.lib.berkeley.edu/TeachingLib/Guides/Internet/**SearchEngines**.html - 28k - Cached - Similar pages

Evaluating Potential Sources

Whenever you use research for a paper, you need to be very careful that the sources you have chosen are legitimate. Inaccurate, biased, or even false information is available in all forms of print or electronic material. Indeed, in the age of information we live in, with the prominence of the Internet and the seemingly limitless opportunities for information it offers, you must be more careful than ever to evaluate the sources you find and to engage your critical thinking skills to assess their accuracy and reliability. As an example, many instructors refuse to accept Wikipedia as a source because it allows anyone to add information to the entries posted on its site. Many people, intentionally or otherwise, post misinformation, and corporations have been known to add or change content to make themselves appear in a more favorable light.

Here is a set of questions to use as guidelines for evaluating whether to include specific sources in your documented or research paper. If you answer "no" to any of them, you may want to decide against using the source, or at least check with your campus librarian to see if it is legitimate.

Questions for Checking the Reliability of a Source

1. **Is the source up to date?** Are there more current sources available with the same information? It is essential to use the most up-to-date

and legitimate sources in your paper to support your ideas. If your sources don't have credibility, then neither do you.

2. **Is this a scholarly or academic resource?** You want to check the origin of your source and make sure the information is objective and not slanted in order to sell a product or a particular point of view on a controversial issue. Is the source privately or publicly funded? In general, you are better off using sites that end in .edu (education sites such as college Web sites) or .gov (government resource sites), or sites run by reputable companies or nonprofit organizations as opposed to for-profit .com sites.

3. **Does the author have the correct credentials for writing knowledgeably on this subject?** Do not assume that having an M.D. or Ph.D. automatically gives a person credibility in any field; make sure the author is writing from his or her field of expertise. Check what field the author's degree is in and see if that matches the content of the material. You can also check the job that the expert holds to see if it relates to the subject. You can even conduct a Google or Yahoo search on the author to check his or her background. If the author's background seems unrelated to the subject, then that person is probably not an expert you should use.

4. **If statistics and numbers are included in a source, who commissioned the study or conducted the research?** For instance, if you are researching the effects of tobacco industry advertising on middle school students, you should look for unbiased sources of information and carefully evaluate the accuracy of studies commissioned by the tobacco industry itself.

5. **Can you verify the information contained in a source?** If numbers and statistics are involved, doublecheck the data using one or more other sources.

6. **Does the author provide secondary research of his or her own to support ideas and claims?** Are these sources credible? Choose a few key facts, and run a Google search to test them against what other sources say.

7. **Does the author present different sides of an issue even if strongly advocating a particular stance?** Check your source against others that come up in an Internet search on the subject. Of course, many sources will have a particular bias on a subject, but if a source or author simplifies an issue or doesn't address counterarguments, he or she could be oversimplifying his or her argument, and using it would hurt your credibility.

Again, if you answered "no" to any of these questions, you may want to reject the source. You don't want the sources you've used in your paper to damage your credibility and ideas in any way. Sources should be there only to support and strengthen your claims.

Once you have determined that a source is reliable, you want to ask more specific questions about its content. Here are some questions to ask in order to evaluate whether a source provides unbiased information and/or well-supported arguments.

Questions for Evaluating the Content of a Source

1. What **assumptions** does the author make in his or her arguments?
2. What **biases** are evident in the author's claims and point of view?
3. Who paid for or sponsored the author's research?
4. What **point of view** is the author putting forward?
5. Has he or she included the major counterarguments and objections to the claims he or she is making?

APPLYING CRITICAL THINKING

PURPOSE   IDEAS   SUPPORT   ASSUMPTIONS BIASES   CONCLUSIONS   POINT OF VIEW   ANALYSIS

When you evaluate sources, you look at the strength of the **ideas**, reasoning, **support**, and **conclusions** provided by writers for their arguments. You want to look for examples, reasons, and details that support the points they are making. You need to be aware of their **biases** (personal opinions) and **assumptions** (information they take for granted) that might affect the reliability of their arguments. You also need to consider the counterarguments—what people who argue for a different stand might say against their conclusions on the issues.

Integrating Sources into Your Paper

As you begin to incorporate sources into your writing, be sure that they serve as backup for your own ideas and for the expository purpose of your essay. You want to let expert opinion, statistics, and other valuable nuggets of information you gleaned from your research work for you: Don't let your voice, your purpose, your ideas, and your arguments get lost in the background. The research is support; it should not speak for you.

When you synthesize ideas from sources into your arguments, you should smoothly weave together your own ideas and the quotes, summaries, and paraphrases of the other sources you use to support your ideas. When you blend your ideas with the ideas and support from other sources, you develop the purpose of your paper and the support for your ideas in the most effective way.

Every time you include a piece of information from a secondary source, whether it is a summary (a condensed statement of the author's main ideas in your own words) of an idea, a concept or argument, a paraphrase of a particular section, or a direct quotation (using an author's exact words, whether just a phrase, a whole sentence, or an entire passage) from a source, remember to frame that reference on both sides with your own analytical setup, interpretation, and conclusions.

Cross Reference
See Eight Steps for Writing a Summary, Chapter 17, for more on summary and paraphrase.

The Analytical Ice Cream Sandwich Revisited

The Analytical Ice Cream Sandwich is the building block for good analytical research and documented writing. Whenever you are given an assignment that involves secondary research and analysis of your sources, use it to ensure that each time you bring in a text reference (summary, paraphrase, or direct quote), you frame it with your own analytical interpretation of what is being said by the author and analysis of the significance of the implied or direct message(s) it contains.

You can also use the Analytical Ice Cream Sandwich to critique the techniques (style, writing, tone, and language) the author uses to develop point(s). See Chapter 17, p. 337.

Cross Reference
See the sample documented paper with integrated sources and Ice Cream Sandwiches in Chapter 19.

Twelve Steps for Writing a Research or Documented Paper

The following guidelines will help you work through the process of writing a research paper:

Step One: **Select your subject.** Unless your topic is assigned, pick a subject that interests you. Remember, you'll be working with this subject for the next several weeks. Also, make sure it's a subject that can be researched with relative ease—nothing too obscure.

Step Two: **Prewrite to narrow your subject down to a manageable topic.** Most subjects are too broad to cover in a short research paper and need to be narrowed down through a process of thinking about and fine-tuning one or more aspects of the general subject.

▶ **NOTE**   If you do not know a great deal about your chosen subject, you may have to do Step Three before you can adequately prewrite.

Step Three: **Survey your topic by doing preliminary reading.** Get an overview of your topic by reading background articles and getting a sense of the issues and subtopics related to it. You may need to narrow your topic and the scope of your paper still further after you've done some preliminary research, if you find that your subject is more complex than you anticipated.

Step Four: **Write a preliminary thesis statement.** A good thesis statement presents an argument that can be proved and supported by the facts and information gathered through research. You should have an analytical purpose to prove.

Step Five: **Brainstorm, freewrite, and organize ideas, questions, and subtopics to develop your thesis statement.** Think of this stage as a chance to develop *how* you will go about structuring your paper and what kind of information you will need to find for the subtopics and categories you brainstorm on the basis of your thesis statement.

Step Six: **Prepare a working outline.** Taking the ideas you generated in step five, create a rough outline, and determine the main subheadings for your paper. Ask yourself, *What do I want to say? How will I develop my arguments? What support will I provide?* Be sure to put your preliminary thesis at the top of your outline.

Cross Reference
See sample outline on pp. 119–120.

Step Seven: **Conduct research, and take notes.** Begin researching for sources. Be sure to record all bibliographical information in your notes for each source you locate and decide to use. A brief listing of what is required for books, newspapers, magazines, and Web pages follows. For more detailed information about a variety of sources, see Compiling a Works Cited List on pp. 375–385.

> **Books:** name of authors(s), title of book, place of publication, publisher, year of publication
>
> **Newspapers:** name of author(s), title of article, title of newspaper (name of city and state if local paper), date of publication (day, month, year), edition (if more than one), section and/or page number(s)
>
> **Magazines:** author(s) name, title of article, title of magazine, date (day, month, year), page number(s)
>
> **Web pages:** Note that not all this information will be available for every Web page: name of author(s),

page title, Web site title, publisher or sponsor, date of publication (day, month, year), date of access (day, month, year); if you use a database to access the page, note the name of the database.

▶ **TIP**   Keep your notes sorted alphabetically by the authors' last names to make it easier to create your bibliography or Works Cited page later.

Step Eight: **After research, review your notes carefully** to see if you have any gaps in your research. Use your preliminary thesis and your rough outline to assess your gathered notes. *Go back to research any gaps you've discovered.*

Step Nine: **Re-outline your paper, fine-tuning the structure and organization and modifying your arguments and your thesis (if necessary) on the basis of any newly discovered information.** Add more details to your outline if necessary, noting carefully which sources you will use in which sections of your paper for support of your ideas. In addition to structuring your paper and developing a helpful Table of Contents for your major categories, you will also be planning when and how to use the sources you've found.

Step Ten: **Write the first draft of your research paper using your revised outline.** (Isn't it amazing that your first draft doesn't come until Step Ten of this process? Much of the work for a good research paper happens long before you sit down to write a draft. Procrastination is deadly in the research process.) Your introduction should lead into and then present your thesis (argument). The body of your paper should develop and support your thesis using the sources you have identified. Your conclusion should sum up and reiterate your thesis. Be sure to cite all your sources, using the documentation format required by your instructor, to avoid plagiarism (see How to Avoid Plagiarism on pp. 355–359).

Step Eleven: **Prepare your bibliography or Works Cited page.** Again, check with your instructor. Follow the instructions for the documentation format assigned (see MLA documentation format in Chapter 19; for other formatting styles, refer to the relevant handbooks).

Step Twelve: **Revise, edit, and proofread your paper.** Check for unity, coherence, organization, support, and details, and then fine-tune your introduction, thesis, and conclusion.

Doublecheck format and accuracy in all references (summary, paraphrase, or direct quotes). Check especially for punctuation errors within your citations. Use a dictionary and the spell-checker, and consult the thesaurus to find synonyms for words you have overused. Add transitions where needed within and between paragraphs.

▶ **TIP**   If you can put your draft away for at least two days before doing step twelve, you will see errors you didn't see before and make a clearer and more accurate assessment of your paper. You may want to visit your college's tutoring or writing center to get some objective feedback on your ideas, organization, and use of secondary sources for support (another good reason not to procrastinate in the research process).

Before you start work on your research paper, create a timeline using the following checklist. Write a target date for each task, and then fill in when you actually complete that stage.

TWELVE STEPS CHECKLIST

Due date for your paper (to hand in to instructor): _____

Step One: Select your subject.

Targeted date of completion: _____

Actual date of completion: _____

Step Two: Prewrite to narrow your subject.

Targeted date of completion: _____

Actual date of completion: _____

Step Three: Survey through preliminary reading.

Targeted date of completion: _____

Actual date of completion: _____

Step Four: Write a preliminary thesis statement.

Targeted date of completion: _____

Actual date of completion: _____

Step Five: Brainstorm, freewrite, and organize ideas.

Targeted date of completion: _____

Actual date of completion: _____

Step Six: Prepare a working outline.

Targeted date of completion: _____

Actual date of completion: _____

Step Seven: Conduct research and take notes.

Targeted date of completion: _____

Actual date of completion: _____

Step Eight: Review your notes and check for gaps.

Targeted date of completion: _____

Actual date of completion: _____

Step Nine: Revise your outline and fine-tune content.

Targeted date of completion: _____

Actual date of completion: _____

Step Ten: Write your first draft.

Targeted date of completion: _____

Actual date of completion: _____

Step Eleven: Prepare your bibliography/Works Cited list.

Targeted date of completion: _____

Actual date of completion: _____

Step Twelve: Revise, proofread, and edit your paper.

Targeted date of completion: _____

Actual date of completion: _____

(LO 4) PLAGIARISM

Plagiarism is taking someone else's words, research, or even ideas and using them as if they were your own without giving credit to the original source. Some people are tempted to cheat by the ease of getting information (even full papers) written on any subject from the Internet and intentionally use someone else's work as if it were their own. By doing so, they are committing plagiarism, the most serious and damaging act possible in one's academic career. Even if a person isn't caught cheating immediately, the plagiarized work can be discovered later in his or her academic or professional career with very damaging consequences.

Some people commit "accidental" plagiarism by not correctly documenting and citing the source(s) from which they obtained information. Even if a person does not intend to cheat, this sloppy scholarship can still seriously damage academic credibility. Penalties for plagiarism vary from course to course and campus to campus, and they range from just a failing grade for that particular paper to expulsion from the institution.

Each person's writing style and voice is as unique as one's fingerprints or handwriting. An instructor very quickly gets a sense of your style and voice (and level of writing and vocabulary ability), and when you plagiarize a phrase, sentence, passage, or whole paper, red flags go up immediately in the instructor's mind. All the instructor has to do is plug a suspect phrase—even a partial sentence—into a Google search, and up pops the original source for the article or prewritten essay you plagiarized from. Moreover, most campuses have purchased software designed to spot plagiarism in student essays and automatically search for the original source on the Internet. As the possibilities for plagiarism using the Net increase, so do the methods for spotting those instances. It's just not worth risking your academic (and potentially your professional) career.

How to Avoid Plagiarism

Just buckle down and do the work and the research yourself. If you find a great source that says what you want to say, then use it well in your paper, giving a specific citation for each idea or word used from that source. Let the expert support your own brilliant ideas and arguments; that's more impressive in the long run, anyway.

Avoiding plagiarism starts with being aware of what it is and then taking the precautions necessary to document and cite all your sources, even if you just gained an insight or idea from another person. Take careful notes, and mark direct quotes as well as summarized ideas with the page numbers they came from. In the process of searching for secondary sources, especially when using the Internet, be sure to take detailed notes about the source information of any piece you are even considering using in your paper. Make sure that you use your own words and sentence constructions and even your own style when you paraphrase or summarize the ideas of others and that you credit the original source clearly to avoid plagiarism.

Avoiding "Accidental" Plagiarism

Many students intentionally cheat and copy ideas or words without giving credit to the original author. Some students, though, are guilty of just being ignorant of the rules for citing sources or maybe even of dismissing that nagging feeling that they might be improperly using other people's ideas. Never try to claim ignorance as an excuse. You are in college now; be responsible and scholarly, and always give credit for others' ideas or words. You are stealing someone else's intellectual property when you plagiarize. It is a serious offence with serious consequences. To avoid the type of accidental plagiarism that usually happens when you think you are using sources in a fair way, use the following definitions and guidelines:

Types of Accidental Plagiarism (or at least the types that most students don't realize is plagiarism):

1. **Using the annotated instructor's edition of a course textbook is a form of plagiarism.** With so many textbooks available for sale on the Internet through Amazon, Craigslist, and so on, it is easy to come across an annotated instructor's edition of your course textbook. The annotated instructor's edition has the answers to most of the exercises in your text. The insights that appear in these editions are meant for your instructors only. If you buy an annotated edition of your textbook for any class, reading the sample answers before you write your own answers constitutes cheating and plagiarizing. If you get an instructor's version of a textbook by accident, exchange it immediately for a student edition. If you are caught using an instructor's edition, you will be subject to disciplinary action by the college.

2. **Using words, phrases, visuals, or even *ideas or concepts* from a source you read on the Internet without citing it is plagiarism.** Again, the bottom line is that if you didn't have an idea that you used in your paper *before* you read other sources, then you need to cite the source(s) that gave you that idea—even if you phrase the idea in your own words in your paper. Some students claim that they had a specific idea before they read a source that just happened to have the same ideas. So they say, "Well, I already was thinking that way, or beginning to, before I read that article, so it is just a coincidence." Be careful about this argument though. It is rare for people to have very similar fleshed out ideas. Instead of having to defend the fact that you just "coincidentally" came up with the same idea as that of a noted scholar, why not just cite that scholar and add credibility to your claim? Be careful, too, that the brilliant idea you put in your paper didn't come from something you read a while back: If you learned it from somewhere (no matter how long ago), you need to research that original

"somewhere" and give credit where credit is due. The sole exception is when a fact is "common knowledge." A common-knowledge fact is something that most people can be expected to know. For example, if you mention that George Washington was our first president and that his home was in Mt. Vernon, you wouldn't have to cite a source (unless you didn't know that information before you began your paper). Rule of thumb: When in doubt, always cite the source.

3. **By far, though, the most common form of "accidental" plagiarism is the result of poor paraphrasing skills.** This type of "accidental" plagiarism occurs when students actually cite a source, but the amount of material they use from that source, or the overall writing style—i.e., use of words, phrases, and writing patterns—is too close to the original (without using quotation marks). Be careful about relying too much in your paper on someone else's words or ideas. Basically, if you use too many of the same phrases or words from the original and do not use quotation marks, it is considered plagiarism *even if you cite the source.*

Examples of Attempted Paraphrasing: What Is Plagiarism and Not Plagiarism

The following examples are student attempts to paraphrase an excerpt from Mark Clayton's "A Whole Lot of Cheatin' Going On" (see pages 426–429 for the whole essay). Versions A and B are examples of "accidental plagiarism," and version C is done correctly and is not plagiarism. Study the differences.

Paraphrase Versus Plagiarism

Original Source Excerpt (paragraph 23 from the original article):

Such savvy borrowing may be lost on some educators, but others, like librarians, are catching up. "Students are finding it so easy to use these sources that they will dump them in the middle of the papers without any attribution," says John Ruszkiewicz, an English professor at Texas. "What they don't realize is how readily [professors] can tell the material isn't the student's and how easy it is for instructors to search this material on the Web" (434).

Student Version A → Plagiarism

Students borrowing from the Web may be lost on some educators, but some teachers and librarians are catching up. Some students use chunks of other sources right in the middle of their papers without citations. But what these students often don't realize is how easily professors can tell the material isn't the student's and how the instructors can easily search and find this material on the Web too.

This paraphrase is an example of plagiarism because the student uses many of the same phrases as the original passage and the same overall style and structure as the original author with just a few substitution words or phrases (without using any quotation marks and without citations).

Student Version B—Attempted Paraphrase → But Still Plagiarism

According to Mark Clayton, students borrowing from the Internet may be missed by some teachers, but others are catching it. Students find it easy to use these sources and will put them in their papers without citations or credit. However, they don't realize that professors can tell the material isn't the student's and that it is easy for them to search the Web and find this material too.

This paraphrase is an example of "accidental" plagiarism because the student has combined a couple sentences, substituted a few words, but still has used the same overall structure with minor substitutions and has given a nod to the original author with a tag line but still does not have a proper parenthetical citation anywhere in the paraphrase.

Student Version C—Appropriate Paraphrase → *Not* Plagiarism

According to Mark Clayton's article, "A Whole Lot of Cheatin' Going On," many students are using the Internet to research sources on topics they write about, but they are using these sources in their papers without giving any credit to the original authors. Clayton also points out that teachers and librarians are figuring out what's going on and can recognize when it is not the student's own work. Furthermore, teachers can find the sources themselves on the Internet and prove that the student has plagiarized (434).

This student has paraphrased using his or her own words and sentence constructions, and the student has accurately reflected the author's ideas and cited him correctly both with a tag and a parenthetical citation.

Here are guidelines for recording source information for print, online, and other media sources in your notes:

LO 5 Guidelines for Accurately Recording Source Information

1. **Note the name of the person(s) or organization** who wrote the material or conducted the study.

2. **Write a summary of the information** you may want to use, with specific sections that are particularly relevant paraphrased in more detail (it is best to take notes on the information in your own words—noting the particular page numbers and sections where the summarized and paraphrased information came from).

3. **Write down any exact quotations** that you think you may want to use because they are worded so perfectly that you can't sum up the information better. Be sure to include the exact page number(s) for each direct quotation you record and the full name of the author or the person the author is quoting in the article. Remember, if the author quotes someone else and you decide to use that quotation, then you will need to cite it as an indirect quotation in your paper—see MLA documentation format in Chapter 19.

For Internet-based sources, do the following as well:

4. **Record** where, how, and when you found the Web site.

5. **Record** the complete URL.

6. **Note** where on the site you found the information (page, section number, etc.).

▶ **NOTE**   As you search for sources, remember to consult the checklist earlier in this chapter in order to evaluate their credibility.

ACTIVITY 18-1   Avoiding Plagiarism

Directions: *Go to your library either in person or online and find an academic article or essay. First, use the Guidelines for Accurately Recording Source Information above and write in the correct source documentation on the lines below.*
Answers will vary.

_____

_____

Then, on a separate sheet of paper, either summarize the article in one or two paragraphs of your own words, or paraphrase one paragraph of it. After you have summarized or paraphrased, go back over your draft to make sure that you have used your own words, style, and sentence constructions, not those of the original author. Report your findings here.

_____

_____

_____

_____

To check your progress in meeting this chapter's objectives, log in to www .mywritinglab.com, go to the **Study Plan** tab, click on **Using Sources with Integrity** and choose **Research Process** from the list of subtopics. Read and view the resources in the **Review Materials** section, and then complete the **Recall**, **Apply**, and **Write** sets in the **Activities** section.

19 Documentation:
Using Modern Language Association (MLA) Format

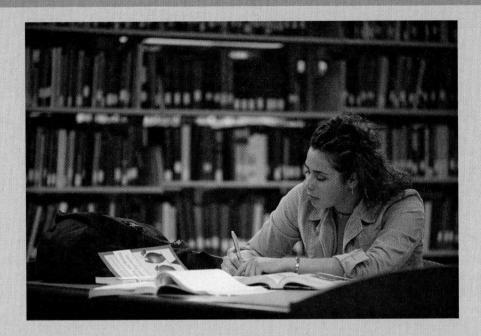

THINKING CRITICALLY

Look at the picture above. Then answer the questions that follow.

1. Do you think it is important to cite sources in a paper when you use them? Why, or why not?

   _____

   _____

2. Do you think it is helpful to use a consistent format for citing sources in a paper? Why, or why not?

   _____

   _____

LO 1 USING MODERN LANGUAGE ASSOCIATION (MLA) FORMAT

MLA style is the standard documentation format used in the United States for writing in English and the humanities (literature, philosophy, history, art, etc.). There are several other documentation styles used by various disciplines and publishers. For instance, APA (American Psychological Association) is the standard for writing in the social sciences, psychology, sociology, criminology, health sciences, business, economics, and some education departments. (For guidelines on how to use APA style, see the *Publication Manual of the American Psychological Association*, or search for APA guidelines online.) Since most English courses and courses in the humanities assign MLA style for documenting sources, this text includes an overview of that system.

Following is a brief introduction to using MLA format. For a more detailed and complete description of MLA style, consult the *MLA Handbook for Writers of Research Papers*, due out in a seventh edition in spring 2009, or a current writer's handbook that includes a full section on MLA documentation format. You can also access information on MLA format online. Go to www.mla.org or search for "MLA format" using a search engine such as www.google.com to find MLA guidelines, tips, and software that will help you format a paper using MLA guidelines and that includes templates for the Works Cited page. The description of MLA style shown here includes the updates published in the *MLA Style Manual and Guide to Scholarly Publishing*, 3rd edition (2008).

The three main principles of MLA format include the use of in-text citations, endnotes, and a Works Cited list that provides detailed publishing information for each source cited in the body of the paper.

LO 2 Formatting Your Paper

Here is an outline of the general MLA guidelines for formatting a paper:

Paper: Use standard 8.5″ × 11″ paper with margins of 1 inch on all sides.

Font: The preferred font for MLA is 12 point, usually Times Roman or Courier (check with your instructor for a preference).

Spacing: Double space throughout the paper, including the title page, Works Cited list, and endnotes page.

Numbering: Number all pages, including the first page, with a heading that includes your last name and the page number, like this: Garcia 8. Place this heading in the upper right corner of each page, including the Works Cited page, half an inch from the top of the page.

▶ **NOTE** Use the "header/footer" feature of your word processing program to set these preferences.

Titles: Italicize the titles of books when using MLA style. For shorter works such as magazine articles and short stories, use quotation marks around titles.

Title page: Do not create a separate title page when using MLA format unless your instructor requests one, in which case get specific formatting directions. In general, a basic title page should be in 12-point font; include the title about ⅓ of the way down the page, followed by your full name, the class name, the instructor's name, and the date. All of this information should be centered and double spaced.

First page: The standard MLA title page is the first page of the paper typed as follows: In the top left corner, type your full name, your instructor's name, the course name, and the date. Double space these lines. Double space again, and then center your paper's title. Capitalize the first, last, and all significant words in the title. Do not italicize your title, and only use italics or quotation marks if you are including the name of another published work in your title, for instance:

Turmoil in the Minds of the Characters from *The Sound and the Fury*

Double space all titles longer than one line. If you have a title and a subtitle, separate the title from the subtitle with a colon, for instance:

Speaking Havoc: Turmoil in the Minds of the Characters from *The Sound and the Fury*

Tables and figures: Label all tables numerically (e.g., Table 1, Table 2, etc.), and always include a short caption (e.g., A Rise in Insanity Cases in the 1890s). Label all images, drawings, and other nontextual material numerically (e.g., Fig. 1, Fig. 2, etc.), and always include a short caption (e.g., A Typical View from the Asylum Window).

WORD PROCESSING

TYPING FORMAT FOR ESSAYS

Paper	8½ × 11 inch white paper.
Line spacing	Use double spacing through the entire paper, including heading and title—with no extra spaces between them or between paragraphs.
Margins	Leave one-inch margins at the top, bottom, and both sides of the paper. Justify left margins, but, unless otherwise requested, do not justify right margins.
Titles	Modern Language Association (MLA) format does not require a title page (if your instructor requests a title page, get instructions for the desired format).
	If your instructor does not want a title page, then leave a one-inch margin at the top of the first page; and on the left-hand side at the top, place your full name, your instructor's name, the course name and number, and the date submitted. Start each item on a separate line. See the sample paper in correct MLA format at the end of this chapter (pp. 386–391).
	Then, press the return button once (remain in double space), and center the title. In the title, capitalize the first word, last word, and all words in between, unless they are an article or a preposition.
	If you have a title and a subtitle, use a colon between the title and the subtitle.
	Do not make the title bold or increase the font size.
	Do not underline your title or use italics or quotation marks unless citing the title of another work (see Italics on next page). See the sample title format in the model paper at the end of this chapter.
Page numbering	Page numbers should be in the upper right corner of each page, one-half inch from the top of your page and flush with the right margin. Include your last name, a space, and then the page number. Use the headers and footers function on your computer if using word processing.
	Do not put in a comma or *p.* or *page* between your last name and the page number; just one space should separate them.
Fonts	Use 10- to 12-point type and a standard-style font (fonts most commonly used include Times New Roman, Arial,

Helvetica, Courier, and Palatino). Check with your instructor for particular preferences.

How to use . . .

Italics	Use italics for the titles of the following sources: books, films, journals or magazines, book-length poems, Web sites, online databases, television and radio broadcasts, CDs, record albums, performances, and works of art.
Tabs/ indentations	Indent five spaces (one tab) every time you start a new paragraph (including in dialogue), with no extra spaces between paragraphs. Indent 10 spaces when inserting a block quotation of more than four lines (see page 367).
Spacing/ punctuation	**End punctuation** (periods, question marks, and exclamation marks): Insert no space before the mark, and type one space after.
	Commas, semicolons, colons: Insert no space before the mark, and type one space after it.
	Parentheses, brackets, and quotation marks: Insert one space before the opening mark and one space after the closing mark.
	Hyphens and dashes: Do not insert a space on either side.
	Ellipses: Insert one space before the first period. The exception is when a complete sentence is followed by an ellipsis. In that case, the period that ends the sentence is placed before the ellipsis, with no space before it (since it is end punctuation). Insert one space between each of the three periods that form the ellipsis. After the ellipsis, insert one space. The only time you don't insert a space afterward is when a closing quotation mark comes next. In that case, there is no space after the last period in the ellipsis.
	Slashes: When using a slash to separate lines of poetry, insert a space on both sides of the slash. When using a slash between two words (e.g., either/or), do not insert any spaces.
Visuals in your document	Some papers, especially papers written for non-English courses across the curriculum, will require you to add visuals such as charts, graphs, or even photographs. If so, be sure to lay out the visuals in a clear format with a text explanation below the visual. See Chapter 20, Analyzing Visuals, for types of visuals and techniques for writing about them.

Five Word Processing Tips

Make friends with your computer! The best way to make typing your documents on a computer easier is to practice and take advantage of the many shortcuts computers offer. Here are five tips to help make your experience go more smoothly.

1. **Save often, and back up your files.** Back up your files! Save them on your hard drive and on a separate disk, memory stick, or CD. You may even want to send them to yourself as an e-mail attachment in case of an emergency. Be sure to *save your document every five minutes* or so to avoid losing it in case of a power outage or other disaster.

2. **Label all documents carefully.** *Create an effective folder system* to store your files, and label them as specifically as possible. Create a folder for each of your classes. Then, label each document for each assignment and even assignment drafts that you've created for that course:

   Folder: English 101

   > **Document 1:** Narration Essay Draft, 5-23-10

   > **Document 2:** Final Narration Essay Draft, 5-28-10

   Include a brief description of the assignment and the draft date of each document.

3. **Control AutoFormat.** You can decide if you want to use AutoFormat or if you want to turn it off. It is there to work for you, not to work against you (check in the Format drop-down menu for the AutoFormat function). Go to your Edit button and click Undo Autoformat if it is doing things you don't want it to do.

4. **Get to know your toolbar.** Take the time to take a thorough tour of your toolbar—it's designed to help you.

5. **Use spell-check and grammar check.** However, don't completely trust these tools; they are not perfect, so doublecheck anything you're not certain about in a dictionary and a grammar handbook. Remember, spell-check will always give you a correctly spelled word, but it may not be the word you want at all.

Cross Reference

See Chapter 29 for more tips on using spell-check.

Example: I took a *brake* from work today.

[The italicized word should be "break."]

Finally, always print an extra copy of your final draft, and keep a spare copy for yourself (even the most dedicated instructors have lost essays—it is your responsibility to have a backup copy). Before you submit your work, do a last-minute check through the hard copy for spelling and typo errors, overall format, and the quality of the printing before submitting the essay.

Incorporating Quotations

All quotations must be cited. This means you need to include the last name of the author and the page number(s) of the work the quoted information comes from in parentheses immediately after the quotation. (However, online sources often don't include page numbers. See page 374.) In general, end punctuation goes *after* the parenthetical citation, except in the case of a long quotation that is set off in a block without quotation marks. (See In-Text Citations on pp. 369–375 for further details.)

Quotations from Prose

Four lines or less: If a quotation is four lines or less in length, include the lines within the body of the text, surrounded by double quotation marks. If the quotation includes a quotation from someone else within it, use single quotation marks to indicate where the original double quotation marks were. Provide a parenthetical citation at the end of the quotation, before the period.

Single quotation

When Daniel Meier speaks of his job as a teacher of small children, he writes, "My work is not traditional male work. It's not a singular pursuit" (91).

Quotation within a quotation

According to Greg Critser, author of "Supersize Me," the founder of McDonald's was at first reluctant to supersize: "Wallerstein could not convince Ray Kroc, McDonald's founder, to sign on to the idea. . . . 'If people want more fries,' Kroc would say, 'then they can buy two bags'" (98).

More than four lines (block quotation): If a quotation is more than four lines in length, set it off from the main body of the text in an indented block form one inch or 10 spaces from the left margin, double spaced, and do not use quotation marks. Place the parenthetical citation after the period in a long quotation.

Block quotation

George Orwell, in "A Hanging," writes,

> One prisoner had been brought out of his cell. He was a Hindu, a puny wisp of a man, with a shaven head and vague liquid eyes. He had a thick, sprouting moustache, absurdly too big for his body, rather like the moustache of a comic man on the films. Six tall Indian warders were guarding him and getting him ready for the gallows. Two of them stood by with rifles and fixed bayonets, while the others handcuffed him, passed a chain through his handcuffs and fixed it to their belts, and lashed his arms tight to his sides. (2)

Quotations from Poetry

Three lines or less: If you are quoting three lines or less from a poem, include the lines within the body of the text, with each line break indicated by a slash with a space on either side of it. The parenthetical citation should be placed *before* the final period. In the citation include the numbers of the lines you are quoting. The first time you do this, include the word *line* or *lines* before the number(s). For subsequent citations, just include the line number(s).

Example

In Madeline DeFrees's poem "Balancing Acts," she writes, "At 47, Hope's driven to find her feet in construction. / She crawls the hip roof of her house like a cat burglar" (21).

Three lines or more: If you are quoting three lines or more from a poem, set the quotation off from the main text in an indented block form one inch or 10 spaces from the left margin, double spaced, and do not use quotation marks. The parenthetical citation should follow the final period.

Example

In Edna St. Vincent Millay's poem "To Elinor Wylie (in answer to a question about her)," she writes,

> Oh, she was beautiful in every part!—
> The auburn hair that bound the subtle brain;
> The lovely mouth cut clear by wit and pain,
> Uttering oaths and nonsense, uttering art
> In casual speech and curving at the smart (1–5)

Indicating Editorial Information

Sometimes when you are quoting writers and citing information, you need to insert notes to explain some of the information or to note existing errors within the quoted material. Certain conventions for doing this are outlined below.

Indicating errors in an original source: If there is an error in a quotation you are using from a primary or secondary source (grammar, spelling, etc.), indicate you are aware of the error by placing the word "sic" (Latin for "thus") in brackets immediately after it, so your readers will know it is not your error.

Omitting words, phrases, or sentences from a direct quotation: First, be sure that the word(s), phrase(s), or even sentence(s) you are omitting from the direct quotation does not change the author's intended meaning. Then use the following guidelines for how to indicate what information has been omitted or changed.

1. To omit one or more words or a part of a sentence from an original quote, use an ellipsis (a series of three periods with spaces between them):

> "Shima deliberated on the color of her gown for the winter ball for over an hour."

becomes

> "Shima deliberated on the color of her gown . . . for over an hour."

2. To omit one or more sentences from a quotation, use an ellipsis with an extra period (a total of 4 dots):

> "Shima deliberated on the color of her gown for the winter ball for over an hour. She couldn't decide whether she wanted to be traditional or a rule breaker. Finally she decided on a very traditional cream-colored gown."

becomes

> "Shima deliberated on the color of her gown for the winter ball for over an hour. . . . Finally she decided on a very traditional cream-colored gown."

3. To insert clarifying words or information: Use brackets around words, phrases, or needed tense changes that must be added within a quotation to provide clarification for the reader or make the tense or form consistent.

> "Kyle and Emily always argue[d] about the choices for dinner."

LO 3 IN-TEXT CITATIONS

For every piece of information, idea, or reference used in your paper that comes from someone other than yourself, whether you are paraphrasing, summarizing, directly quoting, or just alluding to an idea that you gained from someone else, you must include a parenthetical citation. Usually, this means including the name of the author(s) and/or the title of the work and the relevant page number(s) in parentheses immediately after the information you are using. This brief citation refers to a Works Cited list at the end of the paper, which provides the reader with detailed information on each source. However, depending on the source, the exact rules for citation vary. Consult the following list for how to include each in-text citation correctly.

Cross Reference
See Compiling a Works Cited List on pp. 375–85.

▶ **NOTE**   A parenthetical citation is followed by a period, except in the case of a longer quotation that has been indented, in which case the citation follows the period.

Cross Reference
See Incorporating Quotations, p. 367.

Print Sources

Text by One Author

Author named in text: If you name the author in your introduction to a quotation, paraphrase, or summary, include both his or her first and last name the first time you mention him or her in your paper, and include only the page number in the parenthetical citation:

> Mary Clearman Blew describes the setting by saying, "The hills lay bare under the sweep of the galaxy, waiting from the beginning of time until the end" (33).

If you use the author's name again in the body of the text, use only the last name.

Author not named in text: If you do not name the author in the sentence in which you paraphrase, summarize, or quote him or her, then list the last name of the author and the page number of the original source from which it came in your citation:

> A writer describes the setting, saying "The hills lay bare under the sweep of the galaxy, waiting from the beginning of time until the end" (Blew 33).

Text by Two or Three Authors

Authors named in text: If you choose to use two or three authors' names in the body of your sentence to introduce source information, use their full names, in the same order of credit given in the source, and include only the page number(s) in the citation:

> The fishing crew of John Wyman, Bob Williams, and Bill Myers agreed that "there's nothing better than catching the wild Coho salmon after they have made their trek up the river" (44).

Authors not named in text: If you do not name the authors in the body of your text, include their names in the citation. Separate the names of two authors by "and" and the names of three authors by a comma and then an "and"; then add the page number(s) for the quotation or reference:

> The salmon fishers agreed that "there's nothing better than catching the wild Coho salmon after they have made their trek up the river" (Wyman, Williams, and Myers 44).

Text by More Than Three Authors

If a source has more than three authors, you can either list the authors' names in your introduction to the quotation or in the parenthetical citation. Or you can list the first author's last name and the Latin words "et al." (meaning "and others") and then the page number in the parenthetical citation:

> The return "of the wild salmon every summer in Alaska causes a boost in the local economy and a flood in the seafood market of high quality and delicious meal options" (Jordan et al. 226).

Two or More Works by the Same Author

If you use more than one work by the same author, include an abbreviated version of the specific title you are referencing in your in-text citation. Place the shortened title after the author's last name and a comma. Follow the title with the page number.

> When the character first realizes she's in love, she struggles with the emotion: "Your love is newly born, the first page in a blank notebook" (Allende, *Paula* 77).

If you use the author's name in your introductory sentence, do not include it in the parenthetical reference:

> When the character first realizes she's in love, Isabel Allende describes the girl's struggles with the emotion: "Your love is newly born, the first page in a blank notebook" (*Paula* 77).

If you use both the author's name and the title of the work in your introductory sentence, then just put the page number in the citation:

> When the character in *Paula* first realizes she's in love, Isabel Allende describes the girl's struggles with the emotion: "Your love is newly born, the first page in a blank notebook" (77).

Two Different Authors with the Same Last Name

If you are using two or more sources whose authors have the same last name, be sure to include enough additional information in your citations to distinguish between them. You can do so by using their first initials, or by using their whole first names if they share the same first initial: (B. Smith 22) or (Brenda Smith 22).

Works with No Author Listed

If you use a work whose author is not named, include the first one to three words of the title (or the whole title if it is short) in the parentheses followed by the page number(s):

> The "general notion is that people learn abuse only through modeling and there are no genetic factors" ("Abuse as a Cycle" 38).

▶ **NOTE**   Make sure that the one to three words you use to indicate the title are alphabetized the same way in the Works Cited list.

Work from an Anthology

When you quote a selection from an anthology (a quotation from a story, article, essay, or poem from a collection of such works by various authors), cite the name of the author, not the name of the editor of the anthology. The editor and anthology information will be provided in the Works Cited list. For example, if you were quoting Linda Pastan's poem "Marks" from the anthology *Literature: An Introduction to Reading and Writing*, editors Edgar V. Roberts and Henry E. Jacobs, your citation would look like this:

She writes, "My daughter believes / in Pass/Fail and tells me / I pass" (Pastan 814).

Works with Editors or Translators

When you use information from a work that has an editor or translator, but no named author, use the editor's or translator's name in your citation, followed by the page number(s):

The anonymous poem encourages readers to "Live life to its absolute fullest" (Roberts and Jacobs 68).

▶ **NOTE**   In the Works Cited entry, you will indicate that this poem is from an anthology and Roberts and Jacobs are the editors of that anthology (alphabetized by Roberts' last name in your Works Cited list).

▶ **NOTE**   If the work has been translated into English by a translator, but the original author's name is provided, then use the original author's name and only list the translator in the Works Cited entry:

In *One Hundred Years of Solitude*, the character Colonel Aureliano Buendia says, "We leave Macondo in your care . . . try to have it in better shape when we return" (García Márquez 105).

Works by a Corporation, Government Agency, or Other Group Author

If you are referencing a work by a group, use the name of the organization followed by the page reference in the citation. If the organization is mentioned in your introductory sentence, include just the page number(s) in parentheses:

According to a study conducted in 2007 by the Department of Transportation, "Most people who carpool do so less than four times a week" (4).

If the organization is not mentioned in your sentence, include its name and the page number in your parenthetical citation:

In fact, "Most people who carpool do so less than four times a week" (Department of Transportation 4).

Multiple Sources for the Same Piece of Information

If you want to indicate that you have obtained the same information from several different sources, list the last names of the authors in the citation, each followed by the relevant page number and separated by semicolons:

Several studies have proven that child abuse is a cycle with violence passing from parents to children, who, in turn, abuse as parents (Smith 19; Clay 89; Misho 245).

Classic Novels

If you cite a famous literary work that is available in several versions or editions, it is helpful to add the chapter number after the page reference to help readers find the quotation in their edition of the text: (Bronte 47; Ch. 6).

Verse Dramas/Plays

Instead of citing page numbers for plays, give the name of the play in your sentence, and then cite the act, scene, and line numbers, separated by periods in the parenthetical citation. Do not use Roman numerals.

In William Shakespeare's famous play *Hamlet,* the main character, Prince Hamlet, says in apology for his somewhat-accidental murder of Polonius, "Sir, in my heart there was a kind of fighting / That would not let me sleep" (5.2.4–5).

Poetry

If you use the name of the poet in your introductory sentence, then in the citation, list the line number (or numbers):

In T.S. Eliot's poem "The Lovesong of J. Alfred Prufrock," the opening seems like an invitation: "Let us go then, you and I" (1).

If you do not mention the author in your introductory sentence, then cite the author's last name and the line number(s) in your citation:

The narrator in the poem says, "Let us go then, you and I" (Eliot 1).

Indirect Citations

If you use a quotation that originally came from another source (if you quote someone quoting someone else), then use the abbreviation "qtd. in" to illustrate that it is an indirect quote. Use the full name of the person you are quoting in the body of the sentence before the quote and then use the name of the author of the source you are using in the parenthetical citation, preceded by "qtd. in":

> Austin Levors argues that "we are all accountable for the future of our next generation" (qtd. in Blanchard 564).

> ▶ **NOTE**   In the Works Cited page, this entry will be listed alphabetically under the name of Blanchard along with the name of his book or article and the publishing information. The purpose of a Works Cited list is to record sources *you* used, not the sources your sources used.

Reference Entry from a Dictionary or Encyclopedia

If the entry you are referencing does not credit a specific author, then use the title of the entry in your citation:

> Bioluminescence is light produced by a chemical reaction within an organism ("Bioluminescence" 203).

> ▶ **NOTE**   The Works Cited entry will be alphabetized under "Bioluminescence," followed by the name of the encyclopedia or dictionary with publication information.

Sacred/Religious Texts

Since there are different versions and translations of most religious texts, you will need to identify which version you have used in your Works Cited list. In general, though, it is not mandatory to give the version of the religious text you have used in your parenthetical citation; instead, use the book, verse, and line numbers. For instance, for a quotation from the Bible, you could simply put the chapter and verse numbers: (Revelation 10.14). It is also acceptable to include an abbreviated code for the version of the Bible you are citing, for instance (KJV, Genesis 1.1–5). "KJV" stands for King James Version. See the MLA Web site for abbreviations of other Bible versions. Again, be sure to cite all publishing information for the religious text version you used in your Works Cited list.

Electronic Sources

Electronic sources from databases, CD-ROMs, or the Internet must be cited in your paper. Give the author's name(s) if provided; if not, give the title of the material. If the electronic source is paginated, then provide a page number.

Author Named in Source

For electronic sources, if the work has an author and uses page numbers, then use the standard rules for parenthetical citations outlined above:

> Women often forget to take care of themselves when they are pregnant (Anstor C1).

Author Not Named in Source

If the work has no author but does have a title and page numbers, then use a shortened version of the title in the citation:

> People just have a natural sense of what part of the country they should live in for their tastes ("Knowing Where" 38).

Page Numbers Not Included in Source

If the source does not include page numbers but does use paragraph numbers, include the relevant paragraph number(s) in your parenthetical citation. If there are no page or paragraph numbers, just use the author's name in the citation.

> People just have a natural sense of what part of the country they should live in for their tastes ("Knowing Where" par. 5).

No Information Available

If there is no article name, no author, no page numbers or other information and you are using just a fact or statistic from a Web site, then include the address of the Web site in your parenthetical citation:

> It is highly likely that children who were abused by their parents may abuse their own children as well, a "vicious cycle" (www.abuse.com).

Remember, all information you use from any source must be documented so that you avoid plagiarizing and provide your readers with the information necessary to view your sources. Electronic sources are the most commonly plagiarized, often unintentionally, due to a lack of knowledge about how to cite them accurately.

LO 4 COMPILING A WORKS CITED LIST

Every work or idea that you cite parenthetically in your paper must also be included in the Works Cited section at the end of your paper. Here are some guidelines for formatting your Works Cited page using the MLA format.

Formatting Your Works Cited Page

1. Start your list on a new page at the end of your paper, with the title Works Cited centered one inch below the top of the page (but be sure to have your last name and the page number in the right-hand corner as in the other pages of your paper). Do not bold the Works Cited title, put it in quotation marks, or make it a larger font.

2. Insert a double space between the title and the first entry and between and within all subsequent entries.

3. Align the first line of each entry flush with the left margin of the page, and indent each subsequent line of the entry five spaces (one tab) from the margin (sometimes called the "hanging indent format"). Do not number the entries.

4. Alphabetize the Works Cited list by authors' last names. If a work has a corporate or group author, list it alphabetically by the first word of the name of the organization. If a work does not have an author, alphabetize by the first word of the title (but ignore "A," "An," or "The").

5. If you have two or more works by the same author, then use three hyphens "---." in place of the author's name in the second and subsequent entries by the same author.

6. If a work has an editor or translator, be sure to include that information. If a work has a named author, list that name first, then the title, followed by either the abbreviation "Ed." for editor, or "Trans." for translator and then that person's first and last names, followed by a period.

> Allende, Isabel. *Paula*. Trans. Margaret Sayers Peden. Print.

If there is no author, list the name of the editor or translator first, followed by either the abbreviation "ed." or "trans." then the title and the publication information:

> Wafer, Harold, trans. *Gilgamesh*. Weston: Weston, 1969. Print.

Format for the Most Common Works Cited Entries

For source types not included here, check the *MLA Handbook*, MLA Web site, or a composition handbook with a comprehensive MLA section.

Print Sources

Print sources such as books, magazines, journals, and newspapers usually provide thorough publication information. Be sure to follow the guidelines listed below for Works Cited entries for print sources.

Books   There are six basic units of information to include for book entries:

- Names of author(s)
- Book title
- City of publication
- Publisher
- Year of publication
- Medium of publication

1. **Names of author(s):** Provide the author's full name, last name first, followed by a comma, and then the first name (followed by middle initial or name if provided). If there are two or three authors, list all of them, in the same order they appear in the source. For all authors except the first one, write their names in the usual first and last name order. Use a comma and the word "and" between the names of authors. If there are four or more authors, list the first one, last name first, and then use "et al." to identify the other authors. Follow the name of the author(s) with a period and one space.

2. **Title of book:** Provide the complete title, including the subtitle if there is one. Separate the title and subtitle with a colon and a space. Put the title in italics. Capitalize the first, last, and all principal words of the title. Follow the title with a period and one space.

3. **City of publication:** Provide the name of the city of publication (usually found on the title page or copyright page). If more than one city is listed, use the first one listed. For cities outside of the United States that are not well known, add the abbreviation for the country or province. Follow the city of publication with a colon and a space.

4. **Name of publisher:** Provide the name of the publishing company. Shorten the names of publishers by deleting "A," "An," or "The" at the beginning or "Co.," "Inc.," "Pubishers," "Press," "Ltd.," or "Books" at the end. For university presses, change the "University" to "U" and the "Press" to "P": e.g., Harvard UP or U of Oregon P. Use shortened titles for major publishers—for instance, use "Pearson" for "Pearson Education." Follow the name of the publisher with a comma and a space.

5. **Year of publication:** Give the year of publication. If several years are listed, provide the most recent. If no publishing year is listed, then use the most recent copyright listed. End with a period after the year.

6. **Medium of publication:** Add the medium of publication at the end of the entry: Print.

Sample Entries

Book by one author:

> Sedaris, David. *Dress Your Family in Corduroy and Denim*. New York: Little, 2004. Print.

Book by two or three authors: Reverse the name of the first author only:

> McClendon, Ruth, and Leslie Kadis. *Reconciling Relationships and Preserving the Family Business: Tools for Success*. New York: Haworth, 2004. Print.

Book by four or more authors: Name only the first author listed and then add "et al." (for "and others") or you may choose to list all the authors in the order they appear in the original source:

> Durrant, Sam, et al. *Postcolonial Narrative and the Work of Mourning*. Albany: State U of New York P, 2004. Print.

Book with no author (alphabetize by the work's title):

> *New York Public Library American History Desk Reference*. New York: Macmillan, 1997. Print.

Two or more works by the same author: If you have two or more works by the same author, use --- for the author's name for the second book. Alphabetize by the title, for example:

> García Márquez, Gabriel. *Chronicle of a Death Foretold*. Trans. Gregory Rabassa. New York: Avon, 1970. Print.
>
> ---. *One Hundred Years of Solitude*. Trans. Gregory Rabassa. New York: Ballantine, 1982. Print.

Articles from Scholarly Journals Seven basic units of information are needed for journal articles:

- Names of the author(s)
- Title of the article
- Journal name
- Volume/issue number
- Year of publication
- Page number(s) of the article
- Medium of publication

1. **Names of the author(s):** Use the same guidelines for authors as specified in the section on books on p. 377.

2. **Title of article:** Provide the complete title of the article in quotation marks. Include the subtitle if there is one, separated from the main title by a colon and a space. Capitalize the first, last, and all principal words in the title. End the title with a period inside the quotation marks and one space after the last pair of quotation marks.

3. **Name of journal:** Give the full name of the journal, in italics. No punctuation follows (see next step).

4. **Volume (and issue) number:** Provide the volume number and, if there is one, the issue number (separated by a period): e.g., 21.7. No punctuation follows (see next step). Do not include volume and issue numbers for magazines and newspapers.

5. **Year of publication:** Put the year of publication in parentheses after the issue number. Follow the last parenthesis with a colon.

6. **Page numbers:** Provide the page numbers of the article from the journal (beginning and ending pages). End the entry with a period.

7. **Medium of publication:** Add the medium of publication at the end of each entry: Print.

Sample Entry

> Vasishth, Neal. "The Trouble with Pedagogy." *Pedagogical News* 28.6 (2005): 32-46. Print.

Magazine Articles Six basic units of information are needed for magazine articles:

- Names of the author(s)
- Title of the article
- Magazine name
- Day, month, and year of publication
- Page number(s) of the article
- Medium of publication

1. **Names of the author(s):** Use the same guidelines for authors as specified in the section on books on p. 377.

2. **Title of article:** Use the same guidelines as those for the titles of scholarly journal articles above.

3. **Name of magazine:** Give the full name of the magazine, in italics. No punctuation follows (see next step).

4. **Publication date:** Provide the day first (if the magazine you are citing is published more frequently than once a month). Then provide the month and year (no punctuation between them). Months are abbreviated. Put a colon after the date. 22 Feb. 2004:

5. **Page numbers:** Provide the page numbers of the article from the magazine (beginning and ending pages). End the entry with a period.

6. **Medium of publication:** To the end of each entry, add the medium of publication: Print.

Sample Entry

> Haygood, Rachel. "The Complexities of Shadow." *Speed Online* 14 Apr. 2005: 16-25. Print.

Articles, Editorials, and Letters from Newspapers   Six basic units of information are needed for newspaper articles:

- Names of author(s)
- Title of the article
- Newspaper name
- Day, month, and year of publication
- Section letter or number and page number(s) of the article
- Medium of publication

1. **Names of author(s):** Use the same guidelines for authors as specified in the section on books on p. 377.

2. **Title of article:** Use the same guidelines as those for titles of scholarly journal articles on page 378.

3. **Name of newspaper:** Give the full name of the newspaper, in italics. No punctuation follows (see next step).

4. **Day, month, and year of publication:** Provide the day first, then the month and year (no punctuation between them). Abbreviate all months except May, June, and July. Follow the date with a colon: 22 Feb. 2004:

5. **Page number(s):** Provide the section letter (such as A or F) and the page number(s) of the article from the newspaper (beginning and ending pages). End the entry with a period.

6. **Medium of publication:** To the end of each entry add the medium of publication: Print.

Sample Entry

> Haygood, Rachel. "The Complexities of Shadow." *The Monrovia*
> *Times* 14 Apr. 2005: A8. Print.

▶ **NOTE**   If the entry from the newspaper is an editorial, type the
word "Editorial" after the name of the article, followed by a period and
a space. If it is a letter to the editor, type the word "Letter" after the author's name, followed by a period and a space.

Selection from an Anthology   A selection from an anthology (a poem,
story, play, essay, or article) must include the original work's author and title
as well as the name of the anthology and the editor(s) of that anthology.
Here is the information needed in the order it should appear:

1. **Names of the author(s):** Use the same guidelines for authors as specified in the section on books on p. 377.

2. **Title of the selection:** Give the name of the selection in quotation
   marks, followed by a period (period goes inside the quotation marks)
   and a space.

3. **Title of the anthology:** Give the name of the anthology, italicized and
   followed by a period and a space.

4. **Names of the editors:** Provide the name of the editor or editors, preceded by "Ed." for one editor or "Eds." for more than one. Use the regular order for names: first and then last name. Follow with a period
   and a space.

5. **City of publication:** Provide the city of publication, followed by a
   colon and a space.

6. **Name of publisher:** Provide the name of the publisher, followed by a
   comma and a space.

7. **Year of publication:** Give the year of publication, followed by a period
   and a space.

8. **Page numbers:** Give the page numbers for the selection, followed by a
   period.

9. **Medium of publication:** To the end of each entry add the medium of
   publication: Print.

Sample Entry

> Dillon, Kim Jenice. "A Thin Neck to Snap." *Sisterfire: Black*
> *Womanist Fiction and Poetry.* Ed. Charlotte Watson Sherman.
> New York: Harper, 1994. 11-31. Print.

Articles in Reference Books   If the author's name is given, provide that first, then the title of the article in quotation marks, the title of the work it came from (in italics), the name of the editor(s) (preceded by Ed. or Eds.), the number of volumes, and the publication information:

> Scott, Loretta. "George Washington." *Encyclopedia of Presidents*. Ed. Campbell Kingley. 2 vols. New York: Cirius, 2005. Print.

▶ **NOTE**   Do not include page numbers.

If the author is not named, begin the entry with the article title.

> "George Washington." *Encyclopedia of Presidents*. Ed. Campbell Kingley. 2 vols. New York: Cirius, 2005. Print.

Citing an Introduction, Foreword, Preface, or Afterword   If you cite one of these elements in your paper, start with the name of the person who wrote the part you are citing (last name first). This might be the author of the whole work, or a different author who wrote the Introduction or Foreword. Then give the name of the part (e.g., Foreword), followed by a period. Next provide the name of the book (followed by a period), the author of the book (first name first), the publishing information, and the page numbers:

Sample Entry

> Hoene, Jennifer. Introduction. *The Literary Nature of Philosophy*. Sandra Johanson. Boston: New World, 2005. v–xii. Print.

Media Sources

You have to cite information for media the same way as you do for print and electronic sources.

Paintings, Sculptures, or Photographs   State the artist's name first, putting the title of the work in italics. Follow with the year of composition and the medium of composition, such as Photograph or Watercolor. If it belongs to a museum or gallery, list the name and the city:

> Gericault, Theodore. *Raft of the Medusa*. 1819. Oil on Canvas. Musée de Louvre, Paris.

Films   Begin with the title of the film, italicized and followed by a period; then give the name of the director (followed by a period), the name of the distributor (followed by a comma), and the year of release (followed by a period). Add the medium of publication: Film.

> *Blade Runner*. Dir. Ridley Scott. Warner, 1991. Film.

Interviews   If you conduct an interview, specify whether it was an in-person or telephone interview and the date the interview took place:

> Rowling, J.K. Personal interview. 25 June 2005.

If it is a *published interview* conducted by someone else, give the name of the interviewee, the name of the interviewer, the date of the interview, and any other pertinent information (e.g., the call letters of the radio or television station the interview was originally broadcast on or the print publication it appeared in), followed by the medium of publication.

> Wiesel, Elie. Interview with Ted Koppel. *Nightline*. ABC. WABC, New York, 18 Apr. 2002. Television.

Electronic Sources

Three different kinds of electronic sources are databases supplied on CD-ROM or DVD disc, databases accessed online, and Web sites accessed through search engines such as Google. The three sections below discuss each one. When the work you are using is an article or other piece from an online magazine, newspaper, or scholarly article, first refer to the entries for these sources when they appear in print (see pages 376–83 for the basic information to include.)

CD-ROM and DVD Databases   When citing CD-ROM or DVD databases that are accessible through a computer, be sure to list the author's name, if available; the title of the material; the medium of publication (e.g., CD-ROM); the vendor's name; and the date of electronic publication.

> *All Movie Guide*. CD-ROM. Ottawa: Corel, 1996.

> Anstor, Marylee. "Nutrition for Pregant Women." *New York Times* 12 Apr. 1994, late ed.: C1. *New York Times Ondisc*. CD-ROM. UMI-ProQuest. Oct. 1994.

If a CD-ROM is accessed through a periodically published database such as ProQuest, then be sure to include the name of the author, title of the material (in quotation marks), name of the print periodical the material originally appeared in (if applicable), date the material was originally published (if available), page number(s) of the original print article (if available), name of the CD-ROM, publication medium (CD-ROM), name of the database used to access the material, and electronic publication date:

> Levens, Elaine. "Telling the Stories." *Storytellers Inc.* 15 Apr. 2004: 22–26. *Story Magazines Ondisc*. CD-ROM. GRCC-Proquest. Nov. 2005.

Online Databases   When you cite sources from online databases, include as many of the following elements as possible:

1. **Names of author(s):** If the name of the author (or authors) is provided, start the citation with it, last name first.

2. **Name of article or entry:** Provide the title of the piece. Also, if no author is listed for an article, alphabetize the entry by the material's title.

3. **Name of source:** Include the name of the source—magazine, newspaper, etc. Next list the date the material was first published in print using the format day month year.

4. **Page numbers:** If the page numbers of the source are given, place them after the source name and a colon. If pages are all in one sequence of numbers, give them all: for example, 1–10. If page numbers aren't in sequence, give the first page number followed by a plus sign. No space comes between the two: 2+. If no page numbers are listed, use the abbreviation *n. pag.*

5. **Name of database and medium of publication:** Provide the name of the database in italics. Then list the medium of publication: Web.

6. **Date the source was accessed:** Include the date you accessed the source, for example 7 Dec. 2008. Abbreviate the names of all months except May, June, and July.

Sample Entry

> Fargo, Emmanuel. "Why Settle for Second Best?" *Education Review* Mar. 2005: n. pag. *Academic Search Elite*. CD-ROM. Web. 20 May 2006.

Internet: Source from a Web Site   Give as much information as necessary to direct the reader to the original online source. Include all of the following information that is available:

1. **Names of the author(s):** If there is an author credited (or authors) start the citation with it, last name first.

2. **Title of the article:** Provide the full title. If there is no author listed for the material, alphabetize the Works Cited entry under this title.

3. **Name of Web site:** Provide the name of the Web site, in italics, if it is different from the title of the article.

4. **Version or edition number:** If such a number is given, provide it: Rev. ed., for instance, means "revised edition."

5. **Publisher or sponsor of the Web site:** If not given, use the abbreviation n.p. for "no publisher."

6. **Date of publication:** If not given, use the abbreviation n.d. for "no date."

7. **Medium of publication:** Web.

8. **Date of access:** Give the date you accessed the site. Use the day month year format.

9. URL: Only provide the URL for sources that readers won't be able to find using the information provided in the citation. For example, if you type the name of the Web site you are citing in the Google search box, you can go to that site, then use the site search feature to find the particular page you are citing. If you can find the source using a method like this, you don't need to include the URL in your citation.

Sample Entry

> Noveck, Jocelyn. "Madonna: An unlikely inspiration for 50-plus set." *AP News.* Associated Press, 16 Aug. 2008. Web. 18 Aug. 2008.

Again, many professional Web sites and nonprofessional, private Web sites do not provide all the information listed above. The key is to include as many of the nine elements as possible in the same order as they are listed. For complicated or difficult-to-access online sources, go to www.mla.org for more information on citing online and Internet-based sources.

LO 5 ENDNOTES

In general in MLA format, it is best to avoid adding notes with supplementary information in your paper: If it's worth saying, why not put it in the body of your paper? However, you can add endnotes in MLA format (see "Content Notes" in the current edition of the *MLA Handbook* for more details). When you have additional comments or information that you want to include in your paper, but they might interrupt the flow of your ideas, include them in endnotes that have been numbered consecutively throughout your paper. Put the number for the endnote in the body of your paper at the end of the phrase or sentence containing the information you will elaborate upon in the endnote. Place the number after the punctuation mark and raise it slightly above the line, with no space before the number and no punctuation after it:

Even before the fighting broke out, the war had started economically.[1]

Formatting Your Endnotes Page

At the end of your paper, begin a new page with the centered heading Notes (do not put the heading in quotation marks, underline it, or make the font bold or larger). The Notes page is double spaced like the rest of your paper. For each note listed in your paper, list the number and add the note. For each note, indent five spaces from the left margin, raise the number of the note slightly above the line, leave one space, and then write the note. Any lines that carry over from the note should start at the left margin:

Notes

[1]For more details about the economic battles that were taking place at this time, see Colin Mather, *A Time of Unrest* (New York: Marigold, 2004) 64-98. Print.

For more details on using endnotes in MLA and sample Notes pages, go to **www.mla.org** or Section 6.5.1 in the *MLA Handbook* (7th ed.).

Sample Documented Student Paper

Bayne 1

Trina Bayne

Professor Reynolds

English 101

5 May 2008

Plagiarism: The Cost of Too Much Information and Not Enough

Do you know exactly what plagiarism is? Many students do not. Colleges agree that plagiarism, specifically using someone else's words, ideas, or original work as if they were one's own without giving proper credit, is a problem that has only gotten worse due to the ease of finding sources and pre-written term papers on the Internet. Unfortunately, too many students are not given the support they need to know what plagiarism is in the first place and how to avoid it. Colleges and universities should create specialized orientations as well as ongoing workshops to inform students of the causes and effects of plagiarism and to instruct them in the correct ways to use and document sources in their essays and other written and oral work.

Bayne 2

Numerous studies, as well as the experience of professors in the classroom, have indicated that plagiarism is on the rise. Several forms of plagiarism have been growing due to the ease of finding information on the Internet. Indeed, "Technology has made it easier for students to cheat . . . and makes the likelihood of getting caught much lower . . . professors are less likely to be able to locate the incriminating needle in the vastness of the Web's haystack" (Lee 1). Some of the types of plagiarism that students have been committing include using part or all of essays and term papers posted on free essay sites including "freeessays.com" and "cheaterhouse.com," using facts and details found through key word searches and not citing the original source, cutting and pasting passages or entire articles from Internet sources without providing citations or using quotation marks for direct quotes, re-wording quotes using students' own words, claiming the ideas as their own, and not giving the original sources credit. An article titled "Faculty Perceptions of Plagiarism" points out that the rise of Internet plagiarism has "brought these rising statistics to the forefront: 10% of students admitted to engaging in such behavior in 1999, rising to 40% in a 2001 survey in which the majority of students (68%) suggest[ed] this was not a serious issue" (Liddell and Fong 1). This increase shows that students have begun to plagiarize more and more and that their attitudes about plagiarism have become more casual.

Many students do not realize that they have committed plagiarism because they do not know exactly what it is. In general, most students realize that when they copy a passage, word for word, they are plagiarizing. In an article called "Plagiarism: Do Students Know What It Is?" professors conducted a survey asking students questions related

Continued ▶

to different types of plagiarism to see what students believed constituted cheating:

> The results indicate that students know that the act of using
> someone else's words as if they were their own does indeed constitute plagiarism. Students at all levels gave similar answers.
> However, students were less certain about the concept of using
> someone else's ideas, with 40% of students not acknowledging that
> this was plagiarism. (Dawson and Overfield 2)

Somehow, students have gotten the idea that as long as they are not using an author's exact words, then it is not cheating to use his or her ideas. In addition, "Similar uncertainty was shown with regard to the concept of using someone else's results as their own and of sharing work with someone else and pooling ideas. Getting ideas from a textbook was not seen as plagiarism" (2). Based on this study, students tend to think that as long as they are not lifting exact words, then they are not cheating using someone else's ideas or results.

Students who are not truly aware of what constitutes plagiarism need more guidance; however, intentional plagiarism is a different story. Once all students have been informed and have clear information about the different forms of plagiarism and how to avoid it, then colleges have a right to impose harsh punishments on those who plagiarize. Some people would argue that it is a student's responsibility to research and know the rules of plagiarism and how to cite sources correctly, but isn't it a college's job to inform students and teach them the rules in the first place?

Colleges and universities need to offer initial orientations to new students that go over the definitions of plagiarism and tell them explicitly how to avoid it by correctly giving credit to any

Bayne 4

sources or ideas they use. Then, colleges should offer ongoing work-shops on documentation and avoiding plagiarism. Such workshops could be offered regularly in on-campus tutoring or writing centers. Predictably, some people will argue that the costs for colleges of offering such orientations and ongoing workshops is a concern. However, the need to get to students early in their college career and then reinforce the rules is evident: A 1998 study from *Who's Who Among American High School Students* found that "80 percent of college-bound students admitted to cheating on their schoolwork. Alarmingly the percentage of students actually *caught* cheating is a mere 5 percent, the study showed" (Lee 1). Students are leaving high school knowing they have cheated and not getting the guidance and rules they need to avoid doing so.

Once colleges have taken these relatively inexpensive steps to help students avoid plagiarism, the benefits will far outweigh the costs of losing students through disciplinary actions and the dam-age caused to colleges' reputations. Besides the orientations and workshops, colleges will also need to invest in software that helps teachers spot cases of plagiarism. A number of software programs and Internet antiplagiarism sites are available to help colleges and universities catch students who intentionally commit plagiarism. John Barrie, the creator of Turnitin, a program that matches stu-dent papers suspected of containing plagiarized passages or ideas with the passages or articles they have been plagiarized from, says, "What you really have here are students using the Internet like a 4.5 billion-page cut-and-paste encyclopedia" (qtd. in Lee 1). Lee responds to Barrie's insights by adding, "while he [Barrie] believes the Internet has exacerbated the problem, he also believes the

Continued ▶

Internet will solve it, through programs such as Turnitin, which he invented in 1996" (1). Therefore, colleges and universities will be able to take back control over this rampant problem through the very means that caused its increase in the first place.

The final benefit that colleges and universities will gain from taking a proactive approach to educating students about plagiarism and its many forms and educating them about how to avoid it will be to their integrity as institutions. Investing the money it would take to inform students and to go after those who blatantly break the rules will result in the reinstatement of their reputations as institutes of higher learning and places of integrity. Matthew S. Willen writes about the value of educating students about a moral approach to writing and documentation and avoiding plagiarism. In his article, "Reflections on the Cultural Climate of Plagiarism," he points out that colleges must take an active role in creating a climate that belittles the value of plagiarism. He encourages colleges to change the way they present writing to their students by showing them how to "value the process of writing—which includes invention, drafting, collaboration, revising, and editing—and not simply the final product as what is essential to their learning" (1). Students need to value what they can gain by going through all the stages of the writing process to produce thoughtful, well-crafted papers based on their own ideas and research. Furthermore, he emphasizes,

> We need to stress that writing doesn't simply document what they know on a topic; its processes enable comprehension of the topic. From a pedagogical perspective, the real crime of plagiarism is less that it is dishonest than that it precludes learning. (1)

Bayne 6

More than anything, as the old cliché goes, cheating only cheats the cheater. Actually, it hurts the colleges too: their reputations and their ability to offer students a chance to really learn for themselves.

Plagiarism is certainly an escalating problem at colleges and universities nationwide. Many students are not fully aware of the definitions of plagiarism and/or have lost sight of how serious an offense it is. Many do not know that plagiarizing results in loss of learning. Colleges and universities must choose to take a proactive approach to tackling this problem though educating students about it and cracking down on those who intentionally choose to cheat. Both the students and the colleges themselves will reap the benefits of a plagiarism-free learning experience.

Continued ▶

Bayne 7

Works Cited

Dawson, Maureen M., and Joyce A. Overfield. "Plagiarism: Do Students Know What It Is?" *Bioscience Education Journal* 8.1 (2006): n. pag. Web. 31 July 2008.

Lee, Grace. "Plagiarism 101." *ReadMe.* Dept. of Journalism, New York U, 28 Apr. 2004. Web. 28 July 2008.

Liddell, Jean, and Valerie Fong. "Faculty Perceptions of Plagiarism." *The Journal of College and Character*. NASPA, Florida State U, 2007. Web. 28 July 2008.

Willen, Mathew S. "Reflections on the Cultural Climate of Plagiarism." *Liberal Education* 90.4 (2004): n. pag. Association of American Colleges and Universities. Web. 26 July 2008.

PEARSON

To check your progress in meeting this chapter's objectives, log in to www.mywritinglab .com, go to the **Study Plan** tab, click on **Using Sources with Integrity** and choose **Research Process** from the list of subtopics. Read and view the resources in the **Review Materials** section, and then complete the **Recall**, **Apply**, and **Write** sets in the **Activities** section.

20 Analyzing Visuals

The Conversation

Wayne Buck

LEARNING OBJECTIVES

In this chapter, you will learn to

 LO 1 Think and write critically about various visuals.

LO 2 Analyze various types of visuals.

LO 3 Become a visual detective.

THINKING CRITICALLY

Look at the picture above. Then answer the questions that follow.

1. What is going on in this picture?

_____

_____

2. What are some possible messages the photograph conveys?

_____

3. What clues helped you to read these messages?

_____

4. What is your intellectual response to this photograph?

_____

5. What is your emotional response (if any)?

_____

393

LO 1 VISUAL COMMUNICATION AND CRITICAL THINKING

Visuals are an essential part of human communication. They are particularly important now when so many forms of visual communication abound in American culture: art, TV, movies, the Internet, advertising, and even camera phones. It is easy to overlook the importance of applying your critical thinking and analysis skills to visuals, but sometimes a visual can deliver a more effective argument or evoke a more immediate emotional response than a sentence or essay can and in a shorter amount of time. Like words, visuals represent ideas and arguments that can be thoughtful and truthful, misleading, or even deceitful. Visuals often have a clearly intended thesis, or argument, that the creator wants the viewer to infer. Artists, photographers, and advertisers employ particular visual approaches and include specific visual clues to help impart their intended messages. Therefore, reading and writing about visuals requires you to engage the same critical thinking and analysis skills you engage in writing about other authors' ideas and arguments.

Visuals *imply* the messages their creators intend, and viewers of the images *infer* these meanings from the visuals.

Visual (and sender)	**Viewer (receiver)**
↕	↕
Implies a message	*Infers* a message (based on clues)

APPLYING CRITICAL THINKING

PURPOSE	IDEAS	SUPPORT	ASSUMPTIONS BIASES	CONCLUSIONS	POINT OF VIEW	ANALYSIS

Imply/implication: To imply means to hint that something is so, to say it indirectly. When artists imply what they want to say in works of art, they make choices about what they will and will not include in order to convey their message. They might present an image from an unusual angle, place contrasting images together, omit parts of an object, or add elements you would not expect to see.

Inference: To infer information from a visual involves tapping into your ability to "read between the lines" and figure out what an artist means based on clues in his or her work of art. When you are thinking critically about visuals, you need to look for clues that indicate the point the artist, photographer, or painter is making.

Use your **analysis** skills to break down all parts of the image and evaluate implications and inferences.

Visuals invite a dialogue between themselves and the viewer. An image sends a message, but the viewer creates his or her own version of the message through an intellectual and emotional response to it. Viewers bring their own personal history, knowledge, and associations to the reading of visual clues just as they do to reading written text.

When you study visuals, you must study all the clues they present. Like words, visuals can have clear **denotative**, or exact, meanings, and they can have **connotative**, or emotional, meanings and associations. You need to fill in the blanks, draw conclusions, and tap into your intellectual and emotional responses (if any) to the image. You must also study the form and conventions of the image and what choice of medium the artist has made in order to interpret its messages and implied arguments. Sometimes, you must even study what is left out and why.

THINKING AND WRITING CRITICALLY ABOUT VISUALS

There are many parallels between analyzing a visual and analyzing text:

1. Visuals have a message: a thesis or argument. They have a **purpose.**

2. Visuals express a particular **point of view** and can display the **biases** of the artist or creator.

3. Visuals include clues (or details) related to their main point and are designed to impart those clues as effectively as possible.

4. Visuals can appeal both to the viewer's intellect and emotions.

5. Visuals may need to be viewed in their historical or cultural contexts in order to be fully understood. You must **analyze** their parts.

The ideas of logos and pathos apply to visual arguments, just as they do to arguments made in writing. **Logos** is an appeal to reasoning and logic. For instance, most academic writing appeals to logos. Many photographs, especially documentary or news photographs, also appeal to logos. **Pathos** is an appeal to emotion. Advertisements are notorious for using visuals to appeal to our emotions in order to sell products.

Being a Visual Detective: Asking Questions

Much of the work of a good visual is done in a way that is subtle. Therefore, be sure to ask specific questions when you are analyzing visuals. Turn on your visual detective skills, and don't just look at images passively. Ask questions as you view them: *"What?" "How?" "Why?" "Who?" "When?" "Where?" "So what?"* Also, pay attention to every detail: size, color, shape, medium, approach, content, background, and historical or cultural hints within the image.

ACTIVITY 20-1   Applying Questions to an Image

Directions: *Look at the photo, and answer the questions that follow. If needed, refer to the information provided earlier in this chapter for help.* *Answers will vary.*

Annie Musselman (anniemusselman.com)

1. Does this photograph appeal more to your sense of logos (logic), pathos (emotion), or both? Explain your answer.

_____

_____

2. Answer briefly (in a few words or a short sentence) each of the analytical detective questions for this photograph: *What* is this a picture of? *How* is the image organized? *Why* did the photographer arrange

the picture this way? *Who* is/are the subject(s) of the picture, and who is the intended audience? What details stand out, and why?

_____

_____

_____

3. How do the color, shapes, and background of this photograph add to its message?

_____

_____

TYPES OF VISUALS

Before you can become good at critically analyzing visuals, you have to become familiar with the most common types of visuals. This chapter will focus on photos, film, TV, advertising, drawings, pictures, and sculpture because these forms, like essays, have ideas and arguments, and they can be studied for message and technique, just like good expository writing.

Photographs

Photographs are a powerful form of visual communication. In many ways, they are like paragraphs: They pack a big message into a small space and develop the message through details and structure. It is possible to have multiple reactions to and interpretations of photographs, since a dialogue is created between them and you the viewer. It is important to keep in mind that the photographer, like a writer, determines what information you receive. He or she makes decisions about what to include and what not to include in a photograph. You are viewing an image that has been created to make a specific point or to evoke a particular emotional response. Also, digital editing and manipulation can make photographs show whatever photographers want them to. They can easily be made to lie, although we often assume they show the truth.

Thinking Critically About Photographs

A photograph should be analyzed for its composition (the arrangement of visual elements and the decisions made in that process) and content (what's in it and the meaning evoked by it). The historical and social context of a photograph should also be carefully examined. There are specific elements of photographs you should look at and terms you should be familiar with that are used for analyzing photographs and the techniques photographers use to create their message.

Terms, Elements, and Message

Photographs convey messages and emotions through their images. The following terms and elements conventionally are used to talk about the medium of photography. Some terms deal with the composition of a photograph, and some terms deal with specific visual effects in the overall picture. Finally, the last set of terms deal with the thematic elements of a photograph—the messages.

Composition terms

Composition: The overall arrangements of all of the elements that make up the entire image

Central focus: The object or objects that are most prominent and clearly in focus

Subject: The main person or object in the photograph

Setting: The physical surroundings and background of the picture

Background: The background of the photograph may or may not be in focus

Angle: The point or angle from which the photographer took the picture, the visual point of view

Visual elements

Focus: Some objects in an image may be sharp and clear, and some may be less sharp and clear, or out of focus.

Light/lighting: Some objects may be brighter than others. Some may be darker; some may be highlighted. Is the light natural or artificial? Is the light direct, harsh, or soft?

Shape: There are two types of shape to consider—the shape of the whole photograph (such as rectangular, square) and the shapes within the composition.

Texture: The feel of the paper the photograph is printed on or the appearance of the texture of the image.

Theme/message terms

Theme: The main idea of a photograph

Intention: What the photographer intends to convey with this image

Audience: The target audience for the image

Social and historical context: The social and/or historical background or context for the image

Questions to Ask

When you look at a photograph, ask yourself the questions listed here. Note that they relate directly to the terms and elements described above and ask you to consider the photographer's intentions in composing the image, the message he or she wants to convey.

1. What is my overall reaction to this image?

2. Is the photographer appealing to logos (logic), pathos (emotion), or both?

3. Is there a particular social or historical context for this picture? If so, what effect does that have on my reaction to or understanding of the message(s)?

4. Does there seem to be an intended audience for this photo, or does it appeal to a broad audience?

5. Have I considered the composition elements of the photo and what effect they have on my reading of this picture?

6. Have I considered the visual effects such as lighting, setting, and focus and what effects those elements have on my reading of this picture?

7. What thesis or argument is conveyed through the image?

ACTIVITY 20-2   Analyzing a Photograph

Directions: *Look at the photograph below. Then answer the questions that follow.*   *Answers will vary.*

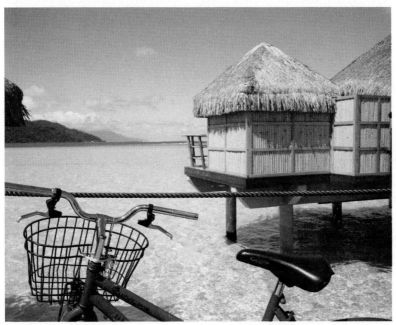

Annie Musselman (anniemusselman.com)

1. What mood is created in this photograph? Are there any social messages? Personal messages? _____

    _____

2. Why do you think the photographer chose to include just a partial image of the bicycle? _____

    _____

3. Choose three of the terms from Terms, Elements, and Message above, and describe how they are used in this photograph and what effect they have on the overall message it conveys. _____

    _____

ACTIVITY 20-3   Analyzing and Writing About Photographs

Annie Musselman (anniemusselman.com)

Directions: *On a separate sheet of paper, write a paragraph that provides a detailed, objective description of the photo above. Think of it as a verbal sketch, as though you were describing the photo for someone who could not see it. Summarize and describe the scene and the impression that the photograph presents. Then answer the questions that follow.* Answers will vary.

1. What is the theme, or controlling idea, in this picture?

    _____

    _____

2. What associations or concepts come to mind when looking at this picture?

    _____

    _____

3. What composition choices did the photographer make, and what visual elements did he include that influence the overall effect of this photograph? Refer to Terms, Elements, and Messages on page 398 for help in analyzing form and techniques. Be specific.

    _____

    _____

4. What social message or argument is suggested by this photograph?

    _____

    _____

5. What details helped you draw these conclusions?

    _____

    _____

6. Write a paragraph that develops the theme evoked by the picture but using words and written description instead. Make sure that your topic sentence states the same kind of message or point that the picture communicates.

    _____

    _____

    _____

TV and Film

Television shows and films are complex visuals. You have to engage your critical thinking skills in order to move from being a *passive* watcher to an *active* "reader" if you want to go beyond just enjoying them to understanding the messages they convey and the techniques used to impart those messages. Television shows and films communicate important social messages and serve as "mirrors" of society; whether in the form of documentaries, reality shows, or dramas, they reflect values and culture. Therefore, they should be read the same way you would read a story, article, or novel: with the intention of exploring the author's (the director's and producers') messages and techniques for delivering those messages.

Thinking Critically About Television and Film

How the camera records the scenes being acted out or happening in real life is an important part of understanding TV and films. As in photographs, the TV or movie camera limits what is shown in a particular scene. Directors intend to convey certain messages and try to evoke intellectual and emotional responses from their viewers by making decisions about what they will and will not show them. Be sure to question what you see on the screen, to think about what does not appear there, and to consider the effects on your intellectual and emotional responses to the content. By looking at the techniques used and the point of view and style choices directors make, you'll get a more thorough understanding of the message being presented.

Terms, Elements, and Message

The media of TV and film use specific terms and techniques. Knowing them can help in your analysis of these types of visuals.

Composition terms

Mise-en-scene: Mise-en-scene is a French term used to describe what is in each particular scene: the lighting, costumes, sets, shapes, and characters. It is the composition that fills the frame of the screen.

Camera shots/angles: The way in which cameras are positioned in a film or show creates the point of view, the perspective from which we see everything. Each choice made in a shot creates a particular point of view and attempts to evoke a particular response from the viewer. Here are a few of the most common types of shots used in filmmaking:

The closeup: An up-close shot, for instance showing a character's face only

The extreme closeup: For instance showing just the character's eyes

Medium shot: Showing most but not all of an object or character, full or long shot, for instance, an entire person or group of people in one shot

Pan shot (panning): The camera moves across a scene, for instance, panning across a scene from left to right.

Crane shot: A scene shot from high above, usually an outdoor scene. The camera is set on a mechanical crane and moved up and down as needed.

Tracking shot: The camera moves for an extended period, usually following a character in motion. The camera is set on a dolly or mounted on tracks.

Editing: What is cut out of a film or show, how the scenes are cut and switched, and the decisions made after filming to make the film more powerful or effective (similar to revising a written work).

Elements

Characters: The people, animals, or fictional beings featured in the story are the characters. Pay attention to how the characters are presented, their dialogues, and what they want. Are they likable? Why, or why not?

Soundtrack: Pay attention to the music in the background. What effect does the music have on your response to the scene?

Theme/message

Theme/intention/social and historical context: The themes and messages of the film or show are usually related to society and to human nature. What does this film or show reflect about the culture it portrays and the values of that culture? What is the historical context, if any? Does the film or show argue for social change? How so?

Logos and pathos: Pay attention to both your intellectual and emotional reactions as the film or show progresses. How do these reactions affect your understanding of the messages?

Audience: The target audience for the show or film

Questions to Ask

Here are some general questions to ask yourself as you watch a television show or a film. Be sure to take notes as you watch any show or film that you will write about later:

1. When was the show or film made? Does it reflect current events and values, or is it set in the past in a specific historical period?
2. What does the title mean in relation to the plot, theme, or messages of the film or show?
3. Describe the basic plot or series of events. What happens?

4. Are there any major shifts in the plot or storyline? What are they, and what do they indicate?

5. Who do you think is the intended audience for this piece? What evidence or details lead you to believe this is the intended audience?

6. How does the film or show begin? Why does it begin this way?

7. What is your intellectual response to this film or show? Why? What is your emotional response to this film or show? Why?

8. How do the settings, props, costumes, and soundtrack affect the presentation of the images and plot?

9. How do the camera angles and visual framing of the scenes affect your response to the show or film?

10. What are the messages of the film or show?

ACTIVITY 20-4   Analyzing a Television Show

Directions: *Watch a TV show, and take notes as you watch. Then answer the following questions. Be sure to read through these questions before you watch so you can take notes that will help you answer them.* Answers will vary.

1. What type of show did you watch (news show, reality show, game show, sit com, and so on)?

   _____

   _____

2. What happened in the show? Provide a brief summary:

   _____

   _____

   _____

   _____

3. What themes or social concepts were touched on or developed?

   _____

   _____

4. What techniques did the director/producers use that stood out?

   _____

   _____

   _____

5. What effect did these choices and techniques have on your intellectual and emotional response to the show?

_____

_____

6. Now, review your notes, and write a one or two paragraph critique of the show that explores its strengths and weaknesses and describes the messages and the techniques used to convey those messages. Be sure to incorporate specific examples and details, using your notes.

ACTIVITY 20-5 Analyzing a Film

Directions: *Watch a film, and take notes as you watch. Then answer the following questions. Be sure to read through these questions before you watch so you can take notes that will help you answer them.* Answers will vary.

1. What type of film did you watch (documentary, comedy, romance, drama, and so on)? _____

2. What happened in the film (plot or event)? Provide a brief summary.

_____

_____

_____

_____

3. What themes or social concepts were touched on or developed?

_____

_____

4. What techniques did the director/producers use that stood out?

_____

_____

_____

5. What effect did these choices and techniques have on your intellectual and emotional responses to the film?

_____

_____

6. Now write a short essay about this film focusing on one of these two options:

    a. Write a critique of the film you watched analyzing the film's social messages. Use specific terms and examples of film techniques used by the director, and discuss whether or not those techniques were successful in creating a good film or conveying the intended message(s).

    b. Choose a film that is based on a book you have read. Then compare the way you saw the characters and the story in your head as you read the book to the director's vision of the same story as imparted through the film. Critique the choices made by the director to recreate the story on film. Were the choices effective? Why, or why not?

Advertisements

Advertisements come in many forms: television commercials, billboards, magazine and newspapers ads, even ads at the movie theater. All advertisements have one basic thing in common: They attempt to sell a product to a carefully targeted audience. So analyzing an advertisement is similar to analyzing an author's argument in a piece of persuasive writing. You engage the same kind of analysis skills when you look at an advertisement in order to write about it. Advertisements use various visual details and techniques to generate conscious and sometimes subconscious (below the surface) responses from viewers. They can combine text and visuals or focus solely on visuals or text.

Thinking Critically About Advertisements

In order to think critically about advertisements and analyze both their messages and the techniques used to impart those messages, you need to pay close attention to details and ask questions about everything included in the ad, as well as to what is not included. All advertisements are trying to sell something, so most of them have a direct argument, but many also have implied arguments. Most advertisements use pathos, an appeal to your emotions, to sell their product. Most are selling a particular image and are intended for specific audiences. Note the difference in approaches in advertisements and how they target audiences by gender, social class, economic status, race, age, region, and other factors, depending on the products they are selling. When analyzing advertisements, be sure to check for errors in logic or implied messages that deceive people into thinking that the product might do more than it actually can, such as a new car adding to one's sex appeal.

Cross Reference
Review Chapter 15, Argument and Persuasion, for specific types of logical fallacies.

Critical Thinking Questions to Ask About Ads

Here are some questions to ask when analyzing ads:

1. What product is this advertisement designed to sell?
2. Who is the target audience for the ad? How do you know?
3. What is the direct message of the ad?
4. What are the indirect or implied messages of the ad?
5. What are the visual details that serve as clues to the direct and/or implied messages in this ad? List them.
6. What intellectual response [logos] do you have to this ad?
7. What emotional response [pathos] do you have to this ad?

8. What arguments or appeals are embedded in this ad? Are there deceptive or illogical messages implied?

9. What cultural or historical ideas or norms does the ad tap into? Look especially for references to race, gender, age, economic class, and region.

10. In your opinion, is this an effective ad? Why, or why not?

ACTIVITY 20-6   Analyzing an Advertisement

Directions: *Find an advertisement in a magazine or newspaper, and answer the Critical Thinking Questions above on a separate sheet of paper. Then write a one or two paragraph analysis of the advertisement that first describes it in detail, then identifies its intended audience and direct and implied messages, and finally evaluates the overall effectiveness of its arguments for buying the product. Answers will vary.*

Sculptures, Drawings, and Paintings

Sculptures, drawings, and paintings, like photographs, must be looked at both as a whole and in terms of their details. Look at the types of material (paper, canvas, clay, or stone) they are fashioned from, and look at what is used (ink, charcoal, pencil, paint, hammer, chisel, or mold) to create the images they convey. Sculptures, drawings, and paintings can be realistic (like a still life or a portrait of a person), abstract (based on form rather than a realistic representation of specific objects), or anything in between.

Thinking Critically About Sculptures, Drawings, and Paintings

Sculptures, drawings, and paintings try to capture some truth about life or people. When you write about these visual forms, think of them as narrative or descriptive essays, only created using a visual medium. Mine their messages through the details in their description. What themes and messages do they evoke, and how? What artistic choices did their creators make, and what effects do those choices have on your intellectual and emotional responses to these works of art? Is there a particular historical or social context that adds to their messages? When analyzing a sculpture, painting, or drawing, use the following questions as guidelines for thinking critically about what you are seeing and about the techniques the artist used to create an intellectual or emotional response in the viewer.

Critical Thinking Questions to Ask About Sculptures, Drawings, and Paintings

1. What materials were used to create this sculptures, drawing, or painting? Be sure to note both the type of material (paper, canvas,

cloth, wood) the visual is based on, as well as the material used to create the image.

2. How do the chosen colors, shapes, and types of materials impact the overall effect of the piece?

3. What perspective or point of view is the piece of art presented from? Why? What effect does the point of view or perspective have on your reaction to it?

4. Is the piece realistic or abstract? How does this influence your reaction to it?

5. What is your intellectual response to this piece of art?

6. What is your emotional response?

7. Is there a cultural, historical, or social context that must be considered for deeper understanding of this artwork? If so, explain.

8. What is your personal response to the piece, and what personal associations does it evoke, if any?

9. What are the direct messages and arguments conveyed in this piece?

10. What are the implied messages or arguments?

ACTIVITY 20-7   Analyzing Sculptures

Directions: *On a separate sheet of paper, write a couple of paragraphs analyzing the two sculptures below using the questions above.* *Answers will vary.*

Carved wood, 1968. Douglas L. Cole.

Deliverance. Terra cotta/wood stain, 2006. Paul Metivier.

ACTIVITY 20-8   Analyzing a Drawing or Painting

Directions: *Choose one of the images on pages 410–411 or, a work of art from an art book or the Internet, or a drawing or painting you have seen in a gallery or museum, and answer the questions on pages 408–409. Then write a paragraph about what effect this process had on your viewing of the work of art and your understanding and response to it.* Answers will vary.

_____

_____

_____

_____

_____

_____

_____

_____

Think, Feel, Breathe   Cindy Small (firemonkeystudio.com)

Become a Visual Detective

There are some basic questions you can ask about all types of visuals to begin your process of analysis and figure out the techniques used to convey direct and implied messages. See the Visual Detective Checklist for some general questions to get started in analyzing various forms of visuals.

Niña del Cumpleaños   Cindy Small (firemonkeystudio.com)

VISUAL DETECTIVE CHECKLIST

1. Who is the intended audience (general? specific? if so, list)?

2. Why did the artist use this medium to convey his or her message? Who is the intended audience (General? Specific? If so, list.)

3. What are the strengths or advantages of the type of visual chosen?

4. What are the weaknesses or limitations, if any?

5. What are the *direct* messages of the image?

6. What are the *indirect* or implied messages of this visual?

7. What clues are present as visual evidence of the intended message(s)?

8. Ask *What? How? Why? Who? When? Where?* questions to check for all of the clues. Include any historical or social context you may know about the image.

9. What did you think when you first viewed this image? What did you feel?

10. Does the visual reinforce its intended theme or question it? What is the visual's overall thesis or argument?

ACTIVITY 20-9   Becoming a Visual Detective

Directions: *Choose one of the images from this chapter, and on a separate sheet of paper, answer the visual detective questions on page 412. Then, write a one paragraph analysis of the piece.* Answers will vary.

_____

_____

_____

_____

_____

_____

ACTIVITY 20-10   General Visual Analysis

Directions: *Choose one of the visuals from this chapter. Then follow these steps to reach analytical conclusions about the image you chose.* Answers will vary.

1. Describe the image/visual objectively. What do you actually see (just the facts)? Don't include what you *think* and *feel* about the visual, just what is literally represented. Include details about the medium or type of visual, the format, size, shape, texture(s), colors, and so on. Describe as an observer, but add no judgment.

   _____

   _____

   _____

   _____

   _____

   _____

2. Is there any background information you can provide: historical context, cultural clues, visual type, or genre?

   _____

   _____

3. Now focus on your subjective response to the image. What thoughts are provoked by it? What feelings (if any) are evoked?

   _____

   _____

4. What associations come to mind when you look at this visual? Why?

_____

_____

5. Focus on the details of the image and the conscious choices made by the artist. What effects do these details and choices have on you?

_____

_____

6. List a couple of specific examples of the details that served as visual clues that led you to a particular thought or emotion:

_____

_____

7. What ideas or concepts are represented in this image?

_____

_____

8. What is the thesis or argument implied by this visual?

_____

_____

9. After considering all of your answers so far, what do you think are the main messages of this image, and who is the intended audience?

_____

_____

10. Is the visual successful in imparting its message or unsuccessful? Why?

_____

_____

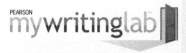

To check your progress in meeting this chapter's objectives, log in to www.mywritinglab.com, go to the **Study Plan** tab, click on **Readings and Visuals for Thinking and Writing** and choose **Critical Thinking: Responding to Text and Visuals** from the list of subtopics. Read and view the resources in the **Review Materials** section, and then complete the **Recall**, **Apply**, and **Write** sets in the **Activities** section.

21 Writing About Stories and Essays

THINKING CRITICALLY

When critics review a play, they not only talk about whether the play was enjoyable, they also talk about the classic elements it should contain and whether they were executed well, including the writing, the acting, the sets, the costumes, the lighting, and so on.

How is a critic's job of reviewing a play similar to a student's job of critiquing another writer's story or essay? What do you think is similar? What kinds of things do you think you would look at when writing about an author's writing?

Continued ▶

_____

_____

_____

_____

LO 1 WRITING ABOUT STORIES AND ESSAYS

Analysis essays written about a story or essay go beyond just a summary of what happened. Instead, you interpret and analyze what the author's intended messages are and the techniques the author used to get his or her message across to the reader. Engage your critical thinking skills when you write about stories and essays. The skill of analysis is particularly essential in writing about fiction.

If you are writing an analysis essay for your instructor and classmates on an essay or story you have all read, then do not *summarize* the story or essay, since your audience has already read it. Instead, focus on interpreting the story's meaning. Show what the author's main messages are, and analyze the techniques and style choices the author made to convey those messages.

APPLYING CRITICAL THINKING

 PURPOSE IDEAS SUPPORT ASSUMPTIONS BIASES CONCLUSIONS POINT OF VIEW ANALYSIS

Inference involves tapping into your ability to "read between the lines" and figure out, or infer, what someone means based on clues found in what they say or write. For instance, in a short story, you would use information about the setting, the characters, the plot, and maybe repeated images as clues to *infer* the message and **purpose** the author means to convey through telling the story.

Interpretation involves decoding an idea so you understand its meaning. When you interpret an author's ideas, you explain them using your own words. You need to interpret and understand an author's ideas before you can **analyze** their importance and evaluate them. When you read a short essay, you need to be sure that you clearly understand the **ideas** the author is discussing before you can evaluate whether they are valid or important.

However, if your analysis essay is for a broader audience who may not have read the original work, you may need to include a brief summary of the story first (see Chapter 17, pp. 330–331, Eight Steps for Writing a Summary).

Before you begin writing your analysis of an assigned or chosen essay or story, ask yourself the following questions:

1. What is the most important message the author wants to get across to the reader?

2. What are some of the secondary messages or ideas developed in this piece?

3. Are there any implied messages or ideas? If so, what are they?

4. How does the author's tone affect the overall impression made by the essay or story?

5. What specific writing techniques did the author use?

6. Are the style and writing techniques used effective or not? Why, or why not?

Further questions to ask if you are analyzing a fictional story include:

1. What is the plot? What happens, and how does the action build and resolve or not?

2. Who is the main character (protagonist)? Is there something he or she wants?

3. Is the setting (physical place and/or historical setting) of the story significant?

4. Is there any symbolism in the language or in the action of the story?

LO 2   STRUCTURE OF AN ANALYSIS ESSAY

Introductory Paragraph

In the first paragraph of your analytical essay, begin with a general introduction to the subject and to the direct or implied message(s) (two to four sentences). Then, add an analytical thesis statement that presents your opinion of what are the main messages of the piece.

If you are writing about fiction, it helps to include a plan in your thesis statement that outlines how you will organize your essay. For instance, you could focus on individual characters (one paragraph at a time), you could discuss the progression of the story and its themes in the order events occur, or you could examine the author's writing style and techniques (such as symbolism, diction, and so on).

Body Paragraphs

Each body paragraph should have an analytical topic sentence based on your thesis and elements of the essay or story you are analyzing. For instance, if your essay focuses on analyzing the main characters, you could have a topic sentence for each main character that relates to the thesis statement. If you are writing an analysis based on the progression of events in the story, you could explain how the author leads up step by step to an analytical message. Then again, if you are focusing on the writing techniques used by the author, you could discuss style and language choices, such as the use of particular words or symbols, in order of their importance.

After the topic sentence, you should provide support statements, examples from the essay or story, and analysis of those examples. Each example from the essay or story needs to be interpreted (translated by you to explain what this part of the essay or story illustrates) and analyzed for its meaning (the direct and implied messages in the story).

In general, you need about two quotations from an essay or story for each body paragraph in order to provide adequate support for your thesis. Every time you use a quotation from the essay or story, you need to structure it in the following way.

LO 3 The Ice Cream Sandwich Technique for Framing Quotations

Cross Reference

See Chapter 17, pp. 336–339. The Ice Cream Sandwich: Framing Facts and Sources.

- **Top cookie:** First, you need a general analytical statement, one or two sentences, to set up the quotation.

  > **Example:** In "The Discus Thrower," by Richard Selzer, the doctor in the story is intrigued by his patient's sense of pride.

Cross Reference

The following examples are in MLA citation format— see Chapter 19 for how to integrate quotations correctly.

- **Ice cream filling:** Next, you need to incorporate the quotation and then a citation.

  Use a colon: You may connect a quotation of one to three sentences in length to your general analysis sentence (top cookie) by using a colon and then the quotation. To use a colon to set up a direct quotation, the sentence in front of the colon must be a complete sentence and must set up the idea(s) within the quotation to follow:

  > **Example:** In "The Discus Thrower," by Richard Selzer, the doctor in the story is intrigued by his patient's sense of pride: "His face is relaxed, grave, dignified" (96).

  Use a tag: You may use a simple tag:

  > **Example:** Selzer writes, "His face is relaxed, grave, dignified" (96).

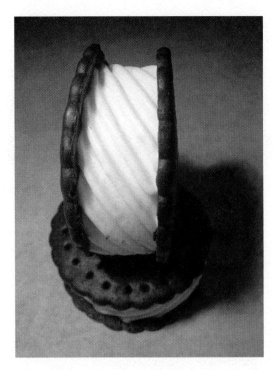

Weave the quotation: Or you may weave a piece of a quotation from the story or essay into your own sentence:

> **Example:** The doctor describes the patient's face as "relaxed, grave, dignified" (96).

- **Bottom cookie:** Finally, you need one or two sentences that interpret what the quotation is saying and analyze its significance (what this excerpt demonstrates, why it's important).

> **Example:** This description of the patient creates an image of dignity and grace. The doctor realizes this poor patient still has dignity and pride and a need for respect, even though there is little left to him physically.

Again, it's a good rule of thumb to include at least two full ice cream sandwiches (with specific references to the story, essay, or article) for support of your thesis in each body paragraph.

Concluding Paragraph

You will need a concluding paragraph that restates your thesis (not the same words, though; say it a different way) and sums up and concludes your essay's main points.

Use the following critique form to check that you have included all the elements of a good analytical essay.

ANALYTICAL ESSAY CRITIQUE FORM

Overall

                Done well   **Needs work**

1. Is the essay analytical (does it include interpretation, commentary, and analysis of the message/s)? _____ _____
2. Does the essay avoid merely summarizing the story or essay? _____ _____
3. Does the essay stay focused on proving the thesis? _____ _____

Introduction

4. Is the title interesting, appropriate, and typed in the correct format? _____ _____
5. Does the general introduction lead smoothly into the thesis? _____ _____
6. Is the thesis statement clear (is it a clear presentation of the story's message)? _____ _____
7. Is a plan of development included in the thesis (e.g., did you organize your paragraphs by themes or ideas, characters, the author's style and writing techniques, and so on)? _____ _____

Body

8. Do the body paragraphs have clear topic sentences? _____ _____
9. Does each body paragraph include support, examples and quotes from the story or essay (about two quotations per body paragraph)? _____ _____
10. Is each quotation tagged or woven into your own sentence? _____ _____
11. Is each quotation framed with your analysis—set up and then interpreted (ice cream sandwich technique)? _____ _____
12. Are quotation marks and punctuation handled correctly? _____ _____
13. Is there a concluding analytical sentence in each body paragraph? _____ _____
14. Are transitions used well, both within and between paragraphs? _____ _____

Conclusion

15. Does the concluding paragraph sum up your points well without introducing new ideas or analysis? _____ _____

Citation Format (MLA)/Grammar/Spelling

16. **Citation format:** Every time a quotation is used, is it followed by parentheses containing the author's name and/or a page number and a period outside the parentheses? _____ _____

17. **Circle grammar errors you see in this paper:** spelling errors; fragments; run-ons/comma splices; pronoun disagreement; reference fault errors; errors in verb use; commas, semicolons/colons, quotation marks, and apostrophes; point-of-view shifts; faulty parallelism; passive voice constructions.

18. Other types of grammar or sentence-level errors you noticed in this draft:

_____

Comments:

_____

_____

Sample Student Story Analysis Essay

Read the original essay " 'Just Walk on By': A Black Man Ponders His Power to Alter Public Space," by Brent Staples, in Chapter 22 first, in order to fully understand this student's analysis of the piece.

Smith 1

Martin Smith

Professor Johnson

English 090

11 October 2009

Judged by Appearance Only

People view each other based on a variety of factors, including race and gender, and sometimes they act in ways that are judgmental and prejudiced. Brent Staples, a black man, focuses on how he is seen by others and how he solves the problem of discrimination in " 'Just Walk On By': A Black Man Ponders His Power to Alter Public Space." In this story, Staples explains why some people are scared of him and what steps he takes to prevent people from seeing him as a threat.

Thesis

Continued ▶

Smith 2

Topic sentence

Throughout the story, Staples focuses on the subconscious, and sometimes conscious, behavior that people exhibit. This behavior involves acting differently toward and being afraid of those who look different. This behavior reflects the biased nature of all humans. People often focus first on the differences of others before they look for com-

Concluding sentence

mon ground. So, people tend to choose to be close to people who are like them, and they often choose to think the worst of people who are differ-

ent.

Topic sentence & top cookie

Staples' first encounter with prejudice was with a 20-year-old white woman on a deserted street in Hyde Park, Chicago. Staples

Quotation = ice cream

writes, "As I swung onto the avenue behind her, there seemed to be a discreet, un-inflammatory distance between us. Not so. She cast back a

Bottom cookie

worried glance" (88). Even before Staples says a word or makes a move, the woman reacts to him in a negative and worried manner. This reac-

Analysis

tion shows that she fears him based solely on his appearance. However, the fact that it was night and a lonely street is important too. She probably felt scared even before seeing Staples. However, Staples goes out of his way to alleviate this woman's fear. He has gotten into the habit of crossing to the other side of the street just to help women feel safer at night if he is around them.

Topic sentence & top cookie

In another instance of being judged by his skin tone, Staples

Quotation = cream filling

brings up a time when he was rushing to work: "One day, rushing into the office of a magazine I was writing for with a deadline story in

Bottom cookie

hand, I was mistaken for a burglar" (89). Since Staples was moving quickly, it gave the appearance that he was going to do something bad or had already committed a crime. Like "the speed of an ad hoc posse" (89), security chased him. And as Staples says, they "pursued me through the labyrinthine halls, nearly to my editor's door . . . I had no way of proving who I was" (89). In the first place, Staples should have

Smith 3

acted more professionally by not running, and he should have stopped when he realized he was being pursued. However, he was an employee at this place, and it's not all that unusual for people to run in the halls when they are in a hurry. Staples implies that he was pursued because he was black. A white man or woman running down the hall probably would not have gotten security's attention. These types of unfair and unpleasant experiences happened to Staples on a regular basis, just for being a black man.

Therefore, staying in the shadows or modifying his own behavior to appear non-threatening became Staples' way of dealing with the prejudice of people who feared him. Choosing to avoid problems before they happen, he says, "I now take precautions to make myself less threatening. I move about with care, particularly late in the evening" (89). This decision to stay in the shadows and appear less threatening seems to work well for Staples; he discovers quickly what puts the people who are frightened by his appearance at ease. He avoids uncomfortable situations whenever possible, and, when he does come across unsuspecting "victims," he whistles tunes from Beethoven or Vivaldi (89). By whistling classical tunes, he puts frightened white people at ease. Staples demonstrates a strong ability to adapt to the situations he encounters.

In this story, Staples demonstrates some everyday instances of prejudice and brings to light the unkind and biased ways in which some people act. He also shows that he has chosen to respond to prejudice thoughtfully and with grace and humility instead of bitterness and anger. A man's power to alter public space can come from within him, despite the way he is viewed by others.

Analysis

Concluding sentence

Topic sentence & top cookie

Quotation = ice cream

Bottom cookie
Analysis

Concluding sentence

Restatement of thesis

ACTIVITY 21-1   Story Analysis Assignment

Directions: *Choose one of the stories or essays from Chapter 22 or a different story or essay that your instructor assigns or that you have chosen. Then, use the Six Steps to Active Reading in Chapter 2, and read the piece. Next, write an analytical essay using the suggestions in this section for structuring and developing your analysis. Finally, use the critique form in this chapter for self- and peer reviews of your essay draft.*

ACTIVITY 21-2   Analysis Essay Assignment

Directions: *Choose one of the stories or essays from Chapter 22, and complete one of the essay assignments listed at the end of it.*

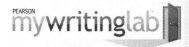

To check your progress in meeting this chapter's objectives, log in to **www.mywritinglab .com**, go to the **Study Plan** tab, click on **Readings and Visuals for Thinking and Writing** and choose **Critical Thinking: Responding to Text and Visuals** from the list of subtopics. Read and view the resources in the **Review Materials** section, and then complete the **Recall**, **Apply**, and **Write** sets in the **Activities** section.

Reading Selections and Critical Thinking Tasks

Polar Opposites   Cindy Small

THINKING CRITICALLY

Reading an essay or story requires you to engage actively in your reading, much like studying a work of art. What details and messages stand out in the mixed-media picture above?

_____

_____

Be sure to engage your critical thinking skills as you read the following selections, and complete the reading reflection and critical thinking questions that follow each one.

APPLYING CRITICAL THINKING

PURPOSE   IDEAS   SUPPORT   ASSUMPTIONS BIASES   CONCLUSIONS   POINT OF VIEW   ANALYSIS

Here are some questions you can ask as you read that will help you think critically about what an author is saying.

1. What is the author's **purpose** or goal in this reading selection? What does he or she set out to explain, argue, or prove?

2. What are the implied or stated questions being addressed in this reading selection?

3. What **ideas** and **support** (evidence, data, experience, or facts) does the author use to develop his or her purpose or goal for the reading? Is the support adequate? Convincing?

4. Does the author present alternative **points of view** when needed?

5. What **assumptions** does the author make in this reading selection? (Assumptions are ideas or reasons the author takes for granted and upon which he or she bases judgments or develops his or her reasoning.) Are the assumptions valid?

6. What are the implications, consequences, and **conclusions** of the author's reasoning and/or ideas and arguments (direct or implied) in this selection? Use your **analysis** skills to evaluate them.

   Also, refer to the strategies for active reading in Chapter 2 as needed.

A Whole Lot of Cheatin' Going On

Mark Clayton

Mark Clayton is a writer whose research and writing about the increasing instances of plagiarism and other forms of cheating in colleges and universities have caused a stir in the academic world. Ironically, this article about plagiarism is often used and not cited in essays and summaries that can be purchased online for students to use as their own work.

1   Sitting in the glow of his computer screen at 2 a.m. on Oct. 26, 1998, John Smolik, a University of Texas freshman, fires off an e-mail message to an online debate over academic cheating on the Austin campus.

2   Many of the 100-plus student messages argue that cheaters only hurt themselves. Not so says Mr. Smolik's missive, labeled "reality check!" "Cheating is an answer," he writes. "It might not be a good answer, but nonetheless it is an answer."

3   Actually, Smolik "disagrees with cheating" and was simply playing devil's advocate, he said in a recent interview. But he allows that his provocative message put forward a widely shared view. And researchers agree.

4   Across America, college students and college-bound high-schoolers appear to be cheating like there's no tomorrow, student surveys show.

5   The Center for Academic Integrity in Nashville studied 7,000 students on 26 small-to-medium-size college campuses in 1990, 1992, and 1995. Those studies found that nearly 80 percent admitted to cheating at least once.

6   "We've seen a dramatic increase in the more explicit forms of test cheating" and illegitimate "collaboration," says Donald McCabe, associate provost at Rutgers University in Newark, who founded CAI and did its studies.

7   He and others blame poor role models and lack of parental guidance for the growing acceptance of cheating in colleges. Easy access to the Internet, with its vast and often hard-to-trace resources, is another factor.

8   Add to that a pervasive change in societal values, and students can easily be snared if they lack a strong moral compass—as well as a campus where peers and administrators take a firm stand against dishonesty.

9   "Nobody cheated [in the 1960s] because of the peer pressure and like-lihood of being turned in," claims Johan Madson, associate provost for student affairs at Vanderbilt University in Nashville. "Students of this generation are reluctant to turn their classmates in. They feel everyone ought to have their own right to do their own thing."

10   The problem is hardly limited to college campuses. Critics also point to widespread cheating in high school as a reason for colleges' current woes.

11   *Who's Who among American High School Students,* which lists 700,000 high achieving students, surveyed these top performers last year and found that 80 percent said they had cheated during their academic careers. Joe Krouse, associate publisher of the listing, says it is "the highest level we've ever seen."

12   Mr. Krouse taps adult behavior as a factor. "Because adults and role models in society do it, some students may have used those examples to rationalize cheating," he says. In a survey conducted in 1997–98, he also found that 66 percent of the parents of these top students said cheating was "not a big deal."

COLLEGES ARE WATCHING MORE CLOSELY

13   Whatever the reason for cheating, its sheer volume is capturing the attention of more than a few schools. Most, chary of their images, down-play dishonesty, unwilling to air dirty laundry in public. Yet a few are confronting cheating by making it highly public—on campus, at least.

14   The University of Texas is the nation's largest university with about 50,000 students. It has roughly 180 academic-integrity cases pop up annually, says Kevin Price, assistant dean of students. The school is trying to raise the profile of integrity issues during orientation with skits, a 10-page handout on plagiarism, and a newsletter called the *Integrity Herald* for faculty.

15   Another sign of academic stirring: the Center for Academic Integrity, founded in 1993, already has 175 member schools and is drafting a framework of principles that could be applied nationwide to lower student cheating.

16   Schools like Stanford University, Georgetown University, the University of Delaware, and a half-dozen others are also buffing up or introducing new honor codes.

17   But Mr. Madson at Vanderbilt University says what is most needed is for students themselves to take charge and reject the attitude that cheating can be justified.

18   Students say time and workload pressure are major factors spurring academic dishonesty, followed by parental pressure. "It's definitely what you get assigned—and how long you have to do it—that right there determines whether you're going to cheat," says Smolik, the University of Texas freshman.

19   Anne-Elyse Smith, another freshman at Texas, reasoned in an online debate that it may not be smart to cheat, but it could be educationally valuable.

20   "People should hold themselves accountable to a standard at which they are comfortable, and get out of the education what they can," she wrote. "If that involves looking at one answer on a quiz, I think the person is more likely to remember that one answer since they had to resort to cheating to obtain it."

A LITTLE IMAGINATION, A LOT OF HIGH TECH

21   Whether copying another student's homework, cheating on a test, or plagiarizing an essay, cheating is limited only by imagination—and technology. Some program their calculators with formulas, but rig them to show an empty memory if an instructor checks.

22   But what alarms some campus officials the most is the Internet's proven potential for explosive growth in negative areas such as pornography—and the possibility that plagiarism could be next. Web sites sporting names like "Cheater.com" and "School Sucks" offer tools for rampant plagiarism at the click of a mouse. "Download your workload" the latter site suggests, boasting more than 1 million term-paper downloads.

23   Such savvy borrowing may be lost on some educators, but others, like librarians, are catching up. "Students are finding it so easy to use these sources that they will dump them in the middle of the papers without any attribution," says John Ruszkiewicz, an English professor at Texas. "What they don't realize is how readily [professors] can tell the material isn't the student's and how easy it is for instructors to search this material on the Web."

24   Anthony Krier, a reference librarian at Franklin Pierce College Library in Rindge, N.H., is one such literary bloodhound. Last semester, he investigated nine cases of plagiarism, three of them involving the Internet. One student had downloaded and passed off as his own a morality essay, apparently unaware of the irony, Mr. Krier says.

25   Some colleges are fighting back with explicit warnings, more detailed orientations, and classes on how to cite sources—and lawsuits. Boston University sued five online "term-paper mills" in 1997. The case was rejected by a federal judge last month. School officials vow to refile.

26   Last fall, the dean of the school's College of Communication, Brent Baker, wrote a letter to students urging them to protect their "good name" by reviewing carefully the school's code of conduct. To drive home the point, he attached a listing of 13 unnamed cases and the penalties— probation, suspension, and expulsion—meted out.

27   Likewise, the 152 reports of academic dishonesty for 1997–98 at the University of Southern California in Los Angeles "is higher than previous comparable years beginning in 1991," wrote Sandra Rhoten, assistant dean in the office of student conduct, in a letter in the campus newspaper describing violations and sanctions assessed.

28   "We had a full-blown, two-year campaign [starting in 1995] to educate people about the problem," Ms. Rhoten says in an interview. "Sometimes faculty feel alone in this. We're reassuring them that we take this seriously too."

THE EXPECTATION OF HONESTY

29   Being blunt is the idea. Talking about the expectation of honesty is constant. And along with explicit warning shots, freshmen at USC are getting more intensive and detailed training in what constitutes plagiarism and other forms of cheating, Rhoten says.

30   The school passes out brochures on plagiarism, has regular coverage in the student paper on cheating cases, and has beefed up orientation courses with training to explain subtler issues like unauthorized collaboration—the largest area of student honor violation at USC and many other campuses, Mr. McCabe and others say.

31   For instance, Lucia Brawley, a senior majoring in English at Harvard University in Cambridge, Mass., does not believe cheating is a big problem at her school. But when asked about the collaboration issue, she is less sure.

32   "With people I know in the sciences, there's so much to do and so little time, they help each other," she says. "You go to a lecture today, I'll go next week. You do the reading this week, I'll do it next week. It's a gray area."

33   Ultimately, though, it is students who will have to uphold academic integrity themselves, many say.

34   The University of Virginia has a student-run honor code whose "single sanction" for violators is expulsion. It is one of the nation's strictest. Even after more than a century, it remains controversial on campus. Of 11 cheating cases last semester, five resulted in expulsion. But the code has also created an atmosphere of trust that means students can take unproctored exams. "Many of our alumni attribute their success in life to this school's honor code," says Cabell Vest, a graduate student who chairs UVA's honor council.

35   At Vanderbilt, which also has a strict code, 20 academic dishonesty cases are under review, Madson says—triple the number a few years ago. But he is confident the school is creating an atmosphere less tolerant of cheating. "You just can't have an academic enterprise that isn't based on integrity and honesty," he says. "Nobody wants somebody building bridges to take shortcuts."

Reading Reflection Questions   *Sample answers are provided.*

1. List at least three of the reasons (causes) that the author offers for the increase of student cheating over the past 45 years.

   adults and role models cheat, Internet cheating sites, parents say it isn't a

   big deal

2. How has technology, specifically the Internet, affected cheating/plagiarism? Provide some specific examples from the article.

   It makes it too easy: There are sites like Cheater.com and SchoolSucks.com

   that provide full essays to plagiarize.

3. How are colleges/universities responding to this increase in cheating? Provide a couple of specific examples.

   orientations, handouts on plagiarism, lawsuits

4. T/F _____*T*_____ Clayton sees a connection to changing societal values and an increase in plagiarism.

5. T/F _____*F*_____ The most successful students graduating recently rarely cheated (less than 10 percent of them).

6. _____*C*_____ Which of the following is *not* one of the types of cheating that students do that Clayton discusses?

   a. copying another student's homework
   b. cheating on a test
   c. working with a tutor
   d. plagiarizing an essay

Checking Vocabulary

Define each of the following words by figuring out their meaning using context clues in the reading selection. If you cannot work out the meaning of a word, refer to a dictionary.

7. provocative (paragraph 3): *thought-provoking*

8. provost (paragraph 6): *administrator*

9. plagiarism (paragraph 14): *presenting someone's work as your own*

10. collaboration (paragraph 30): *working together*

READING CRITICALLY

Answers will vary.

1. What is the author's **purpose** or goal in this reading selection?

   _____

   _____

2. What are the implied or stated questions being addressed?

   _____

   _____

Continued ▶

3. What specific **support**, details, and examples does the author use to develop the purpose or goal for the reading?

_____

_____

4. What inferences does the author include in this reading? (Inferences imply "if this, then this" types of cause-and-effect analysis.)

_____

_____

5. Who is the intended audience, and how did you reach that **conclusion**?

_____

_____

Writing Assignments

1. Write a classification essay (see Chapter 10) that categorizes types of cheating. Use examples from Mark Clayton's essay as well as those from your own experiences.
2. Write a cause-and-effect analysis essay (see Chapter 13) on cheating. Be sure to look at both causes and effects, and bring in references to Clayton's essay as well as to your own experiences.
3. Write an argument essay (see Chapter 15) that proposes possible solutions to the problem of cheating at your own campus. Come up with a specific plan of action.

"Just Walk On By": A Black Man Ponders His Power to Alter Public Space

Brent Staples

Brent Staples is an editorial writer for _The New York Times_. He has a Ph.D. in Psychology from the University of Chicago. He won the Anisfield Book Award for his memoir, _Parallel Time: Growing Up in Black and White_.

1   My first victim was a woman—white, well dressed, probably in her early 20s. I came upon her late one evening on a deserted street in Hyde Park,

a relatively affluent neighborhood in an otherwise mean, impoverished section of Chicago. As I swung onto the avenue behind her, there seemed to be a discreet, uninflammatory distance between us. Not so. She cast back a worried glance. To her, the youngish black man—a broad six feet two inches with a beard and billowing hair, both hands shoved into the pockets of a bulky military jacket—seemed menacingly close. She picked up her pace and was soon running in earnest. Within seconds she disappeared into a cross street.

2   That was more than a decade ago. I was 22 years old, a graduate student newly arrived at the University of Chicago. It was in the echo of that terrified woman's footfalls that I first began to know the unwieldy inheritance I'd come into—the ability to alter public space in ugly ways. It was clear that she thought of herself as the quarry of a mugger, a rapist, or worse. Suffering a bout of insomnia, however, I was stalking sleep, not defenseless wayfarers. As a softy who is scarcely able to take a knife to a raw chicken—let alone hold one to a person's throat—I was surprised, embarrassed, and dismayed all at once. Her flight made me feel like an accomplice in tyranny. It also made it clear that I was indistinguishable from the muggers who occasionally seeped into the area from the surrounding ghetto. I soon gathered that being perceived as dangerous is a hazard in itself: Where fear and weapons meet—as they often do in urban America—there is always the possibility of death.

3   In that first year, my first away from my hometown, I was to become thoroughly familiar with the language of fear. At dark, shadowy intersections, I could cross in front of a car stopped at a traffic light and elicit the *thunk, thunk, thunk, thunk* of the driver—black, white, male, female—hammering down the door locks. On less traveled streets after dark, I grew accustomed to but never comfortable with people crossing to the other side of the street rather than pass me. Then there were the standard unpleasantries with policemen, doormen, bouncers, cabdrivers, and others whose business it is to screen out troublesome individuals *before* there is any nastiness.

4   I moved to New York nearly two years ago and I have remained an avid night walker. In central Manhattan, the near-constant crowd covers the tense one-on-one street encounters. Elsewhere, things can get very taut indeed.

5   After dark, on the warrenlike streets of Brooklyn where I live, I often see women who fear the worst from me. They seem to have set their faces on neutral, and with their purse straps strung across their chests bandolier-style, they forge ahead as though bracing themselves against being tackled. I understand, of course, that the danger they perceive is not a hallucination. Women are particularly vulnerable to street violence,

and young black males are drastically overrepresented among the perpetrators of that violence. Yet these truths are no solace against the alienation that comes of being ever the suspect, an entity with whom pedestrians avoid making eye contact.

6   It is not altogether clear to me how I reached the ripe old age of 22 without being conscious of the lethality nighttime pedestrians attributed to me. Perhaps it was because in Chester, Pa., the small, angry industrial town where I came of age in the 1960s, I was scarcely noticeable against a backdrop of gang warfare, street knifings, and murders. I grew up one of the good boys, had perhaps a half-dozen fistfights. In retrospect, my shyness of combat has clear sources. As a boy, I saw countless tough guys locked away; I have since buried several, too. They were babies, really—a teen-age cousin, a brother of 22, a childhood friend in his mid-20s—all gone down in episodes of bravado played out in the streets. I chose, perhaps unconsciously, to remain a shadow—timid, but a survivor.

7   The fearsomeness mistakenly attributed to me in public places often has a perilous flavor. The most frightening of these confusions occurred in the late 1970s and early 1980s, when I worked as a journalist in Chicago. One day, rushing into the office of a magazine I was writing for with a deadline story in hand, I was mistaken for a burglar. The office manager called security, and with the speed of an ad hoc posse, pursued me through the labyrinthine halls, nearly to my editor's door. I had no way of proving who I was. I could only move briskly toward the company of someone who knew me.

8   Relatively speaking, however, I never fared as badly as another black male journalist. He went to nearby Waukegan, Ill., a couple of summers ago to work on a story about a murderer who was born there. Mistaking the reporter for the killer, police officers hauled him from his car at gunpoint and but for his press credentials would probably have tried to book him. Such episodes are not uncommon. Black men trade tales like this all the time.

9   Over the years, I learned to smother the rage I felt at so often being mistaken for a criminal. Not to do so would surely have led to madness. I now take precautions to make myself less threatening. I move about with care, particularly late in the evening. I give a wide berth to nervous people on subway platforms during the wee hours. If I happen to be entering a building behind some people who appear skittish, I may walk by, letting them clear the lobby before I return, so as not to seem to be following them. I have been calm and extremely congenial on those rare occasions when I've been pulled over by the police.

10   And on late-evening constitutionals I employ what has proved to be an excellent tension-reducing measure: I whistle melodies from Beethoven and Vivaldi and the more popular classical composers. Even steely New Yorkers hunching toward night-time destinations seem to relax, and occasionally they even join in the tune. Virtually everybody seems to sense that a mugger wouldn't be warbling bright, sunny selections from Vivaldi's "Four Seasons." It is my equivalent of the cowbell that hikers wear when they are in bear country.

Reading Reflection Questions   *Sample answers are provided.*

1. Explain exactly what Brent Staples means by his title to this piece. Explain how this title relates to his message in the essay.

   He had to learn to change his behavior so people, particularly women,

   wouldn't be afraid of his appearance—also, he learned to let go of being angry.

2. Explain how Staples is sometimes perceived by women on the street. Then explain how Staples has adjusted his behavior and dealt with the problem. Provide specific examples from the essay.

   He is seen as a threat based on his skin color/appearance. He has learned to

   cross the street, whistle classical music, etc. to put women at ease.

3. What is the author's tone and overall viewpoint in this essay? How has he chosen to react to the stereotype he gets judged by? What is his attitude?

   His tone is patient and understanding, though disappointed. His attitude

   is surprisingly understanding.

4. What does Brent Staples mean by the word *victim* when he writes "My first victim was a woman"? *It's ironic—she wasn't really a victim, but she*

   felt like she might be, based just on his appearance.

5. T/F ____*F*____ Staples' tone is angry in this essay.

6. ____*C*____ Which of the following best describes his purpose in this essay?
   a. To display his anger at the rudeness of strangers
   b. To tell readers that it's hard to get along with coworkers
   c. To explain the extra steps a black man has to take to put some white people at ease in public situations
   d. To compare and contrast living as a black person or a white person in the United States

7. What does Staples mean by the last line, "It is my equivalent of the cow-bell that hikers wear in bear country"? Who would the "hikers" represent in this essay? Who would the "bears" represent? Why a cowbell?

He is a hiker who wears a cowbell so that bears won't see him as a threat

(white people = the bears; bell—like the classical music he whistles = un-

threatening).

Checking Vocabulary

Define each of the following words by figuring out their meaning using context clues in the reading selection. If you cannot work out the meaning of a word, refer to a dictionary.

8. impoverished (paragraph 1): *poor*

9. uninflammatory (paragraph 1): *not challenging/threatening*

10. vulnerable (paragraph 5): *at risk*

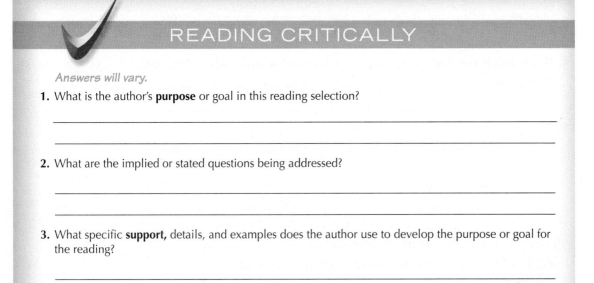

READING CRITICALLY

Answers will vary.

1. What is the author's **purpose** or goal in this reading selection?

_____

_____

2. What are the implied or stated questions being addressed?

_____

_____

3. What specific **support,** details, and examples does the author use to develop the purpose or goal for the reading?

_____

_____

4. What inferences does the author include in this reading? (Inferences imply "if this, then this" types of cause-and-effect analysis.)

_____

_____

5. Who is the intended audience, and how did you reach that **conclusion**?

_____

_____

Writing Assignments

1. Write a narration/description essay (see Chapters 7 and 8) that describes a time when you were stereotyped or judged based on your external appearance (e.g., race, gender, style, age, size, and so on).

2. Write a story analysis essay (see Chapter 21) that focuses both on how Staples uses specific writing techniques and style choices to achieve his purpose or message in this piece and analyzing his direct and implied messages in this article.

3. Write an argument essay (see Chapter 15) that comes up with a specific plan of action for educating children at an early age (grade school) regarding stereotyping based on race.

One Man's Kids

Daniel R. Meier

Daniel R. Meier is a teacher and a writer. He has written articles and books related to teaching, including _Learning in Small Moments: Life in an Urban Classroom_ and _Scribble Scrabble—Learning to Read and Write: Success with Diverse Teachers, Children, and Families._

1   I teach first graders. I live in a world of skinned knees, double-knotted shoelaces, riddles that I've heard a dozen times, stale birthday cakes, hurt feelings, wandering stories, and one lost shoe ("and if you don't find it my mother'll kill me"). My work is dominated by 6-year-olds.

2   It's 10:45, the middle of snack, and I'm helping Emily open her milk carton. She has already tried the other end without success, and now

there's so much paint and ink on the carton from her fingers that I'm not sure she should drink it at all. But I open it. Then I turn to help Scott clean up some milk he has just spilled onto Rebecca's whale crossword puzzle.

3   While I wipe my milk- and paint-covered hands, Jenny wants to know if I've seen that funny book about penguins that I read in class. As I hunt for it in a messy pile of books, Jason wants to know if there is a new seating arrangement for lunch tables. I find the book, turn to answer Jason, then face Maya, who is fast approaching with a new knock-knock joke. After what seems like the 10th "Who's there?" I laugh and Maya is pleased.

4   Then Andrew wants to know how to spell "flukes" for his crossword. As I get to "u," I give a hand signal for Sarah to take away the snack. But just as Sarah is almost out the door, two children complain that "we haven't even had ours yet." I stop the snack mid-flight, complying with their request for graham crackers. I then return to Andrew, noticing that he has put "flu" for 9 Down, rather than 9 Across. It's now 10:50.

5   My work is not traditional male work. It's not a singular pursuit. There is not a large pile of paper to get through or one deal to transact. I don't have one area of expertise or knowledge. I don't have the singular power over language of a lawyer, the physical force of a construction worker, the command over fellow workers of a surgeon, the wheeling and dealing transactions of a businessman. My energy is not spent in pursuing, climbing, achieving, conquering, or cornering some goal or object.

6   My energy is spent in encouraging, supporting, consoling, and praising my children. In teaching, the inner rewards come from without. On any given day, quite apart from teaching reading and spelling, I bandage a cut, dry a tear, erase a frown, tape a torn doll, and locate a long-lost boot. The day is really won through matters of the heart. As my students groan, laugh, shudder, cry, exult, and wonder, I do too. I have to be soft around the edges.

7   A few years ago, when I was interviewing for an elementary-school teaching position, every principal told me with confidence that, as a male, I had an advantage over female applicants because of the lack of male teachers. But in the next breath, they asked with a hint of suspicion why I chose to work with young children. I told them that I wanted to observe and contribute to the intellectual growth of a maturing mind. What I really felt like saying, but didn't, was that I loved helping a child learn to write her name for the first time, finding someone a new friend, or sharing in the hilarity of reading about Winnie the Pooh getting so stuck in a hole that only his head and rear show.

8   I gave that answer to those principals, who were mostly male, because I thought they wanted a "male" response. This meant talking

about intellectual matters. If I had taken a different course and talked about my interest in helping children in their emotional development, it would have been seen as closer to a "female" answer. I even altered my language, not once mentioning the word "love" to describe what I do indeed love about teaching. My answer worked; every principal nodded approvingly.

9   Some of the principals also asked what I saw myself doing later in my career. They wanted to know if I eventually wanted to go into educational administration. Becoming a dean of students or a principal has never been one of my goals, but they seemed to expect me, as a male, to want to climb higher on the career stepladder. So I mentioned that, at some point, I would be interested in working with teachers as a curriculum coordinator. Again, they nodded approvingly.

10   If those principals had been female instead of male, I wonder whether their questions, and my answers, would have been different. My guess is that they would have been.

11   At other times, when I'm at a party or a dinner and tell someone that I teach young children, I've found that men and women respond differently. Most men ask about the subjects I teach and the courses I took in my training. Then, unless they bring up an issue such as merit pay, the conversation stops. Most women, on the other hand, begin the conversation on a more immediate and personal level. They say things like "those kids must love having a male teacher" or "that age is just wonderful, you must love it." Then, more often than not, they'll talk about their own kids or ask me specific questions about what I do. We're then off and talking shop.

12   Possibly, men would have more to say to me, and I to them, if my job had more of the trappings and benefits of more traditional male jobs. But my job has no bonuses or promotions. No complimentary box seats at the ball park. No cab fare home. No drinking buddies after work. No briefcase. No suit. (Ties get stuck in paint jars.) No power lunches. (I eat peanut butter and jelly, chips, milk, and cookies with the kids.) No taking clients out for cocktails. The only place I take my kids is to the playground.

13   Although I could have pursued a career in law or business, as several of my friends did, I chose teaching instead. My job has benefits all its own. I'm able to bake cookies without getting them stuck together as they cool, buy cheap sewing materials, take out splinters, and search just the right trash cans for useful odds and ends. I'm sometimes called "Daddy" and even "Mommy" by my students, and if there's ever a lull in the conversation at a dinner party, I can always ask those assembled if they've heard the latest riddle about why the turkey crossed the road. (He thought he was a chicken.)

Reading Reflection Questions   *Sample answers are provided.*

1. What is it that Daniel Meier loves about teaching first graders? Give some specific examples from his essay. *nurturing and consoling them,*

   watching them learn, Winnie the Pooh hilarity, finding a new friend, etc.

2. What does Meier mean by the phrase "The day is really won through matters of the heart" (paragraph 6)? Explain. *helping kids with their*

   day-to-day needs and nurturing them

3. Provide some examples from the essay that prove that Meier is, as he says in his essay, "soft around the edges" (paragraph 6) with his students.

   bandaging dolls, laughing and crying with his students

4. T/F _____F_____ The majority of first-grade teachers are male.

5. T/F _____F_____ Meier hopes to become his school's principal.

6. List two of the "benefits" Meier sees as part of his job (see final paragraph): *being called Daddy or Mommy by his students, knowing the latest*

   kid joke or riddle.

7. T/F _____T_____ Some people question Meier's motives as a male working with young children.

Checking Vocabulary

Define each of the following words by figuring out their meaning using context clues in the reading selection. If you cannot work out the meaning of a word, refer to a dictionary.

8. dominated (paragraph 1): *controlled, guided*

9. transactions (paragraph 5): *business deals*

10. consoling (paragraph 6): *comforting*

READING CRITICALLY

Answers will vary.

1. What is the author's **purpose** or goal in this reading selection?

   _____

   _____

2. What are the implied or stated questions being addressed?

_____

_____

3. What specific **support**, details, and examples does the author use to develop the purpose or goal for the reading?

_____

_____

4. What inferences does the author include in this reading? (Inferences imply "if this, then this" types of cause-and-effect analysis.)

_____

_____

5. Who is the intended audience, and how did you reach that **conclusion**?

_____

_____

Writing Assignments

1. Write a narration/description essay (see Chapters 7 and 8) about one of your favorite elementary school teachers. What makes that teacher stick out in your memory?

2. Write an example/illustration essay (see Chapter 12) about what makes Meier's job more "female" or "feminine" than "male" or "masculine." Provide examples from Meier to back up your analysis.

3. Write an argument/persuasion essay (see Chapter 15) that argues for the need for more male teachers in elementary school. You may want to bring in some cause-and-effect analysis (see Chapter 13) to explain why many men don't choose to teach younger children _and_ what effects (benefits) could come from encouraging more men to enter the career of teaching young children.

The Discus Thrower

Richard Selzer

Richard Selzer was born in Troy, New York, in 1928. He is both a practicing surgeon and a writer. In 1974, after years of being a doctor, he wrote *Rituals of Surgery*, a collection of short stories. He has also published several essays and stories in magazines such as *Redbook*, *Esquire*, and *Harper's*. Many of his essays and stories are in two collections: *Mortal Lessons* (1977) and *Confessions of a Knife* (1979).

1   I spy on my patients. Ought not a doctor to observe his patients by any means and from any stance that he might the more fully assemble evidence? So I stand in the doorways of hospital rooms and gaze. Oh, it is not all that furtive an act. Those in bed need only look up to discover me. But they never do.

2   From the doorway of Room 542 the man in the bed seems deeply tanned. Blue eyes and close-cropped white hair give him the appearance of vigor and good health. But I know that his skin is not brown from the sun. It is rusted, rather, in the last stage of containing the vile repose within. And the blue eyes are frosted, looking inward like the windows of a snowbound cottage. This man is blind. This man is also legless—the right leg missing from midthigh down, the left from just below the knee. It gives him the look of a bonsai, roots and branches pruned into the dwarfed facsimile of a great tree.

3   Propped on pillows, he cups his right thigh in both hands. Now and then he shakes his head as though acknowledging the intensity of his suffering. In all of this he makes no sound. Is he mute as well as blind?

4   The room in which he dwells is empty of all possessions—no get-well cards, small, private caches of food, day-old flowers, slippers, all the usual kickshaws of the sickroom. There is only the bed, a chair, a nightstand, and a tray on wheels that can be swung across his lap for meals.

5   "What time is it?" he asks.

6   "Three o'clock."

7   "Morning or afternoon?"

8   "Afternoon."

9   He is silent. There is nothing else he wants to know.

10   "How are you?" I say.

11   "Who is it?" he asks.

12   "It's the doctor. How do you feel?"

13   He does not answer right away.

14   "Feel?" he says.

15   "I hope you feel better," I say.

16   I press the button at the side of the bed.

17   "Down you go," I say.

18   "Yes, down," he says.

19   He falls back upon the bed awkwardly. His stumps, unweighted by legs and feet, rise in the air, presenting themselves. I unwrap the bandages

from the stumps, and begin to cut away the black scabs and the dead, glazed fat with scissors and forceps. A shard of white bone comes loose. I pick it away. I wash the wounds with disinfectant and redress the stumps. All this while, he does not speak. What is he thinking behind those lids that do not blink? Is he remembering a time when he was whole? Does he dream of feet? Of when his body was not a rotting log?

20   He lies solid and inert. In spite of everything, he remains impressive, as though he were a sailor standing athwart a slanting deck.

21   "Anything more I can do for you?" I ask. For a long moment he is silent.

22   "Yes," he says at last and without the least irony. "You can bring me a pair of shoes."

23   In the corridor the head nurse is waiting for me.

24   "We have to do something about him," she says. "Every morning he orders scrambled eggs for breakfast, and, instead of eating them, he picks up the plate and throws it against the wall."

25   "Throws his plate?"

26   "Nasty. That's what he is. No wonder his family doesn't come to visit. They probably can't stand him any more than we can."

27   She is waiting for me to do something.

28   "Well?"

29   "We'll see," I say.

30   The next morning I am waiting in the corridor when the kitchen delivers his breakfast. I watch the aide place the tray on the stand and swing it across his lap. She presses the button to raise the head of the bed. Then she leaves.

31   In time the man reaches to find the rim of the tray, then on to find the dome of the covered dish. He lifts off the cover and places it on the stand. He fingers across the plate until he probes the eggs. He lifts the plate in both hands, sets it on the palm of his right hand, centers it, balances it. He hefts it up and down slightly, getting the feel of it. Abruptly he draws back his right arm as far as he can.

32   There is the crack of the plate breaking against the wall at the foot of his bed and the small wet sound of the scrambled eggs dropping to the floor.

33   And then he laughs. It is a sound you have never heard. It is something new under the sun. It could cure cancer.

34   Out in the corridor, the eyes of the head nurse narrow.
"Laughed, did he?"

35   She writes something down on her clipboard.

36   A second aide arrives, brings a second breakfast tray, puts it on the nightstand, out of his reach. She looks over at me shaking her head and making her mouth go. I see that we are to be accomplices.

37   "I've got to feed you," she says to the man.

38   "Oh, no you don't," the man says.

39   "Oh, yes I do," the aide says, "after the way you just did. Nurse says so."

40   "Get me my shoes," the man says.

41   "Here's oatmeal," the aide says. "Open." And she touches the spoon to his lower lip.

42   "I ordered scrambled eggs," says the man.

43   "That's right," the aide says.

44   I step forward.

45   "Is there anything I can do?" I say.

46   "Who are you?" the man asks.

47   In the evening I go once more to that ward to make my rounds. The head nurse reports to me that Room 542 is deceased. She has discovered this quite by accident, she says. No, there had been no sound. Nothing. It's a blessing, she says.

48   I go into his room, a spy looking for secrets. He is still there in his bed. His face is relaxed, grave, dignified. After a while, I turn to leave. My gaze sweeps the wall at the foot of the bed, and I see the place where it has been repeatedly washed, where the wall looks very clean and very white.

Reading Reflection Questions   *Sample answers are provided.*

1. What are the direct or indirect (implied) messages in this story?

   that even though this patient was blind and had no legs, he still wanted to

   have respect and had pride/dignity

2. Describe the conflict between the doctor and the nurse in this story with regard to the patient.

   The nurse sees the patient as an annoyance; the doctor is impressed by

   him and admires him.

3. What is it about this patient that intrigues the doctor so? Provide specific examples. *that he still has fight in him and rebellion—like ordering*

   eggs and throwing them against the wall, and asking for his shoes when he

   has no feet

4. T/F _____T_____ The doctor is curious about this patient's unusual ritual.

5. T/F _____F_____ The doctor is annoyed by this patient's stubbornness.

6. T/F _____F_____ The nurse admires the patient's pride.

7. T/F _____F_____ The patient and the doctor become good friends.

Checking Vocabulary

Define each of the following words by figuring out their meaning using context clues in the reading selection. If you cannot work out the meaning of a word, refer to a dictionary.

8. furtive (paragraph 1): *secretive*

9. facsimile (paragraph 2): *a fake version*

10. inert (paragraph 20): *unmoving*

READING CRITICALLY

Answers will vary.

1. What is the author's **purpose** or goal in this reading selection?

2. What are the implied or stated questions being addressed?

3. What specific **support**, details, and examples does the author use to develop the purpose or goal for the reading?

4. What inferences does the author include in this reading? (Inferences imply "if this, then this" types of cause-and-effect analysis.)

5. Who is the intended audience, and how did you reach that **conclusion**?

Writing Assignments

1. Write a story analysis essay (see Chapter 21) that addresses both Selzer's writing technique and style as well as his analytical message (the purpose) of the story.

2. Write a narration/description essay (see Chapters 7 and 8) about someone you know who displayed pride and dignity in the face of an awkward or uncomfortable event or circumstance.

3. Write a process essay (see Chapter 9) that describes step by step a ritual or habit that you have or that someone you know has. Include specific details. What purpose does this ritual serve?

Supersize Me

Greg Critser

Greg Critser is a journalist who writes for *USA Today*. He has written several articles; many of them focus on medical, health, and nutrition topics. His books include *Welcome to Fat Land: How Americans Became the Fattest People in the World* and *Generation R$_x$: How Prescription Drugs are Altering American Lives, Minds, and Bodies*. This reading is from Chapter 2 of *Welcome to Fatland*.

1   David Wallerstein, a director of the McDonald's Corporation, hated the fifth deadly sin because it kept people from buying more hamburgers. Wallerstein had first waged war on the injunction against gluttony as a young executive in the theater business. At the staid Balaban Theaters chain in the early 1960s, Wallerstein had realized that the movie business was really a margin business; it wasn't the sale of low-markup movie tickets that generated profits but rather the sale of high-markup snacks like popcorn and Coke. To sell more of such items, he had, by the mid-1960s, tried about every trick in the conventional retailer's book: two-for-one specials, combo deals, matinee specials, etc. But at the end of any given day, as he tallied up his receipts, Wallerstein inevitably came up with about the same amount of profit.

2   Thinking about it one night, he had a realization: People did not want to buy two boxes of popcorn *no matter what*. They didn't want to be seen eating two boxes of popcorn. It looked piggish. So Wallerstein flipped the equation around: Perhaps he could get more people to spend just a little more on popcorn if he made the boxes bigger and increased the price

only a little. The popcorn cost a pittance anyway, and he'd already paid for the salt and the seasoning and the counter help and the popping machine. So he put up signs advertising jumbo-size popcorn. The results after the first week were astounding. Not only were individual sales of popcorn increasing; with them rose individual sales of that other high-profit item, Coca-Cola.

3   Later, at McDonald's in the mid-1970s, Wallerstein faced a similar problem: With consumers watching their pennies, restaurant customers were coming to the Golden Arches less and less frequently. Worse, when they did, they were "cherry-picking," buying only, say, a small Coke and a burger, or, worse, just a burger, which yielded razor-thin profit margins. How could he get people back to buying more fries? His popcorn experience certainly suggested one solution—sell them a jumbo-size bag of the crispy treats.

4   Yet try as he may, Wallerstein could not convince Ray Kroc, McDonald's founder, to sign on to the idea. As recounted in interviews with his associates and in John F. Love's 1985 book, *McDonald's: Behind the Arches,* the exchange between the two men could be quite contentious on the issue. "If people want more fries," Kroc would say, "they can buy two bags."

5   "But Ray," Wallerstein would say, "they don't want to eat two bags— they don't want to look like a glutton."

6   To convince Kroc, Wallerstein decided to do his own survey of customer behavior, and began observing various Chicago-area McDonald's. Sitting in one store after another, sipping his drink and watching hundreds of Chicagoans chomp their way through their little bag of fries, Wallerstein could see: People *wanted* more fries.

7   "How do you know that?" Kroc asked the next morning when Wallerstein presented his findings.

8   "Because they're eating the entire bagful, Ray," Wallerstein said. "They even scrape and pinch around at the bottom of the bag for more and eat the salt!"

9   Kroc gave in. Within months receipts were up, customer counts were up, and franchisees—the often truculent heart and soul of the McDonald's success—were happier than ever.

10   Many franchisees wanted to take the concept even further, offering large-size versions of other menu items. At this sudden burst of entrepreneurism, however, McDonald's mid-level managers hesitated. Many of them viewed large-sizing as a form of "discounting," with all the negative connotations such a word evoked. In a business where "wholesome" and "dependable" were the primary PR watchwords, large-sizing could become a major image problem. Who knew what the franchisees, with

their primal desires and shortcutting ways, would do next? No, large-sizing was something to be controlled tightly from Chicago, if it were to be considered at all.

11   Yet as McDonald's headquarters would soon find out, large-sizing was a new kind of marketing magic—a magic that could not so easily be put back into those crinkly little-size bags.

12   Max Cooper, a Birmingham franchisee, was not unfamiliar with marketing and magic; for most of his adult life he had been paid to conjure sales from little more than hot air and smoke. Brash, blunt-spoken, and witty, Cooper had acquired his talents while working as an old-fashioned public relations agent—the kind, as he liked to say, who "got you into the newspaper columns instead of trying to keep you out." In the 1950s with his partner, Al Golin, he had formed what later became Golin Harris, one of the world's more influential public relations firms. In the mid-1960s, first as a consultant and later as an executive, he had helped create many of McDonald's most successful early campaigns. He had been the prime mover in the launch of Ronald McDonald.

13   By the 1970s Cooper, tired of "selling for someone else," bought a couple of McDonald's franchises in Birmingham, moved his split-off ad agency there, and set up shop as an independent businessman. As he began expanding, he noticed what many other McDonald's operators were noticing: declining customer counts. Sitting around a table and kibitzing with a few like-minded associates one day in 1975, "we started talking about how we could build sales—how we could do it and be profitable," Cooper recalled in a recent interview. "And we realized we could do one of three things. We could cut costs, but there's a limit to that. We could cut prices, but that too has its limits. Then we could raise sales profitably—sales, after all, could be limitless when you think about it. We realized we could do that by taking the high-profit drink and fry and then packaging it with the low-profit burger. We realized that if you could get them to buy three items for what they perceived as less, you could substantially drive up the number of walk-ins. Sales would follow."

14   But trying to sell that to corporate headquarters was next to impossible. "We were maligned! Oh, were we maligned," he recalls. "A 99-cent anything was heresy to them. They would come and say 'You're just cutting prices! What are we gonna look like to everybody else?'"

15   "No no no," Cooper would shoot back. "You have to think of the analogy to a fine French restaurant. You always pay less for a *table d'hôte* meal than you pay for *à la carte,* don't you?"

16   "Yes, but—,"

17   "Well, this is a *table d'hôte* dammit! You're getting more people to the table spending as much as they would before—and coming more often!"

18   Finally headquarters relented, although by now it hardly mattered. Cooper had by then begun his own rogue campaign. He was selling what the industry would later call "value meals"—the origin of what we now call supersizing. Using local radio, he advertised a "Big Mac and Company," a "Fish, Fry, Drink and Pie," a "4th of July Value Combo." Sales, Cooper says, "went through the roof. Just like I told them they would."

* * * * *

19   Though it is difficult to gauge the exact impact of supersizing upon the appetite of the average consumer, there are clues about it in the now growing field of satiety—the science of understanding human satisfaction. A 2001 study by nutritional researchers at Penn State University, for example, sought to find out whether the presence of larger portions *in themselves* induced people to eat more. Men and women volunteers, all reporting the same level of hunger, were served lunch on four separate occasions. In each session, the size of the main entree was increased, from 500 to 625 to 700 and finally to 1000 grams. After four weeks, the pattern became clear: As portions increased, all participants ate increasingly larger amounts, despite their stable hunger levels. As the scholars wrote: "Subjects consumed approximately 30 percent more energy when served the largest as opposed to the smallest portion." They had documented that satiety is not satiety. Human hunger could be expanded by merely offering more and bigger options.

20   Certainly the best nutritional data suggest so as well. Between 1970 and 1994, the USDA reports, the amount of food available in the American food supply increased 15 percent—from 3300 to 3800 calories or by about 500 calories per person per day. During about the same period (1977–1995), average individual caloric intake increased by almost 200 calories, from 1876 calories a day to 2043 calories a day. One could argue which came first, the appetite or the bigger burger, but the calories—they were on the plate and in our mouths.

21   By the end of the century, supersizing—the ultimate expression of the value meal revolution—reigned. As of 1996, some 25 percent of the $97 billion spent on fast food came from items promoted on the basis of either larger size or extra portions. A serving of McDonald's french fries had ballooned from 200 calories (1960) to 320 calories (late 1970s) to 450 calories (mid-1990s) to 540 calories (late 1990s) to the present 610 calories. In fact, everything on the menu had exploded in size. What was once a 590-calorie McDonald's meal was now . . . 1550 calories. By 1999, heavy users—people who eat fast food more than twenty times a month—accounted for $66 billion of the $110 billion spent on fast food. Twenty times a month is now McDonald's marketing goal for every fast-food eater. The average Joe or Jane thought nothing of buying Little Caesar's pizza "by

the foot," of supersizing that lunchtime burger or super- supersizing an afternoon snack. Kids had come to see bigger everything—bigger sodas, bigger snacks, bigger candy, and even bigger doughnuts—as the norm; there was no such thing as a fixed, immutable size for anything, because anything could be made a lot bigger for just a tad more.

22   There was more to all of this than just eating more. Bigness: The concept seemed to fuel the marketing of just about everything, from cars (SUVs) to homes (mini-manses) to clothes (super-baggy) and then back again to food (as in the Del Taco Macho Meal, which weighed four pounds). The social scientists and the marketing gurus were going crazy trying to keep up with the trend. "Bigness is addictive because it is about power," commented Inna Zall, a teen marketing consultant, in a page-one story in *USA Today*. While few teenage boys can actually finish a 64-ounce Double Gulp, she added, "it's empowering to hold one in your hand."

23   The pioneers of supersize had achieved David Wallerstein's dream. They had banished the shame of gluttony and opened the maw of the American eater wider than even they had ever imagined.

Reading Reflection Questions   *Sample answers are provided.*

1. What are the main messages of this essay (both implied and directly stated)? *that the supersize craze that started at McDonald's has*

   encouraged overindulgence and has spread to other aspects of American

   culture

2. How are statistics used in this article (see especially paragraphs 19 to 21)? What effect do these statistics have in the overall purpose for Critser's essay? *to prove how extreme the portion size has grown*

   _____

3. According to Critser, how did the supersize craze begin, and how widely has it spread? Provide specific examples from the essay.

   with Wallerstein convincing Kroc to increase portion size after trying it

   with popcorn in theaters and after watching customers eat all their fries

   and want more

4. T/F ___*T*___ Ray Kroc, McDonald's founder, was reluctant at first to increase portion sizes.

5. T/F ___*F*___ Burgers have a higher profit margin than do fries and drinks.

6. T/F ___*T*___ David Wallerstein came up with the original idea of increasing portion sizes by selling popcorn.

Checking Vocabulary

Define each of the following words by figuring out their meaning using context clues in the reading selection. If you cannot work out the meaning of a word, refer to a dictionary.

8. gluttony (paragraph 1): *eating and drinking too much*

9. pittance (paragraph 2): *small amount*

10. franchise(s) (paragraph 13): *an individually owned business*

READING CRITICALLY

Answers will vary.

1. What is the author's **purpose** or goal this reading selection?

_____

_____

2. What are the implied or stated questions being addressed?

_____

_____

3. What specific **support**, details, and examples does the author use to develop the purpose or goal for the reading?

_____

_____

4. What inferences does the author include in this reading? (Inferences imply "if this, then this" types of cause-and-effect analysis.)

_____

_____

5. Who is the intended audience, and how did you reach that **conclusion**?

_____

_____

Writing Assignments

1. Write a cause-and-effect essay (see Chapter 13) on the supersize phenomenon as described by Critser in "Supersize Me."

2. Write an example/illustration essay (see Chapter 12) that supports Critser's view about this trend for making everything "bigger"; use examples from Critser as well as examples from your own experiences. Include some narration (see Chapter 7) and cause-and-effect analysis (see Chapter 13).

3. Write an argument essay (see Chapter 15) that develops a specific plan of action for educating children at an early age regarding the supersize phenomenon and its harmful consequences.

A Hanging

George Orwell

George Orwell, born Eric Arthur Blair on June 25, 1903, in Motihari, India, was a famous British writer and journalist. He died in London in 1950. He wrote many essays and stories, but he is most famous for his two novels that critique fascism: *Animal Farm* and *1984*. The following story was written in 1931 and relates to his life in Burma before he left for England.

1   It was in Burma, a sodden morning of the rains. A sickly light, like yellow tinfoil, was slanting over the high walls into the jail yard. We were waiting outside the condemned cells, a row of sheds fronted with double bars, like small animal cages. Each cell measured about ten feet by ten and was quite bare within except for a plank bed and a pot of drinking water. In some of them brown silent men were squatting at the inner bars, with their blankets draped round them. These were the condemned men, due to be hanged within the next week or two.

2   One prisoner had been brought out of his cell. He was a Hindu, a puny wisp of a man, with a shaven head and vague liquid eyes. He had a thick, sprouting moustache, absurdly too big for his body, rather like the moustache of a comic man on the films. Six tall Indian warders were guarding him and getting him ready for the gallows. Two of them stood by with rifles and fixed bayonets, while the others handcuffed him, passed a chain through his handcuffs and fixed it to their belts, and lashed his arms tight to his sides. They crowded very close about him, with their hands always on him in a careful, caressing grip, as though all the while feeling him to make sure he was there. It was like men handling a fish which is still alive and may jump back into the water. But he stood quite unresisting, yielding his arms limply to the ropes, as though he hardly noticed what was happening.

3   Eight o'clock struck and a bugle call, desolately thin in the wet air, floated from the distant barracks. The superintendent of the jail, who was standing apart from the rest of us, moodily prodding the gravel with his stick, raised his head at the sound. He was an army doctor, with a grey toothbrush moustache and a gruff voice. "For God's sake hurry up, Francis," he said irritably. "The man ought to have been dead by this time. Aren't you ready yet?"

4   Francis, the head jailer, a fat Dravidian in a white drill suit and gold spectacles, waved his black hand. "Yes sir, yes sir," he bubbled. "All iss satisfactorily prepared. The hangman iss waiting. We shall proceed."

5   "Well, quick march, then. The prisoners can't get their breakfast till this job's over."

6   We set out for the gallows. Two warders marched on either side of the prisoner, with their rifles at the slope; two others marched close against him, gripping him by arm and shoulder, as though at once pushing and supporting him. The rest of us, magistrates and the like, followed behind. Suddenly, when we had gone ten yards, the procession stopped short without any order or warning. A dreadful thing had happened—a dog, come goodness knows whence, had appeared in the yard. It came bounding among us with a loud volley of barks, and leapt round us wagging its whole body, wild with glee at finding so many human beings together. It was a large woolly dog, half Airedale, half pariah. For a moment it pranced round us, and then, before anyone could stop it, it had made a dash for the prisoner, and jumping up tried to lick his face. Everyone stood aghast, too taken aback even to grab at the dog.

7   "Who let that bloody brute in here?" said the superintendent angrily. "Catch it, someone!"

8   A warder, detached from the escort, charged clumsily after the dog, but it danced and gambolled just out of his reach, taking everything as part of the game. A young Eurasian jailer picked up a handful of gravel and tried to stone the dog away, but it dodged the stones and came after us again. Its yaps echoed from the jail wails. The prisoner, in the grasp of the two warders, looked on incuriously, as though this was another formality of the hanging. It was several minutes before someone managed to catch the dog. Then we put my handkerchief through its collar and moved off once more, with the dog still straining and whimpering.

9   It was about forty yards to the gallows. I watched the bare brown back of the prisoner marching in front of me. He walked clumsily with his bound arms, but quite steadily, with that bobbing gait of the Indian who never straightens his knees. At each step his muscles slid neatly into place, the lock of hair on his scalp danced up and down, his feet printed themselves on the wet gravel. And once, in spite of the men who gripped him by each shoulder, he stepped slightly aside to avoid a puddle on the path.

10   It is curious, but till that moment I had never realized what it means to destroy a healthy, conscious man. When I saw the prisoner step aside to avoid the puddle, I saw the mystery, the unspeakable wrongness, of cutting a life short when it is in full tide. This man was not dying, he was alive just as we were alive. All the organs of his body were working—bowels digesting food, skin renewing itself, nails growing, tissues forming—all toiling away in solemn foolery. His nails would still be growing when he stood on the drop, when he was falling through the air with a tenth of a second to live. His eyes saw the yellow gravel and the grey walls, and his brain still remembered, foresaw, reasoned—reasoned even about puddles. He and we were a party of men walking together, seeing, hearing, feeling, understanding the same world; and in two minutes, with a sudden snap, one of us would be gone—one mind less, one world less.

11   The gallows stood in a small yard, separate from the main grounds of the prison, and overgrown with tall prickly weeds. It was a brick erection like three sides of a shed, with planking on top, and above that two beams and a crossbar with the rope dangling. The hangman, a grey-haired convict in the white uniform of the prison, was waiting beside his machine. He greeted us with a servile crouch as we entered. At a word from Francis the two warders, gripping the prisoner more closely than ever, half led, half pushed him to the gallows and helped him clumsily up the ladder. Then the hangman climbed up and fixed the rope round the prisoner's neck.

12   We stood waiting, five yards away. The warders had formed in a rough circle round the gallows. And then, when the noose was fixed, the prisoner began crying out to his god. It was a high, reiterated cry of "Ram! Ram! Ram! Ram!", not urgent and fearful like a prayer or a cry for help, but steady, rhythmical, almost like the tolling of a bell. The dog answered the sound with a whine. The hangman, still standing on the gallows, produced a small cotton bag like a flour bag and drew it down over the prisoner's face. But the sound, muffled by the cloth, still persisted, over and over again: "Ram! Ram! Ram! Ram! Ram!"

13   The hangman climbed down and stood ready, holding the lever. Minutes seemed to pass. The steady, muffled crying from the prisoner went on and on, "Ram! Ram! Ram!" never faltering for an instant. The superintendent, his head on his chest, was slowly poking the ground with his stick; perhaps he was counting the cries, allowing the prisoner a fixed number—fifty, perhaps, or a hundred. Everyone had changed colour. The Indians had gone grey like bad coffee, and one or two of the bayonets were wavering. We looked at the lashed, hooded man on the drop, and listened to his cries—each cry another second of life; the same thought was in all our minds: oh, kill him quickly, get it over, stop that abominable noise!

14   Suddenly the superintendent made up his mind. Throwing up his head he made a swift motion with his stick. "Chalo!" he shouted almost fiercely.

15   There was a clanking noise, and then dead silence. The prisoner had vanished, and the rope was twisting on itself. I let go of the dog, and it galloped immediately to the back of the gallows; but when it got there it stopped short, barked, and then retreated into a corner of the yard, where it stood among the weeds, looking timorously out at us. We went round the gallows to inspect the prisoner's body. He was dangling with his toes pointed straight downwards, very slowly revolving, as dead as a stone.

16   The superintendent reached out with his stick and poked the bare body; it oscillated, slightly. "He's all right," said the superintendent. He backed out from under the gallows, and blew out a deep breath. The moody look had gone out of his face quite suddenly. He glanced at his wrist-watch. "Eight minutes past eight. Well, that's all for this morning, thank God."

17   The warders unfixed bayonets and marched away. The dog, sobered and conscious of having misbehaved itself, slipped after them. We walked out of the gallows yard, past the condemned cells with their waiting prisoners, into the big central yard of the prison. The convicts, under the command of warders armed with lathis, were already receiving their breakfast. They squatted in long rows, each man holding a tin pannikin, while two warders with buckets marched round ladling out rice; it seemed quite a homely, jolly scene, after the hanging. An enormous relief had come upon us now that the job was done. One felt an impulse to sing, to break into a run, to snigger. All at once everyone began chattering gaily.

18   The Eurasian boy walking beside me nodded towards the way we had come, with a knowing smile: "Do you know, sir, our friend (he meant the dead man), when he heard his appeal had been dismissed, he pissed on the floor of his cell. From fright.—Kindly take one of my cigarettes, sir. Do you not admire my new silver case, sir? From the boxwallah, two rupees eight annas. Classy European style."

19   Several people laughed—at what, nobody seemed certain.

20   Francis was walking by the superintendent, talking garrulously. "Well, sir, all hass passed off with the utmost satisfactoriness. It wass all finished—flick! like that. It iss not always so—oah, no! I have known cases where the doctor wass obliged to go beneath the gallows and pull the prisoner's legs to ensure decease. Most disagreeable!"

21   "Wriggling about, eh? That's bad," said the superintendent.

22   "Ach, sir, it iss worse when they become refractory! One man, I recall, clung to the bars of hiss cage when we went to take him out. You will scarcely credit, sir, that it took six warders to dislodge him, three pulling at each leg. We reasoned with him. 'My dear fellow,' we said, 'think of all

the pain and trouble you are causing to us!' But no, he would not listen! Ach, he wass very troublesome!"

23   I found that I was laughing quite loudly. Everyone was laughing. Even the superintendent grinned in a tolerant way. "You'd better all come out and have a drink," he said quite genially. "I've got a bottle of whisky in the car. We could do with it."

24   We went through the big double gates of the prison, into the road. "Pulling at his legs!" exclaimed a Burmese magistrate suddenly, and burst into a loud chuckling. We all began laughing again. At that moment Francis's anecdote seemed extraordinarily funny. We all had a drink together, native and European alike, quite amicably. The dead man was a hundred yards away.

Reading Reflection Questions   *Sample answers are provided.*

1. What is the main message of this story that George Orwell wanted his readers to understand? *that killing a man is wrong—no matter his crime*

   _____

2. T/F ___F___ According to the narrator, the prisoner's crime was murder.

3. T/F ___F___ This hanging was the first hanging that the soldier/ narrator had witnessed.

4. ___b___ Which of the following best describes the mood or atmosphere of the characters and story?

   a. Light and humorous

   b. Somber and serious at first with relief and laughing at the end

   c. Outraged and angry throughout

5. Which sentence in the story best sums up Orwell's main thesis? Write it here:

   "Suddenly I realized the unspeakable wrongness of cutting a life short . . ."

6. T/F ___T___ The prisoner is a Hindu.

7. Why is the dog important in this story? What function does the dog serve for the plot? *The dog reminds them that the prisoner is a human—he shows*

   the man love and acknowledges him as a human.

8. Why is the fact that the prisoner stepped around the puddle important? What does it signify for the soldier who witnessed this action? *It's strange*

   that even though he is about to die, he steps around the puddle—it triggers

   the realization in the soldier that this man is a living human being.

Checking Vocabulary

Define each of the following words by figuring out their meaning using context clues in the reading selection. If you cannot work out the meaning of a word, refer to a dictionary.

9. sodden (paragraph 1): *very wet*

10. pariah (paragraph 6): *mutt/wild dog/social outcast*

READING CRITICALLY

Answers will vary.

1. What is the author's **purpose** or goal in this reading selection?

2. What are the implied or stated questions being addressed?

3. What specific **support**, details, and examples does the author use to develop the purpose or goal for the reading?

4. What inferences does the author include in this reading? (Inferences imply "if this, then this" types of cause-and-effect analysis.)

5. Who is the intended audience, and how did you reach that **conclusion**?

Writing Assignments

1. Write a story analysis essay (see Chapter 21) that addresses Orwell's writing technique and style as well as his purpose for writing the story. Be sure to use Six Steps to Active Reading (pp. 23–28) to increase your comprehension and ability to analyze the story effectively.

2. Write a narration/description essay (see Chapters 7 and 8) about a traumatic or uncomfortable incident you witnessed and what you learned from the experience. Be sure to frame your essay with an introduction and conclusion that explains what lessons you learned about yourself and others from that incident. Also, be sure to include some dialogue in the correct dialogue format.

3. Write an argument essay (see Chapter 15) that argues for or against capital punishment. Be sure to define your stand clearly, including when and how capital punishment is or isn't justified. Present clear counterarguments to your stand, and address those counterarguments fully. Check with your instructor whether you should or should not conduct and include secondary research on capital punishment. If you do include research, then be sure to cite all sources correctly (see MLA section and Research/Documented Paper information in Chapter 19).

I Wonder: Was It Me or Was It My Sari?

Shoba Narayan

Shoba Narayan has written several articles about travel, food, and life. She holds a B.S. in Psychology and an M.A. in Journalism. Also, her book, *Monsoon Diary: A Memoir with Recipes* (2003) describes growing up in South India. This essay originally appeared in *Newsweek* in March 2000.

1   A sari for a month. It shouldn't have been a big deal but it was. After all, I had grown up around sari-clad women in India. My mother even slept in one.

2   In India, saris are adult attire. After I turned 18, I occasionally wore a sari for weddings and holidays and to the temple. But wearing a sequined silk sari to an Indian party was one thing. Deciding to wear a sari every day while living in New York, especially after 10 years in Western clothes, sounded outrageous, even to me.

3   The sari is six yards of fabric folded into a graceful yet cumbersome garment. Like a souffle, it is fragile and can fall apart at any moment. When worn right, it is supremely elegant and unabashedly feminine. However, it requires sacrifices.

4   No longer could I sprint across the street just before the light changed. The sari forced me to shorten my strides. I couldn't squeeze into a crowded subway car for fear that someone would accidentally pull and unravel my sari. I couldn't balance four grocery bags in one hand and pull

out my house keys from a convenient pocket with the other. By the end of the first week, I was stumbling around my apartment, feeling clumsy and angry with myself. What was I trying to prove?

5   The notion of wearing a sari every day was relatively new for me. During my college years—the age when most girls in India begin wearing saris regularly—I was studying in America. As an art student at Mount Holyoke, I hung out with purple-haired painters and rabble-rousing feminists wearing ink-stained khakis and cut-off T shirts. During a languid post-graduation summer in Boston, when I sailed a boat and volunteered for an environmental organization, I wore politically correct, recycled Salvation Army clothes. After getting married, I became a Connecticut housewife experimenting with clothes from Jones New York and Ann Taylor. Through it all, I tried to pick up the accent, learn the jargon and affect the posture of the Americans around me.

6   Then I moved to New York and became a mother. I wanted to teach my 3-year-old daughter Indian values and traditions because I knew she would be profoundly different from her preschool classmates in religion (we are Hindus), eating habits (we are vegetarians) and the festivals we celebrated. Wearing a sari every day was my way of showing her that she could melt into the pot while retaining her individual flavor.

7   It wasn't just for my daughter's sake that I decided to wear a sari. I was tired of trying to fit in. Natalie Cole had never spoken to me as eloquently as M.S., a venerable Indian singer. I couldn't sing the lyrics of Ricky Martin as easily as I could sing my favorite Hindi or Tamil songs. Much as I enjoyed American cuisine, I couldn't last four days without Indian food. It was time to flaunt my ethnicity with a sari and a bright red bindi on my forehead. I was going to be an immigrant, but on my own terms. It was America's turn to adjust to me.

8   Slowly, I eased into wearing the garment. Strangers stared at me as I sashayed across a crowded bookstore. Some of them caught my eye and smiled. At first, I resented being an exhibit. Then I wondered: perhaps I reminded them of a wonderful holiday in India or a favorite Indian cookbook. Grocery clerks enunciated their words when they spoke to me. Everywhere, I was stopped with questions about India as if wearing a sari had made me an authority. One Japanese lady near Columbus Circle asked to have her picture taken with me. A tourist had thought that I was one, too, just steps from my home.

9   But there were unexpected advantages. Indian cabdrivers raced across lanes and screeched to a halt in front of me when I stepped into the street to hail a taxi. When my daughter climbed high up the Jungle-Gym in Central Park, I gathered my sari and prepared to follow, hoping it wouldn't balloon out like Marilyn Monroe's dress. One of the dads standing nearby

watched my plight and volunteered to climb after her. Chivalry in New York? Was it me or was it my sari?

10   Best of all, my family approved. My husband complimented me, my parents were proud of me. My daughter oohed and aahed when I pulled out my colorful saris. When I cuddled her in my arms, scents from the vetiver sachets that I used to freshen my sari at night escaped from the folds of cloth and soothed her to sleep. I felt part of a long line of Indian mothers who had rocked their babies this way.

11   Soon, the month was over. My self-imposed regimen was coming to an end. Instead of feeling liberated, I felt a twinge of unease. I had started enjoying my sari.

12   Saris were impractical for America, I told myself. I would continue to wear them, but not every day. It was time to revert to my sensible khakis. It was time to become American again.

Reading Reflection Questions *Sample answers are provided.*

1. What are the direct or indirect (implied) messages in this story?

   that the sari represents Indian culture and traditional women's clothing

   and it was important to the author to explore her heritage and to model it

   for her daughter—also, the experiment of wearing a sari for one month af-

   fected the author more than she expected it to

2. List the main reason Narayan chose to wear a sari for one month:

   to model Indian culture and heritage for her daughter and to get in touch

   with her own Indian roots and make America accept her on her terms for a

   change.

3. ___*b*___ Which of the following was *not* presented as a *disadvantage* of her wearing a sari?

   a. Unable to dart quickly across a street

   b. Indian cabdrivers' reactions to her hailing a cab

   c. Riding a crowded subway and worrying about the sari unraveling

   d. No pocket for house keys

4. T/F ___*T*___ Saris are important in Indian culture and heritage.

5. T/F ___*F*___ The author decided to wear a sari every day for the rest of her life.

6. ___*c*___ Which of the following was *not* presented as an *advantage* of her wearing a sari?

   a. Her husband complimented her.

b. Her parents were proud.

c. She could move more quickly while wearing a sari.

d. Her daughter liked her sari.

Checking Vocabulary

Define each of the following words by figuring out their meaning using context clues in the reading selection. If you cannot work out the meaning of a word, refer to a dictionary.

7. languid (paragraph 5): *slow, listless*

8. jargon (paragraph 5): *language of a particular group*

9. venerable (paragraph 7): *honored, respected*

10. sashayed (paragraph 8): *danced/moved*

READING CRITICALLY

Answers will vary.

1. What is the author's **purpose** or goal in this reading selection?

2. What are the implied or stated questions being addressed?

3. What specific **support**, details, and examples does the author use to develop the purpose or goal for the reading?

4. What inferences does the author include in this reading? (Inferences imply "if this, then this" types of cause-and-effect analysis.)

5. Who is the intended audience, and how did you reach that **conclusion**?

Writing Assignments

1. Write a narration essay (see Chapter 7) about a time when you were treated better or worse than usual on the basis of what you were wearing.

2. Write a description essay (see Chapter 8) about a particular item of clothing or object that you or your family owns that illustrates your heritage or your family heritage.

3. Write an argument essay (see Chapter 15) arguing for or against adding a mandatory cultural diversity course at your campus.

Still Hungry, Still Homeless

America Magazine Editorial

America magazine describes itself as a journal of opinion on current events, historical events, spiritual events, family, books, film, and television for Catholic people. This editorial appeared in the magazine's February 5, 2001, issue.

1   One might think that last year's particularly strong economy would have led to a reduction in the number of requests for emergency food and shelter. In fact, however, the year 2000 actually saw a rise in both areas. This was among the sad findings of the United States Conference of Mayors' annual survey of 25 cities around the country, which was released in late December.

2   Officials in the survey cities estimated that requests for emergency food assistance jumped by 17 percent—the second highest rate of increase since 1992. Over half of the people seeking help were children and their parents: a particularly disturbing finding, given the need for parents to be able to provide adequate and nutritious food for their children. A third of the adults, moreover, were employed. This reflects the fact that minimum wage jobs at $5.50 an hour cannot cover the cost of living for most Americans. Mirroring the conclusions of the mayors' report, Catholic Charities USA found in its own year-end survey that its agencies had seen what it termed "a startling 22 percent increase in the use of their emergency services."

3   How could this be, in the face of what many politicians have trumpeted as our unprecedented level of prosperity? Ironically, the mayors' report points out that the very strength of the economy has been partly to blame. Seeing that the earnings of middle-class Americans have risen, landlords have been quick to realize that they can charge much higher rents. But for families at the bottom of the economic ladder, whose earnings did not

increase, the consequence has been an ever more desperate search for housing within their income range; it is a search that has sometimes ended in homelessness. Even those lucky enough to have Section 8 vouchers have discovered that apartment owners often refuse to accept them, knowing that they can command higher prices than the government's reimbursement rate for the vouchers. Thus, in nearly half the survey cities, the report cites housing costs as a primary reason for the increase in requests for emergency food and shelter.

4   Welfare reform has played its part in this bleak scenario. People leaving Temporary Assistance for Needy Families (T.A.N.F.) may indeed have full-time jobs that pay above the minimum wage and yet still not be making enough to lift them above the poverty line. And all too frequently, they are unaware that despite being employed, they may still be eligible for the food stamps (and Medicaid) that could tide them over from one month to the next. Government agencies are not as aggressive as they should be in promoting these programs among the working poor. True, the number of food assistance facilities has increased, but the strain on their limited resources is so great that half the cities report that these facilities must either send people away or reduce the amount of what they can provide.

5   The same situation applies to emergency housing requests. Nearly a quarter of them, says the mayors' report, went unmet. Turned-away families in San Antonio, for instance, found themselves obliged to sleep in cars or parks, under bridges or in already doubled- or tripled-up substandard housing. Even when they can be accommodated, in 52 percent of the cities homeless families may have to break up, with older male youths and fathers sent elsewhere.

6   The outlook for the future is not bright. Almost three-fourths of the survey cities expect a rise in the demand for emergency food. As the officials in Boston put it, "the number of pantries increases every year, and [yet] the requests for assistance have increased by as much as 40 percent." Nor, they add, do they "see any relief in the near future." Again, there as elsewhere, high housing costs, along with low-paying jobs, lead the list of causes for more hunger and homelessness. The answer is implied in the comments of the respondents from Burlington, Vt.: "Without a significant commitment to building a significant number of new and affordable housing units, homelessness will continue to rise." The new secretary-designate of the Department of Housing and Urban Development, Mel Martinez, said at his Senate confirmation hearing that he would try to make more housing available to low-income Americans. We hope that he will act on his words. For many years, however, Congress has shown little interest in this neglected area of American life.

7   In releasing its annual report in December, Fred Kammer, S.J., president of Catholic Charities USA, spoke of its findings as "a story

about . . . escalating need in a land of skyrocketing wealth." He recalled Bill Clinton's promise to "end welfare as we know it." That has happened, but the rise in requests for emergency food and housing calls into question the effectiveness of welfare reform. The real goal, Father Kammer concluded, should be to "end poverty as we know it." Now is the time for Congress to take the strong measures needed to assist the most vulnerable members of society.

Reading Reflection Questions   *Sample answers are provided.*

1. What are the direct or indirect (implied) messages in this article?

   More and more families are needing emergency assistance, and the

   government needs to do something about it.

2. What tone does the editorial have? What effect does it have on the reader?

   an urgent tone—helps convince the reader about how much the problem

   has escalated

3. According to this article, where does action need to take place?

   in Congress

4. T/F ____F____ The homeless people this article describes are solely single males.

5. T/F ____T____ Homelessness has been increasing since the 1990s.

6. T/F ____T____ There has been an increase in the need for emergency food aid.

7. T/F ____F____ When a homeless person gets a job, he or she no longer needs assistance with food or housing.

Checking Vocabulary

Define each of the following words by figuring out their meaning using context clues in the reading selection. If you cannot work out the meaning of a word, refer to a dictionary.

8. unprecedented (paragraph 3): *has never happened before*

9. escalating (paragraph 7): *increasing*

10. vulnerable (paragraph 7): *weak, most susceptible*

READING CRITICALLY

Answers will vary.

1. What is the author's **purpose** or goal in this reading selection?

   _____

   _____

2. What are the implied or stated questions being addressed?

   _____

   _____

3. What specific **support**, details, and examples does the author use to develop the purpose or goal for the reading?

   _____

   _____

4. What inferences does the author include in this reading? (Inferences imply "if this, then this" types of cause-and-effect analysis.)

   _____

   _____

5. Who is the intended audience, and how did you reach that **conclusion**?

   _____

   _____

Writing Assignments

1. Write an argument/persuasion essay (see Chapter 15) about what could be done in your local community to help with food and shelter shortages.

2. Write a one or two paragraph summary of this editorial (see Eight Steps for Writing a Summary, pp. 330–331).

3. Write an example essay (see Chapter 12) about another prominent social problem besides homelessness that you've witnessed in your community.

All the Rage

Dave Barry

Dave Barry, born July 3, 1947, in Armonk, New York, has worked over 25 years as a syndicated humor columnist. His work has appeared in more than 500 newspapers internationally. He has also written several books and had a sitcom called *Dave's World* that aired for four seasons (based on his life and two of his books). In this essay, he explains Parking Lot Rage, Shopping Cart Rage, and other sources of anger that are all the rage.

1   If you do much driving on our nation's highways, you've probably noticed that, more and more often, bullets are coming through your windshield. This is a common sign of Road Rage, which the opinion-makers in the news media have decided is a serious problem, ranking just behind global warming and ahead of Asia.

2   How widespread is Road Rage? To answer that question, researchers for the National Institute of Traffic Safety recently did a study in which they drove on the interstate highway system in a specially equipped observation van. By the third day, they were deliberately running motorists off the road.

3   "These people are *morons!*" their official report stated.

4   That is the main cause of Road Rage: the realization that many of your fellow motorists have the brain of a cashew. The most common example, of course, is the motorists who feel a need to drive in the left-hand lane even though they are going slower than everybody else.

5   Nobody knows why they do this. Maybe they belong to some kind of religious cult that believes the right lane is sacred and must never come in direct contact with tires. Maybe one time, years ago, these motorists happened to be driving in the left lane when their favorite song came on the radio, so they've driven there ever since.

6   But whatever makes these people drive this way, there's nothing you can do. You can honk at them, but it will have no effect. People have been honking at them for years: It's a normal part of their environment. They've decided, for some mysterious reason, wherever they drive, there is honking.

7   I am familiar with this problem because I live and drive in Miami, which bills itself as the Inappropriate-Lane-Driving Capital of the World, and where the left lane is thought of not so much as a thoroughfare as a public recreational area, where motorists feel free to stop, hold family reunions, barbecue pigs, play volleyball, etc. Compounding this problem

is another common type of Miami motorist, the aggressive young male whose car has a sound system so powerful that the driver must go faster than the speed of sound at all times, or else the nuclear bass notes emanating from his rear speakers will catch up to him and cause his head to explode.

8 So the tiny minority of us Miami drivers who actually qualify as normal find ourselves constantly being trapped behind people drifting along on the interstate at the speed of diseased livestock, while at the same time being tailgated and occasionally bumped from behind by testosterone-deranged youths who got their driver training from watching "Star Wars." And of course nobody ever signals or yields, and people are constantly cutting us off, and *after a while we start to feel some rage, OK? You got a problem with that,* mister opinion-maker?

9 In addition to Road Rage, I frequently experience Parking Lot Rage, which occurs when I pull into a crowded supermarket parking lot, and I see people get into their car, clearly ready to leave, so I stop my car and wait for them to vacate the spot, and . . . nothing happens. They just stay there! *What the hell are they doing in there?? Cooking dinner???*

10 When I finally get into the supermarket, I often experience Shopping Cart Rage. This is caused by the people—and you just know these are the same people who drive slowly in the left-hand lane—who routinely manage, by careful placement, to block the entire aisle with a shopping cart. If we really want to keep illegal immigrants from entering the United States, we should employ Miami residents armed with shopping carts; we'd only need about two dozen to block the entire Mexican border.

11 What makes the supermarket congestion even worse is that shoppers are taking longer and longer to decide what to buy, because every product in America now comes in an insane number of styles and sizes. For example, I recently went to the supermarket to get orange juice. For just one brand, I had to decide between Original, Homestyle, Pulp Plus, Double Vitamin C, Grovestand, Calcium or Old Fashioned; I also had to decide whether I wanted the 167-ounce, 32-ounce, 64-ounce, 96-ounce or six-pack size. This is *way* too many choices. It caused me to experience Way Too Many Product Choices Rage. I would have called the orange juice company and complained, but I probably would have wound up experiencing Automated Phone Answering System Rage (". . . For questions about Pulp Plus in the 32-ounce size, press 23. For questions about Pulp Plus in the 64-ounce size, press 24. For questions about . . .").

12 My point is that there are many causes of rage in our modern world, and if we're going to avoid unnecessary violence, we all need to "keep our *cool.*" So let's try to be more considerate, OK? Otherwise I will kill you.

Reading Reflection Questions *Sample answers are provided.*

1. What are the direct or indirect (implied) messages in this story?

   There are too many kinds of rage in the world, and we need to be calmer.

   _____

2. What tone does the author use, and what effect does this tone have on the ideas he presents? *humorous—makes us laugh at ourselves and*

   think about the real problems.

3. T/F ____*F*____ The official report on Road Rage listed that drivers have the brain the size of a cashewnut.

4. T/F ____*F*____ The author thinks Road Rage is appropriate.

5. T/F ____*T*____ Barry pretends to be a person who supports Road Rage for the sake of humor.

6. List two examples of other types of rage that Barry discusses:

   Parking lot rage and shopping cart rage

7. In your own experience, what is the worse type of rage, and why? *Answers*

   will vary.

   _____

Checking Vocabulary

Define each of the following words by figuring out their meaning using context clues in the reading selection. If you cannot work out the meaning of a word, refer to a dictionary.

8. emanating (paragraph 7): *coming from*

9. testosterone (paragraph 8): *male hormone*

10. congestion (paragraph 11): *crowding*

READING CRITICALLY

Answers will vary.

1. What is the author's **purpose** or goal in this reading selection?

   _____

   _____

2. What are the implied or stated questions being addressed?

_____

_____

3. What specific **support**, details, and examples does the author use to develop the purpose or goal for the reading?

_____

_____

4. What inferences does the author include in this reading? (Inferences imply "if this, then this" types of cause-and-effect analysis.)

_____

_____

5. Who is the intended audience, and how did you reach that **conclusion**?

_____

_____

Writing Assignments

1. Write a description (see Chapter 8) and illustration (see Chapter 12) essay about a type of rage you have encountered (you witnessed or you have been involved in).

2. Write an argument essay (see Chapter 15) in which you propose possible solutions for dealing with Road Rage more efficiently.

3. Write a cause-and-effect essay (see Chapter 13) on the subject of road rage.

Barbie Madness

Cynthia Tucker

Cynthia Tucker is a syndicated columnist whose work appears in newspapers internationally. She is the editorial page editor for _The Atlanta Journal-Constitution_. She is a member of the International Women's Media Foundation and the National Association of Black Journalists.

1   When I was 9 or 10, I was steeped in Barbie madness. So much so that I joined the Barbie fan club. My mother still has the membership document

displaying my careful cursive writing alongside the scrawled block letters of a younger sister.

2   Too old to play with baby dolls, I was developing a vicarious interest in high fashion—a world to which Barbie allowed me access. Her overpriced collection of clothes included everything from bridal gowns to swimsuits, all accented by stiletto heels. In fact, her feet were permanently arched so that she could not wear sensible shoes.

3   She wore sheath dresses, capri pants, long gowns. She never got dirty; she never burst a seam (she never bent, of course); she never tripped over those heels.

4   Nor did she ever cause me to believe I would see many real women in the real world who looked or dressed like that. I had never seen a grown woman on the beach in high heels, and if I had—even at 10—I would have thought her nuts. Barbie was fantasy, one of the joyous escapes offered by childhood. My Barbie, white and brunette, never symbolized what I thought anyone ought to look like.

5   After nearly four decades of building a doll with a figure that, by one estimate, gives her measurements of 38-18-34, Mattel is preparing to release a new Barbie of less fantastic proportions. Many parents are breathing a sigh of relief that their daughters will no longer be subjected to such an unrealistic—and possibly damaging—cultural icon. Well, I have good news and bad news for those parents.

6   The bad news is, there will always be damaging cultural icons, plenty of unrealistic representations of women that emphasize youth and a weird voluptuousness/thinness, the combination of which defies physiology. If you think Barbie is the last of them, check out the *Sports Illustrated* swim-suit issue. Check out *Baywatch*. (The syndicated show sells well around the world. Sexism needs little translation.)

7   Now, for the good news: Parents will always have more influence over their children than any doll, any model, any magazine, any movie. Per-haps even more than their children's peers. Don't take my word for it—scientific research has confirmed it.

8   A recent study found that no matter a teenager's economic back-ground, a close-knit family helps prevent risky behavior and encourages educational excellence. Might not attentive parents also provide protec-tion against the sexist influences that permeate the culture?

9   Children learn not just from their parents' rhetoric, but also from their behavior. When a father leaves his family for a younger and more glam-orous trophy wife, he gives his children a much more profound lesson about the value of women than Barbie ever could. So does the mother who constantly applauds her adolescent daughter's popularity with boys.

10   Years ago, Barbie's wardrobe evolved beyond *haute couture* to include professional attire. She also became more ethnically diverse. Now, the doll will get a little nip-and-tuck that widens her waist and de-emphasizes her chest (a bit).

11   But no matter what she looks like, Barbie will never be as important a role model as Mom and Dad are. When Dad coaches his daughter's soccer team or helps her build a treehouse, he gives her a measure of her worth that overshadows even Barbie's bustline.

Reading Reflection Questions *Sample answers are provided.*

1. What are the direct or indirect (implied) messages in this story?

Barbie dolls can influence a girl's perception, but parental influence has

much more power.

2. What are the two main criticisms made about Barbie, according to this article? *unrealistic body standards/damaging cultural icon*

3. _____*c*_____ The main message of "Barbie Madness" is:
   a. Barbie is a harmful toy.
   b. Barbie has no effect on girls' self-esteem.
   c. Parental influence is more important for children's development than the influence of toys like Barbie.
   d. The author wanted to grow up to look just like Barbie.

4. T/F _____*T*_____ Barbie will soon be changed in body proportions (including an enlarged waist).

5. T/F _____*T*_____ Barbie is available in various ethnic types.

6. T/F _____*F*_____ The author thinks Barbie should be banned.

7. T/F _____*F*_____ Ken, the male version of Barbie, is also discussed in this article.

Checking Vocabulary

Define each of the following words by figuring out their meaning using context clues in the reading selection. If you cannot work out the meaning of a word, refer to a dictionary.

8. steeped (paragraph 1): *fully engaged in*

9. cursive (paragraph 1): *formal handwriting*

10. vicarious (paragraph 2): *experiencing something through someone else*

READING CRITICALLY

Answers will vary.

1. What is the author's **purpose** or goal in this reading selection?

_____

_____

2. What are the implied or stated questions being addressed?

_____

_____

3. What specific **support**, details, and examples does the author use to develop the purpose or goal for the reading?

_____

_____

4. What inferences does the author include in this reading? (Inferences imply "if this, then this" types of cause-and-effect analysis.)

_____

_____

5. Who is the intended audience, and how did you reach that **conclusion**?

_____

_____

Writing Assignments

1. Write an argument essay (see Chapter 15) about whether or not Barbie's body proportions should be changed to be more realistic. Provide specific reasons for your arguments.

2. Define (see Chapter 11) and describe (see Chapter 8) a favorite childhood toy of yours.

3. Write a narration essay (see Chapter 7) about a particular childhood memory of yours that involves playing with a toy or toys.

4. Write a cause-and-effect essay (see Chapter 13) related to the images of dolls like Barbie and a child's body image.

Our Tired, Our Poor, Our Kids

Anna Quindlen

Anna Quindlen began her journalism career at the *New York Post* and then became metropolitan editor of *The New York Times*. She contributed to *Newsweek*'s prestigious back page column, *The Last Word*, for many years. Her columns are collected in *Living Out Loud* (1988) and *Thinking Out Loud* (1992). She has written three best-selling novels, *Object Lessons* (1991), *One True Thing* (1994), and *Black and Blue* (1998), and an advice book, *A Short Guide to a Happy Life* (2000). This essay appeared in the March 12, 2001, issue of *Newsweek*.

1   Six people live here, in a room the size of the master bedroom in a modest suburban house. Trundles, bunk beds, dressers side by side stacked with toys, clothes, boxes, in tidy claustrophobic clutter. One woman, five children. The baby was born in a shelter. The older kids can't wait to get out of this one. Everyone gets up at 6 A.M., the little ones to go to day care, the others to school. Their mother goes out to look for an apartment when she's not going to drug-treatment meetings. "For what they pay for me to stay in a shelter I could have lived in the Hamptons," Sharanda says.

2   Here is the parallel universe that has flourished while the more fortunate were rewarding themselves for the stock split with SUVs and home additions. There is a boom market in homelessness. But these are not the men on the streets of San Francisco holding out cardboard signs to the tourists. They are children, hundreds of thousands of them, twice as likely to repeat a grade or be hospitalized and four times as likely to go hungry as the kids with a roof over their heads. Twenty years ago New York City provided emergency shelter for just under a thousand families a day; last month it had to find spaces for 10,000 children on a given night. Not since the Great Depression have this many babies, toddlers and kids had no place like home.

3   Three mothers sit in the living room of a temporary residence called Casa Rita in the Bronx and speak of this in the argot of poverty "The landlord don't call back when they hear you got EARP," says Rosie, EARP being the Emergency Assistance Rehousing Program. "You get priority for Section 8 if you're in a shelter," says Edna, which means federal housing

programs will put you higher on the list. Edna has four kids, three in foster care; she arrived at Casa Rita, she says, "with two bags and a baby." Rosie has three; they share a bathroom down the hall with two other families. Sharanda's five range in age from 13 to just over a year. Her eldest was put in the wrong grade when he changed schools. "He's humiliated, living here," his mother says.

4   All three women are anxious to move on, although they appreciate this place, where they can get shelter, get sober and keep their kids at the same time. They remember the Emergency Assistance Unit, the city office that is the gateway to the system, where hundreds of families sit every day surrounded by their bags, where children sleep on benches until they are shuffled off dull-eyed for one night in a shelter or a motel, only to return as supplicants again the next day.

5   In another world middle-class Americans have embraced new-home starts, the stock market and the Gap. But in the world of these displaced families, problems ignored or fumbled or unforeseen during this great period of prosperity have dovetailed into an enormous subculture of children who think that only rich people have their own bedrooms. Twenty years ago, when the story of the homeless in America became a staple of news reporting, the solution was presented as a simple one: affordable housing. That's still true, now more than ever. Two years ago the National Low Income Housing Coalition calculated that the hourly income necessary to afford the average two-bedroom apartment was around $12. That's more than twice the minimum wage.

6   The result is that in many cities police officers and teachers cannot afford to live where they work, that in Las Vegas old motels provide housing for casino employees, that in shelters now there is a contingent of working poor who get up off their cots and go off to their jobs. The result is that if you are evicted for falling behind on your rent, if there is a bureaucratic foul-up in your welfare check or the factory in which you work shuts down, the chances of finding another place to live are very small indeed. You're one understanding relative, one paycheck, one second chance from the street. And so are your kids.

7   So-called welfare reform, which emphasizes cutbacks and make-work, has played a part in all this. A study done in San Diego in 1998 found that a third of homeless families had recently had benefits terminated or reduced, and that most said that was how they had wound up on the street. Drugs, alcohol and domestic abuse also land mothers with kids in the shelter system or lead them to hand their children over to relatives or foster homes. Today the average homeless woman is younger than ever before, may have been in foster care or in shelters herself and so considers a chaotic childhood the norm. Many never finished high school, and have never held a job.

8   Ralph Nuñez, who runs the organization Homes for the Homeless, says that all this calls for new attitudes. "People don't like to hear it, but shelters are going to be the low-income housing of the future," he says. "So how do we enrich the experience and use the system to provide job training and education?" Bonnie Stone of Women in Need, which has eight other residences along with Casa Rita, says, "We're pouring every-thing we've got into the nine months most of them are here—nutrition, treatment, budgeting. By the time they leave, they have a subsidized apartment, day care and, hopefully, some life skills they didn't have before."

9   But these organizations are rafts in a rising river of need that has roared through this country without most of us ever even knowing. So now you know. There are hundreds of thousands of little nomads in America, sleep-ing in the back of cars, on floors in welfare offices or in shelters five to a room. What would it mean to spend your childhood drifting from one strange bed to another, waking in the morning to try to figure out where you'd landed today, without those things that confer security and happi-ness: a familiar picture on the wall, a certain slant of light through a cur-tained window? "Give me your tired, your poor," it says on the base of the Statue of Liberty, to welcome foreigners. Oh, but they are already here, the small refugees from the ruin of the American dream, even if you cannot see them.

Reading Reflection Questions *Sample answers are provided.*

1. What are the direct or indirect (implied) messages in this story?

   that homelessness is increasing, especially among women and children, and we

   have not done enough to help

2. How does the title get featured in the conclusion of the article, and for what purpose? *a quote from the Statue of Liberty—she says they are*

   here already, the homeless, and we need to help them

3. According to Quindlen, how much has the number of homeless families and children who need shelter at night increased in the last 20 years?

   from 1,000 families to 10,000 kids

4. According to the article, what is the "simple" solution to the homeless-ness problem? *affordable low-income housing*

5. T/F ____*T*____ Homeless kids are twice as likely as nonhomeless kids to repeat a grade.

6. T/F _____*T*_____ The author argues that welfare reform has actually increased the homeless problem.

7. T/F _____*T*_____ The average cost of an apartment, according to
Quindlen, requires nearly twice the current hourly wage.

Checking Vocabulary

*Define each of the following words by figuring out their meaning using context clues
in the reading selection. If you cannot work out the meaning of a word, refer to a
dictionary.*

8. claustrophobic (paragraph 1): *fear of being in a confined space*

9. flourished (paragraph 2): *thrived*

10. supplicants (paragraph 4): *people asking for something*

READING CRITICALLY

Answers will vary.

1. What is the author's **purpose** or goal in this reading selection?

_____

_____

2. What are the implied or stated questions being addressed?

_____

_____

3. What specific **support**, details, and examples does the author use to develop the purpose or goal for
the reading?

_____

_____

4. What inferences does the author include in this reading? (Inferences imply "if this, then this" types of
cause-and-effect analysis.)

_____

_____

5. Who is the intended audience, and how did you reach that **conclusion**?

_____

_____

Writing Assignments

1. Write an argument essay (see Chapter 15) that poses a solution to combating homelessness in your city or town.

2. Write a one to two paragraph summary of this essay using Eight Steps for Writing a Summary (pp. 330–331).

3. Write a narration/description essay (see Chapters 7 and 8) describing an incident you were part of or that you witnessed related to poverty and the effects on the youth in our society.

To check your progress in meeting this chapter's objectives, log in to www.mywritinglab .com, go to the **Study Plan** tab, click on **Critical Thinking** and choose **Critical Thinking: Responding to Text and Visuals** from the list of subtopics. Read and view the resources in the **Review Materials** section, and then complete the **Recall**, **Apply**, and **Write** sets in the **Activities** section.

23 Sentence Parts

Green Man   Hank and Richard Galmish

THINKING CRITICALLY

Sentence parts are like a mosaic: Individual pieces fit together to make a coherent whole and create an overall message, each piece adding to the meaning. What sentence parts do you already know before reading this chapter? List all the sentence parts you can think of here.

_____

_____

_____

_____

_____

_____

LO 1 THE BUILDING BLOCKS OF SENTENCES

The individual components of sentences are the building blocks. All sentences must have at least a **subject** (the *what* or *who* the sentence is about) and a **verb** (the action of the sentence) and convey a complete thought. However, there are many other parts to a sentence—phrases, articles, noun determiners, coordinating and subordinating conjunctions, and conjunctive adverbs—which, like a mosaic, can be fitted together to express what you want to say.

APPLYING CRITICAL THINKING

| PURPOSE | IDEAS | SUPPORT | ASSUMPTIONS BIASES | CONCLUSIONS | POINT OF VIEW | ANALYSIS |

When you are making choices about which elements to include when **constructing a sentence**, you need to ask yourself the following questions:

1. What is my **purpose** for this particular sentence? What do I want to say?

2. What **ideas** and information do I need to include in this sentence?

3. Who is my target audience? How can I best put the parts of the sentence together to convey my ideas to this audience?

Then, use your **analysis** skills to break the sentence back down into its parts and make sure that you have constructed it correctly. Check that the sentence contains a verb and a subject, expresses a complete thought, and is written in the correct tense.

SUBJECTS AND PREDICATES

A **sentence** is a group of words that expresses a complete thought. Every sentence contains at least a subject (a noun or a noun plus its modifiers) and a predicate (a verb, or a verb plus its modifiers). When the modifiers are stripped from the subject and the predicate, leaving only the noun and the verb, the noun is called the **simple subject** and the verb is called the **simple**

predicate. The simple subject and the simple predicate are the two most basic building blocks of the sentence.

SUBJECT	PREDICATE
\u00A0	\u00A0

SUBJECT   PREDICATE

The gray-haired **dog/** *limped* slowly to its dog bed.

SIMPLE SUBJECT   SIMPLE PREDICATE

dog   *limped*

The Subject

The main, simple, subject of the sentence is *dog*. *Gray-haired* describes the dog. *The* describes the rest of the words in the subject. When a word describes another word, it is called a modifier. *The gray-haired dog* is the complete subject.

The Predicate

What did the dog do? It *limped*. That action is the verb, the simple predicate. How did it limp? *Slowly*. This word describes how the dog limped; it modifies the verb. The verb plus the modifier and the other words that complete the meaning of the verb make up the complete predicate: *limped slowly to its bed*.

ACTIVITY 23-1   Simple Subjects and Predicates

Directions: *Underline the simple subject in each sentence, and mark it with an S. Then double underline the simple predicate (the verb) in each sentence, and mark it with a V.*

1. A large <u>bird</u> <u>flew</u> across the sky.

2. <u>He</u> <u>knew</u> he was trouble.

3. Her <u>legs</u> <u>were folded</u> beneath her.

4. In the story, the <u>hero</u> <u>must have jumped</u> from one roof to another.

5. Suddenly, the <u>puppy</u> <u>leaped</u> for the ball.

Subjects

The **subject** is one or more words that indicate *who* or *what* is doing the action of the verb. The subject can be a noun or noun phrase, a pronoun, a gerund phrase, or the implied *you* of a command. In the following sentences, the subjects are in **bold** font, and the verbs are in *italics*:

> **Kenneth** *called* the fire department last night. (noun as subject)
>
> **She** *didn't use* a recipe for the cake. (pronoun as subject)
>
> **The old theater building** *created* an old-fashioned feel to the neighborhood. (noun phrase as subject)
>
> **Its stubby legs** *took* it slowly across the room. (noun phrase as subject)
>
> *Grab* the keys. (implied you as subject)
>
> **Knowing she could change** *kept* her motivated. (gerund phrase as subject)

1. **The subject can be a noun, a noun phrase, or an infinitive.**
   - **Noun as subject.** A **noun** can be a person, place, thing, idea, or state of existence.

Nouns at a Glance

Common nouns	name general categories or types: *object, person, navy, tornado*
Proper nouns	name specific people or items: *The Lincoln Memorial, Sherman Alexie*
Abstract nouns	are not related to specific details: *love, fear, faith, happiness, beauty*
Concrete nouns	are related to specific sensory details: *brittle, soft, sweet, whistling, stone*
Singular nouns	name one of something: *child, Tom, Columbia River*
Plural nouns	name more than one of something: *children, tables, clouds, movies*
Collective nouns	name several items grouped as one collective item: *team, family, group*
Count nouns	can be counted as individual units: *girl, friend, dog, couch*
Noncount (mass) nouns	cannot be counted as individual units in English: *sand, vegetation, education, flour, biology, anger, blood*

   - **Noun phrase as subject.** A **noun phrase** is a noun plus its modifiers, the words that describe it.

> **Most people** *sleep* at night. (The noun is *people*. The word that describes it is *Most*.)

- **Infinitive as subject.** Phrases beginning with *to* can be subjects.

> *To be happy* is something most people want.

- **Nouns and noun phrases can be joined to form a *compound subject*.** A compound subject is made of two or more nouns or noun phrases joined with the word *and* or *or*.

> **Clara and Soroa** *caught* the morning train. (Compound subject)
> **Clara's cousins**, Jerith and Mathew, *arrived* on the late train. (Subject)
> **Either the eastbound train or the westbound train** *will arrive* first. (Compound subject)

2. **The subject can be a pronoun.**

   A **pronoun** is a word that replaces a noun that was mentioned previously: *I, you, he, she, it, we, they, this, that, these,* and *those* are pronouns. Pronouns can also be indefinite, or a pronoun that refers to one or more unspecified beings, objects, or places: for example, *everyone, someone, anybody, both, few,* and *many*.

> The couple was married in Hawaii. **They** *had planned* the wedding a full year in advance. (The pronoun *They* replaces *the couple* from the first sentence.)

3. **The subject can be a gerund phrase** (an *-ing* phrase that serves as the subject of the sentence).

> **Taking the test early** *is* sometimes a bad idea. (*Taking the test early* is the subject, a gerund phrase; *is* is the main verb of the sentence.)

4. **All sentences must have a subject, but in commands, the subject *you* is implied.**

   The subject *you* is implied in a command or request directly stated to someone.

> **(You)** *Run!* (*You* is implied; *Run* is the verb.)
> **(You)** *Eat* the cake. (*You* is implied. *Eat* is the verb.)

▶ **NOTE**   The subject doesn't always come first in the sentence. Sometimes other words come before the subject of a sentence. For instance, the second sentence in the example below starts with a **transition**, that is, a word that shows the relationship between the two sentences. The subject follows it. To find the subject, identify the verb, and then ask who or what performed the action of the verb.

The laundry **waited** to be washed. Next to the basket, *the washing machine* **sat waiting.**

ACTIVITY 23-2   Identifying Subjects

Directions: *Underline the subjects in the following sentences. Be careful not to underline all the nouns—only the noun functioning as the subject. If the subject is implied, write "implied" at the end of the sentence.*

1. <u>Patrick</u> took three classes this semester.
2. <u>He</u> says he has to balance work and school.
3. His best <u>friends</u>, Chris and Mike, like to take at least four classes a semester.
4. However, <u>students</u> make choices based on their lives outside of school.
5. In fact, be sure to think about your work and home life first.   *Implied (you)*

Predicates

All sentences must have at least one verb or verb phrase. A **verb** is the action of a sentence—it can be a physical action, a mental action, or a state of being.

Physical Action

Hannah *kicked* the ball. (*kicked* is the simple predicate; *the ball* describes what she kicked. The complete predicate is *kicked the ball.*)

Hannah *kicked* the ball and *ran* behind it. (compound predicate; the two verbs are in italics. The complete compound predicate is *kicked the ball and ran behind it.*)

Mental Action

I *thought* about taking a trip. (*thought* is the simple predicate)

State of Being

I *am.* (simple predicate)

Verbs function in different ways, depending on their role in a particular sentence:

1. Some verbs can stand on their own as the main verb of a sentence.

> **My dog** *eats* three times a day. (simple present tense verb)
>
> **Clara's sisters** *called* all their friends to invite them to the party. (simple past tense verb)

2. Some verb forms need auxiliary, or helping, verbs, to complete them.

A **verb phrase** is two or more words working together to create the action (verb) for the sentence.

> The new campaign *was created* today. (*Created* can't be a main verb on its own in this sentence.)
>
> She *has been waiting* for a new mission. (*Waiting* can't be a main verb on its own.)
>
> When *will* he *arrive*? (*Will* adds the meaning of "the future" to the verb *arrive*.)

There are three verb forms that can't be the main verb of a sentence without some helping verbs. They are the *to* form, the *-ed* form in certain cases, and the *-ing* form:

- **to + Verb (Infinitives).** In an infinitive, the word *to* comes before the plain form of the verb: *to walk, to run, to eat*. The infinitive can't be used alone as the main verb of a sentence—you couldn't write, *The child to eat cake*. Infinitives don't give enough information about when something is happening in order to be used as the main verb. In predicates, they normally follow the main verb.

> Emily **had promised to cook** dinner for Kyle. (*Had promised to cook* is the whole verb phrase.)
>
> The meeting **was scheduled to occur** at noon on Tuesday.

> ▶ **NOTE**   Avoid *splitting your infinitive* by putting a word in between the "to" and the verb:

> **Incorrect:** Phoebe wanted *to boldly go* where no woman had gone before.
>
> **Correct:** Phoebe wanted *to go boldly* where no woman had gone before.

To verbs can also act as the subject of a sentence:

> *To run a marathon* **takes** true determination.

- ***-ed* Verbs (Past Participles).** To indicate the past tense of most verbs, *-ed* or *-d* is added to the plain form. If there is no helping verb (such as *is, was, has,* or *had*), then the verb is in simple past tense form. A verb in the simple past can act as the main verb of a sentence. In other cases, the *-ed* form of a verb must be helped by an auxiliary verb. A helping verb plus an *-ed* verb forms a perfect tense.

Simple past tense:	She *cooked* lasagna. She also *made* a nice salad.
Present perfect:	She *has wanted* to have a party for all her friends for years. (*has* adds the meaning of "the present" to *wanted*)
Past perfect:	She *had planned* to throw a party for her colleagues, too. (*had* adds the meaning of "the past" to *planned*)

- ***-ing* Verbs (Gerunds).** Verbs that end with *-ing* are called gerunds. An *-ing* form is never a complete verb by itself—you wouldn't say My *boyfriend washing his car.* In predicates, a form of the verb *to be* is needed before the gerund to indicate an action that *was, is,* or *will be* continuing. An *-ing* word can also serve as a subject, without the auxiliary verb.

> He **is** *having* a hard time understanding. (*is* adds the meaning of "the present" to the gerund)
>
> Yesterday, he *was hoping* to take the test. (*was* adds the meaning of "the past")
>
> He *will be studying* for the test all night long. (*will be* adds the meaning of "the future")

Remember: Gerunds can also serve as the subject of the sentence— see Subjects above.

3. **Verb tense indicates time—past, present, and future.** (See Verb Tense at a Glance below for more information.)

Verb Tense at a Glance

Think of tense as a timeline that starts on the left, in the past, and moves to the right, in the future.

Past	Present	Future
←———— I walked	I am walking	I will walk ————→

X---------present progressive----------- Y ------------future progressive----------Z

Here's a chart that shows the past, present, and future tenses of the verb *walk*:

Tense	Past	Present	Future
Simple	She walked.	She walks.	She will walk.
Perfect	She had walked.	She has walked.	She will have walked.
Progressive	She was walking.	She is walking.	She will be walking.
Perfect Progressive	She had been walking.	She has been walking.	She will have been walking.

▶ **NOTE**   For most verbs in the present tense, use the base form (as found in the dictionary) for the first person subjects *I* and *we*, the second person subject *you*, and the third person plural subject *they*. For the third person singular subjects *he, she,* and *it,* add *-s* or *-es*.

> **Example:** base form: *walk.*
>
> **First person, second person, third person plural:** I walk. You walk. They walk.
>
> **Third person singular:** He walks. She walks. It walks.

Base Forms: *To Be* Verbs

Since there are many irregular verbs in English that don't follow this pattern, be sure to consult a dictionary and/or grammar handbook for correct verb forms. Here are the three irregular verbs that are most common and a chart showing how they change with different tenses.

Base Verb	Present singular	Present plural	Past singular	Past plural
Be	I am	We are	I was	We were
	You are	You are	You were	You were
	He/she/it is	They are	he/she/it was	They were
Have	I have	We have	I had	We had
	You have	You have	You had	You had
	He/she/it has	They have	He/she/it had	They had
Do	I do	We do	I did	We did
	You do	You do	You did	You did
	He/she/it does	They do	He/she/it did	They did

Irregular Verbs

Here is a list of some of the most common irregular verbs in English.

Base Form	Simple Past Tense	Past Participle
awake	awoke	awoken
be	was, were	been
bear	bore	born
beat	beat	beat
become	became	become
begin	began	begun
bend	bent	bent
beset	beset	beset
bet	bet	bet
bid	bid/bade	bid/bidden
bind	bound	bound
bite	bit	bitten
bleed	bled	bled
blow	blew	blown
break	broke	broken
breed	bred	bred
bring	brought	brought
broadcast	broadcast	broadcast
build	built	built
burn	burned/burnt	burned/burnt
burst	burst	burst
buy	bought	bought
cast	cast	cast
catch	caught	caught
choose	chose	chosen
cling	clung	clung
come	came	come
cost	cost	cost
creep	crept	crept
cut	cut	cut
deal	dealt	dealt
dig	dug	dug
dive	dived/dove	dived

Continued ▶

Base Form	Simple Past Tense	Past Participle
do	did	done
draw	drew	drawn
dream	dreamed/dreamt	dreamed/dreamt
drive	drove	driven
drink	drank	drunk
eat	ate	eaten
fall	fell	fallen
feed	fed	fed
feel	felt	felt
fight	fought	fought
find	found	found
fit	fit	fit
flee	fled	fled
fling	flung	flung
fly	flew	flown
forbid	forbade	forbidden
forget	forgot	forgotten
forgive	forgave	forgiven
forsake	forsook	forsaken
freeze	froze	frozen
get	got	gotten
give	gave	given
go	went	gone
grind	ground	ground
grow	grew	grown
hang	hung	hung
hear	heard	heard
hide	hid	hidden
hit	hit	hit
hold	held	held
hurt	hurt	hurt
keep	kept	kept
kneel	knelt	knelt
knit	knit	knit
know	knew	know

Base Form	Simple Past Tense	Past Participle
lay	laid	laid
lead	led	led
leap	leaped/leapt	leaped/leapt
learn	learned/learnt	learned/learnt
leave	left	left
lend	lent	lent
let	let	let
lie	lay	lain
light	lighted/lit	lighted
lose	lost	lost
make	made	made
mean	meant	meant
meet	met	met
misspell	misspelled/misspelt	misspelled/misspelt
mistake	mistook	mistaken
mow	mowed	mowed/mown
overcome	overcame	overcome
overdo	overdid	overdone
overtake	overtook	overtaken
overthrow	overthrew	overthrown
pay	paid	paid
plead	pled	pled
prove	proved	proved/proven
put	put	put
quit	quit	quit
read	read	read
rid	rid	rid
ride	rode	ridden
ring	rang	rung
rise	rose	risen
run	ran	run
saw	sawed	sawed/sawn
say	said	said
see	saw	seen
seek	sought	sought

Continued ▶

Base Form	Simple Past Tense	Past Participle
sell	sold	sold
send	sent	sent
set	set	set
sew	sewed	sewed/sewn
shake	shook	shaken
shave	shaved	shaved/shaven
shear	shore	shorn
shed	shed	shed
shine	shone	shone
shoe	shoed	shoed/shod
shoot	shot	shot
show	showed	showed/shown
shrink	shrank	shrunk
shut	shut	shut
sing	sang	sung
sink	sank	sunk
sit	sat	sat
sleep	slept	slept
slay	slew	slain
slide	slid	slid
sling	slung	slung
slit	slit	slit
smite	smote	smitten
sow	sowed	sowed/sown
speak	spoke	spoken
speed	sped	sped
spend	spent	spent
spill	spilled/spilt	spilled/spilt
spin	spun	spun
spit	spit/spat	spit
split	split	split
spread	spread	spread
spring	sprang/sprung	sprung
stand	stood	stood
steal	stole	stolen

Base Form	Simple Past Tense	Past Participle
stick	stuck	stuck
sting	stung	stung
stink	stank	stunk
stride	strod	stridden
strike	struck	struck
string	strung	strung
strive	strove	striven
swear	swore	sworn
sweep	swept	swept
swell	swelled	swelled/swollen
swim	swam	swum
swing	swung	swung
take	took	taken
teach	taught	taught
tear	tore	torn
tell	told	told
think	thought	thought
thrive	thrived/throve	thrived
throw	threw	thrown
thrust	thrust	thrust
tread	trod	trodden
understand	understood	understood
uphold	upheld	upheld
upset	upset	upset
wake	woke	woken
wear	wore	worn
weave	weaved/wove	weaved/woven
wed	wed	wed
weep	wept	wept
wind	wound	wound
win	won	won
withhold	withheld	withheld
withstand	withstood	withstood
wring	wrung	wrung
write	wrote	written

ACTIVITY 23-3   Identifying Verb

Directions: *Underline the verbs in the following sentences. If there is an auxiliary verb, be sure to underline that as well.*

1. Patrick <u>had taken</u> three classes last semester.

2. He <u>says</u> he has to balance work and school.

3. His best friends, Chris and Mike, <u>like</u> to take at least four classes a semester.

4. However, students <u>have</u> to <u>make</u> choices based on their lives outside of school.

5. In fact, <u>be</u> sure to think about your work and home life first. *Implied (you)*

APPLYING CRITICAL THINKING

PURPOSE   IDEAS   SUPPORT   ASSUMPTIONS BIASES   CONCLUSIONS   POINT OF VIEW   ANALYSIS

Analysis involves breaking down an **idea** and working out the meaning of the individual parts and how they relate to the whole. Use your analysis skills to choose the correct tense to use as you write. Ask the following questions to determine *when* the action of the sentence is taking place, and then ensure that you have used the correct tense.

1. Am I writing about something that happened in the past and then stopped?

   If so, use the **simple past**: Manny **went** to the store yesterday.

2. Am I writing about something that happened and stopped before another past event?

   If so, use the **past perfect**: Although he **had brought** a grocery list, he still **forgot** to buy milk.

3. Am I writing about something that started before but still happens?

   If so, use **the present perfect tense**: She **has wondered** for a long time what it would be liked to be married.

4. Am I writing about something that is happening now?

   If so, use the present or present progressive tense. She **is leaving** now.

5. Am I writing about something that hasn't happened yet but will happen in the future?

If so, use the **future tense**: By tomorrow, I **will know** how it feels to be married!

6. Am I writing about something that will start in the future, continue, and then stop at a particular time?

If so, use the **future perfect**: According to her grand plan, she **will have been married** for a couple of years before she has children.

ACTIVITY 23-4   Correct Verb Forms and Tenses

Directions: *Choose the correct verb form and tense of the verb in brackets to fill each space in the following paragraph:*

Last year, I [to travel] ____*traveled*____ to Europe. The cities I saw [to be]

____*are*____ famous travel destinations. I [to love] ____*loved*____ the city

of Paris. I remember I [to be] ____*was*____ determined to go to the top of

the Eiffel Tower, even though I [to be] ____*am*____ afraid of heights. Once

at the top, I [to look] ____*looked*____ out over the whole city. Almost every-

one [to have] ____*has*____ a desire to travel. However, my desire [to

increase] ____*increased*____ on this trip, and I next [to go] ____*went*____ to

London so I could [to explore] ____*explore*____ that famous city. I must [to

admit] ____*admit*____ that I [to be] ____*was*____ also enchanted by this

city. I [to enjoy] ____*enjoyed*____ the friendly people and the history of the

city. I had [to see] ____*to see*____ the Tower of London, of course, and Tower

Bridge. Both of these cities [to be] ____*will be*____ in my heart forever.

Inside the Predicate: Objects

An **object** in grammar is usually part of the predicate, and it is the object of the action, or the receiver of the action. A **direct object** is the receiver of action within a sentence, as in "He hit the ball." Therefore, the direct object refers to the person or thing receiving the action of a transitive verb.

The **indirect object** identifies to or for whom/what the action of the verb is performed. In the sentence, "She sent Anders the letter," "letter" is the *direct object* as it is directly affected by the action (sending), and "Anders" is the *indirect object* as he receives the letter.

Here are some additional things to keep in mind about objects:

1. Some verbs describe an action that doesn't include a receiver:

> The sun **rises**. The moon **sets**.

2. Other verbs do require (or can have) a receiver:

> The potential employer **took** new applications once a month.

The verb *took* needs a receiver, which is called the **object of the verb**. What did the potential employer take? New applications. *Applications* is the object of the verb *took*.

3. Pronouns can take the place of nouns.

> The company **will take** more applications soon. It **will advertise** next month.

In the second sentence, *it* replaces *the company*.

4. Sometimes the subject acts on an object *to* or *for* someone or something else. That someone or something else is called the **indirect object**.

> Too much exercise *can cause* **problems** for one's back.

To find the direct object, you would ask "What can too much exercise cause?" The direct object is *problems*. To find the indirect object, ask "Problems to or for whom?" In this case, the word *for* is in the sentence. The indirect object is *one's back*.

ACTIVITY 23-5   Identifying Direct and Indirect Objects

Directions: *Underline the direct objects and indirect objects in the following sentences. Mark DO over the direct objects and IO over the indirect objects.*

1. Loc gave Saed the answer.

2. Jackson tossed his laundry into the hamper.

3. Chico gave Maria a ring.

4. Sal provided a place for them to meet.

5. Aretha ate the pizza quickly.

PHRASES

A **phrase** is a group of related words without a subject and a predicate. You saw at the beginning of the chapter that a subject can be a noun phrase, which includes a noun and all its modifiers:

The sparkling ocean stretched for miles in every direction.

A noun phrase can also act as the object of a verb:

She wanted to swim in *the blue green sea.*

Two of the **verbals** (forms of verbs that function as other parts of speech such as a gerund or an infinitive and are usually part of a phrase) that you studied earlier can also be considered noun phrases: one is the gerund phrase:

Swimming in the ocean is refreshing.

and the other is the infinitive phrase:

To swim in the ocean takes strength and skill.

A noun phrase can also be the object of a preposition, which is discussed in the next section.

Prepositions and Prepositional Phrases

Prepositions are words that connect nouns and pronouns to other parts of a sentence. Prepositions indicate relationships in time, place, and direction and also signal connections such as cause and effect or addition: *before, after, above, below, across, because of,* and *in addition to.* A **prepositional phrase** begins with a preposition (see chart below) and ends with a noun, pronoun, gerund, or clause, the "object" of the preposition.

The **subject** of the film *is* the problem of child labor in some countries.

The prepositional phrases underlined above help guide you through the meaning of the sentence. (The subject of the sentence above is in bold font, and the verb is in italics.)

Visualization/Memory Tip: Think of a cat and a set of two large tubes or pipes: Prepositions are anything the cat can do in relation to those two tubes (for instance, the cat can go *around* the tubes, *toward* the tubes, *over* the tubes, *on* the tubes, *in* the tubes, *between* the tubes, and so on). Of course, there are many prepositions that don't work with the cat/tubes example; for instance, a cat cannot be "of" the tubes. This is just a memory trick (mnemonic device) to help you recognize many common prepositions.

The Most Common Prepositions in English

about	down	outside
above	during	over
according to	except	past
across	except for	plus
after	excepting	regarding
against	for	respecting
along	from	round
along with	in	since
among	in addition to	than
apart from	in case of	through
around	inside	throughout
as	in spite of	till
at	instead of	to
because of	into	toward
before	like	under
behind	near	underneath
below	next	unlike
beneath	of	until
beside(s)	off	unto
between	on	up
beyond	onto	upon
by	on top of	up to
concerning	opposite	with
considering	out	within
despite	out of	without

You should try not to end your sentences with a preposition.

Example	Cara is who Steve is having dinner with.
Rearranged	Cara is the one with whom Steve is having dinner.
Or even better	Steve is having dinner with Cara.

However, there are cases where there is no other way to rearrange the sentence.

It was something he couldn't stop thinking *about*.

The cat wants to come *in*.

Prepositional phrases include a preposition, the object of the preposition, and any modifiers of the object. The entire prepositional phrase functions as a modifier in the sentence.

That mean mother *of hers* is always looking *for more to be mad about*.

Of hers modifies *mother* and so is part of the subject. Put another way, *of hers* modifies a noun, so it is an adjective. *For more to be mad about* modifies a verb, so it is an adverb. Adjectives and adverbs are discussed later in the chapter.

ACTIVITY 23-6 Identifying Prepositional Phrases

Directions: *Underline the prepositional phrases in the following sentences:*

1. Laci rode the bus with her friends to arrive with the rest of the class.
2. The raccoon arrived at the back door of his house looking for food.
3. Supreeda changed her mind because of the cost and other factors.
4. She called him back before he got back to her.
5. She decided to be bold instead of waiting around.

Participles and Participial Phrases

Participles are verb forms that can either be part of the main verb or can function as adjectives or adverbs. Present participles end in *-ing: leaving, heaving, ringing.* Past participles usually end in *-ed* or *-d: hated, performed, laid.* However, some participles are formed irregularly with endings such as *-n* and *-t: forgiven, taken, spent, brought.*

Part of main verb: Chester *was having* second thoughts.

Daniel *was defeated* in the tennis match.

As adjective: The *defeated* player shook hands graciously with his opponent.

As adverb: I saw JoAnn *looking at* Tim with a playful expression.

Participial Phrases use the *-ing* form for present participle, and the past participle phrase usually ends in *-ed, -d, -n, or -t*: elec*ted*, dele*ted*, chose*n*, and sen*t*.

I saw Daniel *trying to hit* her serve.

The *elected* official will take her office in the fall.

ACTIVITY 23-7   Identifying Participles and Participial Phrases

Directions: *Underline the participles and participial phrases in the following sentences:*

1. Iman caught Joed staring at his watch during their date.
2. Regina had said no before realizing that it might be a good idea.
3. Frustrated, Tam tried one more time.
4. Alieu had taken ten classes so far.
5. The frazzled woman took her case to a lawyer.

Adjectives and Adjective Phrases

Adjectives are words that modify nouns and pronouns (the adjectives below are italicized; the nouns they modify are in bold).

Modifying nouns: The *skinny* **dog** looked thin and scared.

Modifying pronouns: **They** were very *thin*.

Descriptive adjectives can take three forms:

1. **The positive form, used to** express simple descriptions such as *red, heavy, tiny, flat, beautiful*:

   The *new* **car** looked good.

2. **The comparative form, used to** compare two things such as *lower, smarter, more functional, less useful:*

> Trina has a *newer* **car** than her boyfriend's.

3. **The superlative form, used to** compare three or more things such as *largest, dirtiest, most functional, least useful:*

> She had the *newest* **car** on the block: newer than any of her neighbors' cars.

An **adjective phrase** is a phrase that modifies a noun or pronoun:

> The **woman** *parking the car* is my mother.

The adjective phrase describes *woman*, a noun.

ACTIVITY 23-8   Identifying Adjectives and Adjective Phrases

Directions: *Underline all the adjectives and adjective phrases in the following sentences.* **Tip:** *It might help to circle all the nouns first.*

1. The smelly sock on the tile floor kept people out like a strict guard.
2. The ancient book from Stella's library was a rare item.
3. The playful kitten playing with the wool sock batted the white fuzzy friend for hours.
4. The large black luxury car pulling into the driveway impressed the curious guests.
5. The loud obnoxious music was coming from the student's backpack, and we were sure it was a banned electronic device.

Adverbs and Adverb Phrases

Adverbs are words that modify verbs, verb forms, adjectives, and other adverbs to indicate *how, where, when,* or *how much.* Many adverbs end with *-ly,* but not all. The adverbs below are in italics; what they are modifying is in bold font.

> Modifying verbs: Lori **spoke** *loudly.*
> Modifying verb forms: Troy had *barely* **noticed** the child hiding in the back.

> Modifying adjectives: It was a *very* **fancy** dinner.
>
> Modifying other adverbs: The dog ran *very* **quickly**. Who knew he could run *this far*?

Like adjectives, adverbs have three forms. The adverbs below are in italics; what they are modifying is in bold font.

1. Positive: *quietly, smoothly, slow, awkward/ly, intensely*

> She **limped** *awkwardly*.

2. Comparative: *quieter, smoother, slower, more awkwardly, more intensely*

> She **limped** even *more awkwardly* when she noticed she was being watched.

3. Superlative: *quietest, smoothest, slowest, most awkwardly, most intensely*

> She **limped** the *most awkwardly* after a few people laughed.

An **adverb phrase** is a phrase that begins with a preposition and functions as an adverb:

> The casserole was **full** *of vegetables from her garden*.

The adverb phrase *of vegetables from her garden* modifies *full*, an adjective.

ACTIVITY 23-9   Identifying Adverbs and Adverb Phrases

Directions: *Underline the adverbs and adverb phrases in the following sentences:*

1. The shopper moved <u>speedily</u> through the sale aisle.
2. David had finished his meal <u>extremely</u> quickly.
3. The traffic moved <u>slowly</u> along the interstate.
4. The music played <u>quietly</u> in the lobby.
5. The children grabbed <u>greedily</u> at the free candy.

ACTIVITY 23-10   Identifying Adjectives and Adverbs

Directions: *Underline the adjectives and adverbs in the following sentences. Then circle the nouns, verbs, verb forms, or adverbs they are modifying.*

1. Leslie's brand-new convertible car raced quickly along the highway.
2. The family nobly honored the recently departed head of the extended family.
3. The sandy beaches and warm breezes of Hawaii easily calmed the weary traveler.
4. The man with the eye patch made the imaginative child nervous as he looked very cautiously from behind the building.
5. The last movie played promptly at 7:00 in the remodeled theater.

ARTICLES AND OTHER NOUN DETERMINERS

The **articles** *a*, *an*, and *the* are a type of **noun determiner**—a word that signals a noun is to follow; the choice of an article is determined by the context and the type of noun that follows.

1. **A and *an* are indefinite articles used for general description nouns.**

   - Use *a* when the noun that follows starts with a consonant or a consonant sound: *a car, a sheep, a place, a united front* (the *u* sounds like a consonant, *y*, so use *a*).
   - Use *an* when the noun that follows has a vowel or a vowel sound: *an Englishman, an orange, an elevator, an honor* (the *h* is silent; the word begins with a vowel sound of *o*, so use *an*).

2. ***The* is a definite article.**

   Use *the* when the word that follows is a specific noun (not a general descriptor): **the** best place to shop, **the** champion racehorse, **the** movie to watch.

   Cross Reference
   See Chapter 32 for more about when to use an article.

3. **Other noun determiners** include the following:

   - **Demonstratives:** *this, that, these, those*
   - **Possessives:** *my, our, your, his, her, their, its*
   - **Cardinal numbers:** *one, two, three, and so on.*
   - **Miscellaneous:** *all, another, each, every, much, and so on.*

ACTIVITY 23-11   Identifying Articles and Noun Determiners

Directions: *Underline the articles and noun determiners in the following sentences:*

1. The digital recorder kept an accurate record of the meeting.
2. Taking every class available in college is not a good idea.
3. That person over there is alone.
4. One of these tools should do the trick.
5. Your teacher is a very helpful mentor.

LO 2   CONJUNCTIONS

A **clause** is a group of words containing a finite verb. A clause can be **dependent**, which means it cannot stand on its own as a complete sentence, or **independent**, which means it is a complete sentence. *Coordinating conjunctions, subordinating conjunctions,* and *conjunctive adverbs* help correctly join two clauses. If the clauses are both independent (two complete sentences, each with its own subject and verb), use a coordinating conjunction with a comma or a conjunctive adverb with a semicolon. If one of the clauses is dependent on the other, use a subordinating conjunction.

Coordinating Conjunctions

Coordinating conjunctions connect two independent clauses using a comma and a coordinating word. The ***only seven* words** that can be used along with a comma to connect two independent clauses are the following coordinating conjunctions:

For	And	Nor	But	Or	Yet	So

A simple mnemonic device for remembering these seven words is the acronym FANBOYS, which consists of the first letter of each.

▶ NOTE   Be careful not to assume that whenever you use one of these seven words in a sentence, they are serving as a coordinating conjunction. You may be using the word "and," for instance, in a list of items such as *bread, cheese,* **and** *mustard,* in which case the word "and" is not coordinating two independent clauses.

ACTIVITY 23-12 Identifying Coordinating Conjunctions

Directions: *Underline the coordinating conjunctions in the following sentences. Check to make sure that the word is functioning as a coordinating conjunction.*

1. *It must be one of the seven words listed on page 502.*
2. *It must be preceded by a comma.*
3. *It must be between two independent clauses.*

If the word is one of the seven words listed above but does not fulfill one of the other two criteria needed to be a coordinating conjunction, do not underline it.

1. The neighborhood decided to take action, <u>so</u> they started a clean-up campaign.
2. People said they were interested, <u>but</u> only a few volunteered at first.
3. Several of the neighbors were willing to work, <u>and</u> that was enough to get the ball rolling.
4. The strongest and youngest took the job of clearing the debris, <u>for</u> that task required physical strength.
5. They agreed not to let the children lift big objects, <u>nor</u> would they let them handle sharp debris.
6. Their neighborhood had been used as a dumping ground, <u>so</u> they had a lot to do.
7. They had to decide if they would take things to the dump or pay someone to move the trash. *Correct*
8. They decided to take the debris to the dump, <u>but</u> they needed a truck.
9. They didn't have enough money for a truck rental and the dump fees. *Correct*
10. Then, the children sold lemonade for two days, <u>and</u> they raised the money needed.

Subordinating Conjunctions

Subordinating conjunctions connect dependent (or subordinating) clauses to independent clauses. If the dependent clause is first, be sure to use a comma after it. If it follows the independent clause, do not use a comma.

Dependent clause first: *Because* she always supported her students, Jaeney decided to contribute to the scholarship fund.

Dependent clause second: Jaeney decided to contribute to the scholarship fund *because* she always supported her students.

The twenty most common subordinating conjunctions are listed below.

TWENTY MOST COMMON COORDINATING CONJUNCTIONS			
after	before	though	whether
although	if	unless	which
as	once	until	while
as though	since	when	who
because	that	whereas	whose

Conjunctive Adverbs

Conjunctive adverbs are words that can also connect two independent clauses, but they are not coordinating conjunctions: They are adverb transitions. Conjunctive adverbs are also used at the beginning of a sentence to help connect it to a preceding sentence or paragraph. Here is a list of the most common conjunctive adverbs:

CONJUNCTIVE ADVERBS		
consequently	moreover	therefore
furthermore	nevertheless	thus
however	otherwise	

When a conjunctive adverb appears between two clauses, a semicolon sets it off from the clause that comes before it, and a comma sets it off from the clause that comes after it.

Kathleen wanted to win the race; *consequently*, she trained for weeks.

Ty wanted to compete, too; *however*, he injured his knee.

ACTIVITY 23-13   Identifying Subordinating Conjunctions and Conjunctive Adverbs

Directions: *Underline the subordinating conjunctions and/or conjunctive adverbs in the following sentences:*

1. While I ate my breakfast, I thought about my work schedule.
2. I couldn't seem to wake up; therefore, I bought a coffee before getting on the bus.

3. I read the paper and drank my coffee <u>until</u> I got to work.

4. My boss is strict about breaks; <u>nevertheless</u>, I took an extra one on the day I stayed late.

5. <u>Before</u> Ethan could finish his essay, the teacher called time.

ACTIVITY 23-14   Identifying Coordinating and Subordinating Conjunctions and Conjunctive Adverbs

Directions: *On the lines provided, label the word in bold font in each sentence as either a coordinating conjunction (**CC**), a subordinating conjunction (**SC**), or a conjunctive adverb (**CA**).*

SC   **1.** **Although** I know it's bad for me, I allow myself the indulgence.

CA   **2.** Chocolate has sugar; **nevertheless**, it has healthy properties, too.

CC   **3.** Chocolate has antioxidants, **and** dark chocolate has a lot of them.

CA   **4.** Chocolate is certainly one of my favorite treats; **however**, other candy tempts me as well.

CC   **5.** Sugar contributes to tooth decay, **yet** candy is a favorite treat.

CA   **6.** I try to maintain a healthy diet; **however**, I crave dessert at night.

CC   **7.** I could try eating more fruit, **but** that's just not the same somehow.

SC   **8.** **Because** most candy features sugar or corn syrup, it is full of calories.

SC   **9.** I think I will still allow myself these treats **since** we're all entitled to one vice in life.

SC   **10.** **As** far as vices go, candy is low on the dangerous list.

ACTIVITY 23-15   Create Your Own Sentences Using Coordination and Subordination

Directions: *Create five sentences of your own on the **subject of weather** using both coordination and subordination. Three should include either a coordinating*

conjunction, *a subordinating conjunction, or a conjunctive adverb. The other two are your choice. Refer to the tables earlier to identify possibilities.*
Answers will vary.

1. Use a **coordinating conjunction:**

   _____

   _____

2. Use a **subordinating conjunction:**

   _____

   _____

3. Use a **conjunctive adverb:**

   _____

   _____

4. Your choice:

   _____

   _____

5. Your choice:

   _____

   _____

ACTIVITY 23-16   Identifying Parts of Speech

Directions: *In the following excerpt from Diane Ackerman's "Chocolate Equals Love," mark the various parts of speech or connecting words in the following way: Circle all subjects; underline all verbs, and double underline all prepositions or prepositional phrases.*

We can thank the Indians of Central and South America for chocolate's bewitching lusciousness. As the Spanish explorer Hernán Cortés found, the Aztecs worshipped chocolate (which they named *cacahuatl*) as a gift from their wise god Quetzalcoatl. Aztec soldiers and male members of court drank as many as 2000 pitchers of chocolate every day. They spiked their drink with vanilla beans and spices, and they drank it bubbly thick from golden cups. Adding chili peppers gave it bite. The Aztec leader Montezuma required a chocolate ice, made from pouring syrup over snow that runners brought to him from the nearest mountain.

To check your progress in meeting this chapter's objectives, log in to www.mywritinglab .com, go to the **Study Plan** tab, click on **Sentence Constructions and Common Sentence Errors** and choose **Subjects and Verbs, Parts of Speech—Phrases and Clauses, and Consistent Verb Tense** from the list of subtopics. Read and view the resources in the **Review Materials** section, and then complete the **Recall, Apply,** and **Write** sets in the **Activities** section.

Box Cars   Tom Shugrue

THINKING CRITICALLY

As you learned in Chapter 23, sentences contain certain essential
parts. These parts can be rearranged to create different sentence structures and achieve sentence variety, which keeps writing interesting.
Once you know the parts, you can arrange them in different ways in
order to get your desired effect. List any other sentence parts besides
the **subject** and **verb** that you can remember off the top of your head.

_____

_____

_____

_____

_____

_____

LO 1 COORDINATION AND SUBORDINATION

In order to achieve sentence variety in your writing, you must fully understand the functions of coordination and subordination. They are crucial because they allow you to combine independent clauses in different ways in order to make sentences more effective and interesting.

Coordination

When two independent clauses of equal importance are joined, they form a **coordinate sentence**. They can be joined in two ways.

1. **Coordinating conjunctions:** Use one of the **FANBOYS** (*for, and, nor, but, or, yet, so*) and a **comma** to combine the two independent clauses.

> The news report said the weather was turning blustery, *so* Hannah went back for her hat and gloves.

2. **Conjunctive adverbs:** Use one of the conjunctive adverbs (followed by a comma) after a semicolon to combine two independent clauses. Some commonly used conjunctive adverbs include *however, therefore, thus, moreover, furthermore, otherwise, nevertheless,* and *consequently*.

> Mahmoud slammed the oven door; *consequently*, the cake fell.

Subordination

When one clause is less important (needs less emphasis) and can be made into a dependent clause, then it is **subordinate** or *dependent* on the independent clause. Use subordinating conjunctions to mark the beginning of the dependent or subordinate clause. Some of the most common subordinating conjunctions are *because, since, if, after, although, until, while, as, as though, before, once, that, who, whose, which,* and *whereas*.

> The map indicated we were getting close *although* we couldn't see a sign of civilization.
>
> *Even though* we were starving, we decided to keep driving to the next town.
>
> *Since* Trinh ate all the eggs, we couldn't have pancakes this morning.

ACTIVITY 24-1   Sentence Combining Coordination
and Subordination

Directions: *Combine each of the following pairs of sentences into one grammatically correct sentence using either coordination or subordination as indicated.*
Answers will vary. Sample answers are provided.

Example:	**a.**	Good eating habits are part of a long-term health plan.
	b.	It is important to teach children about nutrition early.

Coordination: Good eating habits are part of a long-term health
plan, **so** it is important to teach children about nutrition early. (*coordinating conjunction*)

Subordination: Good nutrition, **which** is important an important
part of a long-term health plan, should be taught
early to children. (*subordinating conjunction*)

1. The Internet has made finding particular music and songs easy. For a
small fee and sometimes for free, one can download music.

The Internet has made finding particular music and songs easy, and for a

small fee and sometimes for free, one can download music.

2. Many organizations offer sports camps in the summer. Children on
summer break can choose from a variety of sports, including soccer
and baseball.

Many organizations offer sports camps in the summer, which allows

children on summer break to choose from a variety of sports, including

soccer and baseball.

3. Salmon is a healthy and delicious seafood option. It provides high levels of omega-3 fatty acids.

Salmon is a healthy and delicious seafood option, for it provides high levels

of omega-3 fatty acids.

4. Chihuahuas are one of the smallest breeds of dogs. Toy Chihuahuas
are particularly tiny.

Chihuahuas are one of the smallest breeds of dogs, of which toy

Chihuahuas are particularly tiny.

5. Chilies come in many varieties. They range from mild to fiery hot.

Chilies come in many varieties, and they range from mild to fiery hot.

6. Seattle has become famous for coffee. It is also famous for computer software.

Seattle has become famous for coffee; furthermore, it is also famous for computer software.

7. Some people prefer to write with pen and paper. Some prefer composing directly on the computer.

Some people prefer to write with pen and paper, but some prefer composing directly on the computer.

8. It is important to stretch one's muscles before exercising. Stretching helps avoid major injuries.

It is important to stretch one's muscles before exercising since stretching helps avoid major injuries.

9. The new restaurant was a hit. It featured homemade tortillas and crunchy tacos.

The new restaurant was a hit, and it featured homemade tortillas and crunchy tacos.

10. Palm trees are associated with Southern California. The palm tree is not native to California.

Palm trees are associated with Southern California although the palm tree is not native to California.

LO 2 SENTENCE TYPES

A **sentence** is a group of words that expresses a complete thought and contains at least one independent clause. An independent clause includes, at a minimum, an implied or stated subject and a main verb; it expresses a complete thought. Sentences can have distinct purposes and different structures.

Sentence Purposes

Sentences can have the following four purposes (the verbs are in italics, and the subjects are in bold in the sample sentences below):

1. **Declarative:** They make a statement or declaration.

> The new hybrid **cars** *are* better than ever.
> Both the hybrid **sedans** and the **SUVs** *drive* well and *get* good mileage.

2. **Interrogative:** They ask a question.

> Will **you** *buy* a hybrid car?

3. **Imperative:** They give a command.

> *Try* a test drive of one of the new models. *(subject is the implied **you**)*

4. **Exclamatory:** They express a strong emotion or sentiment.

> The newest **hybrids** *are* spectacular!

ACTIVITY 24-2   Practicing Sentence Types

Directions: *Write one sentence of your own for each of the sentence types. Be sure to punctuate them correctly.*   Answers will vary.

Declarative:

_____

Interrogative:

_____

Imperative:

_____

Exclamatory:

_____

SENTENCE STRUCTURES

There are four basic sentence structures (the subjects in the sample sentences below are in bold, and the verbs are in italics):

1. **Simple Sentences:** Simple sentences have one independent clause.

> The **banks** *are lowering* the interest rate.

2. **Compound Sentences:** Compound sentences have two or more independent clauses.

> The **banks** *are lowering* the interest rate, and **people** *are beginning* to buy new houses again.

3. **Complex Sentences:** Complex sentences have at least one independent clause and at least one dependent clause (in any order and number).

> The housing **market** *is starting* to get busy again since the interest rate dropped.

4. **Compound-Complex Sentences:** Compound-complex sentences have at least two independent clauses and at least one dependent clause (in any order).

> The **realtors** in my neighborhood ***have** jumped* on the bandwagon, and **they** *are pushing* for even more sales because the rates will surely rise again soon.

ACTIVITY 24-3 Practicing with Sentence Structures

Directions: *Create each sentence using the sentence structure indicated.*
Answers will vary.

Simple Sentence:

_____

Compound Sentence:

_____

_____

Complex Sentence:

_____

_____

Compound-Complex Sentence:

_____

_____

To vary your writing, you can combine dependent clauses with independent clauses (coordination and subordination) in various patterns to achieve a variety of sentence types. Think of the train in the photograph at the beginning of the chapter. You can create a variety of train types (of different lengths) using combinations of independent and dependent clauses (boxcars) hooked together with their appropriate coordination or subordination hook.

Engage your critical thinking skills to decide on the best sentence type to express your ideas in the context of your writing assignment. The types of sentences you use will depend on what you are discussing and who you are writing for. Here are a few possible combinations (DC = dependent clause, IC = independent clause):

1. Two independent clauses (joined by a coordinating conjunction)

> IC   +   IC
>
> Selling a home is stressful, *but* it helps to hire a realtor.

2. A dependent clause in front of an independent clause

> DC   +   IC
>
> When I sold my home, I tried doing it on my own at first.

3. Independent clause followed by a dependent clause

> IC   +   DC
>
> The stress of waiting for an offer was intense when I first advertised the sale of my house.

4. A dependent clause followed by an independent clause and a dependent clause

> DC   +   IC   +   DC
>
> When I didn't get an offer for over a month, I finally hired a realtor *because* I needed professional help.

See how many types of sentences you can create as you experiment with coordination and subordination (review Chapter 23 for more on coordination and subordination).

ACTIVITY 24-4 Sentence Combining Practice

Directions: **Step One:** *Write a paragraph that describes where you live using 8–15 simple sentences.* **Step Two:** *Go back and revise your original paragraph, and combine some of your sentences using coordination and subordination to achieve sentence variety.*

Original Version

_____

_____

_____

_____

_____

_____

_____

Revised Version

_____

_____

_____

_____

_____

_____

LO 3 SENTENCE VARIETY

When crafting longer pieces of writing, such as paragraphs and essays, you should vary your sentences in length, type, and rhythm. Readers get tired of short, choppy sentences, and your style and tone suffer, too. Use a variety of sentence lengths to keep your reader interested and your style strong. Similarly, change the structure of your sentences in your paragraphs and essays to avoid a monotonous style, tone, and rhythm.

One way to achieve sentence variety is to go back to some of your original, simple sentences and add more details and examples. For instance, if you had a sentence which read *I like to snorkel,* you could vary it in length and style by simply adding more details: *I like to snorkel because of the intense connection it provides me with nature through the many sea plants and animals I get to see first hand.*

Another way is to combine sentences through coordination and subordination to create more complex sentences, as we have been practicing in this chapter and in the preceding one. For example:

> **Before:** I like to snorkel. Sea turtles are the most exciting creatures to see while snorkeling.
>
> **Revised with coordination:** I like to snorkel, and sea turtles are the most exciting creatures to see underwater.
>
> **Revised with subordination:** Though I like to see all kinds of plants and animals when I snorkel, sea turtles are my favorite.

You can also achieve more variety in your writing by including sentences that are *declarative, interrogative, imperative,* and *exclamatory.*

> I really enjoy snorkeling. Have you ever tried it? You have to try snorkeling in Hawaii. It is the best spot to snorkel by far!

APPLYING CRITICAL THINKING

PURPOSE	IDEAS	SUPPORT	ASSUMPTIONS BIASES	CONCLUSIONS	POINT OF VIEW	ANALYSIS

In order to achieve sentence variety in the revision stage of your writing, engage your **analysis** skills. Go through your draft again, and read each sentence carefully. Make sure that you have expressed your thoughts clearly, used correct grammar, and all the parts of the sentence work together to express what you want to say. Then, see if you can incorporate some of the following suggestions for making your sentences more interesting and expressive:

Five Tips for Achieving Sentence Variety

1. Doublecheck the entire piece to make sure you have a good balance of short and long sentences.

2. Try adding some additional information (words or phrases) to your shorter, simpler sentences.

3. Try using different types of sentences: statements (declarative), questions (interrogative), commands (imperative), and exclamations.

4. Try combining some of your sentences to create compound, complex, or even compound-complex sentences, using coordination and subordination.

5. Vary the style and rhythm of your sentences. Read the sentences aloud to find out if they sound interesting or could benefit from some of the changes listed above.

Before and After Revising for Sentence Variety

Before (no variety)

Making soap at home is a fun hobby and can be used to make beautiful gifts. Soap making involves following a step-by-step process and caution. Most soap is made by combining fats with lye. Some soaps use animal fat and some use vegetable fat. Also, some soap is cold processed some hot processed. In the cold process, lye is dissolved in water, and then fatty oils are stirred in. However, the cold process requires very exact measurements for the lye and oils. In the hot process, the lye and the oils are boiled together to a temperature of 80-100 degrees Celsius. The measurements don't have to be as exact in the hot process because the heat will adjust the balance until saponification occurs (the fat changes into soap). Next, the soap starts to thicken. At that point, one can add essential oils or fragrances to the soap. Finally, the liquid is poured into a mold and allowed to cure for a day to up to a month, depending on the process used.

After (revised using the five tips for achieving sentence variety)

Have you ever thought of making your own soap? *[Change in sentence type for variety]* Making soap at home is a fun hobby and can be used to make beautiful gifts. Soap making involves following a step-by-step process, and one needs to use extreme caution when working with harsh ingredients such as lye. *[Use of coordination to combine two sentences]* In fact, most soaps are made by combining fats, animal fats or vegetable fats such as olive oil, with lye. Also, some soaps are cold processed, while some are hot processed. *[Use of subordination to combine two sentences]* In the cold process, lye is dissolved in water, and then fatty oils are stirred in; however, the cold process requires very exact measurements of the lye and the oils. *[Subordination]* In the hot process, the lye and the oils are boiled together to a temperature of 80-100 degrees Celsius, and the measurements don't have to be as exact as in the cold process because the heat will adjust the balance until saponification occurs (the soap sets up). *[Subordination]* Next, the soap starts to thicken, and, at that point, one can add other essential oils such as moisturizing jojoba oil or fragrant oils such as peppermint oil to the soap. *[Use of coordination to combine two sentences]* Finally, the liquid is poured into a mold, and the soap is allowed to cure for a day to up to a month depending on the process used. Try making your own soap today! Beautiful, handmade soap makes a perfect gift.

ACTIVITY 24-5   Practicing Sentence Variety

Directions: *Using the five tips on page 516, rewrite the following paragraph to achieve more sentence variety.* Answers will vary.

Alfred Hitchcock made many classic American movies. Most of his films were in the genre of horror. However, many would say they should be considered psychological thrillers. One of the most famous films of his career was *Psycho.* However, some would argue that either *Vertigo* or *Rear Window* hold their own against *Psycho* in terms of being his best film. Two more films by Hitchcock that stand out are *North by Northwest* and *The Birds.* Two lesser-known films include *Strangers on a Train* and *Shadow of a Doubt.* These two lesser-known films are actually two of his best. Almost all of his films feature an everyday person who has to overcome unusual, often deadly circumstances. Sometimes Hitchcock even has us rooting for the bad guys. Without a doubt, the most noteworthy aspect of Hitchcock's films is the tension he creates and the eerie atmosphere he creates on film.

_____

_____

_____

_____

_____

_____

To check your progress in meeting this chapter's objectives, log in to www.mywritinglab .com, go to the **Study Plan** tab, click on **Sentence Constructions and Common Sentence Errors** and choose **Varying Sentence Structure** and **Combining Sentences** from the list of subtopics. Read and view the resources in the **Review Materials** section, and then complete the **Recall, Apply,** and **Write** sets in the **Activities** section.

Correcting Major Sentence Errors

Beach Stones

LEARNING OBJECTIVES

In this chapter, you will learn to

 Spot and correct sentence fragments.

 Spot and correct run-ons and comma splices.

THINKING CRITICALLY

The parts of a sentence come together to make complete sentences, but you can't just put the parts together randomly, like stones on a beach. If you don't have all the necessary parts, or if you have too many parts without the correct punctuation, you can end up with a major construction error. If you are missing a necessary sentence part, you will have a sentence fragment; if you have enough parts for more than one sentence but have improper or no punctuation, you will have a comma splice or a run-on.

On the basis of what you learned in Chapters 23 and 24, what are the two main sentence parts that will determine if you have a complete sentence?

_____

_____

_____

LO 1 FRAGMENTS

A **sentence fragment** is exactly that: a fragment, a piece of a sentence posing as a complete sentence. It starts with a capital letter and ends with a period, but it does not express a complete thought. Though we often use fragments in everyday speech and when reporting the speech of others in written dialogue, college essays generally require the use of grammatically complete sentences.

See the following box for a list of errors that can cause fragments:

Common Errors That Create Fragments

1. **Missing subject:** leaving out the *subject* of the sentence

2. **Missing, incomplete, or incorrect form of verb:** leaving out the *verb,* using an *incomplete verb*, or using the *wrong form of a verb*

3. **Including a subordinating word or phrase before the subject and the verb:** adding a word or phrase which makes a clause *dependent* on another clause for meaning

---

Check your writing carefully for these three common errors that lead to sentence fragments.

1. Missing a subject

> **Forgot to close the car door.**
>
> [Subject missing: *Who* forgot to close the car door?]
>
> *Mahad* forgot to close the car door.

2. Missing the verb, using an incomplete verb, or using the wrong form of a verb

> **A good variety of dining options in the cafeteria.**
>
> [No verb. Add one to make the sentence complete.]
>
> A good variety of dining options *is* available in the cafeteria.

> **Margaret studying for the test.**
>
> [Incomplete verb: add the helping verb *is* or *was* before *studying*.]
>
> Margaret *is studying* for the test.
>
> Margaret *was studying* for the test.

> **The machine running the elevator.**
>
> [Wrong form of verb: change to *runs* or *ran*.]
>
> The machine *runs* the elevator.
>
> The machine *ran* the elevator.

3. **Including a subordinate word or phrase before the subject and verb (makes the word group a dependent clause)**

> **Since she travels every spring.**
>
> [Subordinating word: the word *Since* makes this a dependent clause. Either delete the word *Since*, or add an independent clause before or after it.]
>
> ~~Since~~ She travels every spring.
>
> Since she travels every spring, she has accrued a great deal of frequent flyer miles.

Identifying Sentence Fragments

A complete sentence contains a subject and a verb and does not have a subordinating word or phrase before the subject. Here are three steps you can use to identify sentence fragments:

Three Steps for Identifying Sentence Fragments

1. Find the verb.

2. Find the subject.

3. Check for a subordinating word or phrase.

Cross Reference

See p. 483 for more on verbs.

1. **Find the verb.** Since the verb is usually easy to find because it indicates the action or state of being (physical action or mental/emotional action) in a sentence, find it first. If there is no verb (or if an auxiliary verb is needed), then you have a sentence fragment. Ask yourself, "What is happening in this sentence?" For example:

> **The kitten in the living room.**
>
> [*What* is the kitten doing in the living room? The sentence needs a verb.]
>
> The kitten *is sleeping* in the living room.

If the verb is an *-ing* form (verbal), make sure there is an auxiliary or helping verb (a *to be* verb such as *is, was, are,* or *were*) in front of it. For instance:

> **Tom *taking* a nap.**
>
> [The above sentence needs a helping verb.]
>
> Tom *is taking* a nap.
>
> OR, change the *-ing* form to a regular verb:
>
> Tom *takes* (or *took*) a nap.

Cross Reference

See p. 480 for more on subjects.

2. **Find the subject.** Ask yourself, "*Who* or *what* is the subject of the action/verb I found?" If there is no noun serving as the subject, then the word group is a sentence fragment. For example:

> **Takes the bus almost every day.**
>
> [*Who* is taking the bus? *Who* is the subject of this sentence?]
>
> *Lori* takes the bus almost every day.

> **Exception:** The one exception is when the subject is implied, as in the word *you* in a command. For example:

> **Don't drop that glass.**
>
> [Although not stated, the subject of this sentence is the implied: "You"]
>
> (You) Don't drop that glass.

3. **Check for a subordinating word or phrase that creates a dependent clause.** When you put a subordinating conjunction such as *whenever* in front of the subject of a sentence, the sentence becomes a dependent clause. It is incomplete because it now depends on the addition of more information to make sense, for example:

Cross Reference

See p. 482 for more on the "implied you" subject.

> **Whenever she works on weekends.**
>
> [The word *whenever* makes this a dependent phrase. Either delete the subordinating word *whenever*, or add an independent clause before or after the phrase.]
>
> ~~Whenever~~ She works on weekends.
>
> *Her partner complains* whenever she works on weekends.
>
> Whenever she works on weekends, *her kids don't get to see much of her.*

Here are a few of the most common words that indicate the beginning of a dependent clause or subordinate phrase:

because	as	believing that
since	on	hoping that
when	in	especially
whenever	every time	
if	knowing that	

Cross Reference

See p. 503, for a more complete list of subordinating words and a more in-depth explanation of using subordination.

Correcting Sentence Fragments

When you have spotted a fragment caused by one or more of the errors discussed above, use that error or set of errors as a key to fixing the problem.

1. **Missing verb**

> **Fragment:** Rainfall on the streets. [Missing a verb, so add one]
> **Revised:** Rainfall *puddles* on the streets.

> **Fragment:** The kids playing on the lawn.
> [Not a complete verb, so add an auxiliary verb or change the verb form]
> **Revised:** The kids are playing on the lawn.
>   The kids play on the lawn.

2. Missing subject

> **Fragment:** Needs to find a good career. [Missing a subject, so add one]
> **Revised:** *Clay* needs to find a good career.

3. Dependent clause

> **Fragment:** Because I rowed yesterday.
> [Dependent clause due to the word *because*—delete the word *because*, follow it with a comma and an independent clause, or precede it with an independent clause followed by a comma]
> **Revised:** ~~Because~~ I rowed yesterday.
>
>   Because I rowed yesterday, *I will rest today.*
>
>   *I will rest today* because I rowed yesterday.

ACTIVITY 25-1   Identifying and Correcting Fragments I

Directions: *Using the three-step test for fragments, list which type or types of error created each fragment below. Some items may have more than one error.*

1. *Missing a subject*
2. *A missing, incomplete, or incorrect form of verb*
3. *Subordinate word or phrase before the subject and verb*

Then, add or delete words to fix the fragment and rewrite it as a complete sentence. You may need to add more information for the sentence to make sense.
Answers may vary. Sample answers are provided.

Example: Ate the salad.   Error Type(s) ____1____

Corrected: *Cameron ate the salad.*

1. Knowing that homemade spaghetti   Error Type(s) ____3____
   sauce is the best.

   Corrected: *Homemade spaghetti sauce is the best.*

2. My mom always making her sauce   Error Type(s) ____2____
   from scratch.

   Corrected: *My mom always made her sauce from scratch.*

3. Garden tomatoes being the essential   Error Type(s) _____2_____
ingredient.

   Corrected: *Garden tomatoes are the essential ingredient.*

4. Since the sauce is made mostly   Error Type(s) _____3_____
from tomatoes.

   Corrected: *The sauce is made mostly from tomatoes.*

5. Fresh herbs essential to the overall   Error Type(s) _____2_____
taste.

   Corrected: *Fresh herbs are essential to the overall taste.*

ACTIVITY 25-2   Identifying and Correcting Fragments II

Directions: *Review the following word groups. If a word group is a complete sentence, write S on the line provided. If it is a fragment, write F, and then revise it to make it into a complete sentence. You may add or delete words to fix the fragments.* Answers may vary. Sample answers are provided.

____F____ **1.** The Statue of Liberty, a miraculous engineering achievement.

   The Statue of Liberty is a miraculous engineering

   achievement.

____F____ **2.** The statue, completed in 1886, covered with a thin copper skin, located in New York Harbor.

   The statue, completed in 1886, covered with a thin copper

   skin, is located in New York Harbor.

____S____ **3.** The copper skin is less than the thickness of two pennies.

   _____

____F____ **4.** Spectacular views available from the observation deck.

   Spectacular views are available from the observation deck.

____F____ **5.** Designed by the French sculptor Frederic Auguste Bartholdi.

   The statue was designed by the French sculptor Frederic

   Auguste Bartholdi.

ACTIVITY 25-3   Identifying and Correcting Fragments III

Directions: *In the spaces provided after the paragraph, mark F for a fragment and S for a complete sentence. You should find seven fragments. After you have marked each word group, revise five of the fragments in the second part of the exercise.*

[1]The Statue of Liberty is an American icon. [2]Because she is known as a symbol of freedom and liberty. [3]The statue was dedicated on October 28, 1886. [4]Given to America by the people of France. [5]Commemorating the American Revolution and America's friendship with France. [6]The statue itself was constructed in France. [7]Then dismantled and shipped to America in several crates. [8]The statue was reassembled and mounted on a pedestal built especially for it on an island in New York Harbor. [9]Proclaimed a National Monument on October 15, 1924. [10]The care of the statue was then transferred to the National Park Service. [11]In 1956, the island the statue was built upon was renamed "Liberty Island." [12] In 1965, Ellis Island becoming part of the monument as well. [13]In 1986, the Statue of Liberty was newly restored. [14]Reopening to the public on July 5,1986. [15]The Statue of Liberty will always represent everything good that America stands for.

1. _____S_____   5. _____F_____   9. _____F_____   13. _____S_____

2. _____F_____   6. _____S_____   10. _____S_____   14. _____F_____

3. _____S_____   7. _____F_____   11. _____S_____   15. _____S_____

4. _____F_____   8. _____S_____   12. _____F_____

Now, pick five of the fragments you found above, and rewrite them below to make them into complete sentences by adding the needed subject, fixing or adding the needed verb, or by removing the word that makes them a dependent clause.
Answers may vary.

1. _____

_____

2. _____

_____

3. _____

_____

4. _____

_____

5. _____

_____

ACTIVITY 25-4   Identifying and Correcting Fragments IV

Directions: *Add the needed words or even a complete additional independent clause to the following fragments to make them into complete sentences. You may also need to change the tense of a word to correct a sentence.*

Answers will vary. Sample answers are provided.

1. Knowing it was time to go to school.

   Knowing it was time to go to school, Nolan got his shoes on quickly.

2. Counting his money.

   Timothy was counting his money.

3. To take someone's advice well.

   You must be humble to take someone's advice well.

4. Finding her way to the store.

   Finding her way to the store, Lela stayed on the sidewalk the whole way.

5. Learning to ride a bike.

   Learning to ride a bike requires patience.

RUN-ONS AND COMMA SPLICES

A **run-on**, sometimes called a *fused sentence,* occurs when you combine two or more independent clauses (complete sentences) with no punctuation to separate them. See Chapter 23, "Sentence Parts," for more about what makes an independent clause or a complete sentence. Use your analysis skills to check for the necessary parts of a sentence and to make sure you don't have two or more independent clauses that need stronger punctuation to join them.

Example of a run-on/fused sentence:

Rain brings flowers spring is stunning.

[This group of words is a run-on because it includes two full sentences, each with a subject and a verb.]

Rain	**brings**	**flowers**	**spring**	**is**	**stunning.**
(subj)	(verb)	(obj)	(subj)	(verb)	(obj)

A **comma splice** is a particular type of run-on that occurs when you combine two or more independent clauses (two complete sentences, each with a subject and a verb) with just a comma.

> **Example of a comma splice:**
>
> **Rain brings flowers, spring is stunning.**
>
> [This word group is a comma splice because it contains two full sentences, each with its own subject and verb, on both sides of the comma.]

Correcting Run-ons and Comma Splices

Here are four ways to fix run-ons and comma splices:

Four Ways to Fix Run-ons and Comma Splices

1. **Use ","** + coordinating conjunction (FANBOYS).

2. **Use "."** or **"!"** or **"?"** (add a final punctuation mark).

3. **Use ";"** and sometimes a **":".**

4. Make one of the sentences into a dependent clause by adding a subordinating word.

---

1. **Add a coordinating conjunction** (FANBOYS—For, And, Nor, But, Or, Yet, So) after the comma. A comma with a coordinating conjunction is equal to a period.

   > Rain brings flowers, and spring is stunning.

2. **Change the comma into a period** (or an exclamation point or a question mark if the first independent clause is a question).

   > Rain brings flowers. Spring is stunning.

3. **Change the comma into a semicolon or a colon.** A semicolon can be used to combine two independent clauses that have a strong content

connection, but use semicolons sparingly to indicate a powerful connection between two complete thoughts.

> Rain brings flowers; spring is stunning.

A colon can also be used between two independent clauses if the second clause *answers* or *explains* the first one.

> I like spring rain for one reason: It brings flowers.

Cross Reference
See Chapter 26 for more on using semicolons and colons.

4. Turn one of the independent clauses into a dependent clause by adding a subordinating word.

> Since it rains a great deal in the spring, we get stunning flowers.

Cross Reference
See p. 504 for more on subordination.

ACTIVITY 25-5   Correcting Run-ons

Directions: *Fix the following run-on (fused) sentences by (1) adding a comma and a coordinating conjunction (For, And, Nor, But, Or, Yet, So), (2) adding a period, or (3) adding a semicolon or colon.*
Answers will vary. Sample answers are provided.

1. Homemade chili is the best it's especially good with roasted corn.

   Homemade chili is the best; it's especially good with roasted corn.

2. The kitten chased after the moth she was determined to catch it.

   The kitten chased after the moth. She was determined to catch it.

3. On Saturdays, we go to the park on Mondays we go to work.

   On Saturdays, we go to the park, and on Mondays we go to work.

4. Baseball is an all-American sport basketball is a close second.

   Baseball is an all-American sport, but basketball is a close second.

5. Snow is wonderful it's so pretty.

   Snow is wonderful: It's so pretty.

ACTIVITY 25-6   Correcting Comma Splices

Directions: *Fix the following comma splice sentences by (1) adding a comma and a coordinating conjunction (For, And, Nor, But, Or, Yet, So), (2) adding a period, or (3) adding a semicolon or colon.*
Answers will vary. Sample answers are provided.

1. Homemade chili is the best, it's especially good with roasted corn.

   Homemade chili is the best; it's especially good with roasted corn.

2. The kitten chased after the moth, she was determined to catch it.

   The kitten chased after the moth. She was determined to catch it.

3. On Saturdays, we go to the park, on Mondays we go to work.

   On Saturdays, we go to the park, and on Mondays we go to work.

4. Baseball is an all-American sport, basketball is a close second.

   Baseball is an all-American sport, but basketball is a close second.

5. Snow is wonderful, it's so pretty.

   Snow is wonderful: It's so pretty.

ACTIVITY 25-7   Correcting Run-ons and Comma Splices I

Directions: *Mark each sentence RO for run-on (no punctuation between two independent clauses), CS for a comma splice (two independent clauses joined with only a comma), or C if the sentence is correct. Then fix the run-ons and comma splices, using one of the methods listed in the box titled Four Ways to Fix Run-ons and Comma Splices.* *Answers will vary. Sample answers are provided.*

___RO___ 1. The Alamo, located in San Antonio, is one of the most famous sites in Texas it was originally named Mission San Antonio de Valero.

   The Alamo, located in San Antonio, is one of the most

   famous sites in Texas. It was originally named Mission San

   Antonio de Valero.

The Alamo

_CS_   **2.** Original construction of the mission began in 1724, in the early 1800s the Spanish stationed a cavalry unit at the former mission.

Original construction of the mission began in 1724, and in

the early 1800s, the Spanish stationed a cavalry unit at

the former mission.

_C_   **3.** The Spanish soldiers began calling the building the Alamo, the Spanish word for "cottonwood."

_____RO_____ **4.** In 1836, the battle took place that made the Alamo the famous site it is today it was part of the revolution against Spanish rule in Texas.

In 1836, the battle took place that made the Alamo the

famous site it is today. It was part of the revolution

against Spanish rule in Texas.

_____CS_____ **5.** On February 23, 1836, Santa Anna's Spanish army entered San Antonio, the Texan revolutionaries fought from within the Alamo.

On February 23, 1836, Santa Anna's Spanish army entered

San Antonio, and the Texan revolutionaries fought from

within the Alamo.

_____C_____ **6.** The revolutionaries held out for 13 days against Santa Anna's army, but they were fighting against overwhelming numbers.

_____

_____

_____RO_____ **7.** Thirty-two additional volunteers joined the Alamo defenders on the eighth day of the siege this brought the total to nearly 200 fighters facing a vastly higher number of Spanish soldiers.

Thirty-two additional volunteers joined the Alamo defenders

on the eighth day of the siege. This brought the total to

nearly 200 fighters facing a vastly higher number of

Spanish soldiers.

_____RO_____ **8.** David "Davy" Crockett, well-known frontiersman and former congressman, was one of the famous defenders of the Alamo, a renowned knife fighter and western hero, Jim Bowie, was another.

David "Davy" Crockett, well-known frontiersman and former

congressman, was one of the famous defenders of the

Alamo. A renowned knife fighter and western hero, Jim

Bowie, was another.

___CS___ **9.** The final assault on the Alamo took place on March 6, 1836, and the battle was over, Santa Anna's army finally overwhelmed the defenders.

The final assault on the Alamo took place on March 6,

1836, and the battle was over: Santa Anna's army finally

overwhelmed the defenders.

___CS___ **10.** It is a myth that no one inside the Alamo survived, there were about 20 survivors, including women and children and one male slave.

It is a myth that no one inside the Alamo survived, for

there were about 20 survivors, including women and

children and one male slave.

ACTIVITY 25-8 Correcting Run-ons and Comma Splices II

Directions: *In the spaces provided below the paragraph, mark RO for run-ons, CS for comma splices, and S for correct sentences. You should find four comma splices and five run-ons.*

Franklin Delano Roosevelt Memorial, Final Room and Statue

[1]The Franklin Delano Roosevelt Memorial is well worth visiting. [2] It was dedicated on May 2, 1997, it is one of the newest memorials in Washington DC. [3]The Memorial is located near the famous Cherry Tree Walk by the Tidal Basin the location is not far from the Jefferson Memorial. [4]The memorial pays tribute not only to Roosevelt but also to a difficult time in America's history. [5]Moreover, the memorial design balances history and sentiment. [6]The memorial is set up like a journey, one wanders through granite "rooms" that tell the stories of FDR's terms as president. [7] The walls are made of red South Dakota granite they enclose each section of the memorial with open passages between them. [8]There are four "rooms" in the monument, each represents one term in Roosevelt's twelve-year presidency. [9]The rooms are arranged in chronological order a visitor literally walks through the memorial as if embarking on a historical journey. [10]In each of the rooms, water is used to symbolize the state of the nation at the time. [11]The water becomes increasingly chaotic as the country becomes more chaotic, for instance, during the Great Depression era segment of the memorial, the water is falling over rocks in a waterfall suggesting "troubled waters" or difficult times. [12]One room features a bronze relief of FDR's funeral march in that room the water is completely still. [13]Moreover, in that room, even the huge, decorative stones around the memorial are completely organized; in the other rooms, they seem to be more disorganized or stacked randomly. [14]People who walk through the memorial are drawn to the natural water and stone they are encouraged to touch both as they pass through. [15]The memorial leaves a lasting impression of both the man and the times during which he was president.

1.	S	5.	S	9.	RO	13.	S
2.	CS	6.	CS	10.	S	14.	RO
3.	RO	7.	RO	11.	CS	15.	S
4.	S	8.	CS	12.	RO		

Now, pick five of the run-ons and/or comma splices you found above and revise them by adding the needed punctuation or joining word.

1. _____

_____

2. _____

_____

3. _____

_____

4. _____

_____

5. _____

 To check your progress in meeting this chapter's objectives, log in to www.mywritinglab .com, go to the **Study Plan** tab, click on **Sentence Constructions and Common Sentence Errors** and choose **Fragments** and **Run-Ons** from the list of subtopics. Read and view the resources in the **Review Materials** section, and then complete the **Recall**, **Apply**, and **Write** sets in the **Activities** section.

26 Comma, Semicolon, and Colon

Frank and Ernest

PERIODICALS

QUESTION MARKICALS AND SEMI-COLONICALS →

THAVES

LEARNING OBJECTIVES

In this chapter, you will learn to

 Use the comma correctly.

 Use the semicolon correctly.

 Use the colon correctly.

THINKING CRITICALLY

Punctuation is essential to imparting meaning. What do you think it would be like to read a paragraph with no punctuation marks? Why?

_____

_____

_____

_____

_____

_____

_____

LO 1 COMMA

The comma (,) is the most common form of punctuation. It serves several functions in writing and helps your readers understand your ideas and sentences. **Commas** clarify, make distinctions, or create the pauses that help your readers follow your sentences and ideas.

Five Comma Rules

There are five basic rules of comma use, and if you keep them in mind, the mystery of comma use will be solved. Try not to use the "comma by instinct" approach: There really are consistent rules for comma use.

When you are editing your writing, check to see if the commas you have used fall into one of these categories, and if they do not, then remember the old rule: "When in doubt, leave it out." A comma where it doesn't belong usually causes more problems than leaving it out does.

Rule 1

Use a comma before a coordinating conjunction in order to combine two independent clauses to create a compound sentence.

Independent clause + , + FANBOYS + independent clause

▼

(Coordinating conjunctions)

Use the mnemonic device (memory trick) FANBOYS (**F**or, **A**nd, **N**or, **B**ut, **O**r, **Y**et, **S**o) to recall them. These are the only seven words in the English language that can be used after a comma to combine two independent clauses (when you use any other word, you end up with a comma splice).

The computer graphics course is fun, and the professor is excellent.

Many students want to take the course, but it is already full.

▶ **TIP**   The comma comes *before* the coordinating conjunction. Also, be careful not to place a comma automatically as soon as you see one of the FANBOYS. These words need to have an independent clause (with a subject and a verb) on *both* sides for the comma to be used. Otherwise, they are part of a compound subject or a compound predicate, and in that case, you don't use a comma:

> Maya took the course last year and said it was great.

There is only one subject in this sentence: *Maya*. There are two verbs that both relate to the subject: *took* and *said*. The word *and* links two parts of a compound predicate, and no comma is needed.

Rule 2

Use a comma to separate the items in a series (a list of three or more items) or a list of coordinate adjectives.

1. **Using commas with items in a series.** Commas help separate distinct items within a list of items:

> **Item + , item + , item + , and item**

> Maya has taken several other computer courses, including Computer Programming, Software Tools, and Web Site Development.

Placing the last comma before the "and" is one of the comma rules currently in debate. Some people argue that a comma replaces the word "and" so the last comma before an item in a series isn't necessary. However, there are cases when a reader could get confused by the absence of a comma before the last item in the series, so it's usually a good idea to put it in. Consistency and clarity are the rules of thumb. For example:

> I went to the movie with my cousins, Marco, and Sofia.

Without the second comma, the reader would not know whether Marco and Sofia are the names of the speaker's cousins or the names of two other people who accompanied the speaker and the speaker's cousins to the movie.

2. **Coordinate adjectives versus cumulative or compound adjectives**
   - **Coordinate adjectives:** If two or more adjectives before a noun indicate separate qualities, use a comma between them. In other words, you are listing the separate qualities:

> Marco thought it was a poignant, thought-provoking, inspiring movie.

▶ **TIP**   If you can change the order of the adjectives and replace each comma with the word *and*, then you are dealing with coordinate adjectives:

> Marco thought it was a thought-provoking and inspiring and poignant movie.

- **Cumulative adjectives:** If the adjectives are working together in order to describe something or modify each other in stages, then *do not* use commas:

> Author Betty Friedan pointed out the inequities of traditional gender roles.

No comma should come between *traditional* and *gender* because the words function as cumulative adjectives. "Gender roles" functions as a single unit, and "traditional" describes that unit.

▶ **TIP**   Try adding "and" between the adjectives or reversing their position. If the sentence changes meaning or sounds wrong, then the adjectives are cumulative adjectives and should not be separated by a comma. For example:

> Author Betty Friedan pointed out the inequities of traditional and gender roles.
>
> Author Betty Friedan pointed out the inequities of gender traditional roles.

Inserting *and* between *traditional* and *gender* changes the meaning of the sentence, and "gender traditional roles" sounds wrong. Here is another example of a sentence containing cumulative adjectives:

> Even today an impenetrable glass ceiling blocks career advancement for women in certain professions.

Again, you wouldn't want to change the order of *impenetrable* and *glass* in this sentence. Cumulative adjectives should sound right in the particular order in which they appear: They are not interchangeable. You wouldn't say "glass impenetrable ceiling."

- **Compound adjectives:** If two adjectives are used together to make one descriptor, then they become a compound adjective, and you should use a hyphen between them instead of a comma.

> **Coordinate adjectives:** The lilac bushes were covered with lavender, blue, and pink blossoms. [Three separate qualities/colors, so use commas]
>
> **Compound adjective:** The lilac bushes were covered with lavender-blue and pink blossoms. [Lavender-blue is one color, so use a hyphen, not a comma]

> **Coordinate adjectives:** The small, modern hospital provides excellent care for patients. [Small and modern are two separate qualities, so use a comma]
>
> **Compound adjective:** The small-animal hospital provides excellent care for dogs and cats. [Small-animal is one quality, so use a hyphen]

Rule 3

Use a comma after introductory material (an introductory dependent clause, an introductory prepositional or participial phrase, or an introductory single word for emphasis or transition).

> **Dependent clause + , + remainder of sentence**
>
> **Introductory phrase + , + remainder of sentence**
>
> **Introductory word + , + remainder of sentence**

A comma sets off the introductory word, phrase, or clause from the rest of the sentence. To find introductory material, look for the main subject and verb and see what comes before them.

1. Introductory dependent clause

Use a comma between the end of an introductory dependent clause and the remainder of the sentence. A dependent clause begins with a subordinating word, such as *though, because, since, when,* or *if.*

> *If the weather is good,* I go jogging in the park.

However, if a dependent clause comes after an independent clause, then a comma is not required:

I go jogging in the park *if the weather is good.*

Cross Reference

See p. 503 for more about subordinating words.

2. Introductory prepositional phrase

Use a comma after a prepositional phrase that comes at the beginning of the sentence. A prepositional phrase begins with a preposition such as *on, in, before,* or *after*:

Before heading out to jog, I do some warm-up exercises.

If, however, a prepositional phrase comes after an independent clause, *do not* use a comma:

Cross Reference

See p. 495 for more about subordinating words.

I do some warm-up exercises *before heading out to jog.*

3. Introductory participial phrase

Use a comma after a participial phrase that comes at the beginning of the sentence. A participial phrase begins with a word ending in *-ing*:

Jogging through the park, I feel a little creaky at first.

4. Introductory word for emphasis or transition

Use a comma after a transitional or emphatic word that comes at the beginning of the sentence:

Eventually, I hit my stride and feel totally energized.

5. Direct address

When you begin a sentence by directly addressing someone by name or title, use a comma after the name or title:

Daniel, have you ever served on a jury?

▶ **TIP** If the direct address comes at the end of the sentence, you will need a comma before the name or title. If the direct address comes in the middle of the sentence, use two commas, one before and one after the name or title:

Have you ever served on a jury, *Daniel?*

With all due respect, *Your Honor,* the prosecution objects.

Dear Ashley, I hope you win the case. [Also used in an informal letter greeting]

6. Yes and no statements

Use a comma after a *yes* or a *no* that begins a sentence:

> *Yes,* I was proud to serve as a juror.

7. Tag lines for dialogue or quotations

Use a comma after a tag word or phrase that comes before a quotation or a dialogue in your sentence:

> *The lawyer asked,* "What caused you to trip and fall?"
> *Walt Whitman wrote,* "Justice is always in jeopardy."

> ▶ **NOTE**   Sometimes the comma can be omitted after introductory material if there is a short clause or a phrase that causes no danger of misreading.

> *Without a doubt* jury duty is a solemn responsibility.

However, it's acceptable to use the comma there, too.

> *Without a doubt,* jury duty is a solemn responsibility.

Rule 4

Use a comma to set off interrupters—words, phrases, or clauses that "interrupt" a sentence between the beginning and end of an independent clause (IC).

> **Beginning of IC + , + interrupter + , + end of IC**

1. Dependent clause interrupter

Use commas before and after a dependent clause that interrupts an independent clause:

> Mary decided, *after she discovered the high cost of housing,* to share an apartment.

> ▶ **TIP**   Imagine taking the middle clause out of the sentence, using the two commas like two handles you can grab to remove the interrupting clause. The sentence should still make sense if you removed the interrupting clause.

> Mary decided to share an apartment.

2. Transitional words and phrases or parenthetical interrupters

Use commas before and after transitional words or parenthetical interrupters.

> Most of her friends, *however*, had already made other housing arrangements.

> ▶ **TIP**   You can also imagine these commas as handles you can use to remove the transitional word or phrase or the parenthetical interrupter. Test to make sure your sentence still makes sense without the deleted word(s).

> Most of her friends had already made other housing arrangements.

> ▶ **NOTE**   Use commas around parenthetical or side information instead of using parentheses when the information is still fairly important and when you are using parenthetical citations in more formal writing (see Chapter 19 for more on parenthetical citations).

3. Appositive interrupters

Use commas before and after appositive interrupters (nouns or phrases that rename or categorize nearby nouns):

> Mary heard that Brianna, *a friend from college*, was looking for an apartment mate.

4. Nonrestrictive clauses

A nonrestrictive adjective clause starts with a relative pronoun (*who*, *whom*, *whose*, or *which*) or with a relative adverb (*where* or *when*). The information conveyed by this type of clause is not essential for identifying the subject of the sentence. That is, the clause doesn't *restrict* the subject.

> Mary, *who had always enjoyed Brianna's company*, was delighted to learn that she was interested in sharing an apartment.

In this instance, the relative pronoun *who* introduces a nonrestrictive clause; you do not need the information in this clause to identify the subject, Mary. The clause provides extra, nonrestrictive information.

▶ **NOTE: RESTRICTIVE CLAUSES**   When the information in the relative pronoun statement or adverb statement is necessary in order to *restrict* or identify the noun/subject, then *do not* use commas:

The friend *whom Brianna had been sharing an apartment with* was moving to a different town.

The clause "whom Brianna had been sharing an apartment with" *restricts* the noun, "friend," by clearly identifying a particular person.

5. Tag lines that interrupt a dialogue or a quotation

Two commas are used to set off tag lines that interrupt a dialogue or a quotation in the middle of the sentence.

"My friend is leaving next month," *Brianna explained,* "so you could move in then, if you like."

▶ **TIP**   You even need a comma if the tag comes at the end:

"That should work out perfectly," *Mary said.*

▶ **NOTE**   Note that the comma comes *inside* the quotation marks in both cases. Do not use quotation marks or a comma with an indirect quotation:

Brianna *said that* she was looking forward to sharing the apartment with Mary.

Rule 5

Use commas according to conventions for dates, locations, numbers, and titles and to avoid confusion. Here are some examples of commas used to indicate date, location, number, and title.

1. Dates

Abraham Lincoln was born *February 12, 1809.*

Charles Darwin was born *February 12, 1809,* the same day Abraham Lincoln was born.

[Note that the comma is required to be placed also after the year if more information follows, as in the second example above.]

2. Addresses/Locations

Darwin grew up in a large, comfortable home in *Shrewsbury, England*. Lincoln grew up in *Hardin County, Kentucky*, in a one-room log cabin.

[Notice the required comma after *Kentucky*.]

3. Numbers

There are more than *10,000* species of birds in the world.

4. Formal titles

Don Kroodsma, *PhD*, analyzes how and why birds sing.

Use commas to prevent confusion and to distinguish between repeated words or phrases:

The recent oil spill can only be described as *a disaster, a disaster* that seriously damaged the environment and cost the lives of many birds.

Because of bird-rescue efforts after the oil spill, some oil-coated birds that were not expected to *survive, survived*.

When Not to Use a Comma

- Do not use a comma to separate a subject from its verb.
- Do not use a comma to separate verbs that share the same subject.
- Do not automatically place a comma before every *and* and *but*. Check to be sure that these words have a subject and a verb on both sides (in other words, that they link two independent clauses).
- Do not place a comma between the verb and the direct object.
- Do not place a comma before a dependent clause that follows an independent clause (unless the comma is necessary for reading clarity).
- Do not place a comma after *especially* or *such as*.

ACTIVITY 26-1   Correcting Misused Commas

Directions: *Delete the misused or unnecessary commas in the following sentences:*

1. The tomato is an amazing, and delicious vegetable.
2. Actually, the tomato, is really a fruit, not a vegetable.
3. The heirloom tomato is an old-fashioned variety, and tastes especially delicious.
4. Heirloom tomatoes come in a variety of colors, such as, red, purple, yellow, and green.
5. I grow my own tomatoes, because home-grown tomatoes taste better than store-bought tomatoes, and are rewarding to grow.

ACTIVITY 26-2   Adding Commas and Comma Rules

Directions: *Each of the 10 sentences below needs one or more commas. Place the commas where they belong in the sentences. Then, write the number of the rule that applies for each added comma or commas.*

1. Mount Rainier is near Auburn, Washington, and looms over the skyline.

   Rule ____5____

2. Mount Rainier has a snow cap year round, and it is almost 15,000 feet high.

   Rule ____1____

3. Mount Rainier is a favorite location for locals and tourists who like hiking, camping, and snow sports.

   Rule ____2____

4. The mountain, a recognizable icon for anyone living in the Seattle area, is like a watchful parent overlooking the city.

   Rule ____4____

5. When Mt. St. Helens erupted in the 1980s, many in Seattle worried about the status of Mount Rainier.

   Rule ____3____

6. Mount Rainier is home to a variety of wildlife, including deer, bears, and various birds.

   Rule ____2____

7. Though many think of it as merely a mountain, Mount Rainier is actually a volcano.

                                                        Rule _____3_____

8. Mount Rainier is a dormant volcano now, but it could erupt in the future.

                                                        Rule _____1_____

9. Seattle and its surrounding towns, Tacoma and its surrounding towns, and many other communities would be affected by an eruption.

                                                        Rule _____2_____

10. Since Mt. Rainier is so high, only experienced hikers should try to reach its summit.

                                                        Rule _____3_____

ACTIVITY 26-3   Add, Delete, and Move Commas I

Directions: *Add, delete, and move commas as necessary in each sentence below. If you add or move a comma, write the rule that applies in the space provided. If you delete a comma, briefly explain why in the space provided.*

1. The difference between these two drinks, according to the barista, is the amount of foam included.

    Reason for change: *Rule 4* _____

2. Max was afraid of spiders, and he didn't like mice either.

    Reason for change: *Rule 1* _____

3. Rox, on the other hand, argued that the practice should be twice a month.

    Reason for change: *Rule 4* _____

4. Gurpreet said, "I prefer homemade meals."

    Reason for change: *Rule 3* _____

5. On the last Saturday of the month, we will begin practice for our softball league.

    Reason for change: *Rule 3* _____

6. The team members felt that they weren't being heard, and that their coach did not respect them.

    Reason for change: *Misuse of Rule 1: second clause dependent* _____

7. Anabelle, pretending that she hadn't noticed the new car next door, asked her parents when they would be getting a new family car.

    Reason for change: _Rule 4_ _____

8. Dorothy liked cappuccinos, and her sister loved lattes.

    Reason for change: _Rule 1_ _____

9. Robert said, that he preferred iced tea to coffee any day.

    Reason for change: _Misuse of Rule 3: this is an indirect quote_ _____

10. Make sure to apply time-management skills, note-taking skills, and revision skills.

    Reason for change: _Rule 2_ _____

ACTIVITY 26-4   Add, Delete, and Move Commas II

Directions: *Add, delete, and move commas as necessary. Consult the Five Comma Rules if you need help.*

In many different ways, the Internet has changed the way higher education works. The Internet is clearly here to stay, but it has really only been an active part of our lives since the 1990s. Especially when writing research papers, students have come to rely heavily on information, available on the Internet. This amazing wealth of information, though, comes with certain risks. For instance, a great deal of information, that pops up, on the Internet is inaccurate. Many people rely on the facts, statistics, and expert testimonials they find online. Students should be cautious, however, because some sources are unreliable. It is important to doublecheck all sources for credibility, and accuracy. Another problem arises when students fail to cite Internet sources or cite them incorrectly, and, that mistake can lead to plagiarism, a serious academic crime.

APPLYING CRITICAL THINKING

| PURPOSE | IDEAS | SUPPORT | ASSUMPTIONS BIASES | CONCLUSIONS | POINT OF VIEW | ANALYSIS |

When you are constructing sentences and making choices about using commas, ask yourself the following questions:

*   What is my **purpose** for this particular sentence, and how can I best construct my sentence and use commas to achieve my purpose?

- How can commas make my meaning clearer?

  Then *break down the particular parts* of the sentence, using your **analysis** skills to make sure that you have constructed the sentence correctly and used comma(s) correctly.

SEMICOLON AND COLON

The semicolon and the colon are stronger marks of punctuation than is the comma. The semicolon and the colon are used to separate clauses, clarify meaning, or provide emphasis.

LO 2 Semicolon

The **semicolon** (;) is used to separate related clauses and phrases that are of equal importance. The semicolon is one of the most abused, misused, and neglected punctuation marks in the English language, but when used correctly (and sparingly), it functions as a specific and powerful punctuation mark.

There are only two rules for using the semicolon.

Rule 1

Use a semicolon between two independent clauses when the second clause has a strong connection to the first, and they are equally important.

Use a semicolon instead of a comma with a coordinating conjunction when you want to emphasize to your reader the connection between the two independent clauses.

> **Independent clause   +   ;   +   independent clause**

> Angel Falls is a scenic wonder; from the top of a mountain in
> (SUBJ) (VERB)
>
> Venezuela, the waterfall plunges more than 2,640 feet.
>   (SUBJ)   (VERB)

Note that each of the two independent clauses in the example could function as a complete sentence with a subject and a verb; however, the semicolon emphasizes the connection between the two clauses more than a period or coordinating conjunction would. Here is another example:

> The remote location of Angel Falls enhances its mystique; the waterfall is hidden deep in the jungle.

Cross Reference

See pp. 527–529 for more about comma splices.

Sometimes a student will mistakenly use a comma to link two independent clauses in a sentence, thus creating a comma splice. To correct the comma splice, the student can either add a coordinating conjunction after the comma or replace the comma with a semicolon.

Often, a semicolon is followed either by a transitional expression or word (see pp. 114–116 for a list of common transitional words or expressions) or by a conjunctive adverb, followed by a comma.

> Angel Falls is the tallest waterfall in the world; however, Victoria Falls in Zimbabwe is known as the world's largest waterfall.

CONJUNCTIVE ADVERBS OFTEN USED AFTER A SEMICOLON (AND FOLLOWED BY A COMMA)

however	therefore	furthermore	moreover	consequently
also	finally	certainly	next	then
besides	conversely	likewise	subsequently	similarly
otherwise	indeed	meanwhile	thus	specifically

▶ **TIP**   The semicolon should be used sparingly for maximum effect. It is a gem, so use it when it is the perfect punctuation mark, not when a period would do.

Rule 2

Use a semicolon to separate complex items in a series.

When a sentence contains numerous lists that already have commas in them, use semicolons to separate these lists.

> **Item 1, with internal punctuation; item 2, with internal punctuation; and item 3, with internal punctuation.**

Do you remember Rule 2 for commas to separate items in a series (see p. 538)? This semicolon rule is very similar except that you use semicolons when the items you are listing have subcomponents separated by commas:

> In the United States, travelers can observe impressive waterfalls in Yosemite National Park, California; Colonial Peak, Washington; Glacier National Park, Montana; and Niagara Falls, New York.

If only commas had been used, a reader might become confused and think the sentence was listing the locations of eight waterfalls instead of four.

▶ **TIP 1**   Note that you include a semicolon before the "and" that comes before the final item listed.

▶ **TIP 2**   If the sentence had not included the states in which the waterfalls are located, you would use only commas: Yosemite National Park, Colonial Peak, Glacier National Park, and Niagara Falls.

Here's another example:

> Other dramatic waterfalls include Dettifoss, a glacier-fed waterfall in Iceland; Kaieteur Falls, a broad waterfall in the rainforest of Guyana; and Iguazu Falls, a cascading waterfall in Argentina.

When Not to Use a Semicolon

- Do not use a semicolon after the phrases *especially* and *such as*.
- Do not use a semicolon after a coordinating conjunction (FANBOYS).
- Do not use a semicolon before the words *because* and *since* if they introduce a dependent clause after an independent clause.
- Do not use a semicolon before a list of words or items that follows an independent clause (use a colon).

ACTIVITY 26-5   Adding a Semicolon

Directions: *Add semicolons where they belong in the following sentences:*

1. Several poems were selected, including "Stopping by Woods," by Robert Frost; "Forgiveness," by Madeline Defrees; "Yesterday," by Marie Howe; and "God's Grief," by Ellen Bass.
2. The World Series is the climax of the baseball season; the series combines the pleasures of tradition and suspense.
3. Suzanne loves to eat salads; she eats at least one a day.
4. Garlic is a versatile herb; it can enhance the flavor of many different foods.
5. We took the scenic route; it was longer but more relaxing.
6. Known for their memorable personalities, our grandmother's pets included Houdini, the amazing disappearing housecat; CoCo, the famous singing poodle; and Ginger, the ball-catching terrier.
7. Good advice is hard to come by; bad advice is everywhere.
8. Cat owners are creative; dog owners are easy going.
9. Bruce didn't fight it; he let his son Jin choose a puppy.
10. Take a minute to think about the day; minutes disappear quickly.

ACTIVITY 26-6   Adding or Deleting a Semicolon

Directions: *In each of the following sentences, add or delete a semicolon, or change the semicolon to a comma:*

1. The birthday party was great;everyone had fun.
2. The birthday cake was delicious,/ and the music was lively.
3. People danced to such popular songs as/ "Irreplaceable" by Beyoncé.
4. Emma received some awesome gifts, including; CDs, books, and DVDs.
5. Emma will never forget this party;however, her parents may wish to forget how much work it was.

APPLYING CRITICAL THINKING

| PURPOSE | IDEAS | SUPPORT | ASSUMPTIONS BIASES | CONCLUSIONS | POINT OF VIEW | ANALYSIS |

When you are constructing sentences and making choices about using the semicolon, ask yourself the following critical thinking questions:

*   What is my **purpose** for this particular sentence, and how can I best construct my sentence and use a semicolon to achieve my purpose?
*   Will a semicolon make my meaning clearer or add emphasis to a cause-and-effect relationship between two clauses?

    Then *break down the particular parts* of the sentence using your **analysis** skills to make sure that you have constructed the sentence correctly and used a semicolon correctly.

 Colon

The colon (:) is used inside a sentence to clarify meaning, provide emphasis, or introduce information. There are several rules for using a colon, but it basically indicates that a list or explanation is to follow.

Rule 1

Use a colon between two independent clauses when the second clause explains, summarizes, or answers the first one.

The contestants in the singing contest all had the same dream: They
    (SUBJ)   (VERB)   (SUBJ)
wanted to become famous.
(VERB)

Each independent clause in the example could function as complete sentence. The second clause explains the first one. It's true that a period or a comma followed by a coordinating conjunction would work here, and even a semicolon would work between the two clauses. The colon, however, is the *best choice* because it is the most specific and exact form of punctuation in this case. The colon helps the reader see the explanation relationship between the two clauses. Here's another example:

The contestant had two choices: She could sing a popular song or perform a song she had composed herself.

> ▶ NOTE   When a colon separates two independent clauses, the second independent clause usually begins with a capital letter.

Rule 2

Use a colon after an independent clause that is followed by a word or phrase that answers or explains the idea set up in the independent clause.

The contestants in the singing contest all had the same dream: to become famous.

[Colon followed by a phrase]

The contestants in the singing contest all had the same dream: becoming famous.

[Colon followed by a phrase]

The contestants in the singing contest all had the same dream: fame.

[Colon followed by a single word]

The contestant had two choices: to sing a popular song or perform her own song.

[Colon followed by a phrase]

> ▶ TIP   An independent clause must come before the colon.

Correct: The <u>judges</u> <u>cited</u> two main factors: the originality of the winner's song and the energy of her performance.

Incorrect: Two main factors for judging: the originality of the winner's song and the energy of her performance.

Rule 3

Use a colon after an independent clause that introduces a list of items.

When planning our trip to Montana, I started a list of items to take on hikes: water, energy bars, first-aid kit, raingear, insect repellent, and sunscreen.

We also started getting in shape for mountain climbing: taking long walks, lifting weights, eating healthy foods, and getting enough sleep.

▶ **TIP 1**   Be sure that the clause that comes before the colon and that the list is independent. It should have both a subject and a verb and not be introduced by a subordinating conjunction.

Correct: We wanted to climb several mountains in Montana: Blue Mountain, Heaven's Peak, and Rising Wolf Mountain.

Incorrect: Several mountains to climb in Montana: Blue Mountain, Heaven's Peak, and Rising Wolf Mountain.

▶ **TIP 2**   Don't use a colon after words and phrases such as *such as* and *including*. Think of these words as replacements for a colon; they serve the same function.

Correct: We also scheduled other activities, such as fishing excursions, horseback riding, and museum visits.

Incorrect: We also scheduled other activities, such as: fishing excursions, horseback riding, and museum visits.

Rule 4

Use a colon before a quotation if an independent clause is used to set up the quotation.

In *Travels with Charley*, John Steinbeck wrote: "Montana is a great splash of grandeur."

Miscellaneous Uses

There are several miscellaneous uses for the colon.

- **In greetings:**

  To Whom It May Concern:
  Dear Mr. Ortiz:

- **To show hours and minutes:**

  6:05 P.M.

- **In titles and subtitles:**

  Angels and Ages: A Short Book about Darwin, Lincoln, and Modern Life

- **To show ratios:**

  The odds were 4:1 that the new drug would be effective.

- **In bibliography or works cited formats:**

  Upper Saddle River: Pearson, 2010.

Cross Reference
See Chapter 19 for information on documenting sources.

When Not to Use a Colon

- Do not use a colon after *especially, such as, consisted of, including,* and other words or phrases that indicate a list will follow.
- Do not use a colon after a verb that sets up a list of objects.
- Do not use a colon between book and verse or act and scene (in MLA style). Use periods instead:

  Correct: Genesis 4.2
  Incorrect: Genesis 4:2
  Correct: *Phantom of the Opera,* 1.3 (or I.III)
  Incorrect: *Phantom of the Opera,* 1:3 (or I:III)

ACTIVITY 26-7   Adding a Colon

Directions: *Add colons or another appropriate punctuation mark where they belong in the following sentences:*

1. Keep in mind several skills when learning to drive:frequently looking in your rear-view and side mirrors, paying attention to the speed limit, and staying focused on the road.

2. In *Macbeth*, in a key early act and scene (1.4), we see the beginning of the dangers of blind ambition.

3. The odds were 5:1 against the new horse.

4. There is one factor that really tells how you did in a course: your final grade.

5. Elijah had one particular gift: he was a fantastic dancer.

ACTIVITY 26-8   Adding or Deleting a Colon

Directions: *Add or delete colons where needed in the following sentences:*

1. Jack enjoys: cooking Italian food, playing the piano, and swimming in the ocean.

2. Tara wanted two things from her new job: a good salary and full benefits.

3. When I'm on vacation, I look forward to simple activities, such as: relaxing, eating delicious food, building sandcastles, or just reading a good book.

4. The teacher had requested that the college bookstore order the textbook *Geography: An Introduction to the Field.*

5. To prepare for her trip, she needed to buy the following items: a suitcase, a travel towel, a small alarm clock, and a travel guide.

ACTIVITY 26-9   Adding a Semicolon or a Colon

Directions: *Add a colon or a semicolon to the following sentences where needed. Choose the best, most specific choice for each.*

1. Recently our small town suffered a great loss: the death of a magnificent beech tree.

2. Gracing the front lawn of the public library, the beech tree had been there for as long as I can remember: The tree must have been over a hundred years old.

3. A local historian even wrote a book featuring the tree: *What the Tree Saw: Tales from a Small Town.*

4. Every part of the tree was beautiful: the smooth gray trunk, the muscular branches, the burgundy-colored leaves.

5. Everyone loved that tree: children who hung from its branches, students who sprawled in its generous shade, and workers who ate their lunches on nearby benches.

6. The tree was like an extension of the library: Patrons greeted the tree like an old friend when they arrived and bid it a fond farewell when they departed.

7. It was a sad day when the town had to say goodbye for the last time: The tree was dying and would have to be cut down.

8. At 10:00 a.m., when the power saws roared into action, a crowd gathered to pay its respects, including Keisha Smith, the library director; Ruth Poritz, the reference librarian; Carlos Rodriguez, the children's librarian; and townspeople of all ages.

9. When the tree was gone, I had double vision: My eyes viewed an unfamiliar swath of sky, but my mind's eye filled the space with a leafy canopy.

10. Today, children dance on a broad stump; next to it, a tiny, lovingly tended beech tree dreams big dreams.

ACTIVITY 26-10   Adding Comma, Semicolon, and Colon

Directions: *The comma, the semicolon, and the colon are three punctuation marks that are often confused. For each sentence of the passage, insert the correct punctuation mark—comma, semicolon, or colon—in the appropriate blank. Review the rules if you get stumped.*

> **, (comma) ; (semicolon) : (colon)**

Email ___,___ short for electronic mail ___,___ has transformed business ___;___ the way employees communicate on a day-to-day basis is forever changed. Of course ___,___ the main standard for employee communication still exists ___:___ face-to-face meetings. Many simple questions and memos ___,___ however ___,___ can be handled through email ___;___ it's convenient and quick. Employees rely on email ___,___ and they are expected to use it.

Though email ___,___ in general ___,___ has been a blessing ___,___ many people find that it is also a curse because of the huge number of emails they receive and the "spam" (junk email) that floods their inboxes. Some employees may receive as many as 1 ___,___ 000 emails per working day ___;___ that adds up to an incredible number at the end of each year. Moreover ___,___ the task of reading emails adds to a person's daily workload ___;___

many employees complain they were better off without email___,___ so some companies are looking into restricting unnecessary emails. Despite the drawbacks of email, one conclusion is unavoidable___:___ email in the workplace is not going away any time soon.

APPLYING CRITICAL THINKING

| PURPOSE | IDEAS | SUPPORT | ASSUMPTIONS BIASES | CONCLUSIONS | POINT OF VIEW | ANALYSIS |

When you are constructing sentences and making choices about using colons, ask yourself the following critical thinking questions:

- What is my **purpose** for this particular sentence, and how can I best construct my sentence and use a colon to achieve my purpose?
- Am I using a colon after an independent clause to list items? Am I using a colon to separate two independent clauses, where the second clause answers the first?

Then, *break down the particular parts* of the sentence using your **analysis** skills to make sure that you have constructed the sentence correctly and used a colon correctly.

To check your progress in meeting this chapter's objectives, log in to www.mywritinglab.com, go to the **Study Plan** tab, click on **Handbook of Grammar, Mechanics, and Style** and choose **Commas and Semicolons, Colons, Dashes and Parentheses** from the list of subtopics. Read and view the resources in the **Review Materials** section, and then complete the **Recall, Apply,** and **Write** sets in the **Activities** section.

27 Other Punctuation

THINKING CRITICALLY

Do you think punctuation is important? Why, or why not? What function does it serve for the reader?

_____

_____

_____

_____

_____

_____

_____

_____

ⓛ LO 1 END PUNCTUATION

As its name implies, end punctuation comes at the end of a sentence. There are three types of end punctuation: the period, the question mark, and the exclamation point.

Period

A **period** (.) is used to end a statement. You should use a period under the following circumstances:

1. **Use a period at the end of a complete sentence (independent clause).** The sentence can be a statement or an indirect question:

   > Coldplay is his favorite band. [Statement]
   >
   > He asked me if I'd like to go to the Coldplay concert. [Indirect question]

2. **Use periods with some abbreviations (not all abbreviations require periods; check a dictionary if you are unsure).**

   Mr.   Ms.   etc.   e.g.   R.S.V.P.   B.C.   A.D.
   A.M. (or a.m.)   P.M. (or p.m.)   Dr.   Ph.D.

   ▶ **NOTE**   Some of these abbreviations are acceptable without the periods: AM, PM, BC or BCE, AD or ACE.

ACTIVITY 27-1   Adding the Period

Directions: *Add a period where needed in the following passage:*

Mr. Jannson was my favorite high school teacher. He really cared about his students. Also, he took the time to really get to know us. I learned so much from him. Mr. Jannson's heart was in his work, too. My good friend Dr. Shepard agrees that having a passion for one's job is what makes someone good at what he or she does. It was certainly true about my favorite high school teacher.

Question Mark

A **question mark** (?) is used at the end of a sentence to indicate that a question is being asked. Use a question mark when a sentence is a direct question.

Do you think Coldplay is better than Radiohead?

Do not use a question mark if the sentence is an indirect question:

I asked my friend if she liked Coldplay better than Radiohead. [Period, not a question mark]

Using the Question Mark with Quotations or Dialogue

Be sure to check if a question mark is part of a quotation or a piece of dialogue (whether you are quoting a question or a person is asking a question) or if you are asking a question about a quotation. If it is part of a quotation or a piece of dialogue, the question mark goes inside the quotation marks.

She asked, "Are the Radiohead tickets already sold out?"

If you are asking a question about a quotation, the question mark comes after the closing quotation marks:

Who was it that said, "Music is the universal language"?

ACTIVITY 27-2   Adding, Moving, or Changing the Question Mark

Directions: *Add or move the question mark, or change it to another form of punctuation as necessary in the following passage.*

"Do you plan to join us tonight?" Heather asked. However, Jonah didn't answer her. Later he asked her if she knew what time it was? She wondered if he cared about her at all?.What did it mean that he ignored her sometimes? Also, she wondered, what poet or songwriter wrote, "Love is a battlefield?"?

Exclamation Point

Use an **exclamation point** (!) to show emphasis, to express strong emotion—excitement, surprise, disbelief—or to indicate a strong command.

I'm starving, and that stew smells delicious!
You scared me to death!
I can't believe he gave us a pop quiz the day before spring break!
Stop—it's a red light!

▶ **NOTE**   Try not to overuse the exclamation point, or it will lose its power! See what I mean?! Too much!

ACTIVITY 27-3   Adding or Replacing the Exclamation Point

Directions: *Add the exclamation point, or replace it with a different type of punctuation mark as needed in the following passage.*

"Earthquake!" she shouted. Chuck knew they had to stay calm!. So he helped her move slowly to a safe doorway!. However, right when they got to the front door, they heard someone outside yell "Run!" That's when they started to feel a little more panicked.

ⓛⓞ② APOSTROPHES

The **apostrophe** (') is used to indicate contractions (words in which certain letters have been omitted) and to show possession (who or what owns something).

Apostrophe and Contractions

Use an apostrophe to indicate the omission of one or more letters when words are combined to form a contraction. Place the apostrophe where the missing letter(s) would be: *it's (it is)* or *haven't (have not)* or *would've (would have)*. Contractions may not be appropriate for formal, academic writing. **Check with your instructor to see if contractions are allowed in your essay or if a more formal academic tone is preferred. It may depend on the assignment or type of essay you are writing or on your target audience.** See Chapter 30 for more about tone and word choice.

Common Contractions

aren't	are not
can't	cannot
could've	could have
couldn't	could not
didn't	did not
doesn't	does not

don't	do not
hadn't	had not
hasn't	has not
haven't	have not
he'd	he had/he would
he'll	he will
he's	he is
I'm	I am
isn't	is not
it'd	it had/it would
it'll	it will
it's	it is
let's	let us
mightn't	might not
might've	might have
mustn't	must not
she'd	she had/she would
she'll	she will
she's	she is
shouldn't	should not
should've	should have
there'd	there had/there would
there'll	there will
they're	they are
'twas	it was
wasn't	was not
we'll	we will
we're	we are
weren't	were not
what'd	what had/what would
what's	what is
won't	will not
wouldn't	would not
would've	would have
you'll	you will
you're	you are

▶ **NOTE**   Be careful when you use the following contractions. They sound like other words that have different meanings (see Commonly Confused Words, p. 620).

they're	= they are	vs.	there	= adverb
you're	= you are		your	= possessive pronoun
who's	= who is		whose	= possessive pronoun
it's	= it is		its	= possessive pronoun

▶ **SIMPLE TEST**   If the word can be said aloud as two words, then it is probably the contraction you want.

Correct: The car needs new tires, and *it's* not getting good mileage. [The car needs new tires, and *it is* not getting good mileage.]

Incorrect: The car needs new brake pads, and *it's* windshield is cracked. [The car needs new brake pads, and *it is* windshield—oops, wrong word; use "its," possessive pronoun, instead—*its* windshield is cracked.]

Apostrophe and Possession

Add an apostrophe to a noun or indefinite pronoun to indicate possession. (But don't add an apostrophe to an already possessive pronoun such as *his, hers,* or *its.*)

Sam's essay about her most embarrassing moment was hilarious.
[The apostrophe indicates the essay belongs to Sam.]

Someone's dirty dishes are in the sink.
[The apostrophe indicates that dirty dishes belonging to someone are in the sink.]

1. **Singular possession.** Use an apostrophe before the added *s* to indicate possession.

The hummingbird's wings can beat up to 78 times per second.
[The apostrophe indicates that the wings of the hummingbird can beat up to 78 times per second.]

History's lessons are always being relearned.
[The apostrophe indicates that the lessons of history are always being relearned.]

Dr. Ortega is *everyone's* favorite professor.
[The apostrophe indicates that the favorite professor of everyone is Dr. Ortega.]

If the singular noun already ends with the letter *s*, then add an apostrophe and another *s*.

Each of the *octopus's* eight arms has two rows of suction cups.
[The singular noun *octopus* ends with an *s*, so add an apostrophe and another *s*.]

▶ NOTE   Don't use apostrophes with pronouns that are already possessive.

Correct: Is this textbook yours or mine? Its cover is torn.

Incorrect: Is this textbook *your's* or mine? *It's* cover is torn.

2. **Plural possession.** Use an apostrophe after the *s* that indicates a plural, possessive noun.

Many of the *trees'* branches broke during the ice storm.
[Refers to two or more trees—the only way to know this is by the placement of the apostrophe.]

The *artists'* paintings are on display in the main gallery.

[The placement of the apostrophe indicates that there is more than one artist.]

▶ NOTE   If the form of the noun is already plural, add an apostrophe and an *s*.

The *women's* locker rooms are on your right.

▶ NOTE   Don't use an apostrophe to make nouns plural.

Correct: There are several news Web sites that I check every day.

Incorrect: There are several news Web site's that I check every day.

3. **Possessive and compound nouns.** Place an apostrophe at the end of compound nouns in order to indicate possession.

> My *brother-in-law's* jokes are pretty lame.
> [The apostrophe goes at the end of the compound noun; you do not write *brother's-in-law*.]

With two brothers-in-law, you make the word "brother" plural by adding an *s*; then just use apostrophe and an *s* after "law" (only one law but two brothers).

> My *brothers-in-law's* favorite joke is so lame that they are the only ones who laugh.

4. **Possession and proper names.** Add an apostrophe and an *s* to single proper names to show possession.

> *Shanika's* job interview went very well.
> [There is only one Shanika, so the apostrophe goes before the *s*.]
> *Professor Wang's* letter of recommendation helped Shanika get the job.

If a proper name ends in *s*, usually you show possession by adding an apostrophe and another *s*.

> *Chris's* dream is to become a marine biologist.
> [The name *Chris* already ends with an *s*, so add an apostrophe and another *s*.]
> *Henry James's* novels are psychologically complex.

However, if the pronunciation would be awkward with the added *s*, it is acceptable to omit the extra *s* (both ways are acceptable).

> The New Testament includes descriptions of *Jesus'* [or *Jesus's*] disciples.

If the proper name is plural, put the apostrophe after the *s*.

> *The Steinbergs'* house is always full of neighborhood kids.
> [Adding the *s* makes the name *Steinberg* plural to indicate a whole family, not one person, and the apostrophe after it indicates their joint possession of the house.]

5. **Joint possession.** If two or more people share a possession, then add an apostrophe and an *s* only after the last name.

> Are you riding in *Lamont* and *Whitney's* car?
> [The car belongs to both of them, so the apostrophe goes after *Whitney*.]

If people individually (separately) possess things, use an apostrophe and an *s* for each one.

> Are you riding in *Lola's* car, *Ethan's* car, or *Kenji's* car?
> [There should be three cars, so the apostrophes are used to indicate individual possession.]

Apostrophe and Plurals

Use an apostrophe to indicate plural numbers, letters, and symbols and to indicate the plurals of words used as an item. (Due to the dynamic nature of grammar—rules change with use, and word processing has also affected these rules—it is now acceptable to use an apostrophe or to omit the apostrophe in many of these cases. You may choose to add the apostrophe or leave it out, but be consistent in your choice.)

> The Federal Aviation Association announced that mechanical defects on two *747's* had been corrected.
> [It's acceptable to use *747s*.]
>
> My preschooler, who is learning to write, complains that *M's* and *N's* look too much alike.
>
> The two *A's* I got last semester raised my GPA.
>
> For the arithmetic worksheet, the kindergarten teacher printed the *+'s* and *−'s* in different colors.
>
> When making an oral presentation, try to avoid nervous verbal mannerisms such as *uh's*, *um's*, and *you know's*.

Apostrophe and Missing Letters or Numbers

You can use an apostrophe to indicate letters or numbers that are missing from words in dialogue, slang, or colloquial speech. Remember, you should only include slang or colloquial words such as these in dialogue; these words are inappropriate in academic writing.

> "Y'all come in now. I'm *fixin'* to serve up some three-alarm chili."
>
> My grandmother said, "We went through some tough times during the 30's, but we never doubted that things would get better."

When Not to Use an Apostrophe

- Do not use an apostrophe with possessive pronouns (*his, hers, its, ours, yours, theirs, whose*).
- Do not use an apostrophe to form plurals that do not indicate possession.

ACTIVITY 27-4 Apostrophe Practice I

Directions: *Add, delete, or move the apostrophe in the following sentences as needed. Write C for correct if the use of the apostrophe is correct.*

_____ **1.** "They're going to visit for three days," his sister said. "Don't forget to clean up Ryan's room."

___C___ **2.** Today's TV shows are much more action packed.

_____ **3.** My college's cafeteria is open until 10:00 p.m. Is yours open that late?

_____ **4.** The Hendrickson's pets were lost while they were on vacation.

_____ **5.** The children's books were new, and they didn't cost too much.

_____ **6.** The cats' were sleeping on her front porch.

_____ **7.** The bosses' rules were posted on the bulletin board.

_____ **8.** The 6's and 7's on all the uniforms were in a different font.

_____ **9.** All the C's on Julio's report card were in his math and science classes.

_____C_____ **10.** It's important to realize that we can't see all the leaves'
colors until late fall.

ACTIVITY 27-5   **Apostrophe Practice II**

Directions: *Place the apostrophe where needed in the following passage. There are 15 apostrophe-related errors.*

Last summer I took a car trip with my sister Bella, her husband Miguel, and their six-year-old son Luis. Our destination was Garden of the Gods Park in Colorado Springs.

The areas geology is fascinating. Silhouetted against the dramatic backdrop of snow-capped Pikes Peak are giant formations of red rock. Hogbacks, tilted ridges of sandstone, assume strange shapes with whimsical names such as "Kissing Camels."

We started by taking an inexpensive, 20-minute guided bus tour of the park. The busses left every half hour, so we didnt have to wait long. I was relieved that the buses air conditioning worked (unlike the broken AC in Bellas and Miguels car). The guides narration was very informative, as she described the geology, ecology, and cultural history of the region.

After a pleasant lunch on the cafés terrace, which offers great views of the rock formations, we hiked Ridge Trail. Its only a half-mile hike, so Luis could keep up, and we were glad to stretch our legs. We kept a sharp eye out for rattlesnakes, which lurk in the rocks nooks and crannies.

Next, we spent time at the Nature Center, which offers a variety of educational, hands-on exhibits. A series of geology murals illustrates how the park would have looked billions of years ago. I was impressed by the quality of the murals artwork, and Luis liked the pictures of dinosaurs. I was also impressed by the childrens programming at the Nature Center, which included Junior Ranger activities (complete with an official-looking badge and certificate for kids). One exhibit demonstrates how the magpie builds its nest. Luis's favorite exhibits were the life-size replica of a buffalo and the "Talking Rock."

I know some people find family road trips stressful, but our's was truly memorable. I'd recommend Garden of the Gods as an excellent vacation destination for folks of all ages!

LO 2   QUOTATION MARKS

Quotation marks (" ") are used to indicate direct quotations or dialogue (written or spoken), to indicate some types of titles, and to define words or to use them ironically.

1. **Use quotation marks around direct quotations.** Use quotation marks when you are directly quoting someone else's words in your writing. Enclose all words that are quoted directly from another source in a pair of **double quotation marks**, one set at the beginning of the quotation and one set at the end:

> John Sawhill said, "In the end, our society will be defined not only by what we create but by what we refuse to destroy" (56).

> ▶ **NOTE**   Remember to include a page citation for sources. See Chapter 19 for correct MLA citation format.

When there is a quotation within a quotation, use **single quotation marks** around the internal quotation:

> Describing her rival writer Lillian Hellman, Mary McCarthy said, "Every word she writes is a lie, including 'and' and 'the.'"

2. **Use quotation marks to quote prose or poetry.** Use the following information to help you use quotation marks correctly when you quote from prose or poetry.

   • **Introducing quotations.** If you are quoting a complete sentence, use a tag to introduce the quotation followed by a comma. If, however, you are introducing a quotation using a complete sentence of your own, use a colon. Be sure to start the quotation with a capital letter.

> **Tag:** James Baldwin said, "The challenge is in the moment; the time is always now" (83).
>
> **Introductory sentence:** James Baldwin said it best: "The challenge is in the moment; the time is always now" (83).

- **Quoting partial sentences.** If you quote only part of a sentence, then don't start the quotation with a capital letter.

> James Baldwin said that "the time is always now" (83).

- **Leaving words out of a quotation.** If you leave out part of a quotation, use an ellipsis (three spaced dots) to indicate where the omitted word or words were deleted.

> Frederico García Lorca wrote, "There is nothing more poetic and terrible than the skyscrapers' battle with the heavens that cover them. Snow, rain, and mist highlight, drench, or conceal the vast towers, but those towers . . . shine their three thousand swords through the soft swan of the fog."

- **Adding words and phrases.** If you add a word or phrase for clarification within a direct quotation, put brackets around the insertion.

> Tom Paine wrote, "What we obtain too cheap, we esteem too lightly; it is dearness [high cost] only that gives everything its value."

- **Quoting lines of poetry.** If you quote lines of poetry in your own sentences, use slashes to indicate where the original line breaks were.

> Poet Maya Angelou wrote, "The caged bird sings with a fearful trill / Of things unknown but longed for still" (1).

- **Quoting four or more lines of poetry.** If you quote four or more lines of poetry or prose, set the quotation off in a block by indenting 10 spaces from the left margin and omit quotation marks.

> Maya Angelou wrote:
> The caged bird sings with a fearful trill
> Of things unknown but longed for still
> And his tune is heard on the distant hill for
> The caged bird sings of freedom. (1)

3. **Use quotation marks with dialogue.** Quotation marks are used in writing to indicate when someone is speaking. Here are some tips for using quotation marks with dialogue.

- Put the actual words spoken by the person in quotation marks.
- Use commas to set off tags at the beginning, middle, or end of the dialogue.
- Start a new paragraph whenever you switch speakers or characters in dialogue, even if the line is only one word long.

> "So what did you think?" she asked.
>
> "The special effects were awesome!" he said. "I was surprised that the 3-D glasses worked so well."
>
> "I know," she said. "The 'look' of the movie was very original. The plot—not so much."
>
> "I hear you," he said. "Been there, done that."

4. **Use quotation marks for specific types of titles.** Use quotation marks around the titles of short stories and poems (not book-length epic poems, though), chapter titles, essay titles, magazine article titles, television episodes from series, and song titles.

> **Story title:** "What You Pawn I Will Redeem" by Sherman Alexie
>
> **Poem title:** "Where the Sidewalk Ends" by Shel Silverstein
>
> **Magazine article title:** "Four Ways of Looking at Breakfast" by Thomas Fuller
>
> **Television episode title:** "No More Mister Nice Guy"
>
> **Song title:** "I Will Always Love You" by Dolly Parton

> ▶ NOTE   Titles of books, epic poems, plays, movies, CD/albums, TV shows, and magazines are all italicized.

5. **Use quotation marks around words that are being singled out for definition or to indicate irony.** When you are going to define a word or intend to indicate you are speaking ironically, use quotation marks.

> The word "miscreant" refers to a person who is dishonest or unkind.
>
> School and work leave little time for anything else: My "free time" is used for running errands and doing chores.

Punctuation and Quotation Marks

Place commas and periods inside quotation marks if you do not include a page citation.

"Wildwood," a short story by Junot Díaz, won the O'Henry Award.

William Strunk said, "Omit needless words."

However, if you include a citation, the punctuation goes after the citation.

In his eulogy for Eleanor Roosevelt, Adlai Stevenson said, "She would rather light candles than curse the darkness, and her glow has warmed the world" (McCarthy 63).

[The period should not go inside the closing quotation: Place the period after the citation and after the last parenthesis.]

▶ **NOTE**   When you use the semicolon and the colon in your writing, they should be placed after the quotation marks. For instance:

The ad described the apartment as "dirt cheap": It turned out to be more dirty than cheap.

See Chapter 19 for details about correct citation format. Also, review the rule on p. 561 about placing the question mark inside or outside the quotation marks.

ACTIVITY 27-6   Adding Quotation Marks I

Directions: *Place quotation marks where needed in the following sentences. Write a C if the sentence is correct without quotation marks.*

_____ 1. The title of William Faulkner's novel *The Sound and the Fury* is based on a famous line from Shakespeare that says that life is the following:

"A Tale told by an idiot, full of sound and fury, signifying nothing."

_____ 2. "Stop now," said the mother, trying to keep her children safe, "and look both ways before crossing."

_____ **3.** The head of security asked "When is it appropriate to yell the word 'Fire' in a crowded theater?"

_____ **4.** Which poet said "Bad writers imitate; good writers steal?"

_____ **5.** Suzanne Paola's poem "Prayer to Seal the Womb Door" is about the sorrows of miscarriage.

___C___ **6.** He asked where he should leave his coat.

_____ **7.** "Too Many Online Options" was the title she created for her article in *The Current*.

_____ **8.** One of the most famous poems ever written is Dylan Thomas's "Death Be Not Proud."

_____ **9.** Elvis Presley's song, "Love Me Tender," is a classic.

_____ **10.** "Should I act?" is something Hamlet's character asks himself several times during the play *Hamlet*.

ACTIVITY 27-7   Adding Quotations Marks II

Directions: *Add quotation marks where needed in the following paragraphs.*

When I was a child, I played a game with the kids in my neighborhood called "Ding, Dong, Ditch." Though it wasn't a nice game, it was one we loved to play. One time it got me into a great deal of trouble. We had to run up to a neighbor's door, ring the doorbell, and then run away before he or she could catch us. When it was my turn, I rang old man Perkins' door. However, before I could run away, I saw him open the door. "Oh no," I said under my breath.

"Susie Finkle," he said, "I see you, and I am going to call your mother."

"Please don't tell my mother," I pleaded with him, turning to face him now that I was caught.

"Well, you need to learn an important lesson about respect, young lady." He shook his finger at me, his lips tight-clamped together.

Later, when I got home, my mother said, "I want to talk to you Missy." I knew I was in trouble when my mother called me "Missy."

LO2 PARENTHESES

Parentheses (()) are used for setting off information or citations. Parentheses can be used in a number of ways:

1. **Use parentheses to set off nonessential information.** Use parentheses to set off nonessential information or side comments in the middle of a sentence.

> The school's science teacher (who also coaches the soccer team) has really gotten the kids excited about science.

If the information in a side comment is relatively important, it is preferable to use parenthetical commas to set it off (see Commas, Rule 4, p. 542).

> The storm, which included high winds and hail, caused widespread power outages.

▶ **TIP**   You can test to see if parentheses or commas work best around a word or phrase by reading the sentence without those words to see if the sentence still makes sense.

2. **Use parentheses to set off numbers or letters in a list or series.**

> If your clothes catch on fire, follow these three simple steps: (1) Stop moving, (2) drop to the ground, and (3) roll to extinguish the flames.
>
> When administering CPR, remember your ABC's: (A) **A**irway (check the airway), (B) **B**reathing (provide rescue breathing), and (C) **C**irculation (check pulse to determine if chest compressions are needed).

▶ **NOTE**   Only certain style formats, for instance, writing for business or science, encourage the use of numbers or letters with parentheses. Writing in the humanities usually involves using full words to list items (such as "first," "second," "next," and so on).

3. **Use parentheses to indicate formal citations.** Use parentheses in formal citations when documenting sources. See Chapter 19 for the correct MLA format.

> As H. L. Mencken observed, "The cure for the evils of democracy is more democracy" (Corcoran 36).

4. **Use parentheses to indicate abbreviations.** Use parentheses around the letters serving as an abbreviation of a full name. Use the full name, and follow it with the abbreviation in parentheses so that readers know what the initials stand for when you use them again:

> The Federal Drug Administration (FDA) has not yet approved the new medication.

ACTIVITY 27-8   Adding or Deleting Parentheses

Directions: *Add or delete parentheses as needed in the following passage:*

My schedule (of classes) was easy to remember (I like it when I get an easy schedule. The classes were listed as follows: 1) Math at 9:00 a.m. 2) English at 10:00, 3) Science at 11:00, and 4) Drama at 1:00. I also read that "Students must pay for their classes by the third day to keep their schedules" (School Handbook, 26.

LO 2 HYPHEN

The **hyphen** (-) is used to combine or divide words. Here are some examples of the uses for the hyphen.

1. **Use a hyphen (-) to form compound words.** Check your dictionary to be sure that the compound word you're using is usually hyphenated. Some are not. Here are some commonly hyphenated compound words.

> **Fractions** such as *one-third, two-thirds, one-fourth*
>
> **Numbers** that are spelled out between twenty-one and ninety-nine
>
> **Compound nouns** such as *mother-in-law* or *brother-in-law*

2. **Use a hyphen with compound modifiers.** Use a hyphen with compound modifiers, usually adjectives, which are used together as one descriptor before a noun.

The bank approved the store owners' application for a *short-term* loan.
[Here *short-term*—a compound adjective—modifies the word *loan*.]

The *well-liked* professor was awarded tenure.

▶ **NOTE** If a compound modifier is not followed by a noun, then omit the hyphens.

The bank loan would enable them to keep the store open in the *short term*.

The tenured professor was *well liked*.

3. **Use a hyphen to join letters, prefixes, and suffixes to a word.** Here are some examples of common prefixes that require a hyphen:

Letters before words: T-shirt, B-team, S-curve, A-frame, J-bar, C-note

***Self-* before words:** self-addressed, self-control

***All-* before words:** all-knowing, all-seeing

***Ex-* before words:** ex-husband, ex-mayor

Usually the prefixes *anti-*, *pro-*, *co-*, and *non-* do not require hyphens unless the prefix ends in a vowel and so does the root word, for example, *anti-inflammatory*, *co-owner*, *non-union*, *de-emphasize*, *re-cover* (to cover again), *re-create*, and *co-ed*.

4. **Use a hyphen when dividing words at the end of a line.** It is preferable not to divide words at all, but if you do, be sure to follow these guidelines:

- Divide words at syllable breaks.
- Don't leave fewer than three letters at the end of a sentence before the hyphen or have two or less letters only on the next line.

   Dividing words is rare these days since computers automatically wrap words over to the next line. Some textbooks still divide words at the end of a line, but in your papers, you should avoid dividing words and let the computer format them for you.

ACTIVITY 27-9 Adding Hyphens

Directions: *Add a hyphen where needed in the following sentences. If the sentence is correct, then write C on the line provided*

_____ 1. Dan wanted to reconnect with his family.

_____ 2. She accused him of being antisocial during the party.

___C___ 3. The preamble to the constitution is moving.

_____ 4. Spain has the most striking bluegreen water.

_____ 5. Kimiko's six year old brother ate all the ramen.

___C___ 6. She sat with all of the three year olds.

_____ 7. The magazine had prounion bias.

_____ 8. The ever changing look of Annika's hair made her unique.

_____ 9. The premade lemonade tasted like paint stripper.

___C___ 10. Previewing a chapter before reading it helps comprehension.

LO 2 DASHES

Dashes (—) are used to help information stand out, to add emphasis. (If your keyboard doesn't include a dash (—), use two hyphens together to create one.)

Dashes can be used around a phrase in the middle of a sentence or at the end of a sentence. They enclose material like parentheses do, but dashes are used to emphasize the material inside them, not to de-emphasize it. At the end of a sentence, a dash can work much like a colon, but it is more informal.

> Generally speaking, I'm a great supporter of tradition, but I draw the line—and I suspect I'm not alone in this—at the tradition of spring cleaning.
>
> Early autumn—when the morning air is crisp, and the first red leaves appear—is my favorite time of year.

▶ **NOTE** Material enclosed by dashes can be removed, and the sentence will still make sense.

▶ **NOTE**   Dashes are considered an informal punctuation mark. In more formal writing, use commas or colons instead of a dash.

ACTIVITY 27-10   Adding or Deleting Dashes

Directions: *Add or delete dashes in the following passage:*

The circular saw ‾ an essential tool for wood working ‾ has many uses for working on home projects. One use—is cutting lumber for various projects. Also—it's important to follow safety precautions while using it ‾ it can be a dangerous tool if used incorrectly.

LO 2 SLASH

A **slash** (/) is a diagonal line slanting from right to left that is used to indicate a choice between words or line breaks in quoted excerpts from poems.

1. **Use a slash between two words to indicate there is a choice of using either.**

   yes/no   and/or   either/or

2. **Use a slash to indicate line breaks when you quote two or three lines of poetry within your own sentence.**

   > The first three lines of "Juke Box Love Song," a poem by Langston Hughes are: "I could take the Harlem night / and wrap around you, / Take the neon lights and make a crown" (24).

ACTIVITY 27-11   Using a Slash

Directions: *Write three sentences that use words that are sometimes combined with a slash to show that either could be used.* *Answers will vary.*

Example: *The test featured a yes/no answer format.*

_____

_____

_____

_____

_____

LO 2 ELLIPSIS

An **ellipsis** (. . .) is used to indicate that words, phrases, or even complete sentences have been omitted. An ellipsis consists of three periods with spaces between them, with a space before the first one and a space after the last one.

1. **Use an ellipsis to signify where words have been omitted in a quotation.** An ellipsis is used to indicate where you have omitted words within material you are quoting. Be careful not to change the author's intent when omitting a word or words in the middle of a phrase or sentence. An ellipsis is not needed at the beginning or end of a quotation if you are quoting part of a sentence or a phrase.

   For example, here is an excerpt from Amy Tan's novel *Joy Luck Club*:

   > My mother believed you could be anything you wanted to be in America. You could open a restaurant. You could work for the government and get good retirement. You could buy a house with almost no money down. You could become rich. You could become instantly famous.

   Here is the same passage with some of the text removed as indicated by the use of an ellipsis:

   > My mother believed you could be anything you wanted to be in America. You could open a restaurant. You could work for the government and get good retirement . . . You could become instantly famous.

2. **Use an ellipsis to indicate a cutting off or trailing off of a sentence in dialogue.**

   > Noticing her frown, he hastily added, "Oh, never mind . . ."
   > OR
   > "Hold on a minute . . . ," Eliot interrupted. "That doesn't make sense!"

ACTIVITY 27-12   Using Ellipses

Directions: *Choose one of the readings from Chapter 22, and copy five sentences from it. Then remove at least five words from one of the sentences using an ellipsis and without changing the original meaning of the passage.* Answers will vary.

_____

_____

_____

_____

_____

_____

LO 2 BRACKETS

Brackets ([ ]) are similar to parentheses, only square as opposed to curved, and they are used to set off information.

1. Use brackets to add a word or comments to a direct quotation.

> In the words of Thomas Wolfe, "It [New York City] was a cruel city, but it was a lovely one."
>
> One of the goals stated in the first sentence of the U.S. Constitution is to "provide for the common defence [sic]."

▶ **NOTE**   The word *sic* (Latin for "as is") in brackets is used to show that a word in a quotation has been quoted exactly, even if it is incorrect or misspelled.

2. Use brackets when you need to set off material that is already in parentheses.

> (The conductor reminded the orchestra to play *sotto voce* [quietly] during the vocalist's solo.)

ACTIVITY 27-13   Using Brackets

Directions: *Choose one of the reading selections from Chapter 22 and quote two sentences from it, adding a word or phrase of your own in brackets.*
Answers will vary.

_____

_____

_____

_____

_____

_____

_____

ACTIVITY 27-14   Practicing with Punctuation

Directions: *Choose the appropriate punctuation mark from the list below to fill in each of the blanks in the paragraph that follows.*

. period	? question mark	/ slash
, comma	! exclamation point	- hyphen
; semicolon	" " quotation marks	[ ] brackets
: colon	' apostrophe	— dash

Be sure to take precautions when you fly to avoid deep vein thrombosis _____[___DVT___]___. Several activities can prove to be life _____-_____ saving measures. You should exercise as you fly to help avoid DVT. You can do foot lifts, knee lifts, ankle turns, forward bends, and upper-body stretches_____._____ Severe DVT can be dangerous_____;_____ it is important to be aware of the symptoms. Knowing what to watch for can save a person_____'_____s life. Keep a mental yes_____/_____ no checklist when you fly. If you start to experience any of the following symptoms, don't say to your-self, _____"_____Oh_____,_____ I'm just being silly._____"_____ Symptoms include tenderness or redness _____,_____ pain or swelling, fever, sudden cough, or joint soreness. If you feel the symptoms _____—_____ whether you consider them serious or not_____—_____ do the following_____:_____ let your flight attendant know right away_____!_____ Why risk putting your life in danger_____?_____

APPLYING CRITICAL THINKING

| PURPOSE | IDEAS | SUPPORT | ASSUMPTIONS BIASES | CONCLUSIONS | POINT OF VIEW | ANALYSIS |

When you are constructing sentences and making choices about punctuation, ask yourself the following critical thinking questions:

- How can punctuation make my meaning and **purpose** clearer?
- What are the best choices I can make for punctuation in this sentence? A period? An apostrophe? Quotation marks? A colon or a semicolon?
- Am I sure I've used this punctuation correctly?

Then, *break down the particular parts* of the sentences using your **analysis** skills to make sure that you have constructed the sentence correctly.

To check your progress in meeting this chapter's objectives, log in to **www .mywritinglab.com**, go to the **Study Plan** tab, click on **Handbook of Grammar, Mechanics, and Style** and choose **Final Punctuation, Apostrophes,** and **Quotation Marks** from the list of subtopics. Read and view the resources in the **Review Materials** section, and then complete the **Recall, Apply,** and **Write** sets in the **Activities** section.

28 Correcting Common Shift and Construction Errors

Tilted House   Tom Shugrue

LEARNING OBJECTIVES

In this chapter, you will learn to

 Find and correct construction and shift errors in your sentences.

THINKING CRITICALLY

Look at the picture above, and then answer the following questions:

How would looking at this picture of a destroyed house be different if the viewer was a stranger and not the owner of the house?

_____

_____

_____

What you see depends on who you are and your relationship to what you are viewing. In writing, a sudden change in the structure of your sentences or a shift in point of view can interfere with your readers' ability to understand your point or can change the meaning of the sentence completely.

LO 1 CONSTRUCTION AND SHIFT ERRORS

This chapter covers some of the most common construction and shift errors people make when writing, explains what the errors are, and shows how to fix them.

SUBJECT–VERB AGREEMENT (S–V AGR)

A verb must agree with its subject in number. A singular subject requires a singular verb, and a plural subject requires a plural verb.

> **Singular subject:** The *restaurant* **is** open until 10:00 p.m.
> **Plural subject:** Most *restaurants* **are** open until 10:00 p.m.

Subjects composed of collective nouns, singular nouns ending in *s*, or certain nouns that refer to measurements require singular verbs.

- **Collective nouns** (words that include a group but can act as a singular noun) take singular verbs:

> The *band* **plays** during halftime.

- **Singular nouns** ending in *s* still take singular verbs:

> *Physics* **is** a field that demands skills in math.
> *Measles* **is** a serious illness in children.

- **Nouns referring to measurements** such as time, weight, and money usually take singular verbs:

> The twenty *dollars* **goes** to Beth.
> The extra five *pounds* **looks** good on her.

Subject–Verb Agreement Errors

A **subject–verb agreement** error occurs when a writer uses a singular noun with a plural verb or a plural noun with a singular verb. For the subject and the verb to "agree," both must be in singular form or both in plural form. Errors often occur in subject–verb agreement in the following situations:

- When a verb comes before the subject
- When words come between the subject and the verb
- When the subject is an indefinite pronoun
- When a sentence has a compound subject

Here's how to avoid these errors:

1. **Verb before the subject** (the verb is in bold font, and the subject is in italics).

> **Incorrect:** There **is** many *birds* in our yard.
>
> **Corrected:** There **are** many *birds* in our yard.

2. **Words coming between the subject and the verb** (often prepositional phrases).

> **Incorrect:** *One* of the students **were** in the bookstore this morning.
>
> **Corrected:** *One* of the students **was** in the bookstore this morning.

The subject of the sentence is the word *one*, and because the subject *one* is singular, the verb should also be singular. The subject is not *students*, which would require the verb *were*. A noun at the end of a prepositional phrase, such as *students*, can never be the subject of a sentence.

> ▶ **TIP**   To avoid mistaking part of a prepositional phrase for the subject, try crossing out all the prepositional phrases in a sentence to find the subject, and check if the verb agrees with it. For example, you could cross out the prepositional phrase "of the students" in the incorrect example shown above.

One ~~of the students~~ **were** in the bookstore this morning.

Doing this clearly shows the disagreement between the singular subject *one* and the plural verb *were*, indicating that you should correct the sentence by changing *were* to *was*.

3. **Indefinite pronouns as subjects taking singular or plural verbs.**

   Indefinite pronouns function as general nouns rather than as substitutes for specific nouns. Some indefinite pronouns take singular verbs, and other indefinite pronouns take plural verbs. Listed below are some of the most common indefinite pronouns that require singular verbs.

   > *another, anybody, each, either, everybody, everyone, everything, neither, no one, nothing, one, something*
   > **Example:** *Everybody* **is** going to the concert.

   Here are some of the most common indefinite pronouns that require plural verbs.

   > *all, both, few, many, most, some*
   > **Example:** *All* **are** welcome to attend the reception.

   Writers often make the mistake of using plural verbs with singular indefinite pronouns.

   > **Incorrect:** *Everyone* **like** to eat good food.
   >
   > *Each* of the customers **order** food from the menu.
   >
   > **Corrected:** *Everyone* **likes** to eat good food.
   >
   > *Each* of the customers **orders** food from the menu.

4. **Compound subjects taking plural or singular verbs.**

   Compound subjects can take either singular or plural verbs, depending on the subjects. Subjects joined by *and* generally take a plural verb:

   > **Incorrect:** *Fruit and cheese* **tastes** good together
   > **Corrected:** *Fruit and cheese* **taste** good together.

When subjects are joined by *either . . . or, neither . . . nor,* or *not only . . . but also,* the verb agrees with the subject closer to the verb:

Incorrect: Neither Rob nor *Jim* **want** to wash the dishes.

Neither the kids nor *Jim* **want** to wash the dishes.

Neither Jim nor the *kids* **wants** to wash the dishes.

Corrected: Neither Rob nor *Jim* **wants** to wash the dishes.

Neither the kids nor *Jim* **wants** to wash the dishes.

Neither *Jim* nor the *kids* **want** to wash the dishes.

ACTIVITY 28-1   Subject–Verb Agreement

Directions: *Correct the error in subject–verb agreement in each of the following sentences. Cross out the incorrect word(s), and write the correction above the word(s) you deleted. Answers will vary.*

1. One of the most exciting sports in the United States ~~are~~ *is* recreational parachuting, also known as skydiving.

2. After jumping from an aircraft, the skydiver, whose pack contains both main and backup parachutes, ~~fall~~ *falls* freely for awhile before opening the main parachute.

3. During freefall, a skydiver who maximizes wind resistance, spreading both arms and legs, ~~maintain~~ *maintains* a horizontal position while falling at speeds of up to 60 mph.

4. The sensations of freefall ~~does~~ *do* not resemble the sudden sinking feelings of a rollercoaster ride; rather, skydivers describe the experience as "floating with support."

5. Though some parachutes are dome shaped, the rectangular parachute, which is simple to steer and facilitates gentle landings, ~~consist~~ *consists* of a series of tubular cells.

6. Steering lines, which are attached to the right and left sides of the parachute, ~~gives~~ *give* the skydiver some control over the direction and speed of descent.

7. For beginning skydivers, there ~~is~~ *are* several different training methods available, including tandem training and Accelerated Free Fall (AFF) training.

8. Neither the tandem method nor the AFF method ~~require~~ *requires* first-time skydivers to jump alone; trainers jump with them.

9. Generally speaking, anybody over the age of 18 ~~are~~ *is* allowed to skydive, and many skydiving enthusiasts are in their 60s, or even older.

10. Although there ~~is~~ *are* substantial risks associated with the sport, skydivers are willing to accept the dangers in order to experience the thrill of "flying."

PRONOUN–ANTECEDENT AGREEMENT (PRO AGR)

A **pronoun** (such as *he, she, it, we, they,* or *our*) takes the place of another noun or pronoun used earlier in a sentence or in a preceding sentence. The noun or pronoun to which it refers is called the **antecedent.**

My *boss* communicates well, and *she* is always fair.

In this example, the pronoun *she* refers to the noun *boss*; *boss* is the antecedent of *she*. A pronoun must agree with its antecedent in **number** (singular/plural), **gender** (male/female), and **person** (first, second, or third).

My *great-grandfathers* were farmers, and *they* both raised dairy cattle.

The plural, third-person pronoun *they* agrees with its antecedent, the plural noun *great-grandfathers.*

My *great-grandfather* was a farmer, and *he* raised dairy cattle.

In this example, the singular, third-person, masculine pronoun *he* agrees with its antecedent, the singular noun *great-grandfather*.

Pronoun–Antecedent Agreement Errors

Pronoun agreement errors occur when a pronoun "disagrees" with its antecedent. Often writers create pronoun agreement errors in an attempt to avoid using gender-specific language. However, the rules of pronoun usage relate to the logic of singular and plural balance. If the noun is singular, then the pronoun that refers to that noun must be singular. If the noun is plural, then the pronoun must be plural.

> **Incorrect:** A student can get *their* books at the campus bookstore.

The subject *student* is singular; therefore, using the pronoun *their* (which is plural) creates a pronoun error. There are two ways to fix this error.

1. Make the pronoun singular:

> A student can get *his or her* books at the campus bookstore.

2. Make the subject plural:

> Students can get *their* books at the campus bookstore.

Cross Reference
See pp. 663–665,
Avoiding Sexist Language

▶ **NOTE**   Making the subject plural helps avoid two problems related to sexist language: using unnecessarily gender-specific language, and using the split pronoun, *his or her*.

▶ **NOTE**   If the singular subject *is* gender-specific, then be sure to use a gender-specific pronoun.

> A boy scout must keep *his* uniform clean.
> A ballerina must have *her* shoes custom-made.

It's a matter of logic: When gender *is* specific, use a gender-specific pronoun. When gender *is not* specific, don't use a gender-specific pronoun.

ACTIVITY 28-2 Pronoun Agreement

Directions: *Fix the pronoun agreement error in each of the following sentences. Cross out the error, and write the correction over it. If you change a pronoun or antecedent, remember that you may have to change the verb, too.* Answers will vary.

1. Reading aloud to a young child benefits ~~them~~ *(him or her)* in many important ways.

2. For a child, stories are magical, and ~~it comes~~ *(they come)* alive in the child's imagination.

3. Cuddled in a parent's lap at story time, a child feels secure and relaxed, which helps ~~him~~ *(him or her)* focus on the book.

4. Illustrations are important, too, as ~~it provides~~ *(they provide)* clues about what is happening in the story.

5. Reading aloud builds vocabulary: The child may hear an unfamiliar word as the adult reads aloud, and ~~their~~ *(its)* meaning becomes clear in the context of the story.

6. Looking at the printed words, the child begins to understand that ~~it corresponds~~ *(they correspond)* to spoken words.

7. Discussing the book also promotes oral language proficiency, as children learn to express ~~his or her~~ *(their)* thoughts about the story.

8. To build knowledge, a nonfiction children's book is helpful because ~~they provide~~ *(it provides)* information about the real world.

9. A parent who reads aloud to ~~their~~ *(his or her)* children fosters lifelong love of reading as well as enhanced academic achievement.

10. An adult may remember favorite stories from childhood for many years, and ~~they look~~ *(he or she looks)* forward to sharing those stories with another generation of children.

PRONOUN REFERENCE (PRO REF)

A pronoun should clearly refer to its antecedent, the noun it is replacing.

Pronoun Reference Errors

A pronoun reference error occurs when a pronoun does not have a clear connection to its antecedent (the noun it refers to). The antecedent can be *ambiguous* (it is unclear which noun is the antecedent), *vague* (the antecedent is often completely missing), or *too broad* (there is no specific antecedent).

1. **An ambiguous pronoun reference** error occurs when there are two or more possible antecedents for a pronoun. To fix this type of reference error, revise the sentence to distinguish which antecedent you meant to refer to.

> **Example:**   Julie told Mayra that she needed to take her test at the Testing Center. [Who needs to take the test, Julie or Mayra?]
>
> **Corrected:** Julie told Mayra that she *was planning* to take *the* test at the Testing Center.

2. **A vague pronoun reference** error occurs when the antecedent for the pronoun is completely missing. To fix this type of reference error, you need to fill in the missing noun or subject.

> **Example:**   At this coffee shop, *they* never provide enough free coffee refills. [Who does *they* refer to? *Coffee shops* is not the antecedent.]
>
> **Corrected:** At this coffee shop, *the servers* are always very busy, and *they* never provide enough free coffee refills.

3. **A broad pronoun reference** error occurs when a relative pronoun (most commonly *who, whom, whose, which, these, those, that,* and *this*) is used without a clear noun to refer to. The relative pronoun may refer to a whole group of words, or even a whole sentence, instead of referring back to one clear noun antecedent. To fix this type of pronoun reference error, supply the missing noun or replace the relative pronoun with a noun.

> **Incorrect:** The landlord did not allow pets, which many tenants did not like. [The relative pronoun *which* refers to the entire situation of pets being prohibited, which creates ambiguity.

> Do the tenants referred to not like pets or not like the policy prohibiting pets? In order to correct this broad pronoun reference error, an antecedent for *which* must be supplied or the sentence restructured to indicate a clear subject.]
>
> **Corrected:** The landlord did not allow pets, a policy which many tenants did not like.
>
> OR
>
> The landlord did not allow pets because many tenants objected to them.

The pronouns *this, that, these,* or *those* can cause pronoun reference errors when they are used to refer to a whole sentence or a situation described in a previous sentence. The error occurs because the pronoun has no clear, specific noun antecedent. Usually, this type of reference error requires you to insert a noun or a noun phrase after the pronoun.

Examples

> *This* is the reason for our trouble.
> [What is the *this* that is the reason for our trouble?]
>
> *That* is the one I want.
> [What is the *that*?]
>
> *These* (or *those*) are the ones I want.
> [What are the *these*?]

Corrected

> *This* lack of funding is the reason for our trouble.
>
> *That* puppy is the one I want.
>
> *These* (or *those*) puppies are the ones I want.

▶ **TIP**   When a reference error is caused by using a pronoun like *this* or *that*, think of adding a "fill in the blank" answer after it. Answer the question, "This *what*?" or "That *what*?"

ACTIVITY 28-3   Correcting Pronoun Reference Errors

Directions: *Rewrite the sentences below to correct pronoun reference errors. You may need to add nouns or rewrite sentences completely to fix the errors. Answers will vary. Sample answers are provided.*

1. Before putting the vase on the shelf, he dusted it.

   He dusted the vase before putting it on the shelf.

   _____

2. I did not go to the party, which was depressing.

   I felt depressed because I did not go to the party.

   _____

3. When my dog kept barking at the cat, I put it in the other room.

   I put my dog in the other room because it kept barking at the cat.

   _____

4. A commercial interrupted the reality show on television, but we were tired of watching it anyway.

   A commercial interrupted the reality show on television, but we were

   tired of watching that show anyway.

5. I checked the weather forecast yesterday, but they didn't predict this downpour we're having today.

   I checked the weather forecast yesterday, but the meteorologist

   didn't predict this downpour we're having today.

POINT-OF-VIEW (POV) SHIFTS

In Chapter 1, the term *point of view* was used to refer to a writer's perspective on a subject. In grammar, however, **point of view** determines the pronouns you use in essay writing. While it is possible to switch among points of view within an essay, you generally use personal pronouns associated with a single point of view: *first person, second person,* or *third person.*

1. First person

> **Singular:** I, me, my, mine, myself
> **Plural:**   we, us, our, ours, ourselves

First-person point of view is most commonly used in narrative writing.

> **Example:** *I* went on a vacation with *my* family this summer. *We* took *our* favorite car, but two days into the trip, *our* car broke down.

2. Second person

> **Singular and plural:** You, yours, or implied you/imperative (command form)

Second-person point of view is most commonly used for rhetorical questions (a question you ask to interest your readers) in an essay introduction. In general, avoid using second-person point of view when writing essays except in rhetorical questions. Be careful not to use the pronoun *you* to refer to people in general. Use the second person only when specifically addressing the reader. For example:

> **Example:** Do you think you pay too much for your college textbooks?

3. Third person

> **Singular:** He, she, him, her, his, hers, himself, herself, it, its
> **Plural:**   They, them, their, theirs, themselves

Third person is the preferred point of view for most essays.

> **Example:** Author Alice Walker met Martin Luther King, Jr. during the early 1960s. *He* inspired *her* to become active in the civil rights movement, and *she* participated in the 1963 March on Washington.

Indefinite Pronouns

See Chapter 32 for an in-depth coverage of pronouns. For all indefinite pronouns except *one*, third-person personal pronouns may be used with the indefinite pronoun to maintain a consistent point of view.

> **Example:** *Anyone* who wants to use a gym locker is required to bring *his or her* own padlock.
>
> Michael and Janine joined the other musicians for a jam session; *both* brought *their* own guitars.

The indefinite pronoun *one* can refer to the writer or people in general.

> **Example:** *One* would think that the library would stay open all night during finals.

This sentence suggests that the writer thinks the library should stay open all night. The sentence also implies that other people are likely to agree.

The possessive form of one is *one's*. For example: "One should be attentive to *one's* personal hygiene." (Note that *one's*—unlike *hers, ours,* or *theirs*—includes an apostrophe.) Do not mix the indefinite pronoun *one* with personal pronouns or general nouns such as *a person*, especially in the same sentence.

> **Incorrect:** *One* should not neglect *his or her* studies.
>
> *One* should not neglect *their* studies.
>
> *A person* should not neglect *one's* studies.
>
> **Correct:**   *One* should not neglect *one's* studies.

> ▶ **NOTE**   Avoid using the words *man* or *mankind* to represent people in general. These terms are no longer used to refer to both men and women (but, of course, you can use *man* if you are talking about one particular man). Instead, use terms such as *humans* or *humanity*. (See Avoiding Sexist Language in Chapter 30.)

Avoid Incorrect Point-of-View Shifts

Though it is possible to employ more than one point of view in an essay, be sure that the switch is logical and actually needed grammatically. The most common point-of-view shift error involves switching to the second-person pronoun *you*. In casual speech, people often use the generic *you* to mean "people in general." However, in formal writing, this substitution is not acceptable.

> **Incorrect:** *I* had a wonderful time collecting shells on the beach. When *a person* looks carefully at low tide, *you* could see many different kinds of shells.
>
> **Correct:**   *I* had a wonderful time collecting shells on the beach. When *I* looked carefully at low tide, *I* could see many different kinds of shells.

> ▶ **NOTE**   Many teachers suggest using the third-person-plural point of view in most college writing to avoid both point-of-view shifts and other agreement errors.

POV shift error (indefinite pronoun shift to second person):

One can get *your* classes paid for by financial aid.

Pronoun agreement error (plural pronoun for singular noun):

A *student* can get *their* classes paid for by financial aid.

Both errors fixed by substituting a plural noun for the subject and using a third-person plural pronoun:

Students can get *their* classes paid for by financial aid.

ACTIVITY 28-4   Correcting POV Shifts

Directions: *Correct the POV shift errors in the following sentences. Be sure to stay in the point of view that is used first in the sentence.* Answers will vary.

1. When there's a good sale, I enjoy shopping for clothes, but it's
    frustrating when ~~you~~ [I] can't find the right size.

2. When one works in customer service, it is important to be polite at all
    times, but rude customers can try ~~your~~ [one's] patience.

3. To meet your deadline for this project, you may need to put in some
    extra time at the office, but ~~one~~ [you] will not have to work more than
    45 hours per week.

4. When starting to diet, people are able to exercise self-restraint, but
    ~~one's~~ [their] resolution tends to falter after a few weeks without chocolate.

5. Many claim to believe in honesty, but few would claim that
    ~~he or she has~~ [they have] never told a single white lie.

6. Everybody deserves a second chance, especially when ~~one~~ [he or she / the person] admits
    making a mistake and apologizes for it.

7. When planning their vacation in Maine, they considered driving up
    to Canada, but ~~you'd~~ [they'd] need a ~~passport~~ [passports] to cross the border, so they
    rejected that idea.

8. Anyone who is interested in volunteering at the animal shelter
    should write ~~their~~ [his or her] name on the list.

9. If one notices that the car is making an unusual noise, ~~you~~ *one* should
    have the car checked immediately by a qualified mechanic to make
    sure it is safe to drive.

10. With this benefits package, a person's health insurance coverage
    begins right away, but ~~one's~~ *his or her / the person's* dental coverage does not begin until
    three months later.

ACTIVITY 28-5   Correcting Subject-Verb and Pronoun Agreement Errors and Point-of-View Shifts

Directions: *Fix errors in subject-verb agreement, pronoun agreement, and point of view in the following passage. Cross out the errors and write corrections above them. You will find a total of six errors. Answers will vary.*

In her book *Alex and Me*, scientist Irene Pepperberg, who has a Ph.D.
and other impressive credentials, ~~offer~~ *offers* a fascinating account of her 30-year
relationship with Alex, an African gray parrot. Until recently, scientists
assumed that a parrot, whose brain is no bigger than a walnut, could not
understand human language, and that ~~they~~ *talking parrots* were only mimicking the
words of their owners. Based on her observations of Alex, however,
Pepperberg concluded that an African gray parrot that interacts with
people ~~are~~ *is* capable of understanding as well as speaking. According to the
author, Alex also could count and identify colors. Like apes, ~~an African gray parrot lives~~ *African gray parrots live* a long time (up to 50 years), and their social groups in the
wild are large and complex. Pepperberg speculates that the parrots' ability
to perform complex cognitive and linguistic tasks ~~are~~ *is* at least partially
attributable to these factors of longevity and socialization. The book is
highly entertaining, and ~~you~~ *readers* will be touched as well as amazed by the
anecdotes about Alex. For example, when Pepperberg picked up Alex at
an animal hospital, after he had undergone surgery, he looked at her and
said, "Wanna go back."

FAULTY PARALLELISM (//)

Parallelism (or parallel structure) involves using a consistent grammatical form or word form in sentences that have a series of verbals or phrases in order to keep them in balance. Faulty parallelism occurs when the same grammatical form or structure is not used throughout. When this happens, the form changes and the sentence becomes unbalanced.

> **Incorrect:** When we're on vacation, we *swim* in the ocean, *run* on the beach, and *hiking* in the mountains.

The last verb in this list of three verbs is *hiking,* which uses an *-ing* form of the verb, while the first and second verbs use the base forms. To correct this error, simply change *hiking* to *hike.* Or, if you prefer to use *-ing* verbs, then change *swim* and *run* to *-ing* verb forms by restructuring the sentence.

> **Corrected:** When we're on vacation, we *swim* in the ocean, *run* on the beach, and *hike* in the mountains.

OR

> When we're on vacation, we like *swimming* in the ocean, *running* on the beach, and *hiking* in the mountains.

Sometimes, problems with parallelism occur with whole phrases, especially when comparisons are being made.

> **Incorrect:** Page didn't know *whether to give* Jacob her new toy or *if she should keep* it for herself.

The phrases *whether to . . .* and *if she should . . .* are not parallel constructions. Choose one or the other to create the comparison. Here is one way to correct the sentence.

> **Corrected:** Page didn't know *whether to give* Jacob her new toy or *keep* it for herself.

Note that when there are two infinitive phrases (*to give, to keep*), the "to" does not need to be repeated.

Here are two other ways to correct the parallelism error in the original sentence.

Corrected: Page didn't know *if she should give* Jacob her new toy or *if she should keep* it for herself.

OR

Page didn't know if she should *give* Jacob her new toy or *keep* it for herself.

ACTIVITY 28-6   Correcting Faulty Parallelism

Directions: *Rewrite the following sentences to correct errors in parallelism.*
Answers will vary. Sample answers are provided.

Example: The babysitter prepared a snack, washed the dishes, and reading a story.

Revised: The babysitter prepared a snack, washed the dishes, and read a story.

1. Receiving gifts can be fun, but to give gifts can be challenging.

   Receiving gifts can be fun, but giving gifts can be challenging.

   _____

   _____

2. When selecting a gift, consider three factors: the nature of your relationship with the person, money you have for gifts, and the amount of time you have to shop.

   When selecting a gift, consider three factors: the nature of your relation-

   ship with the person, the amount of money you have budgeted for gifts,

   and the amount of time you have to shop.

   _____

3. Whether the person is a close friend or an acquaintance that you have known professionally, your choice of a gift should reflect the person's interests and preferences.

   Whether the person is a close friend or a professional acquaintance, your

   choice of a gift should reflect the person's interests and preferences.

   _____

4. You can gather clues about a person's interests by asking the person directly, check with mutual friends who know the person better than you do, or observing the person's clothing and home.

   You can gather clues about a person's interests by asking the person

   directly, checking with mutual friends who know the person better than

   you do, or observing the person's clothing and home.

5. The gifts you purchase for close friends and family probably cost more than the gifts bought by you to give casual friends or colleagues, but sometimes the perfect gift for a loved one is not expensive at all.

   The gifts you purchase for close friends and family probably cost more

   than the gifts you buy for casual friends or colleagues, but sometimes

   the perfect gift for a loved one is not expensive at all.

6. Of course, the cheapest approach is not to buy a gift but making a gift; unfortunately, many people lack the skills and they are not having the patience needed for this approach.

   Of course, the cheapest approach is not to buy a gift but to make a gift;

   unfortunately, many people lack the skills and patience needed for this

   approach.

7. Sometimes shopping is the hardest part of the process: You may know what you want to buy but not knowing where to find it.

   Sometimes shopping is the hardest part of the process: You may know

   what you want to buy but not know where to find it.

8. You may prefer the convenience of online shopping, but if the gift-giving occasion is rapidly approaching, shipping and delivery of the item may take too long or be costing too much money.

   You may prefer the convenience of online shopping, but if the gift-giving

   occasion is rapidly approaching, shipping and delivery of the item may

   take too long or cost too much money.

9. Maybe what you need is a shopping buddy—someone who is liking to help, loves to shop, and has good judgment.

   Maybe what you need is a shopping buddy—someone who likes to help,

   loves to shop, and has good judgment.

10. Finding the perfect gift for a friend can be stressful and it can be taking a lot of your time, but seeing your friend's happiness when the gift is opened can be almost as much fun as receiving a gift yourself.

    Finding the perfect gift for a friend can be stressful and take a lot of

    time, but seeing your friend's happiness when the gift is opened can be

    almost as much fun as receiving a gift yourself.

DANGLING AND MISPLACED MODIFIERS (DM AND MM)

A **modifier** is a word or word group that *refers to* or *modifies* a nearby word or word group. Errors in modifiers occur when the nearby word or word group is not directly stated (so the modifier is "dangling" without anything to connect to) or the modifier is in the wrong place and therefore isn't close enough to the word or word group it is supposed to modify (a misplaced modifier).

Dangling Modifiers

Dangling modifiers are missing a home base: The word they intend to modify is missing in action. As a result, dangling modifiers are often unintentionally funny. This example illustrates the dangers, and the humor, of dangling modifiers:

Example: Galloping across the finish line, the crowd cheered loudly.

Clearly, the writer meant to describe race horses galloping across the finish line, but by failing to include the noun *horses*, the sentence unintentionally creates the humorous image of people ("the crowd") galloping across a finish line.

Revised: The crowd cheered loudly as the horses galloped across the finish line.

OR

As the horses galloped across the finish line, the crowd cheered loudly.

▶ **NOTE**   Dangling modifiers often occur due to an introductory phrase not being followed by a needed subject. A possessive noun does not count as such as subject. For example:

Incorrect: After examining the patient, the doctor's recommendation was to continue the prescribed treatment.

Correct: After examining the patient, the doctor recommended continuation of the prescribed treatment.

ACTIVITY 28-7   Correcting Dangling Modifiers

Directions: *Edit the following sentences to correct dangling modifiers. You may need to add a subject, change words, or rearrange the sentence.* Answers will vary. Sample answers are provided.

1. While trying to study, the jackhammers made a terribly distracting noise.

    While trying to study, I found the noise of the jackhammers terribly

    distracting.

2. Having agreed only reluctantly to the blind date, it was a pleasant surprise to discover that my date was smart and funny.

    Having agreed only reluctantly to the blind date, I was pleasantly

    surprised to discover that my date was smart and funny.

3. Out of breath after only a few minutes, the treadmill needed to be reset at a lower speed.

    Out of breath after only a few minutes, I needed to reset the treadmill

    at a lower speed.

4. Having searched through every file, the missing documents could not be found.

   Having searched through every file, we could not find the missing

   documents.

5. Hiking up the mountain trail, a large bear suddenly appeared.

   When we were hiking up the mountain trail, a large bear suddenly

   appeared.

6. Holding a half-eaten cupcake, the little boy's shirt was covered with frosting.

   The little boy was holding a half-eaten cupcake, and his shirt was covered

   with frosting.

7. Lost in a pleasant dream, the ringing alarm clock was totally ignored.

   Lost in a pleasant dream, I totally ignored the ringing alarm clock.

8. Seeing the disappointed faces of people leaving the box office, it was obvious that tickets for the concert had already sold out.

   When we saw the disappointed faces of people leaving the box office, it

   was obvious to us that tickets for the concert had already sold out.

9. Rereading the paragraph several times, the meaning was still unclear.

   The meaning of the paragraph was still unclear to me even after I reread

   it several times.

10. While taking college classes, the part-time job at the café helped pay her bills.

    While she was taking college classes, the part-time job at the café

    helped pay her bills.

Misplaced Modifiers

A **misplaced modifier** is in the wrong place in a sentence, so the reader thinks it modifies the wrong word or cannot figure out what it is modifying.

> **Example:** I was chased by a dog wearing my pajamas.

Okay, it's bad enough to be chased by a dog, but it adds insult to injury if he's wearing my pajamas! The modifier *wearing my pajamas* is in the wrong spot: It is closer to *dog* than to *I*.

> **Revised:** Wearing my pajamas, I was chased by a dog.

Single-word modifiers such as *often* and *almost* are often misplaced:

> **Example:** I almost made $200 for the lawn-mowing job.

So did the job not happen? If the writer means that he or she made almost $200 for the job, then the modifier needs to be placed immediately before the word (or words) being modified:

> **Revised:** I made almost $200 for the lawn-mowing job.

ACTIVITY 28-8   Correcting Misplaced Modifiers

Directions: *Rewrite each of the following sentences to correct the misplaced modifier. You may need to completely restructure the sentence.*   Answers will vary. Sample answers are provided.

1. The patient was referred to a cardiac specialist with symptoms of heart disease.

   The patient with symptoms of heart disease was referred to a cardiac

   specialist.

2. Dressed in a suit and tie, she thought her boyfriend looked especially handsome.

   She thought her boyfriend looked especially handsome dressed in a suit

   and tie.

3. Pausing to sign autographs, they caught a glimpse of the famous actor.

   They caught a glimpse of the famous actor pausing to sign autographs.

   _____

4. The wrestler was 6'3" with long hair and a mustache weighing 204 pounds.

   Weighing 204 pounds, the 6'3" wrestler had long hair and a mustache.

   _____

5. Covered with grated parmesan cheese, I love any type of pasta.

   I love any type of pasta covered with grated parmesan cheese.

   _____

6. When driving late at night, coffee helps prevent drowsiness.

   Coffee helps prevent drowsiness when a person is driving late at night.

   _____

7. She decided she wanted to be an astronaut when she was seven years old.

   When she was seven years old, she decided she wanted to be an

   astronaut.

8. The student added sulfur to the test tube smelling like rotten eggs.

   The sulfur, smelling like rotten eggs, was added to the test tube by the

   student.

9. Professor Jenkins is teaching a course on criminal behavior at Fairview College.

   At Fairview College, Professor Jenkins is teaching a course on criminal

   behavior.

10. The scientist explained how the spider traps its prey spinning a new web each night.

    The scientist explained how the spider, spinning a new web each night,

    traps its prey.

ACTIVITY 28-9   **Correcting Dangling and Misplaced Modifiers I**

Directions: *On the line before each sentence, write **DM** if the sentence includes a dangling modifier and **MM** if it includes a misplaced modifier. Then revise the sentences to correct the errors.*

   _MM_   1. The actress was offered many comedy roles, but she only said she would accept dramatic roles.

   The actress was offered many comedy roles, but she said

   she would only accept dramatic roles.

DM   **2.** Flipping through the magazine, an article about animal rights caught my eye.

An article about animal rights caught my eye as I was

flipping through the magazine.

DM   **3.** Hopelessly lost, and having neither a map nor a GPS in the car, the only alternative was to keep looking for familiar landmarks.

Hopelessly lost, and having neither a map nor a GPS system

in the car, we felt that our only alternative was to keep looking

for familiar landmarks.

MM   **4.** The frightened puppy was rescued by a kind pedestrian without a collar.

The frightened puppy without a collar was rescued by a

kind pedestrian.

MM   **5.** The antiques dealer bought a chair from the distinguished gentleman with decorative carving.

The antiques dealer bought a chair with decorative carving

from the distinguished gentleman.

DM   **6.** Tired of studying all day, a quick bike ride was energizing.

Tired of studying all day, she found that a quick bike ride

was energizing.

DM   **7.** Making sandwiches for the children, the squirrels kept running up to the picnic table to beg for bits.

As I was making sandwiches for the children, the squirrels

kept running up to the picnic table to beg for bits.

MM   **8.** Sucking her thumb, the father carried the sleepy toddler to the car.

Sucking her thumb, the sleepy toddler was carried to the

car by her father.

DM   **9.** Without knowing his size, it was not possible to buy him clothes for his birthday.

Without knowing his size, she knew it was not possible to

buy him clothes for his birthday.

____MM____ **10.** Wearing a spooky Halloween costume, the neighborhood was terrorized by Marcus.

Wearing a spooky Halloween costume, Marcus terrorized

the neighborhood.

ACTIVITY 28-10 Correcting Dangling and Misplaced Modifiers II

Directions: *Underline misplaced and dangling modifiers in the following paragraph. Then write **MM** over the underlined word or phrase if it is a misplaced modifier or **DM** over the phrase if it is a dangling modifier. You should find seven modifier errors.*

Built to honor George Washington, the Washington Monument is the world's tallest stone structure and <u>nearly</u> [MM] stands 560 feet high. Made of marble, granite, and sandstone, <u>visitors</u> [DM] are impressed by both the monument's height and its simple beauty. Constructed between 1848 and 1884, <u>architect Robert Mills</u> [DM] was the monument's designer. Formally dedicated on February 22, 1885, <u>hundreds of people</u> [DM] gathered at the the site to hear commemorative speeches. Climbing the 897 steps to the top, the <u>monument</u> [MM] had over 10,000 visitors during the first six months after its dedication. From the top of the monument, visitors can <u>almost</u> [MM] see the entire city. Flashing intermittently, <u>people</u> [MM] can also observe the light at the summit that keeps planes from getting too close to the monument.

PASSIVE VOICE CONSTRUCTION (PASS)

As a grammatical term, "voice" refers to verbs. Verbs can be in the active or passive voice. When a verb is in the **active voice**, the subject performs the action. When a verb is in the **passive voice**, the subject experiences the effect of the action. Passive voice includes a form of the verb "to be" and a past participle.

Whenever possible, avoid using *passive* voice construction and opt for *active* construction to write clear, powerful sentences. An active verb construction is easier for readers to understand because the active voice places the emphasis on *who* is doing the action:

> **Passive voice:** The ball *was thrown by* Thomas.
>
> **Revised to active voice:** Thomas *threw* the ball.

Not only does the active voice construction sound cleaner, it is also clearer since the "doer" of the action (Thomas) is emphasized and not buried at the end of the sentence. Here is another example of passive voice construction:

> **Passive:** The puppy that was selected by the children was wagging its tail.
>
> **Changed to active:** The children selected the puppy that was wagging its tail.

ACTIVITY 28-11   Changing Passive Voice to Active Voice I

Directions: *Rewrite each of the following sentences in the space provided, changing the sentence from the passive voice to the active voice.* Answers will vary.

1. The cupcakes were baked by Kim for the birthday party.

    Kim baked the cupcakes for the birthday party.

    _____

2. In the middle of the flower garden, a hole was dug by the chipmunk.

    The chipmunk dug a hole in the middle of the flower garden.

    _____

3. The dead tree was chopped down by Tomas, and he split the wood into logs.

    Tomas chopped down the dead tree and split the wood into logs.

    _____

4. When the band members came onstage, they were greeted by loud applause.

    Loud applause greeted the band members when they came onstage.

    _____

5. The compromise proposed by the union was rejected by the management.

   The management rejected the compromise that the union proposed.

   _____

6. A compelling argument in support of gun control was presented by the author.

   The author presented a compelling argument in support of gun control.

   _____

7. At the regional dog show, the grand prize was won by Chica the Chihuahua.

   Chica the Chihuahua won grand prize at the regional dog show.

   _____

8. The answer to the complex math problem was computed by Angela in record time.

   Angela computed the answer to the complex math problem in record time.

   _____

9. The tree house was constructed by Tamara for her niece and nephew.

   Tamara constructed the tree house for her niece and nephew.

   _____

10. The travel arrangements were made by Hector three months before the trip.

    Three months before the trip, Hector made the travel arrangements.

    _____

ACTIVITY 28-12   Changing Passive Voice to Active Voice II

Directions: *Rewrite the following passage in the space provided, changing each sentence from the passive to the active voice.* Answers will vary.

In 1761, a musical instrument known as the glass harmonica was invented by Benjamin Franklin. Empty glass bowls of graduated sizes were nested within one another by Franklin to create his instrument. A hole was drilled in each bowl by Franklin so the bowls could be mounted on a horizontal spindle. A foot pedal operated by the performer caused the bowls to turn. Musical tones of different pitches were produced when the performer's moistened finger was pressed against the revolving, different-sized bowls.

For a brief time, the popularity of the glass harmonica was great, and music featuring the instrument was written by composers such as Mozart and Beethoven. The sounds emitted by the glass harmonica were ethereal; as the high-pitched tones bounced off a room's walls, listeners seemed to be surrounded by the delicate music.

After Franklin returned from Europe with his new invention, the instrument was played by him in the attic of his house while his wife slept downstairs. When the unique sounds of the glass harmonica were first heard by her, she "awakened with the conviction that she had died and gone to heaven and was listening to the music of the angels."

In 1761, Benjamin Franklin invented a musical instrument known as the glass harmonica. To create his instrument, Franklin used empty glass bowls of graduated sizes, nested within one another. Franklin drilled holes in the bowls and mounted them on a horizontal spindle. The performer operated a foot pedal that caused the bowls to turn. By pressing a moistened finger against the revolving, different-sized bowls, the performer produced musical tones of different pitches.

For a brief time, the new instrument was very popular, and composers such as Mozart and Beethoven composed music featuring the glass harmonica. The instrument emitted ethereal sounds; as the high-pitched tones bounced off a room's walls, the delicate music seemed to surround listeners.

When Franklin returned from Europe with his new invention, he started playing it in the attic while his wife slept downstairs. When she first heard the unique sounds of the glass harmonica, she "awakened with the conviction that she had died and gone to heaven and was listening to the music of the angels."

APPLYING CRITICAL THINKING

| PURPOSE | IDEAS | SUPPORT | ASSUMPTIONS BIASES | CONCLUSIONS | POINT OF VIEW | ANALYSIS |

Once you have drafted and revised your work, use your **analysis** skills to break your sentences down into their particular parts to make sure you have constructed them correctly and haven't made any of the errors discussed in this chapter.

Ask yourself the following questions:

- **Have I switched point of view when I shouldn't have** (from first person—*I, me us*; to second person—*you*; or to third person—*he, she they*)?
- **Does each verb agree with its subject** (are the verb and the subject both singular or both plural)?
- **Do pronouns agree with their subjects** (are the pronoun and the subject both singular or both plural)?
- **Are pronoun references clear** (is it clear to which noun a pronoun refers)?
- **Are my sentence structures parallel** (do they stay consistent throughout the sentence)?
- **Are my modifiers attached and in the right place** (are the words they modify included in the sentence)?
- **Did I avoid passive voice construction?**

To check your progress in meeting this chapter's objectives, log in to www .mywritinglab.com, go to the **Study Plan** tab, click on **Handbook of Grammar, Mechanics, and Style** and choose **Subject-Verb Agreement, Pronoun Antecedent Agreement, Parallelism, Misplaced or Dangling Modifiers,** and **Consistent Verb Tense and Active Voice** from the list of subtopics. Read and view the resources in the **Review Materials** section, and then complete the **Recall, Apply,** and **Write** sets in the **Activities** section.

Frank and Ernest

ERNIE'S LOOKING UP THE MEANING OF "PALINDROME."

AHA!

DICTIONARY

THAVES

© 2003 Thaves. Reprinted with permission. Newspaper dist. by UFS, Inc.

LEARNING OBJECTIVES

In this chapter, you will learn to

LO 1 Learn tips to improve your spelling.

LO 2 Distinguish commonly confused words.

LO 3 Use a dictionary and a thesaurus.

LO 4 Use capitals, numbers, and abbreviations correctly.

THINKING CRITICALLY

Explain what this cartoon is about. What is funny about it?

_____

_____

_____

_____

_____

This chapter will give you tips on how to choose the right words and how to use a dictionary or a thesaurus for help in spelling words correctly. It will also provide tips on how to abbreviate words and how to use numbers and capitalization correctly in your writing.

LO 1 TEN TIPS FOR SPELLING IMPROVEMENT

Though not everyone is a "natural-born speller," correct spelling is important in your writing. If you make spelling mistakes in a final draft, your readers may still understand what you mean, but they may lose respect for your ideas and consider your arguments less credible. If you want to be taken seriously as a writer, then you have to take correct spelling seriously, too. My friend Walter, who teaches composition, always says to his students, "I don't take off for spelling in essays, but I do take off for misspelling!"

Spelling Tip 1: Use a Dictionary

During the revision and editing stage of your writing process, use a dictionary to doublecheck any word that you are not 100 percent sure is spelled correctly. *When in doubt, look it up.*

Spelling Tip 2: Check for Correct Pronunciation

Some spelling errors occur because some words are not spelled the way they sound or are pronounced. Here are a few examples of words that are commonly mispronounced and, consequently, misspelled: *accidentally* (not "accidently"), *athletics* (not "atheletics"), *disastrous* (not "disasterous"), *February* (not "Febuary"), *government* (not "goverment"), *mathematics* (not "mathmatics"), *publicly* (not "publically"), *temperament* (not "temperment"), and *wondrous* (not "wonderous").

Spelling Tip 3: Do Not Confuse Homophones

Some spelling mistakes occur as the result of confusing two **homophones**, words that sound the same, or nearly the same, but have different meanings and sometimes are spelled differently. Here are some examples:

affect/effect

complement/compliment

break/brake

right/write/rite

See Commonly Confused Words later in this chapter (p. 620) for a more complete list of homophones, and use the list to avoid spelling errors.

Spelling Tip 4: Use Rules for Making Words Plural

Some plural forms of words are commonly misspelled. Watch for them. Here are a few rules that will help you spell plurals correctly:

1. **Most nouns are made plural by adding a final s:** *cat/cats, dog/dogs,* and *apple/apples.*
2. **Nouns ending with an s, x, ch, or sh need es to form the plural:** *boss/bosses, ax/axes, crutch/crutches,* and *dish/dishes.*
3. **If a noun ends with a y with a consonant in front of it, then change the y to an i, and add es to form the plural:** *beauty/beauties* and *city/cities.* However, always keep the y when you are making a family's name plural: *the Murphys.*
4. **If a noun ends with y with a vowel in front of it, then keep the y and add an s to form the plural:** *boy/boys* and *ray/rays.*
5. **If the noun ends with an o, add either an s or es.** It's best to consult a dictionary if you're not sure whether the word you're spelling ends in s or es: *solo/solos, piano/pianos, hero/heroes,* and *tomato/tomatoes.*
6. **If a noun ends with an f, or an f followed by a silent e, then change the f to a v, and add es (for words ending with an f) or s (for words ending with an f followed by a silent e):** *leaf/leaves, self/selves, wife/wives,* and *knife/knives.* However, for some words ending with an f, the plural is formed just by adding s: *chief/chiefs* and *proof/proofs.* Consult a dictionary if you are not sure which ending is correct.
7. **There are many irregular plurals in English, and most of them are well known from regular usage.** Here are a few examples: *child/children, man/men, woman/women, tooth/teeth, mouse/mice, deer/deer, moose/moose, sheep/sheep, datum/data,* and *medium/media.* When in doubt, consult a dictionary.

Spelling Tip 5: Distinguish Between *ei* and *ie*

Learn the correct spelling of words containing *ei* or *ie*. Pay attention to the previous letter and the sound of the word to figure out whether "i" goes before "e" or vice versa. There are some simple rules you can follow.

1. **When the sound you want to make is ee as in see, then use i before e:** *believe, chief, grief,* and *yield.*
2. **When the combination is preceded by a c, the spelling is almost always ei:** *receive, deceiving, ceiling,* and *conceit.*
3. **When the word has an ay sound, as in bay or way, then the spelling is almost always ei:** *neigh/neighborhood,* and *weigh/weight.*

▶ **TIP**   Remember the famous saying taught in grammar school: " 'i' before 'e' except after 'c,' " or when it sounds like an *ay* as in *weigh* or *neighborhood*. Even this rule has exceptions: *caffeine* and *seize*, for example. So, remember to consult a dictionary when you have any doubts.

Spelling Tip 6: Learn the Rules for Adding Suffixes and Prefixes

Adding Suffixes

1. **When adding the *-ing* suffix, in general, drop the silent *e* at the end of a word:** *become/becoming, come/coming, hope/hoping, scare/scaring,* and *surprise/surprising*. However, there are a few exceptions, such as *dye/dyeing* and *shoe/shoeing*.

   When the word ends with a *y*, then retain the *y*: *cry/crying, enjoy/enjoying, lay/laying,* and *study/studying*.

2. **When adding the *-ible* suffix, drop the silent *e*:** *force/forcible*.

3. **When adding the *-able* suffix, the silent *e* may be dropped or kept, so consult a dictionary if you are unsure:** *advise/advisable, argue/arguable, manage/manageable,* and *change/changeable*.

4. **A final silent *e* that is preceded by another vowel is always dropped when adding any suffix:** *argue/arguable* and *true/truly*.

5. **When a word ends with a *y* and is preceded by a consonant (and the suffix added is not *-ing*), then change the *y* to an *i* before adding the suffix:** *happy/happiest/happier, pity/pitiful,* and *ugly/uglier/ugliest*. However, when the *y* is preceded by a vowel, keep the *y* and add an *s*: *delay/delays, enjoy/enjoys, toy/toys,* and *valley/valleys*.

6. **When you are adding a suffix to a word that ends in a consonant, you often need to double the consonant first:** *cancel/cancelled, grip/gripping, grip/gripped, sad/saddest, occur/occurrence, refer/referred,* and *scar/scarring*. But there are exceptions (such as *deep/deepened, cancel/canceling,* and *crawl/crawler*), so consult your dictionary when in doubt.

Adding Prefixes

Adding a prefix to a word does not typically require a change in the spelling of the base word, but if the base word starts with a vowel, a hyphen may be needed. Again, when in doubt, consult your dictionary.

appear/disappear	eminent/preeminent
operate/cooperate	educate/re-educate
spell/misspell	emphasize/re-emphasize
usual/unusual	

Spelling Tip 7: Keep a List of Your Errors

Keep a list of your own repeat offenders—frequently misspelled words—in a spelling log or journal. Just being aware of your most frequent errors will help you eradicate them eventually.

Spelling Tip 8: Be Familiar with Some of the Most Commonly Misspelled Words

Consult the following list for some of the most commonly misspelled words in college essays: *believe, conceive, curiosity, definitely, disastrous, environment, forty, friend, interrupt, irrelevant, license, mathematics, medieval, necessary, occasion, precede, professor, receive, tendency, themselves, thorough,* and *weird.*

Spelling Tip 9: Be Aware of Common Letter Groupings

Be aware of common letter groupings, such as *qu, ei, ie, au, ch, ou, th, sh,* and *gh.* Note patterns, and keep them in mind: *quiet, quite, receive, diet, launch, those, should,* and *tough.* Use these patterns as spelling tips.

Spelling Tip 10: Use Spell-Check

Use the spell-check function on your computer, but be careful. See the Rewards and Dangers of Spell-Check on the next page.

ACTIVITY 29-1   Trying out the Spelling Tips

Directions: *Correct the spelling errors in the following paragraph. Refer to the ten spelling tips above for help. You should find 12 spelling errors in this paragraph.*

About a year ago, a ~~freind~~ *friend* persuaded me to go to a yoga class. I had always thought that yoga was a little ~~wierd,~~ *weird* and I couldn't ~~concieve~~ *conceive* of con-torting myself into pretzel-positions. Besides, I hadn't exercised in months and was in ~~pityful~~ *pitiful* shape physically.

But when my friend described some of the physical and mental benefits, he piqued my my ~~curosity,~~ *curiosity* so I decided to give the class a try. I was nervous at first, but I soon discovered that most of the exercises were ~~managable,~~ *manageable* even for me. The hour-long class provided a ~~through~~ *thorough* workout. I was disap-pointed when the next class was ~~canceled.~~ *cancelled* I even started doing yoga at home most mornings. Now I depend on yoga instead of ~~caffiene~~ *caffeine* to jump-start my *definitely*

day. I would definately recommend yoga to people of all ages. For me, yoga

truly   *hoping*

has truely been a gift—a gift I would like to share. That is why I am hopeing

to become certified as a yoga instructor next year.

THE REWARDS AND DANGERS OF SPELL-CHECK

Spell-check is certainly a gift to writers, but don't fall into the habit of always believing what spell-check suggests. You need to be sure you are using the right word in the right context. Spell-check will always suggest a correctly spelled word, but it might not be the word you intended, and the word suggested by spell-check may mean something completely different. Many spell-check programs automatically indicate (by a red underline, for example) a misspelled word as soon as you've finished typing it. In some word processing programs, you can use your computer mouse to right-click the word, and spell-check will offer possible correct spellings. When in doubt, though, consult your dictionary to doublecheck. Here is a list of the rewards and dangers of using spell-check programs.

The Rewards

1. **The spell-check function can help you spot many of your spelling errors.**
2. **The spell-check function is convenient,** requiring just a mouse click. In some word processing programs or computer systems, spell-check operates automatically.
3. **The spell-check function offers a fairly extensive collection of correctly spelled words.**

The Dangers

1. **Spell-check may not point out words in your essay that are spelled correctly but not used correctly.** For example, spell-check would not identify these two errors:

   Incorrect: My brother suggested that we play "Monopoly," but I get *board* with *bored* games.

   These two italicized words should be interchanged.

> **Corrected:** My brother suggested that we play "Monopoly," but I get *bored* with *board* games.

2. **Spell-check may suggest words that are correctly spelled but do not fit the context of your sentence:**

> **Example:** I'm not sure whether I should take a biology course, but I'm *definantly* taking physics.
> **Spell-check suggestion:** I'm not sure whether I should take a biology course, but I'm defiantly taking physics.
> **Intended correct spelling:** I'm not sure whether I should take a biology course, but I'm *definitely* taking physics.

In this example, the writer misspelled the word *definitely*, meaning "without a doubt," but spell-check incorrectly substituted the word *defiantly*, meaning "in a challenging or disobedient manner."

> ▶ **NOTE** Be careful not to automatically click "Replace" for words suggested by spell-check. Look carefully, and when in doubt, consult a dictionary to make sure you are choosing the right word for the context of your sentence.

3. **Spell-check does not include every word you might use.** Sometimes spell-check wrongly identifies correctly spelled words (such as proper names with unusual spellings) as errors. Consult a dictionary or other resource, as needed.

As you can see, spell-check is a wonderful tool. Far too often, however, students rely too heavily on spell-check and run into trouble. Use this tool with caution: Apply critical thinking, and have a good dictionary handy as a backup.

ACTIVITY 29-2 Testing Spell-Check

Directions: *Using a computer that has spell-check installed, write a paragraph of your own and deliberately misspell five words, preferably words with difficult or uncommon spellings. Then, use spell-check to fix the spelling of the words. Use a dictionary to doublecheck a word's spelling, if necessary. Then answer the following questions in the spaces below. Answers will vary.*

1. Was spell-check's first suggestion for each of your misspelled words accurate? If not, list the inaccurate suggestions, and explain why they were wrong.

   _____

   _____

2. When you mistyped the word, did spell-check automatically identify it (for example, by underlining it in red)? Did you try "right-clicking" on the word for instant suggestions for the correct spelling? If so, how did that go? _____

   _____

3. Did you use a dictionary? If so, how did it help?

   _____

   _____

LO 2 COMMONLY CONFUSED WORDS

Often, spelling mistakes result from writers confusing one word with another that sounds like it (a homonym). Some confusion also results from using the wrong form of a word, using slang, or using a word that is spelled correctly but in the wrong context.

Here is a list of some of the commonly confused words that most often show up in student writing. Consult this list to make sure that you haven't used a word that sounds like the word you want but is incorrectly spelled.

a/an

Both these words are indefinite articles (see p. 501 for more on articles). Use *a* when the word following it starts with a consonant sound, and use *an* when the word following it starts with a vowel sound (*a, e, i, o, u*) or a silent *h*. When the *h* is not silent, use *a*. Sometimes an initial vowel has a consonant sound; when this is the case, use *a*.

> Lil ate *an* apple from Hallie's fruit bowl, and Hallie thought it was *an* honor to provide her with a treat. Neither was interested in eating *a* banana.
>
> The author is currently writing *a* history of the Iditarod, *a* unique dog sled race that began in 1973.

a lot/allot/alot (misspelling)

a lot is a two-word phrase (an article and a noun) that means *a great deal* or *many*. The phrase is best used only in informal writing.

allot is a transitive verb meaning *to divide something up* or *to portion* or *to allow*.

alot is a common misspelling of "a lot." It is not a legitimate word.

> Marge didn't want *a lot* from life: She just wanted what was *allotted* to her.

accept/except

accept is a transitive verb (see p. 484 for more on verb forms) that means *to agree* or *to receive*.

except is either a verb meaning *to exclude* or *leave out* or a preposition meaning *other than* or *apart from*.

> Sandy decided to *accept* all the gifts from Sam *except* the new pet lizard.

adapt/adopt

adapt is a verb meaning to *adjust* or *to fit or make suitable*.

adopt is a verb meaning to make something or someone one's own.

> Martin had to *adapt* his viewpoint to match his wife's state of mind so they could *adopt* the newborn kittens.

advice/advise

advice is a noun meaning *a suggestion or recommendation*.

advise is a verb meaning *to suggest, give a recommendation*.

> I *advise* you not to listen to all of your parents' *advice* when you have a new baby.

affect/effect

affect is a verb meaning *influence* (think "a" for action).

effect is a noun meaning *a result* (think "e" for ending), or it can be a verb if used to mean *to bring about*.

> Monique's strong academic goals *affected* her success and created long-lasting, positive career *effects*. The new rules *effected* a change in policy.

afraid/frightened

afraid is an adjective, usually followed by the preposition *of* or the word *that*; *afraid* means "filled with fear, regret, or concern."

As a child, I was *afraid of* the dark.

He was *afraid that* he would not have enough time to study.

frightened can be an adjective, meaning "filled with fear" or "alarmed"; *frightened* can also function as a verb, meaning "made afraid."

The *frightened* dog hid under the bed.

The loud crack of thunder *frightened* the dog.

aggravate/irritate

aggravate is a verb meaning "to make worse."

irritate is a verb meaning "to annoy, anger, inflame, or to chafe."

Winston was *irritated* by the rash on his arm, but he *aggravated* the itching by constantly scratching it.

all ready/already

all ready is an adjective phrase meaning "prepared."

already is an adverb used in expressions of time.

We were *all ready* to leave for the airport, but we realized that our ride had *already* left.

all right/alright (misspelling)

all right is an adjective or an adverb, depending on the context, and means "agreeable, satisfactory."

alright is a misspelling of "all right" and should not be used.

Kelly was *all right* after she found out that many students confused words and their spellings.

allude/refer

allude is a verb meaning "to call attention to something *indirectly*."

refer is a verb meaning "to describe something in a particular way."

In her speech, Susan didn't *refer* directly to the Bible, but she *alluded* to it.

allusion/illusion

allusion is a noun meaning "an indirect or casual reference" or "a specific reference to a well-know artistic or literary work."

illusion is a noun meaning "an unreal perception" or a "visual trick."

Houdini often included *allusions* to famous lines from Shakespeare before he performed one of his famous *illusions*.

among/between

among is a preposition used for referring to *more than two* people or things.

between is a preposition used for referring to *two people or things*.

The money was divided *among* the nieces and nephews, but the furniture was divided equally *between* the son and the daughter.

bad/badly

bad is an adjective used to describe a negative attribute of a person or a thing.

badly is an adverb used to describe a verb or action in a negative light. A descriptive linking verb—such as *look, seem, smell, sound*, or a form of the verb *to be* (am, is, were, etc.)—uses *bad* instead of *badly*, but other verbs require the adverb *badly*.

It was a *bad* idea to act *badly* on the first day at my new job. I felt *bad* about complaining, but the office refrigerator smelled *bad*, and something needed to be done about it.

beside/besides

beside is a preposition meaning "by the side of" or "next to."

besides is an adverb meaning "in addition to."

Besides waiting for him for over two hours, she had to stand *beside* a smelly dumpster.

board/bored

board is a noun meaning "a wooden plank."

bored is a verb meaning "being in a disengaged mindset, uninterested."

Sharif was so *bored* by the lecture that he wanted to hit his head against a *board*.

brake/break

brake is a noun meaning "an instrument for stopping a vehicle" or a verb meaning "to stop a vehicle."

break is a noun meaning either "a rest period" or "a fractured bone or object," or a verb meaning "to separate something(s) into two or more pieces" or "to exceed a record or violate a rule."

Mohammad decided to *brake* suddenly so he didn't *break* the bumper on his car or any of his bones as a result.

can/may

can is a verb meaning "to be able to."

may is a verb meaning "permission to do" or "possible to do."

Since Valery *can* eat anything she wants, she *may* ask you if she *may* have more cookies.

cannot/can not/can't

cannot is the correct spelling of the negative form of "can."

can not is a common misspelling of "cannot."

can't is a contraction for "cannot"; it is less formal and is used mostly in dialogues.

Marisela *cannot* believe her ears whenever her daughter Soroa says, "I *can't* do it, Mom."

capital/capitol

capital is a noun meaning "the location or seat of a government (states and countries)"; the word also can refer to wealth, or an uppercase letter, or the death penalty (capital punishment).

capitol means the actual building where the state or country's government meets.

When Jane visited an elementary school in Washington, D.C., she learned that students had taken a tour of the U.S. *Capitol* building and had also memorized all of the *capital* cities of the United States.

coarse/course

coarse is an adjective meaning "rough" either in texture or attitude.

course is a noun that can mean "a class," "a curriculum," "a direction for a journey," or "one part of a several-part meal."

Lee didn't accept *coarse* language in his workshop. He did let people work with *coarse* material like sandpaper, though.

Ilona took a special *course* on French cooking and learned to make a full five-*course* meal. She now wants to continue on her *course* to receive a full culinary degree.

complement/compliment

complement is a noun meaning "something that completes or coordinates with something else" or a verb meaning "to complete."

compliment is a noun meaning "a positive statement about something or someone" or a verb meaning "to give a positive statement about something or someone."

Craig gave Joan a *compliment* about the way her aqua-colored blouse *complemented* her eyes.

conscious/consciousness/conscience/conscientious

conscious is an adjective meaning "able to feel, think, or be aware."

consciousness is the noun form meaning "awareness" or "knowledge."

conscience is a noun meaning "a person's sense of right or wrong, morals."

conscientious is the adjective form of "conscience" used to describe a person.

Lily had a guilty *conscience* about what she had done, but Shima wasn't even *conscious* of her inappropriate behavior.

Mikhail's acute *consciousness* allowed for him to become a more *conscientious* student.

could have/could've/could of

could have is the helping verb *could*, meaning either "might" or "having the ability to," plus the main verb *have*.

could've is the correct contraction form of "could have" and is used in informal writing only.

could of is a misuse/misspelling of "could have"; do not use it.

Kate decided her students needed a reminder not to use "*could of*" in their papers instead of "*could have*." After class, Marta declared, "I *could've* done without that lesson!"

desert/dessert

> **desert** can be a noun meaning "a dry, arid place, usually with sand and little vegetation"; as a verb, desert means "to leave or abandon."
>
> **dessert** is a noun meaning "the last course in a meal, usually sweet."

> The Mojave *Desert* is probably the most prominently featured *desert* in Hollywood movies. Often, the hero is *deserted*—wounded and horseless—in the *desert* by his enemy.
>
> Bev enjoyed a delicious New York cheesecake as *dessert* after dinner.

> ▶ NOTE   A memory trick to remember how to spell *dessert*: You want *two* helpings of it after dinner. So, remember to include *s* twice when you spell *dessert*.

device/devise

> **device** is a noun that means "an object, mechanical, electric, or electronic, created for a particular purpose."
>
> **devise** is a verb meaning "to create a plan or think up something."

> The spy *devised* a way to escape that involved creating a *device* that would blow up the lock on his cell door.

effect/affect (see **affect/effect**)

either/neither

> **either** can be an adjective or pronoun meaning "one of two people, things, or concepts"; *either* can also be an adverb introducing "the first of two alternatives."
>
> **neither** is the negative version of "either": "not one of . . . "

> Nguyen planned to order *either* a taco or a burrito for lunch but later decided to have *neither*, asking instead for a hamburger.

> ▶ NOTE   If more than two things or people are involved, use *any* instead of *either*—for example, Nguyen wasn't sure she liked *any* of the choices on the menu.

except/accept (see **accept/except**)

explicit/implicit

> **explicit** is an adjective meaning "directly expressed."
>
> **implicit** is an adjective meaning "implied but not directly expressed."

> The rules of board games are usually *explicit*, but the rules of life tend to be *implicit*.

farther/further

farther is an adjective, adverb, or noun meaning "more distance."

further is an adjective or noun meaning "more."

Francisca needed *further* proof that walking improves heart health before she would commit to walking a little bit *farther* every day.

fewer/less

fewer is an adjective or noun meaning "less" and is used only for things that can be counted.

less is an adjective or noun that refers to an "amount" or "specific value or degree." It is used with nouns that cannot be counted.

To diet successfully, it helps to consume *fewer* calories and take in *less* fat.

good/well

good can be an adjective that is used to describe a person or thing in a positive way; *good* can also be a noun meaning "positive."

well is an adverb, noun, or adjective used to describe positive attributes. When used to describe a person, "well" focuses on health or state of being and feelings, while "good" focuses on character or personality.

Sibyl is a *good* person. She is feeling *well* now, after her long bout with pneumonia. She can dance almost as *well* as she used to before her illness.

hanged/hung

Both *hanged* and *hung* are past tense forms of *hang*.

Use **hanged** only as a past-tense of the verb *hang* when referring to an execution.

Use **hung** for all other past-tense forms of "hang."

In the novel, the prisoner was *hanged*, and, afterward, a sign that stated his crimes was *hung* over the gallows.

hear/here

hear is a verb meaning the physiological act of *hearing*.

here is a noun that indicates a physical or symbolic place.

Eduardo, did you *hear* that loud noise? I think it is coming from behind *here*.

▶ **TIP**   Remember that the word "hear" has the word "ear" in it.

hole/whole

hole is a noun that means "an opening."

whole is a noun or an adjective that means "complete."

> Pedro, there must be a *hole* in Napoleon's stomach because I can't believe he ate the *whole* pie.

imply/infer

imply is a verb meaning "to suggest a secondary meaning, to suggest indirectly."

infer is a verb meaning "to deduce, or to draw a conclusion."

> I didn't mean to *imply* that he was stingy, but I did *infer* from his comments that he won't be joining us on the trip.

its/it's

its is a possessive pronoun indicating ownership.

it's is a contraction for the words "it is."

> *It's* a fact that this dog loves *its* bone.

lay/lie

lay is a transitive verb meaning "to put or place." It is followed by a direct object. *Lay* is the present-tense form of the verb. *Laid* is the past-tense form and the past-participle.

lie can be a noun meaning "false statement," but it also can be an intransitive verb meaning "to recline or rest." *Lie* is the present-tense form of the verb. *Lay* is the past-tense form, and *lain* is the past participle.

> The robber *had laid* his gun on the floor of the car, but he grabbed the gun out of the car when the police officer approached. The officer ordered the robber to *lay* down the gun and *lie* on the ground with his hands behind his back. After handcuffing the robber, the officer *laid* the gun in the trunk of his cruiser, while the robber *lay* on the ground. The robber *had lain* there for only a few minutes before back-up arrived.

lead/led

lead has two pronunciations and two meanings: (1) pronounced *led*, it is a noun meaning a "type of metal" and (2) pronounced *leed*, it is a noun or verb meaning to "show the way" or "to make follow."

led (rhymes with *bed*) is a verb and is the past tense form of definition 2 of *lead* above.

David asked Traci to *lead* the way to the kitchen so he could inspect the *lead* pipes, so Traci *led* him there.

loose/lose

loose (pronounced *loohs*, with a final *s* sound) is a noun or adjective meaning "not attached," "roomy, unbinding," or "not exact."

lose (pronounced *loohz*, with a final *z* sound) is a verb meaning "to fail" or "to not be able to keep or to find something."

We knew we would *lose* the match since Iliana managed to *lose* her lucky socks and her confidence the day before the match.

She must have a *loose* interpretation of sports fashion to wear such *loose* shorts.

passed/past

passed is a past tense verb meaning "to go by" or "to have achieved," such as a goal or test.

past is a noun or adjective used with time meaning "in a previous time, not current."

Sophia *passed* Brad on the way to take her last test. Later, she told him that she had *passed* the exam. Now her *past* fears related to passing the test have been laid to rest.

precede/proceed

precede is a verb or adjective meaning "something that comes before."

proceed is a noun or a verb meaning "to go forward" (action).

Winter *precedes* spring, but when spring arrives, we will *proceed* with wearing lighter clothing.

principal/principle

principal is a noun for "the head position of a school" or an adjective meaning "first, most important."

principle is a noun meaning "a basic truth, moral law, or assumption."

Andy always acts on the *principles* he learned from his parents. Because of his good moral sense, he would make a great *principal* for my son's elementary school.

▶ **TIP**   The princi*pal* is the one you hope would be your "pal."

quiet/quit/quite

quiet is a noun, verb, adjective, or adverb meaning "silent, or with little or no sound."

quit is a verb meaning "to stop or give up."

quite is an adverb meaning "very, entirely, completely."

> The crowd suddenly went *quiet* as the band walked onstage. Saito *quit* talking to Dolly and turned toward the stage, and it was all *quite* magical.

raise/rise

raise is a noun or a verb. The noun *raise* means "an increase in salary." The transitive verb *raise* means "to move or lift something up to a higher position."

rise is a noun meaning "an increase," and it is an intransitive verb meaning "to go (or come) up."

> After Val decided to *raise* her expectations and work her hardest, she finally got her *raise*.

> We *rise* at sunrise and hope not to see another *rise* in gas prices.

right/rite/write

right is a noun meaning "a moral," "guaranteed condition," or "the opposite of left"; it can also be an adjective meaning "appropriate" or "correct"; it can even be a verb meaning "to make something correct, fix."

rite is a noun for a "ritual or ceremonial act, literal or symbolic."

write is a verb meaning "the creation of words or symbols on a surface."

> Lisa knew she had the *right* to make the *right* choice for her own life and to set things *right* with Sam, so she made a sharp *right* turn into the next street to go back and talk with him yet again.

> In California, learning to surf is a *rite* of passage for many teens.

> The textbook title *The Write Stuff* is based on a pun—learning to *write* stuff (essays) the *right* way.

than/then

than is a conjunction used for comparison of two or more unequal items.

then is an adverb related to a particular period in time or a conjunction meaning "therefore."

My three-year-old daughter first asked if I was older *than* Grandpa; *then* she asked if I was older *than* Grandma.

that/which/who

See the discussions of restrictive versus nonrestrictive clauses on p. 543 and pronouns on p. 482 for more help on these.

that can function as a relative pronoun that introduces a restrictive clause—a clause that limits or restricts the meaning of the words that are modified. The clause is essential to the meaning of the sentence.

Did you try the new restaurant *that* Will told us about?

which can function as a relative pronoun that introduces a nonrestrictive clause, a clause that is not essential to the meaning of the sentence.

Washington, D.C., *which* is lovely in the fall, is not really a state or a city: It's a district.

who is a relative pronoun used to refer to a person; *who* is used to convey both essential (restrictive) and non-essential (nonrestrictive) information.

Restrictive: Maria is the one *who* knows how to make perfect Mexican wedding cookies from scratch.

Nonrestrictive: Maria, *who* grew up in Mexico, knows how to make perfect Mexican wedding cookies from scratch.

their/there/they're

their is a plural possessive pronoun.

there is a noun, an adverb, or an impersonal pronoun. Use it to indicate a place or direction and as a pronoun to start sentences.

they're is a contraction for the words "they are."

Did Anna and Liz finish *their* paperwork so we can go to lunch?

Do you want to go *there* for lunch? *There* is an excellent lunch menu.

Cindy and Allen are my cousins; *they're* the ones who live in Virginia.

threw/through/thru

threw is the past tense form of the verb "throw."

through is a preposition indicating passage or movement, often from one side to another; and it is also an adverb meaning "finished" or "done."

thru is a common misspelling of "through," and it should not be used in formal writing.

> Heather *threw* the pen to Abby.
>
> Sothera is *through* with love since she has gone *through* the rocky passage of heartbreak too many times.

to/too/two

to is a preposition used to indicate direction or movement.

too is an adverb meaning "also," "in addition," or "very." With the first two usages, it is always preceded by a comma at the end of a sentence or surrounded by parenthetical commas in the middle of a sentence.

two is a noun or adjective used to indicate the number that comes after one and before three.

> Jim went *to* his new classroom.
>
> After Emma and Dominic moved *to* Arizona, Ann and Dale moved there, *too*. Carlene and John were *too* happy to complain about them all coming at once.
>
> It was lucky that Becky, *too*, was able *to* get *two* weeks of vacation during the busiest time of the year.

waist/waste

waist is a noun meaning the middle part of a person's body.

waste can function as a noun or a verb. The noun can refer to a failure to use something wisely; the verb can mean "to squander something."

> Juliette, even though she has had two children, has a tiny *waist*.
>
> It is a *waste* of time to watch television.
>
> I ordered the gift online because I didn't want to *waste* my energy by checking a bunch of different stores.

weather/whether

weather is a noun used to indicate climate conditions.

whether is a conjunctive adverb, similar to "if," used in clauses to indicate conditions.

The *weather* conditions for the Labor Day weekend in Lake Chelan were favorable.

Whether he liked it or not, Josh's parents made him stick with his piano lessons.

were/we're/where

were is a past-tense form of the verb *to be* (the plural form of *was*).

we're is a contraction for the words "we are" or "we were."

where is a noun indicating a direction or a place.

The kindergarteners *were* eager for snack time.

We're ready to serve the milk and cookies now.

Where do you want us to set the cookies?

Home is *where* the heart is.

who/whom

Both *who* and *whom* are used to refer to people. Use **who** as the subject of a sentence (subjective case) and **whom** as the object (objective case). To test whether **who** or **whom** should begin a question, try answering the question by using a personal pronoun.

Who was William Shakespeare? [*He* was a playwright.]

The pronoun "he" is in the subjective case, so "who" is correct.

Whom did you invite to the party? [I invited *him*.]

The pronoun "him" is in the objective case, so "whom" is correct.

▶ **TIP**   Remember the "m" in *whom* like the "m" in *him*.

who's/whose

who's is a contraction for "who is" or "who has," and **whose** is used to indicate possession.

Who's ready to read *Hamlet*? *Whose* book is this?

would have/would of (misuse)

would have is the correct spelling for this verb tense phrase and **would of** is an incorrect usage of the verb tense.

Caroline *would have* been sad if she had missed the concert.

your/you're

your is the second person possessive pronoun.
you're is the contraction for the words "you are."

Did you take *your* medicine yet?

You're not looking too well.

You're welcome.

ACTIVITY 29-3   Commonly Confused Words

Directions: *Underline the correct word for each bracketed choice below.*

I'm not a morning person, and getting ready for school on time used to seem like [a, <u>an</u>] overwhelming challenge. When my alarm clock rang, I usually hit the snooze button and [<u>lay</u>, laid] in bed for another 20 minutes. Especially when I'd gotten less [then, <u>than</u>] six hours of sleep, I needed several cups of coffee just to get going. While drinking my coffee, I'd [waist, <u>waste</u>] time watching news shows on television. Before I knew it, it was almost time to leave, so I'd skip my shower and frantically rummage [threw, <u>through</u>, thru] my drawers to find some clothes. As I ran out the door to catch the bus, I made a wild grab for my books and papers, which never seemed to be where I had [lay, <u>laid</u>, lain] them the previous day. I was always [frightened, <u>afraid</u>] of forgetting something important, and I often did. Since I hadn't showered, I worried all day that I looked [<u>bad</u>, badly] and maybe even smelled [<u>bad</u>, badly], [to, two, <u>too</u>]!

I'm happy to report that I have found a way to [brake, <u>break</u>] these bad habits by following a few simple time management strategies. I try to get [a, <u>an</u>] hour more sleep each night than I used to, which helps reduce brain fog in the morning. Most importantly, I get organized the night before, making sure that I am [already, <u>all ready</u>] for school the following morning. After checking the weather forecast, I [<u>lay</u>, lie] out my clothes and collect my school materials. When everything is properly organized, morning chores no longer seem like such [a, an] heavy burden. I also have found [a, an] use for the kitchen timer in the mornings: When I pour my coffee, I set the timer for 15 minutes so I don't [lose, loose] track of time. When the timer dings, I make myself turn off the television, [whether, weather] I want to or not, and take a shower. Then I have plenty of time to get dressed and catch the bus. I no longer have to run the [hole, whole] way to the bus stop.

It may sound silly, but my entire outlook has changed because of this new morning ritual; [its, it's] enabled me to take charge and feel in control. I [cannot, can not] believe how these time management strategies have [effected, affected] the rest of my life. When I get off to a good start in the morning, I seem to have [fewer, less] problems all day. I only wish that I'd made this change in my morning routine years ago; I could [of, have] spared myself [a lot, alot, allot] of anxiety. Of [course, coarse], my particular time management strategies might not work for everyone, but I think it would be worthwhile for any student to get organized and [device, devise] his or her own morning ritual.

LO 3   TIPS FOR USING A DICTIONARY

A **dictionary** is a reference text (or online version of a reference text) that gives the pronunciation and definitions of words. It is a good idea to buy a comprehensive college dictionary and/or to use an online version. Be sure that your dictionary is no more than five years old and that it features American spellings and usage.

There are also specialized dictionaries available in hard copy and online for particular subjects such as biology, history, or psychology, as well as dictionaries that give a word in one language and then the word in another language, for instance a Spanish–English dictionary (be careful not to depend on these for accurate translations).

During the writing process it is best to postpone using the dictionary until the revision and editing steps. If you are writing your first draft and keep stopping to look up words (for spelling or for word choice), you may lose your train of thought, and the delay may lead to a stall in generating ideas and details. Instead, after you have written at least one full draft, go back and use a dictionary to check your word choices. See if the words you're using are appropriate in terms of their denotations (exact meanings) and connotations (associated meanings), spelling, tone and style, and context.

Anatomy of a Dictionary Entry

A dictionary entry has several parts: the word's pronunciation, part(s) of speech, meaning(s), origin(s) (etymology), related forms, synonyms, and antonyms. Here is an example of a typical dictionary entry from dictionary.com for the word *formidable*.

---

for·mi·da·ble [**fawr**-mi-*duh-buh*l]

–adjective
1. causing fear, apprehension, or dread: *a formidable opponent.*
2. of discouraging or awesome strength, size, difficulty, etc.; intimidating: *a formidable problem.*
3. arousing feelings of awe or admiration because of grandeur, strength, etc.
4. of great strength; forceful; powerful: *formidable opposition to the proposal.*
Use **formidable** in a Sentence
See images of **formidable**
Search **formidable** on the Web

Origin:
1400–50; late ME < F < L *formīdābilis* causing fear, equiv. to *formīd-* (s. of *formīdāre* to fear) + *-ābilis* <u>-able</u>

—Related forms
for·mi·da·ble·ness, for·mi·da·bil·i·ty, *noun*
for·mi·da·bly, *adverb*
non·for·mi·da·bil·i·ty, *noun*

—Can be confused: <u>formative</u>, *formidable.*

—Synonyms
1. dreadful, appalling, threatening, menacing, fearful, frightful, horrible.

—Antonyms
1. pleasant.

TIPS FOR USING A THESAURUS

A **thesaurus** is a text that provides **synonyms** (words that have very similar meanings) and sometimes **antonyms** (words that have opposite meanings). You can buy a hard copy or use an online version.

When revising your writing, you may find that you have used certain words too often in your essay or that you need a better, more precise, or just more interesting word than the one you have used. At those times, a thesaurus can be a great help.

When using a thesaurus, you have to be particularly careful to check the connotations (associated meanings or more subtle meanings) of a word to make sure you have used the *best* word for your intended meaning. It's a good idea to use a dictionary in tandem with a thesaurus to check the synonyms listed and make sure the one you choose has the right meaning.

Anatomy of a Thesaurus Entry

A thesaurus entry lists the word in bold, names its part of speech, and then lists its synonyms and sometimes its antonyms. Here is an example of a typical thesaurus entry:

Main Entry:	formidable
Part of Speech:	*adjective*
Definition:	horrible, terrifying
Synonyms:	appalling, awful, dangerous, daunting, dire, dismaying, dreadful, fearful, fierce, frightful, horrific, imposing, impregnable, intimidating, menacing, redoubtable, shocking, terrible, terrific, threatening
Antonyms:	feeble, friendly, harmless, nice, pleasant, powerless, weak
Main Entry:	formidable
Part of Speech:	*adjective*
Definition:	difficult, overwhelming
Synonyms:	all-powerful, arduous, awesome, challenging, colossal, dismaying, effortful, great, hard, impressive, indomitable, intimidating, labored, laborious, mammoth, mighty, murder*, onerous, overpowering, powerful, puissant, rough go, rough*, staggering, strenuous, tall order, toilsome, tough proposition, tough*, tremendous, uphill
Antonyms:	easy, not hard, pleasant, trivial

* = informal/non-formal usage from *Thesaurus.com*

Sometimes a thesaurus will list words that are not clear synonyms or antonyms of the target word but have related or contrasting meanings. If you are not sure how to interpret an entry, make sure to check the key provided in the thesaurus.

A thesaurus can come in very handy when you are writing your essay draft and several of the same words come up again and again. For instance, consider the following synonyms for the word "said":

acknowledged	disclosed	proclaimed
added	divulged	professed
addressed	droned	ranted
admitted	elaborated	reassured
advised	emphasized	refuted
advocated	entreated	related
affirmed	exclaimed	repeated
agreed	explained	replied
alleged	exposed	responded
announced	expressed	resumed
answered	indicated	retorted
argued	inferred	returned
asserted	implied	reveal
assured	instructed	snapped
attested	lectured	sneered
avowed	maintained	solicited
began	mentioned	specified
called	moaned	spoke
claimed	mumbled	stated
commented	murmured	stressed
complained	muttered	suggested
confided	narrated	thought
cried	noted	threatened
debated	objected	told
decided	observed	urged
declared	petitioned	uttered
denounced	pleaded	vowed
described	pled	whispered
dictated	pointed out	yelled
directed	predicted	

Each of these words imparts a particular connotation for *how* a person *said* something.

ACTIVITY 29-4   Using Synonyms

Directions: *Fill in each blank using the most appropriate synonym for* said *listed above.* *Answers will vary. Sample answers are provided.*

1. "It's not like stealing," ___argued___ Karen. "That $100 bill was just lying on the sidewalk outside the bank."

2. "You're right," Jim _____agreed_____. "It's not wrong to take money you find in a public place."

3. "But it's still not our money," _____objected_____ Rodney. "It might belong to someone who really needs it."

4. "That's true," _acknowledged_ Jim, "but we don't know who that person is, so there's no way to return the money. Let's just take it and get out of here."

5. "Hold on a minute," _____urged_____ Rodney. "The person who dropped the bill probably uses this bank. We could give the money to a bank official, and maybe the person would check back to see if anyone found the bill."

ACTIVITY 29-5   **Using a Dictionary and a Thesaurus in Combination**

Directions: *First use a thesaurus to look for an alternative word for each of the words listed below. Then, use a dictionary to provide the meaning for the new word you chose. Write your findings in the spaces provided.* *Answers will vary.*

1. **Eliminate**

   Thesaurus word you chose: _____

   Dictionary meaning: _____

   _____

   _____

2. **Reinforce**

   Thesaurus word you chose: _____

   Dictionary meaning: _____

   _____

   _____

3. **Ludicrous**

   Thesaurus word you chose: _____

   Dictionary meaning: _____

   _____

   _____

4. **Good**

Thesaurus word you chose: _____

Dictionary meaning: _____

_____

_____

5. **Difficult**

Thesaurus word you chose: _____

Dictionary meaning: _____

_____

_____

6. **Superstition**

Thesaurus word you chose: _____

Dictionary meaning: _____

_____

_____

7. **Intention**

Thesaurus word you chose: _____

Dictionary meaning: _____

_____

_____

8. **Optional**

Thesaurus word you chose: _____

Dictionary meaning: _____

_____

_____

9. **Temporary**

Thesaurus word you chose: _____

Dictionary meaning: _____

_____

_____

10. **Control**

Thesaurus word you chose: _____

Dictionary meaning: _____

_____

_____

LO 4   CAPITALIZATION

Capital letters are used for the first word of a sentence, of course, but there are other basic rules for capitalization that you should know.

Capitalization Basics

The basic rule is that capital letters are needed when you are using a specific name or label. So, if a word describes a general object or category, the initial letter of the word is not capitalized, but if the word describes a specific person, place, or thing—one particular, named object—the initial letter is capitalized. Therefore, common nouns are not capitalized, and proper nouns are capitalized. (For a review of nouns, see p. 481.)

Here are some general categories of words that need to be capitalized.

1. **Capitalize the first word of a sentence and the first word of a sentence used in a direct quotation.**

> In *The Waste Land*, T. S. Eliot described April as the cruelest month.
>
> Edna St. Vincent Millay said, "April comes like an idiot, babbling and strewing flowers."

- *Do not capitalize* the first word of the second part of an interrupted or continuing quotation: "April," said Edna St. Vincent Millay, "comes like an idiot, babbling and strewing flowers."

2. **Capitalize the pronoun *I* and the names of specific people.**

> Here are some famous people I'd love to meet: Toni Morrison, Jimmy Page, Mae C. Jemison, Bill Gates, Sandra Day O'Connor, and Stephen Hawking.

3. **Capitalize the names of nationalities, cultural or ethnic groups, and languages.**

> Cambodian, Italian, Canadian, Mexican American, Nigerian, Hebrew, Asian American, Swahili, Japanese, Portuguese, African American, Greek, Russian

If a prefix comes in front of a word that is usually capitalized, keep the formal name capitalized: *un-American, anti-American,* and so on.

4. Capitalize formal and informal titles for specific persons or positions.

> Chancellor Merkel, Uncle Robert, Senator Feinstein, United Nations Secretary-General Ban Ki-moon

- *Do not capitalize* a title if it follows a proper name—Angela Merkel, chancellor; Robert, my uncle; Dianne Feinstein, senator.
- *Do not capitalize* nouns that refer to family relationships—for example, mother, father, mom, dad, grandfather, grandmother, aunt, and uncle—unless they are being used as proper names:

> My *grandfather* was a real character. He used to play tricks on *Grandmother* to make her laugh. My *father* was their only child. I love to hear *Dad* tell stories about his childhood. I also love the story of how my mom and dad met. He says it was love at first sight, but *Mom* said it took awhile. My *mother's* sister, *Aunt Rose*, claims my *mother* had a crush on my *father* before he even noticed her. My *uncle*, Ed, says it took months for *Dad* to get up his courage to ask her out.

5. Capitalize names of specific places (including continents, countries, regions, states, counties, cities, parks, and streets).

> Antarctica, Europe, Ghana, Brazil, the Middle East, New England, North Dakota, Oregon, Boone County, Hong Kong, Seville, Tampa, Forest Park, Hollywood Boulevard, Bourbon Street

6. Capitalize the names of days, months, and holidays.

> Tuesday, August, Thanksgiving, Valentine's Day, Memorial Day, Mother's Day, Veterans Day, Presidents Day

- In general, *do not* capitalize the seasons (summer, winter, spring, and fall). However, if they are part of a specific event or title, they are capitalized: *Spring Fling, Winter Festival,* and so on.

7. **Capitalize the names of religions, religious titles used for specific individuals, holy texts, and holy days.**

> Buddhism/Buddhists, Christianity/Christians, Hinduism/Hindus, Islam/Muslims, Judaism/Jews, Taoism/Taoists, the Dalai Lama, Father Morris, Reverend Adams, Rabbi Hirshfeld, Tipitaka, Bible, New Testament, Rig Veda, Qur'an, Talmud, Tao-te-Ching, Easter, Ramadan, Yom Kippur

8. **Capitalize the names of specific organizations (including businesses, government institutions, political groups, and academic or cultural institutions).**

> General Motors, Whole Foods, Cub Scouts, Boys and Girls Clubs of America, National Endowment for the Humanities (NEH), Democratic Party, Republican Party, Amnesty International, Parent Teacher Association (PTA), Association of Higher Education, Library of Congress

Capitalize abbreviations (or acronyms) for companies, institutions, and organizations: NBC, AARP, NATO, FDA, UPS, and so on (see Abbreviations later in this chapter for more examples).

9. **Capitalize the names of historical periods, events, or historical documents and holy texts.**

> Iron Age, Italian Renaissance, Industrial Revolution, Age of Enlightenment, First World War, Cold War, Battle of Waterloo, Reformation, Fall of Constantinople, Norman Invasion, Treaty of Versailles, New Deal, Code of Hammurabi, Emancipation Proclamation, Gutenberg Bible, Bill of Rights

- Do not capitalize *centuries*: the seventeenth century and so on.
- *Lord* and *God* are usually capitalized and so are pronouns that go with particular supreme beings: the *Lord* and *His* teachings, the *Goddess* and *Her* ways.

10. **Capitalize the names of monuments, buildings, and famous objects.**

> Eiffel Tower, St. Louis Arch, Stonehenge, Empire State Building, Taj Mahal, Alhambra, Rockbridge High School, Crown Jewels

- *High school, middle school,* and *elementary school* are not capitalized if they are not part of the name of a specific school.

> Next year my brother will be a senior at Rockbridge *High School*. The year after next, he will graduate from *high school*.

11. Capitalize the names of specific brands or trademarks.

> Levi's, Mercedes-Benz, Dunkin' Donuts, Betty Crocker, Black & Decker, Disneyland, Apple Inc., Google

12. Capitalize the titles of books, magazines, articles, stories, poems, plays, films, TV shows, albums, CDs, songs, and works of art.

In titles, capitalize the first and last word and all significant words in between except articles (*the*, *a*, and *an*) and prepositions (*of*, *in*, *on*, and so on):

> *The Brief Wondrous Life of Oscar Wao*, *US Weekly*, "Three Quick and Easy Meals," "The Tell-Tale Heart," "The Road Not Taken," *Streetcar Named Desire*, *Avatar*, *Survivor*, *Led Zeppelin IV*, "We Are the World," *The Scream*

ACTIVITY 29-6   Capitalization Practice

Directions: *Underline the letters in the following paragraph that should be capitalized. Refer to the rules above for help.*

Every summer our family attends the fourth of july celebration organized by the local branch of veterans of foreign wars (vfw). It is the most popular celebration in springfield county, and people from many small towns come to enjoy the food, the music, and the fireworks. The greenfield high school athletic field provides ample space and parking for the festivities.

The celebration opens with a few short speeches by local citizens. One year a high school principal, ms. higuchi, spoke about her parents. As asian immigrants to the united states, principal higuchi's mother and father cherished the freedoms of their adopted country and inspired their daughter to follow her dreams. Another year one of our neighbors, a former hippie who has an american flag painted on his volkswagon van, spoke about the importance of free speech. He pointed out that it is not un-american to disagree with government policies, as diversity of opinion strengthens, rather than undermines, democracy. Last year, professor ashley jackson, a professor of history at a local college, gave a short presentation about the history and symbolism of the liberty bell.

This year, the president of the springfield historical society, who was dressed in an eighteenth-century costume, kicked off the celebration by reading aloud quotations from heroes of the american revolution. He ended by quoting benjamin franklin, who said, "without freedom of thought there can be no such thing as wisdom; and no such thing as liberty without freedom of speech." Then a popular local singer, who performed on the television show american idol, led the crowd in a stirring rendition of the song "god bless america."

NUMBERS

Rules for using the correct format for numbers vary according to context. The following standards will work for most academic writing.

1. Spell out numbers zero through ten and numbers that can be written using one or two words.

> At the bakery, we had to choose among ten different kinds of cookies and eight kinds of cake.
>
> So far, twelve hundred citizens have signed the petition.

> ▶ **NOTE**   For business or technical writing, use numbers for all numerals ten and above.

2. Spell out numbers that begin a sentence, no matter how large the number.

If possible, however, revise the sentence so you don't need to start with a number. Make sure to use commas correctly in numbers over one thousand.

> Twenty-seven hundred and fifty fans clapped and cheered loudly when the band came onstage.
>
> When the band came onstage, 2,750 fans clapped and cheered loudly.

3. For extremely large numbers, use a combination of figures and words.

> The national debt now stands at $12.4 trillion.

However, if it is not a round number, you'll have to use all figures.

If the national debt were divided equally among U.S. citizens, each person's share would be $40,315.65.

4. Use figures for dates, years, and times.

July 6, 2002, 11:25 A.M.

5. Use figures in addresses.

The White House, 1600 Pennsylvania Avenue NW, Washington, D.C. 20500

6. Use figures for exact measurements and specific identifications.

The General Sherman Tree in Sequoia National Park is 274 feet tall; at the base of the tree, the trunk is 36 feet wide.

The football player is 6'5" tall and weighs 265 pounds.

Tonight we're staying in room 274 at the Holiday Inn on Interstate 91.

The Channel 22 meteorologist predicts a foot of snow for our area.

I have to finish reading Chapter 12 of the textbook because there may be a pop quiz tomorrow.

Please turn to page 74, and read Act 3, Scene 2 of the play.

For homemade salad dressing, use a 1:3 ratio of oil to vinegar—for example, 1/4 cup oil and 3/4 cup vinegar.

Nearly 65 percent of people polled say that the governor is doing a good job.

Because of the two A's I earned last semester, I now have a 3.7 GPA.

The icy roads remained treacherous, as the temperature hovered around 32°F.

The job has a 40-hour workweek but sometimes requires overtime.

ACTIVITY 29-7   **Numbers Practice**

Directions: *Correct the errors in numbers usage in the following sentences. Underline the error(s) in each sentence, and then write the correct form(s) in the space provided. If the sentence has no errors in numbers usage, write "correct."*

1. The novel—a fantasy story about a boy wizard—has sold more than four hundred million copies worldwide, making the previously unpublished author a billionaire.

    400 million

2. Initially rejected by many publishers, the novel eventually earned the author an advance of two thousand five hundred dollars.

    $2,500

3. Targeted for children nine or ten years of age, the book soon became popular with readers of all ages.

    Correct

4. In the years that followed, the author wrote six more books about the boy wizard; the final book was released on the twenty-seventh of July in 2009.

    July 27, 2009

5. 6,000,000 copies of the sixth book in the series were sold in the United States within the first twenty-four hours of its release.

    Six million, 24

6. The largest U.S. book retailer reported that the last book in the series broke the record for pre-orders, as more than five hundred thousand copies were preordered.

    500 thousand

7. The address of the U.S. publisher of the books is five hundred East Broadway, New York, NY 10012.

    500

8. The books can be challenging for young readers; one book in the series is seven hundred sixty-six pages in length.

    766

9. In chapter nine of the last book, on page five hundred, a central mystery of the plot is finally solved.

    9, 500

10. The author has given several live television interviews, most recently on Channel ten, when she spoke at length about her creative process.

    10

LO 4   ABBREVIATIONS

Although abbreviations are common in casual writing, they are less acceptable in academic writing. These are the most commonly accepted categories of abbreviations.

1. **Titles or Academic Degrees**
   - **Mr./Mrs./Ms.** These abbreviations are acceptable when used as titles before a person's last name.
   - **Academic Titles/Degrees.** Abbreviated academic titles and/or degrees are used *after* a person's name:

> B.A. (Bachelor of Arts), M.A. (Master of Arts), B.S. (Bachelor of Science), M.F.A. (Master of Fine Arts), Ph.D. (Doctor of Philosophy), R.N. (Registered Nurse), M.D. (Doctor of Medicine), C.P.A (Certified Public Accountant)
>
> W. E. B. DuBois, Ph.D.; Shan Shan Sheng, M.F.A.; Christiaan Barnard, M.D.

> ▶ **NOTE**   The title *Professor* is usually spelled out: Professor George C. Gross.

   - **Government/Military/Religious Titles.** Abbreviate governmental, military, and religious titles when they are used *in front* of someone's complete name. If only a person's last name is given, then use his or her full title.

> Sen. Daniel Inoue of Hawaii has served eight terms in the U.S. Senate. Senator Inoue serves as Chairman of the U.S. Senate Committee on Appropriations.
>
> Rev. Martin Luther King, Jr. said: "Nonviolence is a powerful and just weapon." Reverend King went on to describe nonviolence as "a sword that heals."

2. **Countries, States, or Cities**
   - **States/Countries/Cities.** In addresses, abbreviate the state and country. In sentences, spell out the names of cities and states.

> Johnson Space Center, 2101 NASA Parkway, Houston, TX 77058 U.S.A. Astronauts are trained at the Johnson Space Center in Houston, Texas.

▶ **NOTE**   Abbreviate United States only when used in an address or used as an adjective.

> In the United States, astronauts are trained at the Johnson Space Center.
>
> NASA, the National Aeronautics and Space Administration, manages the U.S. Space Program.

3. Common Acronyms

Acronyms are composed of the first letter of each word of a name that includes two or more words. Acronyms designating agencies, businesses, or institutions are commonly used in writing and speech. These types of acronyms do not require periods between the letters.

> AAA (American Automobile Association), AP (Associated Press), ASAP (As Soon As Possible), CEO (Chief Executive Officer), CIA (Central Intelligence Agency), CPR (Cardiopulmonary Resuscitation), DOD (Department of Defense), EST (Eastern Standard Time), FDA (Federal Drug Administration), FTE (Full-Time Equivalent), GPS (Global Positioning System), HDTV (High-Definition Television), HMO (Health Maintenance Organization), IT (Information Technology), IV (Intravenous), MADD (Mothers Against Drunk Driving), NASA (National Aeronautics and Space Administration), NPR (National Public Radio), NRA (National Rifle Association), PIN (Personal Identification Number), RAM (Random Access Memory), TDD (Telecommunication Device for the Deaf), VA (Veterans Administration)

Use these abbreviations when using the following terms with **numbers:** A.M. or a.m. (ante meridian), P.M. or p.m. (post meridian), and MPH or mph (miles per hour).

4. Latin Expressions

> The following Latin terms are abbreviated only when they appear inside parentheses: c. or ca. (approximately), cf. (compare), e.g. (for example), etc. (and so forth), et al. (and all others), i.e. (that is), re. (concerning), and vs. or v. (versus).

> The Great Pyramid (completed c. 2580 BCE) is the largest of the pyramids.
>
> Perennial flowers (e.g., iris, peonies, and daylilies) bloom again each spring.
>
> In the winter, outdoor activities (sledding, skiing, ice skating, etc.) can combat cabin fever and chase away the blues.

In the main body of a sentence, use complete words and/or their English equivalents.

> Many items are on sale now: clothes, linens, kitchenware, furniture, and more.

5. Documentation Formats (such as MLA or APA)

The following abbreviations are commonly used in documenting sources using MLA, APA, or other styles. (See Chapter 19 for specific MLA documentation information.)

> vol. for "volume," vols. for "volumes," trans. for "translator" or "translated by"

ACTIVITY 29-8   Abbreviation Practice

Directions: *Underline the correct word(s) or abbreviation for each bracketed choice. Refer to the rules above for help.*

1. [Reverend, Rev.] Adam Clayton Powell, Jr., an influential civil rights leader during the 1930s, was elected to the [United States, U.S.] House of Representatives in 1944.

2. *Masterpiece Classic*, a popular [Public Broadcasting Service, PBS] television show, often features dramatizations of Jane Austen novels.

3. Women's Medical College was founded in 1867 by Elizabeth Blackwell, [Medical Doctor, M.D.].

4. High-protein plant-based foods—[for example, e.g.,] legumes, tofu, and other soy products—play an essential role in a healthy vegan diet.

5. Barbery, Muriel. *The Elegance of the Hedgehog.* [Translated by, Trans.] Alison Anderson. New York, NY: Europa Editions, Inc., 2008.

Active Spelling

You need to be active in your spelling choices:

- **Use a dictionary.** If you are not sure how a word is spelled, use the spelling tips in this chapter and/or consult a dictionary.
- **Beware of homophones.** If the word you are using is a homophone (a word that sounds like another word) check that you have used the correct spelling so that readers will know what you mean. Consult a dictionary or the list of commonly confused words in this chapter to be sure.
- **Keep a list of your most common spelling errors.** Be aware of the spelling errors you most commonly make (keep a list of corrections received from instructors), and check for them when you proofread your writing.
- **Use spell-check.** Use the spell-check feature on your computer. Remember: If a word is *spelled correctly* but *used incorrectly,* spell-check will not indicate this.

To check your progress in meeting this chapter's objectives, log in to www.mywritinglab. com, go to the **Study Plan** tab, click on **Handbook of Grammar, Mechanics, and Style** and choose **Spelling, Easily Confused Words, Capitalization,** and **Abbreviations and Numbers** from the list of subtopics. Read and view the resources in the **Review Materials** section, and then complete the **Recall, Apply,** and **Write** sets in the **Activities** section.

Tone, Style, Word Choice, and Usage

'Word up homey.'

THINKING CRITICALLY

Look at the cartoon above. Word choice has a powerful effect on how readers understand ideas in writing. How do the word choices for the graffiti on the right differ from those on the left, and what makes this funny?

_____

_____

_____

_____

Continued ▶

_____

_____

_____

_____

When you write, you should choose your words wisely, use the right tone for your audience, and be careful to avoid usage mistakes.

LO 1 THINKING CRITICALLY ABOUT TONE AND STYLE

Tone and style are important elements in writing essays. Tone and style together create your writing "voice." **Tone** reflects your manner or attitude, and **style** includes the choices you make about language, diction, and sentence structure. The way you employ these elements helps establish your voice in writing. Writing styles can be as distinct as fingerprints. In fact, some teachers say that after a few weeks of class, students could turn in their essays without names on them, and the teachers would be able to figure out who wrote each paper on the basis of the distinctive voices evident in each of the essays.

The tone and style choices you make affect the way a reader hears or responds to your ideas and the credibility and effectiveness of your ideas. Some writers create style, tone, and voice patterns in their essays unconsciously; they don't think about the distinctive voice they have created through their choices. However, it's important to become aware of these choices and *evaluate critically* whether these are the best choices for your assignment and audience.

When deciding on a particular tone for an assignment, remember that the tone you use reflects your attitude toward the subject and the arguments you are making. Also, be sure to think about your audience when choosing the most effective and appropriate tone for your essay. Your tone may be formal, serious, informal, playful, mocking, sarcastic, or impartial and detached.

Emailing, Texting, and Audience

Also, when you are composing a work- or school-related email, do not use the kind of language or spelling you would use while texting a friend. For example, when you email a friend, you will most likely use a casual, informal tone and word choices (maybe even texting style shortcuts such as "cuz" or "B4." However, when you email your instructor, your tone should be more formal, polite, and respectful (yes, even in an email).

APPLYING CRITICAL THINKING

PURPOSE   IDEAS   SUPPORT   ASSUMPTIONS BIASES   CONCLUSIONS   POINT OF VIEW   ANALYSIS

Consider the following questions before you begin writing, and then make conscious choices about tone and language as you write your drafts:

1. What is my topic, and what kind of tone would be most appropriate for the subject matter, **ideas**, and arguments that I want to make?

2. What attitude do I want to portray in this essay (for example, serious/formal, playful/informal, sarcastic/mocking, and so on)?

3. Who is my intended audience? What tone would be most effective for getting my message across to my intended audience?

4. What is my **purpose** in this essay? What tone and style choices would be most effective for the messages and arguments I want to convey?

As you revise your essay draft, check again to make sure that the style and tone of your writing are appropriate and are the most effective choices for your topic, your audience, and your arguments and conclusions. For instance, a formal research paper on breast cancer would require a serious tone. However, a personal narrative essay about your first time snowboarding might be more casual and informal.

Here is an example of inappropriate tone in an academic paper that evaluates Diane Ackerman's essay "Chocolate Equals Love":

> Diane's essay talked about how awesome chocolate is.

Revised:

> Diane Ackerman's essay "Chocolate Equals Love" explores the benefits, the pleasures, and the history of chocolate.

Formal Style and Tone Versus Academese

Even when you are writing a more formal academic paper, avoid **academese**: writing that uses pompous multisyllabic words and unnecessarily complicated sentence structures. Academese is filled with passive voice constructions (see pages 608–609 for more on passive construction) and contains overly complex language or jargon. Here is an example:

> Facilitation of the deliberations of the collaborative, strategic-planning body was assumed by individuals possessing requisite levels of professional expertise and relevant experience.

Translation into a more reasonable tone and style:

> Senior staff led the meetings of the planning committee.

The bottom line is that academese doesn't make you sound smarter if your readers don't understand what you are trying to say—and sometimes even when they do. Successful writing communicates ideas clearly. Strengthen your tone and style by consciously choosing the best voice and language for your arguments and your intended audience.

> ▶ **NOTE**   Using a complex word in and of itself is not a bad idea. Just be sure that the word you choose is the best one to convey your intended meaning and that, overall, the passage is not too complex for your intended audience. See the vocabulary-building section on p. 675 for more on using complex words and expanding your vocabulary.

Doublespeak, a kind of language that deliberately distorts or disguises meaning, can be similar to academese. Doublespeak typically contains *euphemisms*, deliberately vague or indirect words used in place of words that might be considered overly direct, unpleasant, or offensive. For example:

> **Corporate downsizing and outsourcing have resulted in job flexibility or termination.** (Employees have been fired or have lost their job security because the management is restructuring the business or using cheaper labor.)

> **The mission to neutralize the target resulted in some collateral damage.** (A government operation to kill an enemy agent caused unintended deaths or injuries of innocent bystanders.)

ACTIVITY 30-1   Tone

Directions: *The following sentences are from a letter to the editor of a campus newspaper. Rewrite each sentence to change the overly informal tone to a tone that is more appropriate for an academic paper.* Answers will vary. Sample answers are provided.

1. The college library is all run-down and looks really, really bad.

   The college library building is in a serious state of disrepair.

2. In the lobby, the rug is all raggedy, and the dim lights are annoying.

   In the lobby, the carpet is threadbare, and the lighting is poor.

3. Those armchairs on the first floor, where people hang out and read, are dirty and ratty and broken down.

   The upholstered chairs in the first-floor reading area are stained, frayed,

   and sagging.

4. The bathrooms are disgusting, and they're always out of paper towels and stuff.

   The restrooms are poorly maintained and often lack paper towels and

   other supplies.

5. The college has to have a library, but this place is the pits.

   The library is important, but the current state of the building sends the

   opposite message.

ACTIVITY 30-2   Revising to Eliminate Academese

Directions: *Read the following paragraph about methods for coping with the stresses of a new job. In the space provided, rewrite the paragraph to eliminate academese and make the passage readable for a general audience. You may need to look up some of the words in a dictionary in order to translate them.* Answers will vary. Sample revisions are provided.

Visualization of successful workplace performance is a prerequisite for actualization of professional goals. Systematic analysis of the relative urgency of work-related tasks is necessary for the development of an effective strategy for fulfilling professional obligations in a timely manner. An incremental approach is recommended for assignments characterized by significant breadth or complexity. For documents that are deemed critical for the implementation of a given project, it is considered prudent to make appropriate arrangements for duplication of such documentation. Avoidance of lapses in punctuality is achieved through strict compliance with contractually specified arrival times.

Picture yourself succeeding in your job, and you will. Set priorities, and do the most important things first. Break large tasks into small steps. Make copies of important documents. Get to work on time.

LO2 WORD CHOICE

Word choice, sometimes referred to as **diction**, is exactly that: You make a conscious *choice* when you are selecting each word. Pick the best word for the idea you are expressing based on the content of the sentence and where the word will appear. Think about your intended audience as you choose your words. Will you need a formal word or an informal word? Will you need to use language that a general audience can understand, or should you use discipline-specific terms for a specialized audience? Is your tone academic or more casual? How should that affect your word choices? For example:

> **Intended audience:** Local school board
>
> **Inappropriate diction:** The school board is crazy to even think about cutting art classes. There are lots of better ways to solve our money problems.
>
> **Revised:** I urge the school board to preserve the arts program and to seek alternative strategies for balancing the budget.

Many words have both literal and implied meanings. Primary, or literal, meanings are called **denotations**, and secondary, or implied, meanings are called **connotations**. Think of the denotation of a word as the exact, or surface, meaning of a word; think of connotations as the "baggage," or associations that come with that word. The denotation of a word is like the tip of an iceberg that shows above the surface of the water, and the connotations, which often impart the most meaning, are the base of the iceberg under the water's surface. Some words have very few connotations, while others are rich with connotative associations. For instance, consider the following two signs:

Which language is more effective? Both signs advertise a residence for sale, but *house* is a more denotative word while *home* is full of connotations. *Home* is where the heart is; it's apple pie, Mom, comfort, and everything we associate with the bigger concept of *home*. So, make word choices carefully in order to get the maximum effect, and be sure the words you choose are conveying (both on the surface and more subtly) exactly what you mean to say.

Choose the language that achieves clarity and accuracy in both your sentence and your overall essay. When you use effective diction, your ideas are communicated successfully.

Slang

Slang is casual language consisting of informal words that are not listed as "real" words in the dictionary (though they might be listed as slang). The old saying "*Ain't* ain't a word 'cause it ain't in the dictionary" is partially true: It isn't a real word, but it is listed in most dictionaries—as slang. It's fine to use slang in casual social speech or emails between friends or even in dialogue in narration essays. However, in most cases in essay writing, you should convert slang into more conventional word choices.

> **Slang:** The author's first novel was a bust, and the critics were cold, but her next novel was kickin, and the critics were blown away.
>
> **Revised:** The author's first novel was unsuccessful, and the critics judged it harshly, but her next novel was excellent, and the critics were impressed.
>
> **Slang:** At the beginning of the story, the guy is all hung up on this hottie, but he majorly blows it, and she tells him to hit the road.
>
> **Revised:** At the beginning of the story, the character is in love with a beautiful woman, but he makes a serious mistake, and she ends the relationship.

Jargon

Jargon is the language used in a specific field. Jargon has its place, and if one is writing for an audience familiar with the jargon of that field, then it's fine to use it. Otherwise, it needs to be translated into more general language. For instance, if you worked in a computer repair store, you could leave a list of instructions for your coworkers that would be filled with jargon that they would understand but a new computer owner would not.

> **Jargon:** The search engine allowed him to download jpegs loaded with megapixels onto his hard drive.

> **Revised:** The Internet search engine he used allowed him to save extremely large picture files onto his computer.

Dialect

Dialect is language that reflects the speech (word choice and accent) of a certain region or culture. Dialect can reflect a specific region of a country such as a Southern dialect in the United States, or it can reflect a particular economic group or cultural heritage.

> **Dialect:** I reckon the dogs are fussin' at a critter down yonder.
>
> **Revised:** I think the dogs are barking at some animal over there.

Although you would not use dialect in an academic paper, it would certainly be appropriate to use it in dialogue to communicate information about a person or character speaking.

Foreign Words

Foreign words that are used without a specific purpose can be confusing. If you decide to use a foreign term in your sentence, be sure it is one your intended audience will recognize. Otherwise, use the English version of the term, or define it in parentheses:

> **Foreign term:** When he saw her reaction to his remark, he realized he had made a *faux pas*.
>
> **Revised:** When he saw her reaction to his remark, he realized he had made a *social blunder*.
>
> **With definition:** When he saw her reaction to his remark, he realized he had made a *faux pas* (*social blunder*).

There are times when it is appropriate to use slang, dialect, technical jargon, and foreign words in dialogue or in direct quotations, but in general, you should not use them in formal academic writing.

ACTIVITY 30-3   Slang, Dialect, Foreign Words, and Tone

Directions: *Read the following paragraph from a student's essay entitled "A Day in the Life." In the space provided, rewrite the paragraph so it has a more appropriate tone and more appropriate word choices for a general audience. Make* *sure to eliminate slang and translate foreign words. If necessary, consult a dictionary or online resources.* Answers will vary. Sample revision is provided.

Last week I was working and studying 24/7. Plus my computer went all wonky, and I had to pull an all-nighter to finish my research paper. So on Saturday I called my homie Victor to blow off steam. He agreed it was wack that I never get to just zone out and catch some z's. We decided to go shoot hoops and pump iron at the gym. Afterward, we went to his crib and spent the afternoon hanging out and playing video games. It felt good to chill. We nuked some popcorn, but I was still starving, so I asked Victor if I could get more eats. He said "mi casa es tu casa," so I raided his frig and made a sick sandwich that put me in a food coma. It was a sweet day.

I had to spend most of my time working and studying last week. My computer was not operating properly, and I had to work all night to finish my research paper. So, on Saturday, I called my friend Victor to complain. He agreed it was too bad that I hadn't had any time to relax or sleep. We decided to play basketball and lift weights at the gym. Afterward, we spent the afternoon at his apartment, relaxing and playing video games. It felt good to take it easy. We prepared some popcorn in the microwave, but I was still very hungry, so I asked Victor if I could have more to eat. He said, "My house is your house," so I got some food from his refrigerator and made a great sandwich. I was so full I could scarcely move. It was a wonderful day.

Clichés

Clichés are expressions that have been used so often they have become stale and no longer communicate their intended meanings. Originally, they effectively conveyed powerful images or ideas to readers, but through repeated use, they have lost their effectiveness, no longer conjuring any images or ideas.

Most clichés are metaphors or similes. **Similes** make implied or direct comparisons between two similar things in order to convey an idea. **Metaphors** are implied comparisons to other things.

Emily Dickinson wrote, "'Hope' is the thing with feathers—/That perches in the soul."

In the above example, the metaphor implicitly compares "hope" to a "bird."

Similes are comparisons that use the specific words *like* or *as:*

> Anna Akhmatova wrote, "Summer's ardent rustling / Is like a festival outside my window."

This simile uses *like* to compare the rustling of summer leaves to the sounds of a festival.

> In "Names of Horses," Donald Hall describes how a horse's neck "rubbed the window sill / Of the stall, smoothing the wood *as* the sea smooths glass."

This simile uses *as* to compare the repetitive action of the horse's neck to the repetitive action of ocean currents; the simile also compares the smoothness of the wooden sill to the smoothness of sea glass.

Often, famous metaphors and similes from literature pop up in student writing. However, many of these similes have lost their effect over time and should be avoided. Instead, create a fresh comparison of your own. Who knows, maybe it will be so good that everyone will want to use it, and it, too, will become a cliché one day. Here are some of the most overused clichés:

> I've been *busy as a bee* preparing for the party.
>
> For a moment, he didn't respond to the insult, but it was the *calm before the storm.*
>
> She never gets stage fright; she's always *cool as a cucumber.*
>
> My grandmother exercises every day, so she's *fit as a fiddle.*
>
> After his girlfriend broke up with him, he was *sadder but wiser.*
>
> Wearing old jeans, he *stuck out like a sore thumb* at the fancy reception.
>
> Sitting close to the cozy fire, I was *snug as a bug in a rug.*
>
> He describes his volunteer work at the shelter as a *labor of love.*
>
> She reached down to pick up her briefcase, but it had *vanished into thin air.*
>
> I checked once again to make sure I had my car keys: *better safe than sorry!*
>
> The high school reunion was a real *trip down memory lane.*
>
> As a lawyer, she's *tough as nails* and *drives a hard bargain.*
>
> The plant he had forgotten to water was *dead as a doornail.*
>
> My husband *slept like a log,* but I *didn't sleep a wink.*

In the revision stage of your writing process, check to make sure that clichés haven't crept into your writing—they can get in automatically and be hard to spot. Here is a list of some of the most common clichéd phrases in English—be sure to look again at the very common clichés used in the sentences listed on the preceding page, too.

Common Clichés

add(ing) insult to injury	green with envy	rise to the occasion
better half	heavy as lead	sharp as a tack
beyond a shadow of a doubt	hit the nail on the head	sink or swim
	in this day and age	smart as a whip
bottom line	last but not least	sneaking suspicion
brave as a lion	light as a feather	straight and narrow
cold, hard facts	nose to the grindstone	tears streamed down
come to grips with	paint the town red	tried and true
crazy as a loon	pale as a ghost	untimely death
crying over spilled milk	pass the buck	walk the line
deep, dark secret	pretty as a picture	wax eloquent
drunk as a lord	quick as a flash	white as a sheet
face the music	red as a rose	work like a dog
few and far between	right as rain	worth its weight in gold
flat as a pancake	rise and shine	

ACTIVITY 30-4   Revising Clichés

Directions: *Rewrite each of the following sentences to eliminate the cliché, replacing it with fresh imagery.* Answers will vary.

Example: After their narrow escape, his face was white as a sheet.

Revised: After their narrow escape, his face was pale as moonlight on a frozen lake.

1. My roommate had to sew on the button for me because I'm *all thumbs.*

   _____

2. The client didn't like our proposal, so it's *back to the drawing board.*

   _____

3. My neighbor's three-year-old child is *cute as a button*.

_____

4. The party was supposed to be a surprise, but Frank *let the cat out of the bag*.

_____

5. It was *easy as pie* to install the new computer software.

_____

6. Some of my so-called friends are unreliable, but Monique is *true blue*.

_____

7. He's feeling *down in the dumps* because he didn't get the job.

_____

8. My brother likes to keep his apartment *neat as a pin*.

_____

9. The midterm exam was a *wake-up call* for students who expected the course to be easy.

_____

10. My mother works too hard; I have to remind her to *stop and smell the roses*.

_____

LO 3 AVOIDING SEXIST LANGUAGE

Language is dynamic: It evolves with culture. It used to be acceptable to use gender-specific terms such as *man* or *mankind* to stand for all people, but due to political and societal changes in the last few decades, the use of such language is now considered sexist.

Use Gender-Specific Terms Only When Appropriate

The key to avoiding sexist language is to use logic: Use gender-specific terms only when the subject really is gender specific. **Gender-specific terms** are words that refer to a specific gender. For instance, the terms *men* and *he* refer to males, and the terms *women* and *she* refer to females.

Each member of the women's basketball team put on *her* uniform.

The man with the clipboard raised a whistle to *his* lips.

If your subject is not gender specific, use inclusive (non–gender-specific) language.

> Fans roared *their* approval as the home team scored another point.

Non–gender-specific terms are neither male nor female; they are neutral and therefore include both sexes. Some examples of gender-neutral terms are *people, one, humanity,* and *humankind.* Plural pronouns such as *they, them,* or *their* are also gender neutral. When you use terms like *people* or *humans,* you can use the plural pronoun *their.* If you use singular terms such as *a person* or *one* as your subject, then you'll need to use *he or she* instead of *they* to avoid a different type of mistake, a pronoun agreement error (see pp. 589–599 for more on pronoun agreement). In general, the easiest way to avoid a pronoun agreement error is to use the plural forms of non–gender-specific terms and the corresponding plural pronouns.

> **Singular:** Any student who wishes to change majors should consult *his or her* faculty advisor.
>
> **Plural:** Students who wish to change majors should consult *their* faculty advisors.

Don't Assume an Occupation Is Exclusively Male or Female

Another kind of sexist language use arises from stereotyping certain occupations as being primarily for women or for men. Consider the following example:

> **Sexist language:** Demand for qualified nurses remains high, and a student who graduates with the R.N. degree can be optimistic about *her* job prospects.
>
> **Revised:** Demand for qualified nurses remains high, and students who graduate with the R.N. degree can be optimistic about *their* job prospects.

Here's another example:

> **Sexist language:** When discussing treatment options with a physician, make sure that *he* answers all of your questions about possible side effects.
>
> **Revised:** When discussing treatment options with a physician, make sure that *he or she* answers all of your questions about possible side effects.

Both sentences stereotype men and women. Of course, men can be nurses, and women can be doctors. Careers are not limited to a single gender. Along the same lines, be careful not to write *male nurse* or *woman doctor*—just say *nurses* or *doctors*, and then use the plural pronoun *their*.

Use Parallel Terms for Men and Women

Be careful not to have double standards. For instance, if you are writing about high school students, don't call the males *men* and the females *girls*. Instead call them *boys and girls* or *men and women*. Be consistent and fair in your use of terms.

Here are some gender-specific terms that are already obsolete and some non–gender-specific terms that can be used to replace them.

Gender-Specific Term	Inclusive Term
man or mankind	humans, humanity, people, humankind, human beings
fireman	firefighter
policeman	police officer
mailman	mail carrier, postal carrier
weatherman	meteorologist, weather forecaster
salesman	sales associate
congressman	representative, senator, legislator
foreman	supervisor
chairman	chairperson, chair
businessman	business person or exact title (e.g., sales manager)
manpower	staff, personnel, workers
to man	to operate, to staff
man-made	handcrafted, human-made
male nurse	nurse
female doctor	doctor

ACTIVITY 30-5   Revising Sexist Language

Directions: *Rewrite each of the following sentences to eliminate sexist or inappropriately gender-specific terms.*   Answers will vary. Sample answers are provided.

1. The fire at the apartment complex was intense, and firemen struggled to contain the blaze. _The fire at the apartment complex was intense,_

   and firefighters struggled to contain the blaze.

2. Gusty winds hampered efforts to extinguish the blaze, and the rain fore-casted by local weathermen arrived too late to help dampen the flames.

   Gusty winds hampered efforts to extinguish the blaze, and the rain fore-

   casted by local meteorologists arrived too late to help dampen the flames.

3. Other fire departments sent reinforcements, as the small town did not have enough manpower to contain the fire.

   Other fire departments sent reinforcements, as the small town did not

   have enough personnel to contain the fire.

4. Two people who had escaped the fire, a young man and an eighteen-year-old girl, spoke to a local television reporter on the scene, express-ing their shock and disbelief.

   Two people who had escaped the fire, a young man and a young woman,

   spoke to the media, expressing their shock and disbelief.

5. Every parent viewing the news broadcast that night hugged her own kids and breathed a sigh of relief that no children or adults were harmed in the fire.

   Parents viewing the news broadcast that night hugged their own kids and

   breathed sighs of relief that no children or adults were harmed in the fire.

TEN USEFUL ESL TIPS FOR NON-NATIVE SPEAKERS

Here are ten grammar tips that are useful for both non-native speakers and those students who need to brush up on their grammar usage.

Tip 1: Check for Count Versus Noncount Nouns

Count nouns name items that can be counted as individual units:

> dog/dogs, cat/cats, boy/boys, girl/girls, flower/flowers, window/windows, cracker/crackers, street/streets, nut/nuts

Noncount (or **mass**) nouns name items that cannot be counted as individ-ual units:

> food, rice, flour, water, sugar, peace, life, death, furniture, milk, wood, cotton, leather, beauty, chess, evidence

Tip 2: Check for Article Use and Definite Versus Indefinite Articles

Articles (sometimes called *determiners*) are divided into two categories: **definite**, or specific, *the*, and **indefinite**, or nonspecific, *a* or *an*, *some*, or no article at all.

1. **Definite articles:** Use *the* to refer to particular or specific common nouns (singular or plural) and noncount nouns that are specific because the noun was previously identified:

   > *The* sandwiches we ordered were delicious.
   >
   > Let me pay for *the* food this time.

   OR, because the noun is identified by a modifier:

   > *The* best vegetarian pizza has caramelized onions on it.

   The is also used with some proper nouns:

   > *The* Smiths just moved to New Mexico.
   >
   > They used to live in *the* Midwest.
   >
   > We took a riverboat cruise on *the* Mississippi.
   >
   > *The Columbia Tribune* is known for its lively editorials.

2. **Indefinite articles:** Use *a* or *an* with singular countable nouns that are generic or are nonspecific because the noun was not mentioned previously:

   > She asked if he would like to get *a* cup of coffee sometime.

   OR, because the noun's identity is not important to the context:

   > He scribbled his phone number on *a* scrap of paper and handed it to her.

   OR, because the noun has no restricting modifier:

   > A few days later, they went to *a* movie together.

Use *some* with plural nouns or noncount nouns that refer to a particular or specifiable quantity:

> *Some* roses are very fragrant, but others have no fragrance at all.
>
> The orchids need *some* water, but not too much.

Do not use any articles with noncount common nouns that are generic and nonspecific and have no particular quantity or identity:

> She sprinkled *sugar* on the cookies while they were still warm.

Tip 3: Choose the Right Preposition or Prepositional Phrase

Getting prepositions right is difficult since many are learned through use and familiarity with a language, but some logical rules do apply for using some prepositions. The most easily confused prepositions are those related to *space* and *time*.

1. Space: Think location versus direction.

> **Location:** Use *at*, *on*, or *in*
>
> They had a picnic *at* [location] the park.
>
> They sat *on* [surface] a blanket because the grass was damp.
>
> He put the leftover food *in* [enclosed] the basket.
>
> **Direction:** Use *to*, *onto*, or *into*
>
> They ran *to* [direction] the car when it started to rain.
>
> Muddy water splashed *onto* [surface] her new jeans when she got out of the car.
>
> They carried the picnic basket and other gear *into* [enclosed] the house.

2. Time: Use *at* for an exact point in time, *on* for a particular day or date, and *in* for months, years, centuries, and longer periods.

> The baby was born *at* 1:30 A.M. *on* Sunday.
>
> My parents were married *in* 1974.
>
> The play is a period drama set *in* the nineteenth century.

3. **Prepositional phrases:** A prepositional phrase cannot be used as the subject of a sentence. Instead, use a noun or add a subject pronoun after the prepositional phrase.

> **Incorrect:** *In my apartment complex* has a nice community room.
>
> **Correct:** My apartment complex has a nice community room. OR *In my apartment complex*, there is a nice community room.

Tip 4: Avoid Mixing Subordination and Coordination

Use a subordinating clause with a comma, or connect two clauses with a coordinating conjunction, but do not use both (see Chapter 23 for more on sentence combining).

> **Incorrect:** *Although* I went to bed early, *but* I was still tired in the morning.
>
> **Correct:** *Although* I went to bed early, I was still tired in the morning.
>
> OR
>
> I went to bed early, *but* I was still tired in the morning.

Tip 5: Be Sure to Use Subject Pronouns

If you have used a noun subject in a sentence and don't want to repeat the subject in the next sentence, be sure to use a pronoun to represent the original noun in your second sentence.

> **Incorrect:** I'm taking upper-level physics this semester. *Is* a challenging course. [no subject pronoun]
>
> **Correct:** I'm taking upper-level physics this semester. *It is* a challenging course. [subject pronoun added]

Tip 6: Use *It* or *There* Correctly with Deferred Subjects

In English, when a subject is deferred (placed later in the sentence than is usual), the usual subject spot has to be filled with *it* or *there*.

> **Incorrect:** *Is* not good to use a cell phone while driving.
>
> **Correct:** *It is* not good to use a cell phone while driving.
>
> **Incorrect:** *Are* risks even when drivers use hands-free cell phones.
>
> **Correct:** *There are* risks even when drivers use hands-free cell phones.

Tip 7: Be Familiar with Idioms

Idioms reflect the customary speech patterns of a given language. They are particular ways of saying things that develop in a specific region or in a language that don't translate directly or easily into another language. Idioms are learned over time through immersion in a language, and the incorrect use of an idiom is often an indicator that the writer is not a native speaker. Many mistakes in idiom usage come from the misuse of prepositions (see Tip 3 on page 668) or verbal phrases.

Verbal phrases are formed when a verb is combined with an adverb or preposition to create a new meaning. Most verbal phrases are idioms, and they are used more in informal conversation or informal writing than in formal essays. However, even when used in informal writing, verbal phrases are written in a particular order.

Here's a list of verbal phrases that form some of the most common idioms in English.

Common English Idioms

ask out	fill in	put
break down	fill out	away/back/off/on/out/up
break up (with)	fill up	quiet down
bring up	find out	run across/into/out
burn down	get along (with)	show off/up
burn out	get away (from or with)	shut off/up
burn up	get back in/on	speak out/up
call back	get out/over/up	stand up (for)
call off	give back/in/up	stay in/off/up
call up	go out (with)	stop up
catch up (with)	go over	take after/in/off/out/over
check in	grow up	take care (of)
check out	hand in/out	tear down/up
check up (on)	hang out/up	think on/over
come out	have on	throw out/up
cross out	help out	try on/out (for)
cut (it) out	keep on/out/up	tune in/out/up
cut up	leave out	turn down/off/on/out/up
drop in	look after/into/out/over/up	wake up
drop off	make up	watch out (for)
drop out (of)	pass out	
figure out	pick out/up	

Tip 8: Check Your Use of the Infinitive and the Gerund Verb

An **infinitive** is a verb with the word *to* in front of it. It indicates action *after* the time of the main verb, indicates an *effort*, or indicates a *purpose or intention:*

> **Infinitive (action after):** I decided *to paint* the garage.
>
> **Infinitive (indicates effort):** I tried *to paint* the whole garage in one day.
>
> **Infinitive (indicates purpose):** I went downtown *to buy* more paint.

A **gerund** uses an *-ing* verb form. Generally speaking, gerunds tend to present facts rather than intentions. A gerund may also indicate an experiment:

> **Gerund (fact):** I finished *painting* the garage before dark.
>
> **Gerund (experiment):** Try *painting* an entire garage in a single day.

Check to make sure you've used the infinitive and gerund forms of verbs correctly.

Tip 9: Be Careful About Commonly Confused Words

Be careful not to use a word that sounds like another one (a homonym) but isn't the right word for what you want to say. Use the correct spelling. See p. 620 for a list of some of the most commonly confused words in English.

> **Incorrect:** All of *they're* friends *accept* Kiyoshi came to the party.
>
> **Correct:** All of *their* friends *except* Kiyoshi came to the party.

Tip 10: Use an English as a Second-Language Dictionary and Use It Well

Travel or minimal translation dictionaries tend to oversimplify a word's meaning or give very few definitions. Choose a good, complete English as a Second Language (ESL) dictionary. A complete dictionary will give you more specific meanings and connotations so you can pick the best English word for the context of the sentence you are writing. Also, see if it contains a list of idioms so you can check your verb phrases to make sure they are correct.

ACTIVITY 30-6   Fixing ESL Errors

Directions: *In the space provided, rewrite the following paragraph to correct common ESL errors. Refer to the ten tips in this section for help.*   Answers will vary. Sample answers are provided.

Last summer I visited my cousin Rosario in the Austin, Texas. I had a great time sightseeing and hanging up with her. My favorite activity was watching bats! During spring and summer, a huge colony of Mexican free-tail bats lives at downtown Austin. They're home is a Congress Avenue Bridge. Each evening on dusk, 1.5 million bats emerge from under the bridge to forage for the food. They consume about 30,000 pounds of mosquitoes and other insects each night.

At first when Rosario invited me to watch the bats, I felt like turning her off. The bats sounded scary of me. But Rosario said, "Its not scary at all!" Although I could of said no, but I decided to trust my cousin. In Saturday evening, my aunt gave us a ride and dropped us in the bridge. In joining crowds of tourists lining the sidewalks near the bridge. As it grew darker, an occasional bat flitted passed, and we could here faint, squeaking noises. Suddenly, bats started streaming out from under the bridge, raising like a dark cloud onto the sky. We watched for more than the half hour. Was quiet an amazing sight!

Last summer I visited my cousin Rosario in Austin, Texas. I had a great time sightseeing and hanging out with her. My favorite activity was watching bats! During spring and summer, a huge colony of Mexican free-tail bats lives in downtown Austin. The home of this colony is Congress Avenue Bridge. Each evening at dusk, 1.5 million bats emerge from under the bridge to forage for food. They consume about 30,000 pounds of mosquitoes and other insects each night.

At first, when Rosario invited me to watch the bats, I felt like turning her down. The idea of watching bats sounded scary to me. But Rosario said, "It's not scary at all!" Although I could have said no, I decided to trust my cousin. On Saturday evening, my aunt gave us a ride and dropped us at the bridge. We joined crowds of tourists lining the sidewalks near the bridge. As it grew darker, an occasional bat flitted past, and we could hear faint, squeaking noises. Suddenly, bats started streaming out from under the bridge, rising like a dark cloud into the sky. We watched for more than a half hour. It was quite an amazing sight!

To check your progress in meeting this chapter's objectives, log in to www.mywritinglab .com, go to the **Study Plan** tab, click on **Handbook of Grammar, Mechanics, and Style** and choose **Standard and Non-Standard English** from the list of subtopics. Read and view the resources in the **Review Materials** section, and then complete the **Recall, Apply,** and **Write** sets in the **Activities** section.

"My teacher said the school has tough new standards and I need to improve my vocabulary. What's 'vocabulary'?"

THINKING CRITICALLY

Look at the comic strip above. Then answer the following questions.

What effect does word choice and level of vocabulary have on your impression of people or of their ideas or level of intelligence? Provide one example of a time when someone's vocabulary choices affected your impression of him or her in a positive way or in a negative way. Then, explain why.

_____

_____

LO 1 VOCABULARY BUILDING

Did you know that the average educated person knows about 20,000 words and uses about 2,000 different words a week? William Shakespeare, arguably the greatest English-speaking writer, had a vocabulary of between 18,000 to 25,000 words, back when people were happy to have an average of 5,000 words. Why is having a better vocabulary important? Studies have shown that having a better vocabulary increases your success in school and in your career. It also improves your understanding of other people's ideas and arguments in both verbal and written forms. Having a command of language is a form of power. Most highly successful business and political leaders of the world have impressive vocabularies and a clear command of the English language.

The best way to increase your vocabulary is to make a conscious decision to work on building it up daily. Write new words and their definitions in a notebook as you learn them and then use them when you speak and write. The more you use new words in your day-to-day life, the faster your personal vocabulary will grow. Don't be afraid to take some risks and make some mistakes as you try out new words. However, try not to use an awkward or overly formal or complex word where a simpler one would be better. As Mark Twain once said, "Never use a five dollar word when a ten cent one will do." However, using too many simple words won't necessarily generate more complex arguments and reasoning. Find the right balance for your purpose and audience.

Five Tips for Building Your Vocabulary

Tip 1: Keep a Vocabulary Log or Vocabulary Journal. Every time you read or hear a new word, write it in your log, note where it came from (a textbook, lecture, the radio, and so on), write down what you think it means, look it up in a dictionary (immediately or as soon as you get a chance), and write down the relevant definition(s). Using a new word helps you remember its meaning, so write a sentence using the new word. Be sure to review your log regularly to brush up on your new words list.

Sample Entry

> **pseudonym:** I heard this word in my Victorian literature class when my teacher explained that George Eliot was the <u>pseudonym</u> of Mary Anne Evans.
>
> **My definition:** a fake name
>
> **Dictionary definition:** pseu•do•nym (**sood**-n-nim) *n.* bearing a false name; a fictitious name; *esp*: PEN NAME
>
> **Used in a sentence:** Mary Anne Evans used the pseudonym George Eliot because she was a woman writing in a man's world.

Tip 2: Make a conscious effort to use new words. If you use a word more than a few times, it becomes "yours" and a natural part of your own vocabulary. Again, be sure that you are using the word correctly.

Cross Reference
See Chapter 29 for tips on how to use a dictionary or thesaurus and sample entries for each.

Tip 3: Make friends with your dictionary and your thesaurus. Consult a dictionary and a thesaurus regularly to learn new words and to find synonyms for words you tend to use all the time so you can add variety to your vocabulary.

Tip 4: Learn Latin roots, prefixes, and suffixes. A large percentage of words in English are derived from Latin word parts. Becoming familiar with the meanings of these common **prefixes** (word beginnings), **roots** (common word bases), and **suffixes** (word endings) makes it easier to understand new words. For instance, the Latin prefix *de*, meaning *away* or *from,* is used all the time, in words such as *derail* (go off the tracks) and *depart* (go away from). The Latin root *tact* means *touch*, as in *tactile* (relating to the sense of touch). The Latin suffix *ism* means *belief*, as in *pacifism* (belief in settling disputes peacefully).

Tip 5: Use the Internet. The Internet puts a world of vocabulary tools and vocabulary-building resources at your fingertips. You can look up roots, prefixes, and suffixes as well as definitions of words and **homonyms** (words that sound alike but don't mean the same thing), **synonyms** (different words that mean the same thing), and **antonyms** (words that mean the opposite of each other) in various online dictionaries and thesauruses. Just use your favorite search engine (such as Google, Ask, or Yahoo!) and plug in a word to see what happens!

ACTIVITY 31-1 Keeping a Log

Directions: *Begin your own vocabulary log. Keep track of new words that you hear or read this week. Look up the meanings of the new words in your dictionary, and then use them in sentences of your own. Use a separate notebook for your vocabulary log, and try to keep it with you throughout the day: You never know when a good word will come along.*

ACTIVITY 31-2 Vocabulary Practice

Directions: *Write down two words that appear somewhere in this chapter that you did not know before reading this section.* Answers will vary.

1. _____

2. _____

Look up their meanings in a dictionary (online or hard copy):

3. _____

4. _____

Use each word in a sentence of your own:

5. _____

6. _____

 _____

ACTIVITY 31-3 Vocabulary-Building Techniques

Directions: *Complete the following tasks for each word listed below:*

1. *Use an Internet search engine (Google, Ask, or Yahoo!) to look up the meaning of the word.*
2. *Briefly summarize the definition(s) of the word that you find online.*
3. *Write your own definition(s) of the word.*
4. *Create a sentence of your own using the word.*
5. *Try to use the word in conversation or writing this week.*

   1. retaliate

   Online definition(s): take revenge for a perceived wrong; action taken

   in return for an injury or offense; to respond in kind to an injury or affront

 _____

My definition(s): _____

Used in a sentence: _____

_____

2. **scintillating**

Online definition(s): *brilliantly clever; marked by high spirits or* _____

excitement; emitting or reflecting light in a flickering manner _____

My definition(s): _____

Used in a sentence: _____

_____

3. **nonchalant**

Online definition(s): *marked by blithe unconcern; indifferent;* _____

behaving as if detached _____

My definition(s): _____

Used in a sentence: _____

_____

4. **beguile**

Online definition(s): *influence by slyness; to deceive or delude; to* _____

charm or captivate; mislead by means of pleasant or alluring methods _____

My definition(s): _____

Used in a sentence: _____

_____

5. **vacillate**

Online definition(s): *sway unsteadily from one side to another;* _____

waver between conflicting positions or courses of action _____

My definition(s): _____

Used in a sentence: _____

_____

SYLLABLES

Syllables are the number of sounds in a word. For instance, the word *dog* has only one syllable, but the word *Labrador* has three syllables: *lab-ra-dor*. Syllables help you pronounce words correctly. When you look up a word in the dictionary, you will see it broken down into syllables through the use of hyphens, dots, or slashes. For example, the word *irritable* could be shown in several ways: *ir-it-a-ble*, *ir.it.a.ble*, or *ir/it/a/ble*.

PRONUNCIATION

Pronouncing words correctly isn't just about breaking a word into syllables. Dictionaries also provide phonetic (spelling by how a word sounds) pronunciation guides, to help you pronounce words correctly. The following pronunciation guide will help you identify the most common consonant and vowel sounds in English.

PRONUNCIATION GUIDE

Consonant sounds		Short vowel sounds		Long vowel sounds	
b	bed	a	ham	a	say
d	dog	e	ten	e	she
f	fur	i	if	i	hi
g	goat	o	lot	o	go
h	her	oo	look	oo	school
j	jump	u	up	u (yoo)	use
k	kick				
l	leaf				
m	man				
n	no				
p	power				
r	row				
s	saw				
t	tea				
v	vase				
w	way				
y	yes				
z	zero				
ch	channel				
sh	shop				
th	that				
th	thick				

ACTIVITY 31-4   Practicing Pronunciation

Directions:

1. **Pronounce** *each of the following words aloud.*
2. **Break the word into syllables** *using dashes or dots, and write it in the space provided.*
3. **Look up the word in a dictionary.** *Make sure you have pronounced it correctly and divided it into syllables correctly. Then read the definition(s) of the word.*
4. **Write a brief definition** *in your own words.*

1. **incandescent**   *in-can-des-cent*

   My definition: *when something hot is shining or someone is feeling really emotional*

2. **reconnaissance**   *re-con-nais-sance*

   My definition: *information you collect or things you find out about your enemy*

3. **phlegmatic**   *phleg-mat-ic*

   My definition: *laid back (not emotional)*

4. **alleviate**   *al-le-vi-ate*

   My definition: *making something better*

5. **supercilious**   *su-per-cil-i-ous*

   My definition: *snobby, looking down on other people*

LO 2 CRITICAL THINKING AND CONTEXT CLUES

Sometimes when you are reading it's not possible to stop and look up a word you don't know in a dictionary or on the Internet. Also, it may be impractical to look up *every* word you don't know at first glance. At those times, it is best to figure out a word's meaning as much as you can by using the context clues that surround it.

Using **context clues** involves engaging your reasoning and critical thinking skills to find clues that come before and after a word, in the same sentence or surrounding ones, and putting them together to figure out the meaning of the unfamiliar word. So, as you are reading, when you come across a word you don't know, don't skip over it or get frustrated. Instead, use context clues and your critical thinking skills to figure out the word's meaning. Figuring out a word's meaning using context clues is a skill that you get better at with practice. Moreover, you'll remember the new word better if you have to figure out its meaning yourself, and this will help build your personal vocabulary as you read more.

Critical Thinking and Visualization

Think of a jigsaw puzzle that is missing a piece. By studying the pieces surrounding the missing piece, you can figure out pretty accurately what that missing piece should look like.

Using Context Clues

To figure out the meaning of a word, ask yourself the following questions:

1. **Does the word have a prefix, root, or suffix I know** that will give me a partial clue to its meaning?

2. **What part of speech is the word** functioning as in the sentence? Is it a noun? A verb? An adverb? An adjective?

3. **Is the word followed by a secondary explanation or an example?**

4. **Is there a word used near the unfamiliar word that may mean the same (a synonym) or the opposite (an antonym)** that I can use as a clue?

5. **What details or descriptive words are used in the sentence that I know?** Do they give me clues to this word's meaning?

6. **What idea is being addressed in the sentence that contains the word?**

7. **What is the subject of the whole reading?** How does the sentence that contains this word develop the subject?

8. **What purpose is being developed in this piece of writing?** Does the word in question relate to the overall theme? Does it make sense in that context?

Cross Reference

See Chapter 23 for more on word parts.

If you are *not* able to work out the meaning of the word using these questions, read the next few sentences in the passage, then come back to the word, and try again. Sometimes clues appear later in a paragraph or even in the next one.

Even if you *are* able to work out a word's meaning, it is always useful to go back later and consult a dictionary to make sure you were correct.

ACTIVITY 31-5   Using Context Clues

Directions: *Use the context clue questions to figure out the meanings of the words in bold print in the following passage. In the spaces provided after the passage, write the meaning of each word, and explain how you used context clues to figure it out. Then doublecheck your answers using a dictionary.*

In (1) **retrospect**, I clearly recognize the mistakes I made that morning, but at the time I had no (2) **premonition** of disaster. Hank, my faithful dog and (3) **unwitting** companion in catastrophe, was equally clueless. It was Saturday, and both of us were impatient to get outdoors, so I ignored the (4) **ominous** clouds (that was my first mistake), threw on some baggy jeans (that was my second mistake), and grabbed Hank's leash. Outside, I hastily cuffed my jeans, jumped on my bike, and headed for the park, Hank trotting contentedly by my side.

As we neared the park, a flash of lightning split the sky, releasing a deluge of rain. We had no (5) **recourse** but to turn around and return home. Tail plastered between his legs, Hank whined nervously, hanging back as I struggled to pull the leash without overturning the bike.

Ten minutes later, only halfway home, it happened: As I maneuvered through (6) **inundat**ed potholes, one (7) **sodden** cuff of my baggy jeans unrolled and caught in the spokes of the bike. The next thing I knew, I was sprawled in a puddle, Hank's muddy paws on my chest as he licked the rainwater from my face. Stunned, I lay (8) **immobile** for a moment, contemplating my (9) **ignominious** plight, before cautiously moving my arms and legs, testing for injuries.

Escaping with nothing worse than a few scrapes and a bruised ego, I gingerly walked my bike and Hank the rest of the way home. Later that day, from the comfort of the couch, enjoying a few doggy treats and a cup of cocoa, Hank and I agreed to be a little less (10) **impetuous** when planning future excursions.

1. **retrospect**: *remembering past events*

   Context clues used: *"recognize the mistakes I made that*

   morning . . . at the time" (looking back)

2. **premonition**: *warning, feeling that something may happen*

   Context clues used: *prefix "pre" means "before;" reference to*

   "disaster" and "catastrophe" in the future

3. **unwitting**: _not knowing_

   Context clues used: _prefix "un" means "not;" base word "wit" like_ _"wits" (smarts); synonym "clueless"_

4. **ominous**: _threatening_

   Context clues used: _modifies "clouds," which can show that a storm_ _is coming; words "disaster" and "catastrophe" are threatening_

5. **recourse**: _help in the situation, solution to the problem_

   Context clues used: _sentence structure shows word is a noun;_ _paragraph describes a problem (storm); "only" thing to help_ _solve problem was to find shelter by returning home_

6. **inundated**: _flooded_

   Context clues used: _describes "potholes," which fill with water in a_ _rainstorm; previous paragraph descriptive words "deluge of rain"_

7. **sodden**: _very wet, soaked_

   Context clues used: _descriptive words "deluge of rain . . . inundated;"_ _cuff of "baggy jeans" would tend to sag and unroll when water weighs_ _down the heavy fabric_

8. **immobile**: _not moving_

   Context clues used: _when "stunned" a person tends to remain still;_ _contrasts with "before . . . moving"_

9. **ignominious**: _embarrassing_

   Context clues used: _embarrassing to be "sprawled in a puddle;"_ _descriptive words "bruised ego"_

10. **impetuous**: _acting suddenly without thinking about it first_

    Context clues used: _idea in passage of "mistakes" (ignored clouds_ _and wore baggy jeans that might get caught in spokes); "impatient_ _to get outdoors"_

▶ **NOTE** The reading selections in Chapter 22 include more practice for figuring out the meanings of words using context clues.

Grammar Practice for Non-Native Speakers

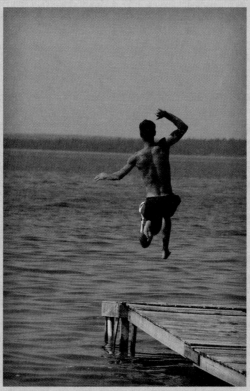

Heading for a Splashdown   Wayne Buck

THINKING CRITICALLY

Look at the picture above. Then answer the question that follows.

Sometimes you have to take risks to learn: Just dive in! How is learning a second language a good example of something that is difficult but rewarding?

_____

_____

_____

LO 1 ARTICLES

The **articles** *a*, *an*, and *the* are determiners that signal that a noun will follow. Some languages do not have articles. In English, *a* or *an* is usually placed before nonspecific nouns to mean *any*, and *the* is placed before specific nouns that are clearly identified (or are the only one).

> We went on *a* vacation to *the* Rocky Mountains.
> [*a* = any; *the* = specific and plural count noun]
>
> Henry wants *a* pizza. He likes *the* pizza I make.
>
> I want *an* egg for breakfast. Please fry *the* egg.

▶ **NOTE**   The examples above show how a general statement uses *a*, but a specific statement uses *the*. In addition, *a* is used for first mention and *the* for second mention of the same noun.

> I bought *a* new car last week.   *The* new car gets very good gas mileage.

However, noncount or abstract nouns and nonspecific plural nouns do not require articles.

> I drink *coffee* for breakfast.   *Coffee* gives me energy for daily activities.

ACTIVITY 32-1

Directions: *Write the correct article: a, an, or the (or X for no article) in the space provided.*

1. Many families turn on _____*the*_____ national news when they get out of bed in _____*the*_____ morning.

2. _____*An*_____ adult may watch _____*the*_____ news and _____*the*_____ weather, but _____*a*_____ child may watch _____*X*_____ cartoons.

3. Although _____*X*_____ adults enjoy _____*X*_____ television, they often have _____*X*_____ work to do around the house.

SINGLE WORD MODIFIERS

Single word modifiers help clarify the meaning of nouns.

Rules for Modifiers

1. Before singular count nouns, use *this, that, another, every, each, neither, either.*

2. Before plural count nouns, use *these, those, some, any, a lot of, many, a few, other.*

3. Before noncount nouns, use *much, any, some, a little, lots of, a lot of, this, that.*

4. Use *any* in questions and negative statements.

5. Use *other* to mean different ones, and use *another* to mean one more or additional ones.

6. Use *the other* to mean a specific different one (or ones).

7. Before nouns, to show possession, use possessive adjectives: *my, your, his, her, its, our,* or *their.*

I don't understand *this* assignment we have today; *every* student is confused.

These homework questions are difficult, but we have *many* days to complete them.

One classmate doesn't have *much* trouble with *his* homework; *another* classmate has *lots of* trouble. I'm not sure about *the other* students.

ACTIVITY 32-2

Directions: *Write an appropriate modifier in each of the blanks in the following passage, using the rules listed above. Answers will vary.*

_____*Many*_____ people prefer to read books about historical events. _____*Other*_____ people don't. _____*Some*_____ people might prefer books about scientific discoveries or current social problems. Of course, a person's age can affect _____*a few*_____ choices for reading topics. _____*Another*_____ thing that can affect such choices is a recommendation from a friend, but _____*each*_____ person has his or her own interests. Interested readers don't have _____*any*_____ problems finding good books.

ACTIVITY 32-3

Directions: *Write this, that, these, or those in the following blanks:*

1. I have _____*this*_____ computer right here. You have _____*that*_____ one over there.

2. I am using _____*these*_____ pencils on my desk. Can you use _____*those*_____ instead?

Write another, or *the other, other,* or *the others in the following blanks:*

3. This sentence has two errors, and the next sentence has _____*another*_____ error.

4. That student registered for summer school, but _____*the other*_____ student with her did not.

5. That college doesn't offer cooking classes, but _____*other*_____ colleges do.

   ▶ **NOTE**   If there is no noun following, you can use *other* + *s*: (#5 . . . but *others* do.)

Write much or *many in the following blanks:*

6. The counselor gave the new student _____*much*_____ information about the campus.

7. The registration forms had _____*many*_____ blanks to complete.

8. Does your instructor take _____*much*_____ time to correct your papers?

LO1 PRONOUNS

Pronouns replace nouns or noun phrases and must agree with nouns in usage, gender, and number.

Subject Pronouns

Subject pronouns identify the doer of the action. They include *I, you, he, she, it, we, you,* and *they.*

> My *parents* bought a house near the mountains. *They* really like the house.
> The *mountain* near my house is beautiful. *It* is covered with snow in the winter.

▶ **NOTE**   English, unlike some other languages, always requires a subject before a verb, even a pronoun subject. However, remember not to repeat the subject.

Correct: *John* has some plans for tonight. *He* is going bowling.

Incorrect: *John* has some plans for tonight. Is going bowling. [subject *He* is missing.]

Correct: *Erika's* hobby is swimming. *She* goes to a pool every day.

Incorrect: *Erika's* hobby is swimming. *Erika she* goes to a pool every day.

Object Pronouns

Object pronouns identify the receiver of the verb action. They include *me, you, him, her, it, us, you,* and *them.* Note the positions in each sentence below where an object pronoun must be used. Objects follow verbs and also follow prepositions.

The teacher *asked* <u>me</u> to give back the papers. She had already *corrected* <u>them</u>.

Theresa *helps* her friends, and they *help* <u>her</u>.

Friendship is important *to* <u>us</u>. We *appreciate* <u>it</u>.

ACTIVITY 32-4

Directions: *Fill in the blanks with a correct subject or object pronoun.*

While my parents lived in another country, _____*I*_____ did not see _____*them*_____ for several years. Finally, my brother and I took a vacation to visit _____*them*_____. While _____*we*_____ were away from home, our friends wrote letters to _____*us*_____ at my parents' address. The mail was slow. We didn't get _____*it*_____ until after returning home. _____*I*_____ missed my friends as much as I had missed my parents. _____*They*_____ both mean a lot to _____*me*_____.

Possessive Pronouns

Possessive pronouns answer the question *whose?* They include *mine, yours, his, hers, its, ours, yours,* and *theirs.*

Some new books are at the bookstore now. *Ours* came in today, but *theirs* haven't arrived yet.

▶ **NOTE**   Do not confuse *its* (no apostrophe/not a contraction) with *it's* (contraction of *it is* or *it has*.)

ACTIVITY 32-5

Directions: *Fill in the blanks with a correct object or possessive pronoun.*

1. Both individuals in a marriage must work at communication. The responsibility is ___*theirs*___.

2. Both partners want their spouse to pay attention to ___*them*___.

3. Researchers in the United States are studying this communication problem and trying to solve ___*it*___.

4. Hopefully new research will help all of us improve relationships. I want to improve ___*mine*___.

Reflexive Pronouns

Reflexive pronouns refer to their noun antecedent for clarification or emphasis. Reflexives include *myself*, *yourself*, *himself* (not *hisself*), *herself*, *itself*, *ourselves*, *yourselves*, and *themselves* (not *theirselves*).

He hurt *himself* when he fell off his bike. The children saw *themselves* in the mirror.

ACTIVITY 32-6

Directions: *Fill in the correct reflexive pronoun for each blank; refer to the list of examples above.*

1. I have been dressing ___*myself*___ since I was four years old.

2. She told ___*herself*___ she would not cry at the movie.

3. He married so that he didn't have to live by ___*himself*___ anymore.

4. The caregiver cooked for the old man and woman because they couldn't cook for ___*themselves*___.

5. My wife and I don't ask for others' opinions. We trust ___*ourselves*___ when making decisions.

Relative Pronouns

Relative pronouns are used to join sentences, making two sentences come together as one. Relative pronouns describe a noun that comes just before them. In the following example, *who* describes John, a noun:

> John likes to play baseball. John is my friend.
>
> John, <u>who is my friend,</u> likes to play baseball. [The relative pronoun *who* is used to join the two sentences.]

▶ NOTE   The clause starting with a relative pronoun cannot stand alone.

> **Incorrect:** John is my friend. Who likes to play baseball.
>
> **Correct:** John is my friend *who* likes to play baseball. OR John, *who* is my friend, likes to play baseball.

▶ NOTE   *who* = people; *which* = animals, things, or ideas; *that* = people, animals, or things.

In the following examples note how the relative pronoun is used to combine two ideas:

Two clauses joined into one with *which*:

> The book on Kennedy is so heavy. I bought it.
> The book on Kennedy, *which* I bought, is so heavy.

Two clauses joined into one with *that*:

> The book on Kennedy is so heavy. I bought it.
> The book on Kennedy *that* I bought is so heavy.

Two clauses joined into one with *whose*:

> The author is famous. *His* book is on Kennedy.
> The author *whose* book is on Kennedy is very famous.

ACTIVITY 32-7

Directions: *Underline the correct relative pronoun for each blank.*

1. Florida is a state (who/<u>that</u>) has many residents who are retired.
2. Florida tourists are people (<u>who</u>/which) like warm weather attractions.

3. People (who/<u>whose</u>) income is low don't have money for entertainment.
4. Florida is a state (whose/<u>that</u>) has a very warm climate.
5. Tourists are people (which/<u>whom</u>/that) every state needs for added income.

▶ **NOTE** *Whom* (object pronoun) can be used as a relative object pronoun, but *that* is now more common.

Punctuating Relative Clauses

There are two kinds of relative clauses, restrictive and nonrestrictive. **Restrictive (essential)** relative clauses are needed to identify a noun clause and have no commas. **Nonrestrictive (nonessential)** relative clauses are *not* needed to give meaning to the sentence and identify a noun. They are set off by commas on both sides as shown in the following example:

John likes to play baseball. John is my friend.

John, *who* is my friend, likes to play baseball.

In this example, the relative clause starting with *who* is not needed to give the sentence meaning.

▶ **NOTE** Nonrestrictive (unnecessary) clauses cannot use *that*; therefore, *which* is used instead:

My neighbor's house, *which* needs a new coat of paint, is older than mine.

LO 1 PREPOSITIONS

A **preposition** is a word that helps show a relationship between two ideas in a sentence. Common prepositions include: *at, for, from, in, on, of, to, with, through, between,* and *by.* A preposition followed by a noun or pronoun becomes a prepositional phrase. A prepositional phrase must not be separated from the rest of the sentence by punctuation.

Correct: He lives alone in a small apartment.

Incorrect: He lives alone. In a small apartment.

Preposition Rules

1. Some prepositions indicate location, as shown in the prepositional phrases below:

on his father's farm	*in* the country	*at* school
by the bus stop	*on* Main Street	

- Use *in* for inside a specific place (*in* his pocket) and *on* for on top of (*on* the table)
- Use *on* for a street without a house or building number (*on* Main St.)
- Use *at* with a house or building number (*at* 1258 Main St.)
- Use *in* for the city and state (*in* San Francisco; *in* California)

2. Some prepositions indicate time, as shown in the prepositional phrases below:

in May	*in* the spring	*on* December 1
at night	*after* school	*by* noon

- Use *in* for months and years (*in* May; *in* 2008)
- Use *on* for dates (*on* Dec. 1) and days of the week (*on* Thursday)
- Use *at* for specific times (*at* 9:00 A.M.)
- Use *from . . . to* for a specific time period (*from* 10:00 *to* 2:00) and *for* for duration (*for* 2 days)

ACTIVITY 32-8

Directions: *Read the following paragraph. Underline all prepositional phrases, and circle the prepositions. You will find 12 prepositional phrases in all.*

I began studying English ⓘn 1999. The English class I took was offered ⓑy the public school ⓘn the evening. Many ⓞf the students ⓘn my class were ⓕrom other countries. The class met ⓞn Tuesday and Thursday evenings ⓕrom 7 to 10 pm. I went ⓣo class ⓦith my husband because he was also learning English. Now the school has grown and moved ⓣo a new building ⓐt 1650 Compass Boulevard. I am proud that our English has improved.

Other Sentence Structure Points to Remember: Gerunds and Infinitives

Gerunds

A gerund is a verb + *-ing:*

Gerunds follow prepositions: interested *in* learn*ing;* tired *of* study*ing*

Gerunds can be the subject of a sentence: <u>Studying</u> is important.

Gerunds can be the object of a sentence: They avoided <u>studying</u>.

Gerunds can be used as modifiers, also called participles: <u>Studying</u> hard, the student passed.

▶ **NOTE**   Certain verbs require gerunds, not infinitives, for the verb following: I *enjoy* learn**ing.** I *avoid* study**ing.**

Infinitives

An infinitive is *to* + a verb. Infinitives separate verbs. Often, infinitives are used after verbs that express feelings.

I want **to** *travel.*   I like **to** *meet* people.   I didn't need **to** *leave.*

Infinitives are also used in place of *that* in sentences showing the will of one person over another:

Correct: They want us *to come* to the party.

Incorrect: They want that we come.

Do not use infinitives with modal auxiliary verbs (helping verbs like *must, should, will, could,* and so on).

Correct: He *should listen* to that advice.

Incorrect: He *should to listen* to that advice.

ACTIVITY 32-9

Directions: *Write a gerund (verb + -ing) or infinitive (to + base verb) for each blank, using verbs from the list below.*

arrive   improve   see   take   register   manage   attend

1. Maria: I am interested in ____*taking*____ a computer class this year.

2. Thuy: I can see why you are interested. It would be helpful. I hope ____*to improve*____ my skills also.

3. Maria: Have you thought about ____*attending*____ a class in the day or evening?

4. Thuy: I want to avoid ____*arriving*____ at work late, so I think I will take a morning class.

5. Maria: That would work for me, too. Let's plan ____*to register*____ for the same course this time.

6. Thuy: Ok. I'll ask my husband ____*to take*____ my daughter to school if the class time conflicts.

7. Maria: ____*Managing*____ time is always a challenge.

8. Thuy: Yes, and the family expects ____*to see*____ us, too.

LO 1 VERBS

Function of Verbs

Verbs are words that show action or join the subject to the rest of the sentence.

1. Verbs indicate the time the action took place—for example, present, past, or future.

2. Verbs begin with a **base** form, which doesn't show time (tense) or person. This is part of the infinitive:

   to understand   to know   to read   to write   to come   to go

   ▶ **NOTE**   An infinitive = *to* + base form of verb. The base form is not the present tense. Never change the base verb in an infinitive by adding an ending.

   Incorrect: to learning

3. Some tenses and verb forms are followed by base verbs:

   Present tense questions and negatives: *Does* he <u>know</u>? No, he *doesn't* <u>know</u>.

Past tense questions and negatives: *Did* she <u>*know*</u>? No, she *didn't* <u>*know*</u>.

Modal verbs: *Could* they <u>*come*</u>? No, they *couldn't* (<u>*come*</u>). *Should* you <u>*call*</u>?

Commands (the **imperative**) also use base verbs:

(You) *Come*.   (You) Don't *call*.

4. A few verbs require base verbs to follow (*make, let, have*):

The teacher <u>*let*</u> him *leave*.

5. Questions can be either "yes/no" type or "information questions" with the words *who, what, where, when, how,* and *why.*

Did you <u>*understand*</u>? (Yes/No)   OR   <u>*What did*</u> you <u>*understand*</u>?

ACTIVITY 32-10

Directions: *Write in any appropriate verb form for each blank.*   *Answers will vary.*

Responsibility in college involves not only completing assignments but also how a student should _____ them. With their busy lives, students often let time _____ without getting homework finished. Some students have their classmates _____ their homework for them. For example, if a student doesn't _____ time to study, he or she may feel pressure and decide to complete the assignment any way possible. Even if a student can _____ help from another person, the other person could _____ mistakes also. Worst of all, copying another person's work can make you _____ your class and give you a bad reputation. Did you ever _____ of this problem? Don't _____ it!

LO 1 Simple Present Tense

Present tense is used for routines (actions that happen anytime or regularly).

▶ **NOTE**   Time words (such as *always, sometimes, once a week*) should help you to decide when to use the present tense.

Action Verbs

Use the base verb for all persons, but add *s* for *he, she,* and *it*.

> I learn, you learn, he learns, we learn, you learn, they learn

Insert *do* or *does* only for questions or negative answers before a base verb.

> *Does* he always <u>eat</u> breakfast?
>
> Yes, he always <u>eats</u> at 8 A.M. [Note *s* for affirmative answer.]
>
> No, he *doesn't* always <u>eat</u> breakfast. [No *s* with negative helping verb.]

▶ **NOTE**   Remember, do not use *do* or *does* for affirmative statements, only for questions and negatives.

> **Correct:** *Do* they always <u>eat</u> breakfast?
>
> Yes, they usually <u>eat</u> at 8:30 A.M.   OR   No, they <u>don't</u>.

ACTIVITY 32-11

Directions: *Fill in a present tense verb to complete each statement or question.*
Answers will vary. Possible answers are provided.

1. Every day my mail ___comes___ at 1 P.M.

   Question: When ___does___ your mail ___come___?

2. Often the mail carrier ___leaves___ me a package.

   Question: What ___does___ he ___leave___?

3. When I'm away, I ___ask___ my neighbor for help.

   Question: Whom ___do___ you ___ask___ for help when you are away?

4. My neighbor never ___forgets___ to help me.

   Question: ___Does___ your neighbor ___help___ you?

Be Verbs

The **be verb** (*is, are, was, were, have/has been*) is followed by nouns, adjectives, and locations. Questions require a form of *be* before the subject, and statements require a form of *be* after the subject.

> *Is he a student?*   Yes, he's a student.   OR   No, he *isn't* a student.
>
> *Is he happy?*   Yes, he's happy.   OR   No, he *isn't* happy.
>   [adjective after *be*]
>
> Where *is he?*   He *is* at school.   He's in the library.
> He *isn't* at home. [location]

▶ **NOTE**   *Be* verbs are also followed by the gerund form (verb + *-ing*), but that is the progressive, not the simple present tense. Use it to show an action in progress. The tense of the *be* verb shows the time, not the main verb + *-ing*: I *am* learning, I *was* learning, I *have been* learning, and so on.

Remember that simple present tense is used for routine actions, not actions in progress.

ACTIVITY 32-12

Directions: *Underline the correct action verbs or be verbs in the sentences that follow:*

1. Austin (is/are) hot but beautiful in the summer.
2. Flowers (blooms/bloom) on many plants.
3. The hotel (has/have) a lovely dining area.
4. My family (likes/like) visiting other places.
5. The attractions of this city (offers/offer) relaxation and good food.
6. Austin (was/were) much smaller when I went there as a child.

ACTIVITY 32-13

Directions: *Form questions with action verbs (do/does + base verb) and be verbs using the sentences in Activity 32-13.*

Answers will vary. Possible answers are provided.

1. Austin/hot in summer: *Is Austin hot in the summer?*
2. Flowers/bloom: *Do flowers bloom in Austin in summer?*
3. Hotel/have/dining area: *Does the hotel have a dining area?*
4. Family/visiting other places: *Does your family like visiting other places?*
5. Attractions of this city/offer: *What do the attractions of this city offer?*
6. Austin/smaller/when you went as a child: *Was Austin smaller when you came as a child?*

Present Progressive Tense

In comparison to the simple present tense, the present progressive shows action in progress or temporary actions happening at this time. The present progressive (also called the *present continuous*) is formed with *be* + verb *-ing*.

> He *is* studying.   We *are* listening.   You *are* writing.   They *are* learning.

Be Verb

The *be* form (*is, are, was, were, has* or *have been*) is called the *helping verb* and combines with the main verb. Continuous temporary actions in the past or present perfect use *be* + verb *-ing*:

> **Past continuous:** He *was* studying when I called.
>
> He *has been* studying hard all year.

Future continuous actions also use *be* + verb *-ing*:

> He *will be* studying until he graduates in June.

Questions

Questions are formed as in the *be* present tense. Move the *be* form in front of the subject.

> *Are they* eating breakfast now?
>
> When *is he* eating breakfast?
>
> *Was* he studying?

Negatives

Negatives are formed by putting *not* after the appropriate form of the helping verb *be*.

> They *are not* (*aren't*) eating breakfast now.
>
> They *have not* (*haven't*) been studying long.

Simple Past Tense

The simple past tense is used for actions that began and finished in the past.

Rules for Simple Past Tense

1. Often a specific time in the past is given, indicated by a time word, such as *ago* or *last* (*week, month, year*).

2. Simple past verbs are regular (add -ed to base verb) or irregular (no -ed but spelling change). Refer to an irregular verb list for study of these past forms.

> He *cooked* breakfast an hour ago.   The flowers *bloomed* last month.
> [completed action]

3. To form questions in the simple past tense, use *did* before the main verb, which takes the base form.

> *Did* he <u>cook</u> breakfast?   *Did* the flowers <u>bloom</u>?   *Did* you <u>call</u>?

4. To form negatives in the simple past tense, use *didn't* + the base form of the main verb.

> He *didn't <u>cook</u>.*   The flowers *didn't <u>bloom</u>.*   I *didn't <u>call</u>.*

▶ **NOTE**   Remember that *was* and *were* (*be* verbs) are used for simple past statements and questions as well.

ACTIVITY 32-14

Directions: *Fill in the correct form of the past tense, including questions and negatives.*

1. He (have) ____had____ to choose a new line of work last year.

2. Working at the automobile factory (be) ____was____ difficult.

3. Last summer his wife (tell) ____told____ him to consider college.

4. When you were a child, (do) ____did____ your family (speak) ____speak____ to you about college?

5. Unfortunately, my parents (not have) _did not have_ the opportunity to attend college.

Present Perfect Tense

Present perfect tense is used to indicate an action that began in the past but continues into the present and even could continue into the future.

▶ **NOTE**   Like the simple past, the present perfect has both regular endings (with -ed) and irregular forms.

Rules for Present Perfect Tense

1. Do not add *been* before the past participle. The present perfect has just two parts.

> **Have or has + past participle:** He *has* worked here for 5 years.
>
> The company *has grown* a lot.

2. Use *has* for *he/she/it* and *have* for all other forms. As with other verbs, the negative is formed by placing *not* after the verb—in this case, after the helping verb, *has* or *have*.

> He *has cooked* breakfast since he was a teenager.   They *have not eaten* yet.

3. Sometimes you use the present perfect for completed actions that are still important.

> We *have* already *eaten*.   They *have never been* to that restaurant before.

4. You also use the present perfect for actions that stop and start (repeated actions) from past to present.

> He *has cooked* for his friends every Tuesday since last year.

> ▶ **NOTE**   Time words, such as *always, never, already,* and so on go between the helping verb and past participle.

5. To form a question, put the helping verb before the subject.

> *Has he* cooked? [subject is *he*]

ACTIVITY 32-15

Directions: *Underline the correct form in each sentence (compare present perfect to simple past, finished actions).*

1. Yesterday I (cleaned/have cleaned) the garage.
2. I (didn't clean/have not cleaned) the garage for two years.
3. We (never used/have never used) the shelves in the back of the garage.
4. We (bought/have bought) our house in 2002.

5. Have you (worked/work) on home improvement yet? (Note the helping verb position for questions.)

Past Perfect Tense

In contrast to the present perfect tense, the **past perfect tense** indicates a past action that occurred before another action in the past. In this case, two verb actions are involved; for the first action that happened, use *had* + past participle.

▶ **NOTE**   It makes no difference which action comes first in the sentence.

> Before I studied this grammar, I *had not understood* the difference in verb tenses.
>
> After I *had practiced* the verb tenses, I improved my writing.

ACTIVITY 32-16

Directions: *Write in the correct answer.*

   _a_   **1.** The present perfect uses a helping verb, which is:
        a. have or has
        b. had
        c. had or has

   _b_   **2.** The past perfect uses a helping verb, which is:
        a. have or has
        b. had
        c. had or has

   _a_   **3.** In the sentence, "I came here after I (action)." use:
        a. had + past participle
        b. have + past participle

Present Perfect Continuous Tense

The present perfect continuous tense emphasizes actions in progress, continuing from past into the present time without interruption. It uses the same helping verbs as present perfect (*have* or *has*) but adds two other changes: the helping verb *been* and *-ing* on the base form instead of using a past participle.

> She *has been taking* Spanish since the tenth grade.

The Past Perfect Continuous tense is used to refer to a continuous, ongoing action in the past which was interrupted by a second action in Simple Past. What is important is the duration of the action expressed through Past Perfect Continuous.

> Keiko *had been waiting* for two months by the time she received the reply.
>
> Doug *had been thinking* about his friends just minutes before they called.

In the preceding examples, the verbs **had been waiting** and **had been think-ing** are in the Past Perfect Continuous tense, and the verbs **received** and **called** are in the Simple Past. The use of the Past Perfect Continuous tense indicates that the actions of waiting and thinking were continuous, and were interrupted by the actions expressed in the Simple Past.

(LO 1) Passive Voice

Sentences with action verbs that focus on the action, not the subject, are called *passive*. For example, we can say "The letter *was sent*" instead of "*John sent* the letter." Use a form of *be* + past participle. The *be* verb controls the time, not the past participle.

> ▶ **NOTE**   If you learn past participles for present perfect with *have/ has*, you will know the past participle form to use with a form of *be* in the passive voice.

John *is sending* the letter.	becomes	The letter *is being sent.* [present progressive passive]
John *has sent* the letter.	becomes	The letter *has been sent.* [present perfect passive]
My friends *send* letters.	becomes	Letters *are sent* by my friends. [simple present passive]

Do not confuse passive voice sentence construction with active voice sentences.

> **Incorrect:** My friend has been sent a letter. [passive voice]
>
> **Correct:** My *friend has sent a letter.* [active voice]

PEARSON

To check your progress in meeting this chap-ter's objectives, log in to www.mywritinglab .com, go to the **Study Plan** tab, click on **Handbook of Grammar, Mechanics, and Style** and examine the list of subtopics underneath. After clicking on a subtopic, read and view the resources in the **Review Materials** section, and then complete the **Recall, Apply,** and **Write** sets in the **Activities** section.

Credits

Index